A History of Finland

A
History of
FINLAND

BY JOHN H. WUORINEN

Published for

The American-Scandinavian Foundation

by

Columbia University Press

New York and London 1965

John H. Wuorinen, Professor of History at Columbia University, is the author of *The Prohibition Experiment in Finland* and *Nationalism in Modern Finland*. He also edited and translated *Finland and World War II*.

The index for this book was prepared pursuant to a contract between the U.S. Office of Education and the American Council of Learned Societies, and is published with permission of the U.S. Office of Education, Department of Health, Education, and Welfare.

To Alfhild

Preface

This book describes some of the main aspects of Finland's position and history during the many centuries before the nineteenth when the country was an integral part of the Swedish realm; offers a summary of the eleven decades from 1808–9 to 1917 when Finland was an autonomous constitutional state in union with Russia; discusses the attainment of independence in 1917–18, the growth of the republic in 1919–39, its involvement in World War II, and the consequences of the war; and delineates, in broad outline, the development of the nation since 1945.

The history here presented moves within the bounds of general political, economic, and (for the period after 1918) international relations aspects of Finland's history. The reason why these areas of the annals of the past were chosen for description and comment is that they are basic in the history of the Finns and compound into a subject quite large enough for a single volume. They are sufficiently extensive, in fact, to impose severe limitations upon the narrative. Considerations of space therefore dictated the omission, regrettably, of some important areas of national and cultural development and concerns, among them literature and the arts.

It has frequently been contended that the history of the past can be successfully studied only after the passage of time has provided a "proper" perspective. Be that as it may, historians interested in foreign affairs, for example, have usually been forced to wait for decades for access to the records of the past. State papers and other necessary documents have all too often been hidden in archives or other repositories closed to researchers for fifty years or more. The purpose obviously is not to provide historians in due time with a "better" perspective but to spread the cloak of secrecy over matters deemed to require secrecy. The extensive documentary material available to students shortly after World War I or the rich stores of German sources obtained after the collapse of Hitler's Germany merely accent the exceptional; they do not in any sense mean that the restrictions ordinarily imposed on the researcher have disappeared.

This brings us to the question whether the historian is impeded or seriously restricted in studying Finland's foreign relations before 1939 and her part in the war after 1939. The question is interesting and pertinent. Several Finnish writers since 1945 have held or implied that the time has not yet come for a definitive description of the complicated events of these years. Some of them can only be put down as pedants whose wordy irresolution invites the surmise that they are really searching for a detour around facts they find forbidding. Others are special pleaders who insinuate or try to prove that Finland before 1939 could be seen, with some justification, as a threat to the USSR and that this was the reason why the Soviets, moved only by considerations of security, attacked Finland in November, 1939. They therefore contend that no final and valid verdict regarding the background of the war and its results can be put forth until "all the evidence is in."

Such interpretations or claims must be dismissed out of hand. They are unsupported by the evidence. They are put forth by authors addicted to distorting irrelevancies or by purveyors of historical make-believe or worse. The facts regarding Finland's foreign policy before 1939 and her position after Soviet military action had imposed war upon the country pose no unusual difficulties for the historian. The facts are etched clearly enough to offer reliable guidelines for a study of the events of 1939–45. The historian therefore has no need to wait for the "sounder" perspective the passage of time allegedly would ultimately provide. The essentials are his for the asking. He need only use them.

I have not hesitated to use them. The results are found in Chapter XI, which summarizes Finland's foreign relations before 1939, and in Chapter XIII, which discusses the circumstances preceding the Soviet attack and sketches the consequences of the war that followed. As far as Finland is concerned, the conclusions dictated by the evidence provide a 1939 balance sheet of aggression that carries only one heading, that of the USSR. To ignore this fact is to sidestep the demands of impartiality and to destroy the focus essential for a correct view of the results of the war.

Work on this volume began over thirty years ago, although most of it was completed and the book was given its present form during the past two years. The award by Columbia University of the William Bayard Cutting Traveling Fellowship not only enabled me to publish a special study, *Nationalism in Modern Finland*, but also gave me an opportunity to survey other aspects of Finland's history. A grant by Columbia's Council for Research in the Social Sciences permitted further study in Scandinavia that yielded much of the material incorporated in this book. A State Department Fulbright grant "to participate in the International Educational Exchange Program of the United States" made it possible for me in 1959 to spend two months in Finland and to learn something at firsthand of the country's post-1945 circumstances.

I must record my indebtedness to several scholars whose works have been especially helpful, or who have extended various personal kindnesses to me, at one time or another, during the past thirty years and more. In offering them my grateful thanks, I would particularly name the following without attempting to indicate the extent to which I am beholden to them: Mr. Erik J. Friis, Editor of *The American-Scandinavian Review;* Mr. Max Jakobson, of the Ministry for Foreign Affairs, Helsinki; Professors Matti Leppo, L. A. Puntila, Pentti Renvall, and Heikki Waris, of the University of Helsinki; Chancellor Bruno Suviranta, of the Graduate School of Business, Helsinki; Dr. Henrik Schauman, Librarian of the Library of Parliament, Helsinki. My colleague Shepard B. Clough, and my former colleague, Harold C. Syrett, the present Dean of Faculty, Queens College, aided me during the early stages of the preparation of the book in a manner that calls for still another expression of appreciation. I am under a special obligation to Dr. Klaus Törnudd, whose exceptionally careful reading of the manuscript eliminated not a few errors and added clarity to many of my generalizations. Neither those named above nor others on whom I have relied in preparing this book are in any way responsible for whatever errors in interpretation or sins of omission or commission may be charged to me.

I wish also to express thanks to Columbia University Press, especially to my editor, Mr. William F. Bernhardt, whose prodigious and discriminating labors greatly improved the manuscript. During the long months of writing my wife has assisted me in a multitude of ways, and this history therefore owes her more than enough to make the dedication hers not only by courtesy but by right.

Columbia University
November 21, 1964   J. H. W.

Contents

Contents

Illustrations follow page 270.

A History of Finland

I

The Country and the People

THE COUNTRY

Historians, geographers, anthropologists, and others have long since pointed out, at times with considerable emphasis, that man has always shown a response to the environment in which he lives; man's habitat has had an unavoidable and many-sided influence on individual and nation alike. This view has been occasionally expressed in terms extravagant enough to make it clear that acceptance of it as a universal "principle" requires abandonment of common sense. Thus the claim that religious conceptions are fundamentally determined by geographical factors can hardly be taken seriously, any more than Strabo's contention, in the first century B.C., that mountain environment encouraged banditry while plains made for natural prosperity. No less open to objection is the well-known notion that physical environment is the determining factor in the formation and perpetuation of "race" as applied, say, to the peoples of Europe in modern times.

But even though physical environment cannot be accepted as a determinant of "race," and geography, climate, and the like cannot be said to furnish the main key to an understanding of differences between European nations in our day, there is no denying their effect upon past historical developments or upon the recent or present economic, social, and political conditions under which men live. That is to say, it is obvious that many aspects of Italian life and culture could not have developed in Greenland—or in Scandinavia, for that matter—and that the civilization characteristic of twentieth-century Netherlands could not well have emerged and flourished in the steppe regions of Asiatic Russia. Environment does impose limits within which a given mode of human life and culture is possible. This is true even of modern industrial societies, although man-dominated environment has increasingly narrowed the area within which man was forced, in earlier days, passively to accept environmental restraints. Geographical environment is still a factor, often merely permissive and not really mandatory, but nevertheless a factor.

These reflections come readily to mind when we contemplate the geographical location of Finland and attempt to appraise the conditions under which the Finns have lived and labored in the past and pursue the complicated business of "man's life in society" in our own day. To what extent have geographical factors played a part in molding the past of the people of this northern republic? How far do the various elements of physical environment explain the life of the nation in our industrial age?

A glance at the map shows that Finland is the most northerly of the European states. It extends north almost to the Arctic Ocean (before the cession of territory to the USSR as a result of World War II, Finland's territory included Petsamo on the Arctic Ocean), and the southernmost parts of the country are considerably farther north than Norway's or Sweden's.

In size, the country ranks fourth among the states of Europe (excluding the USSR). Its area today is 130,160 square miles. The United Kingdom, West Germany, and Italy are considerably smaller; France, Spain, and Sweden are larger. Of the other democracies of Scandinavia, Norway is smaller by some 6,000 square miles, while Denmark is only one-eighth the size of Finland. To carry the comparison a step further: Finland is slightly larger than New England, New York, and New Jersey combined, or Washington and Oregon combined, and somewhat smaller than Minnesota and Wisconsin combined, and about half the size of Texas.[1]

[1] As a result of the Russo-Finnish War of 1939–40 and 1941–44, Finland was forced to cede to the USSR about 18,000 square miles of territory—larger than

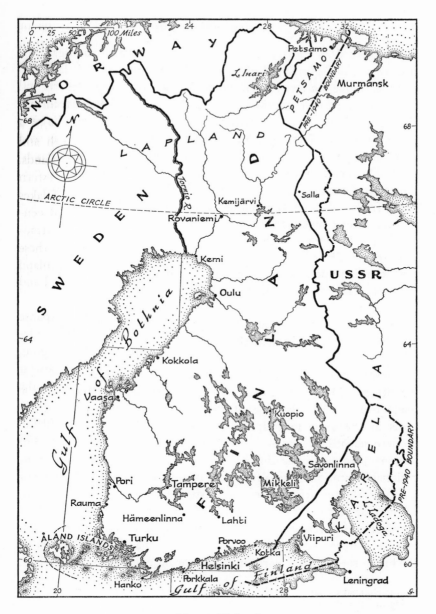

MAP 1. Finland

Nowhere does Finland offer impressive variety of landscape or lush vegetation. Nearly all of the land is low; most of it is less than 600 feet above sea level. Even mountains do not always deserve the name, for most of them do not reach the height of 1,500 feet, and the highest, in the extreme northwest, close to the Norwegian border, is less than 5,000 feet high. Yet variety there is, although it is of a quiet and not of a startling kind. The coastal regions, south and west alike, are fringed by an impressively extensive belt of islands. The open farming country, especially in the southwest and western areas, frequently invites admiration. The tens of thousands of lakes and the river country that are characteristic of a large part of central Finland combine with the extensive forest areas to give attractive scenic diversity that seems especially appropriate to these northern latitudes. Somewhat more than 11 percent of Finland consists of lakes and accounts for the oft-quoted phrase "the Land of the Thousand Lakes."

On the same latitude as the land of the Finns lies the expanse of Siberia north of the sixtieth parallel, the southernmost 600 miles of icy Greenland, and in North America the Hudson Bay region, the southern half of Baffin Island, and the Canadian Northwest Territories. Merely to mention this fact suffices to measure the inadequacy and irrelevance of the classification that places these areas in the same geographical bracket. In the case of Finland, modern scientific farming, up-to-date industries large and small, and in general urban civilization of a high order and political and educational institutions which fully conform to what may be called, for want of a better designation, the western European culture pattern; in the case of the northern reaches of Asia or the North American continent, until relatively recently, primitive modes of existence and culture patterns in the main appropriate to the material aspects of the life of the North American Eskimo or his cousin in north Siberia.

---

all of Denmark—partly in the southeast and partly in the northeast, thus losing direct access to the ice-free Arctic Ocean.

Raye E. Platt, ed., *Finland and Its Geography* (London, 1957), is a good guide in its field. Its historical and other non-geographical sections require some revision. W. R. Mead, the English scholar, is the author of several excellent contributions. See especially his *An Economic Geography of Scandinavia and Finland* (London, 1958).

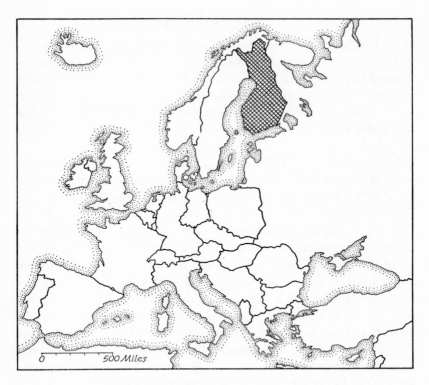

MAP 2. Finland in relation to the rest of Europe

The sharp contrast between a modern progressive nation on the one hand and the simpler societies on the other suggests, if geographical factors are given the weight they seemingly demand, that Finland is something of a puzzle. If we regard the advance of civilization as basically the story of man's increasing control over his environment, the obvious conclusion appears to be that present-day Finland serves as an exceptional illustration of man's victory over obstacles which Nature, usually niggardly and often stubbornly hostile in the far northern latitudes, has placed in his path. The conquest of Nature— or the never-ending challenge offered to its restrictive mandates— seems to have been so successful as to suggest exceptional effort, perseverance, and skill on the part of the people who have, over the centuries, effected it.

There is no denying the importance of human ingenuity, tenacity of purpose, and stamina which have wrought results that may well be said to have often been prodigious. But this is by no means the whole story or the complete explanation for the fact that man has wrested large areas from this inhospitable North European frontier area and has turned them into the home of a modern, progressive, democratic nation. An all-important geographical and climatological fact is also involved. It relates not only to Finland but to Scandinavia as a whole.

Despite the fact that Finland is the world's most northerly country—an independent nation which has, incidentally, a higher density of population than that of any other area of comparable size and location—its climate is considerably less severe than might be inferred. There are no glaciers, no permanent snow, and no permafrost. The prevailing winds are from the southwest and west and bring warmth and moisture from milder regions. The Gulf Stream also is a factor. The relatively large bodies of water to the south and west—the Baltic and its two arms, the Gulf of Finland and the Gulf of Bothnia—add a maritime quality to the climate. In the autumn and the early part of the winter the Baltic remains warmer than the surrounding land masses and delays the fall in temperature. The mean temperature of the coldest month, February, is surprisingly high: in the far north, 12°–5° (all degrees Fahrenheit), and in the southwest, 19°–28°. In July the corresponding figures are 52°–57° in the north and 59°–63° in the south. The growing season when the vegetation foliates and matures is the period when the mean temperature is above 41°. The long days during the growing season compensate to a considerable degree for the absence, normally, of really warm weather. This is especially important because the transpiration of water through the plants, basic in the growth of crops and natural vegetation, proceeds only during daylight.

The result of these factors and circumstances is that the mean annual temperature in the southern part of the country is approximately the same as that of Minnesota, although the winters in Minnesota are likely to be colder and the summers warmer than in south Finland. This is merely one way of saying that, instead of being a semi-Arctic country lying between latitudes that elsewhere (outside of Scandinavia) mean the imposition on man of the restraints of relentless Nature, Finland has been, throughout its recorded history, suitable for human habitation and capable of developing a modern industrial and agricultural civilization. The problem of adjustment to environment has basically been not radically different from the same problem in, say, some of the north-ernmost states of the United States.

Another significant physical characteristic of Finland has long invited the attention of scientists and laymen alike. Well over two centuries ago, in the early 1700s, many Finns and Swedes became aware of the seeming fact that the level of the Baltic Sea was sub-siding. Over the years numerous markings were carved in coastal rocks to indicate changes in the sea level. By the end of the last century, however, it had been definitely established that it was not the subsidence of the sea but literally the uplift of the land that was taking place. Practically the whole country, and especially the western coastal area, is steadily rising from the sea. Investigation and careful measurements taken over the past several decades have shown that elevation proceeds one to nearly four feet every century. The rise is the greatest at the head of the Gulf of Bothnia (three to four feet) and smallest on the south coast where the land rises only about one-third as much. Together with silting caused by the numerous rivers, this constant elevation of the land has added hundreds of square miles to Finland's territory and will in all likeli-hood continue to do so indefinitely. Finland is thus literally a grow-ing country destined to expand westward so long as the geological forces responsible for the rise continue to operate.[2]

THE PEOPLE

Finland's population in 1963 was 4,523,000. The population has been bilingual throughout historic times and remains bilingual today. The two groups are usually referred to as "Finnish-speaking" and "Swedish-speaking," and these designations appear in official statisti-

[2] Fennoscandia in general illustrates the same phenomenon, although the rate of elevation is the highest along the western coast of Finland. Greenland, on the other hand, is slowly sinking. The rate of sinking has been estimated at approximately one to four feet every century. The rate of sinking is greatest on the west and northwest coast and practically nonexistent in the southeast.

cal and other publications. The former is by far the larger group and accounts for about 92 percent of the total, while the "Swedish-speaking" element comes to about 7.5 percent. Other linguistic, ethnic, or "national" elements are altogether insignificant: about 2,500 Lapps in the north (some 7,000 in Sweden and 20,000 in Norway), 1,500 Jews, and smaller numbers of other groups. As these demographic facts suggest, Finland has not been and is not today plagued by race or national minority problems in the ordinary sense of these terms. The constitution of 1919 defines Finnish and Swedish as the two official "national languages of the Republic" and provides that the "educational and economic needs" of the Finns and the Swede-Finns "shall be met on the basis of similar principles."

The language situation in the country is, however, more complex than these facts suggest. More than that, some of its important features are distorted by labels and terminology that have become conventional, especially during the past half-century, despite the fact that they frequently obscure rather than clarify.

The designations "Finnish-speaking" and "Swedish-speaking" are partly inaccurate and misleading. They do not fully define the line separating Finnish-speakers from Swedish-speakers. They merely refer to the fact that at the time of the decennial census somewhat over nine tenths of the population indicated Finnish as the individual's mother tongue or home language, and that slightly less than 8 percent stated that Swedish was theirs (1960 census). In neither category does the declaration regarding mother tongue disclose whether the individual speaks or does not speak the other national language. In other words, these and corresponding figures for earlier decades do not show the extent to which bilingualism prevails among individuals in the two language groups whose "mother tongue" determines the census classification.

Actually practically all educated Finns are bilingual (leaving out of consideration languages other than Finnish and Swedish). While primary schools as a rule do not include or require the teaching of the other native language, all secondary schools irrespective of whether the language of instruction is Finnish or Swedish must, according to law, offer prescribed courses in the other domestic language. Admission to all institutions of higher learning involves the passing of exacting examinations in the other national language, and the same applies to most positions in the civil service. It is understandable that, especially at the higher levels of educational, administrative, and governmental service, rather complete bilingualism is an unavoidable must, and often is markedly more impressive than that found lower down the social or economic scale. The Swede-Finns frequently illustrate more perfect bilingualism than individuals from Finnish-language homes. It has been estimated that well over 40 percent of the Swede-Finns (most of whom are farmers, fishermen, or other so-called lowly folk; "workers" comprise about one third of both language groups) are Finnish-speakers. In 1950, about 159,400 Swede-Finns out of a total of 348,300 were recorded as knowing Finnish also. About 7.7 percent of the Finnish-language group knew Swedish.[3] In Helsinki, the capital, where about 64,000 of the total of 330,500 Swede-Finns live (census of 1960), about 95 percent of the Swede-Finns spoke Finnish as well. Approximately 21,000 Swede-Finns live on the semiautonomous Åland Islands, off the southwest coast of Finland, and have well-nigh completely avoided all inroads of the Finnish language. They thus represent the real hard core of "Swedish-language Finland," but because of their isolation from the main stream of life and development on the mainland they play only a minor part in the nation's daily concerns.

The relative decrease in the number of the Swede-Finns, and the greater degree of bilingualism among them, have been caused in considerable degree by marrying across the language line. It is a significant fact, incidentally, that the term "mixed marriages" is not normally used—and less still in a disparaging sense—in Finland in connection with marriages of individuals whose "mother tongue" differs. In such marriages, bilingualism is obviously clearly involved. In general, however, marriages in this category have meant, over the past several decades, a tendency toward the abandonment of Swedish as the home language. This trend has been reflected especially during the past generation or two in urban centers (Helsinki, Turku, Vaasa, and others) as well as in many rural areas.

Other circumstances have also contributed to the decrease. Among

[3] *Suomen Tilastollinen Vuosikirja* (hereafter referred to as *S.T.V.*), 1958, Tables 21–23.

them is Finnization. The "Finnization" of the Swede-Finns (as the term is used here) means a voluntary acceptance of Finnish by an increasing number of Swede-Finns (or individuals and families who formerly belonged, by commonly accepted criteria, in this group) as the home language or "mother tongue." The process began well over a century ago as the nationalist movement obtained increasing numbers of adherents (see Chapter V) and has continued down to our day. It has at times attained notable proportions and produced impressive results. For instance, about 16,000 families changed their Swedish names into Finnish names on a single day, May 12, 1906, the centenary of the birth of Johan Vilhelm Snellman, the great patriot-leader of the mid-decades of the last century. Those who commemorated the birth of the nationalist leader by legally changing their names were not predominantly Swede-Finns determined to repudiate Swedish by declaring themselves as Finns in language as well as sentiment. Most of the "name-changers" were, in all probability, individuals whose action merely signalized a public and demonstrative acceptance of the "Finnish" nationalist cause, rather than an open renunciation of the Swedish language as such. The changing of family names nevertheless has reflected a slow depletion of the ranks of the Swede-Finns and has represented, over the decades, a growing rather than a decreasing phenomenon. Forty years ago, in 1920, the Swede-Finns numbered 341,000, or about 10,000 more than in 1960.[4]

The problems and complexities of the language situation have been frequently magnified and distorted by historical and "cultural" concepts and interpretations that have enjoyed and still enjoy wider and more general acceptance than they deserve. Historical and other literature, both in Finnish and in Swedish, frequently deals with "Finnish-language culture" as distinguished, allegedly, from "Swedish-language culture." The distinctions which such classifications imply or allegedly establish often rest on "cultural" differences

[4] The official newspaper, the *Suomen Virallinen Lehti*, published an extra issue of 51 pages of four columns each on May 12, 1906, in order to make room for the names changed on that day. Later issues through May contained hundreds of family names that did not get into the issue of May 12. B. Estlander, in his *Elva Årtionden ur Finlands Historia* (Helsinki, 1930), III, 387, estimates that at the time some 100,000 Finnizations of surnames were announced. See also *S.T.V.*, 1923, Table 16; 1962, Table 22.

which have little or no real meaning in the daily round of the farmer, factory worker, lumberjack, clerk or other representatives of the common folk. They can be identified, if at all, only by sophisticates familiar with the romanticized, finespun conceptions of dedicated language nationalists.

As far as the Swede-Finn group in general is concerned, the vocal spokesmen and defenders of the "Swedish-language culture" concept have attempted through the years to draw as clear a line as possible between the two language groups. While the line is for the most part of no real consequence in the workaday world, the resolve to insist upon it is frequently demonstrated. Perhaps the most striking illustration of it is the refusal, particularly by dedicated Swede-Finn language nationalists, to accept, especially while abroad, the label "Finn" or "Finnish" and the insistence upon "Finlander" or even "Swede" as the proper designation. The parochialism illustrated by such preferences, while rejected and denounced by some of the outstanding Swede-Finns, shows no signs of disappearing in the near future.[5]

It is a well-known fact that the Finnish language differs greatly from the other languages of Europe. Only Estonian is closely enough related to Finnish to enable a layman to discern a common linguistic base. Hungarian is often mentioned as a relative of Finnish. Actually the relationship is very remote, being about as close as that between English and Persian. Because of the exceptional isolation of the Finnish language, and because of the fact that the world of the learned long assumed—and the fanciful constructions of the dilettante still take for granted—that language denotes and offers a measure of racial relationship, the attempts to explain the origin and background of the Finns, the speakers of this unique language, led long ago to the formulation of racial concepts and conclusions that have

[5] Among the many Swede-Finns who have refused to accept the "Finlander" label are such prominent figures as the sculptor Ville Vallgren, Marshal Mannerheim, General Erik Heinrichs, and others. There are additional evidences, needless to say, of the lack of unity among the Swede-Finns. This is illustrated in politics by the fact that Swede-Finn strength in Parliament is usually measured by the Swedish People's party strength—in 1962, 14 seats out of 200—and is normally not considered to include the 4 Socialist and the 2 Communist Swede-Finns (as of 1962).

persisted down to our own day and still continue to baffle and mis-
lead. The question is, in some respects, one of the most surprising
"racial" problems among the nations of modern Europe.

Few questions relating to the peoples of Europe have received
more attention than that of the "races" in Europe. Especially during
the past century, the literature dealing with it has grown to considerable proportions. The conclusions formulated by the scores of
contributors to this literature represent a bewildering array of facts,
half-truths, interpretations, contradictions, and illogical claims. Probably because the problem appears in the last analysis to be insoluble,
scientists dealing with it have been led to distinguish, by using different criteria, "races" which vary in number from three or four to
over thirty. Many of the writers in the field have confused "race"
with language, real or assumed cultural differences, and the like.
Relatively few have fully recognized the fact that, whatever the
so-called original racial background of a given people may have been,
thousands of years of migrations, wars, and peaceful intercourse have
all too often produced an intermixture destructive of distinctive
biological characteristics that alone can form, in any meaningful
way, the basis of racial differentiation.

While archaeological and other studies have shown that man has
inhabited Finland for nine thousand years or more, the present
population can in all likelihood be traced mainly to settlers who
probably came beginning as early as the second millennium B.C.
and continued to settle in Finland until the sixth century A.D. Whence
they originally came has not been definitely explained, and probably
never will be, any more than the distant origins of the French or
the English or the Germans will ever be reduced to conclusions free
from assumptions plain and fanciful.

The speculation concerning the racial background of the Finns
is old, and its history during the past two centuries is not lacking
in interest. In common with the trend elsewhere in Europe, eighteenth-century Finnish writers, for instance, were inclined to establish, among others, relationship with the Jews. The lost tribes of
Israel furnished a tempting and convenient point of departure for
imaginative interpretation and claims along this line. It did not take
long, however, before supposed philological and other contacts

between the Finns and Jews or other peoples of antiquity gave way to interpretations pointing in a different direction.

Toward the close of the eighteenth century, philologists discovered certain similarities between English, German, Latin, Greek, and other European languages on the one hand and Sanskrit on the other. In the early 1800s, Sanskrit was pronounced the mother of the other languages, and the term "Indo-European" languages was introduced into European philology. By the middle of the century, comparative philology and other studies had led to the concept that an "Aryan" people of a distant past had been the source of most Europeans and that this relationship was "racial" and could be identified by linguistic evidence. The search for their original home became a concern of the scholar. Before long, "scientific" conclusions as well as popular assumptions came to be based on the view that Asia was the homeland of the Aryans. In the sixties Friedrich Max Müller, a German savant who enjoyed enviable scholarly prestige, felt able to declare that there was a time "when the first ancestors of the Indians, the Persians, the Greeks, the Romans, the Slavs, the Celts and the Germans were living together within the same enclosure, nay, under the same roof." [6] It goes without saying that neither the enclosure nor the roof has ever been located and the chances are altogether that they will forever remain as elusive as they were a century ago.

By about 1890, the search for the original "homeland" of the

[6] Quoted in F. H. Hankins, *The Racial Basis of Civilization* (New York, 1926), p. 17. See the first two chapters of Hankins for a survey of this problem. Friedrich Max Müller (1823–1900) published his conclusions in 1861. In another work, published in 1888, he vigorously protested against the notion that language could be or should be identified with race. He said: "I have declared again and again that when I say Aryas . . . I mean simply those who speak an Aryan language. The same applies to Hindus, Greeks, Romans, Germans, Celts and Slavs. When I speak of them I commit myself to no anatomical characteristics. . . . I assert nothing beyond their language when I call them Hindus, Greeks, Romans, Celts and Slavs; and in that sense . . . only, do I say that even the blackest Hindus represent an earlier stage of Aryan speech and thought than the fairest Scandinavian. This may seem strong language, but in matters of such importance we cannot be too decided in our language. To me an ethnologist who speaks of Aryan race, Aryan blood, Aryan eyes and hair is as great a sinner as a linguist who speaks of a dolicocephalic dictionary or a brachycephalic grammar." *Biographies of Words and the Home of the Aryas* (London, 1888), p. 121.

"Aryan" people had come to include other, non-Asian parts of the world. Already by 1870, Asian origins had been challenged, and various areas in Europe—for the most part the southern Baltic region or the eastern parts of Europe—were claimed to be the original center of dispersion. Even northern Africa was brought into the picture. Also—and this was more important—the physical characteristics and mental attributes of the mythical "Aryans" had been catalogued by the end of the century in increasing detail by scientists of fertile imagination and by popularizers of robust daring. They were described in flattering terms as blond, tall, narrow-faced, longheaded, and endowed with mental qualities and other abilities greater than those of other "racial" groups. During the past two or three generations the interest in the "Aryan" has fathered abundant progeny, the racialism of Nazi Germany being only one of its more recent manifestations. While scientific study has long since exploded the Aryan myth, many of its basic concepts still enjoy wide popular, uncritical acceptance.

The interests in the racial background of the Finns, during the nineteenth century, followed much of the pattern furnished by the study and speculation concerning the origins of Europeans in general. In Finland, also, philological studies prepared the ground for conclusions and yielded the evidence considered most significant. But more than elsewhere, perhaps, the problem of origins was colored by what may be called a nationalist approach, for the decades that witnessed the emergence of real interest in this question were the very decades during which the modern Finnish nationalist movement was registering its first important gains.

The question of the racial origin of the Finns appeared to be more complicated than that of most other European peoples. Linguistically they represented, as we have noted, an almost completely isolated island among the nations of Europe. Race study in the modern sense still being in its infancy, it was perhaps inevitable that when the question became the subject of serious scholarly concern—roughly, from the 1840s onward—it was the comparative study of language that was assumed to furnish the key to the riddle. An outstanding figure among the many men who sought for the key and ultimately claimed to have found it was a Finnish scientist, M. A. Castrén (1813–52).

Castrén devoted himself to Finnish philology in the hope of being able to throw light upon the distant past of his people and their seemingly obscure relation to the rest of mankind. During a number of years, he made several extensive journeys into European and Asiatic Russia and collected an impressive amount of philological data. He was impelled by strong nationalist as well as purely scholarly ambitions. This appears clear in the light of a statement which he wrote to a friend in the year 1844:

There is only *one* thing by which I have been deeply moved, and I can live only for it. Everything else is of secondary importance. I have decided to prove to the people of Finland that we are not a . . . nation isolated from the world and world history, but that we are related to at least one-seventh of the people of the globe. If the cause of this nation is served thereby, all will be well. . . . Grammars are not my objectives, but without them I cannot reach my goal." [7]

When Castrén presented his findings, in 1849, they were a compound of the aspirations of a nationalist visionary and the conclusions of an able philologist and grammarian.

The conclusions were, briefly, that the Finns should be classified, on philological grounds, with the people of the Turco-Tataric, Mongol, and Manchu-Tungus language groups. It was Castrén's contention that linguistic relationship meant "racial" relationship and he therefore concluded that the peoples who belonged in these language groups had all originated in the Altaic region in Siberia. This meant an Asian and, in popular understanding, Mongolian origin for the Finns. The scientist-patriot had thus seemingly achieved his ambition to establish a relationship between his people and a sizable part of the earth's population.

Later philological and other studies have exploded Castrén's pretentious conclusions regarding the prehistoric past of the Finns. His Ural-Altaic concept still remains what it was when first presented,

[7] See my *Nationalism in Modern Finland* (New York, 1931), pp. 98–100. The letter, dated October 18, 1844, is found in the manuscript collection of the University of Helsinki, "Brev till Joh. Vilh. Snellman II."

namely, a fanciful theory. As one of the leading scholars in the field has put it, "No valid reasons for this classification have yet been produced." [8] In so far as philological and related evidence throws any clear light upon the problem, it points to present-day European Russia as a possible original "home area" of the Finns. But even this conclusion has been challenged by scholars whose claim to distinction is no less impressive than that of the defenders of this locus as the area of original dispersal.

The evidence on which the challenge rests comes especially from anthropologists and ethnologists. The essentials have been summarized, among others, by Professor K. Vilkuna, the well-known member of the Finnish Academy. He has contended for some time that the forebears of the Finns had "in all probability" lived in the Baltic region centuries longer than was assumed earlier, and that any attempt to seek an "original home" in more distant areas means building conclusions on nothing more substantial than pure surmise. Archaeological evidence supports this view. It indicates that human settlement in the east and south Baltic area, whence the Finns gradually began to move to Finland well over two thousand years ago, continued unbroken from about 1500 B.C. to about 400 A.D., that no indication of the kind of migration or movement from farther east that the earlier theories took for granted exists, and that cultural and other contacts during these distant ages, in so far as they can be traced at all, point to the West and to Scandinavia and not to the East.[9]

These findings and conclusions have not sufficed to dispose of the numerous and robust progeny fathered by Castrén and perpetuated by scholars and other writers who have followed, for well over a century, the path marked off by him. The conventional concept of "Finnish-related peoples" still persists, no doubt partly because it has long been a familiar and enticing item on the Finns' romanticist, nationalist bill of fare.[10] Books, periodicals, and the daily press offer

[8] K. B. Wiklund in the *Encyclopaedia Britannica* (14th ed.), IX, 258. See also P. Ravila, "Suomen suku ja Suomen Kansa," in A. Korhonen, ed., *Suomen Historian Käsikirja* (Helsinki, 1949), I, 6–7.

[9] See T. Vuorela, *Suomensukuiset Kansat* (Helsinki, 1960), pp. 5–22.

[10] "Finnish-related peoples" is a concept frequently encountered in the literature in the field. During the past four decades, no less than four major

continuing evidence of the acceptance of the concept of the "Finnish family of peoples" in the inflated, Castrénian sense.

A single illustration will define the contours of the problem. A recent able work in the field, that by T. Vuorela published in 1960, surveys the subject of "Finnish-related peoples" in twelve chapters, each devoted to one of the peoples included in this philologically defined category. They range from the Lapps in the north of the Fenno-Scandinavian peninsula to the Hungarians 1,500 miles to the south and include small groups of peoples who live in faraway northern Siberia. The author's procedure, assumptions, and conclusions regarding the Hungarians are especially revealing. Introducing the Hungarians as the "largest of the Finnish-related peoples," Vuorela summarizes their history over the centuries and describes modern Hungary, depicting the world of the farmer in recent times, folk art, and the like in considerable ethnographic detail. Yet the only reason for the inclusion of the Hungarians in the survey is the relationship between the Finnish and Hungarian languages, which, as we noted above, is about the same as that between English and Persian or Swedish and Persian.[11]

The real meaning of the inflated "Finnish-related peoples" concept can be fully understood if we imagine an English scholar undertaking a study of peoples and nations that, on philological grounds, may be considered related to the English. Proceeding exclusively with the aid of philological evidence, and employing approaches analogous to those we have noted above in the case of the Finns, the English scholar would produce a study of the history and culture of the Iranians, the Albanians, the Swedes, the Lithuanians, and the Hindi-speaking people of India, all of them under the rubric "English-related peoples." A Frenchman engaged upon a similar task and proceeding in the same manner would classify as "French-related peoples," past and present, such nationalities as the

works illustrating this fact have appeared: T. I. Itkonen, *Suomensukuiset Kansat* (Helsinki, 1921); A. Kannisto *et al.*, eds., *Suomen Suku*, 2 vols. (Helsinki, 1926, 1928); I. Manninen, *Suomensukuiset Kansat* (Porvoo, 1929); and T. Vuorela, *Suomensukuiset Kansat* (Helsinki, 1960).

[11] See Wiklund in the *Encyclopaedia Britannica* (14th ed.), IX, 258, and Ravila, "Suomen suku ja Suomen Kansa," in Korhonen, ed., *Suomen Historian Käsikirja*, I, 2; see also M. A. Tallgren and Y. H. Toivonen in G. Suolahti *et al.*, eds., *Suomen Kulttuurihistoria* (Jyväskylä, 1933–36), I, 30–31.

Greeks, the Letts, the Ukrainians, Bulgarians, Armenians, and others. And both the English and the French scholar would present, in support of his "scientific" conclusions, pages and pages showing the actual (or assumed) common root of, or the relationship between, countless nouns—especially nouns—verbs, and adjectives in French, Bulgarian, Ukrainian, Lithuanian, etc.

What are we to conclude, then, regarding the people who inhabit Finland today and their recognizable forebears in historic times? The question, if freed from the romanticist notions which the past few generations have accepted as congenial articles of Finnish nationalist faith, is no more complex than the same question applied to the other peoples in the West European culture area. The earliest "origins" of all of them are obscure and seemingly unknowable. The nations of today, however, can be observed and measured and the conclusions stated in reasonably clear and definite terms.

Finland is no exception. Research and observation have delivered a verdict free from ambiguity. The verdict is, as one would expect, that the Finns and their "racial forebears" are "purely European."[12] More specifically, a study of the physical characteristics of the people of Finland has brought to light that the Finns are relatively tall, being slightly shorter than the Swedes or the Norwegians but somewhat taller than the Danes or the Germans; that they are over-whelmingly blond, in that light and mixed types predominate, only about 6 percent being classified as brunette and less than 2 percent having dark brown or black hair; that they are somewhat more broadheaded than their Swedish neighbors, but less so than the Danes or the majority of the Germans; that the differences between the Swedish-speaking and Finnish-speaking elements of the population are, in so far as they exist at all, small and unimportant; and that blondness, tall stature, longheadedness, and other so-called Nordic characteristics are most frequently found in the western, southwestern, and southern parts of the country, and decrease toward the north and east. At least one of the basic physical charac-

[12] Carlton S. Coon, *The Races of Europe* (New York, 1939), p. 226, and see the maps on pp. 176–77, 252–53, 258–59, 270–71, 294–95; see also J. J. Mikkola, "Oikea Suomensuku," *Historiallinen Aikakauskirja* (Helsinki, 1929), pp. 81–85, and K. Vilkuna's study in *Kalevalaseuran Vuosikirja* (Helsinki, 1948), Vol. 27–28, pp. 244–90.

teristics, stature, has undergone marked change since it became the object of record and study some seventy or eighty years ago. The average Finn today is appreciably taller than his grandfather. The reason is probably a greatly improved standard of living during the past half-century and more.

Finally, the Finns obviously represent, in common with all the other peoples of Europe, a mixture of various strains. The primary strains, the anthropologists claim, are two: the element popularly known as the Nordic, and another, which several anthropologists have designated of late as the East Baltic. Both of the categories are rather arbitrary approximations, needless to say, and stand for no sharp differences. The East Baltic is more prevalent and is distinguished from the former primarily on the basis of a broader head form; otherwise the physical characteristics of the two classifications do not differ conspicuously. The East Baltic element, together with some others, is also found in Sweden and Norway, and while its presence in Denmark is unimportant, Denmark discloses another broadheaded strain that is significant. Except for differences in degree, the peoples of the four Scandinavian nations seem thus to represent pretty much the same physical characteristics.[13]

To sum up, the explanations and assumptions of philologists, or the interpretations formulated by many historians and other writers, have for the most part thrown no real light upon the origin or distant background of the Finns. Not infrequently, they have obscured the problem for the student and baffled and misled the layman. The distant origins of all European peoples, including those of the Finns, are hidden in the impenetrable mists of the faraway past. They are likely to remain forever hidden and the puzzle in-

---

[13] One of the most revealing illustrations of this fact is furnished by the map inside the cover of Coon's study, which also gives an instructive view of Europe as a whole. Of course, such anthropological concepts as tall stature, "Nordic," "East Baltic," and others raise interesting questions. For instance, Coon speaks on p. 73 of the skeletal remains of "an extremely tall man, 181 cm. in height." This is equivalent to 5 feet 11 inches, which in present-day parlance would not be called "extremely tall." H. Lundborg, in his *Svenska Folktyper* (Stockholm, 1919), concludes that 10.7 percent of the Swedes are "pure Nordics." In this case, "tall stature," which is one of the characteristics of this type, is defined as 170 cm. or over (pp. 7–9). This means 5 feet 7 inches or more. It is clear that the percentage of Swedish "Nordics" would drop considerably if "tall stature" were defined as 6 feet or over.

soluble. In the circumstances it is clear that the "racial" classification of the Finns and their place among the other peoples of northern Europe can be defined in only one way. That is to classify according to the abundant available facts that relate to the physical characteristics of the people of Finland. The facts, left to speak for themselves and unmarred by fanciful interpretation, place the Finns in the category of the other northern peoples.[14] Political, religious, educational, and other aspects of Finland's general development in the distant or more recent past merely underscore the same conclusion. This fundamental fact is writ large over the entire recorded history of Finland.

THE MODERN NATION

The distribution of Finland's population is very uneven. Of the total population of 4,523,000 in 1963, somewhat over three fifths lived in the six southwestern and southern provinces, which account for about one fourth of the area of Finland. The huge Lapland province in the far north is most sparsely settled; the Uusimaa province in the south, where Helsinki, the capital, is located, has nearly forty times as many people per square mile as Lapland, and well over ten times more than the Oulu province south of Lapland. Climate, the location of the best farming land, and the development of industry during the past century have combined to produce a result that accounts for the fact that by far the greater part of the population lives south of the line drawn from the head of the Gulf of Bothnia southeast toward Lake Ladoga.

That Finland's population is bilingual has already been noted. The linguistic division rests on no religious or related differences. This

[14] Something of the confusion that still frequently colors the question here discussed is illustrated by several relatively recent official Finnish publications intended for use abroad. Thus *The Northern Countries*, published in Uppsala in 1952 under the imprimatur of the foreign ministries of Denmark, Finland, Iceland, Norway, and Sweden, states in part that "racially [the Finns] have some [*sic*] resemblance to the Scandinavians and some to the Indo-European nations living on the east coast of the Baltic. The nearest relations of the Finns are the Estonians and some Finno-Ugric peoples living in European Russia, but linguistically the Hungarians are also relations of the Finns" (p. 34).

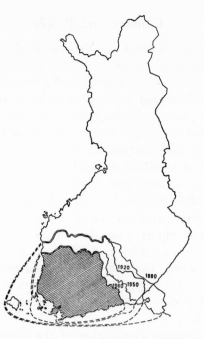

MAP 3. Population concentration in Finland

In 1960, half of the population lived in the shaded area in the map. The corresponding areas for 1950, 1920, and 1880 show how there has been a steady concentration of the population.
From *Introduction to Finland 1963*

is shown by the fact that somewhat over 92 percent of the people belong to the Lutheran Church. Other religious denominations are altogether insignificant. The largest of them, the Greek Orthodox, had 72,100 members (1.7 percent of the total population) in 1962, and other denominations accounted for only 0.3 percent. The number of Finns recorded in the so-called civil registry—which meant that the individuals concerned had no church affiliation—came in 1962 to 244,850 or about 2.5 percent of the population. This fact is especially interesting because it shows that the Socialists, for example, who have traditionally been openly and at times rabidly antichurch and anticlerical, have on the whole found it congenial not to declare themselves out of the traditional church. Much of the membership in the Lutheran Church is purely nominal. The religious unity implied by membership undoubtedly accounts for the fact that church and religion have been, since the sixteenth century, neither the cause of internal conflicts or rivalries nor factors influencing political developments.

Literacy had become general even before 1921 when a law establishing compulsory school attendance between the ages of seven and fifteen was enacted. During the following four decades the ability to read and write became so common as to mean that, as a Finnish scholar has put it, it "had lost its meaning as a measure of the general educational level" of the nation. The extent to which the compulsory attendance law was observed is shown by the fact that, of the 836,800 children in the 7- to 15-year age group obligated to attend school in 1961, only 198 failed, for a variety of reasons, to do so. Secondary and higher education involved, obviously, smaller groups. In 1961–62 secondary schools had 228,400 students, and 17,900 took and passed the final examinations that amount to university entrance examinations. The total enrollment at the universities and at various other institutions of university rank was, in the same year, 28,850.

The city and country distribution of the population has undergone uninterrupted change during the past two generations. The change has meant a substantial absolute, as well as a relative, growth of the urban communities and, in recent years, a marked decline in the size of the farming population. The basic reason for the growth of the city population was, in view of the well-known fact that the birth rate of cities is lower than that of rural areas, migration from the country to the city or to suburban areas sooner or later incorporated into a city. In 1961 the figures showed that the population of the rural areas was 2,733,700 or 60.9 percent of the total. These figures, however, do not adequately distinguish or fully measure the differences between the agrarian and the industrial world. The differences are more fully disclosed by the occupational classes and economic groupings into which the population is divided.

The occupational groups and classes have undergone great changes, needless to say, over the past several decades. Farming was the dominant economic activity when Finland became independent and for several years thereafter. By 1950, however, farming and lumbering combined—they are usually grouped together in Finnish statistics—accounted for only 41.5 percent of the population. In 1960 the figure had dropped to 31.7 percent, and farming alone engaged no more than about 26 percent of the people. Industry, the building trades, commerce, the service trades, and mining had become the source of livelihood for approximately three fourths of the nation. This proportion was substantially greater than the percentage of the urban population. The discrepancy is accounted for primarily by the fact that a considerable number of Finland's industrial establishments (including, incidentally, some of the largest), and therefore the communities in which the labor force and office and managerial personnel lived, were located in areas not yet classified as urban in official statistics although they were not rural but at least suburban in everything but name.

The trend since 1918 is clearly shown by the fact that the "agricultural population" in 1920 numbered 2,061,000 and only 1,408,000 in 1960; that the industrial labor force had grown from 419,000 to 870,000 during the same period and that the main nonfarming labor groups totaled 2,248,000 in 1960; that transportation employed twice as many persons in 1960 as in 1920; and that commerce and trade provided jobs for 106,000 persons in 1920 and 393,000 in 1960. The process illustrated by these figures was speeded after World War II by the fact that a substantial part of the evacuees from the areas ceded to the USSR in 1944 sought and found employment in industrial or related occupations.

Social classes and stratification are not easily identified, except in a broad way, in the democracies of the West. This applies to Finland as well as to her Scandinavian neighbors. To be sure, it is easy enough to distinguish between the Finnish upper social strata and the lowest or between what might be called the upper fringes of the middle classes and the broad middle segments of the lowest groups. It is more difficult, however, to draw the lines sharply. The difficulty is caused by several subtle factors. It stems not only from the vague and differing external criteria suggested by varying income levels or educational accomplishment and degrees, significant by themselves in Finland no less than in the other nations of the North. It grows also from the fact that the individual's own identification of the group or class which he considers his own—and whose ideology and political objectives he on the whole embraces—is frequently determined by preferences and criteria that are at best only imperfectly indicated by statistics or other devices that record the evolution and features of a modern industrial society.

This is merely one way of saying that in Finland as well as in Western democracies in general social stratification involves components the limits of which are at best only loosely drawn. The components and their relationships are, moreover, constantly changing. They therefore underline the impossibility of constructing a scheme or drafting a scale into which the various groups can be easily placed. The broad range of facts and circumstances relating to the so-called class structure of Finland is quite sufficient, however, to enable the sociologist to formulate at least a few satisfactory conclusions. Thus the leading Finnish sociologist-historian, Heikki Waris, has pointed out that the Finnish "body social is, to a decisive degree, a society of the worker and the farmer, that is to say, a society of the common working man." Approximately 50 percent of the working force of the nation could be put in this category in 1960. In that year, the "middle-class" element, incidentally, accounted for well over 20 percent and the farmer class under 20 percent of the total population of the nation.

It is clear that the historian's or the sociologist's categories and classifications of the Finnish people are somewhat academic unless they are related to concrete political and other aspects of the nation's life. If we contemplate Finland's social and economic class structure, we are at once impressed by the fact that, while the republic is, obviously, a laboring man's republic, the majority—the common folk—has not been persuaded so to use its numerical superiority as to give the "working man" a continuing majority in the Parliament, readily usable in the pursuit of labor's objectives; nor has it given labor a decisive say in the composition and policies of the Cabinets of the post-1945 period. Conservatism has similarly failed to reflect the seeming dictates of the class structure. According to a survey in 1950, the Finnish "upper classes" represented approximately 3 percent of the nation's population. Yet it is clear that conservatism as a political force has been, throughout, substantially larger than this percentage suggests. Similar discrepancies between the size of the farmer class and the political influence of the Agrarian party have been recorded since universal suffrage was introduced in 1906, and the same applies to the "middle classes" as well.

Industrialization has wrought profound changes in nearly every aspect of life in Finland during the past two generations. Largely as a consequence of the rapid expansion of an increasingly industrial and urban society, and of the substantial improvement of living standards that has been a conspicuous aspect of the process, egalitarian influences in the middle and upper ranges of education have been especially marked. In the field of school and education no less than in other areas the evidence that Finland has long since become a common man's country is abundant and impressive.

Attendance at a secondary school and success in the examinations upon the completion of the secondary school program—the examinations normally guarantee admission to the universities or other higher institutions of learning—mean in Finland and in the other Scandinavian countries great social prestige and often also marked advantage in obtaining employment. The road leading from the lower social and economic strata to the higher normally runs, we might say, through the secondary school and the matriculation examination that marks graduation. The secondary school therefore stands for a good deal more than an eight- or nine-year school in which instruction—basically in liberal arts subjects—is given. It also offers a measure of societal or class evolution, and therefore indicates the process that has destroyed the earlier privileged position of the classes in school and university and has made it possible for the sons and daughters of the common people freely to acquire the learning and competence required for higher social status and income.

The extent to which the doors of increasing opportunity have been opened ever wider is shown by the following facts. On the eve of World War II (in 1938–39) the number of secondary schools was 222, and attendance was about 53,800. By 1950 the number of schools had grown to 338 and that of the students to 95,000. In 1961–62 the schools numbered 492, attended by 228,400 students. The rapid growth indicated by these figures meant, in the main, the establishment of new schools in nonurban areas, making it easier for country folk to send their children to a school that previously had all too often been out of reach because most of the secondary schools were located in the cities or lesser urban communities. Important as had been the leveling and democratic consequences of the trends regarding secondary schools before World War II—the number of the schools in 1920–21 was only 144; that of the students, 32,500—it is clear that the post-1945 period carried the nation far beyond the markers that had indicated the progress recorded by 1939. The significant growth of the secondary schools is one of the meaningful indications of the speed with which the area of privilege in the field of education has been contracted and opportunity for talent and ambition expanded.

II

Finland in the Middle Ages

Finland's geographical location alone invites the surmise that the country's early history differs in many ways from that of the continental nations of Europe. Such is indeed the case, not only with Finland but with other Nordic nations as well. Many developments that profoundly influenced the history of these peoples came late, in some instances centuries later than in the more southern and western areas of Europe. The spread of the Christian religion and church into the North centuries after both had triumphed in the West is but one illustration of the consequences of the fact that these northern peoples lived far away from the main centers of the Western world.

Man himself came late to Finland. The indications are that the first human settlements appeared between 8000 and 7000 B.C. Who the people responsible for the oldest settlements were we do not know, nor do we know their descendants or successors whose anonymous lives span the silent centuries before the Christian era. They have long offered, and continue to offer, a challenge to archaeologists and other scientists, but they have left no visible trace upon the people and nation we have come to know, in history, as the Finns. They can therefore be left to the obscurity to which the irreversible passing of time has long since assigned them.

In doing so we are following Finnish historians who consider the period before the eleventh century A.D. as belonging, for all practical purposes, in the domain of prehistory. The reason for placing the hither time limits of prehistory as late as the eleventh century is simple and obvious: evidence and source materials essential for historical research and narrative are practically nonexistent before the 1100s. It is only well after A.D. 1000 that the bare outlines of a record deserving the term historical begin to emerge. Even moderately recognizable contours of Finland's political development and religious and economic life do not in fact appear, because of the paucity of sources, until the thirteenth century.

This is probably the reason for the energetic and persevering way in which Finnish historians have seized upon and made use of even isolated facts or seeming facts that are assumed to throw light into the dark areas of the nation's past. Tacitus' *Germania* is a good case in point.

Finnish scholars have long since pointed to Tacitus' *Germania* as a source of information about the Finns. The first Finnish translation of this oft-mentioned (and greatly overvalued) work appeared in 1904; the latest was published, with notes, by an outstanding scholar, Professor E. Linkomies, in 1952.

The *Germania* was written in A.D. 98. It is a lengthy essay—it can hardly be called a detailed study—on the character and customs of the people Tacitus calls the Germans. It has the earmarks of a moralizing tract intended to point out to the Romans their own defects and shortcomings by exalting the virtues of the Germans. Be that as it may, our main interest is the fact that Tacitus speaks also of a people he calls the "Fenni." It is this single word that has led Finnish historians to seize upon the *Germania* as a work that must be mentioned whenever the distant past of the Finns is discussed. As Linkomies puts it: "Tacitus' *Germania* is especially interesting to us because it mentions, for the first time, the name of the Finns, 'Fenni,' in the same form in which it has been used since then and still continues to be used."

Actually, Tacitus devotes three short paragraphs of about one hundred words in all to the Fenni, at the close of his essay. His statement is broadly generalizing and contains nothing that can be connected with the Finns. The suggestion that "Fenni" refers to the Lapps has been made by several commentators. The obvious fact is, however, that Tacitus' mention of the "Fenni" must be dismissed as devoid of substance and meaning, for it throws no light whatever upon the Finns or their early history.

It is thus clear that when we contemplate the early history of Finland—or, for that matter, the early history of the North in general—we must remind ourselves that this history, as we normally use the term, begins very late—not until well into the Middle Ages. Dr. Martin Blindheim, Curator of the Collection of Antiquities at Oslo, has aptly remarked that the Middle Ages in Norway began only "with the official introduction of Christianity, during the early part of the eleventh century." Specifically, Dr. Blindheim points out, in Norway the period spans the years 1030–1537, keeping in mind the obvious fact that historical periods usually imply only an approximation to accuracy.[1]

In the case of Sweden and Finland, the situation is basically the same. It has long been traditional among Swedish and Finnish historians to consider the mid-tenth century as the beginning of the medieval period and 1521 as its close. As we have remarked, nothing approaching even moderately adequate sources for the political or the general history of the country or the people exists until well toward the middle or the end of the thirteenth century. In the case of Finland in particular, it is of special interest that it was the Catholic Church in the land that etched the first and sharpest outlines of the meager historical record of the early centuries of the medieval period.

EARLY SETTLEMENT

Long before Tacitus wrote his *Germania*, Finland had been slowly peopled by newcomers who had emigrated from the lands south of the eastern littoral of the Baltic Sea where, as we have seen, the forebears of the Finns had lived for many centuries. The newcomers appear to have established themselves first in the southwest.[2] The

---

[1] *The American-Scandinavian Review*, December, 1963, p. 355.

[2] The earlier conception was that the Finns had formed clans or tribes during the anonymous ages before they began to people Finland, and that these clans or tribes emigrated, in the course of time, to Finland and gradually took pos-

southern coast remained uninhabited while the southwest and the western coasts developed into areas of fixed communities and trading centers. The small numbers of aboriginal inhabitants, presumably nomadic Lapps, were pushed farther inland and north by the new-comers. Between the close of the eighth century and the end of the first millennium of the Christian era, human habitation included a half-dozen areas in western Finland and parts of the Karelian Isth-mus. They served as centers of further dispersion and expansion during the following centuries along river valleys and lake through-ways. By the early 1500s the northern line of habitation had been pushed some two hundred miles north of the south coast. Along the coast of the Gulf of Bothnia settlements ran for the most part only a few score miles inland, the deepest penetration usually being along the numerous rivers. The modest extent of the process is suggested by the fact that the total population of the country appears to have been only about 400,000 as late as the early sixteenth century.

The process of conquering the wilderness and bringing virgin forest land under the plow was carried forward by enterprising peas-ant folk, although later, after the sixteenth century, the Crown also played an important part in the establishment of new holdings. Ulti-mately villages large and small dotted the coastal countryside while the hinterland for the most part continued to serve as open frontier for the hunter and fisherman. The expanding settlements also in-volved western and ultimately southern coastal areas where people of Swedish speech either had lived of old or appeared as new settlers in the early Middle Ages.

The Finns apparently never developed an advanced political organization we call a state. Their basic organization was in clans, probably consisting at least in theory of descendants of common ancestors. Their religion appears to have been worship of the forces of nature, with probably uncomplicated ceremonial presided over by tribal priests. The various clans were in frequent conflict and war between them was in all likelihood not uncommon. If we are to

---

session of the country. The idea rests on nothing more concrete than guesses. The early settlers were, in all likelihood, individuals or relatively small groups of hunters and trappers seeking new opportunities in the frontier area that Finland then was. See J. Jaakkola, *Suomen Historian Ääriviivat* (Helsinki, 1940), p. 13.

draw conclusions from the rich stores of folk poetry and the like collected, compiled, and published in the eighteenth and nineteenth centuries—the *Kalevala* especially comes to mind—one of their chief contributions was in the realm of the imagination in poetry, in song, in story, in folksay. As regards their civilization in general, we do not know enough about it to detail its aspects or manifestations.

THE "CRUSADE" OF 1157

By the eleventh century, the Roman Catholic Church had entered one of the most significant periods of its history. Under its auspices and leadership, the Western world displayed to an unusual degree man's capacity for devoting, in an age of faith, time and energy to religious purposes. The First Crusade, which Pope Urban II (1088–99) preached before a council assembled in Clermont in 1095, stood for a new achievement of the Church and the Papacy. It marked the beginning of a series of crusades, most of them of no particular importance. It was during this period that Rome consolidated and extended its influence in the Scandinavian North, Sweden included. The accomplishments of the Church in the North were made easier by the fact that the theology and law of the Church had by then been systematized and clearly defined, and that the organization of the ecclesiastical hierarchy had been perfected. The centralized control of the Church had become strong enough to serve its manifold purposes and the clergy had come to play vital parts in many phases of secular life. Secular governments and administration in Europe during these centuries were developed and manned, to a considerable degree, by ecclesiastics using the government of the Papacy as a model, and the expertise of the cleric extended to other mundane concerns as well.

The process of carrying through the conversion of Sweden to the Christian creed required about three hundred years, from the first half of the ninth to the first half of the twelfth century. The conversion of some of the outlying provinces was still going on by 1130. The extension of Christianity to Finland was a part of the process in which English churchmen played a prominent role, especially in its decisive stages. Outstanding among them was Nicholas Breakspear, the son of a poor family who ascended in the hierarchy by his own merits and became Pope Adrian IV (1154–59), the only English Pope.

The political conditions and circumstances in Sweden were very different at the time from those that meet the eye after the national state of the sixteenth century had come into being. Much of the story before the year 1300 remains only partly known because of lack of information or records. The events of the period can therefore mostly be seen or sensed only through legends or partisan claims and counterclaims of chieftains and nobles contending for the crown or other advantage. Dynastic strife is writ large over these obscure pages of Swedish history. The century 1150–1250 seems to have been especially filled with rivalries between contenders for the throne, murders of kings, and other evidence of violence and anarchy.

But this was not all. Provincial separatism or particularism was still strong in this distant age. It frequently challenged and at times practically destroyed the authority of the king, modest at best. The crown was elective and continued elective until well into the sixteenth century. Being elective, it was exposed to challenge, deals, and manipulations often productive not of peace and tranquillity but of strife and periodic upheavals.

The kingdom of Sweden was thus not as yet a united state but a loose federation of provinces. In the federation, each province (*land*) enjoyed considerable local rights and autonomy and had a say in the election, or in confirming the election, of the king. The king was chosen by assemblies of Uppland and other freemen. Upon being chosen, the king proceeded from province to province to receive the oath of allegiance from the assembly of each and swore to uphold the laws of the province. Normally the choice of the king was limited to the members of a single family or dynasty but rivalries between contending families eager to capture the crown often violated the rule. The bloody contest between the houses of Sverker and Erik that spanned most of the century before 1250 strikingly illustrates the consequences of wars fed by dynastic ambitions and offers a measure of the great distance separating the kingship of the twelfth century from the centralized national state that emerged after Gustavus Vasa became king in 1523 and proceeded to lay the foundations of a national hereditary monarchy.

These circumstances were decisive for the developments that brought Finland within the world of Catholic Christendom and turned the country into a part of the Swedish realm. The developments of the eleventh and twelfth centuries invite special attention when we turn to note how these all-important events came to pass.

Until about a generation ago, the interpretations and conclusions of the historian Henrik Gabriel Porthan defined many of the conceptions held by Finnish and other Northern historians regarding Finland during the twelfth and thirteenth centuries. Born in 1739, Porthan became interested in Finnish studies while still a young man. He began his career as a scholar in 1762 when he was appointed lecturer at the Finnish University of Turku, where he became professor in 1777. Until his death in 1804, he contributed a lengthening list of studies dealing with Finland and its people. While he devoted much attention to collecting and publishing materials in the field of folk poetry and the like—his *Dissertatio de Poesi Fennica,* which appeared in five parts between 1766 and 1778, was the first important work in the field—he was also led to historical investigations. His most notable researches appeared in a series of over fifty publications in 1784–1800. He also assisted scores of his students in preparing a large number of historical and other studies. Porthan's prodigious labors left no major aspects of Finland's history untouched—making allowance for the limitations under which historians of the period worked—and he well merited the title "Father of Finnish history" which a later generation bestowed upon him.[3]

Among the problems Porthan tried to solve was that of when and how Finland had become an integral part of Sweden, and the concomitant question of when and how Christianity had been brought to Finland.

Porthan's answers to these and related questions were destined to become the stock in trade of Finnish historians for well over a century after his death in 1804. They have been repeated, in one

[3] See my *Nationalism in Modern Finland* (New York, 1931), pp. 22–26, and the sources listed on pp. 242–43.

form or another, times without number. Perhaps the most important single illustration of Porthan's conception of how historical events had unfolded was given by the first history of Finland published in Finnish by Y. Koskinen in 1869. Because of the prestige this work enjoyed for decades after its publication, the appropriation by its author of the Porthan interpretation turned Porthan's conclusions into virtually unchallengeable verities. Despite the fact that serious historical scholarship over the past generation has questioned and changed Porthan's analyses and conclusions, his conceptions are still widely accepted.[4]

Porthan contended that about the year A.D. 1000 and during the following several decades the Finns, still pagans living outside the limits of the Christian Church, made repeated raids over the southern reaches of the Gulf of Bothnia into Sweden, whose people had become Christian some time earlier. The Finns therefore were a nuisance and a danger to Sweden. In order to remove the nuisance and end the danger, King Erik of Sweden undertook a crusade to Finland, the specific purpose being the baptizing of the Finns. The crusade was launched in 1157 (possibly in 1155). King Erik was accompanied by the English-born Bishop Henry of Uppsala. The crusade was successful. The Finns were defeated, whereupon they submitted and were baptized not far from Turku, in southwestern Finland. Swedish dominion was thus established in Finland and the Roman church, having been introduced as a result of King Erik's crusade, speedily extended its sway. By about the year 1300 most of settled Finland had become a part of Sweden and had thus been included in the expanding Catholic Christian world headed by Rome. Both King Erik and Bishop Henry—Henry was killed shortly after the crusade by a Finnish chieftain—were later canonized. Henry became a national saint of Finland.[5]

[4] Y. Koskinen, *Suomen Kansan Historia* (3d ed., Helsinki, 1933), pp. 39–43; Eirik Hornborg, *Finlands Historia* (Stockholm, 1948), pp. 24–28; J. Hampden Jackson, *Finland* (London, 1940), pp. 26–28; E. Jutikkala, *A History of Finland* (New York, 1962), pp. 20–21.

[5] Another eighteenth-century Finnish historian, Algot Scarin, went so far as to locate the field where allegedly the decisive battle of 1157 took place, and he also identified the well where the defeated Finns were baptized. Both were conveniently located close to Turku, the oldest city in Finland. Scarin's claims rest on no historical evidence whatever.

This simple and seemingly logical account of twelfth-century events has been challenged and revised by twentieth-century scholarship. The reason for the challenge and the revision has been the realization that the earlier interpretations rested on most inadequate and unreliable records. The simple fact is that satisfactory Swedish or Finnish or other sources throwing light upon the events alleged do not exist. The only "sources" for the "crusade" in the 1150s and related matters turn out to be legends of saints compiled in Sweden well over a hundred years later, toward the end of the thirteenth century, and a rambling Finnish folk poem dealing with Bishop Henry and his death which dates from about the year 1400 or possibly earlier. The legends do not describe the undertakings of King Erik and Bishop Henry in Finland. The legend of St. Erik and the poem of the death of St. Henry illustrate, instead, the qualities and characteristics which the Christian conception of the Middle Ages considered appropriate and admirable in a good Christian king and a devoted servant of the Church who had joined hands in doing the Lord's work.[6]

The Church of Rome also is almost completely mute regarding the introduction of Christianity into Finland. Available Church documentation contains no information relating to St. Erik or Bishop (St.) Henry. Only two documents have been found that clearly refer to Finland after the middle decades of the twelfth century (none exist from earlier years). One is Pope Alexander III's bull *Gravis admodum* of 1172 and the other Pope Innocent III's bull *Ex tuorum* from 1209.[7] The *Gravis admodum* shows that Finland is seen as a part of the Christian world in the north, and that the Finns have, according to the impression current in Rome, been remiss in according their priests the honor due them and are more concerned about the things of this world than the salvation of their souls. When threatened by "enemies" (that is, Russians) they repair to the Church and seek solace in the ministrations of the preachers

[6] J. Jaakkola, *Suomen Historia* (Helsinki, 1958), Vol. III, chapters 5–6; R. Rosén, "Varhaiskeskiaika," in A. Korhonen, ed., *Suomen Historian Käsikirja* (Helsinki, 1949), I, 105–10, 125–33.

[7] The former bull is usually considered to have been issued in 1171. Jaakkola, *Suomen Historia, III*, 116–18, seems to offer convincing proof to show that the date is 1172.

whom they look down upon and oppress as soon as the danger has passed. In the future, the bull prescribes, the Finns must be forced to remain strong in their faith and in their allegiance to Christian essentials.

The bull of 1209 relates to the appointment of bishops in Finland. It was addressed to the archbishop of Lund—the seat of the bishop was Danish at the time and remained Danish till 1658—and carries no information regarding the events two generations earlier.[8]

The conclusion that emerges from a consideration of the "facts" pertaining to the alleged crusade in 1157 (or 1155) has been summarized by a Finnish historian—after a thorough consideration of the legend in which King Erik and Bishop Henry are mentioned— as follows:

The only information contained in them which may be considered reliable is probably limited to this: a contender for the crown [of Sweden] by the name Erik undertook, some time in the middle of the twelfth century, an expedition to Finland (the purpose of which is not known), that a servant of the Church by the name Henry was killed while traveling in southwest Finland, and that the lives of the two men were in some way connected. All the other claims, especially those that have served as the basis for various assumptions regarding the relations between Sweden and Finland at the time, must be considered untenable unless they can be substantiated in some other way.[9]

Nothing has so far emerged to support the conclusions of Porthan and other eighteenth-century historians, hitherto uncritically accepted by a host of followers. The conventional story of the "crusade" must be relegated to the domain of historical fiction.

In thus placing the story of the "crusade" of 1157 on the growing heap of historical discards, we are still left with this question: When and how did the Christian Church reach the distant shores of Finland, there to minister to a new-won flock of hardy farmers, hunters, and fisherfolk?

---

[8] See R. Hansen, *Finlands Medeltidsurkunder* (Helsinki, 1910), Vol. I, No. 24, pp. 13–14, and No. 48, pp. 19–20. The well-known Swedish *Erikskrönika* (it dates from the 1320s) also lacks reliable information for the period in question.

[9] Rosén, "Varhaiskeskiaika," in Korhonen, ed., *Suomen Historian Käsikirja*, I, 110.

In answering the question, we are confronted with a few fragments of fact floating in an ocean of guesses plain and fanciful. The
fragmentary facts suffice, however, to draw certain definite conclusions. They clearly indicate, among other things, that the Christian
faith and at least some of the practices associated with the Christian
creed and church had spread to Finland long before the alleged
crusade of the mid-1150s. This is shown, among other things, by the
fact that Christian burial customs—for instance, the east-west direction of the grave—had appeared in southwest Finland at least a
century before the "crusade." The Christian way of burial appears
to have become general in the older settled parts of the country in
the course of the century after about 1050, and had spread far into
southeastern Finland by about 1300. "Primitive" Christianity appears
thus to have existed in Finland long enough before the twelfth century to prepare the ground for the prominent position of the
Roman Catholic Church in Finland, especially during the decades
when it was, for all practical purposes, an autonomous *Ecclesia
Finlandiae* under the direct control of Rome.

THE CHURCH AND ITS LEADERS

When Rome brought Finland within the fold, and well into the
thirteenth century, the Church in Finland was under the direction
of the archbishop of Lund in Denmark (Skåne, with Lund, did not
become Swedish until 1658), who administered the Church during
its important, formative years. While the archbishopric of Uppsala
was established in 1164, Pope Innocent II did not place the Church
in Finland under Uppsala until 1216, and it continued in fact to
carry on, virtually as an autonomous ecclesiastical entity under its
own, local leadership, for several decades thereafter.

It was no accident that the first outstanding figure in Finnish
history was not a lay leader or dignitary but a servant of the Church
—a bishop—who flourished during the period in question. Bishop
Thomas was an Englishman who had been canon in Uppsala and
had preached in Finland. He was called to his high office about the
year 1220—the date is uncertain; the first mention of Thomas' name

occurs in records dating from 1234—and held it for the next twenty-five years. An energetic and resolute churchman, he played a prominent part in solidifying the position of the Church in southwest Finland. He labored hard and long to extend its sway east and north, attempting thereby to provide defenses against clans in the interior still outside the fold and Russians (Novgorodians) intent upon obtaining a foothold in Finland.

Bishop Thomas' episcopacy was notable for another reason. Thomas planned and labored for a quarter of a century under the immediate supervision of Rome and not of the archbishop of Uppsala. The Church in Sweden played no directing part in his endeavors. The circumstances under which the Church in Finland carried on its work therefore turned the Church for the time being into something like an autonomous body whose connection with Rome was direct and not through an intermediary, the archbishop of Uppsala.[10]

The general position of the Church was, broadly speaking, identical with that of the Roman Church elsewhere in Europe. By the early 1300s it had gained two important privileges. In 1219 its property was declared free from the king's power to impose fines or other exactions. By 1250 the principle had been generally accepted that its holdings could not be taxed by the Crown. The members of the clergy could be tried only according to canon law, and not by lay courts but by the Church itself. The Church's authority was not limited, however, to the clergy. It claimed and successfully asserted the right to be the final arbiter and judge of lay matters which were considered to belong to the Church: murder, usury, perjury, heresy, sorcery, and, in general, moral infractions and crimes. It was also the founder and director of such schools as there were. For reasons that will be noted presently, the Church left no deep impression on native higher institutions of learning until after Lutheranism had been introduced.[11]

[10] J. Jaakkola discusses these and related matters during the period in question in *Suomen Historia*, Vol. III.

[11] At the Council of Skeninge in 1248 the Church in Sweden-Finland undertook to enforce one of the most troublesome requirements of the Catholic Church, that of celibacy. The fact that charges of and prohibitions against clerical incontinence had to be repeated on several occasions indicates the difficulties involved.

Throughout much of the Middle Ages, the Church was a species of lay authority or state as well as the all-important saver of the souls of men. Until about the middle of the 1200s the Church in Finland was largely independent of the feeble monarchy, whose pretensions to power did not as yet seriously challenge it. The first recorded taxes in Finland were imposed by the Church and served its needs. The earliest forms of administration grew out of its undertakings and purposes and appear to have represented the only real "government" well into the fourteenth century.

By that time the influence of the Church had grown a great deal, not only because its leaders were on the whole able and energetic men but because the Church in Sweden and Finland was an integral part of the centralized system directed from Rome. Lying on the outer northern rim of the Western world, these lands had been wrested from heathendom long after the Church of Rome had already attained its full vigor. This accounts in all probability for the fact that the Church in the North escaped the destructive and prolonged contests between *regnum* and *sacerdotium* that punctuated the history of France, England, and other rising national states in Europe. No disturbing investiture conflict troubled Rome's supremacy, and no significant heresy emerged, before the Reformation, to challenge prelacy or creed.

While Rome's direction and control of the Church in Finland was at times inadequate and intermittent, it sufficed to give the Church a continuity of purpose and policy that the secular authority of the Crown, frequently destroyed by internal disturbances and wars, could not match. When, in the fourteenth century, the Crown began in Finland as well as the rest of Sweden to replace in secular matters the authority of the Church, it adopted and turned to its own purposes the organization and administrative machinery that the bishops of Turku and their colleagues had developed in carrying on the work of the Church.

During most of the Catholic period, the Church in Finland was coterminous with the bishopric of Turku. The leadership of the Church appears to have been, on the whole, of a high order and included a number of zealous, energetic clerics who labored long and hard in the vineyard. Bishop Thomas has already been mentioned as a most important contributor to the developments that bound Finland solidly to the Mother Church and turned the *Ecclesia Finlandiae* into a virtually autonomous ecclesiastical state directly dependent on Rome. Bishops Bengt (1321–38) and Hemming (1338–66) raised the Church to full stature and on occasion successfully resisted the growing pretensions of the Crown. Magnus Tavast (1412–50) and Magnus Särkilahti (1489–1500) were two outstanding pre-Reformation bishops whose concern for church and flock make their careers memorable. It has been suggested that the reason for the excellent church leadership in Finland was partly the fact that after 1291 most of the bishops, and after 1385 all of the bishops, were native Finns.

Not the least interesting aspect of the early history of the Scandinavian nations is the fact that neither church nor state played an important part in the field of higher education before the Reformation. The Danes, the Finns, the Norwegians, and the Swedes had belonged to the Christian world for several centuries before the first university was founded in the North (Uppsala, in 1477; the University of Copenhagen was founded in 1479, the University of Turku in Finland in 1640, and that of Lund in Sweden in 1666). Higher education and degrees could therefore be obtained only abroad, especially at Continental universities.

Paris was, throughout the Middle Ages, the university most favored by Finnish students. The first Finns to obtain degrees in Paris are mentioned in the records for the year 1313. The number increased gradually after 1350. Some of the Finnish students were prominent at the university, serving among other things as *procurators* of the "English nation" (to which the students from the North belonged) or as lecturers. Between 1313 and 1485, forty-one students from Finland obtained masters degrees at Paris. The indications are that not all aspiring clerics who journeyed to Paris were successful in their academic endeavors, thus illustrating the truth of the saying "You go to Paris in search of the seven liberal arts, and you find the seven deadly sins."

The Charles University in Prague, founded in 1348, was the first university in Central Europe. Within some forty years of its founding, students from Finland began to appear on its roster. Between 1382 and 1404, fifteen Finns received degrees at Prague.

After 1404, German universities attracted a growing number of Finns. Leipzig, Erfurt, Rostock, and Greifswald—all founded between 1409 and 1456—were especially favored. About twenty-five Finns were on the rolls of Leipzig. Erfurt had ten in 1429–47, Rostock had some forty before 1521, and Greifswald had fifteen after 1473.

The total number of Finnish students listed in the records of these universities is one hundred and forty for the period before 1525. The figure is probably smaller than the number of students who actually attended. The enrollment records, some of which have been lost or only partly preserved, appear frequently to have included only the names of degree recipients. Also, the student's place of birth was often omitted or imperfectly entered, and students from Finland were at times identified, understandably, by the word "Suecus" or "de Suecia." Although the figures mentioned are modest, they invite the conclusion that especially the leading Finnish churchmen before the Reformation were men of solid training and intellectual achievements. This circumstance no doubt accounts in large measure for the secure foundations upon which the Church rested until it faced the challenge of the Lutheran innovations in the sixteenth century.[12]

The organization of the Church in Finland corresponded in all essentials to that of the Church elsewhere. The ecclesiastical hierarchy included the lowly parish priest on the one hand and the bishop of Turku, the head of the Church in Finland, on the other. The country remained a single bishopric until 1554. By the early years of the 1300s, there were only some forty parishes and churches, nearly all of them in the old, settled or southwestern part of Finland. New parishes and churches were established over the years; they numbered over one hundred at the opening of the sixteenth century. In 1540, when Sweden and Finland were in the early stages of the changes that led to the Protestant Reformation in the king-

[12] Professor A. Maliniemi's detailed studies of Finnish students at foreign universities during the Middle Ages are summarized in his "Opillinen ja Kirjallinen Kulttuuri Keskiaikana," in G. Suolahti et al., eds., Suomen Kulttuurihistoria (Jyväskylä, 1933–36), I, 557–616. In 1350–1450, the bishopric of Turku sent a larger number of students to Paris than any other bishopric in the North (p. 580). See also H. Holma and A. Maliniemi, Les étudiants finlandais à Paris au Moyen Age (Helsinki, 1937).

dom, 136 parishes comprised the Church. All the early churches appear to have been wooden structures; churches built of stone became general in the thirteenth century. The first Dominican monastery appears to have been founded in the year 1249, and the records indicate that the Franciscan order had extended its activities to Finland by the early 1400s. A monastery and convent at Naantali (Nådendal), founded in 1440 on the rules of the Birgittine Monastery established at Vadstena in 1384, was the last monastic organization in the land. None of the monasteries grew large or important in the religious life of the people; Naantali, for example, had only 60 nuns and 25 monks.

One of the fascinating and still open questions that emerges from a consideration of the Church in Finland—it applies no less to Sweden—is this: By what time had the Church of Rome become sufficiently important and persuasive to brush aside the earlier pagan beliefs and superstitions and to impose its creed and moral code on the common folk? When had the ways of looking at things, the mores, of the laity become sufficiently "Christian" to make them embody and reflect the restraints and mandates of the piety and morality exalted by the creed of Rome? We do not really know, but much in the history of these centuries and later generations suggests that the uncompromising expounders of Catholic verities must have been aware, by the time the Lutheran heresy carried the day, that the vineyard of the Lord still sprouted weeds in disheartening abundance.

THE COUNTRYSIDE AND THE CITY

The majority of the people were freemen usually living in organized village communities. The farms or homesteads of the individual households formed the core of the village. The village was surrounded by the cultivated fields. The arable acreage was periodically divided among the households, each household farming a number of strips into which the land was divided. Farming therefore was necessarily a collective enterprise, the ploughing, planting, harvesting, and rotating of crops being a cooperative undertaking. Pasture land and forest land were similarly held in common. The untamed forests and lakes beyond the limits of the settled areas offered, until well into the modern period, opportunities and rewards prized by the hunter and the fisherman.

The extensive forest and lake regions of eastern, central, and northern Finland also held out opportunities to the enterprising farmer or frontiersman. Peasants willing and ready to face the dangers and hardships of the uncultivated frontier of the interior found a vast wilderness to which the principle "the land belongs to God, the King, and the Crown" did not yet apply. The land was theirs to take and use, without the limitations and encumbrances which time-honored custom or lay or church authority imposed in the communities where men had long ago defined the rules regulating landownership and prescribed the methods of using the land, and where the returns of a man's labor were all too often distressingly meager.

The world of the farmer in the frontier areas differed from that of the south and west. The farmer's first task was to clear the forest land and turn it into arable land. His method was simple. It consisted of felling the trees and cutting the underbrush—the work was usually done in the autumn—and burning the dead trees and bushes in the spring. The homesteader gained a twofold advantage, at relatively little labor: he cleared the land, and he added to its fertility because the ashes increased the yield of the land. After the hoeing or plowing—often superficial—sowing took place and in due time a crop was brought in where the forest had previously held undisputed sway. As soon as the land had been exhausted, the homesteader moved on and repeated the process. Wasteful as this type of land use was—it meant extensive rather than intensive farming—it played an important part in speeding the conquest of the wilderness and the expansion of settlement in the frontier areas.

The usual crops consisted of barley, which appears to have been grown from very early times, and oats as well as rye. Wheat was also grown, but only in some of the southern and southwestern areas. Meadows and pasture land were considered an important part of the peasants' resources; they were held and exploited according to a system of rotation applied to the arable land. The hay crops are often mentioned, in the records of the period, alongside of but separate from the grain crops, especially in connection with the evaluation of a farmstead. The importance attached to hay crops has been seen as a measure of the importance of animal husbandry. The usual farm animals were, as we might assume, horses, cattle, sheep, pigs, goats, chickens, and, especially in west Finland, draft oxen. Reindeer were found among the Lapps in the north. The normal demanding daily round of the peasant was probably seldom broken by concerns or interruptions outside those involved in the daily or seasonal rhythms of his existence. Attendance at church or an occasional visit to a provincial or city fair probably stood out, except in the coastal communities where the sea offered a greater variety of distractions and opportunities, as the main diversions from the usual harsh imperatives of the peasant's life.

We have long since grown accustomed to thinking of cities as the centers of political, administrative, social, and intellectual life, and to seeing them as communities essential for flourishing industry, trade, and commerce. In the Scandinavian lands, especially during the Middle Ages and the first centuries of the modern period, the place of the cities was in all respects far more modest. While they were important in trade and commerce, it was usually the royal castle or manor, or the castles and manors of a handful of leading nobles, that represented the locus of authority and administration. How true this was in Sweden-Finland is perhaps best suggested by the fact that the king and the court had no permanent home or base of operations until the sixteenth century. It was only after Stockholm had at long last become the capital that the king was able to abandon the mode of living and governance that had kept him moving from one royal manor or castle to another, keeping him literally an itinerant monarch, and instead assume the advantages of a royal home and a capital in the modern sense of the term.

The urban communities in Finland were, understandably, smaller and less important than those in Sweden. They did, however, account for the commercial, mercantile, and industrial life of the period, and, while their role pales into insignificance by comparison with the meaning and contributions of Finnish cities in more recent times, they left a deep impression upon life in Finland long before, say, the sixteenth century.

Finnish cities were few and small. In the fourteenth century they numbered only seven. All of them were coastal trading centers. Turku (Åbo) was the largest and most important, but it was hardly more than a village, by modern standards. Its population in the late Middle Ages appears to have been about 1,500. Yet Turku was a busy place. It was the center of the country's religious life; as the residence of the bishop who headed the Church in Finland, as the main administrative center of "Eastland," and as a port through which a large part of the country's foreign trade flowed, it played a larger role in Finland's life than its population suggests.

The Finns' trade with the outside world conformed to the general pattern of trade in the Baltic Sea area. It is interesting to note that approximately 1,400 Arabic coins have been found in Finland, most of them on the Åland Islands. The number of western European coins from the early Middle Ages runs to about 7,000, all of them found on the Finnish mainland. It is thus clear that commercial contacts with the outside world were old and numerous. The main Finnish export article was furs; naval stores appear also to have found a market abroad and remained significant long after the fur trade had declined to insignificance.

Turku illustrated in many ways the main aspects of Finnish cities before the sixteenth century. Its foreign trade connections were mostly with Reval, Danzig, Lübeck, and other Hansa cities. Hanseatic merchants were prominent in its life from early times, as is suggested by the list of burghers that has come down to us from the year 1530. It contains the names of 262 burgher families; of the total, 110 had German names, 94 Swedish, and 58 Finnish. While names by themselves do not necessarily indicate nationality, it is clear that German merchants were prominent in the life of Turku, as indeed they were in Stockholm and other Swedish cities. The same was true of the second largest city, Viipuri (Viborg), where the German element remained not only prominent but held a leading position well into the nineteenth century.

Fairs and markets had early become important in the economic life of Finland, not the least because of the attitude of the Church toward them. Fairs were usually held in the immediate vicinity of a church, in connection with saints' days or other significant events on the calendar of the Church. They were often named for saints; the outstanding among the fairs was that held in Turku, by the cathedral, called St. Henry's Fair. The goods bought and sold ranged from exotic wines from Spain and Portugal to salt, from English woollens and fancy textiles from Flanders to dried cod or fat salted salmon, from high-priced furs to simple wooden utensils, from butter, grain, and hides to ale and draft oxen.

The artisan and his guild were also part of the picture. Workers in leather ranged from cobblers to belt and saddle makers; tailors plied their trade alongside of workers in wood or more precious materials, clockmakers, bakers, candlestick makers, and the rest. The Church played a large and continuing role in developing and providing opportunities for the use of the skills of the artisan. The Turku Cathedral, for instance, under construction and change for generations after 1300, was, as one historian has put it, "almost a kind of continuing trade or vocational school for the artisan" throughout most of the Middle Ages. It provided work for stonemasons, brickmasons, iron and other metal workers, and textile workers, to say nothing of sculptors, painters, goldsmiths, and the like. The apprentice, journeyman, and master, as representatives of the hierarchy of the guilds, continued to flourish for centuries and did not disappear from the scene until the abolition of the last remnants of the guild system in the 1860s.

FINLAND AS A PART OF SWEDEN

In taking a look at the emergence of the Church in Finland and in noting certain features of its position and leadership before the sixteenth century, we have ignored other historical developments. We have also for the moment left aside the important and fascinating question of what the historians mean when they speak of Finland as an integral part of Sweden, meaning that the relationship between what we have come to call Sweden and Finland was that of two constituent parts of the larger whole, the kingdom of Sweden.

We have already dismissed as historically untenable the "crusade" of 1157. In doing so, we have also discarded the notion that Finland had been originally brought to political union with Sweden by force of arms. We have rejected these interpretations not only because of the absence of any contemporary fact or record worthy of being recognized as reliable evidence, but more particularly because they run counter to many basic aspects of later social and political conditions that could have emerged only in a society of free men recognized as the equals of the Swedes with whom they constituted a common kingdom.

Finland became a part of Sweden, as we have seen, centuries before Sweden had become a unified state or, to put the matter differently, before the process of unification had destroyed the province as the basic unit of political organization. The process of union with Sweden—the word "union" is used in a loose sense, without the implication it has when applied to the union of states in more modern times—was begun and carried forward before concepts of law, administrative practices, and political authority had acquired clearly defined meaning outside and independent of the province.

Finland was one of the outlying, peripheral areas of the kingdom slowly emerging as a separate political entity. By the close of the 1300s, Finland had become, we might say, one of the constituent provinces of the kingdom. "Swedish law" was applied in the land by then; the first common law code for the provinces of Sweden proper had been completed only some fifty years earlier (about 1350). In view of the fact that changes in laws and their application in those distant days were slow and at times required generations, it appears correct to say that by 1400 the bonds uniting Finland to Sweden probably were no less close than those that held together the Swedish "lands" across the Gulf of Bothnia. Southwest Finland was in all likelihood more closely connected with Stockholm and the central areas of the kingdom than the northern and western provinces of Sweden itself.

The political and legal rights of Finland's inhabitants offer a telling illustration of the country's relationship to the rest of the realm. The Finns possessed all the rights and privileges enjoyed by the inhabitants of Sweden proper. The law recognized no distinction between Swede and Finn, either during the early generations before the provinces had slowly coalesced and grown into the larger, united kingdom, or later after the hereditary monarchy in the sixteenth century had emerged. The inhabitants east and west of the Gulf of Bothnia were equally "Swedes." Finland itself was considered as one of the provinces of the kingdom and participated in the election of the king, as is shown by an enactment in 1362 that read in part: "As twelve men from each bishopric . . . with their Law man [judge] shall choose the king on behalf of all the people, and as Finland is a bishopric . . . it is reasonable that [the Finns] be given in the future the honor enjoyed by the other bishoprics . . . so that whenever a king shall be chosen, the Law man shall come, with priests and twelve men of the common people, to choose the king on behalf of all the people." The privilege was never questioned while the elective kingship lasted.

Important as participation in the election of the king was—at times it meant, actually, little more than a right to confirm an election already held—it was in some ways of less moment than other rights or prerogatives of mainly local significance. Local government rested in the hands of freemen chosen by their fellow freemen. In the administration of justice, the jury system, resting on long and solid tradition, provided participation by the common folk in the formulation of judicial decisions that often concerned them more intimately than the choice of this or that contender for the throne. Not the least significant indicator of the position of Finland in the kingdom was the fact that the Finns were legally "native Swedes" as regards appointments to public office. Finally, they were represented in the Riksdag from the earliest days of the assemblies that could be called by that name until the Riksdag emerged full-fledged in the seventeenth century, and until the centuries-long connection with Sweden was severed in 1808–9.

These circumstances explain the striking differences between the developments in Finland during the centuries we have reviewed on the one hand and those in the lands south of the Gulf of Finland on the other. When the Teutonic Knights established them-

selves in Estonia and Livonia, the natives lost their lands and freedom and were reduced to the status of serfs. In Finland the course
of events was quite otherwise. The reason is simple and obvious.
There never was a Swedish "conquest" of Finland in the sense in
which the word is normally used. The historical record describes
no conquest resulting in the establishment of an alien rule in the
land; tradition relates or embellishes no events that destroyed the
Finns' freedom and liberties, despoiled them of their lands or other
property, and bound them to a status of the unfree.

This basic fact no doubt explains the absence of the antagonisms
between the Swedes and the Finns which often appear when two
different linguistic or nationality groups are brought into contact
with each other. Other factors unquestionably also were involved.
The Finns and the Swedes had not been living in separate worlds,
safely and securely insulated from each other, before the twelfth
century. Swedes had settled, hunted, and traded in Finland long
before historic times. In the absence of evidence to the contrary,
it appears safe to say that gradual, peaceful penetration rather than
invasion, war, and plunder had characterized the process. Also, no
profound differences existed in the culture of the two groups, in
the stage of social development or economic organization reached
by them. Nor did Finland offer easy and tempting opportunities for
material exploitation. The absence of a strong centralized government in Sweden, the country's backward economic development,
and the lack of valuable natural resources in sparsely populated
Finland account for the absence of mounting economic exploitation
leading to friction and violent clashes of interest. The absence of
war in the relations between Swede and Finn during the seven
centuries that preceded Finland's cession to Russia in 1809 is one of
the remarkable phenomena recorded in the history of Europe.
Common citizenship—the word is admittedly anachronistic when
applied to early centuries of the history of the two peoples—in a
common state and a full sharing of the privileges and burdens of
being subjects of the same Crown offered poor soil for prejudices
and antipathies productive of bloody rivalries. Instead, the historical
experience slowly accumulated in the Middle Ages and greatly ex-

panded during the centuries before the nineteenth gave the two peoples a common heritage whose presence and influence can still be seen in modern Sweden and Finland.

GOVERNMENT AND ADMINISTRATION

In the early days of the development of the power of the Crown, the royal manor and castles appear to have been the centers of administration and supervision. The royal castle—that is, castles controlled by the king; royal residence is not implied—ultimately emerged as the main locus or agency serving the purposes of the monarchy. Finland was divided into several "castle counties." The first three had appeared by the early 1300s. The late date of their establishment is by itself an interesting indication of the late and gradual extension of centralized power in Finland. By the end of the medieval period, they numbered nine. Viipuri and Olavinlinna in the southeastern and eastern frontier areas were especially important because they offered protection against the Russians. The castles were important in peace as well as in war, for they were the seats of government in the ordinary sense of the word. While the castles were usually entrusted to military leaders, they were also held in fief by administrators or favorites deserving consideration, or were run by bailiffs directly responsible to the Crown.

Government and administration under the auspices of the Crown meant primarily the maintenance and manning of the royal castles and the collection of taxes and other dues owing to the Crown. The main concerns of the Crown's governmental function did not cover the decision making and action essential for the normal life of local communities or larger, provincial units. Local government and the general ordering of things belonged to the broad domain of self-government into which King and Crown had not yet intruded. Local government or self-rule involved participation by the common freemen as well as by the nobles who represented the apex of the social and economic pyramid.[13] The latter were less important than

[13] The status of the noble in Sweden and Finland depended, in the main, upon service to King and Crown and the ownership of tax-free land. "The

the former, especially in the interior or frontier areas of the country where the Crown fixed the taxes, or came to an agreement with the inhabitants regarding taxes, and then left them pretty much to their own devices.

An outstanding feature of self-government was the institution of the parish (*pitäjä* in Finnish and *socken* in Swedish). The parish was primarily a judicial district but the parish assembly also handled nonlegal matters. The parish included certain minor officials as well as "judges" who were leading figures in the administration of law or in dealing with other questions pertaining to local government. In the course of time, the parish judges were called upon to supervise the care of roads, bridges, taverns, and the like. In degree as the functions and pretensions of the Crown expanded and taxes and other exactions were increased, new local officials appeared and tended in the course of time to become servants of the "central" government rather than representatives of the authority serving the needs and interests of the local folk.

Records that throw light upon the administration of justice do not begin before the close of the fourteenth century. To be sure, such basic aspects of the administration of law as the jury system had evolved in Finland much earlier, although the first instance of a jury, acting in a case involving disputed village boundaries, is mentioned in Turku as late as 1324. It appears, however, that the institution existed centuries earlier. That is, a number of so-called judge circles, composed of twelve stones arranged in a circle and serving as the seats of jurors, have been found and are still extant in Finland. In some instances, the "judge circle" includes a thirteenth stone, placed in the middle of the circle, on which, presumably, the defendant was seated. The "judge circle" is well known, incidentally, in Scandinavia as a whole and appears to offer proof of a primitive form of jury long before the modern conception of a sworn inquest emerged. The indicting grand jury in criminal cases appears to have

land makes a nobleman" expressed the idea well enough, and certain outstanding offices in the keeping of the Crown similarly bestowed noble title. Full freedom from taxation for military service was decreed in 1279, when the nobles were also divided into three classes of which the knights (*riddare*) were the highest.

been a relatively late part of the developing machinery for administering justice.

The medieval legal conceptions and practices included the ordeal, which was assumed to involve a divine revelation and decision regarding guilt; casting lots and compurgation, which involved the use of oaths; the use of witnesses who testified not regarding the facts but presented evidence regarding the character and reputation of the defendant; and ordeal by water, which meant throwing the defendant into a river or a lake (if he sank, he was innocent). Trial by combat appears not to have been unknown, and the penalties imposed ranged from fines to the loss of ears or nose, or running the gauntlet to hanging or beheading (the theft of a copper kettle was enough to bring in a verdict of hanging). Law and the administration of justice showed, as we might well expect, a robust bias in favor of the local community and against the claims to authority of the "central" government.

Death and taxes were as much a part of life in this distant age as in ours. The system of taxation was, strictly speaking, no system at all, because taxes varied from province to province, in manner of payment, and in type of taxable property. The lack of uniformity in taxation was the result of the fact that the different taxes had originally been based on differing agreements and understandings between the taxing authority and the individual or corporate taxpayer. The tithe levied by the Church appears to have been the oldest recorded tax in Finland. Secular taxation was originally based on the number of adult men in a village or district. Arable land later became taxable wherever agriculture flourished, while the forest and frontier regions were taxed on other bases; farming communities paid taxes on the basis of acreage owned and others according to the adult male population.

Taxes were paid in kind until well toward the end of the Middle Ages. The tax collector of the district or of the Crown therefore had to travel about, collecting the grain, hay, malt, cattle, fish, furs, butter, and the like—butter was a common tax commodity in districts where animal husbandry was important—according to prevailing custom or law. The Crown attempted to commute taxes into money payments—King Erik (1412–39) decreed the crown taxes be paid in money—but met with only limited success, and a large part of the taxes continued to be paid in kind well into the sixteenth century. It was unavoidable under these circumstances that the commodities collected were either used by the king, the court, or local authorities or bartered or sold by them. King Gustavus Vasa (1523–60) was in a real sense the leading merchant of his day because of the large volume of "tax goods" collected and sold under the auspices of his efficient administration.

THE KALMAR UNION

The Kalmar Union united the Danes, Finns, Norwegians, and Swedes under a common crown for well over a century. The union was established in 1397 by Queen Margaret of Denmark (1353–1412). A lady of remarkable talents and personality, she was able to manipulate and make use of dynastic connections and baronial rivalries and politics in such a way as to bring about a union of Norway, Sweden, and Denmark. The union was not destined to last, but it had a significant effect, not the least upon Sweden. The destruction of the union in Sweden as a result of the Gustavus Vasa revolt in 1521–23 ushered in the beginnings of a genuine national monarchy—a hereditary national monarchy at that—and set the nation upon a new course that carried it far from the moorings of the late 1390s.

Margaret was the daughter of King Waldemar of Denmark. She became a queen upon marrying King Haakon VI of Norway, to whom she bore a son in 1370. Six years later, in 1376, upon the death of her father, her son Olav was chosen king. Because of his minority, Margaret became regent of the kingdom. Her husband, King Haakon, died in 1380, and his crown went by heredity to Olav, then ten years old. His mother became guardian of the boy and regent in Norway also. The son came of age in 1385, at the age of fifteen, but died two years later. The "King of Denmark and Norway and Heir to the Kingdom of Sweden"—Olav's father had claimed the Swedish throne, and the son continued the claim in his official title—had thus left an exceptional heritage and opportunity to his mother, Queen Margaret, an ambitious and robust woman then in her thirty-fifth year. She was chosen reigning queen in Denmark, regent of Norway, and assumed the title "Queen of Sweden."

The Norwegian claim to the Swedish throne had been successfully challenged by Albrecht, who had made himself king of Sweden, as the result of a coup, in 1364. The following two decades witnessed a continuing contest between Albrecht and many of the leading barons determined to resist the growing pretensions of the king. The upshot of their machinations was that the Council of State and the nobles recognized Margaret as the regent of Sweden in 1388. Albrecht was captured and put in prison a year later.

Skillfully navigating the tortuous course of royal and baronial politics, Margaret brought forth a grandnephew of hers, Erik— Erik was born in 1382 and was only a child at the time—as candidate for the three thrones. She was successful: Erik was elected king of Norway in 1389, chosen king of Denmark in 1396, and crowned king of Sweden in 1397. A dynastic union had thus been brought about. While the Kalmar Union never became a fully consolidated union of the three kingdoms—each retained its own laws, for instance—it stood for a political entity of impressive outward dimensions, although its combined population probably did not exceed 1,500,000, over one half of the number being Danes.

In some respects, the Kalmar Union brought concrete advantages to the people of the Swedish kingdom. Peace was secured for a relatively long period after 1397. During the early decades of the union, the lawlessness and the exactions of the higher nobility were held within bounds that lightened the burdens of the common folk. After Margaret's death in 1412, however, the union became responsible for policies and developments that imposed burdens on Sweden's inhabitants, the Finns included. In 1426, for instance, her successor Erik became involved in a war with the German Hansa towns. A blockade of Swedish foreign trade, with attendant serious consequences for the nation's economy, was one of the harmful results of the war. Increased taxes, made especially onerous because of declining trade, and the actions of inconsiderate Danish bailiffs used in Sweden to enforce the law and carry out measures considered essential by the Danish king ultimately created opposition culminating in revolts. Outstanding among them was the revolt headed by Engelbrekt, a member of a prominent mining family in the Dalarna province. It began in the summer of 1434 and quickly developed into a Swedish national war of independence against the Danish-controlled union monarchy. The war was not supported by all the Swedes, however. Stockholm, for instance, remained a stronghold under Erik's control, and the Swedish Council of State itself came to an agreement with the king in October, 1434, that favored his cause.

Engelbrekt thereupon had recourse to a move that was destined to have a lasting effect upon the history of the Swedes and the Finns. He convened a meeting of representatives of the nobles, the clergy, the burghers, and the peasants—some historians doubt that the peasants were involved—in an assembly in January, 1435, at Arboga. The Arboga assembly has been called the first Riksdag in Sweden's history. It may be said to have represented the idea that the people had a right to be heard and to participate in measures upholding law and order. The Arboga meeting elected Engelbrekt regent of the realm, although the nobles were by no means united behind him. They favored the setting up of the Council of State as the government of the kingdom, leaving the union king without any real power. A narrow oligarchy sustaining the rights and the privileges of the nobles was thus put forth as the solution of the nation's problems.

Before the problem was solved, Engelbrekt's attempt to carry his campaign through to victory was ended when he was murdered on April 27, 1436. His death did not, however, save King Erik from further trouble. The Norwegians revolted against Erik in 1436, other difficulties emerged, and he was deposed in 1439. While the union was restored two years later when Erik's nephew, Christopher of Bavaria, was elected king of Norway and Sweden (in 1441–42), it again fell apart in 1448 when Christopher died without leaving an heir. The following seventy years witnessed repeated crises caused by attempts to revive or to break the union. Wars, revolts, and conspiracies punctuate the history of the period; Sweden and Denmark were at war through most of the 1450s and intermittently in the 1490s and in 1501–23.

Finland did not occupy the center of the stage during the long decades of conflict and outright war between the supporters and the opponents of the Kalmar Union, but the consequences of the union were reflected clearly enough in Finland as well. Only a few Finnish leaders had attended the discussions in Kalmar in 1397 that resulted in the union, and they had obviously played only a minor part in the legal arrangements involved. While Queen Margaret lived, her grandnephew and successor Erik was at least nominally in charge of the administration of the Finnish part of Sweden—Erik visited Finland twice—with the result that for the time being Finland's connection with the Swedish center of government in Stockholm was loosened. When the Engelbrekt revolt in Sweden challenged Erik's hated rule, west Finland joined the rebels, although some of the Finnish leaders attempted, as did several Swedish leaders also, to shore up the union. In 1438–39, mutinies broke out in central and eastern Finland, partly caused by the uprisings in Sweden. These turbulent years recorded an unplanned change in what might be called the political status of Finland. The so-called Law of the Land (*landslag*) of 1442, promulgated by Christopher, the successor of Erik, provided anew for Finland's participation in the election of the king. Finland had been divided, by 1442, into two judicial provinces, each headed by a Law Man (*lagman*). The law of 1442 stated that both provinces were thenceforth entitled to send representatives to the assembly convened to elect a new monarch, and provided for special procedures designed to safeguard the Finns' interests. If weather or other circumstances prevented the representatives from attending the Uppland assembly at Mora, or if the king could not appear in Finland in person, the Lord High Steward (*Drots*) or some other member of the Council would come in his place, meet with the bishop, deliver the king's solemn oath of assurance, and accept the people's oath of allegiance. These arrangements remained in force for over a century, until the monarchy became hereditary in 1544, but they meant little during the chaotic decades that preceded the end of Sweden's membership in the union.

One of the outstanding leaders of the effort to assert Swedish rights and interests in the Kalmar Union after the 1430s was Karl Knutsson. Co-regent with Engelbrekt in 1435–36, he became sole regent in 1436 and retained the office till 1440. Upon being forced to leave Sweden in 1440, he went to Finland, where he proceeded to secure his own position in the contest against Denmark and maneuvered to bring about a withdrawal of Finland from the union. East Finland, less securely controlled by Stockholm than west Finland, became his base of operations. He was later elected king of Sweden three times—he occupied the throne in 1448–57, 1464–65, and 1467–70—and this circumstance alone suffices to measure the ups and downs of high-level politics during the mid-decades of the union period. After his second forced abdication in 1465—he was replaced by the King of Denmark, Christian I—Karl Knutsson returned to Finland, there to rally the support that later sustained the "national" regents of Sweden and ultimately contributed to the collapse of the Danish cause in Finland as well as in Sweden proper.

The Danish intrigues and plans designed to shore up the union included the use of foreign powers to thwart Swedish purposes. In 1493, for example, the Danish king entered into an alliance with the Grand Duke of Muscovy. Muscovy had by then (in 1478) absorbed Novgorod, the seat of much trouble for and the source of many an earlier invasion of Finland. The Russians launched their invasion in 1495 and, while they failed to take Viipuri, they devastated large areas of eastern and parts of central Finland during 1496. The war was inconclusive and was ended by a peace concluded for six years in March, 1497, which left boundary and related matters where they had been since 1323. The peace was renewed in 1504 for twenty years and for sixty years in 1510. The fact that Denmark had not joined the Russians in the attack on Finland eased the defense position of the country but gave no assurances regarding the future.

While the dangers from the east seemed to be receding, continued union problems and conflicts darkened the horizon. Sweden was almost continuously at war with Denmark after 1503. Some of the castles and areas in Sweden fell into the hands of the Danes, and military and naval operations were extended to Finland as well. After 1505, the Danes raided the coasts of Finland for several years; the raid upon Turku in 1509 was particularly disastrous in that the city was sacked and the cathedral burned. After a few years of uneasy truce, the Danes renewed the war in 1517. Sweden proper was again the main scene of action but Finland also inevitably became involved. Christian II of Denmark, who had come to the throne in 1513, was victorious. The Swedes laid down their arms in 1520—Stockholm surrendered on September 7—the forces that had carried on the fight in Finland surrendered, and the country was occupied by Danish troops after solemn promises that a royal pardon would be extended to all involved in the recent war. Christian II himself was crowned king of Sweden in November. The union had seemingly been reestablished once again, fully under the control of the Danish monarch.

The coronation and the festivities connected with it turned out to be, however, the beginning of the end of the union. The reason was a mass trial, famous in the history of the North, resulting in the execution of over fourscore leading members of Sweden's nobility (including members of the Council of State), high-ranking clerics, and prominent burghers. Immediately after Christian's coronation, members of the Council, noblemen, and Stockholm burghers were called to an assembly in the Royal Castle. The date was November 7. Archbishop Gustaf Trolle, who had been ousted from his see in 1517 by a decision of the Riksdag—the decision had led to the placing of Sweden under a papal interdict and the branding of the Riksdag leaders as heretics—presented, by prearrangement with the king, a lengthy indictment against persons allegedly responsible for the Riksdag decision in 1517, the city of Stockholm, and others. Trolle demanded punishment for the crime against the Church and compensation for the losses suffered by the Church and himself. The company invited to the castle were detained; the accused were brought before an ecclesiastical court the next day, found guilty of heresy, were at once turned over to the secular arm, and were beheaded forthwith in the Stockholm market place. Among the victims of the "Stockholm Blood Bath" were two bishops, many burghers whose only crime was, at the most, that they had opposed the oppressive rule of Christian II, and a large number of nobles many of whom had neither been formally indicted nor brought to trial.

The executions were continued after the main executions in Stockholm and were later extended to the provinces. Among the victims were leading Finnish lords who had sided against Christian and now had to pay the price for having trusted the pledged word of the king.

It is obvious that Christian's action, shocking even in his own day, was intended once and for all to destroy and eliminate the stubborn Swedish opposition to the Danish-controlled union. He was probably sustained in his decision by the fact that Swedish nobles and other leaders had frequently supported, in the past, not the "national" but the Danish cause. He did not realize that in sending scores of honorable men to their graves in the dark autumn days of 1520 he became the gravedigger of the union itself. His bloody resolve brought forth a reaction and a revolt, under the leadership of Gustavus Vasa, destined to free Sweden from the union incubus, so that the country was able to emerge at long last as an independent national monarchy.

III

Finland in Early Modern Times, 1521–1808

GUSTAVUS VASA AND THE REFORMATION

The Reformation in Sweden and Finland differed in several important respects from the developments that challenged and destroyed the Roman Church in some other parts of Europe. Perhaps the outstanding difference was the absence of protest against the real or imaginary abuses and malpractices of the Church. It was not the failings of the clergy or alleged scandals within the Church that created anticlericalism determined to challenge and change the old order. Nor do we find that vital concerns with the Church's teachings, leading to religious individualism or heresy destructive of creed and church, precipitated the trouble. The fact that the Reformation did not foment any kind of social revolt and left no aversion to a "foreign" church also suggests that the change-over from the old to the new was not set in motion and carried through by broadly based dissatisfactions and resentments. The Reformation in Sweden did not come from below. The common people remained on the whole indifferent. They neither rose in revolt against the Church nor bestirred themselves to defend it. The revolt came from above, as a result of the purposes and undertakings of the new national leader, Gustavus Vasa.

When Gustavus Vasa, the leader of the uprising against the Danes, became the king of Sweden in 1523, he found himself as the head of a state hard beset by great difficulties. Stockholm was still in the hands of the Danes, who also held other fortified places, including parts of Finland. The attitude of many of the leading nobles toward the new regime was uncertain, and the Church could not as yet be counted on unqualifiedly to support it. Gustavus Vasa could probably never have carried the day had it not been for the aid of Lübeck, the important Hansa town. Lübeck's support—it consisted of ships, troops, and money—had been dearly bought: extensive, very favorable, and costly commercial privileges had been granted to the city. The royal treasury was practically nonexistent, yet the demands for money and other resources were incessant. The continuing war with Denmark and disturbances and conspiracies at home suggested the long distance separating the dangerous todays from the peaceful tomorrows.

In his attempt to breast the rising tide of financial difficulties, Gustavus Vasa had recourse to new or increased taxes and other levies. He also turned to the Church, insisting upon the use of its great resources. He obtained a contribution from the Church in 1522, took a part of its property as a loan in 1523, forced another contribution in 1524, and thereafter imposed regular levies collected by the bailiffs of the Crown. These measures did not produce the results desired. The real assault upon the Church was begun at the Västerås Riksdag in 1527. The decisions of the Riksdag secured the foundations of the national monarchy, provided the Crown with new financial resources, and actually marked the victory of the Lutheran cause.

The main results of the Riksdag meeting were embodied in the Västerås Edict. The edict sealed the fate of the Catholic Church in Sweden. It provided that the "surplus" property and revenues of the Church be transferred to the Crown and that the nobles could, upon presenting "valid" claims, recover from the Church and religious houses lands given or deeded to them since 1454. The tithe and Peter's pence were henceforth to go to the king. No future ecclesiastical appointment would need confirmation or investiture by Rome. Another ordinance provided that the clergy were subject, in all temporal matters, only to lay courts, and that the "pure word of God" should henceforth be preached throughout the land. The latter provision was the only doctrinal pronouncement of the Riksdag of 1527. The specific acceptance of the Lutheran creed and practice did not come until nearly seventy years later, in 1593. The king was the head of the Church and as such reserved to himself the right to final decisions regarding it.

The results of the Västerås meeting were momentous in Finland as well as in Sweden. The estates previously held by the Church reverted to the Crown. In Finland, some eight hundred homesteads or estates and scores of lesser properties were taken over by the state. The clergy were now paid—the salaries were substantially reduced —for all practical purposes, by the state. The higher clergy in particular were exposed to various exactions and levies. Nor was the movable property of the Church immune. In 1530, for example, the king decreed that one of the bells in each church should be turned over to the Crown; the bell could be kept, however, if the congregation offered a money payment in its place. Most churches appear to have preferred to "buy" back their church bell. Nothing seems to have been too small or trivial for the nosy servants of the king who went about inspecting, searching, and confiscating: used parchment was taken for covers of account books in the king's chancellery; liturgical vessels of silver and gold, as well as vestments, normally considered indispensable for religious services, were prized loot; and in some instances the copper roofs of churches were peeled off, melted, and used for coins or other purposes.

The nobles followed the example of the Crown in despoiling the Church. In taking advantage of the right to recover lands in the possession of the Church since 1454, many a noble paid scant attention to the restrictions defined at the Västerås Riksdag. Nor were ordinary freemen slow to claim and seize whenever possible. Confiscations and appropriations were carried on in a manner that ultimately prompted Gustavus Vasa to issue strict orders against "seizing and snatching, for no reason and without right to do so, the holdings and property of the Church." The monasteries and convents also suffered and ceased to function not long after the Västerås Riksdag had authorized a "redistribution" of property greater than any recorded before the breakup of the Kalmar Union.

When Gustavus Vasa proceeded to lay hands upon the Church, it was in some ways in a markedly vulnerable position. The Church was wealthy. Especially by comparison with the Crown—that is to say, the lay state—it was very well off. It has been estimated that the Church owned well over 13,000 farms or estates by the turn of the sixteenth century and that its annual income was about twelve times the total revenues of the state. In some of the more prosperous provinces, the Church held from one fifth to one third of the homesteads. The over-all figure appears to be about 21 percent, while the Crown held somewhat less than 7 percent and the landowning peasants as distinguished from renters or leaseholders about 52 percent. In Finland, the Church had not gained land in corresponding amounts; over 90 percent of the homesteads were in the hands of landowning farmers. The possessions of the Church were thus extensive and conspicuous enough to expose it to jealousy and attacks by those who wanted to divest it of its wealth.

The Church was vulnerable, by the 1520s, in another sense as well. The deposed Archbishop Trolle, the highest representative of Rome in Sweden, had been conspicuously identified with the bloody business in Stockholm in November, 1520. He was now anathema to every patriotic Swede. Yet the Pope, under the mistaken impression that Trolle could be reinstated and that Christian II would succeed in reestablishing his authority, continued to support both the archbishop and the Danish king. The supporters of Gustavus Vasa found it easy to see opponents of the "national" cause in the spokesmen of the Church and welcomed the opportunity to reduce their influence and undermine the position of the Church.

The Church suffered from still another difficulty. It was almost completely leaderless. The former Archbishop Trolle was an outlaw; two of the leading bishops had been beheaded in Stockholm; two others, including the Finnish bishop of Turku, Arvid Kurki, had died in 1522; two Danish bishops whom Christian II had foisted upon the Swedes had fled the country; and two others were old and unable to carry on. Only one bishop, Brask of Linköping, stood fast as defender of the established Church but was not able to provide the Church with the kind of popular support that alone would have sufficed to give it immunity from the assaults about to be directed against it.

Gustavus Vasa became unavoidably involved in the complicated question of filling the vacant sees. Late in 1522 and in the early months of 1523, some of the cathedral chapters proceeded to elect new bishops who lacked, as yet, proper papal investiture. In the course of the efforts made to regularize the situation, the Swedish Council had occasion to address itself to the papal curia in Rome and urged that native bishops be designated, a new archbishop appointed, and essential reforms within the Church carried out. In the course of subsequent developments, Gustavus Vasa intervened in the situation, forced the ousting of two of the bishops recently chosen, proclaimed the ousted Archbishop Trolle—who continued to enjoy the support of Rome—to be "not only unworthy of the status of a priest but not fit to live," and undertook to fill the vacancies without consulting the Pope. Official connections between the king and the papacy were ended for all practical purposes in May, 1524. Sweden thus became the first state in western Christendom to break away from Rome.

While the developments noted were decisive in bringing about the rupture between Sweden and Rome, religious impulses traceable to Luther were by no means absent. A number of Swedes and Finns had fallen under the influence of Luther's teachings at Wittenberg by the early and middle 1520s. Laurentius Andreae and Olaus Petri in Sweden, and Pietari Särkilahti, Mikael Agricola, and Paavali Juusten in Finland, to mention a few of the leading figures, all performed important service in transmitting the essentials of the Lutheran conceptions and practices to the Swedish realm. Incidentally, the work of these and other men during the decades when the Reformation was carried through affords us one of the many striking illustrations of the fact that Finland's and Sweden's history before the nineteenth century is indeed in many and important ways a seamless garment. It would be misleading, however, to imply that the Lutheran Church emerged primarily as the result of doctrinal reform or changes brought about by zealous clerics. It was King and Crown, as we have remarked, that furnished the essentials for the establishment of the new church.

The Church lost not only most of its property and its earlier leadership in the community but also part of its former ceremonial. The mass was abolished. The colorful processions of earlier days were proscribed; the use of holy water, customary baptism, and extreme unction were no longer allowed; the display and the worship of relics were likewise prohibited. The use of Latin was reduced and ultimately eliminated, and the vernacular took its place. The Lutheran notion that the believer should be given an opportunity to learn the real, inner meaning of Christian precepts placed a new and heavy accent on exhortation and instruction. This became the main purpose and function of the sermon. The sermon could serve its purpose, obviously, only if it was delivered in the vernacular. It therefore followed that the "reformers" of the period placed their confidence in the saving of the Christian community by instruction in the essentials of the faith. This could best be done by translating the Bible and other sacred repositories of the Christian creed and prescription into the vernacular. One of the early accomplishments of Luther was the German translation of the Bible. In Finland, Mikael Agricola, one of the leading men of the Reformation, became the pioneer in the field.

Agricola's first contribution was a primer published in 1542. He was the author of several other religious writings, including a Book of Prayers, and he had translated and published the New Testament by 1548. Another servant of the reformed Church, Bishop Paavali Juusten—Juusten became bishop of Viipuri in 1554, when Finland was divided into two bishoprics, and Agricola became bishop of the Turku diocese—produced a Finnish translation of the catechism and also a collection of psalms. These and other less important beginnings of Finnish sixteenth-century religious literature apparently sufficed slowly to deepen and expand the common man's understanding of the religious and moral injunctions of the gospel of Christ, for they continued to be used for generations after the troubled decades of the Reformation.

If we try to evaluate the meaning and consequences of the Reformation in Finland, we are driven to the conclusion among other things that the generality of the clergy probably remained as ignorant and ill-suited to their offices as they appear to have been before the sixteenth century. Bishop Agricola remarked in the preface to his translation of the New Testament that the priests had taught in the past, and still continued to instruct their charges, "in a manner that is both nasty and lazy." His main purpose in translating the New Testament was, as he put it, to make sure "that not a single preacher or teacher could cover up his laziness by claiming that he did not know either Latin or Swedish."

It is also clear that the schools suffered, for some time, as a result of the Reformation. Discussions among the Finnish clergy, in the late 1560s and the middle 1570s, for instance, disclosed that ill-trained, ignorant students for the ministry had been ordained, that pastors had been appointed who were drunkards, debauched violators of the laws of man and God, and worse. It appears incontestable that a goodly part of the low status of clerics in Finland during several decades after the 1530s was a consequence of the disruptive results of the Reformation not only within the Church itself but also in the schools previously founded and run for and by the Church.

TRENDS IN GOVERNMENT AND LAW BEFORE 1734

It was inevitable that Gustavus Vasa should change and in some degree revolutionize the monarchy and the institutions that had sustained it of old. He introduced a strong personal rule as quickly as circumstances permitted. At the Västerås Riksdag in 1544 he succeeded in having the crown declared hereditary in his own family, thus ending the elective monarchy that had existed since time immemorial. His government was stern and exacting. Landed property being the only important source of wealth and revenue, Gustavus increased the royal domains as well as his own wealth by expropriating and confiscating farms and estates throughout the kingdom. It has been estimated that, by the time he died in 1560, his private holdings included about 5,000 estates and that he had added some 11,000 estates to those of the Crown. The line separating the king's property from crown property was, understandably, most vague at times.

The changes in the monarchy and royal government in general were felt in the Finnish part of the kingdom as well as the Swedish. No revolutionary changes were introduced, but a marked centralization of government was an inevitable consequence of Gustavus' personal rule. His rule was personal especially in the sense that no regular or permanent body of officials or civil servants was developed, and no fixed, well-defined departments of administration were evolved. Gustavus Vasa managed and governed his bureaucracy as if he were running a huge personal business or enterprise; he planned, devised, ordered, directed, scolded, and meted out punishment with seemingly never-failing energy and resolve. Subjects in positions high as well as low felt his anger and had to accept his outbursts of wrath. Typical of the king's ways was his sharp letter to Erik Fleming, his most trusted supporter in Finland, sent to Fleming because of complaints that he and other nobles had imposed illegal exactions and services upon the people. "If you and the many others there," wrote Gustavus, "don't abstain . . . I shall see to it that we find means of ousting you people, in a way that will make your bones rattle, from the bailiffs' houses." Hanging was not an uncommon reward for servants of the Crown found guilty of wrongdoing. The fact that the number of royal bailiffs was multiplied by three during Gustavus' reign offers a measure of the extension of royal jurisdiction at the expense of earlier local, baronial jurisdiction.

Viewing the kingdom as his own possession, Gustavus did not hesitate to make use of its resources in providing for his own kin. He bestowed dukedoms upon his sons. One of his three sons, John, ultimately destined to succeed to the throne, was given most of Finland as a duchy in 1556. Some writers have seen the "Duchy of Finland" as marking the emergence of a separate political organization in the eastern half of the kingdom. While John maintained his court for a few years in Turku Castle and appears to have provided himself with many of the outward aspects of a rule separate from that of Sweden proper, the duchy arrangement never became anything more than a temporary phase in Finland's history. The country never assumed or obtained a status other than that of an integral part of the larger kingdom. The inhabitants of the duchy still took an oath of allegiance to the king; all royal ordinances obtained in the duchy; a separate assembly for the duchy was specifically forbidden; and the king retained the power to appoint the bishops, the "Law Men," and other high officials in the duchy.

John fell out in 1562 with his brother Erik XIV, who had succeeded to the throne two years earlier, was imprisoned in 1563, and remained a prisoner of the king until he succeeded in ousting Erik and ascending the throne in 1568 (he ruled till 1592). The "Duchy of Finland" came to an end when John was imprisoned. The government and administration of the country was again carried on in the manner evolved by Gustavus Vasa: the day-to-day business of government was in the hands of leading Finnish and other nobles who were servants of the king and not independent governors. Henrik Horn in the 1570s and Klaus Fleming later—he was governor of Finland in 1591–97—were outstanding representatives of the Finnish lords in the service of King and Crown during the closing decades of the eventful sixteenth century. In 1581, during the burdensome war with Russia (see pp. 88–89), King John designated Finland as a grand duchy. The new "title" was bestowed on the land of the Finns in recognition of their contribution to the war, but it meant no change in the actual status of the country or of its people.

We have noted that the early stages of the revolt in Sweden against the Kalmar Union—under Engelbrekt in the 1430s—led to the convocation of an assembly that has come to be considered the origin of the Swedish Riksdag. Gustavus Vasa made use of the four-estate Riksdag on seven occasions in pursuing his personal and dynastic purposes. His sons and other successors convened no less than forty-six Riksdags before the 1630s; some of them, like the one Gustavus Adolphus called together in Finland in 1616, were only provincial meetings yet were competent, according to views then current, to advise the king and act for the four estates of the realm—the nobles, the clergy, the burghers, and the peasants. Others included representatives of only two or three of the estates. Gustavus Vasa summoned over thirty such meetings in the course of his long reign. The composition and functions of the Riksdag were gradually regularized only after 1617 when its powers and functions were loosely defined. The Riksdag remained for many years thereafter an inadequate representative of the nation. This is shown by the fact that, beginning in 1627, it became customary to appoint a Secret Committee to handle all important business, the influence of which was out of all proportion to its numbers. It decided questions on behalf of the whole Riksdag and at times replaced it altogether. The membership of the committee was composed of nobles, clergy, and burghers; only rarely could the peasants make their voice heard in its deliberations. Neither the Riksdag as a whole nor the Secret Committee encroached upon the prerogatives of the the Crown until after the end of the disastrous Northern War in the eighteenth century. Meanwhile the central government was reorganized in 1634, in a manner intended to meet the needs and requirements of the time.

The Form of Government of 1634 defined the broad outlines of a strong central government, partly clarifying and confirming practices that had emerged during the preceding two decades, and at the same time provided a clearer prescription of the essentials of local government. The 1634 statute was supplemented in the following year by a general set of instructions for the provincial governors.[1]

The central government in Stockholm was organized in five departments each of which was in charge of a specific area of public business (justice, finance, army and navy, foreign affairs, and the king's correspondence). Each was headed by a state councilor or, in modern terms, a minister. The departments were collegial bodies; they were permanent central offices whose functions and authority were delegated to the department as such and not to any member of it. The State Chancellor was president of the Chancery and as such was in charge of the conduct of foreign affairs as well as the work of offices dealing with domestic matters; he was, as we might put it, foreign minister and minister of the interior. A Department of Accounts administered state revenues and expenditures. Because of the nature of its function, the department was in close and constant contact with provincial governments and therefore stood out, in many ways, as the most important department of the central government. The administration of justice was under the supervision of the

---

[1] "Governor" is a title that Swedish and Finnish usage has tended to shun since the seventeenth century, although "governors-general" were occasionally appointed either in the place of or to supervise *Landshövdingar*. The 1634 Form of Government mentioned only the *landshövding* (*maaherra* in Finnish), which has remained a part of Swedish nomenclature for over three centuries. After 1809, *guvernör* or *kuvernööri* was used in Finland until 1918. Upon becoming independent, the Finns abandoned the Russian-sounding designation and went back to the earlier term.

Lord High Steward (*Drots*), who was the president of the Svea Royal Court.

The "constitution" of 1634 also contained provisions regarding the Riksdag. It may be said that it was only in 1634 that the Riksdag was recognized as a legal organ of the state system. The statute decreed among other things that the decisions of the Riksdag "may be opposed by nobody who owes obedience to King and Realm." It also prescribed that one representative, instead of two or three as had been the case formerly, be sent to the Riksdag from each district. The right of representation and participation in the labors of the Riksdag was often considered a burden rather than a privilege. The farmers, especially in the more distant parts of the kingdom, including Finland, appear to have found it difficult to appreciate the expense involved in sending their representative to Stockholm to attend Riksdag sessions where he could normally only humbly petition, complain, or submissively accept and agree to the decisions of his betters. Often, too, the farmers' representative in Stockholm found himself in dire straits, having been inadequately supplied with money by his district, and dependent for "food money" on the royal or Riksdag purse. In such instances in particular the Crown found it easy to exert pressure upon members of the fourth estate.

The statute of 1634 and certain earlier arrangements were, in some respects, of special significance for Finland. The Chancery had included, after 1620, an official assisted by a clerk whose responsibility was the preparation of matters having to do with Finland. A separate Finnish provincial office was established in the Department of Accounts. From the 1620s onward, proclamations, decrees, and the like were issued in Finnish as well as in Swedish more frequently than formerly.

Provincial and local government was likewise revised. One aspect of the changes is particularly interesting because it reveals a good deal of the simple and as yet informal ways of the older order that was now being changed: the borders of the provinces were for the first time clearly and sharply drawn and the responsibilities and rights of the governors were set down, as was also their strict accountability. The governor was the head of the civil administration in all its branches; he was responsible for the maintenance of law and order and, while he did not act as a judge, he was expected to see to it that the courts administered law in an impartial manner. Later statutes and ordinances elaborated the measures of the 1620s and the 1630s. The administrative machinery that emerged as the result of the innovations noted provided the provincial government with the organs needed to transact the expanding business of the provinces. One of the officials, the provincial secretary, emerged in the eighteenth century as a particularly important personage in whose hands a large part of provincial concerns rested.

The changes and improvements in the area of provincial government were of great importance to Finland. Finland (and other more or less peripheral parts of the kingdom) had provided in the past, because of her relative isolation from the locus of the central government, opportunities for venal and unscrupulous officials whose activities victimized the common folk. While mismanagement and corruption by no means disappeared after the reforms of the 1630s and later, the relatively elaborate and efficient devices for enforcing accountability in offices high and low gave the common people added protection and safeguards against exploitation. A special accounts office was established in Turku. It served as a go-between for Finnish provincial secretaries and the Department of Accounts in Stockholm; the general accounts for Finland were prepared by it.

The Stockholm Blood Bath and the subsequent emergence of the monarchy of Gustavus Vasa had deprived the nobles of much of their leadership and earlier aristocratic prestige and privilege. The dynastic rivalries of Gustavus' sons enabled the nobles to recover some of the lost ground, especially after John III came to the throne in 1568. John issued a charter in 1569 which enumerated and confirmed the special rights—nominal under Erik, John's predecessor —of the nobility. Other charters and arrangements followed. Before long the titled nobility, the counts and the barons, were granted entailed estates and the right to collect and retain certain taxes and revenues. Despite later obstacles and reverses, the noble class succeded in securing and extending its position and special privileges. In 1617, for example, all higher posts in the service of the Crown were specifically reserved to nobles. The reorganization of the

Riksdag in the same year created a separate House of Nobles in which the first estate thenceforth met. The lines separating the nobles from the commoners were at the same time sharply drawn.

The developments affecting the nobles were destined to influence, especially in the seventeenth century, the provincial and local governmental rearrangements we noted in discussing the reforms of 1634 and the years that followed. The leading aristocrats and nobles in general acquired crown lands, control of provinces, supervision of the administration of justice, and other advantages which more frequently than not restricted or rendered meaningless the advantages that the Crown and common folk had presumably enjoyed while the provincial and local governments functioned without interference by the noble governors and other dignitaries. It was not until after 1680 that the Crown succeeded in stemming the tide. The Riksdag of 1680 instituted a large-scale reversion of fiefs and estates to the state. The efforts of the Crown were supported by the three lower estates of the Riksdag. They ultimately resulted in reducing the nobles to an office-holding class without anchorage in the landed property. Some of the holdings of the leading aristocrats of the period had been immense.[2] It was especially the large landowning nobles that were laid low by the decisions of the 1680 Riksdag: all earldoms, baronies, and former royal estates held by them reverted to the Crown, without compensation.

Out of the decisions of the Riksdag came still other results that further undermined the high nobility and correspondingly exalted the power of the king. The reigning king at the time was Charles XI. Charles had succeeded to the throne in 1660, but since he was a minor the country had been governed by a regency from 1660 to 1672. The 1680 Riksdag made it possible for Charles to change the venerable Council of State into a king's council which he consulted only at his own pleasure. The Council became a mere adjunct of royal power. Charles XI became, for all practical purposes, an absolute monarch. The disappearance of the political and economic leadership and prominence of the noble class was thus accompanied

[2] Per Brahe, who headed the administration in Finland in 1637–40 and 1648–54, derived income from about 1,000 holdings in Finland, and his main holding in Sweden comprised some 540 square miles. De la Gardie, one of the leading generals of the day, held 300 estates in 40 parishes.

by the emergence of absolutism. The following forty years were to show the dangers inherent in royal absolutism by imposing immense suffering upon the kingdom and bringing it to the brink of permanent ruin.

The provincial laws or rules had furnished the basis of the administration of justice into the fourteenth century. Sweden's first general "Law of the Land" (*landslag* in Swedish and *maanlaki* in Finnish) was that of Magnus Eriksson, in 1350. It was followed by the Law of the Land of Christopher (1442), although it appears that the latter did not fully succeed to the earlier law until a good deal later. The codes and a special law for the cities from the fourteenth century remained in force until the extensive revision of the law embodied in the Law of 1734. During the centuries between the fifteenth and the eighteenth, however, several changes were effected either by legislation or by custom.

Originally the district as well as provincial judges had been chosen, directly or indirectly, by the people, who, as we have seen, elected even the king until the sixteenth century. The Christopher land law prescribed the process in detail whereby the district judges were chosen. It provided for the selection, by the district assembly, of a jury of twelve men who, with the judge of the province, nominated three potential appointees of whom the king chose "the one whom he wanted and knew to be suitable." When a "Law Man" (judge of the province) was to be chosen, the bishop convened the provincial assembly. The people attending the assembly then selected six farmers (*bönder*) and six nobles (*höfmän*) who, with two priests, designated three possible appointees. The king appointed the one "whom God brings to his mind and whom he understands to be useful to the common people."

An important feature of the administration of justice in the sixteenth century was the fact that it was not sharply separated from general administration. Judges often performed administrative functions; administrative offices or personnel were often involved in handling legal matters and in dispensing justice. The reasons for the absence of differentiation we find embedded in the nature of the monarchy and the institutions by means of which it functioned. The king was the supreme judge as well as the head of the government.

It naturally followed that his appointees were called upon to handle legal as well as other public business. The inquest juries illustrate the confusion, if confusion it was, of the age in these matters. They acted in legal as well as other questions. The two areas of public business were not fully separated until the establishment of new courts of appeal, the Svea Royal Court in Stockholm in 1614 and a similar royal court for Finland in Turku in 1623. Finland's second court of appeal was established in Vaasa in 1776.

Gustavus Vasa changed the traditional practices to suit himself. He held that the appointment of the judges was the king's prerogative and nobody else's. He and his successors saw in judicial as well as other appointments appropriate and useful means for rewarding deserving supporters and favorites, or for obtaining needed services and assistance. Appointment to a judgeship came often to mean nothing more onerous than collecting the income of the office, while the actual function of the judge was performed by a lowly "law reader" who frequently was unfit to do more than announce the verdict of the jury and keep a record of the verdict. The situation did not begin to change for the better until the above-mentioned courts of appeal were established.

Courts of appeal significantly changed the procedures of the lower courts and at the same time imposed more exacting demands upon the judges of these courts. The procedure of the lower courts had been oral; cases were presented and testimony was offered by word of mouth, with but a minimum of written matter being involved. In the courts of appeal, the handling of cases unavoidably meant written records of the procedure and decision of the lower court. This in turn forced the lower courts to meet more exacting qualifications. The courts of appeal, whose responsibility it was not only to handle cases on appeal but to supervise the general administration of justice within their respective districts, themselves began to appoint "law readers" for the lower courts in order to secure the degree of competence deemed essential. The Turku court of appeal appears to have been the first to introduce the practice, which was specifically authorized in the other courts in 1681. The corps of judges also improved toward the end of the century, partly because former officers of the courts of appeal who had acquired competence in the law in the course of their work were increasingly appointed to judgeships.

In degree as the judgeships were held by abler men and men better trained in the law, the role of the jury also underwent change. It came to be appointed, ultimately, by the judge rather than chosen by the people as had formerly been the case. The jury thus lost part of its independence as against the judge, but the fact that the jury in a real sense also became, over the years, a part of the court gave it a special role and status. That is, the jury took part in the process of formulating a verdict, and the verdict of a unanimous jury was accepted, even if the judge found to the contrary, as the verdict of the court. This rule was specifically recognized in the Law of 1734 and applies in Finland today.

THE FARMER IN A CHANGING WORLD

Provincial tax and other records offer some information regarding the size of Finland's population during the Reformation and the following two centuries. We do not know with certainty, however, what the population was before the first census in 1749. The earlier tax records list only taxable farms or homesteads. They seldom yield satisfactory clues regarding the size of the farmer's family. Records of special levies also leave much to be desired. For instance, the immense Älfsborg ransom, paid to Denmark in 1614–20 for the return of the city and fortress on the southwest coast of Sweden, involved a special tax collected throughout the realm on all subjects over fifteen years of age. It might therefore be assumed that the collection of the tax would throw light on the size of the population. A new poll tax, imposed in 1635 on all and sundry in the same age category, raises the same expectation. It turns out, however, that these levies tell us very little because local assemblies or authorities responsible for listing taxable individuals frequently kept very imperfect records. The landless and the very poor, though no doubt numerous, were left outside the tally altogether.

These and other circumstances account for population estimates that vary a great deal. They range from about 250,000 in the 1550s to 400,000 in the second decade of the seventeenth century. The well-known Finnish historian E. Jutikkala, writing in the 1930s, concluded that "when we speak of Finland's population in the 1600s, we are forced for the time being to be satisfied with a figure somewhere between 250,000 and 500,000." [3] Before the nineteenth century the population grew slowly. Wars, famine, and disease took their heavy toll. In 1695–97, for instance, the failure of crops led to the death of untold thousands. Some provinces lost from one fifth to one third or even more of their population. In 1710 the plague appears to have killed a large part of the population of the leading cities, Turku and Viipuri. A decade later, at the close of the disastrous Northern War in 1721, the population had probably shrunk to less than 300,000 souls.

During the century and more after the 1520s when the population increased slightly and at times actually declined, the Church managed to grow. It played a significant role in promoting settlement of the areas where forest and wilderness had held undisputed sway. The parishes of the interior of the country were, in most instances, very large, and their sparse population had been usually but little touched by the ministrations of the Church. The situation began to change in the sixteenth century. Over 70 new parishes were established during the years when the Reformation was carried through. The 1600s witnessed the founding of 119 new parishes (and a score more in the areas obtained from Russia by the terms of the Peace of Stolbova in 1617). Finally, the decades from 1720 to 1809 added 92 parishes to the total. Nearly all the new parishes comprised recent or relatively recent communities and settlements. Meanwhile new administrative units, counties and their subdivisions, had also emerged and testified to the continuing expansion of the settled areas, especially in the northern and eastern parts of the country.[4]

[3] In G. Suolahti et al., eds., Suomen Kulttuurihistoria (Jyväskylä, 1933–36), II, 100. The 1749 census taken in Sweden and Finland is the first general count of heads in Europe. Denmark began a regular decennial census in 1769 and England in 1801

[4] A. M. Soininen's Pohjois-Savon Asuttaminen Keski-ja Uuden Ajan Vaihteessa (Helsinki, 1961) gives an excellent description of the settling of the eastern and central areas of the country in the 1400s and the 1500s. The study includes an eight-page summary in English.

Agriculture had become well established in southwestern Finland centuries before the sixteenth. The strip system of land holding, rotation of crops, common pastures and woodland, and the village comprising a few or as many as a score or more houses were characteristic features of the world in which the farmer was born, lived, and died. The farm was, in the 1500s and 1600s in particular, almost wholly self-sustaining. The main crops were rye and barley. In the 1570s, for example, these two crops represented over 40 percent of the taxes paid (taxes were collected in kind at the time and, for the most part, long thereafter). Oat crops were grown primarily for fodder and probably represented only about one twentieth of the produce delivered as taxes to the Crown. Wheat was also grown but appears to have been unimportant before the 1700s despite efforts made on Crown farms to popularize its cultivation. Hay was obtained mostly from natural meadows.

Cabbage, turnips, peas, buckwheat, hops, hemp, and flax were widely grown by the sixteenth century. The growing of hops was a special concern of the Crown; some of the old provincial laws had prescribed the growing of hops on penalty of a fine. The potato was introduced in the 1730s and slowly gained ground; it had become one of the main crops about two generations later. Tobacco, while used in the seventeenth century, was not grown until early in the eighteenth century and became common more rapidly than the potato. Garden produce was not unimportant. According to a record from 1683, beets, carrots, onions, lettuce, sweet marjoram, anise, parsley, artichokes, and horseradish were grown in southwest Finland. Peter Kalm, the well-known Finnish naturalist and author of the *Travels in North America* (1770) based on his visit to North America in 1747–51, labored energetically during his professorship at the University of Turku to popularize vegetable and fruit gardens, without succeeding, however, in persuading farmers in general that gardens should not grow only cabbage, turnips, and tobacco.

Animal husbandry was an important aspect of farming. Horses were kept in surprisingly large numbers. In east and central Finland nearly one half of the farm animals toward the end of the seventeenth century were horses. They were important as draught animals, as were oxen, which were widely used in certain south and west-central areas of the country. Cattle were valued not only for milk and butter but for meat, hides, and natural fertilizer. Sheep were common possessions of the farmer in the older communities of the southwest; the Turku Castle owned, in 1554, over 200 "English" and some 160 "Finnish" sheep. The wool clip of the former was, if a record from that year can be taken literally, substantially greater than that of the latter. Goats were also common domestic animals—as were pigs—over most of the west and south by the 1650s but had declined in number a century later. Chickens abounded: "Nearly every farmer, cotter and renter keeps a rooster in order to know what time it is at night, and chickens to pacify the rooster." While these words were set down as late as 1827 and cannot be taken as a complete description of the utility of either rooster or hen, they in all likelihood apply to earlier times as well in indicating that barnyard fowl were indeed common.

Considering the climate, the short growing season, and the inadequacy of fodder crops, Finnish farmers seem to have kept more farm animals than was profitable. The perceptive Gustavus Vasa, whose interests and concerns extended even to the minutiae of farming, no doubt made a telling point when he admonished Swedish farmers in 1555 in words that would have been pertinent in Finland as well. "It would be useful," he said in an open letter addressed to them, "if you gave serious thought and consideration to the long months that separate Martin's Mass from Valborg's Mass [from November 10 to April 30] and calculate how much cattle you have and how much fodder you need. If you discover that the fodder is not sufficient for your farm animals, it would be best to slaughter or sell, in order that the animals you keep need not horribly and pitifully starve and die, which can be defended neither before God nor man." [5] We do not know whether Gustavus' exhortation was effective but may surmise that it was disregarded, especially in the areas where natural meadow- or pastureland was abundant and the keeping of cattle therefore relatively easy and common.

The farmer's economy involved a good deal more than the rais-

[5] Quoted in H. Pohjolan-Pirhonen, *Suomen Historia 1523–1617* (Helsinki, 1960), p. 178.

ing of crops or the care of farm animals. The uncultivated forests and wilderness as well as the sea and lakes played an important part in his life. As a hunter and trapper, he levied a toll on the fur-bearing denizens of the forest. The squirrel, ermine, marten, fox, deer, wolves, and bears were all valued for their pelts or furs. The peasant paid part of his taxes in furs, although their importance as taxable commodities sharply declined after about 1550. Seal hunting and fishing likewise loomed large in the picture, especially in coastal communities, as is suggested by the fact that fish products accounted for about 8 percent of the taxes paid in kind in the 1570s. In addition, substantial amounts of fish were exported. The inland lake regions also depended in considerable degree on fishing. Salmon and pike headed the list of valuable catches. Savo, one of the eastern provinces, paid a "fish tax" to the Crown in 1526 of about 375,000 pounds. About 3–4 percent of the taxes in kind around 1530 were paid in salmon.

The world of the farmer suffered at all times from intrusions and exactions from the outside. Taxes on land and other levies took a substantial part of the fruit of his labors. These burdens increased and became heavier as time wore on. The sixteenth century in particular marked a substantial growth in taxes. In this matter as well as in most others, we observe the enterprising Gustavus Vasa at work. A single over-all illustration of his achievement will serve as an example. His revision of the system of taxation, intended to increase to the utmost the flow of income into the coffers of the Crown, approximately doubled the amount of annual taxes collected in Finland between 1530 and 1542.

The expanding business of the royal government required, among other things, more detailed and accurate records of landownership and land taxes. The "land books" compiled annually during Gustavus Vasa's reign listed the farmers in the kingdom and the number of "tax units" for which each was responsible. The first of the books dealing with Finnish districts is for the year 1539; the series covering the provinces as a whole began a few years later. More often than not, the new and more detailed accounts led to increases in the peasants' tax burdens, not the least because some of the levies that had gone to the Church before the Reformation were added to the land tax collected by the Crown (for instance, two thirds of the tithe). The nobles were not affected by these changes because freedom from land taxes was one of the privileges of the noble class. Nearly all of the land taxes and other taxes were paid by the common folk.

This circumstance resulted from no sudden or recent set of exactions arbitrarily imposed upon the lower orders by the higher. It was a consequence of the stratification of society that had proceeded for generations before the sixteenth century and reached its highest stages in that century. The inhabitants of the Swedish kingdom were considered to be divided into clearly defined and recognizable estates, each with special functions and privileges. (The same was true, in varying degree, of the other rising national monarchies of the early modern period.) The nobles served as officials and held the important posts in the army. They enjoyed the most extensive privileges. The clergy and the burghers performed their special functions and enjoyed lesser rewards and privileges. As regards the peasants, the leading historian of their part in the annals of Finland, E. Jutikkala, put the matter admirably and succinctly when he remarked:

It was considered to be the responsibility of the peasants to the state to pay taxes and to provide manpower for the wars of the realm. As a reward for these lowly functions, they needed no other rights than the right to participate in provincial assemblies or in the sessions of the Riksdag when taxes or levies for the army were decided. The peasants themselves submissively accepted the description of the peasant estate used by the other estates: it constituted "the common people responsible for paying taxes" to the Crown.[6]

Swedish and Finnish historians frequently underscore the fact that the Swedes and the Finns never had to accept the oppressed and servile status found over the greater part of western, central, and southern Europe where the feudal system took root and flourished. Their pride in being able to say that the lowly folk in the North have been free throughout their recorded history is understandable. The taint of serfdom did not afflict the Swedes or the

[6] E. Jutikkala, *Suomen Talonpojan Historia* (Helsinki, 1958), p. 103.

Finns during the centuries when it persisted in France, where it was not fully eradicated until late in the eighteenth century; or during the long span of years when it remained an aspect of German life until eliminated in the early part of the 1800s; or during the generations when it bound tens of millions of Russians who remained unfree in law till 1861 and unfree in fact for many years thereafter.

Yet it would be misleading to conclude that the generality of inhabitants of the Swedish kingdom were free and their own masters in the full sense of the word. They had to accept mounting taxes and other demands by Crown and Riksdag over which they had no real control, as well as contentions and claims by the state and exploitation at the hands of the noble landlords that probably often made the realities of existence not only oppressively harsh but close to unbearable.

We have already noted that Gustavus Vasa made use, whenever he could, of the convenient claim that the land belonged to God, King, and Crown. This claim had originally been applied only to the uncultivated forest lands and wilderness. The peasant's farm and other holdings were his and nobody else's. The land he owned carried only one obligation regarding the Crown, namely the land tax.

The theory and conceptions regarding landownership on which the claims of the Crown rested underwent important changes during the 1500s and later. The changes grew out of the acceptance of certain feudal ideas that appear to have reached Sweden mainly from Germany. Basic among them was the contention that the Crown had originally owned all the land and had surrendered only the use of the land to the peasant. The peasant's right of ownership was limited to the use of the land; it did not include title to it or the right to dispose of its product at will. When the Crown imposed a tax on the land, it was merely asserting its rights. The Crown "owned" the tax, and the tax was therefore no temporary or varying impost agreed to at least in theory by the free yeoman but recognizable and continuing evidence of the prior and basic title of the Crown. In time, title and ownership were considered to be divided. The Crown owned the land and its product. The tax paid by the farmer was income collected by the Crown, the proprietor, from its own property. The yeoman had merely the right to live on the land, to cultivate it, and to use part of its product. It was this right, and this alone, that constituted the farmer's "title." [7]

It goes without saying that these theories were never fully applied either in the 1500s or later. They had a good deal to do, however, with the fact that the yeoman's rights of ownership to his land were limited in a number of ways. If he wanted to dispose of his land, he could sell it outside of his own relatives, according to a decree of 1684, only after he had offered it to the Crown. The failure to pay taxes for three years resulted—perhaps more in theory than in practice—in reversion of the title to the state. The farm had to be run and managed according to instructions provided by the Crown (again, theory was often disregarded in practice). The peasant could not turn parts of his holdings over to tenants; in general, he was forbidden to do anything that decreased the area of taxable land. And apart from the practical meaning of these and other restrictions, he was taxed to the limit of his capacity to pay.

Farmers living on land held or owned by a noble were really tenants and normally had to face special exactions. Their taxes and other obligations to the Crown appear to have been substantially reduced as a rule, but the difference was made up by payments and services to the lord. Despite limitations defined in law or by custom, the lord normally demanded week work and other contributions to the limit the traffic would bear, and at the same time attempted to reduce his obligations to the Crown without thereby lightening, needless to say, the burdens of the peasant. We have already noted the increasing accumulation of estates and farms by the nobles after the middle decades of the 1600s. It appears that in the mid-1650s well over one half of the settled areas in Finland were held by the nobles, and that they represented approximately one third of the taxes due to the Crown. Some of the noble holdings had been assigned to barons or other dignitaries living in Sweden—that is, to absentee landlords—whose possessions and interests in Finland were managed by bailiffs whose main interest was the collection of taxes

[7] In this summary I have freely used the excellent discussion of the problem in *ibid.*, pp. 142–50, without attempting to distinguish between the varying terms on which land was held.

and other dues. Many of the grants and gifts to the nobles, however, involved Finnish military and other leaders who had rendered or were rendering important services in Finland in the wars after the middle of the 1500s.

The large-scale post-1680 recapture by the Crown of fiefs, other lands, and concessions made to the nobles during the preceding century and earlier freed the peasant from the growing exactions of the noble on the lands that reverted to the state. It did not, however, wipe out the claims upon him for taxes or other dues. The Crown was not interested, in divesting the nobles of their possessions and privileges, in improving the condition of the peasant, but in securing its own interests and in filling the royal coffers. The royal bailiff or agent charged with responsibility for collecting taxes and safeguarding the interests of the Crown probably seemed every whit as demanding and objectionable in general as the noble's bailiff. And the peasant estate in the Riksdag remained on the whole unimportant. It did not become even approximately the equal of the other estates until a century later, in 1789, when the peasants also gained greater influence in local government as well.

Although the common man lived a life that was meager and in many ways precarious, he enjoyed certain rights which, while all too often limited or disregarded, were never lost or canceled. His rights rested upon rules and ways of doing things that antedated the appearance of the hereditary monarchy or the organization and functions of the Riksdag of the seventeenth century.

Not the least fascinating aspect of the evolution of the Swedish Riksdag is its growth from an irregular assembly of no fixed membership or function into the legislative organ of a national monarchy. Its core in the 1400s was the Council of State, aided by representatives of the burghers and peasants. The clergy as a separate estate did not attend the Riksdag until the reign of Gustavus Vasa, although a few bishops regularly attended as members of the Council of State. Broadly speaking, the Riksdag well into the 1500s carried no more weight and had no more influence than that assured by the leading men or groups who attended its sessions. The Riksdag was normally convened only in exceptional or crisis situations, and the king usually made little or no use of it.

The Riksdag's narrowly restricted authority in law and practice was compensated for by the influence of the provincial assemblies. In taxation, for instance, the essential procedures had been fixed long before Gustavus Vasa appeared on the scene. The "Law of the Land" prescribed that the king had to ask each province for new taxes by turning to the provincial committee composed of the bishop, the "Law Man," six nobles, and six yeomen. The rule or procedure was not always fully observed in practice but the basic principle was followed, and the right of the provinces to consent to taxes was recognized until about the year 1600. As Professor E. Jutikkala has put it, "If tax questions were initially considered by the Riksdag, as was the case with increasing regularity after 1544, the purpose was merely to prepare the matter and define the reasons and justification which were to be submitted to the provincial assemblies." [8] Neither in the provincial assembly nor in the Riksdag was the common yeoman without a voice, although it is clear that his preferences were frequently ignored by the more influential estates.

One aspect of the Riksdag's function, however, gave the estate of the peasants a continuing opportunity to make itself heard. The individual members of the Riksdag, without reference to the estate to which they belonged, had a right to present complaints and petitions from their home district. The complaints of the peasants presented in writing were frequent and often lengthy. They covered a wide range of real or imaginary injustices or malpractices and petitioned the king for redress of the grievances enumerated. And during periods when the Riksdag was not in session, deputations of the peasants often appeared at the court to complain to the king about taxes, the suffering caused by heartless or corrupt bailiffs, or to urge the appointment of a new or the dismissal of an old official. "To go to the king," while often productive of no real relief or improvement, was a time-honored and prized right of the common man that gave him, together with his recognized though modest place in assembly and Riksdag, the status of a free man that high taxes and other exactions did not extinguish.

Gustavus Vasa, who freed Sweden from the overlordship of Danish kings and separated the Church from Rome, also tried to

8 *Ibid.*, p. 98.

free Sweden's economic life of foreign control. His purpose was, specifically, to end the monopoly of Lübeck and other Hansa cities over Sweden's foreign trade. He attempted to direct that trade into new channels by favoring Dutch traders, by attempting to establish trade connections with England, France, Spain, and Portugal, and by stimulating domestic shipbuilding in order to provide the country with tonnage capable of competing with foreign merchants. Navigation acts, a long series of regulations and prohibitions regarding exports and imports, minute prescriptions of what could be bought and sold in domestic markets, and other measures testified to his endeavors.

Gustavus Vasa's ambitious purposes included the further development of existing, and the founding of new, cities in Finland. He was determined to end the Germans' trade monopoly in the Baltic area by obtaining a substantial share of the trade with Russia, hitherto largely in the hands of Reval in Estonia. With this in mind, he issued a Navigation Act in 1550 which also provided for the founding of a new city on the southern shore of Finland. Helsinki (Helsingfors) was the result of these plans. The city never succeeded in becoming the center of the Russian trade Gustavus Vasa had hopefully expected to deflect to Finland, and it remained altogether unimportant until it became, generations later (in 1819), after it had been moved to its present location, the capital of Finland, which by then was living through the first years of its new affiliation with Russia. The oldest cities, Turku and Viipuri, remained the main ports and centers of trade in Finland.

The 1600s witnessed the founding of nearly a score of new cities, most of them on the west coast. While some of them developed into relatively important administrative centers, they remained small; some of them were cities in name only. All of them illustrated the determination of the Crown to control and regulate, fully in keeping with the tenets of mercantilism, the economic life of the new communities. Finland as well as Sweden proper demonstrated the mercantilist conception that the individual can or will conduct his business in a manner benefiting the nation as a whole only when his activities are regulated from above. One of the conspicuous aspects of the intervention of the Crown in economic matters was the granting of special trading privileges to several staple cities which alone had the right to trade with foreigners or enjoyed a monopoly of the purchase and sale of certain commodities.

The failure of Gustavus Vasa and his successors to channel the trade with Russia—or, for that matter, the trade of the eastern Baltic in general—to southern Finnish ports did not mean that the Hanseatics remained in control of the Baltic trade. The earlier preeminence of the Hansa towns was destroyed by developments to which Sweden contributed but little. The Hansa merchants were replaced by the Dutch, who had become a major factor in Finland's foreign trade by the end of the sixteenth century. Viipuri, the trading city on the southeast coast, recorded over one thousand merchantmen coming from or departing for foreign ports between 1584 and 1620; well over one third of the ships were Dutch. By the close of the 1600s the Dutch dominated Baltic trade to a degree reminiscent of the earlier position of the Hansa towns.

In speaking of the consequences of these developments for Finland, a prominent historian has remarked that

the general area of our economic history during the seventeenth century and a part of the eighteenth bears a marked Dutch stamp. The Dutch bought Finnish naval stores; Dutch goods and ways of doing business gained ground in our country. The leading merchants of Turku, Helsinki, Porvoo, and Viipuri were of Dutch descent, Dutch was spoken and written in the business houses of our cities, Dutch seafarers' manuals were used in Finnish waters. Dutch know-how and capital played an important part in the development of our industries. "Dutch" windmills and "Dutch" sawmills were built. Dutch capital gave our lumber trade its start, and a substantial part of our grain trade was in the hands of the Dutch.[9]

Their dominant position was gradually lost only toward the end of the 1700s when the English flag became common in the Baltic and Swedish, Finnish, and other shipping had developed sufficiently to challenge "foreign" competition.

We have already remarked that Finnish cities were small and relatively unimportant well into the nineteenth century. One of the reasons for their slow growth was the frequency of fires. Turku, the

[9] V. Voionmaa, in *Suomen Kulttuurihistoria*, II, 20–21.

unofficial "capital" of Finland, suffered no less than fifteen big fires during the century before 1624. Five of the fires destroyed large parts of the city, and that of 1593 burned it to the ground (the last fire to reduce the city to ashes was in 1827). Pori was destroyed in 1570 and again in 1603, and Viipuri suffered the same fate several times.

The failure of the cities to develop into large and important centers of trade, commerce, and national life in general was caused in part by the fact that foreign trade was largely in the hands of foreign merchants. One of the consequences of this circumstance was the absence, both in Sweden and in Finland, of a strong and influential native burgher class. The native merchants and traders—and artisans also—did not develop into a wealthy class capable of playing the political and social role we associate with the mercantile world of the West. As a group or as the third estate, the burghers in times of national crises stood against neither the increasing exactions of the Crown nor the claims of the Church and clergy. Lowly as the status of the peasant in many ways was, and although his influence upon the political and economic life of the kingdom before the nineteenth century was very limited, the peasant class was nevertheless a more significant political factor in the affairs of state and nation than the burghers. Nothing illustrates this basic fact more strikingly than the success of the king, supported by the peasants, in reducing the power of the nobles in 1680 and later.

WARS AND THEIR CONSEQUENCES

During the generations we have been reviewing, war was a frequent scourge in Sweden-Finland. And even in those distant days war had an aspect we have been accustomed, for the last half-century, to call "modern": it was often total war. It was total in the sense that it was not limited to the fighting forces, whether levies of peasants or paid mercenaries. War entailed as complete a destruction of the enemy as circumstances permitted. Living off his land whenever possible was taken for granted. Killing the population, burning cities and villages, destroying crops and every other form of property, and "appropriating" whatever was useful were common and necessary aspects of war. They were parts of the art of war. Pillaging and laying waste the enemy's land was normally no less important than winning battles or capturing fortresses. War was as heavy a burden as any that weighed down the common people.

During the three centuries before the dismemberment of Sweden in 1808–9, the country was involved in wars that spanned a total of more than eighty years. Some were fought outside the borders of Sweden-Finland—the Thirty Years' War and the Polish and Russian campaigns of Charles XII two generations later come readily to mind—and therefore demanded only two basic exactions: manpower levies and taxes. Heavy as these exactions were, they fell far short of equaling the burdens of the wars that involved directly the domain of the kingdom itself. These wars were fought, more often than not, against the Russians, and wars against the Russians meant—leaving aside the Baltic provinces—that Finland was the first to feel their effects and the first to suffer from their consequences, territorial and other. Especially destructive among the recurring conflicts with the Russians were the wars of 1554–57, the twenty-five years' war from 1570 to 1595 (interrupted, to be sure, by several truces), that of 1609–17, still another war—not long after the Thirty Years' War had ended—in 1656–58, and the long and tragic Northern War from 1700 to 1721. By comparison with these wars, those of 1741–43 and 1788–90 were, we might say, mere footnotes to the long story of earlier wars, although the former resulted in the cession of Finnish territory to the Russian Empire.

Whatever else warfare meant, it always involved armies that had to be raised, maintained, and replenished. The fighting forces of the kingdom rested traditionally on the general obligation of the subject to serve his king and country. It was the common farmer folk, needless to say, that furnished most of the necessary manpower. In time of peace, the farmers were organized into recruiting groups or districts, each of which furnished a given number of men. The buying of substitutes was permitted. The cavalry was composed of volunteers who probably enlisted primarily to escape the hardships of service in the ranks of the infantry or pikemen. In 1630, when Gustavus Adolphus appeared on the scene as one of the leading figures of the Thirty Years' War, Sweden's "domestic" army consisted of twenty-four conscript regiments of 1,000–1,200 men each. Eight of the regiments were Finnish. A reorganization of the army in 1636 fixed the number of regiments at twenty-three; fourteen were Swedish and nine Finnish. In getting ready for the campaign in Germany, Gustavus Adolphus acquired the services of some 30,000 mercenaries, amounting to somewhat less than half of Adolphus' infantry forces. The "domestic" cavalry after 1636 was small, some 8,000 men in all, divided into eight regiments, three of which were Finnish. During the Thirty Years' War, most of Sweden's army consisted of mercenaries, despite ever heavier levies at home.

Finland is no exception to the general rule that boundaries, whether historians call them "national" or "natural" or characterize them in some other way, have been decided by wars. Until the nineteenth century, Finland, being an integral part of Sweden, had of course no clearly marked boundary in the northwest. A political boundary between Sweden and Finland was defined only in 1809. Finland's boundary changes before 1808 were the result of wars, treaties, and arrangements with the Russians, originally of Novgorod, later of Muscovy, and, later still, of the Russian Empire. When the contours of Finland's eastern borders appeared for the first time on the political map of northern Europe, they were defined, in broad terms, by a treaty concluded by Sweden and Novgorod in 1323.

The Nöteborg treaty of 1323 fixed the eastern boundary from the course of the Neva River on the Karelian Isthmus northward, roughly dividing the isthmus. Swinging northward for the length of the isthmus, the line traced a northern and northwestern course which brought it to the upper reaches of the eastern shore of the Gulf of Bothnia, approximately where the present-day city of Raahe is located. Most of the boundary followed an ill-defined course, never fully identified by historians, through hundreds of miles of largely unsettled lake and forest wilderness. All of what is today north Finland and most of east Finland were left east and north of the boundary. As Finnish settlements developed east of the boundary, Sweden claimed the areas. The result was prolonged border disputes that were settled only in 1595.

This boundary settlement of 1595 marked the end of another long

war which began in 1570 and continued for a quarter-century.
While Estonia as well as Finland was directly involved, Finland in
particular suffered from Russian raids and other destruction. Many
settled areas were completely wiped out, others were partly burned,
and helpless farmers and their families were killed or carried into
captivity in Russia. The areas not directly in the path of the fighting
forces or hit-and-run raids of the Muscovites also suffered, especially
from greatly increased taxes, mounting "temporary" dues and assess-
ments, the consequences of a ruthless policy of quartering soldiers
among the defenseless farmers, and the never-ending demands for
transporting and feeding soldiers. Failure to pay taxes and deliberate
abandonment of homesteads by hard-pressed settlers or farmers
became common in some parts of the country. When peace was
concluded in 1595 and the eastern boundary of Finland was redrawn
farther east and extended in the north to the Arctic Ocean, the
respite obtained was destined to last only a few years. Charles IX
(1604–11) renewed the war against Russia in 1609. He left it as a
legacy to his son Gustavus Adolphus (1611–32), whose two decades
of rule were largely devoted to war and resulted in still another
revision eastward of Finland's Russian boundary.

When Gustavus Adolphus ascended the throne—he was in his
seventeenth year at the time—the kingdom was in a precarious situation. South Sweden was in the throes of war against the Danes; in
Livonia, fighting against Poland's forces continued; and in Estonia
and Ingria the war against the Russians was in full swing. Peace
with the Danes was concluded in 1613, at a huge financial cost (the
payment of the Älfsborg ransom, which the Finns of course shared).
The Russian war ended with the Peace of Stolbova in 1617. It
provided among other things for territorial cessions to Sweden, in
the eastern and southeastern Gulf of Finland area (Kexholm and
Ingria), that excluded Russia from the Baltic and gave Finland the
advantage of placing relatively substantial buffer areas between it
and Russia. The arrangements of 1617 also involved, as far as Finland was concerned, a partially adjusted eastern border which was
to last for a century. Its main contours were later redefined, as we
shall see, in a manner that gave Finland most of her nineteenth-
century eastern boundary.

A telling indication of the destructive consequences of the wars of the 1600s was the migration of farmers and other settlers from the east Finland areas that usually bore the brunt of Russian raids and attacks. It has been estimated that in 1656–57, for example, some 4,000 settlers had abandoned their holdings and moved across the border to Russia, hoping thereby to escape the ever-increasing taxes and other exactions of the Crown as well as the ravages of war in general. The Greek Orthodox population of southeast Finland was especially involved in the emigration of the middle decades of the 1600s. While the war years 1656–58 in particular stimulated the migration, it continued intermittently during the rest of the century.

The treaty of 1617 established peace between Sweden and Russia but did not mark the end of Gustavus Adolphus' wars. The war against Poland continued, largely because of dynastic considerations, but it ultimately created no long-range problems or territorial changes for Finland. It was not until the Northern War at the turn of the century brought Sweden face to face with Peter the Great's Russia that the disastrous consequences of war were visited upon the nation in a manner destined to influence its history for generations to come.

The reign of Gustavus Adolphus spanned only a score of years (1611–32). During these two decades his military exploits in the Baltic provinces and Poland, and especially his prominent role in the Thirty Years' War, placed Sweden in the front rank of the Great Powers of the day. After his death in 1632, subsequent events solidified and added to the country's new eminence. Sweden had gained a veritable Baltic empire and stood forth as one of the arbiters of Europe's future destiny. Swedish exploits on the battlefield and decisions at the council table influenced men's lives in the heartland of the continent as well as in the far North.

The newly won preeminence turned out to be only temporary. It was lost, and lost beyond the hope of recovery, within two generations of the close of the Thirty Years' War. More than that, Sweden had to relinquish her overseas holdings in the Baltic provinces. No less ominous was the cession of a substantial part of southeastern Finland to Russia, then rapidly forging ahead under the leadership of Peter the Great. These and other national calamities resulted from the purposes and undertakings of Charles XII, whose disastrous rule began in 1697 and ended in 1718.

Few monarchs have been as highly praised and as roundly condemned as Sweden's Charles XII. August Strindberg, in his play *Charles XII* (1901), remarked that Charles was "the man who ruined Sweden, the great criminal, the champion fighter, the ideal of the ruffians." [10] The great Swedish poet Esaias Tegnér, on the other hand, sang Charles's praises in measures unrestrained. On the centenary of Charles's death in 1818, Tegnér saw Charles as the "greatest son" of Sweden before whose grave History itself "stands uncovered" and beholds how Swedes honor "on bended knee" their hero king now resting beneath the gravestone whose very inscription is Sweden's own poem of the truly heroic.[11] Many historians during the past century and more have shown Charles naïve deference and have held him up as a great national figure; others have dealt with him in a critical spirit, condemning the man and his works as calamitous to state and nation. Poets and popularizers, inspired by nationalist sentiments, have likewise contributed to the ever-lengthening list of appraisals and interpretations. Not the least eloquent commentary on Charles's rule and its consequences, as seen by his own contemporaries, was the repudiation after his death of the autocratic monarchy—which alone had made possible Charles's extraordinary undertakings—and the introduction of a governmental order of things in which the Crown was little more than a rubber stamp.

The reign of Charles XII was almost wholly absorbed in the Northern War. Contrary to the claims of some historians, the war was not forced upon Sweden by a Danish-Polish-Russian conspiracy. It began because Charles, who had become king in 1697 at the age of fifteen, insisted on taking sides against Denmark in a conflict between Denmark and Schleswig-Holstein. By the time the war ended, its consequences, especially for Finland, had become disastrous beyond description.

[10] Quoted in Walter Johnson's *Strindberg's Queen Christina, Charles XII, Gustav III* (Seattle, 1955), p. 93.

[11] "Böj, Svea, knä vid griften/ din störste son göms där . . . / Med blottat hufvud stiger/ historien dit och lär/ och svenska äran viger/ sin segerfana här."

On the eve of the Northern War, the Finnish army consisted of about 15,000 men. New units were formed in 1700, numbering probably 10,000 men. The fighting forces thus totaled some 25,000, or about 6–7 percent of the total population of the country estimated at 400,000. The army of 25,000 represented approximately one fourth of the male population between the ages of sixteen and sixty. During 1700–1709, about 230,000 Swedes and Finns were lost in Poland, Russia, and elsewhere, and estimates indicate that during the second half of the war, in 1709–18, an additional 120,000 lives were lost either in the number killed or wounded or as prisoners. It appears that the annual losses of Finnish lives, during 1700–1718, corresponded to the yearly increment of adult men.

During the first part of the war, actual fighting did not involve Finland. However, the country fell victim to Russian invasion in March, 1710, and by the autumn of 1713 all of it was under Russian occupation, the last Swedish forces having withdrawn in September. Serious as were the losses of thousands upon thousands of lives in campaigns in Poland and Russia, the destruction and lawlessness during the long and harsh years of Russian occupation levied an even heavier toll. Widespread failure of crops added to the misery of the people, many thousands of whom were sent to Russia, there to suffer in wretched captivity from which only a few returned after peace was concluded in 1721. Whoever could escaped to Sweden or sought refuge in the wilderness. Farms and villages abandoned or destroyed—nearly one fourth of the farm holdings were abandoned by their owners or tenants during the war—cities plundered, schools and the university closed or only partly able to function, churches suffering from the results of Russian control and ruthless vandalism, trade and commerce and industry at a standstill, all testified at the war's end to its enormous costs and indicated the immensity of the reconstruction and rebuilding that alone could bring life back to tolerable levels. Finland faced the years of peace with her population greatly reduced—from about 400,000 to under 300,000—for the losses caused directly by the war had been multiplied by epidemics and a particularly destructive plague that ravaged the land in 1710.

The Peace of Nystad, signed on August 30, 1721, added the final touch of injury and disaster. Among the territorial cessions defined by the treaty was a substantial part of southeast Finland (the main territories lost were the Baltic provinces Ingria, Estonia, and Livonia), which Sweden, being at the mercy of the victor, was forced to accept. This territorial amputation further weakened the country and appeared to mark the end of Finland's gradual eastward expansion that had been recorded during the three centuries between the Peace of Nöteborg in 1323 and the Peace of Stolbova in 1617.

Barely twenty years later, long before the scars left by the Northern War had disappeared, war was again upon the country. It was caused by Swedish initiative and began in July, 1741. The war was fought with singular ineptness; a well-known history of Sweden aptly remarks that "never has Sweden fought a more disgraceful war." [12] Most of Finland was evacuated, the Swedish forces steadily retreating as the Russians advanced. "Only by obeying the orders of [Empress] Elizabeth and electing [as the king of Sweden] her *protege,* Adolphus Frederick of Holstein, did the Swedish government succeed in purchasing a fairly acceptable peace [in 1743] after having so wantonly begun this military adventure." [13]

The war not only brought a humiliating end to an enterprise foolishly begun but also led to a further cession of Finnish territory, in the southeast, to the Russian Empire. Its consequences placed the kingdom, for many years to come, in a position of dependency upon the very power the warmongers of 1741 had expected to defeat.

The 1741–43 war marked the last change of Finland's boundaries before 1808–9. To be sure, another war was rashly begun in 1788 against Russia. Gustavus III, the king who then held the throne and ruled as an autocrat, began the war, which threatened to add new disasters to the old. Hostilities were ended in the summer of 1790, however, without any change in Sweden's eastern frontier, and without either the Swedes or the Finns suffering anything like the losses and destruction comparable to those recorded during the calamitous first two decades of the century. Nor did the brief war of

[12] Carl Hallendorff and Adolf Schück, *History of Sweden* (Stockholm, 1929), p. 329.
[13] *Ibid.*

Gustavus III undo the beneficial effects of the reconstruction accomplished during the preceding four decades—that is, since the war of 1741–43—when peace prevailed and recovery from the consequences of the Northern War was recorded on every hand. By the time the century drew to a close, Finland in particular had evidenced growth and development that few could have predicted when Charles XII embarked upon the course that brought misery, destruction, and death to the people he arrogantly ruled and unfeelingly sacrificed in the pursuit of purposes destined, by their very nature, to fail.

PARTICULARIST TRENDS AFTER 1721

A significant feature of Finland's history in the eighteenth century was the gradual emergence of the idea of a Finnish fatherland and the sense of a separate Finnish nationality. The idea was formulated and sustained in the first instance by men of the world of learning. They also developed, among other things, a growing interest in national history.

At the very time when Charles XII was embarking upon the wars that nearly wrecked the Swedish kingdom, an obscure young scholar at the University of Turku—the university had been founded in 1640—was finishing a study published in 1700. The scholar was Daniel Juslenius and his work *Aboa Vetus et Nova* (Turku, Old and New). The study described the then capital of Finland. It was no mere compilation of local history, however, but attempted to provide a "national" history. Earlier writers, folk tales, mythology, chance similarities in words or names, and the like were indiscriminately drawn upon by Juslenius in his construction of a tale, wholly imaginary, of the Finns' national greatness in the past ages. The Finns were set down as descendants of one of the Jewish tribes— considered a wholly plausible background for a people in the days when Juslenius wrote—who had founded, it was claimed, a mighty state under one of Noah's descendants. That the state never actually existed appears to have bothered the young author not at all. An even more bizarre tale was presented in his *Vindiciae Fen-*

norum in 1703. The treatise was a pretentious, militant defense of Finland and its people, offering a boastful cataloguing of the virtues of country and nation. Finland was described as singularly fertile and rich in valuable minerals and its climate uncommonly salubrious. The Finns were blessed, the author contended, with a long list of virtues. Capable of great physical and mental attainments, they were brave, honest, of temperate habits and God-fearing, and had made many contributions to the arts of civilization.

The absurdities of Juslenius were not altogether new, for many of them had been put forth, in less ostentatious form, during the closing decades of the 1600s. The excellencies of one's native province or city was, at the time, a subject frequently chosen by university students in their first effort at scholarly production. The spirit in which such labors were carried on was probably accurately suggested by the author of one of the studies, published in 1694. He wrote: "When nature itself urges us to love our parents who gave us life, how much greater must be our gratitude to our fatherland which has been called, with good reason, the common parent of us all. We must thank her and praise her everywhere and if necessary give our lives for her." [14]

The writings of Juslenius or his predecessors were of small importance as historical contributions. They represent, however, an aspect of the intellectual history of the period. We find in them the first effective expressions of the contention that Finland and its people could claim excellencies inferior to none. They reflected a patriotic attachment to country and nation previously unexpressed and certainly not as yet a part of the nation's literary tradition. Not a few of the unhistorical ideas and absurd contentions expressed by Juslenius became for decades classic models for other writers. Quoted as authority by enthusiastic students, they were found useful, pertinent, and worthy of mention without corrective critical comment by sober historians of a later and presumably more sophisticated age. That Juslenius considered himself a "good Swede" and ended his days as a bishop in Sweden has not prevented Finnish

---

[14] A. J. Pietilä, *Daniel Juslenius* (Porvoo, 1907), pp. 32 ff. E. Ahlman's translation of Juslenius' *Vanha ja Uusi Turku* (1929), especially Chs. II–III, contains excellent illustrations of the author's credulity and pretensions.

historians from seeing in him a main figure in the early history of Finnish national consciousness.

Other developments during the decades after the end of the Northern War in 1721 also sustained and strengthened the new interest in the fatherland. This was true especially of the efforts made on a broad front to regain the economic prosperity destroyed by the war. They rested upon the belief that only by increasing the productivity of farming and reviving industry and commerce could conditions in general be improved. The kingdom's natural resources were written about as never before, the character and earlier history of individual trades were scrutinized, uncultivated areas of the country were investigated and evaluated, and new or improved roads were planned in the hope that greater prosperity might be found.

In these and related endeavors, the University of Turku participated in a manner that ultimately perhaps contributed more to the strengthening of the purposes voiced by Juslenius than to a marked hastening of economic recovery. For instance, historical surveys of towns, provinces, villages, trades, etc.—most of them modest by modern standards of excellence—appeared in increasing numbers as the product of scholarly effort. They dealt for the most part with contemporary conditions and questions; they were descriptions of economic enterprise, administrative organizations, matters relating to church and religion, and the like. During 1730–1800 about one hundred such studies were published. More often than not they reflected a sobriety of approach and seriousness of purpose that placed them, despite factual inadequacies, apart from the fanciful excursions into an imaginary past illustrated by Juslenius. The interest in the fatherland they showed received the approbation of academic authorities and of the leaders of the Church: the head of the university suggested in 1750 that the professors should urge the selection of dissertation topics concerning "our beloved fatherland," and the Cathedral Chapter in Turku emphasized, in 1754, the importance of knowing Finland's history and advised the publication of books on that subject.

As a result of these concerns and interests the history of Finland was placed on a sounder basis than before. They led to a greater knowledge and appreciation of Finland among the educated and

the middle and upper classes in general. While it is easy to exaggerate the significance of these modest historical and related studies,
they appear to have played a considerable part in the discovery of
Finland as a common fatherland and of the Finns as a people separate
from the Swedes. "Patria" began to connote Finland rather than the
kingdom in general and was seen as the larger whole of which the
home town, village, or district was a part. And not less important
was the fact that they provided part of the materials which a later,
more nationalist generation found ready to hand when it proceeded
to construct a national history of more pretentious dimensions. By
the time Henrik Gabriel Porthan appeared on the scene in the 1760s
(see pp. 33, 144) the developments summarized had prepared much
of the ground from which a rich harvest of historical, philological,
and other "patriotic" studies was to be reaped.

In general, these and related interests gradually created Finnish
particularist trends that drew sustenance from many sources. Some
of them can be only surmised but others are obvious enough to
require no extended comment or appraisal.

Geography itself decreed a certain degree of separateness between
Finland and Sweden proper. Until the age of steam in the nineteenth century, communications between Finland and Sweden were
completely severed at certain seasons of the year. As a result, administrative unity and control were at times either limited or nonexistent, and therefore Finland was not as fully a part of the rest
of the kingdom as a glance at the political map of Sweden might
suggest. The absence of easy and regular travel across the frozen-
over Gulf of Bothnia from the Åland sea north to Tornio often
separated Finland from the central administration in Stockholm
and gave longer life to local concerns.

The actual as contrasted with the theoretical functions and importance of the Riksdag also contributed to the same end. Broadly
speaking, the Riksdag became a significant factor in Sweden's government only in the eighteenth century. As a legislative body representing the citizenry of the kingdom it was in many respects conspicuously inadequate. This inadequacy was important to the kingdom as a whole but had a relatively greater bearing upon Finland
than on Sweden proper. While we should keep in mind the fact

that representation in the Riksdag was often considered, before the
nineteenth century, a costly and burdensome obligation rather than
a privilege jealously to be guarded, the fact that the Finnish part
of the realm was usually inadequately represented in the Riksdag was
at times seen as regrettable. Even under the best of circumstances,
members from Finland had no telling opportunity to decide matters
of purely local concern, to say nothing about questions of larger
import, because they were distributed among the four estates. In
each they were a minority that had but little say in questions that
concerned them most intimately, such as taxation, defense, or the
exactions and arbitrariness of Crown officials high and low.[15] The
situation was not basically changed after 1721 when the Riksdag
became, for some fifty years, the repository of governmental power
and the king was reduced to little more than a ceremonial figure-
head.

We have already referred to the internal reconstruction that dominated a good deal of Swedish concerns during the decades following
the close of the Northern War. In this effort, considerable attention
was paid to Finland. Various Riksdag committees investigated the
consequences of the war and ways and means for rehabilitating
the country. Much information was collected; scores of memorials,
complaints, and petitions were received in Stockholm. Many of the
complaints dealt with a grievance by no means new in the 1700s
but seemingly more common by the mid-decades of the century
than formerly, namely, the practice of appointing Swedes to administrative, judicial, academic, and other positions in Finland. The
practice was, understandably, of old standing. After 1721 it became
more common than earlier and created, to judge by the complaints
of the Finns, jealousy and a sense of injury among the gentry and
resentment among the peasantry. Such appointments were, it was
contended, especially objectionable when the appointee knew little
or no Finnish. At the 1738–39 Riksdag, it was alleged among other

[15] It is doubtful, incidentally, that the Finnish representatives in the Riksdag
normally pursued general "Finnish" interests rather than the interests of the
individual estates—nobles, burghers, farmers, and clergy—or the economic
and other concerns of the districts or towns for which they spoke. This is
merely one way of suggesting that it is easy for a twentieth-century observer
of the scene before, say, 1808–9 to see "national" purposes and interests where
actually merely local or class objectives were involved.

things that some customs officials in Finland were inefficient and neglected their duties. "The situation is made worse," according to the charge, by the fact that the customs service in Finland employed "Swedes who do not even understand Finnish. It therefore often happens that goods are incorrectly recorded although they were properly declared, and are confiscated" without any fraud actually being involved. The appointment of Swedes to certain judicial positions was also protested. A judge or official who knew no Finnish was forced to use interpreters, the argument ran, "who feel under no obligation to help the poor Finnish peasant or to see that justice is done. The result is all kinds of errors and confusion, to say nothing of the fact that our own deserving, honorable, and able countrymen are excluded from higher positions." It was demanded that the cause of the difficulties mentioned be removed and that Finns be appointed to the various branches of the central government in Stockholm to facilitate the handling of Finnish business.

The petitions and complaints usually disappeared into the files of the committees appointed to deal with them. However, a Royal Resolution of 1739 recognized the justice of the demand that speakers of Finnish be appointed to judgeships and other offices in Finland "as far as circumstances, the qualifications, and the length of the applicant's previous term of service permit." The resolution did not remove the basic difficulty, for the same grievance persisted after 1739, but it appears to have prepared the way for improved conditions later even though the question of appointments to government or other posts in Finland remained for years a source of irritation. Neither the University of Turku nor the Church escaped involvement, as was shown in 1755 when a new bishop was to be appointed in Turku. The candidacy of one contender for the office was urged on the grounds that he was a Finn—sharp pamphleteering and student demonstrations were also involved—only to meet a pointed rebuke from the king.

It is easy to exaggerate the meaning of the debates and controversies involved in the appointments problem. Many a Finnish historian has seen in it evidence of a deliberate policy of favoring the Swedes at the expense of the Finns and has identified Finnish farmers' and others' complaints and petitions at the Riksdag with genuine grievances that could have been removed by the simple device of appointing a larger number of native Finnish-speakers to public office. They also tend to see in Swedish place-seekers favored individuals tainted with selfish "Swedish" purposes while absolving "native sons" from the same charge. The problem was in all likelihood a good deal more complex than such interpretations suggest. Wirepulling and favoritism undoubtedly were involved in appointments and gave an advantage to aspirants to office who were close to persons and places of influence in Stockholm, but it is difficult to assume that "national" considerations or purposes decided choices and appointments. The way the problem was probably seen by responsible men in Sweden was illustrated by Count Tessin, the chancellor of the University of Turku. In a letter bearing the date February 19, 1757, he deplored the "discord and dissension between the Swedish and the Finnish nations" that had recently been in evidence and denied that discrimination or favoritism determined university or other appointments. "All the inhabitants of the kingdom are subjects of the same state and constitute one people," he declared, and he held that internal jealousies and contention should therefore not be tolerated.[16]

During the closing decades of the 1700s, the problem of appointments and office holding, in the sense in which it had been to the fore, say, in the 1750s, appears largely to have disappeared. It had assumed more manageable proportions probably at least partly because of the prohibition, in 1760, of absentee office holding, ecclesiastical pluralities, and sinecures in Finland. In thus removing a real source of favoritism, inefficiency, and corruption, the prohibition appears to have brought about improvement sufficiently tangible to still earlier criticism and protest.

These and other evidences of Finnish particularism began to emerge at a time when, interestingly enough, Finland was becoming, in some important respects, more rather than less Swedish. The middle and upper classes in the 1700s became, for all practical purposes, Swedish in speech. In the process of Swedization, the schools

---

[16] *Historiallinen Arkisto* (hereafter referred to as *H.A.*), 1889, pp. 449–54; see also *ibid.*, 1878, pp. 185–206, and *ibid.*, 1903, pp. 236–44.

had played a decisive part. It appears that, as long as Latin was the language of education, Finnish was spoken by a substantial part of the classes. After the middle of the 1600s, Latin as the language of instruction began to lose ground, and the process was completed during the 1700s, with Swedish taking the place of Latin. A knowledge of Swedish therefore became a prerequisite for education in Finland as well as elsewhere in the kingdom. Without it, a Finn could obviously not hope to enter the professions or aspire to posts in the service of state or church. This had been true, to be sure, even before the eighteenth century, but the requirement became more impelling during the last hundred years of Finland's union with Sweden. Swedish predominant in the field of education unavoidably meant Swedish as the language of the classes, polite society, and public life in general.

It is easy to understand that Swedish, once acquired, tended to become the dominant and permanent language. According to an observer in 1779, even individuals with modest education "understand and even speak Swedish." By 1800, the gentry in particular illustrated the ascendancy of Swedish. The clergy was likewise influenced by Swedization, but it never became as Swedish in speech as the gentry. The reasons are obvious. The ministers of the gospel —whose mother tongue was in most cases that of their parishioners —were in close and constant contact with the common folk and had to know Finnish. The clergy had used Finnish in religious services even during the Catholic period and had raised the vernacular to the stature of a written language partly before but especially during the first half of the sixteenth century. By the end of the 1700s, the clergy represented, to put the matter in general terms, the only group among the educated classes that was still Finnish in speech. The burgher class, on the other hand, had become largely Swedish in speech by the opening of the 1800s, although a knowledge of Finnish was also common. A considerable degree of bilingualism was unavoidable among the middle and upper classes in view of the fact that some 85 percent of the population was Finnish.

We need hardly add that the greater part of the Finnish-speaking and Swedish-speaking people—the farmers, fishermen, and the like

—lived and died but little touched or troubled by the ascendancy of the Swedish language. Yet the problem was probably sensed by the common folk also. The climb of the common man's son up the educational ladder was difficult but did not depend on the home language of the youth aspiring to rise from the masses to the classes. This is clearly shown by the fact that many distinguished figures— to say nothing of the average educated individual—in the world of learning or in public service before 1800 and later came from Finnish homes. (That is to say, at no time was the Swedish-speaking minority of Finland's population, taken as a whole, the reservoir from which alone the middle and upper classes were recruited or replenished.) A generation usually sufficed to transform the successful Finnish-speaking artisan or shopkeeper into a Swedish-speaking burgher and his son, if he succeeded in school and university, into a Swedish-speaking official or member of the professions. The taking of a Swedish name was usually a part of the metamorphosis. Swedization was often the consequence of even moderate success in business and invariably a part of the process of obtaining an education. The changing of family names into Swedish was by no means uncommon even among the lower classes, especially in urban communities.

It was this general trend toward increasing Swedization that a Finnish observer had in mind when he commented in 1793 that "as recently as the beginning of the present century, the clergy, most of the gentry out in the country, and a great number of the merchants and burghers of the cities spoke Finnish among themselves. How great has been the change since then, and the change has come without any coercion or compulsion. All who have received the education and training of civil servants or attend public schools learn to understand and speak Swedish, and nobody considers this a cause for complaint, any more than those who intend to enter the field of scholarship object to learning Latin." The comment summarized a development and a condition destined to become of outstanding importance not long after Finland's union with Sweden was severed in 1808–9.

THE ANJALA LEAGUE

Finnish historians frequently call attention, in discussing the developments summarized in the preceding pages, to the Anjala League, which, they hold, underscores Finnish separatism and reflects the existence of eighteenth-century independence aspirations significant enough to deserve more than passing mention.

The dissolution of Sweden's Baltic empire as the result of the Northern War meant, as we have seen, not only the loss of the provinces south of the Gulf of Finland but also the cession of a substantial part of southeastern Finland to Russia. Another cession in 1743 contracted Finland's area still further. It therefore seemed, in the eyes of some military men in Finland and other observers, that Sweden could not prevent continued Russian expansion, thus leading to a complete partition of Sweden-Finland, perhaps in the relatively near future. The dire consequences of partition could perhaps be forestalled, some held, if Finland were separated from Sweden without a war with Russia and its independence established under the empire's protection.

The idea that Finland's future security and interests could be safeguarded by such arrangements was naïve and brands its authors as ignorant or unrealistic or both. Among them was one G. M. Sprengtporten. Sprengtporten was an able officer who turned conspirator, fought against his own countrymen in 1789, and ultimately was destined to play an important part in the events after 1808 that defined Finland's position in the Russian Empire. Together with his half-brother J. M. Sprengtporten, he had been involved in the coup in 1772 that started Gustavus III on his career as absolute monarch. Failing to receive the recognition and rewards for his services he felt were due him, he resigned his commission and went abroad, returning to Finland in 1781. His home became the meeting place of scheming officers who proceeded to plan arrangements that would secure Finland's independence under Russia's protection before future military defeats and conquest united the country with Russia without the Finns having a chance to safeguard the interests of the nation. Sprengtporten left Finland in 1786 and entered the service of Russia with the rank of major general. He continued to work for his pet scheme and appeared to be favored by good fortune when war broke out between Sweden and Russia in 1788.

The war was rashly begun in July, 1788, by Gustavus III, without provocation and in deliberate disregard of the constitution, which prohibited the king from starting an offensive war without consulting the Riksdag. The violation of the constitution might have been overlooked by Gustavus III's opponents in Sweden if the war had been successful. It was not; poor generalship, inadequate supplies, and ill-trained forces combined to produce, despite a few battles won and a brilliant naval engagement (Ruotsinsalmi-Svensksund, July 9–10, 1790), a result that spelled defeat. The war also disclosed dissatisfaction among a considerable number of officers that led to trafficking with the enemy and the so-called Anjala League.

A number of the officers serving on the front in Finland appear to have feared, as the result of the war, Russian occupation of the country. They tried to prevent such an eventuality by sending a letter to Empress Catherine a few weeks after the war had begun. In it they held that "the whole nation and especially the people of Finland" desired peace between Sweden and Russia, and proposed, with a naïvete difficult to believe, that the empress guarantee peace by returning to Sweden the areas ceded to Russia in 1743. The incredible proposal led nowhere, needless to say. Gustavus, who as commander-in-chief was with his forces in Finland, got wind of the note and insisted that the officers who had signed the letter pledge themselves to fight the Russians to the last man. The result of the royal demand was not the assurances Gustavus wanted but a document written in justification of the officers' conduct. It condemned the war and urged that peace be concluded with Russia.

The 113 officers who signed the document at Anjala—both Swedish and Finnish officers were involved—contended that Sweden had begun an aggressive war and that therefore "the conviction of the inevitability of war which creates, in a people born to freedom, fighting men who cannot be defeated has vanished." They claimed that the military situation was hopeless enough to make it clear that "it is not thanks to ourselves and our weapons, but thanks to the considerateness of the Russian people, that murder, arson, and destruction have not raged through the length and breadth of our fatherland." It was only because of these considerations, the signers of the statement asserted, that the letter had been forwarded to Empress Catherine. If the empress failed to agree to a peace that Sweden could honorably accept, each signer would consider himself to have been personally attacked by the Russians and would fight to the bitter end.

Upon receiving the officers' reply, Gustavus appears to have been sufficiently disturbed to contemplate abdication but quickly recovered his composure and insisted that the signers redeem themselves by submitting an apology. The king agreed in advance to grant the officers a full pardon. The officers politely refused. In the meantime, Sprengtporten and other like-minded conspirators were working behind the scenes in the hopes of carrying through the goal of an "independent" Finland under Russia's protection. Virtually a prisoner of his own forces and facing a situation that was perilous as well as embarrassing, Gustavus was provided with a convenient out and an excuse for leaving Finland by a Danish declaration of war. He proceeded at once to Sweden, there to organize defenses against the new enemy. The Danish invasion was successfully met, and the Danes withdrew in November. Gustavus could now turn to the Anjala League and its liquidation. A number of the officers were apprehended, tried, and punished. One of the main conspirators was sentenced to death and executed. The dissatisfaction over Gustavus III's rule and undertakings, of which the Anjala episode was but one expression, ultimately culminated in the assassination of the king himself at a masquerade ball in March, 1792. The war against Russia had in the meantime been ended by the Peace of Värälä (August 14, 1790), which reestablished the status quo at the time when the war began two years earlier.

What was the significance of the Anjala League and how important and how widely supported were the Finnish independence aspirations allegedly revealed by the events of 1788?

Henrik Gabriel Porthan, the leading Finnish historian of the day, saw the scheme to detach Finland from Sweden as a "foolish, criminal attempt" detested by all "excepting possibly a few witless adventurers and windbags among our nobility who probably hope they can change their fellow citizens into serfs on the Livonian or Courland model." The common people, Porthan held, "hate the Russians and their protection from the bottom of their hearts, and I would advise that nobody recommend to them the scheme" urged by Sprengtporten and his handful of followers. While opposition to the 1788 war and particularly to the way Gustavus III had irresponsibly begun the war appears to have been widespread in some parts of the country, it implied no support of independence schemes. Such schemes were in fact unknown outside the group of discontented, rebellious officers; the country at large was unaware of them. The clergy remained uniformly loyal to the existing order of things and gave no evidence of an inclination to hold any but properly "patriotic" sentiments toward king and country.

Opposition to King Gustavus III appears to have been fairly widespread among the nobility and was by no means unknown among the burghers. Their opposition did not rest, so far as we can tell, upon aspirations that naturally invite the rubric "national," meaning thereby "Finnish" as distinguished from "Swedish" objectives, whether political or otherwise. The opposition existed before the war, was nourished by the distressing course of the war and the defeatism created by it, and continued after the peace of 1790. In a sense, it culminated in the assassination of the king in 1792. But it would be bold indeed to explain the assassination merely as a consequence of the fumbling separatist intentions of the Anjala group of officers. Many of the officers were in fact not separatists or rebels but men concerned over the breach of the constitution committed by Gustavus when he began the war in 1788, and the convocation of the Riksdag was one of their demands. That men like Sprengtporten and other adventurers were involved and stand forth tarred with the brush of treason does not change the over-all picture. Less still do they invite the conclusion that the people saw in them servants of high purposes worthy of acceptance by the nation.

While it is clear that the Finnish people did not stand behind the

Anjala men and less still supported Sprengtporten and his followers, the Anjala League—and the machinations of a few men after the Anjala group had dispersed in 1788—was interpreted in some quarters at the time, and has been interpreted since, as a Finnish separatist movement. The rank and file of Finland's population remained loyal to the king and harbored no separatist aspirations. Yet this fact has often been overlooked. The reasons were many. Outstanding among them was the skillful manner in which Gustavus III manipulated the situation in 1788–89 and used the Anjala incident in dealing with the opposition groups—primarily the nobles—critical of his policies and especially of the war. Gustavus boldly identified the constitutional opposition in Sweden with "Finnish separatism" and virtual treason. In doing so he exaggerated the extent and importance of the separatists and at the same time made the opposition suspect. The success of Gustavus' tactic was strikingly illustrated at the 1789 Riksdag when, with the support or acquiescence of the three commoner estates, he brushed aside the House of Nobles and forced through several amendments to the constitution of 1772 which further cemented his absolutist rule by placing unrestricted executive powers into his hands. In 1789, the year of the French Revolution, royal absolutism triumphed in Sweden and set the stage for the assassination of 1792. Finland, and the kingdom as a whole, gave no evidence of independence aspirations or movements, either in 1789 or later. The Anjala episode remained an incident of no national import and the purposes of the Anjala group alien to the nation as a whole. It was an enterprise in which the grudges and ambitions of a handful of military men from Finland and Sweden furnished the motive force. It was not an expression of nationalist purposes.

We therefore conclude that what many Finnish writers have seen as evidence of eighteenth-century nationalism or independence aspirations reflected a growing feeling that the Finns "belonged" to a separate geographical area and were linguistically and in other ways different from the Swedes. A species of local patriotism, not yet metamorphosed into nationalism in the modern sense of the word, is what meets our eye as we survey the scene from, say, 1721 to the 1790s. And it is significant that, when less than twenty years after the close of the war in 1790 another war resulted in the partition of Sweden and Finland was annexed by Russia, no Finnish "independence men" on the Anjala model appeared to betray their fatherland and weaken its resistance to the invader by accommodating the enemy.[17]

[17] The literature on the Anjala League and related matters is extensive. See my *Nationalism in Modern Finland* (New York, 1931), sources listed on pp. 243–44, the summary by E. Jutikkala in A. Korhonen, ed., *Suomen Historian Käsikirja* (Helsinki, 1949), I, 616–65, and bibliography on pp. 687–88.

IV

The Separation from Sweden

The long wars that began in 1792 when Revolutionary France became embroiled in war with the western Powers spanned nearly a quarter-century. Their results, as defined by the consequences of the undertakings of the master in aggression, Napoleon, changed among other things the political map of a large part of Europe, set in train events that freed Central and South America from European domination, doubled the size of the United States—witness the Louisiana Purchase—launched England on its course of empire in South Africa, and transformed Russia from an East European into a European Power. In the Scandinavian North the partitions of Denmark-Norway and Sweden testified to the immense ramifications of the upheavals caused by the Corsican's ventures.

The partition of Sweden came in 1808–9, a by-product of the Big Power maneuverings of the day. By the summer of 1807, most of the continent of Europe had been brought to heel by Napoleon, and only England remained to be defeated. A continental commercial blockade was the device that was to paralyze England's economy and thereby bring Albion down. Yet the blockade failed to produce the results desired because wide gaps in it robbed it of its effectiveness. The main gaps were Portugal in the south and Denmark and Sweden—especially the latter—in the north. To close these gaps became one of Napoleon's major objectives. He succeeded in enlisting Alexander I of Russia in the effort, after having defeated Russia in June, 1807.

The essentials of the arrangements of the two emperors were defined at Tilsit in July, some three weeks after Russia's defeat. The conclave would no doubt have been called a summit meeting if the term had then been in use. It resulted, among other things, in a lengthy treaty of peace and friendship and a secret defense and military cooperation agreement. England figured prominently in the designs of the two emperors. An attempt was to be made, with Russia acting as the intermediary, to conclude peace between England and France. If England refused to listen to reason, Russia was to declare herself a supporter, in all respects, of France's demands. If both Powers became involved in war with England, they would at once demand that Portugal, Denmark, and Sweden close their ports to English ships and declare war against the British. If they refused, all three would be treated as enemies.

The three small Powers did refuse to do the bidding of Napoleon and Alexander. Force was therefore to be used to bring them into line. Denmark, however, joined the French camp voluntarily as the result of singularly high-handed action by the British. Denmark having rejected Britain's invitation to enter into a defensive alliance against Napoleon, the English fleet bombarded Copenhagen, forced the city to surrender (September 7, 1807), and carried off the whole Danish fleet. Denmark thereupon went over to the Tilsit coalition (October 30, 1807). Portugal, on the other hand, was occupied by French forces in November. The occupation turned out to be merely the first stage in military operations that led to the invasion of Spain in March, 1808, and a prolonged war that ended only with Napoleon's defeat.

Meanwhile, Alexander I was slow to react to Napoleon's admonitions to proceed to action against England and to compel Sweden to toe the mark. Russia's declaration of war against England came on November 11, 1807. By that time, British ships had been withdrawn from Baltic waters, because of the lateness of the season, and Alexander therefore could look forward to the coming winter months without English naval threat or action in the Baltic. As regards Sweden, Alexander appears to have been reluctant to undertake military action because the recent war against Napoleon and the continuing war against Turkey meant burdens heavy enough— and in the case of Turkey, important territorial objectives in the Balkans—to make it seem prudent to avoid war with Sweden. Recourse was therefore had to diplomatic pressure in the effort to persuade Sweden to join the alliance against England. Gustavus IV of Sweden stubbornly refused and instead proceeded to ready the country for war, hoping to gain enough time to make certain that British aid, expected in the spring of 1808, would be forthcoming. Alexander I ultimately decided to anticipate the situation that would emerge when the British fleet made its appearance and began the invasion of Finland on February 21, 1808.

The fighting forces in Finland that now faced the invading Russians approximated 22,000 men. The Russians appear to have originally committed some 24,000 men to the operation and substantially added to them later. The war went badly for the Finns and the Swedes from the start, partly because the early date of the Russian offensive had robbed the defense of the time needed to complete the preparations that had been planned. A series of retreats, punctuated by a few successful but indecisive battles, led to the Olkijoki armistice on November 11, 1808, and the withdrawal of the defending forces to Sweden where they remained until after the conclusion of peace (September 17, 1809). The former conspirator G. M. Sprengtporten had had a hand, since early in January, in drafting the plans that now began to unfold.

Months before the end of the war the question of Finland's future status had begun to agitate the minds of the leading elements in the country. As we have noted, substantial parts of southeastern Finland had been annexed by Russia in 1721 and 1743 and had become integral parts of the empire. Did the same fate now await the rest of the nation whom the lost war had placed under Russian occupation? It seemed clear that Sweden could not be expected successfully to challenge the verdict of events and recover Finland by military action or by negotiation at the conference table when the peace treaty ending the war would be defined.

Alexander I himself appears to have been uncertain regarding the course to follow. In a proclamation issued on March 15—only five weeks after the beginning of the war—he stated that Finland had been united, in perpetuity, with the Russian Empire. The same statement was repeated on June 5. Political and other considerations, however, led him later to follow a course and to approve a policy which differed sharply in their meaning and consequences from the purposes suggested by the March and June proclamations. The result was an arrangement which enabled Finland to retain her pre-1808–9 constitutional, legal, administrative, and religious institutions with little or no fundamental change: Finland as a part of the Russian Empire was to have the status not of a subject province but of a self-governing, constitutional state, with all the basic instrumentalities essential in such a state—a unique outcome of the war indeed.

Alexander I's new policy began to emerge in June, 1808, while the war still continued, when he instructed the commander-in-chief of the Russian forces in Finland, Count F. W. von Buxhoewden, to arrange for the election of a few representatives of the four estates for the purpose of discussing, in St. Petersburg, the "wishes" and needs of the Finns. The idea created a great deal of unease in the country because it was feared that such a deputation would be considered as the equivalent of a legal assembly of the four estates. The estates could be legally represented only by citizens who had been chosen in accordance with time-honored and clearly defined suffrage laws of the country (that is, laws which had applied in the past to all of Sweden, Finland included, at Riksdag elections).

Having become aware of this view, which obviously reflected the Finns' live concern over the possibility that law and constitution might be violated, the Russian government gave assurances that the deputation would not be considered as representing the estates, and that it was expected merely to make proposals and offer suggestions to the powers that be in the Russian capital. It thereupon went to St. Petersburg. While there its chairman, Baron C. E. Mannerheim —the great-grandfather of Marshal C. G. Mannerheim, who played a major role in Finland's history after 1917—suggested that the estates be convened. Alexander I accepted the suggestion. The first specific indication of his intentions was given by his decision on

December 1, 1808, that questions relating to Finland should hence-forth be submitted directly to him (thus bypassing the ministers of the Russian government) and that a Finnish Diet be convened shortly, in keeping with procedures traditional in the election of members to the Riksdag of Sweden.

THE PORVOO DIET, MARCH–JULY, 1809

The formal call to convene the Diet was issued on February 1, 1809, in the name of the "Emperor and Autocrat of all the Russias" and the "Grand Duke of Finland." This was the first time Alexander called himself Grand Duke of Finland. Elections were hurriedly held in the customary manner, and the four-estate Diet (its members numbered about 125) met in Porvoo on March 25, 1809. On that very day the war ended, for all practical purposes, when most of the last remnants of the Swedish-Finnish forces surrendered. Alexander arrived in Porvoo two days later and formally opened the Diet on the twenty-eighth. On the twenty-ninth, the emperor and the repre-sentatives of Finland participated in a solemn procedure which formally created the self-governing Finnish state.

The first part of the procedure consisted of an Act of Assurance by which Alexander I recognized and bound himself to maintain the constitution of Finland:

We, Alexander I, . . . have desired, by the present Act, to confirm and ratify the religion and fundamental laws of the Land, as well as the privileges and rights which each Estate in the said Grand Duchy in par-ticular, and all the inhabitants in general, be their position high or low, have hitherto enjoyed according to the Constitution. We promise to maintain all these benefits and laws firm, unchanged, and in full force. . . .

After the Act of Assurance had been read to the members of the Diet, it was delivered into the custody of the ranking member of the Diet, the Speaker of the House of Nobles. Thereupon the speakers of the four estates expressed their appreciation of the

Assurance and the estates as a body took the oath of allegiance. They promised "to have and to consider" Alexander I as their lawful monarch (as Grand Duke of Finland) "and to keep inviolate the fundamental laws and the Constitution of the land, such as they are now adopted and in force."

These arrangements and commitments were further solemnized by a decree issued by Alexander less than a week later (April 4).[1] It stated in part that

when We convoked Finland's Estates to a General Diet, and received their oath of allegiance, We desired, on that occasion, by means of a solemn Act . . . to confirm and secure to them the maintenance of their religion and fundamental laws, together with the liberties and rights that each Estate in particular, and all of Finland's inhabitants in general, have hitherto enjoyed.

In hereby promulgating the Act mentioned above to Our faithful Finnish subjects, We also desire to inform them that . . . We consider the oath of allegiance, of the Estates in general, and of the Deputies of the Estates of the Peasants in particular, taken in the name of their fellows as well, to be good and binding on all the inhabitants of Finland.

The Act of Assurance and the decree of April 4, 1809, were later read from the pulpits of all the churches in the country. For the next century and more, copies of both were hung in every church in the land. Until the attainment of independence in 1917–18 these imperial guarantees, to maintain law and constitution inviolate were part of the Finns' conception of one of the decisive events in their country's history and sharply defined their understanding of the nature and basis of Finland's union with the Russian Empire.

The Porvoo Diet did not end its labors until July 19, 1809. Having played its part in the important events that witnessed the Act of Assurance and the decree of April, it had proceeded to discuss a host of questions that the new order of things made pressing. A number of measures dealing with tax matters, financial questions, the military, new administrative organization, and the like were considered and enacted. Alexander attended the ceremonies that closed

[1] This document was in French, as were the other statements by Alexander.

the Diet. In his speech to the legislature he stated (in French) in part that he had convened the Diet in order to

ascertain the wishes and sentiments of the nation regarding its true interests. . . . Completely trusting the loyalty of your character . . . I have allowed perfect freedom in your deliberations. No extraneous influence or authority has dared to cross the threshold of these portals. . . . When you now leave, you still have essential duties to perform. Carry home to your provinces and impress on the minds of your fellow citizens the same confidence which has presided over your deliberations here . . . regarding [the nation's] political existence, the maintenance of your laws, the security of your persons, and the inviolability of your property.

Alexander also predicted that the Finns would be "grateful to Providence" for having "brought about the present state of affairs. Placed henceforth in the rank of nations, governed by its own laws," Finland would in the future remember its former affiliation with Sweden only "in order to cultivate friendly relations after peace has been established." "Externally tranquil, internally free, devoting itself to agriculture and industry under the protection of the laws and morality," Finland would henceforth testify to the success of the new order of things under which the nation would live in the years that lay ahead.

The unhappy war was ended by the treaty of Fredrikshamn on September 17, 1809, almost two months to the day after Alexander I had attended the closing ceremonies of the Diet in Porvoo. By its terms, Sweden formally ceded Finland to Russia, including the Åland Islands, which had long been an administrative part of the Finnish half of the kingdom. The boundary henceforth separating the two sister nations was also fixed and as then defined has remained unchanged, except for details worked out after 1809, down to our own day. These arrangements completed and, as far as could be seen, rendered final the new order of things in Finland. Finland was now a new separate state whose head, the tsar–grand duke, was a constitutional monarch in Finland while he remained the absolute ruler, the tsar of all the Russias, within the empire. Extensive as the powers of the Crown in Finland were, according to the constitution of the country, Alexander I could not legally rule by fiat but would have to accept the Finnish Diet as a partner in legislation—especially in the enactment of important laws, tax measures, changes of the constitution, etc.—and responsible, duly appointed native officials as aids in the governance of the nation. To do otherwise would be to violate Finland's fundamental law and to disregard the bases of "law-bound" society.

THE GOVERNMENT OF AUTONOMOUS FINLAND

Alexander I at Porvoo had not dictated, nor had the Diet been invited to provide, all the governmental and administrative organs by means of which the nation would henceforth be governed. Similarly, the question of how the government of autonomous Finland would maintain such contact as would be necessary with the tsar residing in St. Petersburg had been left open. These and related problems were gradually solved, however. The general pre-1809 governmental and administrative machinery at the local and provincial levels remained, for all practical purposes, unchanged and continued to function as it had before the separation from Sweden. The changes that did emerge related to the higher branches of the government.

The blueprint for the new central government had been drafted in the early spring of 1808 by a special committee of leading Finns appointed by Alexander I. Having been accepted by the tsar, the plan was submitted to the Porvoo Diet; upon approval by the Diet, it was promulgated by the tsar. The plan called for a government council that was to serve in a twofold capacity: it was to be the central government of the nation, and part of it was to serve as the nation's supreme court.[2]

When the government was organized in 1809–11, it had fourteen members. The number grew to twenty by 1820. Part of its mem-

[2] The council was officially designated, in 1816, as the Imperial Senate of Finland. Throughout the Russian period, down to 1917, it was usually called the Senate and its members Senators. In view of the special meaning these terms have in English, we shall call the Senate the Government and its members Ministers. The appropriateness of these designations will become clear as we note the functions and powers of the new central administration.

bers—ten after 1820—constituted the Supreme Court, which was henceforth the successor, in Finland, of the Swedish Supreme Court. The other ten ministers constituted the government proper. Its members were in charge of departments or ministries, such as finance, church and education, interior, agriculture (founded in 1860), trade, public works (also founded in 1860), commerce, industry, justice, war, etc. (The war department was discontinued in 1903; some of the others mentioned appeared only after 1816, the original number of departments having been five.)[3] The members of the government were appointed by the tsar for a renewable term of three years; the appointees had to be Finnish—not Russian—citizens. The Porvoo Diet was given an opportunity to suggest the names of the appointees to the first government but later appointments were made without such recommendations.

The central government also included a number of subordinate central offices. The first to appear was the Medical Directorate (Collegium Medicum) established in 1811. The Post Office and the Directorate of Public Works emerged later in the same year. The Customs Service and the Pilot and Lighthouse Service were founded in 1812. The number of these offices grew over the years as the area of governmental concern and activity expanded; by 1914 they numbered nineteen.

In addition to the government with its ministries, Supreme Court, and central offices, there was still another important and independent official. Designated as the Procurator, he served as an observing, probing public servant whose responsibility it was to ascertain that the members of the government and officials and civil servants performed their functions according to the requirements of the law and that legality and justice in general prevailed. The first incumbent of the post was the nation's leading legal scholar of the period, Matthias Calonius.

The handling of Finnish questions in St. Petersburg did not involve departments or agencies of the imperial government. This

[3] The two sections of the government were called, until 1917, the Department of Justice and the Department of Economy. The latter is obviously a particularly inadequate, not to say clumsy, designation in English. It is of course clear that "Economy" falls far short of covering the areas of governmental function within which the government actually moved.

had been decided when Alexander I resolved, on December 1, 1808, that Finnish matters be thenceforth submitted to him directly. In view of the fact that the tsar–grand duke resided in the Russian capital, it was essential to create a special organization through which Finnish business could be transacted. The solution of the problem was the appointment of a Finnish Secretary of State, with an office and staff in St. Petersburg. The title of the Secretary was changed in 1834 to Minister Secretary of State. This important post was held from 1811 to 1841—a significant, formative period in the history of Finnish-Russian contacts—by Baron Robert Henrik Rehbinder. A special organ, the Finnish Affairs Committee, was also appointed in 1811 to handle Finnish questions preparatory to submission to the tsar. It was dissolved in 1826 but was revived in 1857 and functioned till 1891 when it was finally ended. The State Secretariat and the Minister Secretary of State, on the other hand, continued to perform their function until Finland declared her independence in 1917.

There was one office in the new governmental structure to which the rule that officialdom and civil service should be manned by Finnish citizens did not apply. The office was that of the governor-general. Except for the Finnish adventurer, G. M. Sprengtporten, who had entered Russian service in 1786 and served as governor-general for less than a year in 1808–9, the governors-general during 1809–1917 were, without exception, Russian. The governor-general was the personal representative of the tsar-grand duke. His position was in some respect loosely defined and his functions less imposing than might be assumed in view of the original purpose of his office.

In one respect he was the head of the government. As chairman of the government he presided at its sessions. With few exceptions, the governors-general did not know Swedish (which remained the exclusive official language of the country until 1863), and Russian not being a language in which public business could be transacted, they seldom attended the government meetings. The sessions were therefore usually chaired by a Finnish member of the government, the vice-chairman, who became, in a sense, the premier.

The limited part played by the governor-general in the government by no means marked off the limits of his general position and function. Independent of his loose connection with the central government, he supervised the maintenance of peace and order within the country and watched over the administration as well. "Watched over" is literally correct, for local and provincial government, exclusively manned by Finnish appointees, carried on their business according to pre-1809 law and regulation without any direct interference by the governor-general. He was also the commander-in-chief of the Russian forces garrisoned in Finland. Their number was small throughout this entire period—for instance, it appears to have been about 40,000 during World War I—and they lived completely isolated in a few garrison towns or areas, having little contact with the communities involved, which viewed them as foreigners to be avoided whenever possible. The governor-general was also a go-between to whom certain Finnish and Russian authorities turned if they had business to transact in "the other country." Appointed by the tsar without consultation with the Finns, he had the right to communicate with and submit memoranda to the tsar regarding proposals or recommendations forwarded to St. Petersburg by the Finnish government. He did not enjoy the privilege, limited to the Finnish State Secretariat in the Russian capital, of personally appearing before the tsar to urge policies and measures he might consider important.

It was only during the last score of years of the Russian period—from the middle nineties to 1917—that the governor-general became one of the agencies for destroying Finland's autonomy and carrying forward the purposes of Russification. By that time, however, much of the new order that had emerged in 1809 and the years following had been transformed, as we shall see, by developments that had nothing to do with the original purposes of the governor-general's office.

Not the least significant feature of self-government and autonomy after 1809 was the fact that school, church, and university remained wholly under Finnish control and direction. They thus continued to develop on the bases that generations of pre-nineteenth century life and experience had built. The school system was as yet modest, and half a century was to pass before the first beginnings of a real state-directed national system of education were to emerge. The

Lutheran Church retained its privileged position as state church, undisturbed by the fact that some twoscore thousands of Greek Orthodox citizens had become part of the country's population when the areas ceded to Russia in 1721 and 1743 were reunited with Finland. The University of Turku, moved to Helsinki in 1828, received new and generous grants and other advantages which turned it into a practically new, and certainly vigorous, center of learning destined to play a most important part in the life of the nation after 1830.

As if further to underscore the political and administrative separateness of the Grand Duchy, the customs boundary between the former Finnish part of Sweden and Russia was retained unchanged. Despite efforts made by certain Russian interests in the late 1840s to remove the customs system, which provided Finland with a tariff wall against Russian competition, the customs boundary was retained intact until the 1880s when it was partly modified to meet the new needs of a rising industrial society.

In view of the basic features of the constitution as defined in 1772 and 1789, it is clear that the Crown enjoyed extensive powers in the new Finnish state. As grand duke of Finland the tsar was, to be sure, a constitutional monarch whose function in legislative and other matters was limited in theory, in important respects. Lawmaking involved the participation of the Diet. In legislation relating to economic matters in general, he had the right to issue decrees without consulting the legislature. Customs duties belonged in this category. Measures increasing old taxes or providing for new taxes, however, required the assent of the Diet. The traditional right of self-taxation was thus retained, in principle, unimpaired. Existing taxes, on the other hand—that is, taxes levied as of old in 1809— were automatically continued after 1809. The finances of the state, having on the whole been geared to the yield of traditional taxes before the separation from Sweden, remained on the old basis. All the taxes collected were used for public purposes in Finland; no part of the revenue went to the imperial treasury.[4] The state finances of

___

[4] The main levies in the early part of the 1800s were the land tax (centuries old and the most important tax), the poll tax, various judicial and other fees, a tax levied on home stills, stamp taxes, and customs dues; the last were, for decades after 1809, of very minor importance.

the nation were thus, from the beginning of the union with Russia, independent of those of the empire. While the Diet did not have the right to enforce accountability in the matter of state income and outgo, the Crown was obligated to inform the Diet of the status of the state's finances in order to enable the legislature to ascertain that the public funds had been properly used for the common good.

The competence and powers of the Finnish central government were nowhere defined in complete detail. It had the right to plan and decide regarding all matters which had not been specifically reserved by the constitution to the tsar–grand duke. The area left to its discretion was, in view of the powers of the monarch, far from extensive. It could not alone enact new laws, for legislation involved action by the monarch as well as the Diet. It could not issue decrees dealing with economic matters, nor was it empowered to impose new taxes. Its right to provide for the use of public funds was restricted by the requirements of the state budget. It had the right to submit requests and recommendations—for instance, recommendations for appointments to public posts, which were usually accepted by the monarch—on a variety of matters, including economic and related policies. The drafting of the annual budget was also one of its responsibilities.

While the powers of the government were very limited vis-à-vis the tsar–grand duke, its position in the area of domestic, Finnish matters was quite different. It was in law and in fact the apex of the nation's governmental and administrative organs. It was the national government. Throughout the nineteenth century, and until the chill winds of Russification began to blow hard during the years before World War I, the Finns saw it as a genuine national government, sharply differentiated from everything Russian. That foreign affairs and defense were outside its competence appeared to matter little or not at all. That its decisions were issued in the name of the tsar and not in the name of Finland was an irrelevant formality devoid of real substance. Especially after 1860, when Finland's political autonomy was remarkably extended and seemingly strengthened, and when the economic and general cultural separateness of the country from Russia became ever more marked, it was the government and its distinguished roster of members that were credited with having safeguarded and buttressed the ramparts behind which state and nation had been able, since 1809, to live under the protection of its own laws and constitution.

The Finns had been, before 1808–9, Swedish subjects and citizens in the full sense of these terms. After 1809 they were citizens of Finland, clearly distinguished from the Russians who could acquire Finnish citizenship only according to the Finnish law of naturalization. The law thus placed the Russians in the same category with other aliens. While the constitution as defined in the settlement of 1808–9 did not contain a bill of rights—the same applied also to the Swedish constitution at the time—Finnish citizens continued to enjoy rights and privileges of old standing, solidly anchored in law and custom.

Basic among these rights were personal freedom, equality before the law, which meant immunity to discriminatory enactments and the right to be heard and judged only by regular courts, the right freely to move and select one's domicile, protection against arbitrary action by officials, and the right of petition for redress of grievances. The rights of free speech and free press, as well as of assembly and association, were hedged in by restrictive laws but nevertheless were clearly recognized and not dependent upon arbitrary ruling by individual officials. While property and other qualifications severely limited the right to vote in local or "national" elections—the latter meaning the election of representatives to the four-estate legislature, the Diet—the right to vote was no less clearly recognized after 1809 than it had been during the "Swedish period."

Not the least important right enjoyed by the Finns under the new order had to do with offices and posts in the public service. Only Finnish citizens could be appointed to positions in state or church. While practical considerations led in time to a few appointments in disregard of this rule—the governor-general mentioned above was the outstanding illustration—it remained a strong bulwark against all tendencies to eliminate it and to open the door to alien officeholders.

THE CONSTITUTION OF AUTONOMOUS FINLAND

When Alexander stated in the Act of Assurance that he "desired
. . . to confirm and ratify . . . the fundamental laws of the Land,
as well as the privileges and rights which . . . all the inhabitants
[of Finland] . . . have hitherto enjoyed according to the Constitution," he was understood in Finland to be referring to the constitution of the Swedish realm at the time of the Russian invasion of
Finland. It was this constitution, in force in Finland no less than
in other parts of the Swedish kingdom, that furnished the broad base
upon which the new order of things would henceforth rest. Finland
as an autonomous state can therefore be best understood as a concrete political reality by identifying and understanding the meaning
of the main components of the fundamental law.

The constitution consisted of the so-called Form of Government
of 1772 and the Act of Union and Security of 1789. The Form
of Government, full of contradictions and obscurities, had been imposed upon country and Riksdag by a carefully planned coup d'état
engineered by King Gustavus III. The Act of Union and Security
had been forced through the Riksdag with skill and political
trickery by the same monarch. Taken together, they spelled a
governmental scheme of things over which royal absolutism was
indeed writ large.

The national legislature, the Riksdag, was reduced to a subordinate
position. It could meet only when convened by the king. It could
consider only matters submitted to it by the king and therefore
had no lawmaking initiative or right to legislation by bill. Its say
in matters of taxation was reduced; the king continued to enjoy
a "legal right" to the land tax which the Crown had enjoyed since
the Middle Ages, and the Riksdag's power of decision or veto in
regard to other taxes, such as levies imposed in time of war, was
practically eliminated. While the Riksdag retained the right to be
"informed" regarding the finances of the government, it could not
impose accountability. Foreign affairs and defense remained in the
category of "king's business." All executive functions belonged to the

king "and nobody else." The Council of State was wholly subordinated to the monarch, who was bound, according to the 1772
Form of Government, only by the "law of succession, the law code
of 1734, and this Constitution." The constitution of 1772 was, incidentally, not only a new fundamental law but also an administrative
statute which defined the administrative apparatus in detail and left
all important decisions regarding it in the king's hands.

The Act of Union of 1789 deserves special mention. It was, in a
sense, an addendum to the Form of Government of 1772, some
parts of which were canceled and to which certain new provisions
were added. It further extended the powers of the king. He could
henceforth begin and end war, conclude alliances, and decide regarding "other matters which relate to the welfare of the realm"; in
these and related areas he could proceed as he thought best. He could
also "arrange," according to "His high preference," all of the offices
of the realm. Only "lesser civil servants," the clergy, and judges were
exempt from the Crown's broadly defined powers to dismiss. They
could be deprived of their posts only by legal process.[5]

One of the few restrictions upon the power of the Crown under
the new royal absolutism was the provision that the king was bound
by "the law code of 1734." These words referred to a new common
law code which had been in the process of preparation for over a
century before its final acceptance by the Riksdag on December 13,
1734. The law was promulgated on January 23, 1736, but has long
been known as the "Law of 1734." It was an impressive, outstanding
accomplishment in Swedish legal history. In the words of the
Riksdag decision, the code was henceforth to be "the general, perpetual, and unchangeable law of Sweden." Despite many changes
and additions over the past two centuries and more, parts of it are
still identifiable in the basic structure of law in Finland as well as
Sweden.

During the long centuries before 1808–9 Finland had, naturally,
fully shared the slow evolution of law and the administration of

---

[5] The right of farmers to hold and inherit land, on a basis similar to that
applicable to nobles, was also confirmed, and Crown tenants were given
permanent tenancy rights and the right to become owners by purchase.
Burghers' privileges were also confirmed by the Act of 1789, as were those
of the clergy.

justice which furnished the foundations of the law code of 1734.
After the separation from Sweden, the Law of 1734 acquired—by
accident and not by design—a very special significance. The law
covered nearly all aspects of the life and daily round of the individual. Its 203 chapters provided for matters that ranged from marriage,
property, inheritance, landowning, building, trading, and the like to
crimes and misdemeanors, as well as procedures and rules pertaining
to the functioning of courts of law. It also contained, as an appendix, "some general rules which a judge shall fully observe" ("Någre
almennelige Regler, ther en Domare skal sig aldeles effter rätta").

The common man in all probability neither fully understood nor
appreciated the "constitutional" and administrative consequences of
Alexander I's decisions or the labors of the Porvoo Diet, but he
had no difficulty in realizing the importance of retaining, in the
domain of law and justice, the tested and the familiar ways of yore.
Neither the anonymous many nor the sophisticated few were called
upon to submit, under the post-1809 order of things, to the precepts
of Russian, alien law or the ministrations of judges trained in a
foreign, repellent legal tradition. Therefore the domain of law and
the administration of justice represented, after 1808–9, an area of
human experience and institutional function that remained untouched—for all practical purposes wholly untouched—by alien
influences destructive of rule and practice sanctified by long, native
tradition. The vital areas of man's life in society blanketed by the
Law of 1734 illustrated during the nineteenth century to an exceptional degree the fact that autonomy and self-rule had a very special
meaning and profound significance for the nation at large far beyond
the limits which the "constitutional" arrangements of 1808–9 had
defined.

The Law of 1734 was significant for nineteenth-century Finland
in other ways as well. When it went into effect, a substantial part of
southeastern Finland had been in Russian hands for several years,
having been formally ceded in 1721. Peter the Great permitted these
areas (within which the Law of 1734 obviously did not yet apply)
to retain "Swedish law," which meant the so-called Christopher's
land law of 1442, with later additions and amendments. The additional cessions of southeast Finland in 1743, on the other hand, meant

the inclusion within Russia's borders of districts where the Law of 1734 had been applied for seven years. The question in 1808–9 and shortly thereafter was whether and in what way these eighteenth-century cessions might be "returned" to Finland, and to what extent, if at all, the three variants of "Swedish law" could be rendered uniform.

The answer to the question was given in 1812. Alexander I decreed that the Finnish territories ceded in 1721 and 1743 be united with Finland, becoming integral parts of the Grand Duchy and enjoying the same laws, constitution, and autonomy as Finland. The Law of 1734, together with such changes and additions as had been made after it went into effect, therefore became the basis of the legal order in southeastern Finland as well. Thus all of Finland could build, after 1812, upon the same solid legal and judicial foundations. Legislation and such reordering of the courts and the administration of justice as future needs might indicate would therefore be restricted by no limitations except those imposed by the constitution solemnly recognized as the basic law of the land at Porvoo.[6]

Modern history records few if any international settlements comparable to the result of the labors of emperor and Diet at Porvoo in March–August, 1809, and the arrangements that followed in 1809–12. That the Finnish representatives in Diet assembled readily participated—in the passive, merely advisory way that Alexander I found appropriate—in the task of transforming Finland into an autonomous state is easily understood, given the circumstances created by the victory of Russia's arms. It is Alexander's purpose and objective in setting up the new political order of things which intrigues and puzzles.

[6] The Law of 1734 was published in Finnish by G. Salovius in 1759 and in an expanded and improved version by Matthias Calonius, the leading student of the law in Sweden at the time, in 1808. Calonius and other professors of law at the University of Turku were responsible for the fact that not only the judges but officials and civil servants in general were well versed in the Law of 1734. The same was true during the nineteenth century, thanks to such experts in the law as W. G. Lagus, J. Ph. Palmén, R. A. Wrede, and others. In 1934, the bicentennial of the law, a group of "jurister i Sverige och Finland" published a three-volume work on it. The third volume is a facsimile edition of the original, admirably executed. Its fascinating content appeals to the layman no less than to the expert.

While the answer to the whys and wherefores must be partly tentative, it appears that Alexander's main purpose was to arrange matters in Finland in a manner that would eliminate, or at least greatly reduce, dissatisfaction and resentment over and opposition to the turn things had taken. Russian policy aimed at keeping the people tranquil while the war lasted and to convince the Finns after peace had been concluded that Finland and its citizens were better off than they had been before the separation from Sweden. This could be done, easily enough, by pointing to the actual results of the war. The country had its own, separate government. Its laws, administration, and other traditional institutions were, for all practical purposes, intact. Taxes would henceforth be used only for Finland's benefit. The army formerly stationed in Finland had been disbanded, but its commissioned and noncommissioned officers retained their salaries, fully paid, during the years of retirement. The merchants of the towns had been granted new privileges that broadened the area of their economic opportunity. The clergy also found themselves the objects of special solicitude, and the farmers' lot was eased by the elimination of certain obligations that had previously been theirs. Leading personages in the government and the professions were assiduously cultivated in the hope that they would accept the new order as good and congenial. Developments after 1809 were to show that the broad-fronted policy of pacification was nicely geared to the circumstances of the day, and that it was adequate to produce the results Alexander I considered important.

The policy of pacification was part of a larger purpose, that of turning Finland into a buffer state serving the defense needs of the empire. Russia's strategic boundaries had now been moved to the Gulf of Bothnia and the distant reaches of the Swedish-Finnish border in the northwest. These objectives were, however, not the only ones that explain the whys and wherefores of the 1809 arrangements. Both the nature of the Swedish constitution and Alexander's ideas regarding government, constitutions, and the like were also part of the considerations that made possible the exceptionally favorable status Finland enjoyed after 1809.

It is impossible to imagine that Alexander could have been persuaded to accept a constitutional scheme for Finland more liberal than that defined by the Swedish constitution in force in 1808. The Swedish Riksdag had been riding the crest of the wave for five decades before Gustavus III's coup d'état in 1772, while the Crown had been altogether subordinated to the legislature. By 1789 the roles had been completely reversed. The monarch, as we have seen, dominated the scene. Everything of substance was subordinated to his will. After 1809 the Finnish Diet was the equivalent of the Swedish Riksdag. Its place in the scheme of things—especially its relation to the monarch—was precisely that of the Riksdag under the royal absolutism of the years after 1789. Alexander I could therefore safely accept, without reducing or endangering his own power as "Autocrat of all the Russias," the constitutional order he found in Finland. To perpetuate it by recognizing Finland as a nation "governed by its own laws," as he had done at the Porvoo Diet, did not seem even remotely to jeopardize the tsar's prerogatives and authority.

Alexander I's ideas regarding government also account for his readiness to devise the special status granted to Finland. They were in all likelihood of greater importance than the general nature of the Swedish constitution or the specific manner in which it exalted the monarch and emasculated the legislature. Alexander did not consider a "constitution" a fundamental law or collection of rules and principles designed to limit or divide the monarch's powers or prerogatives. Instead of interpreting the term "constitution" in the manner that has long since become general, Alexander understood something quite different by the term. It meant merely a law which defined and described the governmental and administrative order of things necessary for the carrying on of government. Issuing from the plenitude of the monarch's power, it could in no sense infringe upon the sovereignty of the autocrat.

In this view Finland was, after 1809, "a nation with a constitution" or, to put it differently, a nation whose government was rationally organized; its traditional institutions included, among other things, a four-estate Diet whose function was seen by Alexander as merely advisory. It could be convened and used, at the discretion of the monarch, to serve and support the government. When consulted, the Diet could inform and advise but not decide;

it could petition for but not initiate legislation. The Diet was not an organ whose participation in the formulation of the monarch's decisions and policies was in any sense essential. Without activation by the tsar–grand duke it was nothing. It did not in fact exist unless convened by the tsar; it had no independent power to meet or to dissolve. In a word, it seemed to fit admirably the role which Alexander's political conceptions assigned to it.

It is thus clear that the 1808–9 constitutional and other safeguards of Finland's autonomy were modest in the extreme. The Swedish constitution was, as we have noted, anything but democratic. The heavy accent it placed on the powers of the monarch made possible a "lawful" absolutism in Finland that yielded only slowly to the emerging demands for greater participation, by the Diet, in legislation and policy making. Over half a century was to elapse before the legislature was enabled to perform—at first only within narrow limits—the functions of a lawmaking body.

Coupled with this inadequacy of the fundamental law was another. No statute or charter defining the relationship of constitutionally governed Finland and autocratic Russia had emerged from the Porvoo Diet or Alexander I's plans. As we have seen, Alexander's Act of Assurance confirmed and ratified "the religion and fundamental laws of the land" as well as the rights and privileges that the estates and the Finns in general had enjoyed as of old. His statement at the closing session of the Diet on July 19, 1809, underlined the safeguards of the nation's "political existence," the "maintenance" of the country's laws, the security of the individual, and the "inviolability" of individual property. Important as these and other pronouncements were, they left many matters of vital concern wholly untouched.

Conspicuous among them was the broad and significant area of government. The various arrangements during 1809–16 that established the Finnish government and provided for the office and functions of the governor-general, or those of the Finnish State Secretariat in St. Petersburg, rested upon *ad hoc* decisions and choices by the tsar–grand duke. They did not emerge from a law or statute prescribing by constitutional fiat what was clearly legal and proper and what was not. And it goes without saying that the constitution did not mark off the areas within which the tsar's writ did not legally run in Finland, nor is there any reason for assuming that, if such areas had been fully identified, they would have been considered inviolate either by Alexander or by his successors.

These facts invite the conclusion that after 1809 Finland's constitution could offer at best only few advantages and limited protection against the dangers inherent in the affiliation with the Russian Empire. Later events were to show, however, that the advantages were substantial and the protection on the whole surprisingly strong. The constitution and what it stood for offered a secure anchorage when Finland was increasingly exposed, during the two decades before World War I, to the rising tide of Russification. By the time this tide was running strong, the constitution itself had evolved in a manner that enabled Finland after 1906 to stand forth, because of her internal political institutions, as one of the most democratic nations in Europe.

V

The Nationalist Movement after 1820

ADOLF IWAR ARWIDSSON

While most Finns accepted the separation from Sweden as unavoidable and a good many saw the situation after 1809 as an improvement in many respects upon the past, there were others who hoped that Russia's annexation would not last. They dreamed of a reunion with Sweden; in their view the union with Russia was a great misfortune from which no good could come. In 1812 Napoleon and Alexander, whose agreement in 1807 had led to the dismemberment of Sweden two years later, were again at war. It was hoped that the outcome of the war might cancel the settlement of 1808–9, but much would depend upon the views and purposes of the Swedish government. The shifting currents of opinion and policy in Stockholm were therefore closely followed by the Finns apprehensive of Russia and desirous of reestablishing the old connection with Sweden.

The loss of Finland was not at first considered permanent by Swedish leaders. King Charles XIII said, upon being informed in 1811 by the prominent statesman G. M. Armfelt that he intended to return to his native Finland, "We shall meet again, God helping us, for Finland will return to us yet." Bernadotte, whom the Swedish Riksdag had chosen heir-apparent to the Swedish throne in August, 1810, was fully aware of the fact that in making the choice the Swedes hoped that it would favorably impress Napoleon and gain his support for the recovery of Finland. In 1812, when the French

invasion of Russia "appeared most menacing, Alexander was probably prepared to pay for the cooperation of Sweden by the restoration of Finland. Napoleon made the same tempting offer (in return
for cooperation against Russia) which coincided with the wish of
the majority of the Swedish people." Bernadotte, however, "regarded Finland as an obstacle to a real and lasting peace with Russia,
and contemplated instead the conquest of Norway." [1] By the end
of 1814 Bernadotte could point to the inclusion of Norway within
his domain as "adequate" compensation for Finland. Only two years
earlier, in 1812, he had concluded a treaty with Alexander I which
confirmed the cession of Finland and seemed permanently to seal the
fate of the country as a part of the Russian Empire. The harsh
realities of international politics had thus shattered the hope that the
union with Russia would become only a passing interlude. If the
verdict of 1808–9 were to be changed, new opportunities would
have to be exploited and new sources of strength, sufficient for the
demands of a future day of liberation, discovered.

Even before it had become clear that Sweden had abandoned Finland the Finns appear on the whole to have accepted the verdict
of the war of 1808–9. This is suggested by the views found in
letters and other similar records of the period that have come down
to us. Of the views of the inarticulate common folk little or nothing
is known. Many saw in the grant of autonomy and the retention of
the old familiar constitutional and legal order of things the generous
act of a considerate ruler who wanted to unite Finland to his empire
with bonds of lasting gratitude. Thanks to him the Finns could look
forward to enjoying their time-honored institutions. The Diet of
the nation—a smaller, Finnish version of the Swedish Riksdag—had
been convened not to accept in abject submission the dictates of the
tsar–grand duke but to participate, as was appropriate to a national
legislature, in the making of decisions important to every citizen in
the land. Peaceful growth and orderly development could be taken
for granted in the years that lay ahead so long as the nation enjoyed
the advantages of its new status.

The acceptance of the new status was made easier by a fear of

[1] Carl Hallendorff and Adolf Schück, *History of Sweden* (Stockholm, 1929),
p. 365.

the suffering and disasters that a new war between Sweden and Russia would bring. Quite apart from the losses in life and property that had ever been, at the very least, the result of past wars with Russia, there were other considerations of no small import. Finland as a self-governing, autonomous state invited comparison with its earlier position as a part of Sweden. Finland now enjoyed more than the things for which her spokesmen at many a Riksdag had argued and petitioned. They had urged redress of certain grievances, economic and other. Now an autonomous Finnish government manned by Finns had been created. Place-seeking Swedes, occasionally sources of dissatisfaction and protest in the past, would no longer be a problem. Taxes had been reduced—temporarily, to be sure, but nevertheless reduced. Revenue collected in Finland would not disappear into the royal treasury in Stockholm, where formerly nearly one half of the taxes had normally been forwarded to be spent for purposes frequently of no importance to Finland. And many a leading man of the time had benefited by newly acquired economic or political advantage or both. Acceptance of favors of one kind or another had in some instances disclosed haste in adjusting to the Russian order bordering upon servility that might not stand up well under close scrutiny. Many who were riding the crest of the wave after 1809 could hardly contemplate with equanimity the accountability that a return to Sweden would in all likelihood mean.

The new order seemed tolerable for still other reasons. The establishment of the government in the Finnish capital and of the Finnish State Secretariat in St. Petersburg underscored the fact that Finland stood in direct relation to the tsar–grand duke and had little or nothing, it was easy to convince oneself, in common—beyond the common monarch—with the Russian Empire. The result of the events of 1808–9 therefore came to be thought of by many as having led to submission to the person of the tsar and not as arrangements providing for Finland's incorporation into the empire. As one of the leading personages of the day, Secretary of State G. M. Armfelt, put it, "I have no connection with Russia for I am a Finn and can be nothing else, but I am bound to the benefactor of my country, Tsar Alexander, who has treated me and mine with extraordinary kindness." Armfelt's views were shared by others, especially by persons sufficiently prominent to make them the beneficiaries of the plenitude of imperial favor.

Still another consequence of the events of 1808–9 was seen by many as a promising omen for the future. For centuries before 1809, Finland had been the object of repeated Russian attacks, and Russians had come to be looked upon as the perennial enemy. Neither in history nor in legend did war wear any other visage but the Russian. The situation had now changed, it was believed. Incorporation into Russia would in all probability mean the end of the many wars of the past. Even in an age which was not yet committed, as is ours, loudly and with a stubborn optimism which baffles as well as inspires, to the chimera of a world without war, the likelihood that Finland would henceforth at long last be spared the curse of war was indeed a comforting and reassuring prospect. And this safeguard had been obtained not at the cost of enslavement of a hitherto free people but as the result of a change in Finland's status that offered new advantage and privilege. There was more than rhetoric in the words of a leading military man who said, after appraising the results of Finland's union with Russia: "We are a free people, as heretofore. . . . We are governed according to our own laws. We have chosen our own men to administer justice. . . . If we are permitted [in the future] to enjoy the advantages we now have, Finland will be, considering her position, the happiest country in all of Europe."

Contrasting the lot of his country before 1809 with the present, he summarized the effects of Finland's past situation as a part of Sweden in words which many a Finn probably would have considered altogether appropriate at the time and for many years thereafter:

Finland was the scene of war for centuries. . . . Thousands of persons were killed in every war, to the eternal loss of the country. This is the reason why one third of our country is still uncultivated. When a couple of decades of peace had repaired some of the damage and the population began to grow and material well-being increased . . . war was again upon us. Every peace brought added taxes and burdens—heavier at times than those borne by the Swedes. . . . This was the advantage we derived from [being a part of Sweden]. It is my belief that as long as we enjoy the protection of the ruler of Russia and as long as the Russian monarchy exists Finland will never again become a theater of war. It is in these respects that I consider Finland more fortunate now than [formerly].[2]

There were thus, it seemed, many reasons for finding the new dispensation superior to the old. The actual as well as assumed benefits to Finland of the union with Russia were of course often interpreted in terms of personal advantage. The defeat of Napoleon appeared permanently to seal the cession of Finland to Russia. Sweden had concluded a treaty with Russia, as we noted, which confirmed the cession and therefore removed the possibility of canceling the verdict of 1808–9. These developments made it easy to claim that here indeed was proof positive of the wisdom of compliance. The logic of unchallengeable circumstance had proven compliance to be not merely quick-footed adjustment of stance to fit a new situation but farseeing statesmanship sustained by the dictates of patriotism and a sense of duty. Recent events and future expectations appeared to place a premium upon the new order, which was no hastily contrived improvisation destined to vanish with the emergence of the next Big Power constellation but a solid and on the whole satisfactory reality to which state and nation would henceforth be firmly anchored.

The severance of the centuries-long connection with Sweden also caused a quickening of Finnish patriotism and contributed to a national awakening destined to carry the nation far from the moorings of 1808–9. The strengthening of love of country was part and parcel of the development of a Finnish national consciousness, and it involved, in the first instance, the educated classes who were able to read the signs of the times and understood, at least in general terms, the implications of the union with Russia.

Patriotism is the love of a man for his country. It is, in modern times, both universal and manifold, and merely to take note of its existence is to tell us only that human beings are human. If we seek to be enlightened concerning it, we must know the quality and the purposes of patriotism. In the case of the Finns, it was the cutting

[2] Quoted in Carl von Bonsdorff, *Opinioner och Stämningar i Finland 1804–1814* (Helsinki, 1918), pp. 79–80.

of the connection with Sweden that made it possible—nay, made it essential—for Finnish patriotism to come fully of age. Local and provincial loyalties had to be flattened out and make room for the larger concept of people, nation, and state.

That patriotism was stimulated and strengthened after 1809 was natural, not to say inevitable, given the historical experience extending over hundreds of years that had made the Finns what they were when their country was joined to the giant Russian Empire. The results of the 1808–9 war gave them a new idea and conception of a fatherland—gave them, in a sense, a new fatherland in the literal sense of the word.

The events of 1808–9 placed Finland, for the first time, on the political map of the North. To be sure, the country's boundary with Russia was clear and of old standing. The inclusion in 1812 within autonomous Finland of the southeastern areas that had been ceded to Russia in 1721 and 1743 merely served to reestablish the border with the empire where it had been fixed as far back as 1617. Now another new boundary line had been drawn, for the first time separating Finland from Sweden. Finland now stood forth, with its geographical boundaries sharply marked off, as a separate political entity. Flanked in the west by Sweden, which for the first time in history had become, because of the operation of Big Power politics, "foreign" to the Finns, and in the east by Russia, the nation was henceforth envisioned in sharpened outline as the true fatherland of the Finns. As one of the contemporaries of this event wrote in 1810: "Which do we Finns now consider as our real fatherland, Sweden or Finland? I hold that my fatherland is where I was born, where as a child I imbibed my love of country, and where I grew up and received my upbringing." Another commentator held that "a return to the former union with Sweden was not thought of, and nobody wanted to think of a complete amalgamation with Russia. . . . We considered Finland . . . our fatherland, and felt that Finland was an entity by itself which could no longer become Swedish and ought never become Russian. In other words, we felt that we were Finns, members of the Finnish nation." [3]

[3] A. Schauman, *Från Sex Årtionden i Finland* (Helsinki, 1892–93), I, 19–20; see also my *Nationalism in Modern Finland* (New York, 1931), p. 58.

Such views stimulated the new patriotism upon which a growing number of Finns were to build, during the first few decades of the union with Russia, an ever-stronger sense of national consciousness which not only inspired the articulate leaders of the nation but in time sustained the anonymous many as well.

However acceptable Russia's annexation of the country seemed to some Finns, and however unavoidable it appeared to others who could see no opportunity to change it and therefore accepted things as they were, some of the younger patriots soon came to see the union with Russia in a different light. They regarded it as a national tragedy. To them the union appeared to mean an ever-present and ever-growing threat of political, cultural, and linguistic Russification. Filled with apprehension when they contemplated the future of their country, they cast about for safeguards against the calamity they feared and wanted to escape. They found a safeguard in what might be loosely called internal, national unification.

At the center of their thinking was the idea and conviction that, if the people of the country could be made to sense the danger of Russification and if they could be welded into a nation fully conscious of a separate nationality and distinct culture, the danger beckoning in days to come might be avoided. A strong feeling of national distinctiveness would become the rock upon which the country's fate would securely rest, even if the constitution would at some future date become but chaff in the storm, political autonomy subject to the caprices of imperial policy, and linguistic Russification a real menace to Finns in high station and low. The desired national unity, these young patriots believed, could be built only on linguistic unity.

We noted earlier that the people of Finland have been bilingual since time immemorial. In the early years of union with Russia and until the end of the last century, approximately 85 percent of the population was Finnish-speaking and nearly 15 percent Swedish-speaking, meaning thereby that the group whose home language was Finnish came to well over four fifths, while the people in the Swedish home-language category accounted for about one seventh of the total. Most of the upper and middle classes were at least partly bilingual but Swedish was their "first" language and it was

Swedish that was the language of polite society and education. The mass of the two language groups—which means the common folk who represented the great majority of Finns and Swede-Finns alike —spoke only one language, or had mastered the other only moderately well. Confronted by this internal language division, the patriots proclaimed that it must be eradicated. Because Finnish was the language of the overwhelming majority of the nation, they concluded that it should become the language of all Finns regardless of class or station. Fixing their attention especially upon the middle and upper classes, they claimed that these classes must become fully Finnish in speech. The substance of this creed was expressed by an unknown writer who devised the formula: "We are no longer Swedes, we cannot become Russians, therefore let us become Finns."

The most important early spokesman of the nationalist views was Adolf Iwar Arwidsson, who ultimately became a poet, newspaperman, and historian. Arwidsson was one of the many young Finns who considered the separation of Finland from Sweden a great national misfortune. Well versed in Swedish history and profoundly convinced of the superiority of the culture and institutions of his country over those of Russia, he contemplated with horror the future of Finland as a part of the Russian Empire. The constitutional guarantees granted to autonomous Finland in 1809 he felt to be wholly inadequate. The ease with which the leading elements in the country, as he professed to see them, accepted the new order of things filled him with indignation. In the official classes, he tended to see little more than ignorance, venality, and a selfish chase for pensions, titles, and the like. He desired "to have a real fatherland, to be a citizen of a State, and not a squatter in a rotten province governed by stupid asses and sly foxes."

Determined to arouse his countrymen to the dangers he foresaw and to disturb the tranquillity of both ass and fox, Arwidsson undertook a secret campaign against the powers that be. Unable to use the press in Finland, he dispatched a series of letters to Sweden in 1820. Two were published anonymously in a Stockholm newspaper and circulated in Finland. They contained a wholesale condemnation of the government of Finland, and caused considerable consternation among those most directly affected. In Finland,

Arwidsson had recourse to a less militant method. He founded a newspaper of his own in 1821 and in its pages he prodded his countrymen, as far as prevailing censorship permitted, to a new realization of the needs of the time.

Arwidsson also put forth ideas and theories regarding nationality, many of which became permanent parts of the Finnish nationalist creed of later years. He held that language is the main criterion of nationality. Only a people speaking a common tongue constitutes a national, indivisible whole. A people with a common language is united by ties stronger by far than the bonds through which political or other institutions bind individual human beings together. The highest aim of a nation should be the retention and development of its individuality. This requires the creation and sharing of a common feeling of national consciousness. Whenever a nation fails to retain its individuality, it is guilty of "cowardly, treasonous surrender of the place assigned to it; it has revolted against the Eternal Order" and, having defied it, has forfeited its right to exist. From this it followed, as regards the Finns, that Finnish should become the language of school, society, and government, because it was the language of the great majority of the Finnish nation. The majority of the nation could never become the beneficiary of educational or other advance unless its language replaced Swedish in schools. Nor could the majority feel a vital interest in the government or judicial or other institutions of the land, unless and until Finnish became genuinely the mother tongue of the upper classes.

An important part of Arwidsson's nationalist notions had to do with the new position of his country after 1809. While at first doubtful regarding the meaning and importance of Finland's constitution and self-government as a safeguard, by themselves, against Russification, he came to hold that Finland as a separate constitutional state demanded much more than the sterile efficiency of bureaucratic officialdom. The nation could no longer be satisfied with mere officeholders. It needed statesmen who, inspired by an unselfish love of country and nation, could properly serve the people's needs and purposes large and small.

When Arwidsson urged that "all the Finns ought now to constitute a united whole" and that "every citizen ought to feel deep in his heart that he is a Finn and nothing else," he saw the language barrier separating the classes from the masses as the main obstacle to be overcome. It could be overcome only if the teaching of Finnish and the use of Finnish as a language of instruction became general and if education, instead of remaining a privilege enjoyed by the few—and therefore continuing the process of Swedization—became an advantage enjoyed by all.

It followed, Arwidsson contended, that, unless education solidly founded upon Finnish became truly general and progressive, Finland's future would be dark indeed. Only a nation that enjoyed such education could be "endowed with that strength and perseverance which rulers must take into acount, and which the fatherland can depend upon to give courage in battle and a spirit of devoted sacrifice in the hour of danger." Arwidsson recited with vigor the calamities that befall people unable to retain their linguistic and cultural separateness. Dishonesty and a lack of loyalty characterize the family life of such nations and political subordination to alien peoples is their lot. It was no accident that Arwidsson made Slavic peoples serve as examples of extreme national degradation: "Change us into half-Finns or half-Russians, and we shall soon sink to the level of full-fledged Moldavians, Wallachians, or Serbs."

Arwidsson was forced to leave Finland in 1823 because of his outspoken advocacy of views unacceptable to the government. He emigrated to Sweden where he later became librarian of the Royal Library in Stockholm and the author of several historical works. His collision with the authorities was applauded by like-minded patriots, but for several years his pleas and program went largely unheeded. By slow degrees, however, the Arwidssonian nationalist creed gained ground and, aided by many developments, it was ultimately elaborated into an impressive nationalist movement. The fear of Russification was its main basis.

THE FINNISH LANGUAGE IN SCHOOL AND UNIVERSITY

The nationalist agitation launched by Arwidsson ended with his emigration to Sweden in 1823. Yet the seed he had sown was des-

tined to produce an abundant yield. By the 1840s a veritable nationalist movement had appeared, and by the 1860s the movement
had recorded victories that only the most optimistic could have
predicted in Arwidsson's day. Progress in the field of historical
studies and the teaching of national history; gradual recognition of
the need for introducing on a broader scale the study of Finnish
and the use of Finnish as the language of instruction in schools; the
compilation and publication of a growing body of folklore and the
like; and the accomplishments of patriot-statesmen such as Johan
Vilhelm Snellman carried the "Finnish movement" to goals that
could but seem virtually unattainable in the early years after 1809
and prepared the ground for the ultimate victory of the cause by
the end of the century.

When Arwidsson and others raised their voices declaring that
the middle and upper classes should "nationalize" themselves by
adopting Finnish as their language, they were urging effort that
could not easily be carried through. It was simple enough to claim
that "without Finnish we are not Finns" and that the language of
the majority of the nation "ought to be taught and used more extensively" for the obvious reason that "without its development
we shall never enjoy the advantage of becoming a united people."
It was quite a different matter to become "nationalized" in the linguistic sense so long as education—especially middle and higher
education—remained Swedish. It is therefore not difficult to understand why the nationalist objectives came to include the demand
that Finnish be introduced as a language of instruction as well as a
subject of study in the secondary schools leading to the university
and in the university itself.

An official survey in 1826 showed that Swedish was the language
of instruction in all important schools in the country with the exception of the city of Viipuri in the southeast of Finland, where
German held the field to the exclusion of Swedish. The implications
of the situation were phrased in the same year by the Turku Cathedral Chapter in a statement addressed to the School Commission as
follows: Although "Finnish is the original and true mother tongue
of our country, and therefore of necessity would seem to deserve
careful attention and further development—as is the case among

civilized peoples—little or no attention was paid to it when our educational institutions were founded. Yet a knowledge of Finnish is not only desirable but well-nigh indispensable" in every walk of life. The Cathedral Chapter suggested that Finnish as a subject should be taught "at least in the primary schools," but its suggestion led to no result.

The monopoly of Swedish in classroom and lecture hall was obviously a serious obstacle to educational advance and an injustice toward the great majority of the nation. It could not permanently remain as the sole language of instruction. Change was, however, both gradual and slow. After 1824 clergymen appointed to serve in Finnish parishes were required, for the first time, to present evidence of a satisfactory command of the language of their charges. In 1828 the first lectureship in Finnish was established at the university, and in 1843 Finnish was made a part of the curriculum of the secondary schools. The language was introduced, however, only as a subject of study and not as the language of instruction even in these courses. The first professorship in Finnish was established at the University of Helsinki in 1851, its incumbent being M. A. Castrén. The chair was assigned to Elias Lönnrot, the physician-folklorist, in 1853.

Still another indication of the trend of the times was the decision, in 1858, that doctoral dissertations could henceforth be published in Finnish (as well as Swedish or other languages such as German or French).

Meanwhile the old order was yielding to the new in other ways as well. After 1856, judges appointed to serve in Finnish-language districts had to be able to speak Finnish. Two years later it was decreed that the minutes of county councils in these districts—which meant in most of the country—must be kept in Finnish. And the same year witnessed an achievement which marked the opening of a new era in Finland's educational history: the first Finnish-language secondary school opened its doors in Jyväskylä, in central Finland. That instruction in the school was at first given partly in Finnish and partly in Swedish, that several members of the teaching staff mastered Finnish only in the process of teaching, and that some of the students at the new school were at the outset poorly prepared to study in Finnish suggests something of the difficulties under which Finnish-language secondary schools began to contribute to the process of "nationalizing" the educated classes.

FOLKLORE STUDIES AND THE *KALEVALA*

Several Finnish academic luminaries had already become interested in the collection and study of Finnish folklore during the eighteenth century. Henrik Gabriel Porthan's *Dissertatio de Poesi Fennica* (1766–78) was an outstanding illustration of this interest. Folklore studies remained a respected field of scholarly concern after 1809 and have continued to enjoy marked popularity down to our own day. Yet the decades after 1809 marked an important difference between folklore studies before that date and those that came later. Before the separation from Sweden, folklore, legends, and songs were the concern primarily of scholars of no marked nationalist bent but who often showed more than purely scientific appreciation of their findings. After the separation from Sweden, interest in this field assumed a new aspect: it served to strengthen and sustain Finnish nationalism as a purposeful doctrine. Folklore came to be seen as the embodiment of valued national characteristics and a most important measure of truly indigenous, native culture. "No independent nation can exist without a fatherland, and no fatherland can exist without folk poetry [which is] nothing more than the crystal in which a nationality can mirror itself; it is the spring which brings to the surface the truly original in the folk-soul." A young scholar contended in 1817, in speaking of the folklore collections known at the time, that, if "young Finnish writers" cared more "for the products of their fatherland and tried to develop the literature of their country," a new and splendid field would be open to their efforts. He went on to exclaim that "if we were desirous of collecting our old folk-songs and made of them an organized whole," the result might well be "a new Homer, Ossian, or Niebelungenlied; and adorned by its originality and the honor of its unique development" the Finnish people "would arouse the admiration of the present and of future generations."

The 1820s witnessed the beginning of renewed active interest in Finland's folklore treasures and the publication on a larger scale than hitherto of the materials collected. During and after the twenties, the work of preserving for later generations the remaining songs, poetry, and folksay of their forefathers continued at a quickened pace. One of the important results of these endeavors was a series of four publications by Z. Topelius—the father of the poet and historian—that appeared between 1822 and 1831. In the place of earlier fragmentary compilations Topelius offered lengthy epic poems collected among the common country people. His work proved conclusively that stores of folk poetry—probably rich stores at that —might still be found and salvaged, especially in the eastern part of the country. The man who followed in Topelius' footsteps was Elias Lönnrot (1802–84).

Lönnrot entered the University of Turku in 1822. He soon identified himself with other university students and professors who had begun actively to study and "work for" the Finnish language. Professor Reinhold von Becker, who had recently begun to devote his time and energies to folklore studies, introduced Lönnrot to research in the field. Lönnrot completed his first detailed investigation in 1827, and published four minor collections after several field trips in east Finland and Russian Karelia, in 1828–31. Having completed his medical studies in 1832, he served as physician in a small inland town, meanwhile continuing his work as a rune collector with exceptional vigor and perseverance. The results of his labors were astounding. In a few years he collected from scores of skilled rune singers thousands of items of songs and poems. Lönnrot undertook to weave a complete story out of these materials and produced a connected poem of twenty-five runes containing some 12,000 lines. He named it the *Kalevala* and published it in 1835. A second, enlarged edition of nearly 23,000 lines was published in 1849.[4]

---

[4] The *Kalevala* did not mark the end of Lönnrot's compilation of folk songs and the like. He published the *Kanteletar*, an important collection of some 650 lyric and other poems in 1840, another of folk sayings in 1842, one of riddles in 1844, and a fourth containing poems dealing with magic in 1880. Lönnrot's interests turned ultimately to philology and resulted in a monumental Swedish-Finnish dictionary completed in 1880.

The work of rune collecting continued after Lönnrot had completed the *Kalevala*. By 1922 about 500,000 items of folk songs, poems, and the like had

The *Kalevala*, which begins with a description of the creation of the world, relates at considerable length the adventures of four main heroes. One of the heroes is an old patriarch and minstrel, another a handsome young man who is a skillful smith, the third a reckless, good-natured youth constantly in and out of trouble, and the fourth a slave of prodigious strength whose life is dark and tragic. Skill in the arts of magic and the power of wisdom and song play a decisive part in determining the fate of the individual and the course of events in general. Several heroines enliven the pages of the epic. They range from a beautiful maiden coveted—in vain, to be sure— by an old man to offensive, crude harridans. The close of the last rune tells of the virgin Marjatta who gives birth to a child seen as the Christ child, the "king of Karelia."

To the generation of the thirties the publication of the *Kalevala* was an event of outstanding importance. It was enthusiastically hailed as a relic from what was believed to have been a distant heroic past. It was seen as a Homeric poem which the genius of the people had fashioned in times immemorial and which had been handed down from generation to generation. In the course of the centuries its original unity had been dissolved into thousands upon thousands of fragments which Lönnrot had remarkably recovered and joined into a whole that now stood forth as a mighty monument to the exceptional creative capacity of the Finns in the realm of mind and spirit. The *Kalevala*'s content was thought to be genuinely national; no foreign influences had marred it. It was accepted as a rich storehouse of historical facts as well as a dependable and unique compilation of mythology. It brought to light a fecund poetic genius of well-nigh national proportions that compelled unqualified admiration. Its pages disclosed, it was contended, a fascinating age of novel customs that charmed an age held captive by romanticist appreciation of ancient rusticity and the spell of a culture now revealed for

---

been collected, and a generation later the number had grown to over 1,000,000 (including variants). The *Kalevala* has been translated in full into eighteen languages, among them Swedish (complete translation in 1841), German, French, English (1907), Hungarian, Russian, Spanish, Italian, and Estonian. Babette Deutsch published in 1940 an interesting prose condensation of the *Kalevala* under the title *Heroes of the Kalevala* (Julian Messner, Inc., New York). Francis Peabody Magoun, Jr. translated and published a new prose version of the *Kalevala* in 1963 (Harvard University Press).

the first time. It disclosed the startlingly rich resources of the Finnish language (and was later to play a decisive part in the development of modern Finnish as a literary vehicle). And not least important: the *Kalevala* gave life and inspiration to the rising nationalist movement of the thirties and early forties. Its reception at the hands of the intellectuals of the day and the educated classes in general offers, incidentally, a measure of the extent to which the classes of that time knew Finnish. The *Kalevala* could be read and appreciated only by readers more than moderately versed in Finnish.

Scholarly research during the past two generations and more has demonstrated that Lönnrot himself was, in a special sense, the author of the *Kalevala*. He himself put the matter as follows in 1849:

The order in which the rune-singers sing their poems cannot be completely ignored, although I paid no great attention to it because they differ greatly from one another in this respect. It was this difference . . . which made it impossible for me to consider the arrangement of one superior to that of another. . . . Finally, when no single rune-singer could any longer be considered my equal in knowing the songs, I felt that I had the same right which, I was convinced, the other singers freely reserved to themselves, namely, the right to arrange the songs according as they seemed to fit best; or, in the words of the folk song, "I myself began to conjure, I myself began to sing"—that is, I considered myself to be as good a rune-singer as they were." [5]

The fact that Lönnrot's achievement thus turned out to be not merely that of a collector and compiler but showed him also to be the last and the greatest rune-singer has not robbed the epic of its importance for the growth of Finnish national consciousness. As one enthusiast put it in 1836, the "significance of this treasure of these Finnish poems of antiquity is so great that our native literature has not only been immensely enriched by it but has achieved, through it, almost European distinction. It is not too much to say that our literature has only now shed its swaddling clothes. Finland, the owner and proprietor of these epic poems, will properly learn,

[5] Quoted in A. R. Niemi, *Kalevalan Kokoonpano* (Helsinki, 1898), p. 248. The literature on the *Kalevala* is enormous. F. A. Heporauta and M. Haavio have edited a fascinating collection of twenty-one essays, *Kalevala, Kansallinen Aarre* (Helsinki, 1949)

thanks to her increased sense of self-appreciation, to understand her past and also her future intellectual advance. She can now proclaim to herself: 'even I have a history.' " Another later commentator summarized the matter by remarking that "the *Kalevala* has been a mighty source of strength in increasing our national consciousness and in kindling our faith in the future; in doing so it has sustained the continuing contacts of our educated groups with the larger whole of the nation, has joined the past to the present and has added to our national cultural heritage, and, above all, has stimulated and challenged men of science and poets to formulate ever new interpretations."

Despite the great significance of the *Kalevala* in the development of Finnish national consciousness, and despite the countless stimuli and fructifying impulses it has given to cultural concerns and achievements, it has never become a widely read "people's" book or epic. It took twelve years before the original edition of five hundred copies had been sold. While a handful of intellectuals enthusiastically welcomed the *Kalevala*, the newspapers and periodicals of the day gave it only casual mention, and decades were to elapse before Lönnrot's astonishing work became known—not necessarily read—among the people at large. It has remained, to a large extent, a tome conspicuously displayed on bookshelves, not infrequently impressively bound in leather. It has not become a literary treasure inviting repeated and appreciative perusal by the lay reader.

The reasons are obvious. The language of the *Kalevala* is strange and archaic. Excessive alliteration, stilted rhyme, and repeated use of synonyms create formidable obstacles to easy reading. Repetitiousness and parallelism compound the difficulty. The device used by Lönnrot of having every second line practically repeat in different words the idea or subject of the preceding line, while indicative of the richness of the language to the cognoscenti or the enthusiast, suggests bloated verbosity difficult to digest. The life and world depicted in the *Kalevala* are altogether strange and far remote from the realities of the modern world. No amount of pretentious, romanticized searching for "national" origins of "genuinely Finnish" cultural and other antecedents can hide its primitiveness, which readily suggests a forbidding age far enough in the murky past—if, indeed, it ever existed—to have no historical meaning in modern times.

Two other circumstances appear to have contributed to the same result. First, Lönnrot's great labor and incredible accomplishment in compiling the *Kalevala* have been known ever since the epic was published and are an integral part of its history. Because of the decisive role he played in the creation of the *Kalevala*, the claim that the epic is a "national" product authored by an all-pervasive "national genius" unavoidably raises an insistent question. The question is where the line runs that separates the *Kalevala* as a monument to a dedicated scholar's and rune-singer's achievement from the *Kalevala* allegedly embodying the poetic genius of the Finnish people. The question is not easily answered, but neither can it be ignored. Secondly, representations in painting and sculpture of events and personages in the epic, during the past century and more, have been sufficiently varied to suggest, clearly and emphatically, that purely subjective choices and conceptions have guided painter and sculptor alike. This in turn has underscored the fact that the epic has no anchorage in known historical events.

LITERARY DEVELOPMENTS AND THE NATIONAL AWAKENING

Partly before and partly during the years when Lönnrot was assembling the immense materials that went into the *Kalevala*, a number of poets, novelists, and others furnished new and vital impulses to the nationalist movement. Most of the contribution of these patriots was put forth in Swedish. This was particularly true of the leading poets and literary men of the middle decades of the century. It led some later interpreters of the literary history of the period to claim that the contributions in question were, basically, illustrations of the exceptional flowering of Swedish-language literature in Finland rather than expressions of genuine Finnish nationalist, patriotic attachment to country and nation. Such interpretations miss the mark by a wide margin. They ignore one of the most conspicuous features of the early decades of the Finnish national awakening: practically every aspect of its purposes was stated and urged by men whose natural vehicle of expression was, understandably, Swedish. They were inspired by a profound love of their country and its people and gave expression to their patriotic impulses in a manner that was not a whit less "Finnish" than that displayed by their successors who served the same high purposes of their nation by writing and speaking in Finnish.

This basic fact is strikingly illustrated by the Saturday Society and its members. The Saturday Society began in 1830 as an informal association of university students, graduates, and others with intellectual concerns. Its main purpose was the promotion of patriotic interests and the improvement of the material and cultural life of the nation. Its membership included a large number of the men then living who were destined to prominence, especially in the field of letters and education, during the second and third quarters of the 1800s. The roster included many of the men around whose names the history of one of the most important periods of the Finnish nationalist movement must largely be written.[6]

One of the outstanding results of the Saturday Society's interests and activities was the Finnish Literature Society, founded in 1831. The immediate reason for the organization of the latter society was the desire to assist Lönnrot in the publication of folk songs, poetry, and the like. Its general objectives, however, were more ambitiously defined:

Because it is the Society's aim to work for the cultivation of all subjects that are related to a knowledge of the Fatherland or to the development of the Finnish language, the Society intends to collect all printed and written records concerning Finland's antiquity, mythology, geography, statistics, and the Finnish language and poetry; Finnish songs, old sayings, and antique objects, as well as all publications, irrespective of subject matter, written in Finnish; and whenever possible, to publish works useful for the development of the Finnish language, history, and literature; to give encouragement, by means of prizes, to the writing and translation of books on these subjects by competent authors . . . and

[6] T. Havu, *Lauantaiseura ja sen Miehet* (Helsinki, 1945), is an admirable history of the society, told primarily by means of a series of biographical sketches.

to the study of specific problems related to Finland's history, literature, and language.

The first and greatest single achievement of the society was the publication of the *Kalevala*, made possible by funds raised by the society. During the ensuing years, it became the center of patriotic studies of every description. Beginning in 1841, it published the *Suomi*, a learned compilation that has appeared since that year. As the headquarters for the publication of collections of folklore, innumerable textbooks, dictionaries, and a variety of scientific works, the Finnish Literature Society exerted an influence upon the course of the nationalist movement and the intellectual development of the country which no other organization was able to equal. That the minutes of the annual meeting of the society were kept in Swedish and the presidential addresses at these meetings were delivered in Swedish for a quarter-century after its founding illustrates the fascinating fact, already noted, that the use of Swedish was no obstacle to the pursuit of patriotic goals considered important at the time. Elias Lönnrot, who served as president from 1855 to 1862, appears to have been the first to deliver a presidential address in Finnish in 1857.[7]

Two literary men in particular stand out, during these years, as contributors to the growth of Finnish national consciousness even though they wrote only in Swedish. Both reflected the prevailing patriotic atmosphere and at the same time gave powerful impulses to it. Their contributions were in some respects of greater immediate significance to the nationalist movement than the *Kalevala*.

Johan Ludvig Runeberg (1804–77) matriculated at the University of Turku in 1822. Before completing his studies, he served as tutor in the Finnish countryside, where his interest in the Finnish farmer and his world was greatly stimulated. In 1832 he published the first of a number of poems destined to have a profound influence. The *Elgskyttarne* (The Elkhunters) was a long hexametric poem describing the life of the humble farmer in central Finland. Runeberg saw the lowly tiller of the soil as the embodiment of splendid qualities; in him the poet discovered "patriarchal simplicity, a pro-

<hr />

[7] E. Nivanka, ed., *Pysy Suomessa Pyhänä* (Helsinki, 1961), pp. 40–59.

found manly endurance, an inborn clear comprehension of life's most intimate aspects." *The Elkhunters* gave sharp relief to these and other admirable characteristics and earned it acclamation as the first great national poem of modern Finland. The word pictures in which the poet presented living examples of the life of the Finnish farmer to the upper classes opened new vistas to the patriots. In *The Elkhunters* and other poems, said one of Runeberg's contemporaries, "we recognized ourselves and felt that we were one people, that we had a fatherland and were Finns."

Among the other important contributions made by Runeberg to the growing nationalist spirit of the nation two in particular stand out. Both came in 1848, the first in May and the other in December.

A student festival on Flora Day—May 13—had long been a part of the university tradition. The occasion in 1848 developed into a nationalist occasion the like of which the country had never witnessed in the past. One of the well-known poets and the best speaker of the day, Fredrik Cygnaeus, electrified the thousands present with a compelling oration on the subject "Finland's Name." The climax of the celebration was reached with the singing of "Our Country." The poem had been written by Runeberg in 1846 and set to music in the spring of 1848. It was sung over and over again, with infectious enthusiasm. The dramatic introduction of the song quickly established it as the national anthem of the country. In its Finnish and Swedish versions, it has served as a source of patriotic inspiration for well over a century and gives every promise of remaining permanently one of the main expressions of Finnish love of country and nation.[8]

The quickened patriotic impulses manifest on Flora Day were kept alive and strengthened by Runeberg's *Fänrik Ståls Sägner* (The Tales of Ensign Stål), which appeared in December of the same year. Having kindled the imaginations of his countrymen sixteen years earlier by his *The Elkhunters*, Runeberg now brought forth a collection of seventeen poems—the first of the poems was "Our Country"—which quickly became a veritable storehouse of patriotic inspiration. Augmented in 1860 by seventeen additional poems, the *Tales* dealt with the events and personalities of the unhappy war in

[8] See my *Nationalism in Modern Finland* (New York, 1931), pp. 95–97.

1808–9 that had made Finland a part of the Russian Empire. The poems presented portraits of men and incidents drawn with consummate poetic skill and animated by a deep love of country untainted by chauvinism.

Even a foreigner can hardly read them without being moved to tears by their naive simplicity, by the sheer beauty they shed on noble human striving and suffering, by the faith and reverence with which the poet handles the great issues of life and death . . . by the fiery, self-sacrificing patriotism through which human clay is transfigured into something greater than itself. . . . Noble patriotism has never been more finely expressed than in these poems.[9]

The generation to which the *Tales* were introduced during the Christmas holidays in 1848 instantly recognized the spirit of the poet's message. "We rejoiced, we sighed, we were enraptured [by the poems]," wrote a contemporary, "and our hearts beat faster than before. We felt more than ever that we belonged to a nation worthy of being preserved. This feeling no arbitrary decree could ever hope to suppress." From that day to this, the *Tales* have remained among the vital books of Finnish patriotic literature.

Zachris Topelius (1818–98) was the son of the physician–folklore collector whom we noted among the important predecessors of Lönnrot and the *Kalevala*. While pursuing studies at the University of Helsinki, he lived with the Runebergs and through them came to know the stimulating interests and purposes of the Saturday Society and other similar literary endeavors. After taking his degree in 1840, he became the editor of one of the leading newspapers of the day, the *Helsingfors Tidningar*. Devoted to poetry from childhood, he published verse as well as stories and novels in his newspaper for the next eighteen years. A long series of articles on Finnish history appeared over the years and his publications also included a play and an opera libretto. Three collections of poetry testified to exceptional talent colored by romanticism and a strong love of country. He stood forth in many ways as one of the main popularizers of the national movement. Although he himself never played a direct, active part in carrying the torch of nationalism, he had the skill and

[9] A. Reade, *Finland and the Finns* (London, 1916), pp. 38, 40.

power to bring the meaning and need of it to persons in stations both high and low. He was particularly successful in showing the children and youth of the land what Finland meant and what it demanded of devoted patriotic and enlightened citizenship.

Two of Topelius' contributions were especially significant in carrying the patriots' cause forward. His reader for the primary schools, *The Book about Our Country*, consisted of some two hundred readings dealing with country and nation, half of them devoted to history. It managed to inspire as well as instruct on every page. In his *The Tales of an Army Surgeon* and *Stories for Winter Evenings* (1851–66) Topelius showed himself to be the master of the historical novel. The *Tales* tells the history of Finland —by means of the history of two families over several generations —since the Thirty Years' War. The book has probably contributed, during the past century, more than any other single source to the Finnish Everyman's conceptions of his nation's history. It continues to this day to hold its high place among the leading works of Finnish patriotic literature. As writer and poet for children Topelius has remained popular among the other nations of the North as well. There was more than poetic justice in his appointment, in 1856, to the newly established—the first—chair in Finnish history at the University of Helsinki.[10]

[10] While no professorship in Finnish history had existed before 1856, lectures in the field had been given at least since 1834. Gabriel Rein, Professor of General History in 1834–67, devoted part of his attention to the history of Finland, lecturing only half of the academic year on general history and devoting the rest to Finnish history. Nivanka, ed., *Pysy Suomessa Pyhänä*, pp. 63–65.

VI

The Nationality and
Language Problem, 1863–1914

JOHAN VILHELM SNELLMAN

The Finnish nationalist movement could not permanently be limited to the collection and publication of folklore, discussions regarding the "rights" of the Finnish language, or the endeavors of poets and other contributors to the patriotic message. It had to pass from theorizing and generalized program-making to concrete accomplishment and political change. The central figure in effecting the transition, in carrying the nationalist cause to its main victories during the middle decades of the century, and in defining its later goals was Johan Vilhelm Snellman (1806–81).

Snellman's background was typical of that of many of the nationalist leaders. He came from a Finnish middle-class family. He entered the University of Turku in 1822 and moved to Helsinki in 1828 when the university was reestablished there after the city of Turku had been destroyed by fire in 1827. In Helsinki he became associated with men of Runeberg's and Lönnrot's stamp and the Saturday Society. After he had taken his degree in 1831, he was appointed lecturer in philosophy at the university in 1835 but was forced to leave four years later because of a clash with the authorities over an intended course of lectures on academic freedom. The years 1839–42 he spent abroad—in Sweden, Denmark, and Germany—where he continued his studies, culminating in the publication of his outstanding work, *Läran om Staten* (The Theory of the State), in 1842. Snellman returned to Finland in the autumn of that year. Failing to obtain an appointment at the university, he accepted the post of principal of a boys' secondary school in Kuopio, a small town in central Finland. He returned to Helsinki in 1849, where he quickly established himself as a leading figure in the capital. Appointed to a professorship in 1853, he reached new distinction ten years later when he was appointed a member of the government and shortly thereafter was placed in charge of the Ministry of Finance.

Before leaving Finland in 1839, Snellman had begun a career as a newspaperman which was to last, with some interruptions, for many years. The first result of his journalistic venture was the publication of the *Spanska Flugan* (The Spanish Fly) in the autumn of 1839. It was designed to awaken the public and stimulate the authorities by commenting on the weak spots of the existing order. While the wings of the *Spanish Fly* were clipped by the censor, its buzz was loud enough to annoy and arouse. Snellman's brief first newspaper venture was sufficiently successful to mark the beginning of the end of the romanticist journalism that had held the field in Finland since the twenties. The *Spanish Fly* was not, however, a carrier of the nationalist message. Its function was to sting and irritate, not to preach and instruct.

While serving as a schoolmaster in Kuopio, Snellman established two newspapers in 1844. The *Maamiehen Ystävä* (The Farmer's Friend) appeared in Finnish and was intended for the common folk, whom it provided with useful reading matter. It carried only little direct nationalist argument. The *Saima* addressed itself to the Swedish-language middle and upper classes. Its content and policy quickly made it the leading newspaper in the country. Vigorous in style and not infrequently blunt and even intemperate, the *Saima* presented thought-provoking challenge and real editorial leadership in the presentation of nationalist goals. It formulated a definite program and urged speedy action where its predecessors had all too often been content to offer wordy counsel appropriate to well-meaning romanticist littérateurs. The *Saima* was silenced at the close of 1846 —Snellman had run afoul of the press censor, whose instructions

prohibited political discussions likely to arouse discontent and opposition—but it was succeeded by still another publication, a monthly
review, founded by one of Snellman's friends but edited and controlled by Snellman. The content of the monthly was more literary
than *Saima*'s but its pages carried the message of its predecessor, thus
continuing to put forth the essentials of Snellman's conception of
what was vital for the nationalist cause and for the nation in general.[1]

In energetically and persistently arguing on behalf of the principles he considered vitally important to the people of his country,
Snellman offered a creed the philosophical bases of which he spelled
out with unshakeable conviction. In the life of the individual, he
contended, morality offers the only guide to the good life. Morality
means living and acting according to the dictates of one's conscience
as to what is right and what is wrong. The dictates of one's conscience, however, are subjective and therefore cannot alone serve
as infallible guides of conduct. Human society furnishes the norm for
the individual's action. Work and effort on behalf of the society to
which the individual belongs offer him the guiding star he needs,
and thus enable him to live and achieve in harmony with the demands
of morality.

Man's morality reaches its full stature within state and nation or,
in other words, in politics. In political action, Snellman held, the
citizen is laboring for the good of his nation. If he draws his inspiration from a deep-felt love of country and accepts the spirit of his
people as a directive in his efforts in behalf of the nation, he dis-
charges fully his obligations as a citizen and human being. The spirit
of the nation and the demands it imposes on the individual cannot
always be easily determined. They must be sought in the spirit of
nationalism or sense of national consciousness that animates a people.
It is the sense and feeling of nationalism that must guide the citizen,
the lawmaker, and the statesman and is, in the last analysis, the only
reliable guide for the life and endeavors of the true patriot.

[1] Snellman did not confine himself in the *Saima* or his other writings to the
language or nationality question. He argued on behalf of improved education
and separation of educational institutions from the church, defended the idea
of higher education for women, and dealt extensively with questions of industry, trade, foreign commerce, and the like.

Having thus defined the substance of intelligent citizenship, Snellman indicated what it demanded of all Finns mindful of the welfare and safety of their country. In Snellman's view, language is the basis and the distinguishing characteristic of a nation. It was therefore self-evident that the Finnish nation consisted of the Finnish-speaking majority. In so far as the people of Finland remain a recognizable entity—in other words, continue to exist—they can do so only by remaining Finnish in speech. The Swedish-language middle and upper classes Snellman pronounced to be merely a denationalized appendage of the real Finnish nation. Their duty was to become Finnish in speech and thereby amalgamate themselves with the majority of the nation.[2]

While the Finnization of the classes was demanded by circumstances, the bridging of the linguistic gulf that separated the classes from the masses was seen only as one step toward the ultimate goal. There appears to be no doubt but that Snellman and many another worker in the Finnish nationalist vineyard saw political independence as the desired, ultimate end result of their labors. Commenting in a letter to Snellman on his agitation, M. A. Castrén, the philologist, expressed in the fall of 1844 sentiments that many unquestionably shared:

Go ahead and call forth opposition [to Russia]. But if it is to reach far enough and bring about the results we desire, it must be political—it must be an opposition of the sword. If such an opposition were created at the present time, the result would inevitably be Finland's ruin. . . . I consider all our undertakings nothing less than preparations for revolt. Not that we can expect to engineer such an enterprise singlehanded, but we can bide our opportunities. Russia will sooner or later collide with the Turks . . . and Poland is only waiting for a chance to leap to arms. When the trouble begins, we too shall raise the cry . . . "Down with the Muscovite." But I feel that for the time being we must make no noise. . . . We shall proceed defensively as long as we are too weak to attack the enemy. War is our goal but for the present we can only gather strength. We shall bring forth children; we shall write books; we shall cherish our patriotism and love of country; we shall all labor to

[2] See my *Nationalism in Modern Finland* (New York, 1931), pp. 87–94; M. Juva, "Suomen Kielitaistelun Ensimmäinen Vaihe," in *H.A.*, No. 58 (1962), pp. 364–80.

the best of our ability, and God shall be with us. The Russian will never obtain power over us, least of all spiritual and intellectual power—this I know, for I have seen the terrible barbarism of [Russia].[3]

Over two generations were to elapse before the lofty goal of independence could be reached. Long before that time, however, the nationalist movement had reached some of its important objectives. Outstanding among them was the Language Decree of August 1, 1863, which defined Finnish as one of the official languages of the country. Snellman played a decisive part in bringing about the decree.

Minor measures designed to introduce the use of Finnish in the administration and government of the nation had been put into effect by the opening of the 1860s. In 1856, for instance, provision was made for the appointment of translators in provincial government offices for the purpose of issuing necessary public documents in Finnish. In 1858 it was decreed that Finnish should be, as of 1859, the official language of church and county assemblies in the Finnish parts of the country. These measures, however, left Swedish as the sole official language in the law courts and the central government. The situation changed only with the decree of 1863, which has been called "the cornerstone of the future progress of the Finnish people." Snellman, who had recently been appointed a member of the government, persuaded Alexander II, then on a visit in Finland, to issue the decree, which provided that

1. Although Swedish still remains the official language of the country, the Finnish language is hereby declared to be on a footing of complete equality with Swedish in all matters which directly concern the Finnish-speaking part of the population. As a consequence hereof, documents and records in Finnish shall henceforth be freely accepted at all law courts and administrative offices in Finland.

2. Not later than the close of the year 1883, the aforementioned rights of the Finnish language shall have become fully operative even as regards the issuance of documents and records by law courts and administrative offices; judges and other servants of the state who already pos-

[3] Castrén to Snellman, October 1, 1844, "Brev till Joh. Vilh. Snellman, II" (MS Collection, University of Helsinki).

sess an adequate command of the language may issue records and other official documents whenever they are requested to do so.

The Finnish government was charged with the responsibility of proposing "ways and means for the gradual introduction of Finnish" into the courts and public institutions in general "and for other measures demanded in consequence" of the decree.

The Language Decree of 1863 thus marked a great victory for the cause Snellman and others had carried forward, for Finnish would be fully official, besides Swedish, within two decades. The realization of this goal would not mean, however, the fulfillment of the whole nationalist program. By 1863 it encompassed a good deal more than the purpose secured by the Language Decree. Also, the nationalists were prompted to additional effort by the fact that active resistance to their endeavors had appeared years before 1863 and had become a factor of some consequence by the time Snellman persuaded Alexander II to issue the decree.

The Language Decree was welcomed with expressions of profound satisfaction by the active supporters of the Finnish cause. As a statement in the Diet phrased it in 1877, the decree was "a sort of Magna Carta for the Finnish-speaking part of the nation. It is a document which grants them the privilege of free access to educational opportunity and to all the other advantages of citizenship which our laws and institutions guarantee the other inhabitants of the country." The years after 1863 showed, however, that the application of the decree would in all probability be considerably delayed. This was clearly indicated by a statement of the Diet Committee on Petitions in 1877, when fourteen years had elapsed since the beginning of the process that was to make Finnish official and when only six years remained of the twenty designated as the period within which the full intent of the decree would be carried out. By the decree of 1863 and a subsequent measure two years later, said the committee, "all employees of the Survey and Forestry Office, the Post Office, and the State Bank and the Customs Service must serve the public in Finnish whenever requested. In many instances this provision has not been observed. It would also seem natural that the same obligation should be extended to establishments like the State Railways, and that the spirit and intent of the decrees of 1863 and 1865 ought to be interpreted to mean that, at meetings and on official occasions which have a public and patriotic purpose, the reasonable demands of the Finnish-speaking citizens should not be neglected. [Actually they have] at times received but little accommodation. . . . The causes for dissatisfaction may often be relatively unimportant." If so, merely good will and a desire to be reasonable would have sufficed to remove the reasons for dissatisfaction.

The government itself admitted in 1882 that adequate measures for carrying out the mandate of 1863 had not been taken. In a proposal submitted to the Diet the government stated that "it is probable that a considerable part of our corps of judges still lack a sufficient knowledge of Finnish to use it easily in writing" and inquired "concerning the time which the Diet deems appropriate for the beginning of the full application" of the decree.

The admission of the government made it clear that the powers that be had been resting on their oars and were now taking soundings of the current that was carrying the country close to 1884. The four estates of the Diet held, in their replies, that the application of the language ordinance should not be delayed, although minor adjustments were suggested in exceptional instances where an inflexible insistence upon the letter of the law would work unnecessary hardships. The Diet thus seemed to agree that the reform should be carried out within the time defined by the 1863 decree.

While the Diet registered surprising unanimity in the matter, opposition to the new order appeared in some quarters. It failed to stem the tide, however. An administrative decree, dated December 29, 1883, stated that beginning in 1884 lower courts should use the language of authorities in the district where the court sat; that as a rule the language of the lower courts determined the language of the higher courts; that in cases going directly to the courts of appeal, the courts could freely choose the language used; and that the Supreme Court could decide in each case the language it would use, but beginning in 1885 Finnish translations would have to be provided of all decisions and communications in cases in which Finnish had been originally used by an inferior court or official.

The following two decades witnessed further victories for the Finnish cause. Its proponents had demanded, long before the 1880s, that Finnish and Swedish should have equal status in all branches of the national government and administration. Their demands were met, in the main, in March, 1886, when it was provided that, "with a view to the final establishment of the equality of Finnish and Swedish," all administrative departments and officials "are permitted to use Finnish as well as Swedish" in their correspondence and the handling of their business. Detailed provisions were issued in the next year. They stated that all lower offices and authorities should use the language employed in the minutes and records of the local governing bodies. In bilingual communities, the authorities would decide the choice. In all higher offices, the officials involved could choose either Finnish or Swedish.

The few remaining exceptions in favor of Swedish were removed in 1902 when a decree touching the language of law courts and administrative officials was issued. It prescribed that, in unilingual communities, law courts, civil servants, and other officials should use the language of the community; that in districts comprising localities with differing languages the language of the majority of the localities determined the official language of the district; that an individual litigant or user of the services of public offices might request the use of the language not usually employed by the court or office; that the language of the lower courts determined, in each case, the language of the higher courts; and that, in general, in inter-administrative business the matter at hand should be disposed of in the language of the locality concerned.

Thus the law of 1902 provided, at long last, for the full equality of the two languages. The cause of the Fennomen had registered a decisive victory. The main "language question" after 1902 would turn out to be whether the defenders of the "Swedish cause," who had shortsightedly and stubbornly resisted, for two decades, the clear intent of the law of 1863, would succeed in maintaining that equality.

During the twenty years after 1863, the "language question" continued to serve as a fertile soil for party strife, heated newspaper polemic, and debate among university students, academicians, men of business, the rising organizations of labor, art clubs, theaters, and the like. Practically all groups of men—and women, too—and every walk of life illustrated in some degree the disturbing and divisive effects of the question. The controversy was at times extraordinarily keen and the debate most acrimonious. It ultimately produced a movement and a political party in opposition to the Finnish cause.

These developments invite still another glance at some aspects of the Finnish nationalist ways of looking at things by the middle decades of the century and later.

When the Arwidssons, the Snellmans, and others argued in behalf of their program and purposes, they were either directly or by implication indicting the existing order of things, which they proposed to change in a manner that would be, in some respects, quite revolutionary. Yet the indictment was in one respect curiously imprecise and generalized. Their demand that Finnish become the "national language" of the country was not built on specific cases or individuals who illustrated that injustice and suffering were imposed upon the common folk because Swedish and not Finnish was the official language of the land. That this circumstance often constituted a nuisance, an irritating inconvenience, and a galling encumbrance goes without saying. But specific illustrations of miscarriage of justice and the imposition of unusual burdens or disabilities on the Finnish-speaking population—such as loss of property rights, denial or limitation of the right to vote, difficulties in entering the trades or professions, impairment of the individual citizen's liberties under the law, and the like—traceable to the fact that Swedish was the official language and Finnish was not, were not a part of the bill of particulars offered by the Fennomen. They fought for and ultimately won by contending for a principle.

The absence of specific charges and the reliance of the Fennomen on a generalized indictment create a strong presumption that the day-by-day consequences of the language situation actually bore less heavily upon the average Finn than the nationalists claimed. The main part of their insistent effort was not primarily concerned with righting wrongs specifically affecting the anonymous many;

they were determined that the classes must become "national" by becoming Finnish in language as well as in spirit. It is this circumstance that appears to offer an explanation of yet another aspect of the nationalist argument, namely, the heavy accent placed upon the Finnish language as an abstract concept.

The nationalist literature and agitation abounds in references to the "rights" of the Finnish language, its "lowly status," "humiliating condition," "downtrodden and shameful circumstances," "disgraceful situation," the "oppression" and "indignities" visited upon it in the past, and the like. The language was described and considered as if it were "a person existing in the contemplation of the law," capable of asserting rights or suffering wrongs and damage as do human beings. While the implication no doubt usually was that the "rights," "humiliation," "oppression," and the rest referred to Finnish-speakers and not merely to the language, the deliberate and frequent use of the abstraction suggests once again that the workaday world did not readily provide convincing, concrete, and meaningful instances of the "oppression" of Everyman because of the language situation.[4] The nationalists therefore spoke and argued from and on the basis of lofty principle.

The principle was egalitarian, democratic, and morally unassailable. It placed the requisites of the common good ahead of the interests of the individual. It urged ceaselessly the necessity of love of country and people. Patriotism, national unity, linguistic unity—these were put forth as the high goals for which patriots with capacity for genuine self-sacrificing devotion in the service of the people should ever strive.

The opponents of the Finnish cause frequently contended that the Finnish language was "undeveloped" and therefore could not be used as an official language until some time in the future. This idea

---

[4] K. Vilkuna has pointed out that the archives covering the four centuries since the sixteenth contain "thousands of pages of the records of court sessions" dealing with litigation over fishing rights, an obviously important practical concern of the farmer and fisherman. As far as I have been able to ascertain, the concrete consequences of the pre-1862–1902 language situation, obviously in many senses unfavorable to the mass of the Finnish speakers, left no court-case legacy that could be compared, even remotely, to the situation Vilkuna mentions. See *Tietolipas*, No. 12 (1958), pp. 117–18.

had been frequently put forth years before champions of the "Swedish cause" appeared after the 1850s. It was effectively used by them and seems, in fact, to have been shared by some of the Fennomen as well.

The claim that Finnish was "primitive" and "undeveloped" and therefore could not serve as the language of law, administration, and government or for general cultural and related purposes was a significant part of discussions regarding the aims and merits of the nationalist movement. It is, however, worth special mention because the claim went largely unchallenged, with but little attempt to question or refute it. Yet the challenge was clearly called for and the refutation plainly available to perceptive interpreters of the facts.

The obvious fact was that the problem was not one involving the inadequacies of the Finnish language. The problem was the lack of individuals, whether in the world of learning, administration, the law, or in business, sufficiently energetic and enterprising to become fully masters of Finnish. Religious and theological literature had been available in increasing volume since the middle 1500s. The basic law of the land, that of 1734, had been published in Finnish in 1759. Lönnrot's contributions to his science had led to a growing volume of publications since the 1830s. The first Finnish newspaper had appeared in 1776; a Finnish-language press of modest dimensions had come into being by the 1860s. When Y. Koskinen published his Finnish-language professorial dissertation in 1862, and more especially when he began to publish his history of Finland in 1869—the third edition of his work (1881) was a substantial tome of over 750 pages—he was demonstrating that Finnish, quite sufficient for the writing of a major historical study, was an adequate vehicle in the hands of anyone who had taken the trouble to learn the language.

Not the least fascinating aspect of the language debates and discussions in the days of Snellman and later was the fact that they did not bring to the fore, in response to the claim that Finnish was still too "primitive," any resolute propounder of these obvious relevancies. The contention that Finnish was "undeveloped" was allowed to stand, virtually immune from close scrutiny or outright rejection. It therefore served as cover behind which the unenterprising and the sluggish, as well as the outright opponents of the Finnish cause, could conveniently and safely hide. It also aided the formulators of the Swede-Finn nationalist ideas that began to emerge in the 1850s.

AUGUST SOHLMAN

As we have seen, the Finnish movement involved, during the first decades of its history, only Swedish-speaking upper- and middle-class individuals. Arwidsson's contribution in the early 1820s had been made exclusively in Swedish. Snellman's work was likewise carried on in Swedish; not one of his contributions to the Finnish cause was made in Finnish. Most of the many others who wrote and spoke in behalf of the cause did not know Finnish well enough to use it freely in their endeavors. Their social and linguistic antecedents were on the whole the same as those of the Swede-Finns who ultimately rejected Snellman's program and embraced the later Swede-Finn nationalist creed.

Because the Finnish movement involved, in its earlier stages, only Swedish-speaking upper- and middle-class individuals, it was in the first instance and for many years an "internal" question or problem of the Swede-Finn classes. It was not a movement that set one "nationality," the Finnish, against the other "nationality," the Swedish. Also, Snellman and the other sponsors of the Finnish nationalist movement paid little or no attention, as we have remarked, to the Swede-Finn part of the nation's population as a whole. The Swede-Finn farmer who lived by wresting a modest living from a niggardly soil, or the fisherman who plied the sea or the lakes in the quest of their riches, or the craftsman who worked at his trade in village or city were either ignored or at best glimpsed in passing by the purveyors of the new dispensation. Yet the time was bound to come when the Swede-Finns also would be discovered as a "nationality" and a nationalist movement designed to serve their needs launched.

Much of the essentials for the formulation of a Swede-Finn nationalist creed was furnished by August Sohlman (1824–74), a Swedish journalist whose career included the editorship in 1857–74 of the well-known Stockholm daily, the *Aftonbladet*. Sohlman was both a spirited Swedish nationalist and a "Scandinavian."

Scandinavianism was a movement among university students and professors—intellectuals in general—which aimed at closer cultural and intellectual relations among Norway, Sweden, Finland, and Denmark. It dated from the forties. Some of its supporters were also interested in political and international purposes of larger import. Danish Scandinavians, for example, hoped to enlist the support of their northern neighbors in the solution of the Schleswig-Holstein problem (involving possible difficulties with Prussia). The Swedish Scandinavians included men deeply interested in recovering Finland from Russia. The movement was considerably strengthened by the political constellation in Europe caused by the Crimean War (1854–56). The widening anti-Russian coalition seemed to spell defeat for Russia, leading to at least partial dismemberment of the empire and the possibility of the liberation of Finland.

One of the spokesmen of these optimistic expectations in Sweden was Emil von Qvantén, a Finnish émigré resident in Sweden. An enthusiastic supporter of Snellman's purposes, Von Qvantén advocated Sweden's participation in the war against Russia, which would lead to reunion with Finland in a new Scandinavian state, a greater Sweden-Finland. Sweden and Norway having been under the same crown since 1814, the inclusion of Finland would mean a political entity through which the North would attain greater eminence and prestige.

The ideas of Von Qvantén and reports of Swedish discussions regarding Sweden's foreign policy at the time were circulated in Finland—despite the efforts of the censor—and understandably caused considerable comment. While some of the younger nationalists readily accepted the idea of an autonomous Finland united with Sweden, Snellman and others refused to be carried away by the optimism of Von Qvantén's supporters. To Snellman and his followers the collapse of Russia at the time seemed altogether unlikely and the liberation of Finland therefore a vain hope. Precarious as Finland's position was in many ways, it was preferable for the time being to the risky uncertainties inherent in schemes such as Von Qvantén's.

Sohlman's Scandinavianism had become evident in 1848 when he enlisted in the Danish forces and fought the Prussians. He remained faithful throughout his life to the idea that the North was, in a larger sense, the fatherland of all the Nordic peoples. As a newspaperman he labored consistently for purposes that would bring these nations closer together. In a pamphlet published in 1855 and widely—and secretly, needless to say—circulated in Finland, he reflected upon Finland's general position and the nature and meaning of the Snellman-led nationalist movement, and provided what turned out to be some of the most solid underpinnings of the Swede-Finn nationalist ideology.[5]

In Sohlman's view, the people of Finland represented two separate nationalities, a Finnish and a Swedish. The latter had lived in Finland since ages past. The Swedish-language upper classes were not Finns at all, for they belonged to the Swedish nationality. The Swedish nationality had been, and continued to be, the ruling nationality in the country. In fact, it was only thanks to it that there was a Finland. The Finns had shown themselves to be, throughout history, devoid of the capacity for subjugating their neighbors. No major European nation had played as modest a part in history as the Finns. Being submissive, exceptionally slow in thought and action, they lacked the ability to think clearly and to act energetically and the sense for the practical that enables man to adjust himself to the world about him. Only after the Finns became exposed to the Swedish "spirit" and the influence of Swedish "culture" were they led to the path of progress and their basic character changed and improved. Such Finnish characteristics as faithfulness, diligence, and bravery were the result of long exposure to Swedish "good spirits" and practical common sense. Being members of a race that lacked qualities such as these, the Finns had no culture before being conquered by the Swedes; the culture of Finland in the nineteenth century was the end product of the achievements of the Swedes. All the individuals who stood out as having any importance for Finland's cultural life were members of the Swedish nationality.

[5] *Det unga Finland* (Young Finland), 1855. A second edition was printed in Finland in 1880 and influenced Swede-Finn nationalist extremists during the following decade. Some of the notions summarized here Sohlman had put forth as early as 1846.

These and related racialist notions furnished Sohlman with the basis for evaluating and discarding the program and purposes of Snellman and his followers. Starting from the contention that the Swede-Finn upper classes were not Finns but Swedes, Sohlman claimed that the attempt to merge them with the Finnish-speaking part of the population was stupid and deplorable. The Swedish language should not be "sacrificed" on the altar of a falsely conceived and artificially stimulated nationalism. To do so would mean nothing less than "national suicide." It would be mortifying, silly, and useless: mortifying because Swedes usually clung tenaciously to their language; silly because the nationalist leaders were Finnicizing themselves in the belief that they were making a necessary and noble sacrifice when in fact they were not; and useless because, instead of helping the Finns, they could cause nothing less than irreparable damage to the whole country.

It is thus clear that Sohlman was a Swedish nationalist who saw Finland as a sort of *Svecia Irredenta* and the Swedish-language upper classes as its logical redeemers. It is equally clear that he failed to understand the ideas and fears upon which the Finnish nationalist movement rested. But he specifically raised a question not previously faced by Snellman and others: What is or what should be the relation between the middle and upper classes and the anonymous common folk who constituted the great majority of the Swede-Finns? The question was answered within a few years of Sohlman's analysis of the language problem and related Finnish questions. The author of the answer was Axel Olof Freudenthal (1836–1911), the first formulator, in Finland, of a full-blown "Swedish" nationalist doctrine applicable to the Swedish-language minority.

AXEL OLOF FREUDENTHAL

Freudenthal was the son of a Swede who had moved to Finland in 1798. Originally a student of Latin and Greek at the University of Helsinki, he ultimately devoted his time and energies to Scandinavian antiquities and Old Norse. Appointed lecturer in 1866, he became professor of Swedish language and literature in 1878, a post he held until his retirement in 1904. The remaining seven years of his life he spent living in obscurity in Helsinki. His interest in the nationality and language problem was aroused while still a student at the university in the late 1850s. Coming under the influence of the "Scandinavian debates" of the time, he emerged an enthusiastic "Scandinavian," condemned the aims of the Finnish nationalists as pernicious, and ultimately emerged as one of their outstanding opponents. Following the reasoning of Sohlman, whose contentions he unqualifiedly and uncritically accepted, Freudenthal formulated the ideas which were destined permanently to determine the nationalist Swede-Finn outlook.

Freudenthal held that nationality depends on language; language is not only the most obvious but in "most instances the only clear indication of nationality." Thus neither laws, customs, social institutions, historical factors, nor political factors furnish the basis of nationality. The Swedish-speaking inhabitants should not and could not be called Finns, for they were, Freudenthal contended, nothing less than pure Swedes living in a land that had formerly been a part of the Swedish kingdom. The attempt to carry forward the cause of Snellman and others was therefore sufficiently insane to suggest "Fennomania" as a fitting appellation for their endeavors. Effort and work on behalf of the Finnish-speaking part of the country's population was commendable despite the fact that the Finns constituted a "foreign nation"; circumstances made it, in fact, more or less unavoidable. However, it should not be permitted to undermine the position of the Swedish language in Finland, and least of all should "Swedish men" attempt, by advocating the Finnization of the classes, to decrease the "Swedish" population of the country. The two language groups were different and incompatible; their amalgamation would be impossible for centuries to come. Therefore no useful national policy could be based on the expectation that genuine linguistic unity would some day be attained.

From this it followed, according to Freudenthal, that the Swedes in Finland must at all cost defend and perpetuate the supremacy of the Swedish language in Finland. This was an obligation that must not be ignored, even though the obligation appeared at times to conflict with the Swede's duties as a citizen of the Finnish state. The conflict did not, however, actually exist, for the real interests of Finland required that the future of the nation be placed and retained in the competent hands of the Swedish-speaking classes. They and they alone could maintain Finland's membership in the Scandinavian family of nations, without which all hope of genuine advance and progress would have to be abandoned.[6]

Freudenthal's notion that the people of Finland consisted of two races, the Swedish and the Finnish, and that the former was superior and the latter inferior, was based in the last analysis upon an idea already mentioned: that language is the sole decisive criterion of nationality and therefore of race. However inadequate, not to say absurd, such ideas may seem today, they were in keeping with "scientific" conclusions current a century ago. They enjoyed special immunity from close scrutiny and successful attempts at rebuttal in Finland, however offensive they may have seemed to the many intellectuals—to say nothing of the man in the street—who identified themselves with the Finnish nation and refused to accept the racist division insisted upon by Freudenthal and his followers. The reason is not far to seek. It is a fact that M. A. Castrén had only recently published the results of his extensive philological researches that allegedly proved the relationship between the Finns, the Hungarians, and various lesser groups found in the European and Asiatic parts of the far-flung Russian Empire. Some of these "relatives" of the Finns ("relatives" by Castrén's philological definitions) were backward and primitive even by the most generous standards. They appeared to furnish proof positive and final of the inability of the "Finns" to progress in the arts of civilized living and cultural advance.

It might have been argued that such conclusions were irrelevant as regards the Finns who had lived in Finland since time immemorial and in the course of some two thousand years had become, together

---

[6] I have summarized these developments in *Nationalism in Modern Finland*, pp. 107–27 (see also the sources on p. 259). L. A. Puntila's excellent *Ruotsalaisuus Suomessa* (Helsinki, 1944) offers a lengthy and many-sided analysis of Freudenthal's ideas. Most of them came from Sohlman and from the Norwegian historian Peter Andreas Munch (1810–63). Munch's *Om Finlands Nationalitet og dens Forhold til den svenske* (1855) put forth ideas and conclusions similar to Sohlman's, with whom he also shared the arrogant racist notions later found in Freudenthal's conceptions.

with the other peoples of the North, fully a part of the Western culture area. But the Finnish nationalists in particular could not well have recourse to such argument. To have made use of it in refuting the insolent racist notions of a Freudenthal, galling though they must have seemed to patriots proud of being Finns, would have meant to question and ultimately to reject the conclusions of Castrén. His conclusions were flattering to an uncritical, romanticist age anxious to shore up nascent patriotism by appropriating "scientific" results seemingly proving, as Castrén himself had written, that the Finns were not "a nation isolated from the world and world history" but that they were "related to at least one seventh of the people of the globe." To the extent to which Castrén's claims were taken seriously—and no one had as yet risen to challenge their broader implications—they seemed to prove that the Sohlmans and the Freudenthals were not in error in asserting that what applied to the "relatives" of the Finns applied to the Finns as well.[7] Their assertion, which included, as we have seen, the claim that the Finns had registered cultural and other advance only because they had been fortunate enough to fall under Swedish influence, was therefore allowed to stand without being repudiated by a satisfactory revision of the conclusions of the patriot-scholar Castrén.

Freudenthal's ideas were appropriated by the Swede-Finn nationalists who emerged after the 1860s and had become a significant opposition to the Finnish nationalist movement by the 1880s. They were also embraced, in the main, by the founders of the Swedish People's party that emerged in 1906, the year that witnessed the introduction of universal suffrage and the democratization of the national legislature. While the clumsy racist concepts had largely disappeared, the rest of the Freudenthalian creed remained, on the whole, congenial to the tastes and preferences of the spokesmen of the Swede-Finn nationalists.

The Swede-Finn language and nationalist movement remained largely an upper- and middle-class effort until the 1890s; the Swed-

---

[7] It is an interesting fact that the Castrénian albatross still hangs around the neck of many a Finn who finds it impossible to perceive the need for looking at Castrén's conclusions closely enough to distinguish between his contributions as an outstanding philologist and his romanticized notions regarding the "Finnish-related" peoples.

ish-speaking common folk played no part in it, and the leadership of the movement made no real effort to seek their support. It was not until 1896 that Swede-Finn leaders at long last came to the realization that the "Swedish cause" could no longer be defended without enlisting for it the full support of the Swede-Finn common man. The soundness of this conclusion was more than adequately proven ten years later when the new parliament bill and franchise law, promulgated on July 20, 1906, fundamentally changed the national legislature. The introduction of the single-chamber Parliament of 200 members and the extension of the right to vote to all adult women as well as men made it clear that, unless the Swede-Finn political leaders obtained the support for their cause of the Swedish-speaking farmers, fishermen, laborers, and other common folk, they could not expect to reach even the unpretentious representation that a full utilization of their numerical strength—at the time, nearly 13 percent of the total population—might ensure.

Confronted by this dilemma, the Swede-Finn nationalists had no choice but to accept the consequences of political democracy. Lest "one man, one vote" were to give all the prizes to the numerically strong, they undertook to organize the Swede-Finns as a whole into a political party. As a result, the Swedish People's party was launched in May, 1906. Its program provided a platform on which the Swede-Finn intellectual, farmer, and businessman could stand shoulder to shoulder with the Swede-Finn butcher, baker, and candlestick maker. The main accent of the program was placed—and in the main has continued to this day—on the cultural and language interests of the Swede-Finn group.

EDUCATIONAL ADVANCE

The influence of the nationalist movement upon education was far-reaching. Its consequences were seen in the whole field of educational endeavor, ranging all the way from primary and secondary schools and the university to varied educational enterprises designed to benefit the adult citizen.

A limited amount of schooling had been provided for the bulk of the nation following the Reformation. More substantial advance was recorded in the 1700s when parents were required—after 1723 —on penalty of a fine to see to it that their children learned to read. The literacy of the people was placed on a firmer basis after 1740 when the clergy was obligated regularly to conduct confirmation schools. While the educational system was neither secular nor "national" and was wholly under the control of church and clergy, and while the subjects taught were modest in the extreme, the 1740s marked the beginnings of the attempt to wipe out illiteracy and provided the bases on which a later, more progressive age could build.

As a result of the nationalist movement and in response to the prodding of Snellman and others the question of further educational progress was taken up in a forward-looking, aggressive spirit. The importance of mass education was repeatedly stressed. One of the most frequently recurring ideas of the nationalists was the notion that only by means of popular education could the country be brought to a realization of the needs of the hour and a wholehearted acceptance of the saving spirit of nationalism. As one observer of the passing scene stated in 1857, "Only a high degree of educational accomplishment among the many and not only on the part of the few can possibly save the people from absorption [by Russia]. . . . Extreme effort, work, and struggle in the domain of intellectual advance is required if the Finnish nation is to continue to exist." Snellman put the matter this way: "The right of a nation never extends farther than its might. But might depends not only on material strength. Education also is power, especially in our day, not the least because it makes a nation an integral part of the civilized part of the world." And one of the younger nationalists seconded views of this kind when he stated in 1875 that, "the material strength and resources" of Finland being what they were, the nation "could not possibly attain to importance" among the nations of the world except by virtue of educational advance. "Education is therefore not only important for us; it is the very foundation of our existence." National self-preservation thus required more and better schools and a further expansion of facilities for higher education.

Only the state could provide for the pressing needs increasingly accented. The first steps leading to the establishment of a national, state-directed system of education were taken by the government in 1856. They led to the Act for the Organization of Elementary Schools, passed in 1866. On the basis of this law, a quickly expanding primary school system was built during the ensuing years. After 1874, when the new program was well launched, progress was rapid. The arousing and strengthening of love of country was one of the purposes of the curriculum introduced into the new schools. Reading "suitable patriotic literature" was from the beginning an integral part of the instruction given. The stirring *Tales of Ensign Stål*, various patriotic writings of Topelius, and selections from the *Kalevala* sustained the generations of Finns who attended the primary schools. Table 1 indicates the progress recorded from the mid-seventies to the advent of independence in 1917.

TABLE 1

GROWTH OF PRIMARY SCHOOLS, 1874–1917

| School year | Teachers | | | Pupils | | |
	City	Rural	Total	City	Rural	Total
1874–75	167	272	439	5,920	9,300	15,220
1894–95	691	1,264	1,955	13,400	23,430	36,830
1904–5	975	2,703	3,678	30,450	95,420	125,870
1910–11	1,290	3,740	5,030	37,931	135,162	173,093
1916–17	1,398	4,572	5,970	43,357	157,215	200,572

By far the greater part of the pupils in the primary schools came from Finnish-language homes. In 1910, for example, they accounted for 138,646 out of a total of 173,093, and in 1917 for 174,728 out of a total of 200,572.

While the primary schools ministered to the needs of the many, the secondary schools served relatively smaller numbers who might proceed to graduate studies at the university or professional institutions of higher learning. The renovation of these schools began in the fifties. The avowed purpose was to create as rapidly as possible an educated class Finnish in speech and training in order thereby to bridge the linguistic gulf that had of old separated the classes from the masses. In spite of many difficulties and obstacles—not the least among them was the reluctance of conservative school boards to provide for Finnish-language schools—progress was steady and notable. In 1880 the enrollment in the *lycées* of the country was 3,500; of this number, 1,300 were classified as Finnish-speaking. The corresponding figures were 4,850 and 2,150 in 1890; at the turn of the century, 5,200 out of a total of 8,600 attended Finnish-language secondary schools. By that time the Finnish current was running strong. In 1909–10 the Finnish-language secondary schools accounted for about 70 percent of the total; in 1917 they numbered 15,270 out of a total of 21,970 or approximately 75 percent.

The Finnization of the secondary schools soon changed the composition of the student body at the University of Helsinki. In 1870–72 the number of new admissions at the university came to 516; of this number, 43, or considerably less than 10 percent, were classified as "Finnish-speaking." By 1879–81 their proportion had risen to about one third of the total (178 out of 567); in 1900–1902, 850 out of a total 1,500 were in this group; and in 1910–12 they accounted for well over two thirds of the newcomers (2,206 out of 3,134). The tendency shown by these figures was also observed at the Graduate School of Engineering, founded in 1885.

Originally independent of the nationalist impulses that sustained interest and accomplishment in enlarging education opportunities at levels low, middle, and high was the movement to provide trade and technical schools. Interestingly enough, public authorities appear to have awakened relatively early to the importance of providing vocational instruction to apprentices and others engaged in various handicrafts or industries. An Act of 1842 provided that twenty-five cities in the country establish, with state aid, Sunday schools for apprentices and others engaged in handicrafts. A few of the smaller cities were exempt from the Act. The instruction offered by these special Sunday schools—they appear to have had nothing to do with religious matters—included drafting, writing, geometry, and presumably instruction in some trades. So-called technical trade schools appeared after 1847. They were more ambitious than the Sunday schools. Their entrance requirements called for ability to read and write and knowledge of the principles of religion (probably a very modest requirement). They offered a four-year program of instruction that included drafting, plane geometry, mechanics, physics, chemistry, and mineralogy. The school year was nine months long and daily instruction appears to have run to eight or nine hours. Evening schools providing for vocational instruction—one to three or four hours per evening—also illustrated the trend of the times, as did the technical schools that began to appear in the late 1850s.

A new law of 1885 reorganized the system and introduced uniform "lower" and "higher" trade schools. Both girls and boys could gain admission. The "lower" schools offered instruction on Sundays and one evening a week; the subjects were drafting, arithmetic, business correspondence and bookkeeping, and study of the student's mother tongue. The "higher" schools offered a Sunday and four evenings-per-week program with instruction on a more advanced level in the same subjects plus geometry, composition, and some others. By the mid-nineties, these schools numbered 43, employed 160 instructors, and had 1,500 students. The numbers had grown to 46 schools, 220 instructors, and 2,400 students by the turn of the century; in 1911 the figures were, respectively, 53, 280, and 2,600. In twelve of the schools, instruction was given in both Finnish and Swedish, while twenty-eight were purely Finnish and three were Swedish-language schools.

Not the least interesting illustration of the persistence with which the friends of the Finnish cause were moving forward in their effort to achieve a victory for Finnish in the various fields of the educational and intellectual life of the nation was the emergence of a number of scientific societies. Philology and linguistics, medicine, physics, zoology, botany, history (the Finnish Historical Association was established in 1875), economics, law—in short, a wide range of scientific organizations emerged during the closing decades of the century as testimony to the many-sided accomplishments sustained, in large measure, by the energetic and determined labors of men who responded to the challenge held out to them as a categorical imperative by the nationalist movement. Other examples of the same vital interest and commitment were the Adult Education Society, founded in 1874, and the establishment of the first Folk High

Schools, on the model provided by the Dane N. F. S. Grundtvig, in the eighties. By 1900, twenty-one Folk High Schools were functioning; by 1917, forty. Workers' Institutes—the first appeared in 1899—also bore the stamp of the same general concerns and purposes, although they became important only after 1917. A growing number of Young People's Associations, first emerging in 1881, had become a national institution by the turn of the century, with some 250 local organizations. Nonpolitical, these associations carried their message to high and low throughout the land. They were especially important in enlisting the younger generation of the small farmer class in the effort to create a well-informed, intelligent, and patriotic class of citizens. Originally but little interested in the subtleties of the language problem, they were ultimately important in tipping the scales in favor of the champions of the Finnish cause, as shown by the resolution unanimously adopted by the national assembly of the representatives of the association in 1906. It stated in part that the members of the association "consider themselves duty bound to use Finnish" and that the association would henceforth endeavor to place "Finnish in the position of the principal language of Finland —in other words, shall participate in the effort the purpose of which is the strengthening of our love of country and the raising of the Finnish-speaking part of our population to that position and preeminence which of right belongs to it."

The generation before World War I thus recorded impressive evidence of the advance and achievements of the Fennoman movement. It sustained a rapid expansion of the Finnish-language press. By 1896, fifty-one newspapers were being published in Finnish and forty-four in Swedish. By 1917 the margin of "victory" of the Finnish newspapers was quite wide enough to invite the conclusion that the Swedish-language newspapers still expounding the narrow provincialism of Freudenthal could not in the long run escape the consequences of merely parochial concerns.

The new perils to nation and state that emerged after the beginning of World War I called for loyalties of more generous and demanding dimensions than provincial nationalist conceptions implied. Finnish patriots had in fact been contemplating for several years the possibilities of saving their country from the consequences of Russification and the attendant perils foreseen by Snellman and the other unifiers of the nation. Thanks to the labors of Snellman and the patriots who had embraced his cause, the nation had come of age by the time an assassination, on a sunny Sunday morning—the date, June 28, 1914—in a faraway, unknown provincial capital, set in motion a train of events leading to a great world war and, through it, to the emergence of an independent Finland.

VII

Economic Trends before 1914

Finland's economic development before World War I reflected in many ways the status of the country as an autonomous nation. The separation from Sweden in 1808–9 broke up an economic unity and network of relationships created by generations of historical development. To be sure, the traditional economic connections with Sweden were by no means dissolved overnight. Some of them remained unchanged in one form or another—Swedish money, for instance, continued to circulate until the 1840s—for nearly half a century after the separation. Their disappearance did not mean, however, a speedy or complete economic union with the Russian Empire. In the general economic sphere no less than in the political the contours of autonomy remained clearly defined.

An independent budget, taxation, and finances; a customs boundary corresponding to the political boundary, and periodic customs arrangements between Finland and the empire; a separate monetary system after the 1860s; a policy of Russification after 1890 that, practically speaking, left untouched the broad domain of the nation's economy and did not integrate it with that of the empire; and the fact that by 1914 two thirds of Finland's foreign trade meant trade with non-Russian markets—the result, in part, of Russia's increasing protectionist policies after the 1880s—all underscored the significant fact that "economic autonomy" supplemented and buttressed the nation's position as a separate national and political entity. The war years 1914–18 gradually limited and temporarily ended trade relations with the West and led to increased economic dependence on Russia. This change came too late, however, and did not last long enough to create permanent or insoluble problems for independent Finland after 1918.

THE WORLD OF THE FARMER

The main features of Finland's economy in the early years of the last century remained virtually unchanged until well past 1850. The country was overwhelmingly agricultural. The population in 1811 was 1,053,000; of this total, only about 40,800 lived in cities and only one city, Turku, had over 10,000 inhabitants. Several decades were to pass before Finland began to show indications of the urbanization and industrialization characteristic of modern Finland. Trade and commerce were only modestly developed, as is suggested by the fact that less than 4 percent of the income of the state was derived from customs dues.

Agriculture, the mainstay of the nation, was primitive by the standards of more recent times. Modern methods of farming, diversification of crops, drainage, the use of machinery, and the like had not yet become safeguards against poor crops or the failure of crops. Dairy farming was no less backward than crop farming. Cattle appear to have been kept almost as much for fertilizer as for meat, milk, butter, and cheese production. But primitive as farming conditions were, considerable advance was made during the first half of the last century. Estimates show that, between 1810 and 1850, the annual production of rye increased by more than 100 percent, of wheat nearly 100 percent, of oats to ten times the figure for the early years, and of barley some 300 percent.

The agricultural advance had several causes. One of them was the cumulative effect of efforts made to improve and modernize farming practices, especially after the end of the disastrous and long Northern War in 1721. These efforts were largely a part of the attempt to speed internal improvements and reconstruction throughout the Swedish kingdom in order to raise it from the deep trough of material exhaustion into which it had fallen during the war. In Finland in particular, much thought and labor was expended upon repairing the damage suffered—Finland had been under uninterrupted Russian occupation for over seven years—and rehabilitating the country in every possible way. The government in Stockholm and local authorities in Finland, economists—or savants who passed for such—and other men of learning, as well as experienced men of business and farming, were involved in the effort.

Instruction, advice, and exhortation in the annual *Almanac*, pamphlets, and learned tomes illustrated widespread and continuing interest in general economic welfare and farming in particular. The interest was sustained by the belief that conditions could be improved and economic recovery speeded by increasing the productivity of farming, although the further development of industry and commerce was also considered important. During 1730–1800 approximately one hundred studies by scholars at the University of Turku were published offering surveys of natural resources, trades, economic opportunities, and the like. How to grow better crops, improve the care of cattle and other farm animals, drain land more efficiently, improve roads, and scores of other questions were discussed and suggestions regarding them offered. While understandable professorial inaccuracy of fact or prescription in dealing with matters of this kind was by no means rare, it was more often than not redeemed by sobriety of approach and disarming earnestness of purpose. It was no accident, in view of the serious and prolonged interest in modernizing farming, that the Finnish Economic Society was founded in 1797 and that the first farmers' organization, the Ilmajoki Farmer's Association, was organized in 1803. Others appeared later and played an important part in introducing new farming techniques, improved machinery, better methods of fertilizing, new crops, and the like. The lowly potato, brought to Finland in the 1730s, had conquered most of Finland by the early years of the last century, partly no doubt because of the interest that leading agrarians showed in it as a substitute for the turnip and partly because the potato is the one vegetable which most humans can eat, once they become accustomed to it, every day of the year.

Another reason for the gradual improvement of farming and consequently in the status and condition of the farmer during the nineteenth century was the enclosure movement. Its purpose was to reduce and to eliminate the strip system of landholding. For centuries before the 1800s arable land in Finland as well as the rest of Scandinavia was usually divided into small strips; consolidated holdings were rarely found. Common pasture- and woodland was a part of the system, which often meant that the arable land of a farmer was divided into scores of parcels, at times widely separated. Farming under these conditions was inefficient. So long as they remained unchanged they retarded the introduction of new crops and, in general, more efficient ways of using land.

After lengthy investigation of the problem, enclosure had begun in Sweden-Finland in 1757 as the result of Riksdag legislation. Between that date and 1809, some 15,000,000 acres were consolidated in Finland. By 1848 the figure had risen to 32,000,000 acres. Incidentally, the elimination of the strip system—which continued on a substantial scale to 1890, when enclosure had affected 43,000,000 acres, and was fully completed only by 1917—did not result from the selfish effort of large landowners but from measures enacted under the conviction that the best interests of the ordinary farmer and of the nation as a whole would be served by it. The landless agricultural population lost rather than gained by the enclosures because they limited or eliminated common pasture- or woodland. Landowning farmers benefited. It has been estimated that farm values and productivity were increased by 25 percent as a result of enclosure.

Meanwhile the agrarian scene underwent change in other ways. Until about 1850, the farmer produced nearly all of his food and clothing. Even shoes and the relatively simple agricultural tools in use at the time were normally homemade. After the middle of the century, however, living standards began to improve. Especially among the more well-to-do farmers, larger houses were built, better and more furniture appeared, and farmers' wives showed an inclination, disconcerting to some observers of the passing scene, to sleep till six o'clock in the morning. "Habana sigars," "Pikardo wine," brandy, coffee, sugar, glassware, chinaware, factory-made cloth, and chamber crockery plain and fancy began increasingly to appear in the lists of farmers' purchases at the country stores or in the inventories of their lares and penates.

After the decade of the seventies, the farmer class became the beneficiary of the rising lumber industry. The sale of timber and timberlands put money into the farmer's pocket in quantities that seemed fabulous to many and led him to change many of his former ways of living. Even the teamster and lumberjack shared in the new prosperity; for a while, teamsters in some sections of the country received up to two dollars in daily wages, and ordinary laborers got 50–75 cents, high wages indeed for those distant days. Petroleum lamps came into general use after 1870; the sewing machine—first imported about 1865—found its way into a growing number of homes, and the seamstress became a person of importance who freed the womenfolk from their former bondage to dresses and other articles of clothing previously handed down from mother to daughter, their place now being taken by "modern" cotton dresses cheaply produced by the miracle, the machine; coffee and sugar increasingly became daily articles of consumption even among the lowly, in town and country alike; professional bakers and bakery shops became more common, especially in larger villages; the lowly prune, rice, raisins, and substantial gravies found a permanent place on the menu; pancakes made of "store boughten" wheat flour became something more than a rare delicacy; cigarettes, first manufactured in Finland in 1859, were seen before long on the lips of Everyman; the first bicycle in the countryside was reported in 1890 and became a general means of travel during the next two decades; watch and chain, which had previously graced only the vests of the opulent, became the possession of farmhands as well; factory-made footwear and cloth eliminated homemade shoes and cloth; and even country stores began to carry exotic, fancy brands of conversation aids: port, sherry, brandy, rum, Swedish punch, and others, although the chief stand-bys of alcoholic beverage continued to be *viina* (a type of vodka) and beer.

During the decades from the 1860s to the end of the century, public authority played an important part in raising the farmer to a higher level. Much of the activity of the Finnish government on behalf of agriculture and the farmer from the 1840s onward suggests the motto: "Everything for the people, little by the people." Despite the exaggeration inherent in this phrase, it may be used to bring out the fact that long before universal suffrage was introduced in 1906

—to mention only one aspect of the democratization of the country —government began to serve the interests of the people, the farm folk among them, to a degree unknown in earlier times.

Thus substantial public funds were spent to modernize farming and to provide other services and instrumentalities intended to improve the productivity of the nation's most important economic activity. The first agricultural school appeared in 1840; after 1865, five more began to function. In 1860 a special department of agriculture was established by the government. Money was spent for useful experiments and improvements of various kinds. After 1885 nearly a score of farmers' training schools were founded. Farmers' associations began to appear in larger numbers after 1847 and became increasingly important thereafter. The cooperative idea likewise took root and played a significant part in the developments which began to change crop farming into dairy farming after 1880. By 1900 the annual exports of butter had increased some 400 percent over the figure about 1860 and testified to the speed of the transformation.

Until 1850 approximately 50,000 tons of grain were exported annually; in 1900 the country imported a substantial part of the grain used. By 1914 dairy products had become the second most important item in the exports of Finland and accounted for nearly 30 percent of the total value of exports. In 1911–13 the agricultural self-sufficiency of the country was, according to estimates, only 59 percent. About two fifths of the food consumed by the Finns thus came from abroad. This in itself offered a measure of the distance the nation had traveled during the preceding two generations. The volume of domestic production is shown in Tables 2 and 3.

TABLE 2

MAIN CROPS, 1880–1913
(in hectoliters; 1 hectoliter equals 2.838 bushels)

Year	Wheat	Rye	Barley	Oats	Potatoes
1880	36,400	3,630,000	1,774,000	2,889,000	3,359,000
1896	43,700	4,085,000	2,076,000	6,407,000	6,363,000
1905	54,800	4,071,000	1,874,000	6,364,000	7,296,000
1910	43,700	3,632,000	1,736,000	7,106,000	6,127,000
1913	58,200	3,618,000	1,725,000	7,760,000	6,467,000

TABLE 3

DAIRIES AND PRODUCTION, 1907–1914

Year	Number of dairies	Number of cooperative dairies	Butter production (in tons)	Butter production by cooperatives (in tons)
1907	750	395	12,200	9,500
1909	754	302	12,000	9,400
1910	697	382	11,900	9,700
1912	652	392	12,800	10,800
1913	655	395	13,900	12,000
1914	651	395	13,500	11,800

Source: *S.T.V.*, 1918, Tables 83, 90, 92.

Table 3 illustrates the size of the main dairy industry product during the half-dozen years before the outbreak of the war. It also underscores the part played by the cooperatives in this field.

The exports of butter showed an interesting change during the generation before 1914. In 1880 approximately three fifths of the amounts exported went to Russia and somewhat over one half in 1890. By 1900 Russia's share had shrunk to about one fourth and by 1910 to one fifth. England alone absorbed over seven elevenths of the total exports of this commodity. Germany's share was two to three times as large as Russia's.

The important changes and improvements recorded during the half-century before 1914 left one aspect of the agrarian community untouched. Alongside of the landowning farmer we find large numbers of cotters, renters, agricultural laborers, and others, many of whom constituted a landless, rural proletariat. A government survey of the problem of the landless disclosed in 1901 that approximately one third of the rural population consisted of leaseholders and that about 40 percent of the rural families neither owned nor leased cultivated acreage. Their numbers had grown rather than decreased since 1850, primarily because of the rise of timber and land prices consequent upon the growth of the lumber industries. While increasing attention had been paid to the problem of the landless since the 1880s and the survey of 1901 disclosed its full magnitude, no substantial improvement was registered until the thorough land reform in 1918 and later eliminated the landless group by turning it into a class of independent landowners.

INDUSTRIALIZATION

Improvement in agriculture was matched by developments in the field of industry. In 1809, struggling ironworks surviving from earlier days and textile, glass, and leather industries hardly worthy of the name constituted the meager beginnings of a later machine age. The age of canals and railways was still in the future; as for the steamship, more than two decades were to elapse before the first steamer plied Finnish waters.

The years from 1809 to about 1850 witnessed the modest beginnings of industrialization. But advance was slow. In 1850 the total number of factories—all small—was in the neighborhood of 140; iron, textile, glass, paper, and tobacco factories were the most important. Not the least interesting aspect of the period is the part played by Scots and Englishmen in the founding of factories. James Finlayson, John Barker, W. Crichton, and David Cowie were some of the industrial pioneers from Britain who laid the basis for Finnish industries. Not a few of them bequeathed their names to firms that have flourished down to our own day.

Outstanding among the early British industrialists in Finland was a Glasgow-born Scot, James Finlayson. Born in 1771, he grew up to be a man of a mechanical turn of mind. Among his inventions was an improved wool-spinning machine. Opportunities abroad beckoned in 1811 when he was offered a post as a machine maker in St. Petersburg, the then capital of Russia, where he headed an engineering establishment for several years. A visit to the Tammerkoski rapids in west-central Finland in 1819 led him to petition Tsar Alexander I for the right to establish a manufacturing plant in Tampere for the production of "good machines and tools for the manufacture of the raw material available in the country and to show the inhabitants of Finland how raw materials are processed into finer manufactured goods." Finlayson was a Quaker and therefore also petitioned that Quaker millworkers be granted religious freedom and the right to observe their own social customs. The petition was granted under the date May 20, 1820. He obtained as a free gift a tract of land along the rapids that were to furnish him with power for his factory, and a modest interest-free loan from Finnish state funds.

Finlayson thereupon set to work. He built a small foundry and a substantial building for the manufacture of carding and spinning machines for both cotton and wool. The first state subsidy having proven inadequate by 1823, he asked for another. After a good deal of trouble and delay a second loan was granted in 1826. The condition for the second loan was that Finlayson's establishment be devoted mainly to the production of woollen and cotton yarn and cloth. Production was begun in 1828, a year that marks the beginning of the modern textile industry in Finland. The mill turned out at first to be only moderately successful, and Finlayson sold it in 1835. He returned to Scotland in 1836 and died in Edinburgh in 1852.

After 1850, industrial advance was aided by several factors. Increasing attention was paid to the shortcomings of the antiquated economic laws, privileges, monopolies, and the like inherited from an earlier age. The merits and disadvantages of economic liberalism and protectionism and the advantages of an agrarian as against an industrial economy were debated. Some saw Finland permanently relegated to the status of an agrarian nation, for the country lacked coal and iron and other basic raw materials essential for industry. Others contended that the country's abundant timber, water power, and labor resources offered opportunities for industrial growth and economic advantage more promising than agriculture could be expected to yield. Two government committees were appointed in 1856 to consider measures for developing industries and mining; while their recommendations led to no immediate measures, they added substantially to the discussions that ultimately produced concrete results. Indicative of the trend of the times was the first scientific survey, undertaken on government initiative by a German expert, of state forest resources in 1858.

Changes in the tariff laws in 1859, 1863, 1864, and 1867 eliminated or reduced export and import restrictions and ended duties on grain and several raw materials, including cotton. The trade relations with Russia were eased in 1859 and, while Finland did not obtain export advantages equal to those enjoyed by Russians in the Finnish market, a number of Finnish commodities gained free access to Russian markets. Earlier restrictions on internal trade were swept away in the same year. The guild system with its privileges and restraints on manufacturing was ended in 1868 and the remaining restrictions on free economic enterprise eliminated in 1879. Meanwhile a new corporation law was enacted in 1864 and other measures devised for easier accumulation of the nation's capital resources. State loans at low interest rates were also increasingly granted in the 1860s and later in the effort to aid new industrial enterprises.

Not the least significant reform that benefited industry and other aspects of the nation's economy was the reorganization of the monetary system. Already at the Porvoo Diet in 1809, the point had been made that Finland should have a monetary system independent of Russia's and that a Bank of Finland should be established. The bank was founded in 1811, but nothing came of the idea of a separate currency and the Diet acceded to the use, for the time being, of the Russian ruble as the circulating medium of the country. For the next thirty years, however, Swedish money held its own in Finland and continued to circulate, often to the exclusion of the ruble.

The first step toward a separate monetary system was taken in 1840. In that year the Bank of Finland was reorganized and was given the right to issue ruble currency, the paper to be fully covered by silver, unlike the Russian ruble. The "Finnish" ruble, duly covered, now became the currency of the country. But it was discovered before long that the fluctuations of the Russian ruble tended to have a disturbing effect upon the currency issued by the Bank of Finland and to dislocate economic life in general. It therefore seemed clear that Finland's interests required a monetary system wholly independent of Russia's.

After careful and time-consuming preparation, a separate currency for Finland was announced on April 4, 1860. The unit was defined as the mark (*markka*), divided into 100 pennies. Provision was also made, later in 1860, for the minting of standard silver coins of 1 and 2 marks and smaller coins, the issuance of notes in small and large denominations, and the like. Both the currency itself and the change in the name of the currency, which sharply differentiated it from the Russian ruble, were of great importance—undoubtedly wholly unintended as far as the Russian government was concerned —in giving sharper relief to the separateness of Finland from the empire. The silver standard was introduced in 1865 when the notes of the Bank of Finland were made redeemable in silver. Silver currency was at the same time declared the only legal tender. This decision meant, in fact, that the paper ruble—it had substantially decreased in value, in terms of silver, by 1865—ceased to be valid in Finland. Subsequent decline in the value of silver led to the adoption of the gold standard in 1877–78. The reform then effected placed the Finnish mark, the equivalent of the French gold franc, as an independent unit in the category of European gold currencies. The national currency no longer had any connection with the currency of Russia. The distinction between the two down to World War I was sharply defined by the fact that the gold standard was strictly maintained by Finland until the disturbances set in train by World War I changed the situation.

"Monetary independence" not only accented the autonomy of the country. It also created, as has been suggested, more favorable conditions for industry and general economic life and stimulated the development of banking. The first commercial bank was established in 1862. By 1890 commercial banks numbered six, with a capital of some $26,000,000. By 1913 the number had risen to thirteen, not including branch banks, and their total capital to nearly $185,000,000. Savings banks showed a similar trend; their deposits reached about $65,000,000 in 1913. The postal savings banks began to operate in 1887 and offered still another opportunity for the accumulation of modest savings.

The "industrial age" after 1850 also brought about modernization of transportation and communication. Railroads, canals, the telephone, the telegraph, the postal system, waterways, and roads all represented parts of a development which was changing an agrarian society into an increasingly industrial civilization.

As early as the 1840s the suitability of railroads for Finland was much discussed. The opponents of railroads held that they would be too expensive to construct and could not be used in winter. The speed of trains was considered both unnatural and unnecessary and the natural advantages of canals and waterways in lake-studded Finland sufficiently great to indicate the unwisdom of expending capital upon railroads.

Ultimately the proponents of railroads carried the day. The first line, some 67 miles in length, was opened to traffic in 1862. By 1868 Helsinki, the capital, was connected by rail with the Russian capital. Other lines followed in due time. By 1914 the total mileage in use was about 2,600. Nearly all the lines had been built by the state because private capital in amounts sufficient for as huge an enterprise as railroads was not available. The railroads aided in the spread of new settlements and played an important part, especially after 1870, in the establishment of industries in the rural parts of the country. Furthermore, the Finnish state railways yielded from the start a return of 2–3 percent upon the original investment, and continued to pay the same rate of interest down to World War II. The rails needed before the turn of the century came mostly from abroad; after 1900, locomotives and rolling stock were of domestic manufacture.

In a country as rich in lakes and navigable rivers as Finland, waterways have naturally played a considerable part. Their improvement received much attention after 1840. The first important canal, the Saimaa Canal, some 37 miles long, was completed in 1856. It gave the lake-studded extensive regions of central Finland cheap and easy communication with the outside world. The first Finnish steamship appeared on one of the large inland lakes in 1833. By 1914, over 3,100 miles of improved waterways and canals served the farmer, merchant, and manufacturer. The canals cleared 6,600 ships in 1875, over 31,700 in 1900, and upwards of 40,000 in 1914.

The postal system dated from 1638 but it remained an insignificant branch of the public service until well into the nineteenth century. The Post Office began to use steamships in forwarding mail in 1839, and after 1862 the railroads carried mail as well as passengers and goods. Stamps were introduced in 1856, parcel post in 1867, and post cards in 1871. The sale of money orders was begun in 1881, and six years later, as we noted, the first postal savings banks began to operate.

The first telegraph line, connecting Helsinki with the Russian capital, was opened in 1855. The telegraph system in Finland was constructed, for military reasons, by the Russian government. While it was opened to civilian use in 1858, it remained a Russian institution—the only Russian institution in autonomous Finland, although its personnel was Finnish—till the collapse of the imperial government in 1917. The first telegraph connections with other countries dated from 1869–83, when cables to Sweden were laid. The telephone was introduced in 1880. Private and municipal rather than state initiative was responsible for the earliest telephone companies. The first telephone system was opened in Helsinki in 1882, and spread rapidly after that date. The state took over much of the systems in 1918 and has been a main operator, especially of the long-distance lines, since 1960.

Meanwhile industry, trade, shipping, growth of population, and increasing urbanization were giving additional evidence of the arrival of a new age.

The advent of modern industry was signalized in the sixties and seventies by an extraordinary boom in lumber, the great natural resource of the country. The first steam sawmill was established in 1860; by 1878 steam sawmills numbered 66 out of a total of 249 and became increasingly common thereafter. The use of steam made it possible to locate sawmills at the mouths of rivers on the coast, the lakes and rivers offering efficient low-cost transportation of logs to the mills. Textile, paper, match, cellulose, rubber, margarine, sugar, cement, and plywood factories either appeared as new industrial enterprises or grew from earlier unpretentious establishments into units of considerable size. For example, Finlayson and Company, in Tampere, the leading textile plant, operated 1,000 looms by 1878. Industrial production was valued at nearly $10,000,-000 in 1869 and $20,000,000 in 1876. In 1896 the figure had reached $37,000,000, in 1905 about $69,000,000, and in 1913 about $130,000,-000. By the last year, the industrial labor force had grown from

28,600 in 1885 to 110,500, and some 400,000 people out of a total population of 3,200,000 were directly dependent upon industry for their livelihood.

FOREIGN TRADE

As has been suggested, Finland's separation from Sweden caused no immediate and sharply defined changes in the nation's economic life. The many-sided traditional commercial connections with Sweden appear to have continued practically undisturbed for a decade or more, and Sweden did not really become a "foreign country" in trade matters until the 1840s. During the first generation of the connection with Russia, that country was at best merely able to compete with but not eliminate the former mother country as Finland's foreign trade partner. The center of gravity of foreign trade remained in the cities of the west and southwest coasts. It was only after the 1850s that the southern coastal cities, located closer to St. Petersburg (which became the main gate of Finland's trade with the empire), emerged as important factors because they tapped the resources, previously relatively little developed, of the eastern and southeastern areas of the country.

The commercial connections with the empire depended in considerable degree upon the tariff policies of Russia. The customs boundary between Finland and Russia was eliminated in 1808, before the formal cession of the country by the Peace of Fredrikshamn in 1809, but Finland was turned into a separate customs area in 1812 in order to control Finnish exports and to prevent the inflow of foreign goods into Russia. The arrangement imposed no restrictions on Russian goods reaching Finnish markets and thus implied no reciprocity. A stricter protectionist policy emerged in the early 1820s and continued till 1840. On the whole, however, Finnish exports to Russia were favored well into the 1850s and partly down to the 1880s by the tariffs and other restrictions in force, but the practically free inflow of Russian goods into Finland placed obstacles in the path of her industrial growth until well into the second half of the century. The mid-eighties marked the beginning of the Russian policy that gradually placed Finland, as regards her exports to Russia, in the category of a "foreign" country.

Foreign trade was closely connected, until about the mid-1800s, with shipping. That is to say, Finnish exports—largely naval stores in those days—were carried to foreign markets in Finnish ships, primarily to Sweden, England, Germany, and France. Using local commission agents, the ships—sailing ships, needless to say—would pick up and carry freights in foreign waters for a year or two before returning home with suitable cargo, at times with the holds filled with coffee from faraway Brazil or other necessaries from equally distant places.

The rising lumber industry after the 1860s and expanding industrialization in general changed the picture. The industrial growth noted above stimulated and at the same time was made possible by a growth of the export trade as well as the increased absorptive capacity of the domestic market. In 1913 over $55,000,000 worth of industrial products was sold abroad. The figure represented about two fifths of the value of the total industrial output. Nearly one third of these exports went to Russia.[1] Farm exports exceeded $20,000,000. The former figure represented an eighteenfold increase of industrial exports in 1860 and was three times as large as the total industrial production in 1884.

The volume of foreign trade and the most important areas it involved are indicated in Table 4. The total includes all the countries involved in Finland's exports and imports and is thus larger than the combined figures for the seven countries enumerated. During the years covered by the table, the value of the mark remained stable. The figures therefore justify the conclusion that both annual exports and imports almost doubled during the fifteen-year period (they increased from 233 million in 1890 to 460.7 million in 1910).[2] Russia absorbed somewhat over one third of the total of exports.

---

[1] Access to Russian markets became increasingly difficult over the years. Tariff advantages enjoyed by Finland before 1885 were largely lost in that year. In 1907 the imperial government decreed that Finnish factories, in bidding for army contracts, were to be treated as other foreign factories were.

[2] Table I in J. Paasivirta, *Plans for Commercial Agents and Consuls of Autonomous Finland* (Turku, 1963).

The general trend in the trade with Russia is shown by the following figures: in 1860, Russia took 47.7 percent of Finland's exports; in 1870, 46.9 percent; in 1880, 41.5 percent; in 1890, 39.4 percent; and in 1910, 30.0 percent.

TABLE 4

FOREIGN TRADE, 1895–1910

(in millions of marks)

	1895	1900	1905	1910
Russia				
Exports	51.1	99.2	94.5	109.7
Imports	48.6	57.2	67.9	79.5
England				
Exports	19.3	34.1	29.0	45.7
Imports	36.0	57.2	75.1	85.5
Germany				
Exports	52.5	89.9	101.3	159.7
Imports	10.0	16.8	25.6	34.7
France				
Exports	3.3	5.5	4.6	5.7
Imports	11.0	17.5	20.2	24.6
Sweden				
Exports	9.3	13.1	13.1	19.4
Imports	6.0	7.4	7.6	11.6
Denmark				
Exports	4.4	14.8	12.4	20.9
Imports	16.5	14.9	13.0	10.0
Spain				
Exports	2.0	2.3	1.7	2.3
Imports	5.7	10.0	5.5	9.8
Total				
Exports	142.9	197.7	247.8	290.1
Imports	150.3	270.8	268.2	384.1

The foreign trade developments during the quarter-century before World War I also reflected significant changes in the over-all industrial growth. At the close of the 1880s, agricultural exports accounted for 29 percent of the total; in 1914, despite the notable expansion of the dairy industry during the preceding decade, the percentage figure dropped to 19. The lumber industry was at the top of the list in the late eighties with 45.4 percent but dropped to 22 percent in 1914 (partly because of the war). The paper industry, on the other hand, increased from 10 to 40 percent during the same period. Textiles and metals still remained relatively unimportant; neither reached the figure 7 percent, although the metals industry grew rapidly during the war and accounted for some 10 percent of the exports in 1916.

The part imperial Russia played in the economic changes recorded in Finland during the half-century before 1914 is partly measured by the distribution, in terms of money value, of exports and imports before 1914. Table 5 illumines the relationship between Finland and the empire, although it does not obscure the fact, already noted, that Finland remained conspicuously "autonomous," in terms of her national economy, during the decades before independence was achieved in 1917–18.

TABLE 5

EXPORTS AND IMPORTS, 1865–1913

(in millions of marks)

Year	Exports		Imports	
	Total	Russia's share	Total	Russia's share
1865	40.3	17.2	72.4	33.2
1875	85.4	41.0	157.7	68.3
1885	88.9	61.0	109.0	75.3
1895	142.9	48.6	150.3	50.4
1900	197.7	57.2	270.7	99.2
1905	247.8	67.9	268.2	94.5
1910	290.1	79.5	384.1	109.7
1913	404.8	113.3	495.4	139.5

Until 1880 the sailing ship more than held its own and most of Finland's foreign trade was carried in domestic bottoms. The steamship gained ground after the mid-eighties, however, although the change from sail to steam was much slower in Finland than elsewhere in the North. The first regularly scheduled steamship connection with the outside world—Sweden, Germany, and England—dated from 1868, when English steamers began to maintain regular sailings. In 1883 the Finland Steamship Company was founded and soon became the leader in its field. Early in the nineties, when the company inaugurated regular traffic on the routes to Stockholm, Hamburg, Stettin, and Hull, it owned ten steamships. The introduction of specially constructed icebreakers in 1891 made possible the maintenance of all-important year-round sailings. A further innovation was recorded in 1898 when two passenger-freight steamships built to travel frozen winter routes were introduced in the Hull trade, the cargo service between Finland, Copenhagen, and Hull being especially important. Some 50 percent of Finland's exports and imports were carried in domestic ships after 1900. At the turn of the century, Finland had a merchant marine of 340,700 tons, of which 53,500 represented steamships; by 1914 the figures had grown to 478,000 and 85,500. Also by 1914 the Finland Steamship Company's flag was seen in all the leading West European ports and in the Mediterranean.

The changes wrought by industrialization and its manifold consequences were recorded in significant changes in the size and distribution of the nation's population. The population reached 1,700,-000 in 1870, exceeded 2,000,000 ten years later, grew to about 2,700,-000 by the turn of the century, and approximated 3,200,000 in 1913. After the decade of the seventies, a marked decrease in births was noted. Broadly speaking, the annual increase dropped from about 15 per thousand people in 1870 to about 11 per thousand on the eve of World War I.

Emigration also prevented a more rapid increase in the population of the country than these figures show. Except for the small seventeenth-century emigration to Sweden and to the Delaware region in America, no emigration worth mentioning took place until after the middle decades of the last century. The California gold rush tempted some Finns to leave for the search of riches in faraway America. The Homestead Act of 1862 acted as a magnet after the close of the Civil War, but it has been estimated that only some 12,000 persons had yielded to the lure of the New World by 1880. After 1880, some 2,000 persons emigrated yearly; between 1883 and 1892, the figure reached about 5,000. Thereafter the number grew rapidly. During the years 1901–15, the annual average was about 15,000. Estimates indicated that approximately 380,000 persons had emigrated by the early 1920s. Except for a small minority, the emigrants went to the United States.

Not the least significant change in Finland's population between 1850 and 1914 was the growth of cities. In 1850 the total city population was only 105,000. By 1890 the figure had more than doubled. It grew again by nearly 200 percent between 1890 and 1910. These figures do not tell the whole story, however. They are based upon a conventional statistical distinction between city and countryside which rests on an administrative classification that gives no true picture of the degree of urbanization. Thus there were several among the thirty-two cities of Finland before 1914 that were cities in name only. On the other hand, large industrial and suburban communities did not appear in the list of cities, although they were urban centers in the ordinary sense of the word. Urbanization must therefore be measured in terms of occupations no less than in terms of administrative classification.

The extent to which agriculture lost ground, relatively speaking, after industrialization and urbanization became marked is indicated by the fact that in 1850 over 90 percent of the population depended on agriculture for a living, while a generation later the figure was nearly 75 percent. In 1900 it had dropped to 68 percent and in 1910 to 66 percent. Meantime the industrial labor force had grown from 2,600 in 1850 to 78,000 in 1900 and 110,300 in 1914.

THE RISE OF LABOR

The position of labor also changed in the decades that followed the close of the Crimean War. The stage was being set for the contest, familiar in all lands importantly affected by the coming of machine and factory, between capital and labor.

The rise of the organized wage earner began with reading clubs and similar associations founded in the fifties and sixties for the purpose of enabling the laboring man to become familiar with the history and conditions of his country. Evening schools also appeared and appreciably improved the education of the worker long before the national system of public schools, founded in 1866, began to produce results.

The educational labor clubs were replaced before long by workers' associations, the objectives of which were more definitely connected with the welfare and interests of the growing industrial working class. They remained, however, respectable middle-class organizations in spirit. An indication of the trend of the times was given by the first organized strike, by the typographers' society for higher wages, in 1872. Trade unions began to appear in the eighties with the typographers again in the vanguard. They originated partly in the attempt made by bourgeois friends of the worker to improve the condition of the laborer by organizing individual trades into unions. The unions were free from the militancy of the class-conscious worker we usually associate with labor unions. But before long the tail began to wag the dog, and the workers' associations found it impossible to control the unions. By the nineties, the workers' associations were increasingly absorbed or controlled by the more radical trade unions, which labored for higher pay, shorter hours, and better working conditions and were not averse to using the strike as an instrument of policy.

The formulation of a labor political program and the establishment of a labor press heralded in the middle nineties the emergence of a full-fledged workers' movement. The founding of the *Työmies* (The Worker) in 1895 gave labor an organ dedicated to working-class interests. In 1899 the Labor party of Finland was founded. Its program, the preamble of which had been written by the leading Swedish Socialist leader, Hjalmar Branting, included such well-known Socialist demands as universal and equal suffrage, the eight-hour day, free and compulsory public education, progressive income and inheritance taxes, adequate labor legislation, and measures to improve the condition of the landless agricultural population. Its socialism was the Marxian creed formulated by the Socialists at the Erfurt congress in 1891.

The new party was four years old when it changed its name to the Social Democratic party of Finland. Henceforth Finnish labor proposed to stand on its own feet and to fight its own battles in the political arena. In preparing to tackle and solve the economic, political, and social issues that they considered vital, the Social Democrats proceeded to marshal the resources of the lower classes for the contest they saw ahead. Socialist newspapers were founded and local branches of the party established. Speaker and pamphleteer carried the creed of Marx throughout the length and breadth of the land.

The appearance of the workers' political party organization was seconded by the emergence of labor unions. The trade union movement began to gain momentum after 1890. By the turn of the century some ten national unions had been founded; the printers and the tailors headed the procession, followed by bricklayers, metalworkers, carpenters, stonemasons, painters, and others. The unions were weak by modern standards but they reflected the movement of the times, illustrated in all countries where industrialization and urbanization were changing the old forms of life and ushering in the new world of the factory and the machine. A national federation of labor was planned in 1899 but was not launched, because of personal rivalries and other obstacles, until the formation of the Federation of the Labor Unions of Finland in 1907. The federation took on a strong political coloration from the start and accepted, at its constituent meeting, the Marxian doctrine of the class struggle and a policy of close cooperation with the Social Democratic party. It was also agreed that, while membership in the Social Democratic party was not a condition for membership in the federation, trade unions were expected to belong to the party. The heavy political accent appears to have reflected, in large degree, the fact that until 1906—the year before the federation was founded—the majority of the workers had no vote and therefore were deprived of the chance to exert their influence on political questions. The enfranchisement of the workers and other classes previously deprived of the right to vote was too recent to have led the organized workers to abandon the resolve to use both party and union in the furtherance of the purposes the Marxist program defined as necessary and right.

While the labor union movement grew relatively rapidly after 1905—twenty new unions were founded in 1905-7—it did not succeed in enlisting a large number of supporters. By 1907, the year that witnessed the launching of the Federation of Labor Unions, a total labor union membership of only 26,000 was recorded. The Social Democratic party, on the other hand, had over 80,000 members and had shown itself able, in the first or 1907 election after the introduction of a fully democratic franchise, to obtain the support of 330,000 voters (out of a total of 891,000). That gave it 80 out of the 200 seats in the legislature. The weakness of the labor unions was also shown by the fact that the outcome of strikes between 1907 and 1914 was on the whole against them; the workers won only 15 percent of the strikes, the employers 40 percent, and the rest were ended by a compromise settlement. The Social Democratic party, on the other hand, forged ahead beyond the strong position captured in the 1907 election. After the 1908 election it held 83 seats, in 1909 it climbed to 84 seats, and it reached 86 in 1910. The party retained the same number of seats in the elections of 1911, but in 1913, the last election before World War I, the number rose to 90. Social democracy in Parliament and out was therefore not only important; it was of decisive significance, and seemed to promise that, when conditions would permit the introduction of parliamentary government, Socialists would in all likelihood furnish the country with cabinet leadership. Prior to the war years, however, such a likelihood seemed remote because the Russian government was bent on a policy of Russification that deprived the Socialists no less than the other parties of the opportunity to translate parliamentary strength into effective parliamentary government.

VIII

The War of Independence, 1918

THE MENACE OF RUSSIFICATION

Between 1870 and 1890, several minor attempts to abridge Finland's autonomy had been made. They were warded off, however, and it was not until 1890 that Russia's determination to violate the Finnish constitution became clear. In that year a much-needed reform of Finnish criminal law, enacted by the Finnish legislature and sanctioned by the tsar, was annulled by imperial decree on the grounds that it contained provisions of allegedly "separatist" nature. The management and administration of the Finnish Post Office was placed under the supervision of Russian authorities in the same year, without the consent of the Diet. In 1894 the use of the Russian language was introduced into some of the higher branches of Finland's government. With these measures it became evident that nearly three generations of constitutional government and rule by law were seriously threatened.

The real process of Russification was begun in 1899. An imperial manifesto issued on February 15 of that year placed nearly all Finnish legislation under the surveillance of the Russian government. The constitution and the laws of Finland would henceforth be interpreted in the light of Russian and not Finnish interests and needs. Said the emperor of all the Russias: "While maintaining in full force the prevailing statutes concerning the promulgation of local laws which relate exclusively to the internal affairs of Finland, We have found it necessary to reserve to Ourselves the final decision as to which laws come within the scope of general Imperial legislation." This meant that the constitution and laws of Finland would in the future be "local laws" only and that their importance and scope would be arbitrarily determined in St. Petersburg. If this policy were carried out, Finnish autonomy would soon become a meaningless abstraction.

The manifesto created general uneasiness and consternation in the country. Both the government and the legislature sent a deputation to the Russian capital to call attention to the unconstitutional character of the new policy. The results were nil, for all that was gained by the protests was an unconvincing assurance that the tsar "had given the country the best guarantee for the undisturbed preservation of its internal legislation when he personally undertook to decide, in each instance, whether a matter should be classified as pertaining to imperial legislation."

Protest was not limited to the Finnish government and the Diet. Within a few days of the issuance of the February Manifesto, steps were taken by energetic patriots to produce a national protest. A petition to be signed by the whole nation was speedily drafted. Acting in complete secrecy—the mails, the telephone, or the telegraph could not be used for fear that the undertaking would be discovered by the Russian authorities—the organization necessary for the enterprise was set up and funds collected. On March 5, secret citizens' meetings were held throughout the land, the contents of the petition were read, the signatures of the protestants were affixed, and representatives were chosen to constitute a Committee of Five Hundred to present the protest to the tsar.

The work was completed a week later. The signatures numbered 522,931, which amounted to about one fifth of the total population of the country and included practically all adult men and women. Not the least interesting aspect of the gigantic enterprise was the fact that not until the thousands of copies of the petition had been bound and the five hundred deputies entrained for St. Petersburg did the Russian authorities discover that the country had successfully mobilized its full powers of moral persuasion in protest against the violations of the nation's fundamental law.

The protest brought no relief. The deputation was not permitted to present the petition to the tsar and returned from the Russian capital without having accomplished its purpose. The same fate awaited a committee of distinguished European scholars and statesmen who attempted to intercede on Finland's behalf in June of the same year. The committee intended to present a statement to the tsar pointing out the illegal and unconstitutional character of Russia's policy toward Finland. They said, in part:

Having read and being deeply moved by the Petition of the 5th of March of over half a million Finnish men and women in which they made a solemn appeal to your Majesty in support of the maintenance of their full Rights and Privileges first confirmed by . . . Alexander I in 1809 . . . and subsequently re-affirmed in the most solemn manner by all his illustrious successors, we venture to express our hope that your Imperial Majesty will take into due consideration the prayer of the said Petition of your Majesty's Finnish subjects. It would be a matter of great regret if recent events in the Grand Duchy of Finland should retard the cause of amity among the nations of the civilized world which has in your Majesty so Illustrious an Advocate.

The address was signed by more than a thousand prominent citizens of England, Denmark, France, Germany, Norway, Sweden, Italy, and other countries. Among the outstanding names were those of Joseph Lister, Herbert Spencer, Florence Nightingale, J. Westlake, Emile Zola, Anatole France, Gaston de Paris, the Comte de Broglie, L. Trarieux, Rudolf Eucken, Theodore Mommsen, Hans Delbrück, Henrik Ibsen, Björnstjerne Björnson, Fridtjof Nansen, Verner von Heidenstam, Magnus Mittag-Leffler, Georg Brandes, W. van der Vlugt, and E. Brusa. But the voices of the thousand were no more effective than the protest of the five hundred thousand in stemming the tide of Russification.

Meanwhile the press of the country began to feel the effects of the new policy. Suppression of newspapers, heavy fines, tightening of censorship, forced changes of editors—making continued publication contingent upon the appointment of a new editor—became frequent measures in the attempt to silence the press. Measures of this kind were not very effective, however. Pamphlets and other forms of uncensored reading matter, printed secretly in Finland or smuggled from abroad, appeared as means of anti-Russian propaganda. The censored press was muted, but uncensored pamphlet, tract, and broadside sounded a resonant note of protest audible to all but Russian ears.

Undeterred by Finnish opposition or foreign opinion, the work of Russification continued unabated. An unconstitutional conscription act was forced upon the country in 1901. It provided that Finnish conscripts—who had hitherto served in the separate Finnish army of some 6,000 men—would henceforth serve with Russian troops subject to Russian regulations. The act led to the first real test of strength between Finland and Russia. More than 50 percent of the conscripts failed to appear for the enrollment in the spring of 1902 when the new law went into effect. The upshot of the situation was the abandonment of the attempt to force the Finns to perform military service and the fixing of an annual money payment in lieu of a contribution of soldiers. The Finns had thus succeeded in preventing the enforcement of a law which, if put into effect in its original form, would have meant the incorporation of the fighting forces of the nation in the hated Russian army.

In the meantime, the imperial government hewed to the line of Russification. The use of the Russian language was extended in the upper reaches of the government of Finland, in defiance of law. The teaching of Russian in the secondary schools was materially increased. (No attempt was made to introduce Russian into the primary schools, and Russian was at no time taught in them.) Governors, judges, mayors, city and town councilors, and other civil servants who resolutely refused to recognize the legality of government by imperial fiat were dismissed by the hundreds, and their places were filled either by Russians or by Finns unable or unwilling to resist the pressure from St. Petersburg. By 1904, when the Russo-Japanese War broke out, government according to law had partly been replaced by government by arbitrary decree. The assassination of the Russian governor-general of Finland in 1904 and of another dignitary in 1905 reflected the desperation of the Finns in their unequal struggle for constitutional rights and the freedom of the citizen.

The Russian Revolution of 1905, precipitated by the Russo-Japanese War, brought temporary respite. In November, 1905, the hard-pressed imperial government issued a manifesto which repealed the illegal acts of the preceding half-dozen years and reestablished law and order in Finland. The legislature was summoned to meet in extra session, to resume the work which for several years it had been unable to perform. The most important reform it accomplished under the new and more favorable circumstances that now prevailed was the reorganization of the legislature and the enactment of a new electoral law. Complete political democracy was established. A unicameral parliament, based on equal and universal suffrage—women as well as men were given the right to vote—replaced the antiquated four-estate Diet, and the earlier limitations on the right to vote, based on property, were removed. In other ways, too, government and nation proceeded to repair the damage done since 1899 and got ready for the difficulties which possible renewed Russification would bring in the future.

Trouble was not long in coming. Beginning in 1908, the Russian government introduced a series of measures which gave the lie to the solemn concessions made to the Finns in 1905. Legislative and other matters which might be interpreted as relating to or touching Russian interests were withdrawn from the competence of Parliament. The government was bent to the will of Russia. Beginning in 1910, native-born Russians were increasingly appointed to it. Arbitrary financial levies were imposed; Russian citizens were placed on a footing of equality with Finnish citizens; judges and civil servants who persisted in upholding the laws of the land were imprisoned or exiled; Russian became the official language of the government; and some branches of the public service were subordinated to Russian law. By 1914, orderly processes of government had once again largely disappeared, and the constitution had been shorn of its meaning.

World War I provided additional opportunities for rule by force. Military necessity became an ever-present excuse for disregard of civil rights. Illegal taxes were levied; steps were taken to abolish Finnish citizenship; citizens were frequently apprehended and subjected to Russian law; the budget was twisted to serve Russian ends; and Russian gendarmes became ever more numerous as visible symbols of a policy of oppression intent on breaking down all obstacles. Parliament's appeals to the constitution and its repeated protests against the illegalities committed during the years 1914–17 seemed only to hasten the process of Russification, which was rapidly bringing the country to the status of a subject province governed directly from the capital of the empire. It was not until the Russian Revolution of March, 1917, that the autocratic regime came to an end and the nation was given an opportunity to free itself from the oppressor.

THE INDEPENDENCE MOVEMENT BEFORE 1917

It is doubtful that the Finns nurtured aspirations for political independence before the middle decades of the last century. Even at that time it was the secret dream of the few rather than the avowed ambition of the many. That some of the nationalist leaders considered complete freedom from Russian control as the ultimate objective of the nationalist movement is clear. However, not until Russification became a real menace after 1898 did an independence movement begin to take root. It was secret, needless to say, and was centered in a group styled the Activist Opposition party that came into being in 1904. The purpose of the Activists was to engineer a revolution that would overthrow the tsarist regime and sever connections with Russia; many of them wanted to establish a fully democratic constitution for the country. The Activists represented various parties and drew support from the ranks of labor as well as from other groups. The Russo-Japanese War in 1904–5, which temporarily eased the situation in Finland, gave additional strength and opportunities to the Activists. Secret negotiations with Japanese agents, meetings and subterranean cooperation with Russian revolutionaries and Polish and other non-Russian independence men, preparations for revolt in Finland, and other such activities occupied the Activists.

The arming of the nation was a basic objective of the Activists. In 1905, two yachts and a small steamer, the *John Grafton*, were purchased in England for the transportation of arms and munitions. The *John Grafton*, carrying a cargo of three tons of explosives, 15,500 rifles, and 2,500,000 rounds of ammunition—the cargo was originally partly intended for Russian opposition groups and was paid for by the Japanese—arrived after an adventurous voyage on the western coast of Finland in the fall of the year. It unloaded a part of its cargo, ran aground, and was blown up by the crew when it became clear that the ship could not be floated. The *John Grafton* soon became a magic name among the people, charged with the fascination of mysterious enterprises against the Russian oppressor. The rifles it had succeeded in landing, distributed among trusted folk, became symbols to young and old of the future contest for freedom from Russia. But while another ship, the *Peter*, brought a considerable cargo of guns and munitions in July, 1906, the business of arming the nation never attained important dimensions. When World War I broke out the nation was still nearly completely lacking in the military equipment necessary for revolt or war.

Immediately after the outbreak of the war in 1914, a small group of men began to draft plans for safeguarding the future of the country. The plans were well under way by November, 1914. An emissary was sent to England to prepare the ground for possible English intercession on Finland's behalf. Lord Bryce, Sir Edward Grey, Francis Hirst, the editor of *The Economist*, and others were approached. Early in 1915, a delegation was secretly dispatched to the United States for the purpose of calling the plight of Finland to the attention of American leaders. Armed with letters of introduction from Lord Bryce, Sir Frederick Pollock, and others, the delegation arrived in the United States in March, 1915. Presidents Arthur T. Hadley of Yale, A. Lawrence Lowell of Harvard, and Nicholas Murray Butler of Columbia, former President William Howard Taft, former President Theodore Roosevelt, and John Bassett Moore were among the leading men who were approached and who agreed to "use their influence to obtain guarantees of Finland's autonomy" if the United States would participate in the making of the peace at the close of the war.[1] The effort produced no tangible results, for Finland had become independent by the time the Allies proceeded to make peace in 1919.

Meanwhile some of the younger patriots had embarked upon a more radical policy. Pinning their hopes upon a revolt at home, aided

[1] H. Ignatius, K. Grotenfelt, and others, eds., *Suomen Vapaussota Vuonna 1918* (Helsinki, 1922), I, 137.

by Swedish arms, they began in the autumn of 1914 to work for Swedish support of their plans. Even the possibility of a union between liberated Finland and Sweden was considered. It was hoped that Sweden would provide a considerable number of Finnish young men with opportunity for military training which could not be had in Finland. Inquiries in Sweden soon disclosed, however, that, despite strong sympathies among the Swedes for Finland, such training would have to be sought elsewhere. The Swedish government was thoroughly wedded to a policy of strict neutrality and refused to endanger its neutrality by aiding a dangerous undertaking which could be considered directed against a foreign Power. Unsuccessful in Sweden, the patriots turned to Germany.

After the war had begun most Finnish opinion appears to have been friendly toward Germany or outrightly pro-German. The reason was, basically, that Germany was fighting Russia, and it seemed obvious that Russia deserved to be defeated. The defeat of Russia might, at the least, lead to an improvement in Finland's position as a self-governing nation. It might even open the door to complete independence. This view did not imply acceptance of any "German philosophy" or failure to understand the shortcomings of imperial Germany. The liberal and labor elements—a majority in the national legislature since the parliamentary reform of 1906— considered both Germany and Russia as the main obstacles to a just and peaceful solution of the nationality problems of the day. In both empires, individual liberties and the devices of modern, parliamentary democracy were either rudimentary or nonexistent. In the words of one of the leading younger independence men of the war years, Y. O. Ruuth, "Germany was considered as Russia's tutor in everything having to do with imperialism, militarism, and bureaucracy." Germany's responsibility for causing the great war—it was Germany that had declared war on Russia and France and therefore seemed to stand forth as the sole aggressor—and the rape of Belgium buttressed such conclusions. But all this was secondary to the fact that Germany was at war with Russia. Russia, by her own actions, was Finland's enemy. Russia's enemy could only be, by logic and common sense, a friend—and possibly the savior—of Finland.

In Germany, a group of Finns resident in Berlin had already begun to labor for the cause in November, 1914. Aided by luck and excellent contacts, the independence men soon obtained the ear and support of the German General Staff. By January, 1915—that is, before the revolt began in Finland—they had persuaded the General Staff to accept 200 young Finns to be given limited military training in Germany, the expenses to be borne by the German government. In Finland, the secret organization of the friends of independence had in the meantime been extended and perfected and the recruiting of volunteers for military training in Germany begun. The first volunteers left Finland early in February, and thenceforth increasing numbers of trusted young men were smuggled out of the country. Bound for Germany (through Sweden) they risked life and future in order to become the liberators of the nation.

The Finnish contingent was trained in Camp Lockstedt in Holstein, not far from Hamburg. The course of instruction was at first planned for only six weeks, but it was extended several times. Originally intended as a course in scout activity, the instruction was changed later to provide adequate officer and noncommissioned officer training. The volunteers were organized in May, 1916, as the 27th Royal Prussian Jaeger Battalion. The battalion ultimately grew to about 2,000 men. Its members were drawn from all classes of society; about 40 percent represented university students.

Contrary to the original purpose and agreement, the battalion was sent to the eastern front in June–August, 1916, and participated in engagements against the Russians in June. At the end of August, it became the northermost segment of the German line, on the Gulf of Riga. Dissatisfaction over the turn of events appeared among the volunteers, some of whom began to demand that the battalion be withdrawn from the front. It was transferred to Libau in December. Subsequent attempts to send it to the trenches created resistance and resulted in the sending of some fourscore men to labor service in Germany. The Jaegers returned to Finland in 1918 when developments there indicated that independence would require not only a declaration by the legislature but fighting as well.

Throughout 1915 and 1916, the work of supplying the corps of volunteers in Germany and of preparing the ground for undertakings that would lead the country from Russian oppression to independence was carried on by patriotic men and women. Despite the vigilance of the Russian authorities and soldiery in Finland and the handicaps which the necessity for secrecy unavoidably imposed, an extensive underground organization was perfected. Conservatives, progressives, Socialists, Agrarians, persons in high station and low participated at home and abroad in preparing the uprising which was to take place when Russia's reverses had assumed sufficient proportions to ensure a fair chance of success. Internal division and party squabbles disappeared. The nation was becoming united as never before in the cause of freedom.

The March, 1917, revolution in Russia confused as well as elated the independence groups. The autocratic regime collapsed in Finland shortly after the abdication of Nicholas II. The Russian naval forces stationed in Helsinki began to square their accounts with their officers on March 15; considerable blood was spilled in the process. The Russian governor-general and some of the higher officials were apprehended by the Russian soldiers; a number were summarily shot and others were sent to Petrograd. On March 20 the Russian Provisional Government issued a manifesto which voided the ordinances and decrees that had established the arbitrary, unconstitutional government in Finland since 1898. Political prisoners were freed and the press was unshackled. Finland's self-government was again recognized as resting on and deriving from Finnish law, and promises were given of speedy reform of the Finnish government. Within a week of the collapse of the monarchy, the Finns were able to point to a recapture of the self-rule that had all but disappeared since 1908. The national legislature, elected in 1916, was also convoked. Here was abundant cause for satisfaction.

The revolution also caused uncertainty and misgivings. The sudden collapse of illegal Russian rule and the ease with which the return to the constitution and government by law was seemingly effected endangered the whole independence movement. Contrary to the expectation of many Finns, anarchy in Russia, which they assumed would inevitably follow the downfall of the tsarist government, failed to materialize. The relatively peaceful course of the Russian Revolution in the spring of 1917 appeared to disclose democratic strength in Russia sufficient to allow the transformation of autocracy into a state founded on popular rights. A Russian government founded on popular rights and not paralyzed by internal anarchy would in all likelihood mean opposition to Finnish independence aspirations that could not be left out of calculations. Would it therefore not be best to accept the concessions made by the Provisional Government, to be satisfied with a return to full autonomy, and to abandon the idea of complete independence?

The situation was complicated by the possibility that Germany would not press its Russian campaign hard enough to create a fair chance for the success of a Finnish uprising. Furthermore, the Russian Revolution had come unexpectedly and necessarily created indecision in the minds of many Finns. The crosscurrents of internal politics likewise tossed the cause of independence hither and yon, not the least because the efforts to arm the nation had been only moderately successful. When the legislature convened on April 4, it was by no means clear that the course of events would naturally lead the nation toward independence.

THE DECLARATION OF INDEPENDENCE

The July 1–3, 1916, election had been an unusual electoral contest. Since the preceding election of 1913, the legislature had not been convened, and the conditions in 1916 appeared to justify the conclusion that the new parliament would also be denied the opportunity to perform its proper function. Only 55.5 percent of the qualified voters went to the polls. The Social Democrats, normally the best-organized and best-disciplined party, benefited by the stay-at-home vote. They received 46 percent of the votes cast—376,000 out of a total of 795,200—but captured 103 out of the 200 seats of the legislature and thus emerged, surprisingly, as the majority party in Parliament. The new government, formed on March 26, 1917, was, however, a coalition government. Six of the portfolios were held by Socialists and six by non-Socialists. The government was headed by O. Tokoi, a prominent Socialist and president of the Federation of Labor Unions.

It was the Tokoi-led government, sustained by a Socialist-controlled legislature, that was at the helm when the Finns proceeded to adjust themselves to the consequences of the Russian March revolution.

What the consequences would ultimately be could not be foreseen on April 4 when the legislature convened. The immediate problem was how to secure Finland's vital interests and how to solve the constitutional problem caused by the abdication of Nicholas II, who as Grand Duke had been monarch of Finland as well as the Tsar of Russia. Was the Provisional Government the heir to the powers and prerogatives which Finland's fundamental law had assigned to the monarch? Could the Provisional Government exercise the monarch's power to convene and dissolve the Finnish legislature, grant or refuse promulgation of laws enacted by the legislature? The question of independence also came to the fore, although for the time being it had to be masked as an aspiration cautiously expressed rather than a resolve boldly defined.

By July, 1917, the developments in Russia had led to the conclusion in Finland that the time was ripe for insisting upon broadening the area of the country's self-rule. This could be done, it was felt, by deciding that most of the rights which had formerly been the prerogative of the monarch could henceforth be exercised by the Finns themselves. The rights involved were, broadly speaking, the right to promulgate laws enacted by Finland's Parliament, formally to convene, suspend, or close the sessions of the legislature, and exclusive power of decision regarding foreign affairs and questions relating to military questions or administration.

On July 18, 1917, Parliament enacted a law (the vote was 136 to 55) which stated that "the powers of the monarch [Nicholas II] having ceased to exist, the Legislature of Finland hereby resolves that the following is in force: The Legislature of Finland alone has the power to enact, confirm, and promulgate all Finnish laws, including laws regarding public economy, taxation, and customs duties. The Legislature also has the final power of decision in all other matters which the Tsar–Grand Duke according to rules and regulations formerly in force" had been competent to decide. "The provisions of this law do not apply to foreign affairs, military legislation, or military administration." The legislature also allocated to itself the right to appoint the government and designated the government then in office as the executive power "for the time being."

Having thus substantially expanded the area of the legislature's functions, and having placed the government under the direct control of the lawmaking body (but leaving the vital areas of foreign and military matters wholly in the hands of the Russian government), the Socialist-led Parliament also decided not to submit the "power law," as it has been called, to the Provisional Government in Petrograd for promulgation. The law itself thus became a test of the legislature's real ability to use the broader powers it had boldly defined in the law. The answer was not long in coming: the Provisional Government, holding that the Finns had exceeded their authority, decreed the dissolution of the legislature on July 31. After some hesitation, the decree to dissolve was accepted in Helsinki. Preparations for new elections were thereupon begun. The elections were held on October 1–2.

The electoral campaign was fought partly on the "power law" and partly on other issues. The Socialists, whose purposes included objectives appropriate to militantly class-conscious Marxists, did battle on behalf of the "power law." They confidently looked forward to a continuation of their majority position in the legislature but were grievously disappointed: 108 seats went to non-Socialist candidates, while the Socialists captured only 92 seats (as against 103 in 1916). Premier O. Tokoi and his Socialist colleagues thereupon withdrew from the government, most of them without the formality of a resignation.

The new Parliament convened on November 1. The political situation in Russia changed radically a few days later when the Bolshevik revolution occurred on the seventh. The Bolshevik coup and subsequent events rendered academic the question of whether Finland should strike out on her own only after prior constitutional or other arrangements worked out in cooperation with the government of Russia. The decision to go it alone seemed the only way out. It was announced in a resolution, adopted by the legislature on

November 15, which stated in part that "the Parliament hereby decides to exercise, for the time being, the powers which according to existing rules and procedures previously belonged to the Tsar–Grand Duke." Foreign and military affairs were thus included, as had not been the case with the "power law" of July 18, within Finland's competence. The Bolshevik government in Petrograd did not challenge the resolution, nor did it propose or insist, as the Russian Provisional Government had done in July, that foreign affairs and military matters be considered as still belonging to Russian competence. The resolution thus ended, for all practical purposes, the union between Finland and Russia.

The legislature thereupon proceeded to use its self-imposed "executive powers" by promulgating, on November 16, important laws passed before the war but not yet effective because of the lack of proper promulgation by the Russian monarch. One was the eight-hour law; another reformed the municipal franchise. Both had been demanded for years, especially by organized labor and progressive elements. The legislature also formed a new government. After futile efforts to set up a government including Socialists, Parliament approved, on November 26, a non-Socialist coalition cabinet headed by P. E. Svinhufvud. Premier Svinhufvud was a distinguished patriot and judge who had been sent to Siberia in 1912 because of his uncompromising insistence upon the sanctity of the law. The new cabinet stated in its program pronouncement that its first and main purpose was to issue a proclamation of independence. In forming his cabinet—six of its eleven members were Progressives—Svinhufvud had insisted that its members agree in advance that Finland be declared independent. The formal decision in favor of independence was reached by the government on the day following its formation (November 27). The declaration was submitted to the legislature on December 4 in a proposal for a new constitution which defined Finland as an independent republic. Parliament accepted the declaration on December 6 by a vote of 100 to 88 in the following form:

In view of the fact that the Government has submitted a proposal for a new Constitution which incorporates the principle that Finland is an independent Republic, the Legislature, as the repository of supreme power, for its part accepts the principle and also agrees that the Government shall proceed to the measures which in its judgment are essential for obtaining recognition by foreign Powers of the political independence of Finland.

The Svinhufvud Cabinet proceeded at once to obtain recognition. The Bolshevik government headed by Lenin was the first to accord recognition on December 31, 1917. Germany, Sweden, France, Norway, Denmark, and several others had recognized the new state by January 23, 1918. Finland thus stood forth as an independent nation, free from the affiliation with Russia, whose new masters had voluntarily recognized Finland, without reservations, as a sovereign state free to chart her own course.

INDEPENDENCE ACHIEVED—THE WAR OF 1918

The events of the next few weeks showed, however, that Finland was not in fact free to go her own way and that ominous internal and external obstacles to independence were emerging. The obstacles to the nation's freedom were removed only after a war, at once a civil war and a war of independence, had been fought.

The specific reasons for the war can be indicated by noting that by early December certain revolutionary elements had captured the leadership of the Social Democratic party and had succeeded, partly in cooperation with the Bolshevik regime in Russia, in preparing a revolution designed to bring down the legal government and to replace it by a new, Marxian order of things.

The resolve of the radical groups among the Socialists to overthrow the legal government had been gradually emerging since the October election. After the Bolshevik seizure of power on November 7, the Socialists' determination not to accept the consequences of a minority position in Parliament had become obvious. The Socialist leadership proceeded to set the stage for extraparliamentary measures. On November 12, the Federation of the Labor Unions of Finland, the Socialist Party Committee, and the Socialist Parliamentary Group set up a Central Revolutionary Council of thirty-five members. The council proclaimed a national strike on the next day.

The purpose of the strike—it lasted till November 20—was to exert pressure upon the legislature and bend it to the will of the radicals. During the week of the strike, lawlessness and violence on a large scale spread over many parts of the country; self-constituted Red "forces for maintaining order" made hundreds of arbitrary arrests, "expropriated" property, committed scores of murders, and became guilty of other forms of lawbreaking. The strike was called off only after the Socialist leadership, alarmed at the situation that had developed, had promised the strikers that a Tokoi-led Social Democratic government would be formed (a fraudulent promise and a manifest impossibility, in view of the Socialist minority position in Parliament); that nobody would be held responsible for the breaches of the law during the strike; and that the radical Red police would be advised to keep their weapons (obtained from the Russian forces still garrisoned in Finland). In the proclamation that ended the strike, the Central Revolutionary Council stated that the "fight continues." This meant that "the revolution continues." The Socialist Parliamentary Group issued a proclamation of its own, placing the blame for the strike on the non-Socialist parties in Parliament and accusing them of "the dirtiest form of treason" because they had prevented, it was claimed, the Parliament from functioning during the week of the strike.

The legislature convened on November 21, the day after the strike ended, and proceeded at once to form a coalition government headed by P. E. Svinhufvud, as we have seen. While the Svinhufvud Cabinet had been formed according to normal parliamentary procedure and enjoyed clear majority support in the legislature, recent developments suggested that the Socialists would not genuinely accept the new cabinet and be satisfied with the role of a mere "loyal opposition." This turned out indeed to be the case. The drift toward a Socialist-led revolution continued.

The Central Revolutionary Council had decided by a small majority on November 16—the third day of the national strike—to seize power. The decision was rescinded, however, and the general strike remained only a "dress rehearsal" for the revolution that began some six weeks later. Meanwhile the groups within the Social Democratic party opposed to revolution were brought to heel at a party conference on November 25–27 attended by Stalin. His speech to the conference urged the need of resolute and audacious action on behalf of "Socialist power" and promised Russian aid in removing the obstacles to victory. Stalin's exhortation aided the extremists at the conference in pushing through a resolution which for all practical purposes authorized the Socialist Parliamentary Group and the Socialist Party Committee to proceed, at a time they considered appropriate, to revolutionary seizure of power.

At the time of the party conference, the majority of the Socialist Party Committee members still opposed revolutionary measures as a substitute for democratic, parliamentary procedures. The situation changed at the Party Committee meeting on January 19–22, 1918, when the Committee was enlarged, as a result of the manipulation of resolute extremists, by the inclusion of five new radical members. The revolutionary elements were now in control, especially after the appointment of an executive committee, manned by extremists, to prepare measures for the coup. On January 24 the Red Guards were given orders to stand by. The revolutionaries struck four days later. The executive committee was replaced by a revolutionary government of thirteen members styled the People's Delegation. The civil war was on. The expectation was that Russian aid would be forthcoming quickly and on a scale large enough to secure a speedy victory for the revolution.

When the Svinhufvud Cabinet took office on November 26, 1917, the country could look back, as we have seen, on several weeks of mounting disturbances and lawlessness culminating in the growing anarchy during the days of the general strike. The end of the strike did not mark the end of lawlessness or a return to normal conditions in general. Angry debates in Parliament sustained by the increasingly uncompromising radicalism of the spokesmen of the Socialists; unabated, violent agitation in the Socialist press—often expressed in idiom strikingly searing and vitriolic even when read nearly fifty years later—which frequently threatened direct action and the use of force in carrying through measures urged for the benefit of "the people"; and the increasing pretensions and menace of the workers' "organization for maintaining order"—later called the Red Guards —testified through December and January to the approach of the day when the leaders of the left committed to revolution would strike.

In the face of the growing menace, the legal government was able to proceed only slowly. It had no adequate police force at its disposal. No Finnish army had as yet been created, even though the continued presence of Russian troops in the country and conditions in general clearly indicated the need of a fighting force. Voluntary defense corps—under various names—had been formed since the fall of 1917 in many parts of the country to aid in keeping law and order, but they were neither adequate nor as yet under the direct control of the government. It was not until January 12, 1918, that the Svinhufvud Cabinet was empowered by Parliament to establish— the Socialists opposing—a "strong police force." The action came in direct response to threatening moves by the Red Guards. The Defense corps were placed under government control and command on January 25, but had not been effectively organized or unified when the revolutionaries acted three days later.

The government thus had no army or other force ready to challenge the Peoples' Delegation and the actions of the Red Guards. It had, however, a commander-in-chief, General C. G. Mannerheim. Mannerheim had had a distinguished career in the Russian army and had returned to his native Finland on December 18, only some six weeks before the revolt began. He had been persuaded by Premier Svinhufvud, on January 10, to accept the task of organizing a government force for maintaining law and order, and shortly thereafter he was named commander-in-chief of a fighting force not yet in existence. He left Helsinki on January 18 for Vaasa on the west-central coast of Finland, there to plan for and organize an army.

Vaasa, a provincial city of 22,000 at the time, thus became the center of Mannerheim's activities. It also became the seat of the legal government for the duration of the war. Four members of the Cabinet succeeded in leaving Helsinki and reaching Vaasa only hours before the Reds began the revolt by seizing control of Helsinki on January 28. The "Vaasa government" was strengthened early in March by the arrival of two additional members, including Premier Svinhufvud, who had been hiding in the capital and arrived in Vaasa after storybook adventures that took them through wartime Germany and Sweden before they worked their way back to Finland.

The Soviet government did not officially participate in the war in Finland but Russians and Russian aid played a significant part in the Red revolt. The radical wing of the Socialists and especially the Red Guards saw in the Russian garrisons in the country an important source of strength. The Red Guards were armed by the Russians and were in part led by Russian commissioned and noncommissioned officers, and considerable numbers of Russian "volunteers" fought in some of the battles of the war. The Red artillery, obtained from the Russians, was wholly under Russian command. The Red forces ultimately numbered some 100,000 men. Although the Russian forces involved were, by comparison, small in number, they nevertheless played a substantial role. Something of a measure of their contribution to actual fighting is given by the fact that the Red defense of Tampere, the important industrial city in central Finland, included about 1,000 Russians; that the decisive Rautu engagement at the end of the war (April 5) resulted in the death of 400 Russians and the capture of nearly 700; and that their number on the Karelian front, in February, has been estimated at some 2,100.

The Russians also became involved in the war in situations not of their own choosing. General Mannerheim's initial action was directed against the Russian garrisons in central-western and northern Finland. The garrisons were taken and disarmed; the area thus freed from the Russians became the broad base of operations against the Reds in south Finland. The operation was begun on January 27, with the aid of local defense corps forces composed of civilian volunteers determined to lend a hand in freeing the country from the Russians. Within four days the garrisons in south Ostrobothnia had been taken and about 5,000 Russians disarmed. The northern parts of the country were similarly freed from Russian forces and brought under the control of the legal government by February 7. Mannerheim's forces were in the meantime growing in numbers—most of the 70,000 men under his command when the war ended were small farmers and other ordinary country and city folk—and he could therefore turn to the more demanding task of defeating the Red forces who held most of south and central Finland in their grip. The Reds lost Tampere in south-central Finland on April 6, Helsinki on April 13, and Viipuri in southeast Finland on April 29. The last areas under Red control, on the Karelian Isthmus, were taken by the national forces on May 15. Helsinki witnessed a victory parade by Mannerheim's "people's army" on the sixteenth.

In the victory of the legal government, Germany had played a conspicuous although not a decisive part by giving military aid in the closing stages of the war.

The antecedents of German assistance went back to the early days of independence. Although Finnish independence had been recognized by the Soviet government, tens of thousands of Russian soldiers remained in the country. They and the armed Red Guards paid no heed to constituted authority and carried on, for weeks before the revolt began, in a manner that plainly indicated Russia's determination not to recall, for reasons it considered sufficient, the troops from Finland. The hard-pressed Svinhufvud Government therefore requested that Germany send troops to Finland. Germany replied that no aid could be sent while the preliminary peace discussions with the Russians continued. After the middle of February, 1918—the war of independence was then somewhat over two weeks old—the situation changed. Discussions regarding aid were resumed, and a favorable decision was reached at the German Imperial Headquarters on February 21 by Marshal Hindenburg and General Ludendorff. Germany agreed to send a military expedition to Finland.

The agreement thus concluded had been initiated by the Finnish government without prior consultation with General Mannerheim, who was strongly opposed to accepting German aid. The reason was his firm conviction that the Red forces could be defeated and the Russians ousted from Finland without outside aid. He threatened to resign in protest against the government's decision but reconsidered after he had obtained satisfactory assurances regarding the German troops that were expected.

The conditions Mannerheim insisted upon were stated in a communication to Ludendorff which read in part that "(1) the German troops will be placed, from the moment they land on Finnish territory, under the supreme commander of the Finnish forces, and that (2) the commander of the German Expedition will explain, in a proclamation addressed to the people of Finland, that the Germans have come to Finland not in order to meddle in Finland's internal affairs but in order to aid Finland in her war against the foreign hordes of murderers who have forced their way into our country in violation of law and order." Hindenburg accepted both suggestions without qualification. The preparation for the expedition thereupon proceeded without further difficulty.

The German force landed in Hanko, west of Helsinki, on April 3–5. It numbered some 9,500 men, under the command of Count Rüdiger von der Goltz. A smaller force of 2,500 men under Colonel von Brandenstein was landed at Loviisa, east of Helsinki, on April 7. The Germans began their operations on Finnish soil at the very time when the government forces were registering their decisive victory at Tampere (April 6). The operations preceding the victory at Tampere diluted the concentration of Red forces in south Finland and materially eased the rapid German advance to Helsinki and the capture of the capital by them on April 13.

The war of 1918 caused losses in dead and wounded that seem very modest by comparison with the losses Finland sustained in the two-phase war with Russia in 1939–44. Yet the loss of life was substantial enough to mark the war as a great tragedy and a national calamity. While the record for 1918 is partly inexact, it appears that the estimates of J. O. Hannula in his *Suomen Vapaussodan Historia* (History of Finland's War of Independence) are as accurate as any. The government or "White" forces lost about 5,300 men, of whom some 1,365 are listed, in the official statistics, as victims of murder by the Reds. Most of those killed were farmers, the second largest category being workers and farm laborers. The total losses of the Whites in dead and wounded appear to have approximated 12,600 or some 18 percent of the forces under Mannerheim's command when the war ended.

As regards the losses of the Reds, the estimates vary greatly. The number of men who fell in battle probably reached 5,500. The number of executions at the hands of the Whites seems to have been 2,000–3,000. Between 7,500 and 8,500 Reds thus lost their lives during the war. A still larger number—estimated at 9,500 by L. A. Puntila, in 1963—died as war prisoners in 1918–19.

One of the most pressing problems facing the government in 1918 was that of the Red prisoners, approximately 90,000, who had fallen into the hands of the national army during the war or who were apprehended after the war ended. The available prisons and other places of detention were inadequate to accommodate them. Special prison camps—they ultimately numbered 63—were hastily constructed and other efforts were made to house and feed the Reds. The acute food shortage, which was assuming the proportions of a famine in some parts of the country, and other difficulties in caring for the welfare of the population as a whole unavoidably meant that the conditions in the prison camps were far from satisfactory and indicated from the start the necessity of speedy handling of the cases of the prisoners.

The normal legal machinery of the country was not geared to the demands placed upon it by the tens of thousands of cases which now had to be tried. Parliament therefore passed a law in May, 1918, which provided for the creation of a large number of courts to handle the Red cases. The cases were to be tried according to existing criminal law for crimes committed during the Red revolt, and not for participation as such. The courts were appointed by the Department of Justice.

About 10 percent of the prisoners were released after a preliminary hearing. Some 15,000 were freed on the basis of a decree which stated that "less dangerous" prisoners could be let go at once, with the understanding that they would stand trial later when called upon to do so. Approximately 31,000 were given conditional sentences. Executive pardons on October 30 and December 7, 1918, further reduced the number of prisoners. The first pardon freed and placed on probation all prisoners who had been sentenced to terms of imprisonment of four years or less; it applied to some 48 percent of the persons whose cases had been appealed to the Supreme Court and confirmed by it (95.5 percent of the cases went to the Supreme Court on appeal). The second pardon extended the first to sentences of not more than six years and applied to about 29 percent of the sentences handed down by the court. It also commuted all death sentences to imprisonment for life. These and other measures rapidly liquidated a problem that seemed at the outset to be almost insoluble. By April, 1919—that is, about a year after the end of the war

—only six prison camps remained and the number of inmates had been reduced to about 6,000, among them 45 women. Further presidential pardons followed after 1919, and the prisoner problem could be written off by 1924.

Before the problem of the prisoners—a tragic consequence of the greater tragedy, the war itself—had been solved, many lives were lost. The lower courts passed 403 death sentences, of which the Supreme Court confirmed 245; of these, 125 were actually carried out. The rest were commuted to prison terms. These figures do not show, however, the number of prisoners who lost their lives. Over 8,000 died in prison hospitals and about 2,700 in prison camps. Scarcity of food and inadequate medical care—general throughout the country at the time—accounted for the heavy toll in human lives. The thousands who died after the war had ended offer something of a measure of the immense, calamitous consequences of the Red revolt precipitated by a handful of extremists serving an alien cause.

THE PEACE OF DORPAT, 1920

While the Soviets had not, as we noted, officially been at war with Finland, a state of war had in fact existed between the two countries which could be formally ended only by a peace treaty. The Soviet government at first rejected the contention that the two states had been at war, for no declaration of war had been issued by either. In the original Soviet view, the fighting in Finland had been a civil war in which Russia had not been involved. But quite apart from the question whether the two countries had been at war or not, Finland's independence and the events in the spring of 1918 had created problems involving boundary questions, possible territorial cessions, economic and financial matters, state and privately owned property located in the neighboring country, rights of nationals, and the like. They required solution before normal relations between Finland and the Soviets could be established.

Despite seeming difficulties, the proposal to conclude a treaty was initiated by the Soviet government less than three months after the war ended. Making use of the good offices of Germany, the Russians proposed discussions in the summer of 1918 for the purpose of establishing "normal relations" between the two states. Germany accepted the role of an intermediary and discussions were begun in Berlin on August 2, 1918. They produced no concrete results, partly because of Russian insistence that the two countries had not actually been at war and therefore the questions to be considered involved only economic and financial matters, and partly because of ambitious Finnish demands—they seem naïvely unrealistic in retrospect, to say the least—for the cession of territory along Finland's eastern border.

In September, 1919, the Russians renewed the suggestion that peace discussions be held. Military expeditions, intermittent boundary incidents, and other problems prevented progress for several months. A formal peace conference finally convened in Dorpat, Estonia, on June 10, 1920. Its labors were completed with the signing of the peace treaty on October 14.

The peace treaty was preceded by an armistice signed on August 13 which, in the words of the chief of the Russian delegation, meant "actually the cessation of all military action between the two states." The introductory paragraph of the peace treaty showed that the Soviets had abandoned the fiction that no war had existed. It stated that Finland and the Federated Soviet Republics, "desiring to end the war that later broke out between the two states, and to establish permanent peaceful relations between themselves, and definitely to clarify the relationships that derive from the earlier political union between Finland and Russia, have decided to conclude a treaty for these purposes." The first article of the treaty stated that, after the treaty had gone into effect, "the state of war between the two signatories ends, and the two Powers agree henceforth to maintain mutual peace and good neighbor relations." The peace thus established was not broken until nearly two decades later when the USSR invaded Finland on November 30, 1939.

The Peace of Dorpat further stated that Finland had proclaimed herself an independent republic in 1917 and that the Soviet Union had recognized its independence "within the borders of the [former] Grand Duchy." The treaty contained an important territorial change in Finland's favor, however. The Petsamo area, adjoining the extreme northeastern boundary of Finland, was formally ceded to the republic. The cession was made as compensation for two districts on the Karelian Isthmus ceded by Finland to the Russian Empire in 1864, at which time the empire had agreed to turn over areas on the Arctic Ocean, unspecified as to area and place, to Finland. The agreement had been ignored by Russia until the Soviet leaders recognized it in ceding Petsamo. Economic and financial questions were likewise satisfactorily settled in that all claims by one state on the other were mutually canceled. Petsamo, a number of Finnish islands in the Gulf of Finland, and some other areas were to be demilitarized. The extent of territorial waters in the eastern part of the Gulf of Finland was defined in a manner that left free and open the ingress to Petrograd (Leningrad). Both signatories agreed to labor for the neutralization of the Baltic Sea by means of international agreements. The Soviets proclaimed, in a separate declaration, that East Karelia would be organized as an autonomous area of the Soviet state and "shall enjoy the rights of national self-determination."

BY WAY OF SUMMARY

By the time the Red revolt ended it had become, in the strict sense of the word, a war of independence which turned independence hopefully declared into independence fully achieved.

Several Finnish historians and other writers since World War II have offered a different interpretation. They contend that the purpose of the Socialists who voted against the declaration of independence on December 6, 1917, and of the authors of the later attempt to bring down the legal government by force, was the independence of the nation. The Socialists in general and the Reds in particular, it is claimed, merely preferred different means for reaching the desired goal and therefore did not accept as satisfactory the procedure of the Svinhufvud Government. Such interpretations and claims are, however, refuted by the facts.

The 88 representatives who voted against the declaration of independence by the Svinhufvud Cabinet on December 6 voted for a declaration of their own which the group offered as a substitute for the government declaration. The Socialist proposal stated in part that "the Parliament of Finland expresses the principle that Finland shall be independent." This was merely a declaration of intent and not a bold, unqualified commitment to carry through to independence. The proposal also said that "this independence should be secured, in a conciliatory manner, by means of an agreement with Russia." A committee composed of an equal number of Finns and Russians was to formulate proposals for arranging the relations between the two countries, "the proposals to be submitted, for final approval, to competent state organs" of the two countries. Finally, the appointment of a parliamentary committee of seventeen members was urged "to prepare the said matters and to formulate proposals regarding them for the approval of Parliament."

The wording of the Socialist proposal creates a strong presumption that it was not intended as a genuine declaration of independence, even though Socialist claims and interpretations since 1918 have repeatedly contended that the real purpose of the authors of the 1918 war included Finland's independence and that basically the problem early in 1918 was one of how to reach independence. The unleashing of the revolt in January offers proof positive and final. It showed that differences of opinion as to the means for securing independence were of altogether secondary importance. When the revolt began, four weeks had elapsed since the effort of the Svinhufvud Government to obtain Russian recognition of Finland's independence had met with complete success. The "independence" purpose the radicals were allegedly reaching for had thus been fully accomplished. Whatever differences of viewpoint and preference may have existed before January regarding the manner in which independence could best be established had been brushed aside as meaningless by the time the Reds struck.

The real purpose of the Reds was a political, social, and economic revolution. While they produced no detailed blueprint disclosing the specific nature of the new order they had in mind—they themselves probably had no clear conception of their "new world"—the evidence indicates that they aimed at something more than a pale image of the Communist regime then emerging in Russia.

The question of how extensive the support was that the Red cause enjoyed has been frequently discussed. Obviously no poll or statistical compilation could be attempted at the time. It appears safe to say, however, that while the so-called White cause was embraced by the majority of the people, especially in the area that became the base of Mannerheim's operations, the Red leadership had to contend, in south Finland under Red control, against an underground "internal enemy" from the first days of the war. Also, manpower for the Red Guards was obtained, after the war had begun, for the most part only by exerting pressure on the labor unions, by restricting (after the beginning of March) food ration cards to Red Guard members or others who were employed at some work of "general usefulness," and by introducing, on April 2, compulsory service for all males between the ages of 18 and 55. The revolution did not result from a mass movement expressing resolve to change existing conditions by force; it resulted from the decisions of the extreme radicals who had temporarily captured the Social Democratic party leadership and then proceeded to carry forward the revolutionary purposes of the Red Guards.

The revolt not only failed to enlist mass support; it also failed to get the support of a considerable number of Socialist leaders. V. Tanner, at the time a rising star in the laborite firmament (and later, in 1919–63, one of the outstanding leaders of the Social Democratic party), considered the revolt "a coup against the Parliament chosen in a free election," refused to participate, and unhesitatingly declined a post in the revolutionary government. In his memoirs he mentions a half-dozen other front-rank Socialists who took the same stand, thus showing, as Tanner puts it, that "not everybody had allowed himself to be pushed into lunacy" by the radicals. Among those who joined the revolution there were probably many who shared the view of E. Salin, another well-known Socialist of the time. Salin had strenuously opposed recourse to force yet he joined the revolutionaries. He was reported to have said, after the revolt began, "Having marched in the ranks of the workers for twenty-five years, how could I abandon them now when they are out committing stupidities." It is significant, however, that neither Tanner nor his colleagues who repudiated the revolt actively and publicly opposed it or supported the efforts of the legal government to defeat the Reds and reestablish law and order. They remained mere passive onlookers of the 1918 tragedy although they were destined to play important parts, after the Red revolt had been put down, in the rehabilitation of the Social Democratic party under the republic. As later commentators on the events of the revolt, they often interpreted the cause they had rejected in 1918 in a manner that blurred the real course of events and minimized the revolutionary purposes of the Reds.

The war of independence and its antecedents invite many questions, among which are these: (1) what would have been the consequences of a less rigid Socialist stand regarding promulgation of the "power law" of July, 1917? and (2) what would have been the results for Finland's independence of a Red victory in the 1918 war?

The Socialist-led Tokoi Government had insisted that the "power law" be put into effect without promulgation by the Russian Provisional Government. It had thus refused to proceed "in a conciliatory manner, by means of an agreement with Russia," a position which the Socialist group in Parliament insisted upon as necessary when, five months later, the more vital question of genuine independence was before the legislature. The main reason for the difference in the Socialists' attitude toward the Russian government between July and December appears to have been the change in the Russian government itself as viewed by the Finnish Socialists. The Provisional Government was seen as a "bourgeois" government and therefore suspect. The Bolshevik government, in power after the November revolution, was, it was felt, a "workers' government" championing a cause for which class-conscious Finnish Socialists had labored for decades. Nonrecognition of the Provisional Government's authority up to the limits of discretion was appropriate and good. Readiness to proceed slowly and in friendly cooperation with the Bolsheviks was wise statesmanship contributing to an order of things in which Socialist purposes—defined by December in a markedly more revolutionary spirit than had been the case in July—could be carried to a successful conclusion.

The stand taken on the question of promulgation of the "power law" resulted, as we have seen, in the dissolution of Parliament. Had dissolution been avoided, the legislature with its clear Socialist majority would have continued to serve. Finland would therefore have had a Socialist-led Parliament when the Bolsheviks seized power and also a Socialist-controlled cabinet. It appears safe to surmise that a Socialist-led government sustained by the Socialist majority in the legislature would have found it easy and congenial to cooperate with Lenin and his colleagues. Finland under a Red regime would in all probability have drifted or been forced into the position of a Soviet satellite or worse.

The relations of the revolutionary government with Russia appear to indicate clearly enough the lay of the land. The Helsinki Red government proposed early in February that a treaty regularizing the relations of Finland and Russia be concluded. It was hoped that such a treaty would strengthen the position of the Red government. The Soviets agreed and prescribed that the treaty be concluded in Petrograd. According to former Premier O. Tokoi (Tokoi was Minister of Food in the Red government), one of the two Finnish signatories of the treaty of March 1, 1918,[2] the Finns intended to sign on behalf of "The Republic of Finland." The Russians insisted that they could make concessions only to a nation ruled by the working class, and "they demanded that the name [of Finland] be the 'Socialist Workers' Republic of Finland,' which would mean that the social character of the country would be made clear in its very name." The Finnish representatives had no choice but to accept. The treaty therefore identified Finland by means of a designation insisted upon by the Russians and not freely chosen by the Finns.[3] And while the treaty "clarified" the question of evacuating the Russian soldiers from Finland it did not solve it. The solution was finally provided by the victory of the forces of the legal government, which, to repeat, turned independence hopefully declared into independence actually achieved.

[2] It dealt with boundary questions, the disposition of state-owned property in the two countries, the dismantling of certain Finnish fortifications close to the Russian border, etc. The Russians demanded that they be given full citizenship in Finland (Finns were to enjoy full citizenship in the Soviet Union) but finally accepted, as a substitute, Finnish assurances that Russians would have to meet only "easy requirements" in becoming Finnish citizens.

[3] O. Tokoi, *Maanpakolaisen Muistelmia* (Helsinki, 1947), pp. 200–204.

Government and Politics, 1919–1939

THE REPUBLICAN CONSTITUTION OF 1919

The Svinhufvud Government took up its labors in Helsinki on May 6, 1918, all of its members having returned to the capital by that date. It was confronted by a number of pressing problems, outstanding among which was the drafting of a new constitution. The government had appointed a Committee on the Constitution on March 31, 1917 (only two weeks after the collapse of the tsarist regime), under the chairmanship of Professor K. J. Ståhlberg, consisting of members from all the political parties. Its task was to draft a revised constitution and to propose temporary changes in the existing fundamental law enabling the country to carry on, under the exceptional circumstances created by the coming into power of the Provisional Government in Russia, until a new constitution had been accepted. The committee's labors were completed in October. The draft constitution prepared by it furnished the basis of the government's proposal, presented in conjunction with the declaration of independence on December 6, that Finland should be a republic. The committee specifically suggested the inclusion of provisions for responsible or parliamentary government—that is, executive or cabinet responsibility to the legislative branch—but neither this detail nor the proposal as a whole had passed beyond the stage of discussion in the Parliament's Committee on the Constitution when the Red revolt began on January 28, 1918.

The matter was taken up again when Parliament convened in

May after the close of the war. By that time the background and
the events of the war had changed the situation and had led many
Finns to the conclusion that, while the declaration of independence
labeled Finland a republic, the nation's interests would be best
safeguarded by a monarchical form of government on the Scandinavian model.

The discussion regarding the relative merits of a monarchical or
a republican form of government had emerged during the closing
stages of the war of independence. It was precipitated by individuals with monarchist inclinations who saw the war itself as a
consequence of the "weaknesses" of a republic and as an indication
of the need for a "strong" government whose head would be above
party strife and the contending interests of class or section. Such
views were by no means accepted, however, by all Finns. The bulk
of the nation remained pro-republican. The discussions and debates
in the legislature during the spring and summer showed strong
republican sentiment. The political parties disclosed marked anti-
monarchist feeling. Only one party, that of the Swede-Finns, was
nearly solidly for a monarchy. Many conservatives also were in
favor of a monarchy. The agrarians and the liberal elements were
fairly unanimous in preferring a republic to a monarchy. The Social
Democratic party was out of the picture altogether. The Red revolt
had identified it with the forces that had tried to introduce an alien
Bolshevik regime and robbed it for the time being of all opportunity
to make its influence felt in Parliament. Under normal conditions
the Agrarians, Progressives, and Socialists together would have
mustered ample strength to defeat any attempt to impose a monarchy upon the country.

The disruption of the Social Democratic party was not the only
unusual feature in the situation. German influence was another. The
presence of German troops and the general prestige that Germany
had gained among the people as a result of the military aid given by
Berlin weighed heavily in the scales in favor of monarchy. It seemed
to many that the best guarantees for the country's political future
would be offered by a monarchical form of government, affiliated
with Germany. The result was that the legislature voted in August
in favor of the election of a king. In October, Prince Frederick Karl

of Hesse, brother-in-law of the Emperor William II, was chosen king. Before long, however, the collapse of Germany, culminating in the armistice on November 11, put an end to German ascendancy in Finland. The arrival of Frederick Karl was postponed, and in December he informed the Finns of his decision not to accept the crown. The monarchist movement at once collapsed. The country was free to set its political house in order without outside influence.

Before turning to the adoption of the republican constitution which went into effect in July, 1919, we must take note of a temporary political arrangement made shortly after the close of the War of Independence. The country emerged from the war without an executive head in the narrower sense of the word. On May 18, Parliament chose P. E. Svinhufvud, the Premier of the government, as Chief Executive, the understanding being that Svinhufvud would hold his office only during the time necessary for the establishment of a permanent government. It was Svinhufvud, therefore, who was the head of the state during the months that witnessed the appearance and the collapse of the monarchist movement. Having been closely identified with a policy which internal as well as international developments had discredited by the late autumn of 1918, Svinhufvud resigned as Chief Executive in December. The legislature thereupon chose General Mannerheim to the office. Mannerheim entered upon his new duties on December 12.

Mannerheim had resigned from his post as commander-in-chief of the army two weeks after the entry of the White forces into Helsinki on May 16. The main reason for his resignation was the pro-German policy of the government at the time. During the summer and fall of 1918 he was thus a private citizen without official responsibilities. The growing food shortage, however, which was leading the nation to the brink of starvation, and the consequent pressing necessity to obtain foodstuffs from abroad—which meant purchasing food from or through the Allies—led Mannerheim to accept the post of special emissary to the Allied Powers. When he returned to Finland in December, he could report that 120,000 tons of foodstuffs had been obtained. He also played an important part in preparing the ground for Allied recognition of his country, which had been compromised in Allied eyes by the German rapprochement.

Recognition by Great Britain, the United States, and Japan was obtained in May, 1919.

Meanwhile, return to political normalcy was completed. General elections for a new legislature were held in March, 1919. As we have seen, the Social Democratic party, shorn of the extremist elements that had engineered the revolt, participated in the elections. The Socialists received 80 seats—the exact number they had captured in the 1907 election when the fully free franchise for women as well as men had determined, for the first time, the outcome of a national election—and became once again the largest single party in the legislature. The Agrarians captured 42 seats, the conservative National Union party 28, the Progressives 26, the Swede-Finns 22, and the Christian Workers party 2. The newly elected legislature convened a month later and proceeded at once to fashion a republican constitution.

A bill providing for a republican constitution—it is called the "Form of Government" to distinguish it from other constitutional enactments, of which there are ten in all—was presented by the cabinet to the Parliament on May 13. Incidentally, the government had been reconstituted a month earlier and was composed of Progressives, Agrarians, and representatives of the center group. After lengthy debate in the Parliament and the press, the constitution was adopted on July 17. Of the various parties, the Swede-Finns were especially persistent in opposing the republic. According to the new fundamental law, the first president of the republic was chosen by the legislature. In the election held on July 25 the majority of votes in the legislature—143 out of 200—was cast for Professor Kaarlo J. Ståhlberg, a member of the National Progressive party who had served for several years as the President of the Supreme Administrative Court. General Mannerheim received 50 votes.

The interim office of Chief Executive, held by General Mannerheim during the preceding eight months, now came to an end. The President assumed the duties of his office on July 27, and the country embarked upon its existence as a constitutional republican democracy.

The constitution provided for the following: The President was to be chosen for a six-year term by an electoral college of 300 which in turn was elected by universal suffrage. The successful candidate must receive at least 151 out of the 300 votes. The President had a suspensive legislative veto. The provisions pertaining to the legislature carried over into the republic the unicameral Parliament of 200 established in 1906. Unrestricted universal suffrage likewise remained what it had been since 1906; women and men enjoyed full and equal political rights both as voters and as holders of public office. The legislature was chosen for a three-year period (since 1955, for a four-year term). It was the real seat of governmental power; the constitution stated that power belonged to the people as represented in the Parliament.

This basic principle was illustrated by a specific constitutional provision to the effect that members of the cabinet "must possess the confidence of the Parliament." Ministerial responsibility was thus anchored in the constitution and did not grow out of mere custom and practice. The right of interpellation was likewise definitely fixed. It allowed easy means to the members of Parliament to precipitate debate regarding ministerial policy. Furthermore, Parliament appointed at the beginning of each session a special officer whose duty it was to scrutinize the administration of civil and military affairs. The constitution also provided for a committee on foreign relations that differed from ordinary parliamentary committees. It served a double function: in the first place, it acted as a parliamentary committee that handled foreign affairs. Secondly, it acted as a special adviser to the cabinet and might be called upon to function when Parliament was not in session.

Furthermore, the constitution contained provisions which embedded in the fundamental law the tradition and practice of judiciary independence that had been a fact long before the nineteenth century. It likewise included a bill of rights which contained not only the usual safeguards of individual liberty, the right of free speech, assembly, and the inviolability of property, but others less common. Thus it guaranteed the legal protection of the "labor power of the citizen." In general, the constitution added relatively little, beyond the elements that the emergence of the nation as a sovereign state made necessary, to the substance of government by law that had existed before 1918. Aside from the obvious fact that it provided for a republic, it introduced no startlingly new departures.

PARTIES AND VOTERS

One of the indications of the narrow margin within which Finnish politics moved during the period of autonomy, and likewise an indication of the intensity of the language problem during the closing decades of the last century, was the fact that party alignments before 1890 were primarily determined by the nationality controversy. A "Finnish party" appeared in the 1860s and a "Swedish party" in the 1870s. An attempt in 1880 to establish a liberal party pursuing social and economic purposes and not based on language or nationality objectives failed. By the turn of the century, therefore, modern party organizations were still only in the early stages of their development.

Two outstanding, not to say overpowering, issues dominated the scene at the time. The first was the ominous threat to the country's autonomy and freedom inherent in the policy of Russification pursued by the imperial government. The other was the increasingly insistent demand for amelioration of the condition of the landless rural population and the lot of the growing industrial proletariat and the underprivileged in general. The former called for resolute resistance—it could be, in most instances, only passive resistance, because of the prevailing circumstances—to Russian violations of law and constitution. It was probably supported by practically the whole nation, as shown by the "people's petition" in 1899. The latter involved, as a preliminary condition without which land reform and other progressive reforms could not be carried through, a reform of franchise and Parliament alike in a progressive, democratic spirit.

Except for the labor party founded in 1899 and transformed into the Social Democratic party in 1903, and the Agrarian party established in 1908, these demands and purposes did not become significant planks in Finnish party platforms before the important political reforms of 1906. The pre-1914 party situation was transformed, however, by the political and other consequences of the war in 1918. The new alignments that then emerged grouped the citizenry of the republic into five main parties.

The conservative elements formed the National Union party, representing the right-wing groups among the Finnish-speaking citizens. It claimed to be in a special degree the defender and preserver of the "national" heritage, values, and purposes. The liberals established the National Progressive party. It frequently occupied a centrist position in the general political constellation and was normally found among the advocates of measures and purposes designed to strengthen the democratic process and social reforms. (In Finland, as elsewhere, the liberal cause lost ground, as a political party, during the interwar years and later. In the 1948 election it received only five seats. The party was disbanded in 1951 and its place taken by the Finnish People's party, a liberal representative of middle-class interests.) The Agrarian party was the spokesman of the farmers as a class. The Social Democratic party continued after 1918 as the party of labor. It was considerably weakened by the loss of the extremist elements to the Communists. The Communist party of Finland was founded in Moscow in 1918. It worked through various masked party organizations until it went underground after the outlawing of communism in 1930. The party was revived in October, 1944. It combined with dissident leftist Socialists to form a common party, the Finnish People's Democratic Association (the SKDL), which has remained the "working organization" of the Communists since World War II.

The Swede-Finn "language and cultural" interests were represented by the Swedish People's party founded in 1906. Unbendingly conservative in some matters—the party was uncompromisingly pro-monarchist in 1918—its membership and leaders also included genuine progressives. The heterogeneous membership of the party deprived it of clear-cut economic and social objectives.

The anti-communist agitation and developments in 1929–30 resulted among other things in the emergence of a new right-wing party, the Patriotic People's Movement (IKL), in 1931. Its modest representation in Parliament was obtained largely at the expense of the National Union party.

The unrestricted franchise which the constitution of 1919 provided by continuing the suffrage provisions of 1906 enabled the voters freely to decide directly the party alignments in Parliament and indirectly the compositions of the cabinets, and to register approval or rejection of the domestic and foreign policies of the successive governments. The extent to which the citizenry discharged its duty by actively participating in elections is indicated by two typical elections among the nine held between 1919 and 1939.

In the 1922 election, the total number of persons entitled to vote was 1,487,922. Of this number, 870,860 went to the polls while 617,062 stayed at home and by doing so contributed to the wasted strength of the "easy chair citizens." The number of active voters amounted to 58.5 percent of the citizens who had the right to vote. The election also disclosed a fact which remained more or less constant in Finnish politics before 1939, namely, that the women's stay-at-home vote was larger than that of the men. Only 54.6 percent of the women voters cast a ballot, while 63.1 percent of the men voters discharged their political duty. The election in 1936 followed in the main the pattern set in 1922. The potential voters numbered 1,872,908; of these, 1,178,412 actually voted. The total percentage of voters came to 62.9 percent. Of the men, 67.3 percent voted, and of the women, 59.1 percent. These elections also disclosed another general feature of the Finnish political contests. In the main, urban communities contributed a higher percentage of voters than rural electoral districts. The difference was not great, however, and even the country vote did not drop, in most of the districts, below 50 percent of the theoretical maximum.

The political complexion of the Finns in 1919–39 is shown by the distribution of seats in Parliament and by the changes that the representation of the various parties underwent. Table 6 illustrates the political preferences of the voters.

The Social Democrats captured, as we have seen, the position of the strongest single party in the first election under the republican

TABLE 6

PARTY REPRESENTATION IN PARLIAMENT, 1919–1939

Year	Social Demo-crats	Agrar-ians	National Union	Pro-gres-sives	Swede-Finns	Commu-nists	IKL	Others	Total
1919	80	42	28	26	22			2	200
1922	53	45	35	15	25	27			200
1924	60	44	38	17	23	18			200
1927	60	52	34	10	24	20			200
1929	59	60	28	7	23	23			200
1930	66	59	42	11	21			1	200
1933	78	53	18	11	21		14	5	200
1936	83	53	20	7	21		14	2	200
1939	85	56	25	6	18		8	2	200

constitution. They not only remained in that position through the twenties and thirties but improved it. The voting strength of the party grew, from about 219,000 in 1922 to about 500,000 in the election held in September, 1939. It came not only from industrial workers but from agrarian labor and small farmers also. Because of its prominence, the Social Democratic party represented a decisive factor in the political life of the nation. For a few years after 1918, it suffered from the stigma that was attached to it because of the 1918 war. It is a significant reflection upon the speed with which the alignments of the war of independence were forgotten that the Socialists were able to form a ministry as early as 1926. That is to say, less than a decade after the country had gone through a sanguinary war, it had a ministry—composed exclusively of Social Democrats—headed by the leader of the party which the majority of the nation had blamed for the war. The growing representation of the Socialists in Parliament after 1930 brought them within a reasonable distance of a majority in 1939. The early and complete rehabilitation of socialism during the two interwar decades gave impressive evidence of the success of Finland's internal reconstruction after 1918.

Another heavy weight in the political scales of the nation was the Agrarian or farmers' party, which has always held the loyalty of the majority of the farmer folk. The party has remained the second largest in the legislature. The number of its supporters among the voters grew from 187,000 in 1919 to 263,000 in 1936. In 1939 its representatives in Parliament came close to outdistancing the combined strength of all the other non-Socialist groups. In the course of the twenties and later it contributed several ministries, participated in most of the cabinets, and two of the four presidents of the republic before World War II came from its ranks. The first representative of the party was elevated to the presidency in 1925 and the second in 1937.

The National Union party was and continues to be the main bulwark of conservatism in the republic. From 28 seats in 1919 it grew to 42 seats in 1930—a year that seemed to give conservatism an extra lease on life, as will be seen later—only to lose ground and to finish weaker in 1939 than it had been twenty years earlier.

The National Progressive party was the fourth largest group when the republican constitution went into effect. After 1920 its representation in the legislature steadily declined. Its influence, however, was more important than the number of seats held by it would indicate. On no less than eight occasions between 1919 and 1939, the office of Prime Minister was held by a member of the Progressive party. The first President, Professor K. J. Ståhlberg (1919–25), was one of its representatives; he came within two votes of being chosen for a second term in 1931. The press of the party was excellent and has remained so to date. Its leading organ for many years, the *Helsingin Sanomat*, was easily the best, as it was the largest, newspaper in Finland. That the Progressive party had an exceptionally large number of able men among its leaders was not the least important reason for the significant role of the group whose electoral appeal gave it only 73,600 votes in 1936 when the total vote cast was about 1,173,400. The importance of the Progressives, whose political creed may be broadly characterized as part and parcel of the liberalism that fared ill after World War I in England and elsewhere, was therefore out of all proportion to their numbers. The Progressive party was one of the strong supports of Finnish democratic republicanism.

The party of the Swede-Finns was and is an anomaly in Finnish politics. Resting as it does upon the language and cultural nationalism of the Swede-Finn population as defined and developed by a host of intellectuals and other leaders in the course of the past two generations, it represents the varied and at times contradictory interests of the population segments that compose it. The small farmer, fisherman, and factory worker, the clerk, professor, and industrialist of the Swedish-speaking citizenry often stood side by side on the platform furnished by the party. Until 1936 its voting strength remained fairly constant and approximately represented the proportion of the Swede-Finns to the total population of the country. The decrease in its representation in 1939 marked the beginning of a trend destined to continue after World War II. A part of the Swede-Finn voters have found socialism congenial for many decades; some middle- and upper-class Swede-Finns have in the past abandoned the cause and gone over to other parties, and the indications are that such "defections" will probably continue in the future.

The Communist representation in 1922–29, as revealed by Table 6, in all likelihood indicated the maximum strength of the Communist cause in Finland, although its supporters undoubtedly included not only hard-core Communists but "protest voters" as well. Also, in Finland, as elsewhere, the Communist party appears to have been more successful than other parties in mobilizing its voting strength for elections. While the Progressives, Conservatives, Socialists, and Agrarians succeeded in getting out only about two thirds of their party vote, the Communists were more efficient in bringing their voters to the polls. The evidence in the case supports the conclusion that, excepting the year 1922, when the Communists obtained 13 percent of the vote, the creed of Moscow was never supported in the twenties by more than 10 percent of the population and probably less.

The Patriotic People's Movement (the IKL) was composed of anti-Communists, some of whom were distrustful of democracy, and included citizens who were outright fascist in their political convictions. The IKL never succeeded, however, in capturing more than 7 percent of the representation in Parliament, and in 1939 it obtained only 4 percent of the seats in the legislature. In the early and middle thirties, the party enjoyed publicity at home and abroad which gave it a seeming importance that bore little relation to its real place in the political life of the republic. It did not gain representation in any of the pre-1939 cabinets. During World War II the IKL held one portfolio in the Rangell Government, January 3, 1941–March 5, 1943. The party was ended by legislative fiat in 1944. The IKL leaders, isolated from the supporters of democracy, made themselves heard largely because of a small but harsh party press, a noisy group of articulate representatives in the legislature, and certain acts of lawlessness and violence in the early thirties condemned by the nation as a whole.

Finnish political parties performed three basic functions during the interwar years. First, they served as organizations that instructed the citizens in political questions by urging the wisdom of platform and principle and by propagandizing the electorate in the hopes of obtaining support at the polls. They acted as instruments of political education, not the least by means of the party press. Secondly, they furnished the machinery through which representatives to the national legislature, municipal councils, and the like were nominated and elected. Thirdly, they provided the country in varying degree with cabinet ministers who constituted, as we have seen, the real government of the nation.

THE NATURE AND POSITION OF CABINETS

The first two of the main functions of parties are part of the procedures of a democracy whenever the citizenry is free to make choices and is able to indulge in political activity without let or hindrance. These aspects of party efforts and accomplishments were unmistakable and normal features of the political contests in Finland. The formation and position of cabinets, however, reflected the influence of certain political circumstances that were typical—but by no means unique in Europe in the post-1919 period—of Finland after World War I.

The existence of five major parties meant, among other things, that no party succeeded in becoming a majority party. Coalition cabinets were the unavoidable result. Before 1939 the Social Democrats, the Agrarians, the Conservatives, the Progressives, and the Swede-Finns all held ministerial portfolios at one time or another; only the two extremist parties, the Communists and the IKL, never held cabinet posts during the two decades of the interwar period.

The political complexion of the ministries in 1919–39 may be indicated by the following list of prime ministers and the party from which they came:

August, 1919	J. H. Vennola, Progressive
March, 1920	R. W. Erich, Conservative
April, 1921	J. H. Vennola, Progressive
June, 1922	A. K. Cajander, Progressive
November, 1922	K. Kallio, Agrarian
January, 1924	A. K. Cajander, Progressive
May, 1924	L. J. Ingman, Conservative
November, 1924	L. J. Ingman, Conservative
March, 1925	A. A. Tulenheimo, Conservative
December, 1925	K. Kallio, Agrarian
December, 1926	V. A. Tanner, Socialist
December, 1927	J. E. Sunila, Agrarian
December, 1928	O. Mantere, Progressive
August, 1929	K. Kallio, Agrarian
July, 1930	P. E. Svinhufvud, Conservative
March, 1931	J. E. Sunila, Agrarian
December, 1932	T. M. Kivimäki, Progressive
October, 1936	K. Kallio, Agrarian
March, 1937	A. K. Cajander, Progressive
December, 1939	R. Ryti, Progressive

Eight of the twenty ministries between 1919 and 1940 were headed by Progressives, six by Agrarians, five by Conservatives, and one by a Socialist. During a period that ran to about a decade, Progressives served as prime ministers; for a period of six years, an Agrarian headed the ministry, and a Socialist for one year. The Tanner Ministry was, incidentally, the only single-party cabinet during the period, despite the fact that the Socialists held only 60 seats in the legislature. The five ministries headed by a Conservative lasted in all for only about three years. Conservative leadership was thus markedly less important than the number of Conservative prime ministers suggests.

Until the early thirties, governments were notably short-lived. Their term of office became considerably longer after 1932. Two of the cabinet changes after 1932 were caused not by failure to enjoy support in the legislature but by other events. The Kallio Ministry dissolved in 1937 because of the election in that year which elevated Premier Kallio to the presidency. The reconstruction of the Cajander Ministry in December, 1939, was caused by the Soviet invasion of Finland, and came after Parliament had given a unanimous vote of confidence to the Cajander Government. The criticism occasionally heard during the twenties, that ministries changed too frequently and therefore were prevented from formulating a continuous and forward-looking policy, lost much of its point after 1932. Not the least important reason for the greater stability of cabinets in the thirties appears to have been the fact that the Socialists and the other parties were finding their way to more consistent and many-sided cooperation than before. This was true especially after 1937 when these two main parties, the Agrarians and the Social Democrats, joined hands in forming a government in which each held five portfolios and three were allocated to other parties.

That the Agrarians and the Socialists found it possible to cooperate on behalf of the common good of the nation is not surprising. Both parties labored for objectives that were frequently the same. For instance, the Agrarian party conference in 1921 went on record as favoring, among other things, policies that would prevent socially harmful "money interests" from deflecting the further development of genuine economic and social democracy and that would improve the position of the working class as well as that of the small farmers. In 1932 the Agrarians declared their unbending opposition to communism and to all antidemocratic or fascist movements. A study of the post-1919 Agrarian and Social Democratic party pronouncements shows that the programs of the two parties contained over 100 items that were more or less identical, and about 20 that differed markedly. The most important of their common objectives was, broadly speaking, the further expansion and strengthening of political, social, and economic democracy. The Socialists and Agrarians commanded, as their political strength in elections clearly showed, electoral resources more than sufficient to have sustained, if the war had not intervened in 1939, further and continuing co-operation.[1]

The operation of the cabinet form of government in Finland after 1919 differed in some respects from the functioning of parliamentary government in England, for example. Because of the absence of a two-party system—which means one party in office and the other party assuming the role of an opposition that tries to get into office —the ministries normally were, as we have seen, coalition govern-ments. Coalition ministries ordinarily functioned so long as the majority of the legislature supported the coalition. On some occa-sions, a cabinet failed to resign even when it had suffered defeat on a given measure because it was clear that the combination of groups that gave the adverse vote was such as to exclude the possibility of a new ministry rising from it. Thus some aspects of the technique of the cabinet form of government did not become sufficiently refined to make changes of ministries always follow the simple textbook rules for parliamentary government.

The reason for this situation was that Parliament did not always care to vote a ministry out of office even when superficial considera-tions might have pointed to such action. At other times again, the legislature went out of its way to ditch the ministerial chariot for reasons that could hardly be said to involve important matters of public policy. In other words, it was the lawmakers in Parliament assembled that really made the decision; cabinet immunity from constant scrutiny and the threat of forced resignation did not exist. Vigorous and active use of the legislators' powers against the min-istry was conspicuous and underscored the fact that the center of Finland's political life rested throughout in its lawmaking assembly.

Another feature of the cabinet system in the republic invites comment. After 1919, a trend toward increasing the powers of the cabinet was evident. Expanding social legislation, the economic dif-ficulties of the depression years after 1929, and the threatening in-ternational situation in 1939—to mention a few reasons—called for executive, administrative, and other tasks that necessarily had to be left in the hands of the cabinet. In degree as the scope and functions of the ministerial executive expanded, its position was strengthened.

[1] R. Swento, *Työmies ja Talonpoika* (Helsinki, 1937).

But real power continued to repose in Parliament, which showed at no time before the war an inclination to become docile or unmindful of its part in determining domestic or foreign policy.

THE PROBLEM OF COMMUNISM AFTER 1918

Since the attempt in 1918 to establish a Communist form of government in Finland, the creed and program of Moscow had been suspect in the eyes of the great majority of the people. The Communist party as such was proscribed by a court decision, already noted, and a Supreme Court verdict in 1923 sustained the view that the party was revolutionary in intent, that it aimed at the destruction of the republican form of government, and that it therefore had no legal right to function as a political organization. It did not take long, however, before the Communist elements discovered ways of circumventing the law and the verdict of the court. They had organized the Socialist Workers' party of Finland as early as 1920. The name of the party was changed to Workers' and Small Farmers' party in 1924 and to Socialist Workers' and Small Farmers' party in 1927.

The appearance of the Communists in disguise on the political arena did not escape the attention of the citizenry at large. The Communist representatives in the legislature and the Communist press were characteristically vocal in pursuing the aims of the party, and the organization as a whole did not hesitate to show its colors. That the Communists were able to carry on through the twenties in spite of ample evidence of the antirepublican and revolutionary nature of their political program appears to have two main explanations. The debates in the Finnish legislature show, in the first place, marked indifference toward the Communists, possibly in part because the party was not large enough to seem significant. The highwater mark of its strength was reached in the legislature of 1922. In 1924 its representation dropped from 27 to 18; it rose to 20 in 1927 and to 23 in 1929. The last figure was 11.5 percent of the total number of seats. Secondly, the legislature appears to have assumed the attitude that the question of the illegality of the party —under whatever name it might be disguised—rested with the courts, and that Parliament should not lightly tamper with the suffrage law or attempt to exclude the Communists by changing the laws that guaranteed the right of freedom of speech, press, and assembly.

Until 1929–30, the Communists were therefore able to function in response to dictates that came from Moscow. In 1929–30, however, a series of events occurred which led to the abolition of the party and its disappearance from open participation in the political life of the nation.

In the summer of 1929 the Communists engaged for the first time in what appeared to be undisguised preparation for the revolution they desired. Acting in accordance with procedures used by the Communists in other countries for the organization of a mass demonstration against "war and imperialism" and for the workers' revolution, the Finnish Communists prepared a dress rehearsal to be held on August 1. The purpose of the demonstration appears to have been the creation of disorder which might open the way for the "conquest of the streets." The government later held that the aim had demonstrably been to engineer a revolt and that it had ample evidence showing that no mere peaceful political parade was intended.

The cabinet in office at the time was a Progressive coalition ministry headed by O. Mantere, several of whose party colleagues held portfolios in the ministry. Acting upon the information it had, the government prohibited the holding of the demonstration and likewise forbade the use of the Communist symbol, the red flag. It also saw to it that adequate forces were available to maintain peace and order, if peace and order should be disturbed. The Communist demonstration against "imperialist war" was a failure.

The incident gave the Communists in Parliament ample opportunity for debate. An interpellation addressed to the ministry was used by them as the occasion for charging that the government was intent upon fastening an offensive reactionary servitude upon citizens who prized the sanctity of constitutional immunities and of necessity would defend their liberties. Taking full advantage of the right of unlimited debate that obtained in Parliament, the Communists invoked the fundamental law of the land, although they openly aimed at the destruction of that very law as soon as they succeeded in clamping their system on the country. Freedom was invoked in behalf of a cause that would destroy freedom.

The affair became important because it focused in unusual degree public attention upon the Communist menace. The indignation caused by it, however, would perhaps not have been more lasting than that created off and on during the preceding decade, when secret Communist agents were time and again apprehended and sentenced for treasonable activity, had it not been for the fact that the incident marked the beginning of more conspicuous Communist activity. In November an attempt was made to create a political disturbance because of the hunger strike of certain Communists who had been jailed for treason, and an unsuccessful attempt was made, under the leadership of Communist-controlled labor groups, to engineer a national strike. Meanwhile the parliamentary rostrum was freely used for attacks upon the government and "capitalist reaction." The press reported the speeches and the country grew increasingly disturbed by the seeming threat to its democracy.

Such was the situation by the weekend of November 23, when a Communist organization which functioned under the designation of the "Lapua Young Workers' Educational Association" held a meeting in Lapua, a sizable rural community in west-central Finland. The community and its people had played an important part in supporting the legal government in the war of 1918. It was a typical rural center with a population of solid small farmers, fine primary and secondary schools, successful cooperative enterprises, and active religious organizations. Incidentally, the Lapua Cooperative Society was celebrating its twenty-fifth anniversary over the weekend of November 23, and special preparations had been made in honor of the occasion.

When Communists arrived in Lapua, some 400 strong, they were dressed in conspicuous red shirts and in general made no secret of their political convictions. They were set upon, and some were beaten and roughly handled in general. The tires of cars in which part of them had arrived were slashed and other property damaged. On the evening of Saturday the twenty-third, the meeting of the

Communists was broken up. The same procedure was repeated on the following evening.

The action of the Lapuans aroused widespread interest throughout the country. In general, press and other comment approved of the strong-arm methods used. Within a week, a public meeting was held in Lapua for the purpose of organizing a popular movement against communism. The meeting went on record in favor of "terminating the existence of the Communist party in all its forms" and held that, unless the authorities proceeded to eradicate communism, "there is grave reason to fear" that the government would be forestalled by direct action on the part of the people. A delegation was chosen to present the resolutions to the government in Helsinki. Similar meetings were held elsewhere in the country. Scores of resolutions urging prompt action for the eradication of communism were adopted at the meetings and forwarded to the capital.

The legislature and the cabinet assumed on the whole an understanding attitude toward the rising tide of anti-Communist sentiment. A law was put through which gave the courts the right to declare any society or organization illegal if it labored for objectives condemned by existing law or was contrary to "good morals," or if it continued in disguise the work of an organization which had been pursuing unlawful objectives. An attempt was also made to pass a new press law providing for stricter control of and more exacting punishment for the publication of treasonable matter. The attempt failed; the law was rejected by the legislature in 1930. The Communist press therefore was able to carry on its work, and did so in a manner that was not designed to allay the feelings of the people who considered communism a dangerous enemy and felt that it must be destroyed.

Meanwhile the anti-Communist movement brought forth a national organization established in March, 1930. Its program called for "struggle against Communist and other treasonable activity of every kind" and stated that the organization "proposes, by means of educational propaganda, to expose the true nature of such movements and their effort to end the independence of this country and to destroy its social order based on law." By such exposure the society hoped to obtain the support of the nation and to bring about the end of the Communist movement.

Before long, the failure of Parliament to act quickly and efficiently in putting through legislation that would end Communist activity led to direct action. Late in March, 1930, the defeat of the new press law served as a signal for the destruction of a Communist printing establishment. The guilty persons were apprehended, but when they were tried in court new acts of lawlessness occurred. The authorities were unable to prevent them, largely because an attempt to protect the Communists by a show of force sufficient to prevent further direct action would probably have precipitated a civil war. Direct action therefore ran its course. In July, 1930, some of the Communist representatives were forcibly prevented from attending Parliament; others were apprehended and beaten up. Several kidnapings occurred. Some persons who were in no way connected with communism but who appear to have been objectionable to the direct-action men because of their moderation and condemnation of lawlessness were also kidnaped. Among them were the first President and Mrs. K. J. Ståhlberg, who were taken to a town in eastern Finland and there released unharmed. In the same month, some 12,000 farmers held a mass demonstration in Helsinki and demanded legislation that would once and for all eliminate communism.

Meantime Parliament was dissolved and new elections set for October 1, 1930. Interest in the election was great. The number of voters who went to the polls—it grew from 950,000 in the 1929 election to 1,130,000—established a new record. The results were: the Socialists added 7 to their previous representation and got 66 seats; the Agrarians lost 1 and got 59; the Conservatives grew by 14 and got 42; the Progressives raised their representation from 7 to 11; and the Swede-Finns lost 1 and got 21 seats. The Communist group had been prevented by the law passed in the previous year from participation in the election, and therefore got no seats.

The new legislature proceeded to enact laws designed to end all Communist activity. This meant primarily revision of the local and national suffrage law. The revision was accomplished in November.

The new suffrage law stated in substance that henceforth voters who had belonged, during the year preceding an election, to a party or organization that labored for the preparation or promotion of the overthrow of the political or social institutions of the republic would be denied the right to vote. The local electoral boards were given the power to ascertain whether the parties or electoral groups participating in an election conformed to the requirements of the law.

By 1931 the anti-Communist movement, which apparently was supported in its early stages by the majority of the people, thus reached the goal of outlawing the Communist party. But conditions did not at once return to normal. The main bulk of the adherents of the program left the movement as soon as the country had been freed from communism. A handful of intellectuals, farmers, members of the clergy, clerks, and others, however, proceeded to use the movement as the foundation of an antirepublican organization. They engineered several acts of violence, on occasion prevented the enforcement of law, and in February, 1932, attempted to force the government to do their bidding by organizing the so-called Mäntsälä revolt. The Mäntsälä affair was put down without bloodshed—under the leadership of the conservative President P. E. Svinhufvud—and the period of lawlessness came to an end shortly thereafter. Mäntsälä represented the close of a troublesome chapter of the history of the republic and not the beginning of another.

That the anti-Communist movement lasted as long as it did is partly explained by the hardships that the depression imposed upon large sections of the population. Farmers' discontent took many forms during the years 1929–32. Inflation was urged by some of the small farmers; a moratorium on debts, overdue taxes, and mortgage payments was demanded by others. Not a little of the disregard of law during these years was connected with the economic discontent of the farmer. With the return of prosperity after 1933, the situation changed politically also and the farmer as well as other elements in the population returned to the business of the workaday world.

What remained of the anti-Communist movement after 1932 coalesced into a new party, the Patriotic People's Movement, usually known as the IKL. Strongly conservative or even fascist in sympathies and objectives, its leadership pursued the aim of establishing "strong" government in the place of the "weak" democratic republic. The movement was strong in its suspicion of everything Russian, and some of its newspapers and representatives did obeisance before Berlin and Rome and labored for the introduction of the philosophy and institutions of Hitler and Mussolini. The labor was all in vain. Despite campaigning that made use of prejudice, ignorance, and blatant misrepresentations, the nation remained cool to the new dispensation. In the election of 1933, the party received 14 seats out of 200. In 1936 it was unable to get more, and in 1939 its strength decreased by over one third in that only 8 seats were obtained. If communism before 1930 was unimportant, as many observers maintained at the time and have claimed since, the IKL party was even less important after 1932. Having cleaned out communism, the nation refused to abandon democratic republicanism and gave a decidedly cold shoulder to the IKL and its claims that its leaders held the only keys to the nation's future political well-being.

Communists outside of Finland and their supporters made much of the events of 1930–33. They saw in the anti-Communist movement an embodiment of militant fascism and in the parliamentary legislation of these years the blackest kind of reaction that could but mean the triumph of dictatorship over democracy so long as the legislation barring Communists remained in force. The events after 1933 repudiated this view. If it is at all possible to say that, in the brief period of the first twenty years of the republic, some years were characterized by greater democracy than others, it is correct to say that the years after 1933 witnessed further expansion of a democracy that stayed clear of nazi or fascist practices no less resolutely than it repudiated communism. Nothing proves this more clearly than the political cooperation of the Socialists and the Agrarians after 1936. In 1939, democracy in Finland was in fact strong enough to enable a fully united nation to offer amazingly successful resistance to a formidable Soviet invasion.

GOVERNMENT AND THE CITIZEN

Government in a democracy obviously imposes burdens and restrictions on the citizen and at the same time protects him and intercedes on his behalf in many ways. The laws—constitutional or other—that secure the freedom of the citizen are central elements of the foundations upon which the state rests. They also show in a general way to what extent government exists for the citizen and not the citizen for the state.

The constitution of 1919 contained, as was pointed out earlier, a number of provisions which safeguarded the rights of the citizen. The inviolability of the person, religious freedom, a free press, freedom of assembly and of association were uncompromisingly recognized. They were subject to two limitations only. The first was the general rule that these rights did not extend to persons or associations engaged in treasonable activity or in laboring for the overthrow of the republic. The second limitation was furnished by a principle common to all Scandinavia: the freedoms mentioned are subject to and limited by the demands of morality and considerations of public welfare. These limitations are imposed and interpreted by the courts; they represent no arbitrary means whereby the rights of the citizen can be readily curtailed. The legislation that outlawed the Communist party in 1930 imposed no political disabilities upon citizens who recognized peaceful and orderly change by persuasion and legislative action as the proper rule of democratic society.

The rights of the citizen or of property were interpreted in no inflexible way. Property rights, for example, have come to be considered in a new light during the past several decades. Social and factory legislation, conservation of forests, town planning, state supervision of some forms of business and control of others, or the establishment of a state monopoly like the State Alcohol Corporation testify to the abandonment of the earlier ideas regarding the inviolability of the rights of the individual and property alike. In other words, the demands of social welfare, as understood and interpreted by the lawmakers of the nation, have long since meant the abandonment of undiluted nineteenth-century economic liberalism. This trend was marked before 1919 and was no less conspicuous after 1919. No party advocated a return to the old ways of economic individualism; differences of opinion related to the ways and the extent of restriction and not to the principle of restriction itself.

Even good laws and institutions may bear heavily upon the citizen if their application and work depend upon incompetent or corrupt civil servants and officials. In the main, government, administration, and courts in Finland were and are in the hands of competent personnel. Public opinion, which has been a force of utmost importance since full political emancipation and an extensive press and the like were achieved over half a century ago, demands honesty and impartiality of public servants. Law requires that appointments be based on "merit and ability." The civil service has escaped the blight of party politics and has remained independent of outside influences. As a result, the civil servant may be, and occasionally is, an overbearing officeholder secure in his job, but more frequently he is a good deal more than a mere cog in the machine: an incorruptible and efficient servant of the public.

The administration of justice is in the hands of lower courts, district courts, and supreme courts, of which there are two (one is the Supreme Administrative Court). The judge's tenure of office is for life, subject to removal for incompetence or for crimes. In the rural lower courts, the layman occupies an interesting and important place. These courts are composed of a judge and a number of laymen chosen by the voters. The laymen constitute the jury, but they are not only a fact-finding body. The verdict of the court is always formulated by the judge and the jury together. The jury shares in all the work of the court, and if its decision in a case differs from that of the judge—and is unanimous—it is the lay jury that renders the verdict. This system has traditions that go back several centuries. It has done much to create and sustain the confidence of the people in the lower courts and in the administration of justice in general. The procedure of the courts is less efficient than it might be and the desirability of speedier handling of cases has been stressed over many years. Preparation for introducing greater efficiency has been made for nearly half a century but has not yet resulted in removing all causes for complaint.

The courts are guided by statutory law; "judge-made" law or the use of precedent—in, say, the American sense of the term—is nearly completely absent. The concept "the rule of law" means in Finland—as in the rest of Scandinavia—primarily two things. The first is that law should be applied by courts composed of competent men free from outside influence, able to discharge their duty impartially. The second is that the judgment of the court should be based upon the rules laid down in laws formulated by the representatives of the people. Law is not seen as a mysterious compound of legislative enactments and "judge-made" rules but as a body of principles, directives, and mandates that can be known through the law code by the citizen willing to scrutinize it and capable of understanding ordinary clear exposition. Thus law and the courts do not represent a complicated and obscure science practiced by men who speak a language not comprehended by the citizen. The administration of law still retains, as we might phrase it, especially democratic features that keep it an important part of the processes of self-government, just as a democratic franchise and legislature and the rights of the citizen keep the business of lawmaking a vital part of the same processes.

X

The Economic Scene, 1918–1939

ECONOMIC RECOVERY

The general economic situation of Finland in 1918 was far from good. In some ways, it was more than precarious. The war of independence had caused substantial material losses which could be made good only by the expenditure of funds not easily available. The currency had depreciated, partly because of the pre-1918 connection with Russia and partly because of unavoidable inflation during the war. The establishment of independence furthermore deprived Finland of its most important foreign market. Before 1914, Russia accounted for about 30 percent of Finland's foreign trade. The Russian market was now gone and its loss imposed a serious problem on the nation. The country thus faced a future that only laborious economic readjustment along many lines could secure.

The speed and extent of the economic recovery were illustrated by two aspects of readjustment after 1918. The first related to the financial situation from 1918 to the middle twenties and the second to the adaptation of industry and export trade in general to the conditions created by the loss of the Russian market.

Already in 1917, inflation had cut the prewar domestic purchasing power of the Finnish mark to about one third. Its purchasing power abroad, however, had declined less, or roughly by 50 percent. The discrepancy continued through 1918 and 1919 and resulted, among other things, in a marked rise in imports and a decrease in exports. The purchasing power of the mark continued to fall, both at home and abroad, until 1921, when the mark had dropped at home to only 9 percent of its par value before the war and to 7 percent abroad. After 1921 the situation began to improve. The currency was stabilized and the return to the gold standard was effected in 1925. The value of the mark was then fixed at 13 percent of the prewar mark, which meant that the ratio between the old gold mark and the new was established at 100 to 766.

Deflation and stabilization of the currency were connected, needless to say, with the general financial policy of the country after the war. The unusual demands upon the state treasury during the years 1918–22 could not be met by the income that the existing system of taxation or other sources of revenue provided. Recourse was therefore had to loans. The result was a notable increase of the public debt. At the beginning of 1918, the total state indebtedness was 240,000,000 marks. In the course of the five years from 1918 to 1922, new bond issues brought the state debt to 1,600,000,000 marks, an increase of nearly 700 percent over 1917. After 1922, foreign long-term credits were obtained for refunding operations and other purposes, the mark became stable, and exports began to provide surpluses over imports. State finances as well as the currency had been set in order by 1925.

Meanwhile industry and the world of business in general were adjusting themselves to the new conditions created by independence. By 1918, industrial production had dropped to about 40 percent of the output in 1913. Foreign markets had been largely lost, and domestic consumption had been disastrously limited by the war. Recovery after 1918 was rapid, however. New markets were found in countries in Europe and also overseas which previously had bought little or no Finnish goods, and prewar markets were opened up anew, except in Russia. In 1922 the timber, paper, pulp, and cellulose industries, which represented the main bulk of large-scale industry, reached the level of production in 1913. Domestic consumption likewise expanded, with the result that Finnish industry as a whole appears to have recovered, by 1922, the ground lost as a result of the war years 1914–18. If the number of industrial workers and the number of horsepower used by industry are accepted as a basis for comparison, Finnish industry expanded between 1918 and 1922 by some 25 percent beyond the level of 1913.

Industrial and general economic recovery was reflected in other ways. The extent to which Finland's foreign markets suffered as a result of the war years is best shown by the fact that in 1920, when the return to normalcy was well under way, Finnish exports equaled only those of 1905 and represented some 68 percent of the exports of 1913. In 1921 the percentage was 69, but it rose to 93 in the year 1922. From then on, advance was marked. The exports of 1925 were 40 percent larger than those of 1922 and reflected the fact that the paralysis of the war years had been fully overcome. Tariff legislation in 1919 and 1921 gave moderate protection to home industry and played a part in recovery. That passenger traffic on the Finnish railways grew by nearly 50 percent from 1919 to 1922, and freight by over 50 percent, may be mentioned as further illustrations of the upward swing. In the brief course of a half-dozen years, Finland had set its economic house in order and faced the future free from the handicaps created by the war. In the meantime the nation had undertaken an extensive program of agrarian reform which solved a problem of long standing.

AGRARIAN REFORM

Finland's economic life underwent marked change during the two decades after 1918. In one respect, however, the economic structure remained the same. Agriculture still was the basic industry. The farming population in 1918 was approximately 66 percent of the total. Twenty years later it was still well over 50 percent. The predominance of agriculture during the interwar period depended in large measure upon the results of an extensive land reform inaugurated by legislation in 1918 and carried to completion by the middle 1930s.

During the generation before World War I, attention had been increasingly fixed upon a rural problem of considerable dimensions and significance, that of the landless population. A large part of the rural population did not belong to the landowner class. Years before the attainment of independence, it had become clear that an adequate remedy for the plight of the landless would have to be devised if the nation wanted to eliminate a problem fraught with not only economic but social and political dangers.

The nature of the problem is indicated by the following figures. In 1901, about 24 percent of the rural families were landowners. Some 33 percent were tenants who cultivated land under various lease arrangements. Except for small garden plots approximately 43 percent owned no land. Nearly one fifth (or 18 percent) of the people in the rural regions may be said to have had no home of their own. Furthermore, not a few of the tenants cultivated land on short-term leases which provided no adequate protection as to permanence of tenure or compensation for improvements. In the light of these facts, it is obvious that, despite the notable general economic advance recorded by 1900, Finland entered the twentieth century burdened with a pressing agrarian problem. Some ameliorative legislative measures were taken before 1917. They were inadequate, however—partly because of the pressure of Russification—and it was not until the Russian period had ended that an agrarian reform was carried through.

The first agrarian reform law was enacted in October, 1918. It related to the tenants on land owned by private persons and enabled the tenant to purchase the land he had previously leased. The price for such land was fixed by public authority at the level that prevailed in 1914 in order to avoid gouging because of wartime inflation. The immediate, direct cost of redemption was borne, whenever necessary, by the state. The former tenant was to pay the price of the land purchased in annual installments that ranged from 6 to 8 percent of the purchase price. Two other laws relating to renters were passed in 1921 and 1922. The first provided for the redemption of leasehold properties on land belonging to rural parishes and the second for the redemption of leasehold properties on land owned by the state.

The result of this legislation was that about 117,000 new independent holdings, owned by former leaseholders, were created between 1919 and 1935. This all-important reform was completed, for all practical purposes, by 1935.[1]

Significant as the economic and social emancipation of the tenant class was, it did not eliminate the whole land problem. Another aspect of it remained, namely, the question of how to make it possible for individuals desirous of purchasing land and becoming independent farmers to obtain on reasonable terms land already under cultivation or acreage that had not yet been brought under the plow. This question also had received attention at the hands of public authority before 1914. In 1898 a special Settlement Fund for the Landless Population had been established, and some 14,000 new small holdings and allotments had been created as a result of its work between 1899 and 1920.

After the attainment of independence, legislative provision was made for continued effort along the same line. In 1922 the Law Providing Land for Settlement was enacted. It is usually called the Lex Kallio for Kyösti Kallio, the then Minister of Agriculture, who sponsored it. Kyösti Kallio had sat in the legislature since 1907 and was a farmer by background and a bank president as well as a farmer by profession. He later served as Minister and Prime Minister on several occasions, and was elected President in 1937.

The main purpose of the Lex Kallio was to make the purchase of land easy. It specifically made provision for two kinds of land properties, the allotment and the small farm. An allotment was defined as a parcel of land large enough to provide a building lot for a house, together with sufficient acreage for a fruit and vegetable garden. The maximum size of the allotment was fixed at five acres, but in exceptional cases at more than five acres. Allotments were designed to meet the needs of individuals not primarily dependent on agriculture who wished to supplement their income by small-scale farming and to obtain land for a house.

A farm was defined as a parcel of land, either under cultivation or capable of being cultivated, sufficient to give a livelihood to an "average family" that employed no outside labor, together with enough woodland for the essential needs of such a family. The

[1] K. T. Jutila, "Suomen maatalous ja maatalouspolitiikka 20. vuosisadalla," in *Politiikkaa ja merkkimiehiä* (Helsinki, 1935), pp. 76–84.

maximum of arable land was fixed at 50 acres, and of woodland at 50–180 acres, 50 acres being the most common maximum. These farms were intended to meet the needs of individuals who would be wholly dependent, or nearly so, upon farming.

The opportunity to become the owner of a farm was offered to nearly all persons of twenty-one years or over who did not already hold or lease land which could be turned into an independent farm on the basis of the law of 1918, mentioned above. The applicant had to agree to use the holding within three years for the purpose intended and had to satisfy the authorities that he was not in a position to obtain a farm without the assistance provided by the law. He was likewise obligated to give evidence of ability to farm.

The funds necessary for the purchases of land under the law were advanced by the state. The state also established a special Department of Land Settlement and local Committees of Land Settlement for the purpose of placing adequate administrative and other assistance within the reach of the prospective owner of an allotment or farm. The following procedure in acquiring land under the law was prescribed.

The applicant would forward a written request to the Committee of Land Settlement in the locality in which he wished an allotment or a farm and would indicate the acreage needed (within the maximum established by the law). The local committee would thereupon find out whether the amount and the proper kind of land—either state-owned land or other—was available in the local market. If no state- or privately owned land was available by voluntary sale, the committee would proceed to force the owner of the land desired to sell to the applicant. The owner could not be forced to sell, however, if he held less than 500 acres and if the land he held could be considered efficiently farmed. Owners of more than 500 acres would have to sell a certain percentage of their total acreage. The percentage was fixed on a sliding scale; the maximum that an owner would have to sell ran to 50 percent if he held 12,500 acres or more. The final decision in all cases involving forced sale was formulated by the Department of Land Settlement. It could be appealed to special Land Courts and upon further appeal would be confirmed or annulled by the Supreme Court.

The price of the land was fixed according to the price level that prevailed in 1914. The state financed the whole transaction; no down payment was required. The new owner would liquidate the indebtedness incurred by him in annual payments varying from 7 to 9 percent of the price of his holding. From the seller's viewpoint the transaction meant that the state paid him in cash for the crops, timber, and buildings found on the land sold. For the land itself he would be paid either in cash or in government bonds bearing interest at 7 percent or both, depending on the total value of the land.

The law also established a classification of properties subject to forced sale and fixed the order in which owners could be compelled to sell. Proceeding from the basic principle that land which is demonstrably necessary for efficient agricultural operations should be exempt, it stated that compulsion should be first applied to owners who had, from a moral point of view, no defensible right to own land capable of successful farming. This meant that land owned by lumber companies, for example, was singled out as property most liable to forced sale. In the second category, the law placed all land which either had not been efficiently utilized or had been acquired with a view to speculative gain. The third category consisted of land in the hands of ordinary private owners. In no case did the law contemplate the breaking up of small or of medium-sized holdings if efficiency of cultivation would thereby be impaired.

The Lex Kallio was intended, broadly speaking, not only to make the purchase of land easier. It was also intended to aid in increasing agricultural production and to contribute toward solving the problem of the landless. The law likewise established the important principle that ownership of land carries a moral obligation toward state and nation, and that a failure to recognize this obligation means, in a special degree, the loss of the inviolability of the rights of private property.

The application of the Lex Kallio disclosed from the outset that compulsion was necessary only in a few instances. In the vast majority of cases, sales were effected by voluntary agreement. The available detailed statistics showing the specific consequences of the law relate only to the years before 1932. They show a total of 22,000 sales. Of these, farms numbered 8,200 and allotments 5,450. In

8,350 cases, land had been purchased by farmers whose acreage had not been sufficient for efficient farming, and who therefore needed additional land. It is thus obvious that the Lex Kallio (and another supplementary law enacted in 1922) was less important in creating new holdings than the law of 1918 relating to the redemption of leasehold propetries. It was of great significance, however, in providing a program and in devising machinery for the purchase of land by persons of small or no means who desired to become either farmers or home owners.

The general results of the agrarian reform in 1918–22 were: (1) independent holders had obtained, by 1931, about 3,560,000 acres of land previously owned by private individuals or corporations; (2) during the same period 778,700 acres of state land had been turned over to individual owners; (3) the financing of the reform involved an expenditure of public funds of about $10,000,000 (the unpaid loans from the Settlement Fund amounted to less than $750,000 by the end of 1934); (4) between 1910 and 1930 the landowning population grew by 65 percent and the group of small tenant farmers decreased by 71 percent; (5) in 1937, nearly 90 percent of the farms were held by independent owners, and the problem of tenancy had virtually disappeared.

In 1929 the total agricultural holdings in the country amounted to 6,000,000 acres. These fell into the following groups: farms up to 25 acres, 33.4 percent; those between 25 and 125 acres, 52.1 percent; those between 125 and 250 acres, 8.4 percent; and so-called large farms of 250 acres or over, 6.1 percent. The largest holdings, those of 250 acres or more, decreased both in numbers and in size by about 25 percent between 1920 and 1930, and farms between 125 and 250 acres similarly decreased, the drop being some 10 percent.

THE FARMER IN A CHANGING ECONOMY

Partly as a result of the establishment of new farms and partly because of the introduction of more efficient methods of cultivation, farming expanded substantially between 1918 and 1939. The total area under cultivation grew from 5,000,000 acres to 6,500,000 acres (about 9 percent of the total area of the country). The trend toward dairy farming was conspicuous. Tables 7 and 8 give a picture of the trends between 1920 and 1937.

TABLE 7

PERCENTAGE OF LAND USED FOR VARIOUS CROPS

Year	Wheat	Rye	Barley	Oats	Potatoes	Hay	Other crops	Fallow
1920	0.5	11.5	5.8	19.6	3.5	45.8	3.3	10.0
1925	0.7	11.0	5.1	20.4	3.2	46.4	3.6	9.6
1930	0.6	9.1	5.1	19.2	3.1	51.5	4.0	7.4
1935	2.8	9.6	5.1	18.7	3.3	50.5	4.0	6.0
1937	4.4	9.3	4.7	17.7	3.3	51.7	3.0	5.9

TABLE 8

HARVEST OF MAIN PRODUCTS
(in tons)

Year	Wheat	Rye	Barley	Oats	Potatoes	Hay
1921	20,000	290,000	130,000	500,000	590,000	2,740,000
1931	68,000	350,000	180,000	670,000	1,130,000	3,290,000
1936	140,000	310,000	190,000	690,000	1,430,000	3,700,000
1938	255,900	368,500	207,400	825,650	1,197,800	4,058,300

As regards the money value of the crops raised by the farmers, it suffices to note that, during the years covered by the tables, farming expanded by well over 50 percent. This growth had a good many results. One of them was the increased agricultural self-sufficiency of the nation. A few illustrations will give an idea of the increase. In 1915, nearly all of the wheat consumed was imported; by the closing thirties, roughly two thirds was home-grown. Even such common foods as barley, oats, and potatoes were not grown, in 1915, in sufficient quantities to meet the domestic demand. Twenty years later, imports of these products were only a fraction of the amounts needed annually. Broadly speaking, agricultural self-sufficiency—dependent, to be sure, on imported fertilizers and fodder—was raised to about 85 percent.

Notable as the increase in the raising of food crops was, it represented only one aspect of the advance registered after World War

I. The total yield of animal husbandry was throughout of much greater importance than that of food crops. In the thirties, the former accounted for 65–70 percent of the total agricultural production and the latter less than one third. In terms of cash income, about 75 cents out of every dollar of farm income came from animal husbandry.

This meant dairy farming, which in turn meant that milk, butter, cheese, and the like were writ large on the balance sheet of the Finnish farmer. Milk alone gave him 50 cents out of every dollar earned, and the dollars earned from milk grew by some 40 percent between 1915 and 1937. One of the important reasons for this expanding "milk dollar" was the fact that better care and more scientific management on the part of the farmer enabled the average Bossy to produce annually 6,150 pounds of milk while her maternal ancestor of the World War I period had yielded only 4,400 pounds. Meanwhile Bossy's clan also had increased. If her ancestor had in 1915 belonged to a herd of eleven cows, Bossy in 1937 belonged to a herd of thirteen.

Speaking in general terms, dairy farming produced enough to meet the domestic demand of milk, butter, and cheese and provided considerable quantities for export. Meats and eggs were also exported. In terms of money value, the main exports between 1921 and 1937 amounted to the sums given in Table 9.

TABLE 9

EXPORTS OF FARM PRODUCTS[a]

Year	Butter	Cheese	Meats	Eggs	Hides
1921	295	52	33	4	64
1931	259	54	42	96	48
1936	264	79	62	110	81
1937	283	106	72	125	82

[a] The figures are in millions of Finnish marks. One Finnish mark equaled, during these years, about 2.2 cents.

Excepting butter, the export of these products showed very important increases. It is interesting to note that the production of eggs, which was insignificant down to 1918, became great enough in the course of the thirties to allow exports larger than the combined sales in foreign markets, in the early years of the period, of cheese and meat. This is one of the evidences of the diversification of farming during the twenty years following World War I.

It has been suggested already that the upward swing of farming was attributable not only to the opening of new land for cultivation. The introduction of new methods and increased use of machinery in particular likewise contributed. The following figures, which relate to 1920 and 1930, show the growing mechanization of Finnish farming (which is, as has been pointed out, overwhelmingly small-scale farming). In 1920 the farmers used about 7,000 internal combustion engines or electrical motors as sources of motive power; in 1930 the figure was some 30,400. In the former year, 150 tractors were in use; in the latter, 925. Mowing machines increased from 73,800 to 119,250, threshing machines from 43,200 to 49,200, sowing machines from 14,350 to 24,150, and separators from 141,600 to 170,700. The trend shown by these figures continued in the thirties, especially after the effects of the depression of 1929 had been overcome.

Another factor that contributed to the agricultural advance of the period was the cooperative movement. By the middle thirties, close to 50 percent of the grain sold in the domestic market was handled by cooperatives. Nearly nine tenths of the 700-odd dairies that turned the farmers' milk into butter were cooperative dairies. Over 90 percent of the butter and nearly 60 percent of the cheese exported were inspected, graded, and sold by Valio, the leading cooperative society. About 40 percent of the fertilizers and fodder the farmer purchased and some 60 percent of the seed he used came from Hankkija, the largest central organization of the farmers' cooperative stores and dairies, which also annually sold 45 percent of the farm machinery used and furnished three fourths of the dairies with the equipment they needed. A large part of the farmers' daily purchases at the country store consisted of purchases from a cooperative store, which brought 2 percent returns on purchases—this being the usual dividend—at the end of the year. Finally, his credit needs were often met by cooperative credit societies, of which there were 700 in 1920 and 1,123 in 1938. Run in the interest of the farmer, these credit societies served tens of thousands of them and had not a little to do with the solid financial position of the farmers as a class. The soundness of the cooperative credit societies is shown by the fact that—to mention one example—the total losses recorded in 1938 came to 100,000 marks out of a total annual business of 2,541,000,000 marks.

Statistics that indicate growing acreage or greater yield per acre farmed, and evidence of rising exports or the importance of cooperative enterprises, do not necessarily reflect profitable farming. That is to say, facts of this kind do not by themselves show that the average farmer was able to make both ends meet. They do not give a direct answer to the question: Did farming pay during the post-World War I period?

Before answering this question, passing note should be taken of a feature of Finnish farming which has not yet been mentioned. For the past three generations and more, farming in Finland has been closely connected with lumbering. The lumber industry contributed a significant part of the farmers' income before World War I and continued to do so after the war. The farmer either sold timber or supplemented his income from ordinary farming operations by seasonal work at cutting lumber or transporting it. Most of the work of lumbering was in fact done by landowning farmers. A large part of the agricultural population may therefore be said to have stood with one foot in farming proper and with the other in the lumber industry after 1918. It has been estimated that the farmers received a total income of some $10,000,000 in the best years from the sale of forests and from lumbering, which represented somewhat less than one third of the income derived from animal husbandry.

The broad questions of what the economic position of the farmer was and to what extent the agrarian population obtained a reasonable —or unsatisfactory, as the case may have been—return from its labors have been investigated on several occasions. One investigation was made, for instance, in 1922, when the new agrarian laws were still in the process of changing rural conditions. Another dates from 1929, when land reform legislation had already eliminated most of the conditions that brought it into being. A third was based on a study of the year 1932. At the time, the depression had left a deep impression upon agriculture as well as upon industry, and the survey of 1932 was therefore particularly significant.

During the years before 1914, the debts of the farmer amounted on an average to some 17 percent of the value of his property. Inflation and other factors gave him a more favorable balance sheet during the period immediately after 1918, and by 1923–24 the percentage of debt had dropped to about 9. Expansion, purchases of machinery, the introduction of new methods, and other circumstances raised the figure during the years after 1924. In 1929, when the depression set in, the Finnish farmer was in debt to the amount of 12 percent of the value of the property he owned. The depression brought hard times for the farmer. Lower prices for agricultural products, a notable drop in lumbering and other by-industries of the farmer, and tightening credit drove many a farmer to the wall. Forced sales of farm properties amounted to some 400 in the year 1929. In the following year, the figure rose to nearly 1,000. In 1931 it exceeded 1,600, in 1932 it came to 2,500, and it reached a maximum in 1933, when nearly 3,300 farmers lost their holdings. In 1935 the figure dropped to about 2,000 and declined thereafter. Meanwhile, the percentage of debt rose to about 16 in 1933 and approximated the level reached before 1914.

A clearer picture of the economic position of the farmer was given by the survey of 1932. It showed (1) that out of about 287,000 farmers 34 percent were free from debt; (2) that 37 percent were in debt up to one quarter of the value of the property; (3) that in 20 percent of the cases the debts amounted to 25–50 percent of the value of the property; and (4) that in 9 percent of the cases debts ran to 50 percent or more of the total value of the holding. Of the small farmers, well over one third (34.4 percent) were totally free from debt, and only 6.7 percent of this group had gone into debt to the extent of one half of the value of their property. The large farmers were in a more precarious situation. Only 17 percent of this group were free from debt, and 42 percent carried a debt burden that came to one half of the total value of the property. The main reason for the marked difference between the condition of the small farmers and the large farmers appears to have been the fact that the latter found it more difficult during the depression years to adjust expense—interest charges, wages paid to labor, and cost of living—to the demands of sharply reduced income. The rapid recovery of farming in general from the depression is shown by the fact that, while 9 percent of the farms were heavily in debt in 1932, only 4 percent were in this category in 1935.

The profits made by the farmer varied a good deal from year to year. In the early twenties, profits were reasonably good but soon declined and the average return on the investment dropped to a fraction below 2 percent in 1924. After 1924 the situation improved, and the net return reached 6 percent in 1926. Between 1926 and 1929 it again declined to about 4.3 percent. After 1931 the trend was again upward and gave an average return for 1931–35 of 4.6 percent. The year 1936 was also good and yielded an average profit of 5.8 percent; 1937 was better still and provided the farmer with a 7 percent return on his investment. In 1937 the profit was 5.4 percent on farms of less than 25 acres and ranged to 7.7 percent on farms of over 250 acres.[2]

The evidence thus unmistakably points to the following conclusions. In the first place, the debt burden carried by the farmers was not excessive, and the small farmer in particular lived on a financial basis which did not mean oppressive mortgages and the threat of foreclosure. Even the depression years of the relatively short period 1929–33 failed to expose the majority of the farmers to economic disaster. This appears clear in view of the fact that foreclosures at the height of general economic dislocation (in 1933) did not exceed 3,300.

Secondly, while the profits obtained by the farmer were far from impressive, they appear to have been sufficiently high to make farming pay. Except for the year 1924, when the return on the farmer's capital was slightly below 2 percent, and the depression years from

[2] These generalizations are based on figures and tables in *Unitas*, 1938, No. 4, pp. 101–2, *S.T.V.*, 1938, pp. 98–100, K. T. Jutila's analysis in the work cited in note 1, p. 260, and C. A. J. Gadolin's *Finland av i går och i dag* (Stockholm, 1938), pp. 153–56. The position of agricultural laborers also improved. Between 1914 and 1938 their wages increased by 14–17 times, while the cost of living during the same period was multiplied by only 10½. See J. Laati, *Sosialinen lainsäädäntö ja toiminta Suomessa* (Helsinki, 1939), p. 11; *S.T.V.*, 1938, p. 298.

1929 to 1931, when the return was only 3 percent, the average profit ranged from 4 to 7 percent. Thirdly, it seems that these figures take on added meaning when it is kept in mind that the two decades surveyed in this section were years of important agricultural reform. Nearly 150,00 new farms were established during this period. They usually involved investment of capital and credit transactions the result of which were most seriously felt during the years surveyed. Another twenty years of normal development would in all likelihood have liquidated most of the financial problem created by these transactions.

INDUSTRY—THE PROMISE OF THE FUTURE

While it is abundantly clear that after 1918 agriculture remained the source of livelihood for most of Finland's population, it was industry that held the mortgage on the years to come. The two post-war decades represented, in terms of economic trends, a transition period that changed Finland into a predominantly industrial nation. The trend was indicated by the industrial expansion that took place between 1926 and 1939. In the latter year, industry produced some 80 percent more than in 1926. It has been estimated—perhaps somewhat loosely and optimistically—that in the closing thirties the total value of the output of industry was more than twice the value of agricultural production.

A large part of Finnish industry depends for its operation upon timber, one of the most important of the natural resources of the country. It is therefore essential to take note of the extent of this resource, who owns it, and how it sustains the industrial structure of the nation.

The timber resources of Finland before 1939 were large. The total forest area was close to 65,000,000 acres, of which about 50,000,-000 acres produced industrially or commercially valuable timber. The latter figure represented nearly 70 percent of the whole land area of the country. Finland was therefore exceptionally rich in forests, and with Sweden headed the European nations in the extent of this resource, excepting Russia. Scientific forestry had been in-

tavus Vasa, reigned
3–1560; oil painting by Cor-
us Arendt

John III, reigned 1568–1592; oil
painting by unknown artist

ht: Gustavus Adolphus,
ned 1611–1632; copper
raving by L. Kilian

right: Gustavus III,
ned 1771–1792; copper
raving by F. Gillberg,
r original by L. Pasch

Alexander I, emperor of Russia, 1801-1825, and grand duke of Finland, 1809-1825; oil painting by François de Gérard

Medieval church in Hollola, southwest Finland

dern church in Hyvinkää

K. J. Stahlberg, 1919–1925

L. K. Relander, 1925–1931

P. E. Svinhufvud, 1931–1937

Kyösti Kallio, 1937–1940

Risto Ryti, 1940–1944

Carl Gustaf Emil Mannerheim,
1944–1946

J. K. Paasikivi, 1946–1956

U. K. Kekkonen, 1956–

Church at Seinäjoki, "The Cross of the Plains"; architect, Alvar Aalto

Tuberculosis sanatorium at Paimio; architect, Alvar Aalto

Olavinlinna Castle; situated in the center of the Eastern Lake District of Finland near the town of Savonlinna; built in 1475 as a bulwark against the East

Cathedral of Turku

Lake Saimaa, largest of Finland's sixty thousand lakes

Elias Lönnrot, 1802–1884

Johan Ludvig Runeberg, 1804–1877

Zachris Topelius, 1818–1898

Johan Vilhelm Snellman, 1806–1881

Aerial view of Helsinki

Parliament Building, Helsinki

University of Turku (above): Aerial view; (below): Library

Savonlinna, the center of Finland's Eastern Lake District

Tampere, important industrial center of Finland

troduced in a small way as early as the 1860s, and efficient exploitation of the nation's timber had been translated from an academic
aspiration into an everyday fact before the turn of the century. That
is, the use of the forests was based on a rational, scientific basis well
over two generations ago, and wasteful exploitation unmindful of
future needs had been reduced to a minimum long before World
War I.

It goes without saying that in a national economy such as that of
Finland, where both agriculture and basic industries depend upon
the forest resources of the nation, the question of who owns the
forests is of paramount importance. Table 10 gives the results of

TABLE 10

DISTRIBUTION OF OWNERSHIP OF FOREST LAND

Owners	Supply of timber (in percent)	Annual growth of timber (in percent)
Individual owners	50.6	65.3
The state	37.2	21.4
Lumber companies, etc.	9.7	10.8
Others	2.5	2.5
Total	100.0	100.0

an extensive survey completed as early as 1924. We notice that
about one half of timber acreage representing roughly two thirds of
the annual increment, and therefore two thirds of the amount of
timber available yearly for sale, was owned by farmers and other
private individuals. The state owned well over one third of the
acreage and somewhat more than one fifth of the annual growth.
Lumber companies, paper mills, and the like controlled roughly
only one tenth of both. This meant that "lumber barons" were nonexistent and that corporations had no chance to control the timber
market and to exploit it exclusively in their own interests. On the
contrary, they were dependent upon state sales and the sales made
by private owners for nearly nine tenths of their timber needs. Just
as the "soulless" large landowner did not loom large in agriculture,
so the "soulless" corporation did not assume imposing stature in the
control of forests or timber markets.

Table 11 shows the part that timber played in the industrial life of the nation between 1920 and the late 1930s. For the sake of completeness, exports of unfinished timber are also included. The years 1921–35 are given in annual averages.

TABLE 11

INDUSTRIAL CONSUMPTION OF TIMBER, 1920–1937
(in millions of marks)

Year	Sawmills	Paper and pulp	Plywood	Other	Total	Exports of unfinished timber
1921–25	1,050	270	31	54	1,405	404
1926–30	1,640	535	98	68	2,341	553
1931–35	986	628	106	45	1,765	299
1936	1,370	1,015	164	51	2,600	842
1937	2,074	1,420	206	50	3,750	837

It is evident from Table 11 that the utilization of forest resources by industry expanded greatly. The margin within which further expansion was possible appeared to be ample. As one investigator put it in 1938, in evaluating the importance of timber reserves still untapped, "The industries of the country that use timber as raw material clearly have substantial possibilities for further growth, despite the fact that the exploitation of this basic raw material has greatly increased during the past two decades." [3] Furthermore, the growth of the paper industry and the introduction of the manufacture of rayon suggested future industrial development that provided relatively greater returns from the utilization of timber. To illustrate: 65 percent of the value of sawn timber represents the cost of raw material, in plywood manufacturing 45 percent, but in paper manufacturing only 20 percent, and in the production of rayon only a small fraction. The trend after the early twenties markedly favored the latter industries and indicated further specialization in the same direction by the closing thirties.

The other basic resources of the country during the interwar years may be summarized as follows: Considerable quantities of rich iron ore were found in northern Finland, but the ore was not

[3] *Unitas*, 1938, No. 4, p. 106.

easily accessible and therefore remained unused. Deposits in south Finland were accessible but contained mostly low-grade ore and remained largely untouched. Copper and nickel deposits, on the other hand, were significant. The Outokumpu copper deposits were found in eastern Finland in 1910 and have been exploited since World War I. The production exceeded the needs of the country and yielded exports both of ore and of copper. In 1937 nearly 12,000 tons of copper and some 5,500 tons of copper ore were sold abroad. The nickel resources, located in Petsamo in northeastern Finland, were the largest in Europe. Estimates in the 1930s indicated 3,000,-000–4,000,000 tons of ore. Preliminary work was begun in 1934, and production was started shortly before the outbreak of war in 1939.

Finland has no coal. Water power offers a substitute for coal and exists in abundant quantities. Estimates in the 1930s indicated potential water-power resources amounting to over 2,500,000 horsepower; roughly 20 percent of the total had been harnessed to the service of industries and homes by 1939. Coal and oil imports supplemented water power. Coal imports grew from 1,200,000 tons in 1935 to 2,200,000 tons in 1937 and oil from 140,000 tons to 270,000 tons. Industry also utilized large quantities of the wood refuse of lumber mills and other plants that used timber as raw material.

Despite the absence of the two usual basic supports of modern industrialization, iron and coal, Finland's industry forged ahead rapidly after 1920. Table 12 shows at a glance the rate of change. For the years 1921–35, annual averages are given.

TABLE 12

INDUSTRIAL GROWTH, 1921–1939

Year	Gross value of production (in millions of marks)	Number of workers	Number of horsepower used
1921–25	8,200	135,000	361,000
1926–30	12,300	157,000	502,000
1931–35	11,340	147,000	678,000
1936	16,120	184,000	872,000
1937	21,070	208,000	962,000
1939	26,000	225,800	. . . . . .

The figures in Table 12 show an increase of some 50 percent in the number of workers employed and a growth of about 170 percent in the value of production. What happened to the leading industries of the country during these years is indicated by Table 13. It does

TABLE 13

GROSS VALUE OF INDUSTRIAL PRODUCTION, 1921–1937
(in millions of marks)

Year	Timber industry	Paper, pulp, etc.	Textiles	Food manu- facturing, etc.	Metals and machinery	Total
1921–25	1,992	1,511	895	1,539	924	6,861
1925–30	3,077	2,339	1,157	2,204	1,422	10,199
1931–35	2,171	2,633	1,261	2,138	1,384	9,587
1936	3,095	3,640	1,760	3,010	2,243	13,748
1937	4,399	4,696	2,264	3,454	3,273	18,086

not include such relatively minor branches of manufacturing as furniture, leather, rubber, footwear, glass, cement, bricks, and the like.

Not the least significant fact emphasized by Table 13 is the prominence of industries dependent on timber. Among the major manufacturing establishments, they accounted in 1936–39 for approximately one half of the total value of production. It is also worthy of note that the metal and machine industries, and those classified as food manufacturing industries, grew by 1936–37 to dimensions that placed them ahead of the timber, paper, and pulp industries a decade earlier. Even textile manufactories produced more in 1939 than the traditionally leading industries in the early twenties.

Great as the expansion of metal, textile, and other industries was, it was paper, pulp, and timber that represented the real machine age. They were particularly important in Finland's foreign trade. From 1921 to 1937 they occupied the position shown by Table 14, which includes the main items that accounted for well over 80 percent of the total exports before World War II.

TABLE 14

MAIN EXPORTS, 1921–1937

(in millions of marks)

Year	Timber		Paper and pulp		Dairy products, etc.	
	Exports	Percent of total	Exports	Percent of total	Exports	Percent of total
1921–25	2,471	57.3	1,332	30.9	432	10.0
1926–30	3,290	54.8	1,782	29.7	545	9.1
1931–35	2,283	42.5	2,157	40.2	473	8.8
1936	3,037	42.4	2,900	40.5	538	7.5
1937	4,157	44.8	3,630	39.1	612	6.6

Table 14 gives sharp relief to the dependence of the country upon the industries that rested upon timber. They accounted for over four fifths of the total exports. This circumstance in turn underlines the fact that Finland's industrial life, therefore the economic well-being of its people, was more dependent upon foreign markets —and therefore upon the economic conditions in the world at large —than might seem to be the case. Certainly the number of workers employed by industry gave no indication of the extent to which the economic life of the nation rested upon a basis (foreign markets) that lay outside Finnish legislative or other controls, and was secure only to the extent to which Finland's industry was well managed and its production efficient.

Industrial expansion also played a decisive part in the growth of the means of communication after 1920. Every 100 miles of railroad in 1920 had become about 160 miles by 1939, the total mileage in the latter year being 5,400. The rolling stock had in the meantime doubled. The amount of freight carried by the railroads likewise grew by 100 percent. The number of passengers carried annually declined somewhat, from 24,000,000 to 23,000,000. The reason was the establishment and rapid growth of bus lines and the increased use of automobiles. Where only 4,660 motor vehicles were used in 1923, nearly 56,000 were in use in 1938. The state owned 96 percent of the railroads and received a return of 2–3 percent on its investment.

How were the workers employed by industry affected by the trends noted in the preceding pages? Did the period after 1920 mean improvement in their condition, or was manufacturing success purchased at the expense of the laboring man?

These questions cannot be fully answered because no comprehensive effort has been made to collect complete wage statistics for the period. The official statistical service began to record this aspect of the nation's life in detail only in 1936. But special investigations of the wage problem were made and they cover some of the most important industries of the country. The sawmill industry, for example, has been surveyed for the years since 1924. The important paper and pulp industry was carefully studied after 1928 and the metal and machine industry after 1926. These surveys were sufficiently extensive and the segment of industrial life covered by them broad enough (in 1921 they accounted for nearly two thirds of total industrial production and in 1937 the proportion was slightly larger) to justify certain conclusions regarding the years before World War II.

In the sawmill industry, wages increased on an average by 12–15 percent between 1924 and 1936. The increase in real wages, however, was considerably greater. During these years, the cost of living of the workers in the industry decreased by about 15 percent; most of the drop occurred after the depression of 1929. This meant that in terms of purchasing power the average worker received wages in 1936 that were over 30 percent higher than the wages of 1924. In 1937 his money wages grew by some 13 percent over 1936, while the cost of living rose by less than 5 percent.

The wage trend in the paper and pulp industry was approximately the same. The industry was particularly hard hit by the loss of markets after 1929. While the wage statistics of the years 1928–36 are not fully comparable, it appears that the real wages of the worker increased by some 19 percent. The year 1937 brought a further increase of about 8 percent. The wage situation in the metal and machine industry can be followed in greater detail. Between 1926 and 1936, money wages grew by 15–16 percent. Making allowance for the decrease in the cost of living after 1929, it can be said that the workers in the industry received in 1936 an income that was more than one-third higher than that of 1926.

The general conclusion regarding labor's share in the industrial growth after 1920 is that it became greater and that the worker was appreciably better off in the late thirties than he had been a decade earlier. The depression years, to be sure, resulted in great hardships, but recovery came relatively early and led to a higher wage level than any recorded before 1929. This does not mean that wages in industry had risen, by 1937, to a degree that could be called fully satisfactory from the workers' viewpoint. The general Finnish wage level remained lower than that of many other countries, even if allowance is made for the lower cost of living. The trend after 1932 was such, however, as to bring a very real improvement in the condition of the industrial laborer. In 1938–39 there was every reason for assuming that the improvement would continue in the future.

ORGANIZED LABOR

As we have seen, the first Finnish labor unions were established in 1884. After 1890, attempts were made to weld them into a national federation. Internal conflicts, rivalries among labor leaders, and other factors prevented the formation of a national organization until 1907 when the Federation of the Labor Unions of Finland came into being. Its membership was about 18,000. It grew relatively rapidly during the next decade and included approximately 40,000 members in 1916. In 1917 its membership temporarily rose, under the exceptional conditions at the close of the year, to 170,000.

The war of 1918 disrupted the movement. Organized labor had meant Socialist labor from the start. Both socialism and the cause of organized workers suffered temporary paralysis as a result of the war, and both made a fresh start after the republic was established. The recovery of the Social Democratic party has been noted already, and the story need not be repeated here. The Federation of Labor Unions resumed its work in 1919. At the end of the year, its membership was as great as it had been before 1917. "It was obvious," said one of the labor leaders, in commenting later on the prospects of future growth in 1919, "that this good beginning would have led to speedy expansion, and that the workers would have succeeded in turning their organization into an instrumentality productive of the results they desired, had it not been for the fact that some of the erstwhile leaders of our labor movement who had escaped to Russia [after the war of 1918] began to work against our commendable objectives." [4]

The quotation refers to an aspect of the post-1918 Finnish labor movement which ultimately became of decisive importance. According to testimony furnished by men intimately connected with the movement after 1918, Finnish Communists obtained a foothold within labor organizations and began early to convince many workers that ordinary trade union activity was harmful for labor. They urged that revolutionary organizations devoted to the creation of disturbances and direct action would contribute most to the workers' welfare by preparing the ground for a Soviet republic established with the aid of Russian arms.[5] Labor remained cool, however, to argument and prediction of this sort. The Communist elements thereupon set to work to capture the leadership of the labor unions. Exceptional success attended their effort.

In 1920, Social Democrats and other moderates were voted out of positions of leadership in the Federation of Labor Unions. Communists took their place. The contest for control was carried on all along the line. A new policy in the relations between labor and capital was defined and put into effect by the new leaders. Peaceful bargaining with employers was abandoned. Militant short-time strikes were utilized not only for the purpose of raising the wages of labor or obtaining other concessions—there was no cause to urge the eight-hour day, for it had been established by a national law in 1917—but more particularly with a view to causing trouble pure and simple. Sabotage and the technique of the slowdown were accepted as means whereby the economic machine could be braked or perchance brought to a grinding stop.

[4] E. K. Louhikko, ed., *Suomen ammattiyhdistysten keskusliiton Helsingissa lokak. 19–21 p:na 1930 pidetyn perustavan kokouksen pöytäkirja* (Helsinki, 1931), p. 13.
[5] *Ibid.*, pp. 13 ff.

It did not take long before the results of the new leadership became apparent. Several of the member unions ceased their mutual benefit activity, which had been a conspicuous part of their work for decades, and concentrated their resources on objectives that led to industrial warfare. Moderate members began to withdraw. In 1922 it was decided that the federation join the Moscow International. The decision was not carried out because it would have resulted in the withdrawal of all Social Democrats from the federation. The membership of the federation remained nearly stationary because of uneasiness and indecision among labor groups. The federation could point to no appreciable increase in workers' wages as a result of its activity. In 1926 the Social Democrats emphatically condemned the Communist orientation of the federation and a temporary truce between the Communists and their opponents within the ranks of labor was brought about.

The respite from internal conflict after 1926 enabled organized labor to forge ahead. In 1928 the federation represented 90,000 members. Over 400 collective bargaining agreements, affecting about one third of the membership, testified to the increased use—despite fairly general aversion among the employers to collective bargaining—of peaceful means of determining the conditions under which labor and employers worked together. Having survived the dangers of foundering on the shoals raised athwart its course by Communist leadership, organized labor had set out on a course indicated by markers that did not show the red color of Moscow.

During 1928 and 1929, however, it became evident once again that trouble lay ahead. In 1928 the secretary of the federation was convicted of treasonable activity and sentenced to jail for five years. The conflict within the federation broke out anew, leading to the resignation of all Social Democrats from its executive committee. The Social Democrats withdrew because of their unwillingness to have a hand in an organization that was, in their opinion, sacrificing the worker's welfare for criminal political activity on behalf of a foreign power. The federation itself began to crumble; it lost nearly one third of its membership within a year. In November, 1929, the Communist attempt to engineer a national strike led to clear-cut conflict between the Socialists and the Communists, in that the former officially and openly opposed the strike by prohibiting Social Democrats from participating in it. The strike was a dismal failure and led to the collapse of the federation. By 1930 all but three of the unions that composed the federation had withdrawn from it. Communism had in the meantime been outlawed by a bill enacted by Parliament in 1930. Finnish non-Communist labor found itself once again facing the task of creating a new national organization to take the place of the federation wrecked by Communist leadership.

The new organization was quickly erected on the ruins of the old. Seven unions joined hands in 1930 in forming the Confederation of Finnish Trade Unions (the SAK). Belonging to no political party, the SAK decreed that its member unions could accept affiliation with any political party. Individual members of the unions could join a political party, but only unions that embraced the principles and purposes of the non-Communist labor movement were admitted to the SAK. The socialization of basic means of production was defined—perhaps more as a declaration of principle than as a specific purpose—as one of the goals of the SAK. Support of social legislation designed to aid the wage earner and collective bargaining were likewise accepted as proper objectives and procedures. The confederation joined the western Amsterdam International and cooperated with labor unions in the other Scandinavian countries and also with the International Labor Organization (the ILO).

Free from communism, the confederation enlisted the support of about 15,000 during the first year of its existence. Despite the difficulties created by unemployment and other depression problems in the early thirties, the confederation grew year by year. Its membership approximated 20,000 in 1933, grew to nearly 34,000 in 1935, reached 64,000 in 1937, and topped 70,000 in 1938. In the last year, nineteen unions belonged to the confederation. The movement thus recovered, in the course of a half-dozen years, most of the ground lost in the crucial years 1928–30. The organization in the meantime became a true workers' confederation, free from the handicaps that retarded trade union activity in the course of the twenties.

After the reorganization of 1930, organized labor consistently improved its position. The financial basis of the unions was strengthened and enabled them to pay to their members, in unemployment or sickness benefits, assistance during strikes or lockouts, or for other purposes, well over $2,500,000 during 1930–38, a large sum at the time. Incidentally, in 1938 women constituted 23 percent of the membership of the unions that composed the confederation. In the same year, over 48,000 workers were employed under the terms of 320 separate collectively negotiated wage agreements. Without losing sight of the factors which determine wages but are not related to the strength or weaknesses of labor organizations, it appears safe to conclude that the unions were partly responsible for the higher wage levels after 1933. Twelve categories of wages reported in 1938 showed increases during the preceding four years that amounted to 25–30 percent or more.

The trend of labor-employer relations before the end of the 1930s is indicated by taking note of labor conflicts of the period and their solution. Table 15 shows the extent of strikes and the outcome

TABLE 15

STRIKES AND THEIR RESULTS, 1930–1937

			Settlement		
Year	Number of strikes	Compromise	On strikers' terms	On employers' terms	Working days lost
1930	11	5	2	4	12,100
1932	3			3	2,300
1934	46	30	7	9	89,700
1936	29	17	6	6	35,400
1937	37	21	8	8	183,400

in terms of labor's interests on the one hand and employers' objectives on the other. In the labor disputes important enough to be included in official statistics the workers were on the whole successful in holding their own; while employers' interests prevailed in a greater number of cases than workers', the rule of compromise was applied more frequently than any other, especially after 1934. Compromise effected by bargaining before a conflict precipitated a strike—such cases are not included in the table—also played an important part in reducing open tests of strength (in 1927, for example, 79 strikes, which meant the loss of 1,528,000 working days, were recorded). Collective agreements, often formulated under the leadership of a government mediator, and the growing use of negotiation and compromise contributed much to the fact that the thirties witnessed a better record of relations between wage earners and employers than the twenties.[6]

After two disasters—the paralysis caused by the war in 1918 and the collapse precipitated by Communist tactics and manipulation in 1929–30—Finnish labor organizations found their proper place within the framework furnished by the economic life and institutions of the country. Their growth was not spectacular and by the late 1930s they had a long way to go before they could assume the role that labor unions often played in other lands before World War II. This did not mean, however, that the workers were unusually exposed to exploitation. They were assisted as a class to overcome the consequences of unemployment, sickness, industrial accidents, and the like by a growing body of social legislation. The expanding social and economic services of state and municipality offered many safeguards against economic misfortune and suffering and decreased the exposure to conditions that enlightened public opinion considered socially harmful.

NATIONAL BUDGETS, TAXES, AND DEBTS

Meanwhile the economic life of the nation influenced and was affected in many ways by the banking and credit situation and government financial policy. State revenues and expenditures, foreign and domestic indebtedness, and in general the financial condition of the republic were intimately connected with the economic upward swing of the twenties, the depression after 1929, and the recovery after 1932.

The problem of capital and credit may be suggested by noting

[6] After 1918, the Ministry for Social Affairs furnished, through a group of special labor mediators, its services in the settlement of labor disputes. Arbitration was not prescribed by law but was voluntary, a system that went back to 1889.

that, after economic readjustment following World War I had been completed by about 1924, the money market improved for several years. The accumulation of capital by the banks, as reflected by growing deposits, got under way, and the world of business found it easier to obtain necessary funds. The general trend at the time was indicated by the fact that the official Bank of Finland ("lowest") discount rate, which had risen to as high as 10 percent in 1923, dropped to 9 percent in 1924, 8 percent in 1925, and to 6 percent in the autumn of 1927. The approach of the depression was already reflected in 1928 in the money market when the rate was raised to 7 percent in the autumn of that year. It was lowered after 1931, as the financial crisis eased, industry began to recover, and foreign trade once again recorded surplus exports. The result was that the money market became easier. In 1934 the rediscount rate dropped to 4 percent and remained at that figure till 1939. Farmers, industrialists, and others thus could obtain capital during the middle and closing thirties at a cost lower than it had been at any time since World War I. The earlier dearth of capital had largely become a thing of the past. Finland was moving toward the position of a capital-exporting country.

It is in the light of this fact—which reflected the notable economic growth summarized in a preceding section of this chapter —that the position of the republic as a debtor country, which caused much American comment after 1932, can best be understood. A sound national economy and a rational state budget policy made it possible for Finland to ride the crosscurrents of the depression years and to reach the close of the decade of the thirties with state finances in excellent shape, an unimpaired record as a borrower, and a debt burden relatively lighter than any since the establishment of independence.

The general financial condition of the country may be indicated, in a simplified form, (1) by setting up a balance sheet that shows, in broad terms, the nation's economic relations to the outside world; (2) by drawing a similar balance sheet that records the revenues and expenditures of the national government; and (3) by noting the status of the national debt, domestic and foreign.

The balance sheet that gives the amounts of Finland's payments to and receipts from other countries between 1923 and 1937 is indicated in Table 16. The amounts are annual averages. During

TABLE 16

BALANCE OF TRADE, 1923–1937

(in millions of marks)

Income		Expenditure	
Exports	5,910	Imports	5,610
Shipping freights	290	Interest payments	400
From tourists	180	By tourists	180
Emigrants' remittances	160	Insurance premiums	130
Insurance premiums	120	Other	80
Harbor dues	60		
Other	100		
Total	6,820		6,400
Less Expenditure	6,400		
Surplus	420		

Source: *S.T.V.*, 1938, Table 100, and *Unitas*, 1938, No. 4, p. 140.

these years the average annual surplus was close to $10,000,000. Between 1931 and 1936, it was two to three times this figure. While the surplus was not large, it kept the balance of payments favorable to Finland and enabled the country to escape the difficulties that an adverse balance would have created. The total surplus from 1923 to 1937 approximated $195,000,000 and played an important part in the reduction of the foreign debt.

The balance sheet of the national government assumed the form shown in Table 17 in 1925–39. Both the revenue and the expenditure columns furnish interesting information. As regards income, the effect of the depression stands clearly revealed during the crucial years 1929–32. Revenue dropped at an alarming rate until 1932, having contracted by that time to about three fifths of the revenue of 1928. Not until 1937 did state revenue fully recover the ground lost since 1929.

Expenditures exceeded income even before the depression set in.

TABLE 17

NATIONAL GOVERNMENT REVENUE AND EXPENDITURE
(in millions of marks)

Year	Revenue	Expenditure
1925	3,682	3,952
1927	3,986	3,988
1929	4,432	4,508
1931	3,975	4,245
1932	2,925	3,100
1933	3,300	3,247
1934	4,135	4,100
1935	4,559	4,533
1936	4,870	4,861
1937	5,984	5,998
1938	5,535	5,433

The deficits ranged from roughly $7,000,000 in 1925 to over $800,000 in 1928. Much of the deficit during these years, and later also, derived from so-called capital expenditure and not from current expenditure. This meant that public funds were being used in various ways to increase the assets of the state. Some of the assets acquired were productive of revenue and others not. In 1928 capital expenditures approximated one third of all expenditures, in 1930 about one fourth, and in 1934 over one third. In other words, investment of national funds rather than the yearly expenses of government accounted for much of the deficits before 1939.

The economic conditions after 1929 brought Parliament face to face with the difficult task of keeping state finances sound by curtailing expenses. Shrinking income seemed to make smaller expenses not only desirable but imperative, even if employment and other problems compelled the legislators to appropriate funds for purposes that had not hitherto burdened the budget. The course of action chosen by Parliament is shown by Table 17. Expenditures were pared down year by year until 1932, when conditions had improved sufficiently to reduce the deficit to the small sum of about $500,000. The following year produced a surplus of over $1,500,000. The budget makers once more felt free to expand various kinds of state services, and by 1937 the expense items in the budget were over 90 percent greater than in 1932. The government and the legislators during these years appear to have rejected the notion that economic recovery can be speeded and prosperity held captive by means of lavish expenditure of public money. National finances were handled according to the simpler rule that expanding outgo must be based upon increasing income and that income can be reasonably increased only if and when the sources of revenue permit such action.

An important aspect of the taxation policy and also of the distribution of the cost of government is disclosed by the income and property taxes. The extent to which incomes were taxed is revealed by Table 18, which pertains to 1935, a typical post-depression year. It indicates the categories of income subject to taxation, the total number of persons in each category, the rate of taxation, and the total amount collected from each of the thirteen groups into which Finnish law divided the persons liable to an income levy. The amounts shown in the table are given in dollars, in order to make comparison easier.

The rate of the tax, given in percentages, must be explained at the outset. Within each category, Finnish law provided for two rates. The lower rate applied to the minimum income within the category, and the higher applied to that part of the income in the category which exceeded the minimum. To illustrate: The lowest taxable category covers net incomes from about $220 to about $330. An income of $300 meant a tax computed as follows: The first $220 was taxed at the minimum of .6 percent of the sum, or $1.32. The difference between $220 and the income of $300, amounting to $70, was taxed at 1.6 percent, the maximum percentage within this category, and yielded $1.12. The total tax on an income of $300 was therefore $2.44, and the percentage of the tax .813.

Table 18 invites several comments. In the first place, it is obvious that incomes far down the scale were included among those subject to taxation. Secondly, the number of upper-limit incomes was surprisingly low, in that only twenty persons had net incomes in excess of $33,000. Thirdly, the spread of the tax rate was great; the

TABLE 18
TAXATION OF INCOME, 1935

Net income (in dollars)	Number taxed	Rate of tax percentage	Amount collected (in dollars)
Less than 220	none	none	none
220–330	165,958	0.6–1.6	366,000
330–660	112,132	1–3	735,000
660–990	18,580	2–5	370,000
990–1,320	8,640	3–7	342,000
1,320–1,650	4,135	4–9	272,000
1,650–1,980	2,292	5–11	266,000
1,980–2,970	2,904	6–12	480,000
2,970–3,960	1,034	8–16	313,000
3,960–7,700	954	10–18	598,000
7,700–11,880	177	14–20	253,000
11,880–19,800	96	16–21	243,000
19,800–33,000	34	18–23	158,000
Over 33,000	20	20–	230,000
Total	316,956		

lowest groups paid a little more than one fortieth of the percentage contributed by the opulent twenty in the highest bracket. The former paid on an average $2.00 per income, and the latter approximately $11,500. About 178,000 incomes in the two lowest classes contributed some $1,100,000 in taxes, while less than 1,300 incomes in the five highest yielded $1,382,000.

What this schedule of taxation meant to the taxpayer can be stated in simple terms by noting the following figures:

Net income	Tax paid
$ 300	$ 2.44
600	11.40
1,200	44.40
3,500	331.40
5,000	421.20
10,000	1,538.00
15,000	2,979.32
20,000	3,840.00

City and municipal taxation was limited by law to income taxes only; property taxes constituted the special domain of the national government. The levy imposed from year to year by city or rural authorities varied a good deal as to both amount and locality. Helsinki, for example, imposed an income tax of 8 percent in 1920, 6.5 percent in 1930, 7.9 percent in 1935, and 7 percent in 1937. In Turku, during the same years, the tax was 9.65 percent, 8.5 percent, 11 percent, 10 percent. In some localities the tax was occasionally as low as 5 percent, but the average was between 7 and 9 percent. Local taxation should, of course, be added to the levies of the national government. This meant that Mr. Smith, whom we assume to be a resident in Turku and whose net income was $5,000 in 1935, paid the following tax on his income: $421.20 to the national government and $550 to the municipality of Turku. The total therefore came to $971.20, which represented close to 20 percent of Mr. Smith's income. In Helsinki, where the local levy was 7.9 percent, he would have paid $395 in municipal taxes and a total income tax of $816.20.

It is clear that so-called large incomes were practically nonexistent and that taxation was steeply graduated. The nation was free from those inequalities of the distribution of the income tax burden which placed the main weight on the shoulders of the little fellow. In 1935, out of nearly 317,000 incomes subjected to taxation, less than 1,300 were as high as $4,000. Of the total revenue from income taxes, the 54 incomes of more than $19,800 furnished about 10 percent, and the 1,300 incomes of more than about $4,000 contributed well over 33 percent of the total.

The taxation of property as distinguished from income rested on the same broad principle as the income tax. The nature of the tax is shown in Table 19. (The property subject to taxation and the revenue yielded by the various categories are given in dollar equivalents of the Finnish mark.) As regards the two percentages applicable to each category, they applied to property in the same way as the corresponding percentages, explained above, applied to income.

Table 19 requires no comment beyond the observation that taxation of property rested on a basis which either exempted the small owner from taxation or forced him to pay only a moderate tax. Over 73,000 out of a total of 88,516 paid a tax that amounted to

TABLE 19
NATIONAL TAXATION OF PROPERTY, 1935

Value of property (in dollars)	Number of owners taxed	Rate of tax percentage	Amount collected (in dollars)
Less than 2,200	none	none	none
2,200–3,100	43,035	0.15–0.3	17,200
3,100–6,200	30,222	0.2 –0.6	38,500
6,200–12,400	10,241	0.4 –1.2	53,600
12,400–19,800	2,267	0.8 –2.0	36,000
19,800–26,400	918	1.2 –2.8	28,900
26,400–33,000	509	1.6 –3.6	26,800
33,000–35,200	312	2.0 –4.4	24,900
35,200–59,400	456	2.4 –4.8	62,000
59,400–79,200	177	3.2 –6.4	43,100
79,200–158,400	244	4.0 –7.2	129,300
158,400–237,600	66	5.6 –8.0	78,000
237,600–352,200	45	6.4 –8.4	94,000
352,200–726,000	11	7.2 –9.2	39,200
Over 726,000	13	8.0 –8.0	100,600
Total	88,516		

less than 1 percent and an additional 10,000 paid only a fraction more. The thirteen largest property owners, whose holdings came to $726,000 or over, paid nearly one seventh of the total tax, and the amount they contributed was only slightly less than the sum paid by the 83,500 owners in the first three groups. A nation of small property owners is indicated by the evidence: 85,765 owned property valued at less than $20,000, only 2,751 owned property taxed at more than that figure, and of these only 577 belonged in the $60,000 class. Corporations of various kinds (not including cooperatives and the like) contributed a little over 50 percent of all the income and property taxes collected in 1935.[7]

As regards the broader aspects of taxation, it may be noted that the total annual revenue of the government derived from the following sources. About 23 cents of every dollar of revenue came from income, property, and inheritance taxes. Approximately 17 cents

[7] The figures and Tables 18 and 19 are based on detailed official statistics in S.T.V., 1938, pp. 261–63, 274–82.

represented the net return from various government enterprises, such as the state railways, the postal and telegraph services, forests, interest and dividends on state loans, and the share of the state in the profits of the Bank of Finland. Indirect taxes yielded about 50 cents, and the remaining 10 cents came from miscellaneous sources. The gross revenue of state-run economic undertakings or of undertakings in which the state participated produced a gross revenue in 1937 that amounted to about 16 percent of the total, despite the marked growth of the total revenues of the year.

Leaving capital expenditures aside, the annual income of the national government between 1928 and the late thirties was distributed as follows: Out of every dollar spent, 18.8 cents went for educational purposes; about 19 cents were absorbed by national defense, and a fraction over 14 cents went to interest charges or amortization payments on the national debt. Agricultural improvement and land settlement undertakings received 7.5 cents, the maintenance of peace and order absorbed 7 cents, public health about 7 cents, and the administration of justice a fraction over 4 cents. These services took a total of about 75 cents out of every tax dollar; the remaining 25 cents were used for a variety of other purposes.

Just as it may be said that no man escapes death and taxes, so it may be claimed that no modern state, be it large or small, escapes debts. One of the conspicuous features of the modern state is the fact that it is in perpetual debt, and there appears to be no likelihood that statesmanship will soon free government from this perennial burden.

Finland was no exception to the general rule during 1919–39. The national debt was comparatively insignificant, to be sure. Its size and nature are shown by Table 20. While foreign debt was much more important in 1925 than domestic debt, the position had been reversed by 1937. Regarding the debt as a whole, the high point was reached, as would be expected, during the depression. The notable decrease of the foreign debt and the increase of the domestic debt reflected an improvement in the economy of Finland. The total debt of the country in 1937 amounted to approximately $75,000,000. Of this sum, about $29,000,000 represented foreign debt. At the end of 1938, the foreign debt, including the debt to the United States,

TABLE 20

THE NATIONAL DEBT, 1925–1938

(in millions of marks)

Year	Domestic debt	Foreign debt	Total
1925	761	1,714	2,475
1930	357	2,700	3,057
1933	765	2,742	3,507
1935	1,258	1,908	3,166
1936	1,934	1,185	3,119
1937	2,531	921	3,452
1939	2,595	776	3,371

Source: *Unitas*, 1938, No. 4, pp. 140–45, 1939, No. 1, pp. 6–8; *S.T.V.*, 1938, p. 260.

was reported as about $12,100,000. The revenue-producing assets owned by the state were estimated at nearly four times the value of the total debt and nonproductive state property at roughly one half of the value of the other assets. It was therefore clear that the public debt of the republic in the closing 1930s was small. It amounted in 1937 to less than $20 per capita.

The debt of Finland to the United States stood in a special category. It originated in a great national calamity, the famine conditions of 1918. It grew out of the food purchases made possible by the fortunate circumstance that Herbert Hoover, the United States Relief Administrator in Europe, gave aid to the starving nation when aid was most desperately needed. Strictly speaking, the debt was owed to the United States Grain Corporation and not to the government of the United States. When the original purchase of foodstuffs was negotiated, no definite arrangements for payments were specified. Some payments were shortly made, however, and it was agreed that the debt of $8,300,000 was to be paid in June, 1921; the interest rate was fixed at 5 percent. The debt was not paid in 1921, and a new agreement was therefore needed. In March, 1922, the World War Foreign Debt Commission and Finland funded the debt in a manner that resulted in more liberal terms. The interest rate was reduced, on amounts unpaid prior to December, 1922, to 4.5 percent. During the remainder of the period of payment, fixed at 62 years, Finland was to pay interest at 3 percent for the first ten years and 3.5 percent thereafter. The interest was payable in June and December every year and was regularly paid after the agreement went into effect. The half-yearly payments included a part of the principal also, which stood at $8,150,000 in December, 1939.

The economic development of the nation from the early twenties to the closing thirties may be summed up by saying that it spelled exceptional progress along all lines. An all-important agrarian reform was completed, and the general position of the farmer class was greatly improved. Industry expanded more rapidly than the most optimistic observers could have predicted. In the industrial advance of these years, the worker shared to a greater extent than ever before; his income increased enough to give him a greatly improved standard of living. Finally, the finances of the state were kept in good condition. Both at home and abroad, the state avoided the adoption of default as a policy even when default seemed to promise relief from both domestic and foreign difficulties.

XI

Foreign Relations, 1919–1939

THE ÅLAND ISLAND QUESTION

The basic purpose of Finland's foreign policy after 1918–19 was to defend and shore up the security and independence of the nation. The purpose could be best achieved, in the opinion of governments and Parliament alike, by avoiding conflicts and war with other nations. Such a course was not a matter of choice or preference resting on abstract considerations; it was seen as a necessity dictated by the requirements of basic national interests. The policy followed during the years between the two world wars thus spelled peaceful relations with all nations, large and small. It also meant a scrupulous observance of international commitments and obligations—witness the uninterrupted payments of the debt to the United States during the years when default was the policy chosen by debtor nations of larger pretensions—and, in the event of war between foreign powers, strict neutrality and noninvolvement. The Åland Island question offered the first important measure of Finland's pacific foreign policy.

The Åland Island question arose in 1918 and remained a major problem till 1921. It was brought to the fore by an attempt to unite the islands with Sweden and by Finland's determination to keep them.

The Åland Islands lie between Finland and Sweden, at the mouth of the Gulf of Bothnia, and control the entrance to the gulf. They had belonged administratively and in other ways to the Finnish part of the Swedish kingdom before 1809 and were ceded with Finland to Russia in that year. They became an object of interest to European Powers in the 1850s, during the Crimean War. At the instance of Sweden, the peacemakers at the close of the Crimean War took up the question of the demilitarization of the islands. The result was an international treaty concluded in 1856 whereby Russia agreed not to maintain fortifications or military or naval establishments in the islands.

Demilitarization was observed by Russia until the first decade of the present century. During the years before World War I, however, Russia attempted to free itself from the territorial servitude that demilitarization meant. In 1907 Russia came to a secret understanding with Germany whereby Germany abandoned for its part the demand that the islands remain unfortified. In 1908 a new general international agreement left the situation unchanged, and there the matter rested till the war broke out in 1914. Beginning in 1915, Russia proceeded to erect extensive fortifications on Åland but Britain and France assured Sweden, whose government had become alarmed by the militarization of the islands, that the fortifications would be demolished at the end of the war.

The Åland Islands had thus been intermittently a major item among the international problems of northern Europe long before they became a bone of contention between Finland and Sweden. When the question came to the fore in 1918, however, it involved not only demilitarization but the application of the principle of national self-determination to the Åland population with a view to uniting them to Sweden.

At the time, the resident Åland population was approximately 22,000. It was almost wholly Swedish-speaking, in that only 4–5 percent of the inhabitants spoke Finnish. (In the eastern part of the extensive archipelago which reaches in a more or less continuous belt of islands to the mainland but is not considered a part of the Åland Islands, the Finnish-speaking element was close to 50 percent of the total.) The Åland province was, in fact, more Swedish than any other province of Finland. Down to 1917–18, the inhabitants of the islands had considered themselves a part of the Swedish-speaking population in Finland, had at no time shown separatist tendencies, and had given the Swede-Finns some of their important leaders.

In August, 1917, a secret movement for the inclusion of Åland in Sweden made its appearance in the islands. That the movement was encouraged from Sweden appears definitely proven.[1] While some Swedes had considered the possibility of obtaining the islands already in 1914–15—for instance, there was talk at the time among the Finnish independence men and their Swedish friends of ceding the islands to Sweden in return for military and other aid—and while some Swedish newspapers began to write about the question in the autumn of 1917, Swedish interest in the matter remained dormant for several months. It had not become in any sense marked by January 4, 1918, when Sweden became the first country after Russia to accord unqualified recognition to Finland's territorial sovereignty and independence.

Within about a month, however, the situation changed. In February—the war in Finland had begun late in January—Sweden sent troops to Åland, which was then being successfully freed from its Russian garrisons by Finnish soldiers who received important aid from the local population. Sweden claimed at the time and later that the troops had been sent to the islands to prevent the loss of life and the destruction of property. Acting upon the advice of the Stockholm authorities, which brought the Soviet representative in Stockholm to Åland, the Swedes negotiated with the Finns and the Russians in Åland for the cessation of military operations and the withdrawal of both Finnish and Russian forces from the islands. Because the Finns were prevented from keeping in adequate contact with their command—important instructions to them were either intercepted or delayed in Stockholm—they were persuaded to disarm and were sent home by way of Sweden. The Russians likewise withdrew but without leaving their arms.

In the meantime the Ålanders' agitation for separation from Finland gained ground, partly because of the sympathetic Swedish

[1] This is a controversial question. The Finns assert that the movement was begun in and supported from Sweden. Swedish writers avoid the allegation or deny it. My conclusion is based primarily upon the documents published by J. R. Danielson-Kalmari in his *Ahvenanmaan Asia Vuosina 1914–1920* (Helsinki, 1920; a French edition under the title *La Question des Iles d'Aland de 1914 a 1920* appeared in 1921) and upon the testimony of the Ålander Otto Anderson who lived in Åland in 1917–18. He has told his story in *Les Origines de la Question d'Aland en 1917–1918* (Helsinki, 1920).

response to their cause. A special deputation was sent to Stockholm. It waited upon the king on February 2. On behalf of the Ålanders, the deputation expressed the hope that their province would be "reunited to Sweden" and that the objective would be reached by means of an understanding between Sweden and Finland.

For reasons that are easy to understand, Sweden approved of the aspirations of the Ålanders and undertook to sponsor their cause. On the twentieth of February, the government addressed a communication to the leading Powers which disclosed an active interest in the solution of the Åland question in accordance with the separatist aspirations of the Ålanders. It stated among other things that, in the opinion of the Swedish government, the question of the sovereignty of the islands should be settled between Finland and Sweden, and that the question of the fortification or neutralization of the islands should be settled at the general peace congress at the end of the war.[2]

In the course of a few weeks Sweden had thus committed itself to (1) a military expedition to Åland; (2) a favorable attitude toward the aspirations of the Ålanders and an acceptance of the view that Finland's sovereignty over the islands, which had not been questioned when Finland's independence was recognized, was subject to debate and should be determined by negotiation between the two countries; and (3) the stand that the question of demilitarization would be decided by an international conference.

The Finns emphatically protested against Sweden's policy and procedure. They saw in it nothing less than a thinly disguised attempt to acquire territory belonging to a friendly state. The sending of Swedish troops to the islands was deeply resented as a violation of territorial sovereignty. The disarming of the Finnish troops appeared doubly galling because it had been accomplished in a manner that seemingly implicated responsible Swedish officials. The agitation of the Ålanders was ultimately labeled as treason and the Swedes who gave it direct or indirect support were charged with conniving

[2] This is shown by the British reply to the communication. It is published by Mr. H. Hellner, the Swedish Minister for Foreign Affairs at the time, in *Memorandum rörande Sveriges politik: Förhållande till Finland under tiden från Finlands självständighetsförklaring till det finska inbördeskrigets slut* (Stockholm, 1936), pp. 29–30. H. Gummerus' *Sverige och Finland 1917–1918* (Helsinki, 1936) is highly informative and should be read in conjunction with Hellner's memorandum.

at treason. The application of the principle of national self-determination to a group of 22,000 people was pronounced as an absurd idea destructive of the fundamental interests of state and nation.

Undaunted by Finnish opposition, the Ålanders persisted in their effort. Plebiscites were held that showed them to be virtually unanimous in the desire to be united to Sweden. Supported by the Swedish government, they presented their case at the Paris Peace Conference early in 1919. The conference referred the matter to one of its committees, but no action was taken and the Peace Conference completed its labors without any attempt to find a solution of the problem. Through 1919 and 1920 the question agitated Swede, Finn, and Ålander. At the instance of Sweden, it was brought before the League of Nations in the autumn of 1919. The League proceeded to deal with the matter by submitting two questions to a committee of jurists. One was, in substance: Does the Åland question fall—as Finland contended it did—solely within Finland's jurisdiction? The other related to the demilitarization of the islands. Regarding the first, the decision was against Finland; the answer to the second was that the demilitarization agreement of 1856 was still in force and that the state to which Åland belonged was bound by it. The Council of the League accepted the report.

The Council thereupon resolved to appoint a committee of three to examine the facts in the dispute—the committee was thus to function as a jury weighing the evidence—and to submit its findings to the Council in order to enable that body to formulate a decision "favorable to the maintenance of Peace in that great part of the world." The committee appointed consisted of Abram I. Elkus, an American, Felix Calonder, a Swiss, and Baron Beyens, a Belgian. They visited Sweden, Finland, and the islands, and carefully surveyed the pertinent facts. Their report was placed before the Council on June 20, 1921.

The report held that the islands were clearly under Finnish sovereignty. It rejected the idea of a plebiscite but did not support Finland's contention that the Åland dispute was purely domestic. The question was considered international because it had developed to a point that made it "necessary to submit it to the high authority which the League of Nations represents in the eyes of the world."

The conclusion thus ignored the question of sovereignty as a decisive factor and held that the League could act and prescribe in order to preserve peace. It also implied another conclusion, namely, that the principle that the League had full jurisdiction should be recognized not only by Sweden and Finland, the two parties to the case, but by all interested in the evolution of the League into an organization capable of effectively dealing with situations threatening war.

The report led to further debate before the Council. In the course of it Finland bound herself in advance to accept the Council's decision: Finland "would strictly observe the Covenant and carry out the promises she has made on becoming a member of the League." Sweden hedged: Sweden "is prepared loyally to attribute to the decision of the Council its full value under the Covenant. Nevertheless, future events may take place independently of the will of [Sweden], creating a new situation in the Islands, which it may be impossible to consider as covered by the decision of the Council."

The Council's decision was embodied in several resolutions adopted on June 24, 1921. The decision provided, in substance, that (1) Finland had sovereign rights in the Åland Islands; (2) the islands would be organized as a self-governing province; (3) in order to safeguard the "Swedish nationality" of the islanders, Swedish was to be the language of government, administration, and the schools and the islanders might provide instruction in Finnish only if the separate Åland districts so decided; (4) Finnish citizens from outside the islands might own real estate in the islands and enjoy the rights of citizenship, but could acquire local voting and other rights only after a residence of five years; (5) the President of Finland was to appoint a governor for the islands, but only after prior agreement with the Speaker of the Åland Provincial Assembly; and (6) Finland guaranteed that the islands would be neutralized—that is, freed of any military installations—and would not ever become a source of danger or a threat to any foreign power.

The decision of the Council was accepted, without reservations, by Sweden as well as Finland. Finland had undertaken to accommodate the separatist islanders well over a year before the Council issued its pronouncement. A law enacted on May 5, 1920, provided for extensive rights of self-rule. After the decision of the League, the

Finnish government proceeded to carry into effect the guarantees and provisions put forth in the Council's recommendations of June 24, 1921. The necessary legislation was put on the books on December 9, 1921. A special "guarantee law" was enacted in 1922. Finally, the demilitarization and neutralization of the islands was provided by an agreement signed in Geneva on October 20, 1921. The treaty was signed by Britain, Denmark, Finland, France, Germany, Italy, Latvia, Poland, and Sweden, and went into effect on April 6, 1922.

The system of self-rule in Åland since 1922—it was redefined by a new law in 1952—is democratic and liberal in the strictest sense of the word. Both the machinery of self-government and the areas within which it operates illustrate the broad limits within which the Ålanders are masters of their own house.

The most conspicuous organ of self-rule is the Provincial Assembly of thirty members chosen for a three-year period. The Assembly meets annually. It is empowered to enact laws for the islands except regarding matters reserved to the National Parliament (such as constitutional questions, foreign affairs, defense, criminal law, the administration of justice, the finances of the republic, etc.). The Assembly has the right to initiate, through the national government, legislative measures for consideration by the Parliament regarding matters outside its own competence. The Provincial Assembly also elects the executive, the so-called Provincial Government of seven members headed by a Provincial Councilor who must enjoy the confidence of the Assembly. The organizational arrangements are topped by a Provincial Governor who is in charge of matters of general, national concern. He is appointed by the President of the republic, after prior agreement with the Speaker of the Provincial Assembly.

The costs of maintaining the organizations and personnel required by the autonomy are for the most part defrayed by the Ålanders themselves, but the national treasury has assumed part of the costs —not always with results satisfactory to all concerned—by means of "equalization contributions." The law grants extensive nationality guarantees intended to ensure the continuation of the Swedish language and nationality of the islanders. Swedish is the only official language in Åland; instruction in the Finnish language can be given only if local authorities give their consent; the language of instruction in state-supported schools is Swedish. The acquisition of land or real estate by non-islanders is greatly restricted.

Male Ålanders are exempted from military service and, for all practical purposes, also from "civilian service" which the law permits as a substitute for military service. The special rights and privileges granted to Åland can be altered only with the consent of the Ålanders.

As regards Finland and Sweden, the irritation and friction created by the controversy disappeared surprisingly quickly. By the middle twenties, the Åland problem had ceased to be a source of discussion and debate. Ten years later, Sweden joined hands with Finland in a cooperative effort to cancel the international agreement providing for the demilitarization of the islands. The former parties to an international "law suit" had become active partners in pursuing an objective that the defense needs of both had defined as a common concern.

PROBLEMS OF NEUTRALITY

The unqualified commitment to neutrality as the basic policy after 1918–19 was confirmed by Finland's confidence in the League of Nations and the acceptance of the obligations of membership in the League. The policy was convincingly illustrated shortly after the achievement of independence by the refusal to become involved in a potentially anti-Russian coalition composed of Poland and other border states.

One of the foreign policy alternatives offered to Finland in 1921 was to become a part of the *cordon sanitaire* sponsored by France for the purpose of containing communist Russia. Poland took the lead in the effort to include Finland and the three Baltic states Estonia, Latvia, and Lithuania in the contemplated alliance. Polish efforts resulted in an agreement signed in Warsaw on March 17, 1922. The Finnish Foreign Minister, Rudolf Holsti, attended the drafting of the Warsaw agreement and stood ready to bring Finland into the border-states' bloc. The attempt precipitated lengthy and critical discussion in the Finnish press and Parliament. The cabinet itself was divided on the matter. The result was that Parliament refused to follow Holsti's lead, shelved the question of ratification, repudiated the Foreign Minister by voting no confidence, and forced him to resign. The debate on the question showed an overwhelming majority in Parliament in favor of neutrality as the only safe policy. The defeat of the Holsti policy marked the permanent end of maneuvers to associate Finland with any risky "border-states" policy. The same preference and commitment had in fact been recorded in the fall of 1919 when White Russian and other interests had attempted to entice Finland to join in the Yudenitch effort to take Petrograd. Finland refused to take part in the proposed joint operation and thus recorded a decision that marked, in a concrete manner, the beginning of a neutrality policy that was undeviatingly followed until the Soviet invasion in 1939 forced war upon the country.

Finland's policy of neutrality rested in part on assumptions regarding the League of Nations that turned out to be unrealistic in the long run. The League was seen in the early years of its existence as exerting influence and power which in fact it did not have. The harsh realities beneath the surface of the international order created by the Paris peace settlement and in part contoured after 1920 by the League itself were ignored. The League was not, events were to show, an organization able to secure peace; only a military alliance commanding adequate force and able to act effectively could prevent war or end it quickly once an aggressor had precipitated war.

Contrary to a widely accepted notion during the twenties and the early thirties, League membership meant, by ordinary definition, abandonment of neutrality under certain circumstances and readiness to take action against states unwilling to observe the obligations the League charter imposed. If the obligations of membership were taken literally, no member could actually remain neutral in international situations threatening the peace. Each member undertook "to respect and preserve as against external aggression the territorial integrity and existing independence" of all members. The Council was to decide "the means by which this obligation shall be fulfilled." Also, should a member resort to war "in disregard of its covenants . . . it shall *ipso facto* be deemed to have committed an act of war against all the other members of the League." The League would thereupon indicate the coercive measures to be used against the culprit. They ranged from severance of trade and financial relations to the use of military force.

The international situation and crises before the late thirties did not lead to League decisions calling for an abandonment of neutrality and the use of effective military force or other deterrent coercive action. Poland's aggression against Lithuania in 1920, Lithuania's defiance of the League itself in Memel in the same year, Japanese aggression in Manchuria in 1931, Italian war and conquest in Ethiopia in 1935–36—all were carried through with the aggressor suffering no punishment except exposure to vigorous finger shaking indulged in by onlookers unwilling to defend the aggrieved and punish the guilty. Only after Hitler began to disturb the peace of Europe by his boldly conceived expansionist program did some of the signatories of the Covenant bestir themselves and ultimately accept war as the only means sufficient to strike down the most dangerous warmonger yet to appear in Germany.

Until Hitlerite Germany began to force a new form of aggression upon the European community, Finland's neutrality policy had been, on the whole, an uneventful chapter in the nation's foreign affairs since 1919. The resolve not to deviate from neutrality appeared by the mid-thirties to have been not only a good way but the best way to serve the interests of the republic. Neutrality was an excellent and unassailable policy: it harmed nobody, it threatened the security of no nation, and it met fully the requirements of justice and fair dealing. It was therefore taken for granted that it would yield satisfactory returns by giving the nation immunity to international disturbances creating war.

By 1935, however, it had become clear that the commitment to neutrality as then understood required redefinition. The reason was the new Big Power constellation created by Hitler's actions in 1933–35. Finland's reaction to the results, as seen and measured at the time, of Hitler's unilateral violations of the Treaty of Versailles —the introduction of conscription, the creation of an air force, the remilitarization of the Rhineland, and the rest—was to redefine the meaning of neutrality and its requirements. The new definition was in part a clarification of conceptions held before 1935 and in part an elaboration of a congenial inclination and commitment of old standing involving Finland's Scandinavian neighbors.

In the face of Hitler's "acts of defiance" and aggression in 1934–36, the League of Nations again showed itself to be powerless. This is but one way of saying that the Great Powers whose stand alone decided whether the League could or could not effectively check Hitler's progress along the path leading to mounting international conflicts and possible war did not yet bestir themselves. Finland and her Scandinavian neighbors, observing the rising tide of aggression and international anarchy, noting the failure of economic sanctions in the case of Italy, and concluding that the system of sanctions as it then existed could only lead small nations into dangerous difficulties without assuring them real protection or benefits, redefined their affiliation with the League. They declared, in 1936, that they no longer assumed responsibility involved in sanctions, and served notice that they would henceforth follow a policy of strict neutrality, undiluted by any commitments in advance to take sides, in Big Power conflicts, with one Power or Power group against another. A Scandinavian neutrality bloc had thus emerged. It rested on no treaty imposing neutrality on the four states as an obligation mutually shared; it was grounded in views and understandings shared by good neighbors who had quarrels neither among themselves nor with outside states.

The new definition of neutrality put forth by the Nordic nations was accompanied, as far as Finland was concerned, by a restatement and a sharpened clarification of her Scandinavian orientation. Centuries-long history, preferences deeply rooted in common commitments to democratic ways, and general similarity of outlook had meant, long before the 1930s, full Finnish membership in the Nordic family of nations. The controversy with Sweden over the Åland Islands had not changed the situation, for it turned out to be only a temporary rift quickly mended after 1921. These circumstances illumine the background and clarify the foreign policy purposes of

Finland's joining the Oslo group of nations in 1931 and of the important statement of Premier T. M. Kivimäki in Parliament on December 5, 1935.

Under the pressure of the deepening economic world crisis that began with the panic of 1929, Norway, Sweden, Denmark, Belgium, and Luxembourg signed, in December, 1930, a treaty known as the Oslo Convention. The five signatories agreed to apply the "principles which underlie the activities of the League of Nations in the economic field." In pursuing their common purpose, they declared themselves "prepared to support international cooperation which aims at reducing the barriers to trade and to arrive at a general improvement in the conditions" conducive to better economic relations between nations. Finland, finding the purposes of the five states congenial and hopeful, joined the Oslo group in 1931, and thus expanded the area within which the group attempted to lead the world to a policy of lessening trade restrictions. Finland's Oslo group affiliation also meant association with nations whose policies of peace and avoidance of adventuresome purposes in foreign affairs were wholly above suspicion.

The determination to serve emphatic notice on all and sundry that Finland's foreign policy was directed only toward peaceful goals was shown in an unusual way four years later. Speaking in Parliament on December 5, 1935, Premier Kivimäki held that Scandinavia in general and Sweden in particular

is least likely to become involved in war or other dangerous international complications. Scandinavia therefore has the best chances of remaining neutral. Because Finland's interests also demand, above all, the maintaining of neutrality, it is natural that Finland should align herself with Scandinavia, to which our country is tied, more closely than to any other area, not only by . . . history but by economic and cultural ties and consequently by similarity of outlook as well. Finland considers it her responsibility to maintain an army for her defense (contemplated even in the Covenant of the League) in order to protect her neutrality and independence . . . and in order thereby to aid in maintaining the joint neutrality of all the Nordic countries.

Premier Kivimäki's statement, unanimously endorsed by Parliament, initiated or implied no new foreign policy. It was intended once again to define clearly and emphatically the policy of peace unqualifiedly accepted by Finland no less than by the other Scandinavian democracies: "Friendship toward all and entangling alliances with none." The demonstrative manner chosen to proclaim this position gave it special importance. Its purpose was also to refute once again the claim often put forth by the USSR, despite the clear record of neutrality and repeated assertions over the years by Finnish spokesmen, that Finland was following an anti-Soviet policy and was in fact a tool of "imperialist warmongers."

The Finnish declaration was greeted with expressions of satisfaction in the Nordic countries. It prompted Premier P. A. Hansson of Sweden to remark that Kivimäki's statement, which meant a "declaration of a full acceptance of the Scandinavian peace policy by the Government of Finland," had been greeted "with sincere pleasure by all of Sweden." Referring to the four Scandinavian peoples, he said: "We are situated close to each other, we have a common history and a similar culture, and in the course of development toward a richer life . . . the bonds which unite us have become even stronger. . . . We stand as free nations side by side in the League of Nations . . . but our unity gives added strength to our contributions, dictated both by idealism and self-interest, to the safeguarding of peace and liberty." Finland would have been the last to question or repudiate Premier Hansson's statement.

RELATIONS WITH GERMANY

The relations with western Europe and overseas nations were good after World War I. Germany was, in some respects, an exception. During the first few months of independence—especially between March and November, 1918—relations with Germany were close, largely as a result of the military aid received in the closing stages of the war. Germany's collapse in November ended the Finns' wartime pro-German orientation. During the years of the Weimar republic, relations with Germany were normal and friendly. The coming of Hitler changed the situation. As in the other Nordic countries, the Nazi regime was seen in Finland by all but small groups of extremists as an offensive political system. An adequate measure of the limited extent to which Nazi ideology penetrated into Finland is given by the IKL (the Patriotic People's Movement) in the 1930s. The IKL might be labeled, by loose definition, a semi-Nazi party, although its membership was sufficiently heterogeneous to include substantial non-national-socialist elements. In the 1933 election it captured only 14 seats in Parliament, or 7 percent of the total, and in 1939 only 8 seats or 4 percent.

No pacts or political understandings were concluded with Nazi Germany. Finland's rejection of Hitler's proposal in April, 1939, for a nonaggression treaty—Norway, Sweden, and Denmark had received identical invitations, Denmark alone accepting—indicated unmistakable aversion toward any agreement that might suggest closer relations with Hitler's Germany or that could be interpreted as a modification of the "Scandinavian orientation" emphatically defined in 1935.

RELATIONS WITH THE USSR

The Peace of Dorpat in 1920 did not mark the end of difficulties with the Russians. The relations between Finland and the Soviets during the interwar years, while not marred by major conflicts, were disturbed by occasional friction and problems. They were caused by Russian violations of what the Finns considered to be binding provisions of the Dorpat peace regarding East Karelia; by Finnish volunteer troops that supported local revolts in Soviet Karelia; by the activities of Finnish Communists who had escaped to the Soviet in 1918; and in general by Communist endeavors serving the revolutionary purposes of the leaders in the Kremlin. In the closing thirties more ominous Soviet purposes darkened the horizon when the USSR came forth with demands for Finnish territory—kept secret at the time—allegedly in the interests of Soviet security.

The Dorpat peace treaty provided among other things that Finland would withdraw her forces from the Repola and Porajärvi districts along the eastern border occupied during the attempt, in 1920, of the inhabitants of these districts to seek union with Finland. Article 10 of the treaty stated in part that the provinces in question "will be reunited with the Russian state and will form . . . the autonomous East Karelian area [inhabited by Karelians] that enjoys rights of national self-determination." The details of the arrangements were stated, "for the benefit of the local population" of the districts to be included in the autonomous area, in Article 11. The article provided in part for a complete amnesty for and the freeing of individuals guilty of actions committed because of the recent "state of war or because of political reasons." The treaty also stated that the inhabitants of the two districts were free to move, with their property, to Finland. The right had to be exercised, however, within a year of the coming into force of the treaty.

Developments in 1921–23 showed that the conclusion of the Dorpat treaty did not prevent future difficulty and friction. Uprisings occurred in East Karelia, caused by dissatisfaction over the East Karelian Socialist Soviet Republic and its rule. Several thousand Finnish volunteers, hoping for a union of East Karelia with Finland, took part in the revolts. They failed to improve the lot of the East Karelians and merely succeeded in compromising their own country. As the result of the Karelian problem, Finland was regarded by the Soviets as an aggressor intent on territorial gain. The situation was not eased by Finland's attempt to champion the East Karelians' cause before a larger international forum.

On the occasion of the signing of the treaty, the leader of the Russian delegation, J. A. Berzin, offered three declarations, one of which related to self-government in East Karelia:

The Russian Socialist Federative Soviet Republic guarantees to the Karelian population in the governments of Archangel and Olonets the following rights:

1. The Karelian population in the governments of Archangel and Olonets enjoys the rights of national self-determination.

2. The part of East Karelia inhabited by this population constitutes a territory, autonomous in its internal affairs, belonging on federative principles to the Russian State.

3. Questions relating to this territory are decided by a popular representative body, elected by the local population, which enjoys the right of self-taxation for the needs of the territory, to issue ordinances affecting local interests, and to organize matters of internal administration.

4. The language of the local population is the language of the administration, the jurisdiction and the popular education.

5. The autonomous territory of East Karelia has the right to organize its economic life according to its local needs and in conformity with the general economic organization of the Republic.

6. In connection with the reorganization of the military measure of defense of the Russian Republic a militia will be organized on the autonomous territory of East Karelia with a view to the elimination of the standing army and the substitution for it of a popular militia for local defense purposes.

In the Finnish view, the provision of the treaty and the content of the declaration bound Russia to grant the East Karelians genuine autonomy and "national" and language rights essential for the preservation of the East Karelians as a separate national and cultural entity. This view, which also implied, it was contended, an obligation toward Finland, was held by Finland's government after 1920. It was vociferously urged, especially by the more aggressive nationalist groups among the university students. Failing to persuade the Soviets that its interpretation of the treaty was the correct one, Finland brought the matter before the Hague Court of International Justice. The court refused to consider the question because the Soviets did not recognize its competence to decide the matter. The Assembly of the League of Nations, to which Finland thereupon submitted the case, agreed (on September 24, 1922) that the East Karelian question was important, took note of the stand of Finland in the matter, and suggested, with a view to a successful future solution satisfactory to all concerned, that additional information regarding the question be collected. On the international level, this ended the consideration of the East Karelian question. It remained for several years an irritating question exploited by noisy extremists intent on pressing a case which by its very nature was weak and could not, under any foreseeable circumstances, be successfully pursued.[3]

[3] The Finns' case was especially weak because of the following fact. A careful reading of the Berzin declaration shows that it merely stated what, allegedly, existing conditions in East Karelia already were. In the Russian view, the treaty and the declaration therefore imposed no new obligations regarding the Karelians' self-rule. Incidentally, the French version of the treaty and the declaration uses the future tense in referring to autonomy,

Other indications of Soviet policy and purposes came to the surface after 1920. Many of the extremist revolutionary leaders of the January–May, 1918, revolution in Finland, including the ranking members of the revolutionaries, had escaped to Russia in the closing days of the war, leaving tens of thousands of their followers to face the consequences of their failure to overthrow the country's legal government and constitutional order. The revolutionaries in Russia established the "Communist party of Finland" late in 1918 and proceeded to labor, by means of underground agents and propaganda, for the day when the failure of the 1918 revolt would be canceled by a future victory of the Marxist cause.

In Finland itself, the political activity of the Communists was carried forward, as we have noted, by a party organization functioning under several names. The first was the Socialist Workers' party of Finland, launched in 1920. It captured 27 seats in the 1922 election. The party was dissolved in 1925 by a Supreme Court decision that labeled it a treasonous organization laboring on behalf of a foreign power. The decision did not end the Communists' endeavors, however. While their case was still in the courts, they established a new party, the Workers' and Small Farmers' party. It appeared in time to participate in the 1924 election and obtained 18 seats. The Workers' and Small Farmers' party was recognized, no less clearly than its predecessor had been, as a Communist organization following the leadership of Moscow. It escaped being charged in court with treasonable activity, however, and registered more solid gains in later elections. In 1929 it increased its representation in Parliament to 29. It was outlawed in 1930 after considerable agitation and dis-

language, and the like. The Russian (and Finnish) text states that "the Karelian population *enjoys* the right of self-determination"; the French version: the population "*shall enjoy*" the right. The Russian text: "the language of the local population *is* the language of government"; the French version: the language "*shall be* the language of government." (Italics mine.) See Carl Enckell, *Poliittiset Muistelmani*, II (Helsinki, 1960), 176–78; *Suomen ja Venäjän Välisten Tartossa Pidettyjen Rauhanneuvottelujen Pöytäkirjat* (the Minutes of the Dorpat Peace Conference) (Helsinki, 1921), pp. 137–38; *Suomen Asetusko-koelma* (hereafter referred to as *S.A.*), 1921, No. 21, pp. 64–68. Enckell remarks: "The Finnish Government did not think the errors in translation [in the French version] of decisive importance. The Soviet declarations were considered as promises given to Finland which Finland had a right to insist be fulfilled."

turbances originally precipitated by especially challenging Communist activities in the fall of 1929. Meantime the Communists had succeeded in getting control of several important labor unions and had split the national Federation of Labor Unions.

The actions and intrigues of the Communists, understandably interpreted by non-Communists as evidence of Moscow's determination to interfere in Finland's internal affairs, did not prevent Finland and the Soviets—officially the Union of Soviet Socialist Republics (USSR) after 1922—from reaching agreement regarding a host of practical matters. Treaties and conventions covering fishing rights, the use of coastal and other waters in the Gulf of Finland, Lake Ladoga, and the River Neva, trade and commerce, pilot services, the telegraph, postal and mail services, railroad traffic, and the like were concluded by 1925.

As the Finns scanned the international horizon after 1919, they saw only one Power, the USSR, capable of threatening—and possibly inclined to threaten—their security. It was therefore especially important to take advantage of opportunities and arrangements that seemed to offer assurances of satisfactory relations with Finland's eastern neighbor. Membership in the League of Nations appeared to mean, at least before the emergence of the Hitlerite menace of 1933, a certain degree of protection against unprovoked aggression. More substantial guarantees against developments that might threaten peace were seemingly obtained in 1932 when Finland signed a nonaggression treaty proposed by the USSR. The treaty was renewed in 1934 for a period of ten years. The admission of the Soviets to the League of Nations in 1934 also appeared to expand the area —despite Germany's withdrawal from the League in 1933—within which international complications or threats to peace involving Finland could be avoided or successfully dealt with.

That the USSR had objectives regarding Finland that went well beyond those presumably provided for by the nonaggression pact became clear a few years later. In the spring of 1938, a Soviet emissary, Boris Yartsev, initiated a series of secret conversations in Helsinki with Premier A. K. Cajander, Foreign Minister Eljas Erkko, and the well-known laborite V. Tanner. Yartsev contended that there was a possibility that Germany would attack the Soviet

Union, that the attack would result in German landings in Finland and an invasion of the USSR through Finland, and that the Soviets could not in such an event wait for the enemy to reach the border of the USSR but would meet the enemy on Finnish territory. Because of this possibility, the Soviets now demanded the right to aid Finland and also the right to fortify certain Finnish islands in the Gulf of Finland. The Finns insisted that Finland would fight against any invader, would not abandon her policy of neutrality, and would not permit any foreign power to use Finnish territory as a base for attack against the USSR. Their contention was not changed by the concessions offered in return for Finland's acceptance of the Russian proposal: Soviet guarantee of Finland's inviolability, military assistance, and a favorable trade agreement. The emissary refused to accept the Finns' contention that Finland could successfully repel a German attack and that in any case a German invasion of the Soviet Union through Finland could hardly be considered as a serious possibility.

These discussions, the Russians insisted, had to be kept secret, and the few Finns involved saw to it that word of the Soviet proposals did not leak out. The same was true of the later phase of the discussions which began, again on Soviet initiative, in Moscow on December 8, 1938. By that time Hitler had taken Austria and had carried through the first phase of the dismemberment of Czechoslovakia (the destruction of Czechoslovakia was completed in March, 1939). The Soviet spokesman this time was Anastas Mikoyan. He stated that Moscow had noted with satisfaction Finland's Scandinavian neutrality orientation. Professions of neutrality would not suffice, however, if a third power sought to expand eastward and in doing so violated Finnish territory. Mikoyan therefore proposed that Finland cede one of the main Finnish islands in the Gulf of Finland, the island to be fortified by the USSR. The Finns once again refused.

The USSR returned to the charge a third time in March, 1939, when Foreign Commissar Maxim Litvinov proposed to the Finnish minister in Moscow that Finland lease, for thirty years, four islands in the Gulf that were essential, it was contended, for the defense of approaches to Leningrad. The Finnish reply was again in the negative and pointed out that to lease the islands to the Soviets would

mean a violation of Finland's territorial integrity and neutrality. The
same reply was given to Litvinov's proposal that the islands be exchanged for territory in East Karelia. The Soviets did not abandon
the effort, however. Further discussions were carried on in Helsinki
between Soviet Ambassador Boris Stein and Foreign Minister E.
Erkko. Stein again proposed a lease or an exchange of territory.
The Finnish response once more underscored the determination not
to cede either to the USSR or Germany or anybody else, for to do
so would mean abandonment of neutrality, which the Finns were
determined to defend under all circumstances against any and every
aggressor. On leaving Helsinki on April 6, 1939, Stein made it clear
that the USSR did not accept Finland's negative answer as final
and did not intend to abandon the demand for the islands in the
Gulf of Finland because they were, it was alleged, of prime importance to the security of the Soviets.

The discussions thus ended had been kept strictly secret at the
request of the Soviet government. The Finnish government, the
Parliament, and the public at large knew nothing of the proposals
and intentions of Moscow. The country was therefore unaware of
the fact that when Soviet territorial demands were put forth in
October, 1939—after the Molotov-Ribbentrop pact, the defeat of
Poland, and the dismemberment of Poland by Hitler and Stalin in
September—they were largely repetitions of demands confidentially
but persistently presented since the spring of 1938.

COMMERCIAL TREATIES AFTER 1919

While the Åland island problem was being solved and the relations with the Soviets regularized on the basis of the Dorpat treaty,
Finland was also contending with still another foreign policy question, that of establishing satisfactory commercial treaty relations
with the outside world.

Before 1917, Finland's foreign commerce was regulated by the
treaties which Russia concluded from time to time with other
countries. On only one occasion was exception made to this general
rule. It occurred in 1872, when Finland and Spain concluded a

treaty of commerce which remained in force till 1892. Ordinarily Russia's trade treaties with foreign powers contained special provisions pertaining to Finland. Finnish products in Russian markets were in the main subject to the duties levied upon foreign commodities, but reductions were granted on certain industrial goods. Tariff legislation regulating Finland's trade with Russia was often unfavorable to Finland. This was the case after 1890 when a policy of Russification became the order of the day.

The attainment of independence at once left Finland without regular commercial relations with other states, all the treaties then in force affecting Finland automatically lapsing as a result of the events of 1917–18. The immediate result was that Finnish exports were subjected to whatever duties the various states were inclined to impose. The duties were, in general, the highest provided by their tariffs. Finland's foreign trade was consequently exceptionally handicapped until satisfactory treaties could be concluded. The negotiation of treaties, again, was not an easy task during the years immediately following 1918 because of the general dislocation caused by World War I. The tendency on the part of all countries to protect their domestic markets for the benefit of domestic producers further complicated the situation.

Despite substantial difficulties, commercial agreements were gradually obtained. The first, concluded in 1921 with France, involved exceptional problems because prohibition legislation complicated the importation of one of the most important French commodities, namely, alcoholic beverages. Between 1921 and 1925, twelve other trade treaties were concluded. The countries with which regular commercial relations were established included Great Britain, Germany, Holland, the other Scandinavian states, and the United States; these countries accounted for most of those providing important outlets for Finnish exports. By 1927 Britain absorbed 40 percent of Finland's exports, Germany 16 percent, Holland and Belgium 15 percent, and France some 10 percent. Russia had accounted for 28 percent of the exports in 1913; after 1920, the figure rose to 7 percent once (in 1925) but normally remained below 5 percent. The share of the United States varied between 5 and 8 percent.

XII

Toward a Better Society

Finland's progress in industry, farming, trade, commerce, and the professions illustrated advance and improvement which had the profit motive as its driving force. But there was another side to the picture. Much energy, ingenuity, and substance was expended upon undertakings that aimed not at the gain of the individual citizen but at the welfare of the nation as a whole. Public authority, national and local, paid increasing attention to a wide variety of social and economic problems and sought solutions for them by legislation and the expenditure of public funds. The demands of common welfare, in other words, were increasingly recognized as a guide for national policy and the attempt to meet the demands of the commonweal of the people accepted as an essential objective of statesmanship.

Outside the domain of Parliament and legislative purposes the concept that the interests of the people as a whole should be the active concern of enlightened citizenship likewise gained ground. The cooperative movement is an outstanding illustration of the extent to which enterprising individuals, driven by the unselfish desire to improve the conditions under which many of their fellow citizens lived, were able to contribute to the rising standard of living and to the satisfactions that a rising standard of living meant to the broad masses in particular.

In Parliament and out the Finns thus illustrated a trend general in western Europe. They worked successfully for those over-all objectives that are implied by the rather vague term "the social service state." Both the state or its political subdivisions and quasi-private enterprise, as represented, for example, by the cooperatives, invaded the field which in earlier times had been reserved to "economic individualism."

Several developments during the interwar years contributed toward a "better society" and improved social democracy. Five of them invite special mention: (1) the cooperative movement; (2) the emancipation of women; (3) the prohibition movement; (4) social legislation; and (5) attempts to solve the language problem. These five areas of effort and accomplishment were of unequal importance, but they all illustrate attempts to improve the old and usher in a new and better order of things.

THE COOPERATIVE MOVEMENT

The cooperative movement in Finland had a rather unique beginning. It did not appear as the result of cooperative enterprises founded by the poorer citizens. It appeared because several public-minded middle- and upper-class Finns came to the conclusion, after studying the problem, that the principles of cooperation would produce economically and socially desirable results, and set to work to translate principles into concrete ways of doing things.

Their carefully prepared plan called for the founding, at the start, of a central organization that would give the cooperative movement a directive and advisory organ before any cooperative societies had yet been actually established. The central organization was conceived, in other words, as the founder and promoter of cooperatives. The cooperative movement thus started from the center and spread outward, as it were, and not a little of its later success must be attributed to the blueprint which was prepared at the outset. Most of the blueprint came from the hands of a university professor, Hannes Gebhard, and to him goes much of the credit for the success of the cooperatives in later years. For a generation, Gebhard devoted his time and energies to the cause which he considered of utmost importance to his people.

The Pellervo Society, which began to operate in 1899, for several years determined the whole course of the movement. The society assisted in the starting of cooperatives of various kinds, guided their management whenever needed, aided them in keeping proper records, audited their accounts, and employed advisers competent to spread the cooperative idea and to take a hand in the solution of practical problems. It likewise embarked early upon extensive publishing: general works on cooperation, yearbooks, models for bylaws, ledgers for bookkeeping, handbooks and the like, and two cooperative journals marked the broad area of its endeavors as an effective (but ever-dignified) propagandizer of the cooperative idea. Originally composed only of interested individuals, the society later accepted cooperative societies to membership and finally became wholly the central organ of cooperative societies, although it retained throughout a few hundred individual memberships.

The seed sown by Gebhard and his supporters fell into fertile ground and produced an abundant harvest. In the course of a few years, cooperative shops, dairies, and credit societies or banks came into being. Sustained by a growing number of active cooperators—they approximated 89,000 in 1906 and included well over 300,000 on the eve of World War I—the movement produced the results shown in Table 21 between 1902 and 1918. The membership of some of the main cooperative enterprises grew at the pace shown in Table 22.

TABLE 21

NUMBER OF COOPERATIVE ORGANIZATIONS, 1902–1918

Year	Retail shops	Dairies	Credit associations	Others	Total
1902	34	27		6	67
1906	274	287	143	135	839
1910	452	328	870	639	1,709
1914	415	396	429	835	2,075
1918	585	508	590	1,553	2,705

In less than two decades, the cooperative movement thus became solidly rooted in the economic life of the nation. By 1919 there was every reason for assuming that independence would be no less congenial to the cooperative movement than the trying years since

TABLE 22

MEMBERSHIP OF MAIN COOPERATIVE ORGANIZATIONS, 1902–1918

Year	Retail shops	Dairies	Credit associations	Wholesale associations and affiliated societies
1902	6,000	2,000		
1906	50,000	29,000	5,000	57
1910	37,000	35,000	17,000	139
1914	97,000	42,000	22,000	244
1918	225,000	47,000	29,000	596

the turn of the century had been. Development during the two decades between the wars and the years after 1945 demonstrated the correctness of the assumption. Finland had become a nation of cooperators in the full sense of the term. This is shown by the increase in the number of cooperative enterprises, the expanding ranks of members, and the expansion of the cooperatives in wholesale trade, banking, and other fields (see Table 23).[1]

TABLE 23

NUMBER OF COOPERATIVE ORGANIZATIONS, 1919–1961

Year	Retail shops	Dairies	Credit associations	Others	Total
1919	611	344	596	1,297	3,137
1937	539	676	1,168	4,367	7,473
1945	494	512	941	2,782	4,739
1955	491	358	587	4,397	5,833
1961	473	355	527	2,621	3,936

Sources: S.T.V., 1938, Table 113; 1962, Table 140.

The active membership that sustained the cooperative structure grew by leaps and bounds (see Table 24). Making allowance for duplicate membership, it is obvious that the cooperative idea captured the major part of the nation. The table does not include, incidentally,

[1] For the sake of completeness, the years 1945–61 have been included in the table. If branch stores are included, the retail shops numbered 5,600 in 1945, rose to 8,500 in 1955, and reached 9,200 in 1961.

the membership of the organizations listed as "others" in Table 23, for no information on their memberships is available.

TABLE 24

MEMBERSHIP OF MAIN COOPERATIVE ORGANIZATIONS, 1919–1961

Year	Retail cooperatives	Dairies	Credit associations	Total
1919	301,500	41,500	30,300	372,300
1923	352,300	48,800	64,400	465,400
1930	466,900	74,700	144,400	686,000
1937	562,200	77,200	145,400	784,800
1945	767,600	71,100	177,900	1,016,700
1955	1,039,300	110,150	287,000	1,436,450
1961	1,026,760	185,180	303,950	1,515,990

It may be said that the republic became a cooperators' republic during these years and also that the business of the cooperatives became national in scope. The impressive expansion of the cooperative movement shows that the majority of the Finns actively supported the movement by becoming members of cooperative retail shops or by buying from cooperative shops, eating in cooperative restaurants, frequenting cooperative cafés, or borrowing from cooperative banks or credit societies. According to estimates in 1935, approximately one third of the total retail trade of the country was handled by cooperatives; the same proportion obtained well over two decades later. The cooperatives account for nearly all of the dairy industry, and in others they are of decisive importance. Cooperative manufacturing has for decades expanded along with retail and other trade. Matches, candy, farm and dairy machinery and tools, fertilizers, hosiery, ready-made clothing, and margarine are leading manufactures produced by cooperatives. While the growth of the cooperatives was notable and their role in the life of the farmer and other citizens was great, the cooperatives by no means dominated the economic life of the republic. Industry remained largely outside the cooperative sphere, especially the large export industries—paper, pulp, and timber, for example. The same was true of by far the greater part of the industry that produced for the domestic market. A rough indication of the relative significance of the cooperatives on the one hand and of private industry on the other is furnished by these comparisons: (1) the annual volume of business of the retail cooperatives in 1937 was about twice as large as that of the entire textile industry; (2) it approximately equaled the output of the paper industry; (3) it exceeded by about one fourth the value of the output of the metal and machine industries; (4) and it corresponded to about one fourth of the total value of the entire industrial production.

Three basic reasons seem to explain the rise of the cooperative movement before 1919 and its conspicuous growth after 1919. In the first place, in Finland, and before the turn of the century and for many years later in the other Scandinavian countries as well, the standard of living was modest enough to make small savings an important item in the family budget. The cooperatives offered a chance for more efficient spending of the worker's or farmer's income; they made it possible to stretch the daily wage or the weekly paycheck. They benefited by the unassailable purpose of aiding the consumer. This aim gave the movement a moral justification that private enterprise often seemed to lack and was a source of strength it could ever drawn upon.

Furthermore, the movement enlisted the energies of many unusually competent and unselfish leaders. Able and willing to work hard for a cause they considered worthy of their best efforts, they created businesses large and small that were well run and stood the test of competition with private enterprises. There is no doubt but that the cooperatives were and continue to be efficiently managed. This is shown by the retail shops' exceptionally low running costs. The average cost of management during the interwar years was, in terms of the annual volume of business: in 1920, 4.9 percent; in 1930, 10 percent; in 1935, 8.7 percent; and in 1937, 7.9 percent. Less than 10 cents of every dollar of business done sufficed on an average to defray the expenses of maintaining the retail shop. An enterprise with a yearly volume of business running to $500,000 cost less than $50,000 to run, all expenses included. Efficient management and sound business principles gave the cooperatives an exceptionally good economic position. The depression years from 1929 to 1933 did not cause the bankruptcy of a single cooperative concern.

Also, once the cooperatives weathered the early years of trial, they benefited by the success that success often begets. Having stood the test of exacting and not always friendly competition, and having demonstrated that the cooperative principle is sound when properly and wisely applied, retail cooperatives, sale organizations, and others found increasing favor with the public. Such favor was augmented by means of intelligent and well-directed educational and informational effort. From the start, the advantages of cooperation were urged by means of the printed page as well as by means of good business practices. That the newspaper with the largest circulation in Finland is the *Yhteishyvä* (Common Good), a newspaper of the cooperators for the cooperators, testifies to the success of publicity work that has been carried on for well over two generations.

That the cooperatives contributed to the well-being of the nation is amply demonstrated. They extended to the broad masses of the people the advantages that come from the use of modern techniques, wholesale buying, and a system of credit associations specially designed to meet the needs of the little fellow. They likewise educated a large part of the people in self-government and the management of economic enterprises of various kinds and did much to transform them into more satisfied human beings and better citizens.

THE EMANCIPATION OF WOMEN

The improvement of the position of women in Finland, the extension of their political and social rights, and the attainment by women of full political equality with men rest upon organized effort extending over more than two generations. The emancipation of women from their earlier inferior legal and social position began as early as the 1860s. Their rights to property and their own income were freed from earlier control by husband or father or male guardian in 1864, marriage laws were improved in the same year, and divorce was made easier in 1868. In 1871 the women were given the right to enter the university; the first woman physician was licensed in 1878. In the latter year, inheritance laws were modernized, enabling women to inherit equally with men. It was not until after 1880, however, that the women's emancipation movement began really to gather momentum and to leave an ever-greater impression upon many aspects of the social and economic life of the nation.

In this development, a number of organizations specially dedicated to the cause of women played an important part. The first was the Finnish Women's Association, founded in 1884. It devoted itself to the task of extending educational and related advantages to lower-class women in particular, and at the same time worked for more general legislative reforms. In the course of a relatively brief period, the association became instrumental in obtaining several concessions from the legislature. Between the middle eighties and the close of the century, laws were enacted that gave women the right to enter the national university on the same terms as men; extended the municipal franchise to women; opened the teaching profession to them—women could be appointed to the staffs of normal schools after 1898 and had been admitted to certain instructorships at the university in 1894—and in general erased much of the inequality between the sexes that rested on and was perpetuated by the laws of an earlier age.

Several other women's organizations were founded, especially between 1900 and 1918, and broadened the front of the women's movement. In education and in other fields, new opportunities were increasingly given to women. Posts in the public service were gradually opened to them—women could be appointed to the postal service as early as 1864—and their political rights extended. The first woman factory inspector was appointed in 1903. In 1906, women and men got equal political rights when universal suffrage was established. In the same year, the first regular instructorship at the university was given to a woman, and ten years later a law was passed which provided that women and men teachers should receive equal pay in schools maintained by public funds. The republican constitution of 1919 embodied the principle of full equality and recognized no differences between citizens of the two sexes.

Since 1919, the position and rights of women have been further secured in a number of ways. Over a dozen laws of special importance to women were enacted during the two decades between the wars. The following enactments illustrate the nature and trend of this legislation.

In 1922 a law was passed that defined in a new and liberal spirit the rights and status of unmarried mothers and their children. The law (revised in 1927 and again in 1936) freed children born out of wedlock from the disabilities that had attached to them earlier. The mother was to be the legal guardian of the child, unless the Child Welfare Board found the mother incompetent, in which case the board itself, through its Child Welfare Inspector, was designated as the guardian responsible for providing for the care of the child. The father's responsibility for the child was fixed by the courts (if fatherhood was contested), which also imposed the obligation to support the child until it was seventeen years of age and the right to inherit property equally with legitimate offspring. The mother received support for a period of nine months after birth, in order to enable her properly to care for the child if she kept it.

In 1924 the position of women in the coeducational schools was strengthened by the provision that either the principal or the assistant principal in such schools must be a woman. Two years later, the rights of women in civil service were improved in that women were placed on a footing of complete equality with men in such matters as competence requirements, salaries, pensions, and the like. Some branches of government employ—such as the army, railroads, etc.—still remain, however, wholly or largely in the hands of men. The first woman to be a full professor, on life tenure, was appointed at one of the universities in 1927, and in the same year women scored an important victory when they received the right to become judges and enter the diplomatic or consular service. In 1929 a new marriage law gave the woman equal rights regarding property, guardianship, etc., within the family, and the divorce law was revised so as to remove the lack of equality which in some respects had favored the husband up to that time.

The place of women in the professions and business became secure some fifty to sixty years ago. The trend has been toward greater security and not less since independence was established in 1918. Not only have women held their own in those walks of life that have ordinarily been considered as natural to women; they have also made their own, to an unusual degree, certain vocations that are, in the United States, for example, less commonly thought of as women's professions. For instance, the majority of the dentists in Finland have long been women. In the world of banking also they are very conspicuous, particularly in the offices of the larger banks. The tellers especially are likely to be women. Women architects are also numerous. The only profession worthy of mention that still remains closed to the female half of the Finnish citizenry is that of the Lutheran clergyman. The Lutheran Church has so far managed to retain its masculine purity—a circumstance which may have something to do with the claim of some Finns that the church is in many ways markedly in need of modernization.

For more than fifty years, Finnish women have moved freely on the stage of national politics. Ever since 1906, the feminine contender for public office has been a familiar figure. On the hustings she competes with male candidates, and in Parliament she works with them. Before 1919, between 14 and 24 women captured seats in the election to Parliament; four out of the eight elections between 1906 and 1919 returned over 20 women members. Following the establishment of the republic, their contingent became somewhat smaller until after World War II, as the following figures indicate: 1919, 17; 1929, 15; 1939, 16; 1945, 17; 1954, 30; and 1962, 27.

Most of the women chosen to seats in Parliament belonged to the center or the moderate left-wing groups. The Social Democratic party consistently furnished about one half of the women representatives. In 1927, for example, it accounted for 9 out of 17; in 1930, for 7 out of 11; in 1933, for 8 out of 14; and in 1936, for 8 out of 16. The conservative National Union party never had more than 4 women among its representatives during the years mentioned and reached that figure only once. Whether the preponderantly Social Democratic party affiliation of the women representatives reflected relatively more radical inclinations among the women voters it is impossible to say. In all likelihood it did not. The Socialists—and after 1945 the Communists—were more liberal than the other parties in providing places on the party ticket for women. The voters of the Social Democratic party, irrespective of sex, voted for the ticket and in doing so elected more women to the legislature than the other groups. The first woman to hold a cabinet portfolio was the Social

Democrat Miss Miina Sillanpää, who served as Assistant Minister for Social Affairs in the Tanner Government in 1926–27.[2]

It would be too much to say that the political emancipation of women revolutionized politics or markedly accelerated the speed of change. The women of Finland were the first to illustrate a fact obvious whenever women have become politically the equals of men, namely, that their effort in politics readily fell into the existing party mold and did not produce a new women's alignment. Within the existing parties, however, they appear to have performed fully as intelligently as the men. On the whole, they have been especially ready to sponsor and to vote for social legislative measures. Even in the adoption or rejection of such legislation, however, it was the decision of the party and not the inclination of the individual woman legislator that determined the vote.

The general impression given by two generations of women's participation in the political life of the nation may be summed up by saying that they have been hard-working, conscientious citizens in the performance of their duties. They seemed less inclined than the men to rely, for political success, on such aids as a booming voice or impressive platform behavior. And they were on the whole more modest than the men in claiming that "I have the wisdom, and it will die with me."

OUTLAWING THE CUP THAT CHEERS

When prohibition went into effect in June, 1919, the country embarked upon no hasty experiment. For decades before the republic

[2] Miss Sillanpää's life and career illustrate the transformation that took place in Finland after 1860. A summary of her life reads: "Resident of Helsinki. Born in Jokioinen June 4, 1866. Worked in the Forssa factory 1878–1885. Servant, 1886–1889. Manager of Maids' Home in Helsinki, 1900–1915. Inspector of the Elanto Cooperative cafes and restaurants, 1916–1932. Editor of the *Servants Journal*, 1905–1906, of the *Working Woman*, 1907–1916, of the *Woman Companion* since 1922. Member of the Legislature, 1907–1913, 1917, 1919–1933. Member of the Helsinki City Council, 1919–1925, and since 1930. Assistant Minister for Social Affairs in 1927. Chairman of the Socialist Women's Association. Has held numerous posts of responsibility in the socialist party, among them the chairmanship and secretaryship of 'Working Women's Association.'" L. Ailio and others, eds., *Politiikkaa ja Merkkimiehiä* (Helsinki, 1935), p. 472.

was founded, the cause of temperance had been defended as a sound national policy, and for more than ten years before 1919 the legislative majority—and presumably the majority of the people—had committed itself to the more drastic policy of outlawing intoxicants altogether. Prohibition therefore stood for much more than the victory of a handful of cranks or professional uplifters. It represented the deliberate choice of a large part of the citizenry as the solution of the problem of strong drink.

The problem of strong drink on the eve of prohibition was less serious than it appeared to be in many other countries. Indeed, the prewar temperance movement appeared to have reduced it to dimensions which justified the claim that the Finns were the most sober people in Europe and that the use of liquor in Finland was decreasing year by year. The situation before the war is shown by Table 25.

TABLE 25

PER CAPITA LIQUOR CONSUMPTION, 1896–1910
(Beverage alcohol, in liters of 100 percent)

Country	1896–1900	1901–1905	1906–1910
France	21.3	21.7	22.9
Italy	12.5	15.6	17.3
Switzerland	16.8	16.4	13.7
Belgium	11.7	11.2	10.9
Great Britain	11.6	10.9	9.7
Austria-Hungary	7.5	7.8	7.7
Germany	8.7	8.5	7.5
Denmark	8.8	8.3	6.8
Holland	5.8	5.8	5.0
Sweden	5.4	4.8	4.3
Norway	2.8	2.7	2.4
Finland	2.1	1.7	1.6

The downward trend evidenced by the table continued after 1910, and estimates in 1914–18 indicated that in terms of the consumption of intoxicants during the war years the Finns were three times as sober as they had been in 1910. There seemed to be good reason for holding that, while the prohibition law might be unnecessary because of the seeming success of voluntary abstinence before 1919, it would easily eradicate the remaining problem of drink and would thus usher in a new era. John Barleycorn's progeny—crime, poverty, alcoholism, and the rest of his harmful brood—would become extinct. The nation would be free to fashion its future unhampered by Demon Rum.

In retrospect, the prohibition experiment seems to have been doomed to failure from the start. No provision for enforcing the law was made until a few weeks before it went into effect. In May, 1919, the general supervision of prohibition was centered in the Temperance Department of the Ministry for Social Affairs. The department never became, however, a directing agency in actual enforcement; it never controlled the police, the customs guards, or other organs that were directly involved in the ever-mounting task of compelling obedience to the law.

The inadequacy of enforcement was given sharp relief by the universal disregard of the law. All the evidence relating to the use of intoxicants—drunkenness, violations of the prohibition enactment, crime and alcoholism after 1919—pointed to widespread failure to observe prohibition. Already in 1922 the situation had become bad enough to result in a thorough examination of the prohibition problem. A revision of the law followed the investigation, but the fundamental difficulty remained. Prohibition did not prohibit, and no amount of exhortation by the press, optimistic defense of the law in Parliament, or enthusiastic predictions by professional enemies of strong drink obscured the fact that the Finns liked liquor and were successful in obtaining it, law or no law.

Making full allowance for the unreliable character of the evidence showing that the people would not be weaned from the bottle of intoxicants, it is clear that the figures in Table 26 spell failure to take the law seriously. They show seizure of intoxicants by the authorities, convictions for drunkenness, and detected violations of the prohibition act.

Evidence pertaining to the relation between liquor and crime, and also growing alcoholism during these years, likewise pointed to the conclusion suggested by the table, namely, that smuggling and other sources of intoxicants placed large quantities of alcoholic beverages within the reach of those addicted to the use of "conversation aids." No amount of explanation prevented the conclusion that

TABLE 26
OBSERVANCE OF PROHIBITION

Year	Seizures (in liters)	Convictions for drunkenness		Violations of the prohibition law
		Number	Rate per 10,000	
1921	72,900	30,700	90	11,000
1923	503,800	50,100	144	17,300
1925	557,000	64,300	182	19,800
1928	1,186,000	79,000	220	23,000
1930	1,052,500	88,600	240	35,650

intoxicants were extensively consumed and that the law had failed to achieve its purpose.

As this fact became more obvious, the opponents of the law gained ground. The law had been publicly opposed, from the beginning, by some newspapers and organizations, but for several years their endeavors to defeat it bore no fruit. After 1930, however, opposition became more general. Several unofficial prohibition polls, conducted by newspapers and others in the course of 1931, indicated strong repeal sentiment. Probably the most impressive protest against the continuation of the law was a public address, signed by nearly 120,000 women and presented on May 5, 1931, to President P. E. Svinhufvud. The address urged the scrapping of prohibition and the establishment of some other system of liquor control that would eliminate the evils created by prohibition.

By the autumn of 1931, the leading political parties with the exception of the Social Democrats had directly or indirectly accepted the idea that the prohibition tangle should be straightened out by giving the electorate an opportunity to register its opinion in the matter. In December, 1931, Parliament passed a bill providing for a plebiscite. The bill put three alternatives before the voters: retention of the law without change, modification of the law by legalizing beer and light wines, and complete repeal and the substitution of state-regulated sale of intoxicants for prohibition.

The nation went to the polls on December 29–30 of the same year. The result was an overwhelming repudiation of prohibition. Only

217,208 votes were cast for it, while repeal was supported by 546,332 citizens. Modification in favor of beer and light wines got less than 11,000 votes. Not the least startling aspect of the referendum was the fact that women alone cast 226,820 votes for repeal, or more than the total vote in favor of the retention of the law. It was the women's vote that destroyed prohibition, for if the women had voted solidly for it the outcome would unavoidably have been the defeat of the antiprohibitionists.

The referendum was purely consultative; its only purpose was to ascertain the opinion of the voters. It therefore imposed no direct obligation on the legislature to accept the verdict. The outcome of the referendum was so clear-cut, however, that Parliament could not well ignore it. An extra session of the legislature was convened some three weeks after the results of the vote were known. It enacted a law on January 30, 1932, which repealed prohibition. The effort to legislate liquor out of existence was thus abandoned. The new law went into effect on April 5 of the same year.

The repeal of prohibition did not mean that the sale of liquor would henceforth be fully free. The new liquor law stated in part that "the liquor trade shall be organized in a way that will stamp out the illegal sale of intoxicants and will reduce the use of alcoholic beverages to the smallest possible minimum, as well as prevent drunkenness and its harmful consequences." Accordingly, the liquor business was placed under the control of the State Alcohol Corporation. The corporation was state-owned and state-directed. Since 1932 it has supervised the manufacture, import, and sale of intoxicants and maintained liquor shops, some eighty of which were established by the time the new law went into effect. Their number was later increased. It was only from the state liquor shops that alcoholic beverages could be bought—excepting restaurants, hotels, etc., where liquor could be had for consumption on the premises—after repeal was abandoned. The prices were fixed low enough, from the start, to discourage the use of smuggled goods.

The profits of the state-controlled liquor trade, it was provided, should be distributed as follows: 35 percent was divided between the financing of temperance work for the suppression of possible illegal liquor traffic and the national old age insurance fund; 35

percent was allocated to other unspecified public expenses; and 30 percent was directed to useful public projects in localities where no liquor was sold. The profits accruing for the first two years, however, were used to meet general government expenses. The price-fixing policy of the government was such as to reduce to a minimum the profit made on intoxicants by hotels, restaurants, and the like.

Unsuccessful enforcement and the depression after 1929 may be singled out as the two main reasons for the jettisoning of the prohibition experiment. Of the two, the latter was probably the more important. Most Finns were in all likelihood able long before 1931 to testify to the fact that hotels, restaurants, speak-easies, and bootleggers sold liquor. Yet repeal did not come as a result of the general realization that prohibition did not prohibit. It was the depression that furnished the most telling arguments against continuing the experiment. The contention that prohibition deprived the state of an important source of revenue was heard before 1929, but it was not until 1931 that the law was being repudiated in many quarters because of the conclusion that prohibition was unwise economically. The more satisfactory conditions that have prevailed since 1932 as regards the sale and use of liquor would in all likelihood have been postponed by several years if the depression had not come along to underline the negative consequences of prohibition as a dollars-and-cents proposition. Its enforcement cost too much and the loss of revenue was too great, in view of the shrinking income and the increasing expenses of government during the depression, to justify the continuation of a law that was expensive, ineffective, and not productive of the results expected of it in 1919.[3]

SOCIAL LEGISLATION, 1919–1939

Regulation by public authority of the conditions under which workers could be employed began in Finland with the attempt to protect children against dangers to which they were exposed while at work.

---

[3] I have told the story of Finnish prohibition in *The Prohibition Experiment in Finland* (New York, 1931), and in the *Annals* of the American Academy of Political and Social Science, September, 1932, pp. 216–26.

Regulation of this kind appeared already in the seventeenth century and slowly grew until protection of minors and women against harmful occupations led to more advanced legislative action. In 1868, and again in 1879, minors' and women's work in factories was regulated, but it was not until 1889 that factory legislation in the modern sense began. Additions to the laws then enacted came in 1908, 1909, 1914, and 1916. In 1917 Parliament passed a national eight-hour-day law and in the course of the twenties factory and related legislation was further extended. Additional efforts to improve the conditions under which wage earners worked came in 1934 and 1937.

The main results of factory legislation in 1919–39 may be summarized by noting (1) the provisions under which minors were employed; (2) the restrictions that related to women; (3) provisions for the protection of wage earners against accident and unsanitary or harmful conditions of work; (4) the length of the actual working day; and (5) the enforcement of the factory laws.

No children under fourteen years of age could be employed. Children over fourteen could not be employed at heavy or dangerous work of any kind. They were prohibited from all night work, which meant the hours from 9 P.M. to 7 A.M. The longest permissible working day was six hours, divided by a rest period of at least one hour. Minors between sixteen and twenty could be employed, for a maximum of six hours, from 6 o'clock in the morning; no minor under sixteen years of age could be employed as shop clerk.

In general, women's work was regulated by laws that apply equally to men. Some heavy kinds of work were prohibited to women. In one important respect, women wage earners were placed in a special category. The law provided a recuperation period for all women workers after the birth of a child. In the case of industrial and other female labor the rest period was fixed at four weeks; shop clerks had to be given six weeks in which to recuperate.

All employers had to conform to the general law pertaining to the sanitary conditions under which work was done. The requirements related to washrooms, dressing rooms, lunch periods, proper heating and ventilation, avoidance of unhealthful crowding, adequate safeguards against accidents, and the like. The law covered not only factories, mines, etc., but also offices and shops. It did not apply, however, to work done within the home, and shipping and shipbuilding were subject to special regulations that took cognizance of the character of these occupations.

The eight-hour working day established by law in 1917 applied to practically all employment except farming, hotels and cafés, hospitals, and a few others. The state-owned postal, telephone, and customs services were likewise exempt because of special considerations. The eight-hour law stated that the wage earner might be employed for eight hours per day, and for not more than 96 hours during a two-week period. The law allowed, however, a maximum of 350 hours of overtime in the course of a year. Only 200 of these hours could be agreed upon by employer and worker; the remaining 150 hours required the special consent of the government inspector. All overtime work was paid at a rate from 50 percent to 100 percent higher than the regular wage. In special cases the government could make exceptions in the application of the eight-hour day but only for a year at a time.

The operation of the eight-hour law and the extent to which the right to overtime work was used are shown by Table 27. It is based upon the conditions that existed within eight leading industries, including paper, sawmill, metal, and textile plants, which represent a large segment of Finnish industry.

TABLE 27
THE OPERATION OF THE EIGHT-HOUR LAW, 1925–1937

Year	Number of regular working hours per worker per week	Overtime work hours per worker per week	Total
1925	46.3	1.25	47.55
1930	45.4	1.30	46.70
1937	46.9	2.15	49.05

While industrial employment was based on the eight-hour day —clerks, office workers, etc., also came under the law—the length of the working day on the farm remained unregulated by law. The question of extending the law to farming was debated on several occasions but had led to no result by 1939. Even in the absence of restrictive legislation, however, the working day of farm labor became appreciably shorter than formerly. According to a report issued by the Ministry for Social Affairs in 1939, the length of the working day on the larger farms in the busy summer season was ordinarily ten hours. On the smaller farms the hours ran to somewhat more, but in only exceptional cases to eleven or over. During the winter the working day on the farms was two or three hours shorter than in the summer. These conclusions, based on an investigation of farms that employed outside labor—they therefore did not disclose the conditions on farms that did not use paid outside labor—suggest that the farm laborer's workday tended toward the lower limit established by the law of 1917.

The supervision and controls that the state devised for enforcing factory and related legislation expanded as the legislation expanded. From small beginnings in the eighties, supervision and control grew to substantial dimensions. In 1939 the state or municipalities or rural communities employed over 500 inspectors of various grades to see to it that laws were observed. They were responsible for the inspection of plants and of the conditions under which employees did their work, and had a free hand to consult with employer and employee alike concerning questions that might arise out of the operation of the laws. Failure to observe the laws resulted in notice to the employer, who was given ample opportunity to comply without compulsion. If notice did not result in an improvement of the condition that gave rise to the notice, the case could be taken to the courts for a final decision.

Meanwhile, laws providing for industrial accident insurance, old age and invalidity insurance, maternity aid, and care for needy children and measures designed to relieve the consequences of unemployment were enacted, while the care of the poor, of persons suffering from alcoholism or mental or physical defects, and the search for solutions for housing problems increasingly became matters of public concern. Some of the achievement along these lines had begun before World War I. Most of it became important only after independence and not a little belongs among the successes registered shortly before the war in 1939. Five aspects of social welfare work stand out as especially important.

1. Provision against losses suffered by the worker as a result of industrial and related accidents was first made by a law enacted in 1895. It held the employer responsible for accidents met with in the performance of work. After several other laws had been put on the books in the course of the next thirty years or more, an accident insurance law was passed in 1925 and elaborated in 1935 (it was superseded by another law in 1948).

The law provided for compulsory accident insurance for nearly all types of labor. The cost of insurance was borne by the employer. The benefits accruing to the insured worker were of three kinds: sickness aid for a period of not more than one year, and a modest wage; invalidity aid for life, in the event of complete loss of ability to work, that ran as high as two thirds of the wage but usually was considerably less; and, in the event of death resulting from the accident, a contribution for expenses of burial and payments to dependents up to nearly two thirds of the annual earnings of the deceased. The payments to dependents continued till the children reached the age of seventeen and, in the case of the widow, until she remarried.

The number of wage earners subject to accident insurance was 224,000 in 1920, rose to 300,000 in 1925, exceeded 608,000 in 1936, and had reached 740,500 in 1939. The last figure covered approximately the total wage earning group in the country.

Various sickness benefit associations and funds also operated. The republic did not enact a general sickness insurance law before 1939. The law determining labor contracts—contracts supervised by the state on the terms of which employment is obtained or help hired —stated, however, that all employees were entitled, in the event of illness, to wages for a period up to two weeks. The law in question covered a substantial segment of short-time illness and therefore partly filled the gap which the absence of a general sickness insurance law created.

Toward a Better Society

2. Old age and invalidity insurance became a reality, after many years of preliminary investigation and debate, in 1937 and went into effect in January, 1939. The law covered all persons eighteen years or over. It provided for pensions of all persons sixty-five years or over who had contributed for at least ten years to the insurance fund. The size of the pension varied and was determined by the income of the insured. The maximum was about $240 yearly, and the minimum varied from $25 to $75.

Most of the cost of the insurance was borne by the insured individual and the employer but the state and local governments also contributed. The operation of the insurance plan was in the hands of the National Pension Office, which paid the pensions. Because the law covered all adult persons irrespective of income or participation in other insurance benefits, the pension provisions were more extensive than those ordinarily contained in laws of this kind.

Various private pension funds operated since the turn of the century. Some of these funds, such as the Pension Fund of the State Employees, received contributions from the national treasury. The same applied to unemployment insurance funds, of which there were nine in 1936. Their assistance to unemployed persons usually amounted to a maximum payment of 75 cents per day for a period of not more than 120 days in the course of the year.

Life insurance sold by private companies, which obviously had a bearing upon the problem of the aged and upon that of families left through death without a regular source of income, became increasingly common after the 1918 war. In the early twenties, the total life insurance policies in the country amounted to about $18 per capita. A decade later the figure had risen to $56. In 1937 the total policies in force came to $70 for every man, woman, and child in the nation.[4]

3. State and municipal as well as private voluntary endeavor on behalf of orphans and needy children in general attained substantial proportions after 1919. The Protection of Children Law, enacted in 1936, furnished the legal basis of child welfare work and supplemented the efforts of municipalities and other authorities to provide

[4] *Unitas,* 1938, No. 4, p. 29.

for a wide variety of activity: clubs, summer camps, excursions, health instruction, vocational guidance, and the like. The General Mannerheim Child Welfare League, founded in 1920, was the most important private organization in the field and performed a multitude of services, such as the training of nurses for children, the establishment and maintenance of dental clinics and kindergartens, and the distribution of milk for children. Maternity aid was provided on a national scale in 1936. A law enacted in that year placed financial assistance within the reach of all needy mothers and provided room and board for about 1–2 weeks, depending on the locality. Estimates indicated that some 55,000 mothers were covered by the law and benefited by the financial aid as well as advice and other services provided by the enactment. Maternity aid was later expanded; since 1949 all mothers have received a money grant, prenatal care, and medical and nursing advice. In 1958 the mothers of 95 percent of the children born in that year received maternity aid.

4. The care of the poor by public authority or by private organizations likewise expanded, and ranged from direct distribution of food and the like to the maintenance of bureaus serving the needs of vagrants or institutions for the training of cripples, mentally deficient persons, or alcoholics. By 1939, seven of the leading cities maintained special Legal Aid offices headed by a lawyer appointed and paid by the municipality. The purpose of such bureaus was to provide legal assistance in court and out to citizens unable for financial reasons to retain a lawyer. Similar assistance was also provided by various other organizations.

5. Housing problems in town and country attracted attention years ago, and a number of special investigations of this socially important question were made from time to time. The housing conditions under which agricultural labor and industrial workers lived, and also the housing situation in general, led to several remedial measures after 1919. A rough notion of the margin within which improvement was not only possible but imperative was given by the fact that in Helsinki, for example, a family of six persons lived, on an average, in four rooms in 1930, and a family of three had only two rooms. Congested housing and poor housing in general gradu-

ally disappeared, however, and conditions in 1939 were a good deal better than they had been ten years earlier,[5] although much still remained to be done.

One of the factors contributing to the change was the expenditure of public funds for housing projects. In 1920 a sum of 20,000,000 marks was included in the national budget for loans bearing no interest to municipalities or private building associations. The loans granted ran as high as 30 percent of the building cost, if the municipality provided a free lot and 15 percent of the cost of erecting the building. In 1922 ordinary mortgage loans were included in the policy of stimulating building. Funds were also granted for housing projects in some 150 rural communities. All in all, nearly 100,000,000 marks were set aside to improve housing between 1920 and 1925, and additional sums were expended later. It was private enterprise, however, that accounted for most of the improvements after 1919. The housing projects of the large industrial concerns were in many cases ambitious and created in some instances housing conditions that were close to ideal.

The cost of social legislation and of the various forms of activity and service which attempted to eradicate social and economic maladjustment became greater year by year. The trend was well shown by the fact—to select only one illustration—that in 1935 the national budget allocated nearly 59 million marks for direct social enterprises and administration, nearly 67 million in 1936, over 78 million in 1937, and over 100 million in 1939. The total state appropriations for social welfare purposes in 1938 came to about 645 million. An estimate of the local and private effort in the same field, made by the Ministry for Social Affairs in 1938, led to the conclusion that some 5–6 percent of the annual national income during the preceding decade had been spent for purposes that contributed toward better and richer life for the citizens of the republic.

[5] See *S.A.*, 1926, Nos. 3, 4, 6, 8; *Bank of Finland, Monthly Bulletin*, 1926, No. 8; and J. Laati, *Sosialinen Lainsäädäntö ja Toiminta Suomessa* (Helsinki, 1939), pp. 103–7.

THE LANGUAGE PROBLEM

It was understandable, not to say unavoidable, that the developments on the language and nationalist front from the 1860s to the establishment of independence in 1918 should have bequeathed difficulties and problems not easily or quickly solved. This was illustrated by the fact that the country was barely getting back on an even keel after the war of independence when Swede-Finn attempts emerged to secure rights and privileges considered essential for the linguistic minority.

The decade before 1918 had witnessed increasing evidence, among the leaders of the Swede-Finn nationalists, of an isolationist policy which tended to draw more sharply the lines behind which, it was hoped, the Swede-Finn cause would be secure. The temperance movement was split along language lines; a separate People's Academy was founded; a special "Swedish Day" was set aside in 1908 as a Swede-Finn "national holiday" (the day chosen was November 6, the day of Gustavus Adolphus' death in 1632); attempts were made to prevent land purchases in Swede-Finn localities by Finnish-speaking buyers, etc. Mainly at the instance of Swede-Finn university students, a movement was begun in 1910 to introduce the term "Finlander"—in the place of "Finn"—to designate the inhabitants of the country, thereby avoiding being identified with the Finnish-speaking majority. Plans were also made and funds collected for a separate "Swedish-language" university.

Such divisive endeavors vanished overnight during the trying months January–May, 1918. The Swede-Finns rallied unhesitatingly around the cause of independence and rendered invaluable service to state and nation. The war was barely over, however, when the earlier endeavors reemerged. The executive committee of the Swedish People's party resolved on May 20, 1918, to propose a reorganization of the country's provincial governments that would lead to the creation of purely unilingual administrative and judicial districts. Early in 1919, arrangements were made, under the auspices of the party, for a "Folkting of Swedish Finland." The congress met in

May. The main demands formulated by it were: (1) the position of the two language groups should be defined and safeguarded by the constitution; (2) judicial and administrative areas should be organized along language lines; (3) all state employees should be required to know Swedish; and (4) the future welfare of the nation required, as an "indispensable condition," that "instruction in schools shall be given, for all time to come, in the mother tongue of the pupil." It was also urged that the educational needs of the two groups be satisfied in accordance with common principles.

The extent to which these and related demands were met was indicated by the constitution of July 17, 1919. It provided, in Articles 14 and 75, that

> Finnish and Swedish shall be the national languages of the Republic. The right of Finnish citizens to use their mother tongue, whether Finnish or Swedish, before law courts and administrative authorities, and to obtain from them records and documents in their mother tongue, shall be guaranteed by law, in order to safeguard the rights of both language groups in accordance with identical principles.
>
> The State shall provide for the cultural and economic needs of the two groups in accordance with identical principles.
>
> Every conscript, unless he desires otherwise, shall if possible be enrolled in a unit whose members speak his own mother tongue . . . and shall in such unit receive instruction in that language. Finnish shall be the language of command of the armed forces.

Legislation elaborating these general provisions was enacted in 1921 and 1922. The laws provided that (1) administrative districts should be, "as far as possible," unilingual; (2) a district was unilingual if the minority group represented less than 10 percent of the population of the district, and bilingual if the percentage exceeded ten; (3) in localities classified as bilingual, public authorities and offices, when dealing with an individual citizen, must use the language of the citizen; (4) in all criminal cases, the language of the defendant determined the language of the proceedings and of the court; (5) the classification of districts, by language, was to be reviewed every ten years, on the basis of official statistics. Helsinki, the capital, and Turku were defined as bilingual without reference to the language percentages or proportions defined by the law. Also, all state employees were required to know both Swedish and Finnish. This requirement meant that the civil service personnel was, presumably, bilingual. The Swede-Finn churches were combined in a separate bishopric (in 1924). A Swede-Finn department of education was organized within the national Ministry of Education in 1920.

In pursuance of the Language Law of June 1, 1922, the country was divided, as of January 1, 1923, into language districts. The results were, briefly, as follows: Out of a total of 554 communes (excluding the semi-autonomous Åland Islands, whose population was almost solidly Swedish-speaking), 459 were listed as unilingual Finnish communes and 32 as unilingual Swedish-language communes. There were 109 communes without any Swede-Finn residents and 165 others in which their number was ten or less. The 1922 survey led to the following "language classification" of the larger administrative units and of the judicial districts: of the seven administrative provinces (headed by a governor), four were classified as Finnish and three as bilingual; the lower court districts were either Finnish or bilingual (because of the distribution of the population none was thus placed in the Swedish-language category), while all the superior court districts were classified as bilingual.[6]

The language provisions of the constitution and the legislative measures after 1919 defined the relations between or the "rights" of the two language groups in a manner that naturally invites the appraisal "liberal." That is to say, the minority group—it came to 11.6 percent of the total population in 1910, 11 percent in 1920, and 10.1 percent in 1930—was accorded a status which placed it, in regard to some important matters, on a footing of equality with the majority. Equality and rights had not been exacted by Swede-Finn parliamentary majorities that would not be denied. They had been voted by constitution makers and legislators—among whom the Swede-Finns accounted for less than 15 percent of the votes— persuaded by common sense to recognize that toleration and accommodation of the minority best served the interests of the country as a whole. Mindful of the importance of setting the nation's house in order without increasing internal friction and difficulties, the

[6] See *S.A.*, 1922, No. 337, pp. 1269–77. Åland again stood in a category by itself.

majority let wise restraint instead of mere voting strength render the verdict.

The 1919–22 solution of the language question turned out to be neither satisfactory nor permanent. The history of the language and nationality problem since the 1860s had left, as we suggested, a residuum of ill feeling and intolerance that the achievement of independence did not eradicate. During the interwar years, the spokesmen of the Swede-Finn cause found it difficult to accept some of the interpretations given by Parliament, in the allocation of public funds for educational or related purposes, to the "identical principles" clause in the constitution. They tended in general to insist —not always temperately—that the language clauses of the constitution be interpreted literally. Their stand often meant that the proportionalities be defined as if the circumstances of, say, the early 1920s remained fixed and unchanging. The self-appointed interpreters of the Finnish cause, on the other hand, were prone to display, often in an overbearing manner, a "we-are-the-boss" attitude in demanding, for instance, that the public purse contribute to the "cultural and economic" needs of the majority, not on the basis of a rigid 1:10 ratio, but according to the changing requirements created by the passage of time. Practical considerations, the argument ran, demanded capacity for discerning that the interests of the majority must in many situations be considered paramount and should not be sacrificed by narrow and unimaginative interpretations of the realities of the workaday world.[7]

[7] The literature dealing with the language question during the years 1919–39 is extensive. Adequate samples or summaries of it are found in: *Aitosuomalaisuus. Ohjelmaa ja Päämääria* (Helsinki, 1925); *Suomen Heimo*, a monthly (Helsinki, 1923 ff.); K. S. Laurila, *Kielikysymyksestämme Vieläkin Hiukkasen* (Helsinki, 1927); A. Anderson, *Den Svenska Folkstammens Ställning i Finland* (Helsinki, 1924); J. Hastig, *Vår Nationella Framtidslösen* (Vaasa, 1924); A. Lille, *The New Language Law* (Helsinki, 1921); G. Schauman, *Det Svenska Problemet i Finland* (Helsinki, 1921); E. von Wendt, *Svenskt och Finskt i Finland* (Helsinki, 1925); E. Hornborg, *Den Äktfinska Svallvågen: Den Äktfinska Polemiken i Finlands Universitetsfråga* (Helsinki, 1935); "Språkfrågan vid Finlands Statsuniversitet," in *Svensk Tidskrift*, 1937, H. 5, pp. 319–26; L. A. Puntila, "Kieliryhmien oikeudet ja Kielellinen itsehallinto," in P. Renvall, ed., *Suomalaisen Kansanvallan Kehitys* (Helsinki, 1956), pp. 228–34; *Suomalainen Suomi, passim;* Akateeminen Karjala-Seura, *Suomalainen Valtionyliopisto* (Porvoo, 1926); V. Merikoski, in Finnish Political Science Association, ed., *Democracy in Finland* (Helsinki, 1961), pp. 81–92.

The language nationalists in both camps had little difficulty in the twenties and thirties in discovering reasons for complaint or in exploiting real or imaginary grievances. The "language proportion" among army officers, in the civil service or the diplomatic service, or the extent to which public funds were provided for Finnish-language or Swedish-language public schools in districts defined by law as bilingual, and other factors and circumstances provided continuing opportunities for the extremists on both sides. Outstanding among the subjects of the language debates of the period was the question of "nationalizing"—that is, "Finnicizing"—the University of Helsinki.

A law enacted in 1923 defined the University of Helsinki as a "bilingual" institution. It also provided that the courses and lectures in the various faculties should correspond, as regards the language in which instruction was given, to the ratio of Finnish- and Swedish-speaking students.[8] By the mid-twenties, the demand began to be heard—put forth by spokesmen of the Finnish cause—that the university be turned into a "truly national" seat of learning by requiring that staff and all areas of instruction be Finnish. This demand had occasionally been voiced since 1906. Its supporters in the twenties and later were determined to carry their cause to victory but ultimately had to accept a compromise arrangement. Parliament passed a law in 1937 which provided for fifteen Swedish-language professorships and prescribed that all professors must possess sufficient knowledge of the other national language to give examinations in it.

The law of 1937 fell far short of satisfying the extremists in either group, and the ill-feelings aroused during the years of discussion and debate before 1937 had not disappeared when the nation suddenly found itself facing the Soviet invasion in 1939. That the internal divisions caused by the problem were altogether superficial was strikingly demonstrated by the unanimity with which the whole nation, and especially the groups and classes most directly involved

[8] The classification of students depended on the home language and not on the ability to use one or the other of the "national" languages. The entrance examinations to the university included stiff tests in the two languages and ensured, at the very least, a good working knowledge of both.

in the university controversy, faced the enemy and bore the sacrifices of the war years. The results of the unifying effect of the war, and of the greater moderation engendered by it, were shown in 1948 when the number of "Swedish chairs" at the university was increased to 23. In 1959, "Swedish" professorships and other instructional posts came to 66. The professorships represented approximately one tenth of those at the university (its student enrollment was 13,400 in 1961–62; the proportion of Swede-Finn students was 13 percent in 1959).[9]

The course of the two nationalist movements—of which the language problem was a manifestation—in Finland since 1918 reveals several obvious facts. The controversy did not rest on political or geographical particularism, nor was it kept alive by the conflicts and antagonisms of social classes. Less still was religion involved, for both language groups are overwhelmingly Lutheran. In no sense was the problem one of competing economic interests or systems. Farming, industry, commerce, shipping, and the professions all involved Finns and Swede-Finns alike. These general circumstances account, in large measure, for the disappearance, since the end of World War II, of the agitation and quarrels that held the stage before the war. That the war years also had a salutary effect upon the "language nationalists" has been suggested by a leading student of the Finnish scene in these words: "The wars blunted the edge of the language controversy, and they strengthened even among the Swedish-language element the conception that we all share the same common fate. The wars also increased the desire to take into consideration, in one's activity and endeavors, the needs and requirements of the whole of Finland's democratic society. This new way of looking at things has brought good results in many areas, and it suggests that as regards the problem of linguistic self-rule the trend toward isolationism is waning while the forces making for unity are getting stronger." [10] But however important the war was in erasing pre-1939 difficulties, it appears that the basic reason for the lessen-

---

[9] Some of the available statistics are contradictory. See Puntila, "Kieliryhmien oikeudet ja Kielellinen itsehallinto," p. 232; O. Ketonen and U. Toivola, eds., *Introduction to Finland 1960* (Porvoo, 1960), p. 265; *S.T.V.*, 1962, Table 333.

[10] Puntila, "Kieliryhmien oikeudet ja Kielellinen itsehallinto," p. 234.

ing of friction since 1945 is that the principle of equal treatment of the individual Finn and Swede-Finn, in this question of "language rights," has been observed throughout in a manner that has largely eliminated causes for complaint. And "as regards the technique of administration . . . the system has not caused any difficulties worth mentioning. The right to receive official translation is used to a very small extent by the parties concerned, and the authorities seem as a rule to strive for flexibility in their dealings with parties" from the two language groups. "It is striking that issues concerned with language legislation are very rarely brought to administrative juris-diction for decision, the only exception to this rule being provided by issues associated with communal administration." [11]

[11] V. Merikoski, in Finnish Political Science Association, ed., *Democracy in Finland*, pp. 91–92.

XIII

Finland and World War II

THE OUTBREAK OF THE WAR, SEPTEMBER, 1939

World War II began with the German invasion of Poland on September 1, 1939. The invasion launched the third phase, as it might be called, of Hitler's program of aggression and conquest, the annexation of Austria in March, 1938, being the first and the dismemberment of Czechoslovakia in September, 1938–March, 1939, the second. The Austrian and Czechoslovak undertakings had been carried through without prior arrangements or understandings with another aggressor. In the case of Poland, however, the stage was set by the secret protocol attached to the notorious Molotov-Ribbentrop pact of August 23, 1939. The protocol provided for a joint agreement regarding large areas in east-central and north Europe. It called for a mutually satisfactory division of "spheres of interest" within which the signatories could safely proceed to carry through their territorial and related purposes.

The announcement that a nonaggression pact had been signed by the two dictatorships caused a sensation, partly because Britain and France had lately been attempting to bring the USSR into the common front designed to prevent further aggression by Hitler. The failure of the western Powers to persuade Stalin to join hands with them and the deliberate Soviet choice of what seemed to be a particularly distasteful version of a policy of appeasement underlined the fact that Hitler had once again registered a resounding diplomatic success. Had the secret protocol attached to the agreement been known at the time, the failure of Britain and France to obtain the USSR as an ally would have seemed nothing less than calamitous. The "strictly secret" protocol was an integral part of the treaty of nonaggression, and like the pact itself it needed no ratification and went into effect at once. The text of the document stated in part that the two governments had agreed that "in the event of a territorial and political rearrangement in the areas belonging to . . . Finland, Estonia, Latvia and Lithuania, the northern boundary of Lithuania shall represent the boundary of the spheres of influence of Germany and the USSR. . . . In the event of a territorial and political rearrangement of the areas belonging to the Polish state the spheres of influence of Germany and the USSR shall be bounded approximately by the line of the rivers Narev, Vistula, and San."

The agreement continued: "The question of whether the interests of both parties make desirable the maintenance of an independent Polish state and how such a state should be bounded can be determined only in the course of further political developments. In any event both Governments will resolve this question by means of a friendly agreement."

The possible "territorial and political" rearrangements contemplated by the pact could obviously come about only as the result of the violation of the territorial sovereignty of the countries named by Germany or the USSR or both. Events were to show that the treaty was still another illustration of the use of the "I-take-this-you-take-that" formula well known in the long and often sordid history of international affairs. Hitler began the first phase of the "territorial and political" rearrangements by invading Poland on September 1, and the USSR completed the task by invading eastern Poland on the seventeenth. The details of the division of Poland were completed ten days later, erasing that country from the political map of Europe. Nazism and communism had collected the first fruits of successful cooperation in aggression.

Finland and her Nordic neighbors issued joint and separate declarations of neutrality immediately after the war began. The Hitler-Stalin pact had created no alarm in Finland (the secret clauses were not yet known; they were published only after the war ended). It caused, on the contrary, expressions of satisfaction in many quarters. It was felt that, the two Powers that might threaten Finland's security having joined hands in an important treaty, the peace of the Baltic and Scandinavian area had been made more secure. The feeling was temporarily strengthened by the assurances on August 30 of the German ambassador to Moscow, Count Schulenburg—given to his Finnish colleague in Moscow—that Finland had in no way been involved in the Soviet-German negotiations preceding the signing of the pact. Also, while Finland's relations with the Soviets in the post-1920 era had not been really cordial—Russian-sponsored communism was the main difficulty—satisfactory relations appeared to have been fully secured by Finnish purposes and policies. Both countries had outlawed war as an "instrument" of national policy by 1939; since 1932 they had been bound by a nonaggression pact in force till 1945. Neither had any territorial or other claims upon the other. "Peaceful coexistence"—to use a term that became general after World War II—seemed a reality inviting an optimistic view of the future.

THE MOSCOW DISCUSSIONS, OCTOBER–NOVEMBER, 1939

Most Finns saw the German invasion of Poland on September 1 and the Anglo-French declaration of war two days later as faraway events of no direct effect on Finland. However, Soviet moves in Poland and in the three Baltic states Estonia, Latvia, and Lithuania, together with developments directly involving Finland after October 5, dispelled such optimistic notions and alerted the nation to dangers emanating from the USSR. The Baltic states became ominous illustrations of Moscow's intentions when they were forced, by Soviet pressure, to accept Soviet-dictated military arrangements and concessions. Discussions begun with Estonia on September 25 led to treaties concluded with the three states (Estonia, September 28; Latvia, October 5; and Lithuania, October 11; Lithuania had been assigned to the Soviet sphere by an agreement with Germany on September 28) which placed them under USSR control. In each case the Russians were given the right to occupy certain ports and military and air installations for the duration of the war and to maintain Soviet forces in the areas in question. That the concessions were granted for the duration of the war offered only meager comfort to the three nations, nor could they, knowing their Communist neighbor, take literally the assurance written into each of the treaties that the putting into effect "of the present pact" would in "no way" infringe upon the sovereignty of the countries signing "or, more especially, their economic or political systems." [1]

The Finns, observing the developments south of the Gulf of Finland, had no difficulty in interpreting the meaning of the events that brought the three republics under Soviet domination. It seemed obvious that, no matter what the Russian professions or explanations contended or their promises offered, the admission of Soviet military forces not only exposed these states to the threat of occupation but actually meant occupation. This view was of basic importance when the Finns turned to counter the Soviet move directed against them. It came on October 5 when Finland was invited to discuss, in Moscow, certain unspecified "concrete political questions." The invitation was practically a command, for a reply was requested within two days.

While the "concrete political questions" alluded to in the Soviet invitation were not specified, the invitation recalled to mind the inconclusive three-phase Russo-Finnish secret talks between April, 1938, and March, 1939 during which the USSR had proposed various territorial cessions or lease arrangements, alleging important Soviet defense needs as the reason and justification for the demands put forth. The discussions which began on October 11 and ended, for all practical purposes, on November 8—the Finns thought at the time that they had merely been adjourned—turned out to be a high-level continuation and elaboration of the earlier proposals and counterproposals.

The main Soviet demands, put forth by Stalin himself at the first meeting in the Kremlin October 12, may be summarized as follows: Finland was (1) to accept a mutual-aid pact (the proposal was dropped during the discussion); (2) to lease the Hanko Peninsula

---

[1] The three republics were absorbed into the Soviet Union in the summer of 1940 and thus ceased to be independent states.

in southwest Finland and the surrounding area to the USSR for thirty years, for a naval base, and to provide an anchorage in a bay off Hanko; (3) to cede certain islands in the Gulf of Finland; (4) to accept a change in the Russo-Finnish border on the Karelian Isthmus, involving a substantial area, in order to "increase the security of Leningrad"; (5) to accept the dismantling, as the USSR allegedly stood ready to do, of fortifications on the Karelian Isthmus; and (6) to cede a part of the Petsamo area on the Arctic Ocean in order to correct a boundary previously, the Russians claimed, "clumsily and artificially" drawn.

In return for these concessions, the USSR offered to cede a frontier area of Karelia along the Finnish border. Much was made of the size of the area offered—3,445 square miles, or twice the size of the territories demanded—the implication being that the Soviets offered generous compensation for the Finnish territory it sought to acquire. The offer and later slight modifications of the Russian demands on the Karelian Isthmus failed to convince the Finns that the interests of their country would be served by accepting the Soviet proposals. On the contrary, they held throughout that considerations of Finland's national security and the requirements of absolute neutrality dictated a negative answer to Moscow. Certain minor concessions were offered, however. The Finns agreed to a rectification of the Karelian Isthmus border in a manner that would have moved the border area closest to Leningrad some eight miles farther north, and offered to cede a few islands in the Gulf of Finland. They also stood ready to accept an addition to the nonaggression pact of 1932 which would obligate the signatories to abstain not only from attack but also from aiding, in any way, an aggressor. These concessions were rejected as inadequate by the USSR. The discussions ended when the Finnish delegates left Moscow on November 13. Before leaving, they forwarded a written statement to Molotov expressing the hope that later discussions would lead to satisfactory results.

Neither the delegation nor the country at large believed that the USSR would resort to war, in view of its repeated professions of peace and the commitment to peace (and arbitration in the event of international conflicts) in nonaggression pacts and other agreements. Nor had the Soviets used the threat of force as a tactic in their efforts to force Finland to follow the path chosen by Estonia, Latvia, and Lithuania. This view turned out to be too optimistic, however. The situation became ominous on November 26 when Molotov claimed that Soviet territory had been violated by unprovoked shelling of a Russian village by Finnish artillery. Finnish denials that Finnish artillery could have fired on the village in question were rejected out of hand, as were Finnish claims that only Soviet artillery activity had been verified at the time when the alleged attack had occurred. Finland suggested that the matter be submitted to a commission of arbitration. Finland also stated that "in order to afford convincing evidence of its sincere wish to come to an understanding" with the USSR and to "refute the assertions of the Soviet government that Finland has adopted a hostile attitude" toward the Soviets and threatened Leningrad, "the government is prepared to reach an agreement [with the USSR] regarding the withdrawal of [Finland's] defense forces [on the Karelian Isthmus] to such a distance from Leningrad that they cannot be alleged to be a threat" to the security of the city.

The Finnish proposals led nowhere. Before the communication could be delivered to the Soviet foreign office, the Finnish minister to the USSR received a note from the Kremlin. It illustrated the tactic Hitler had used four months earlier when he attempted to justify the invasion of Poland by contending that Germany had been forced to resort to military operations against Poland because of a Polish invasion of German territory: "As is well known, the attacks by units of Finnish armed forces continue not only on the Karelian Isthmus" but also elsewhere. "The Soviet Union can no longer tolerate this situation. Because of the situation . . . for which [Finland] alone is responsible," the USSR "can no longer maintain normal relations with Finland." American and Scandinavian efforts to intercede and to offer good offices in the attempt to avoid a crisis were accepted by Finland but rejected by the Soviets. Military operations began on November 29 when Russian forces crossed the Finnish border in Petsamo on the Arctic. A full-scale attack was launched on the next day when Helsinki and other cities were bombed and a general Soviet offensive by land, by air, and by sea became a brutal fact. The magnitude of the Soviet operations on the first day of the war showed incontestably that preparations extending over many weeks had preceded the decision to strike.

The Soviet invasion left the Finns with but two alternatives: to fight or to submit. The decision was, unhesitatingly, to fight.

The war thus begun ultimately became two separate wars. The first was a two-phase war fought against the USSR. It lasted until the armistice of September, 1944, and formally ended with the signing of a peace treaty in Paris on February 10, 1947. The second was fought against Germany. It lasted from September 15, 1944, until April 27, 1945, when the last German troops were ousted, after heavy fighting, from north Finland. After having been, according to Finnish interpretations, merely a cobelligerent but in Allied eyes an ally of Germany from June, 1941, till September, 1944, Finland thus became in the last year of the war a cobelligerent of the Allies fighting a common enemy. The obligation to fight in behalf of the Allied cause was imposed by the Soviet-dictated terms of the preliminary peace in 1944. Cobelligerency, costly in lives and property, gave no immunity to later Soviet exactions embodied in a final peace treaty signed in 1947.

THE WINTER WAR, 1939–1940

Finnish military planners and informed opinion in general had proceeded before 1939 on a simple assumption, seemingly justified by the country's policy of peace and the general Big Power constellation in Europe. The assumption was that, if Finland were unfortunately drawn into a war, involvement would come only in connection with a Big Power war. Such a war would mean that Finland could count upon the aid of the adversary of the power attacking the nation. This basic calculation had been rendered meaningless by the Hitler-Stalin agreement and its consequences. Foreign aid therefore appeared only a remote possibility when the Finns girded themselves for the unequal contest on November 30.

The resources available to Finland were modest in the extreme. The Russian attack engaged some 26–29 divisions, each 18,700 men strong, and approximately 2,000 tanks. Finnish defense forces consisted of 9 divisions, of 15,400 men each, and 56 small tanks. The disparity in artillery and other armament was equally great or greater. The whole Finnish army had only 37 antitank guns when the war began. The supply of ammunition was critically low. According to realistic estimates, the infantry had ammunition for only two months' fighting; artillery shells sufficed, probably, for three weeks. The country had modest equipment for only 275,000 men, with the result that a large part of the 400,000 men in the ranks in the closing stages of the war fought in partly civilian garb. The air force was equally inadequate: 30 bombers, 56 fighters, and 59 reconnaissance planes. The superiority of the Soviet fleet was no less obvious, although the severe winter in 1939–40 greatly restricted all naval operations and robbed the USSR of much of its advantage.

While the Finns' striking power had improved by the end of the war, it remained, in terms of armament, woefully inferior to the forces employed by the USSR. Sober estimates placed the number of Soviet planes used to maintain unquestioned air superiority over Finland at about 2,500; Finland was at best able to keep less than 300 planes operating against the enemy. The Finns succeeded in purchasing 425 planes abroad during the war, but most of them reached Finland only after the war had ended. Manpower resources likewise continued throughout the war to give the aggressor a solid advantage which no amount of Finnish prowess or ingenuity could destroy.

Modest as Finland's military establishment and potential were, the nation had one important although intangible resource of incalculable value. It could draw strength from the knowledge that the Soviets had undertaken the invasion without the slightest provocation or justification. The obvious fact that the Finns were the victims of naked aggression, and that the world clearly understood this fact, gave them a great moral and psychological advantage. Max Jakobsson has indicated, in his admirable study of the "Winter War," one aspect of this advantage when he remarks that the government and people alike responded to the Russian attack "with a prosaic concentration on . . . the problems connected with the task of putting the country on a war footing. The record of [November 30] contains no significant manifestations of shock, anger or fear [produced] by the Soviet aggression, no great emotional scenes, no dramatic gestures. It was as if everyone in Finland had deliberately underplayed his part, to produce what could be called a collective understatement." [2] The Soviet attack had the immediate effect of uniting the country as it never had been united before, and immensely steeled the resolve of the whole nation to resist the invader. Difficult as it is to evaluate psychological and moral factors of this kind, there appears to be no doubt but that they were of the greatest importance in sustaining the Finns in the determined effort to keep their country from falling under Soviet domination.

The resolve to do everything possible short of abject surrender to end the war and reestablish peace was underlined by the decision to form a new cabinet immediately after the war had begun. The government in office during the Moscow discussions and when the Soviet attack began was a coalition cabinet headed by the Progressive Premier A. K. Cajander. Premier Cajander and his colleagues had been fully supported by the Parliament through the ominous weeks in October and November. His cabinet was given a vote of confidence endorsing the policy followed during the negotiations with the Soviets. It was not held responsible for the war imposed on the country by Soviet aggression. It was felt, however, that the Cajander Cabinet might be considered an obstacle by the Soviets to renewed discussions to end the war. A new government was therefore appointed on December 1. It began its labors the next day.

The cabinet was headed by a Progressive, R. Ryti, who had served for several years as the governor of the Bank of Finland. Its fourteen members included four Agrarians, four Social Democrats, two Conservatives, and two Swede-Finns. The foreign affairs portfolio went to V. Tanner, the veteran laborite. His appointment would emphatically suggest to Moscow, it was hoped, Finnish readiness to sue for peace at once. The main objective of the Ryti Ministry was to end the war by renewing discussions with the Russians. Unanimously accepting this purpose, the cabinet decided, at its

[2] Max Jakobson, *The Diplomacy of the Winter War* (Cambridge, Mass., 1961), p. 158.

first meeting, to approach the Swedish government with a request for mediation leading to a resumption of negotiations with the USSR. Sweden was also requested to inform Moscow that Finland stood ready to offer new proposals, the implication being that additional concessions to the Soviets might be made. Molotov rejected the Swedish offer of mediation on December 4 and claimed that the USSR was not at war with the Finnish government, having recognized the "Finnish Democratic Government" at Terijoki, a small village on the Karelian Isthmus located a few miles from the Russian border.

The Soviet government showed at the very outset of the war that it was aiming at more than the military defeat of Finland and the acquisition of the territories the Finns had been asked to surrender during the October–November discussions. On the first day of the war, the Moscow radio announced the formation, by the Finnish Communist party, of the "Democratic Government of Finland," at Terijoki. The village had been abandoned by Finnish troops and was one of the first to be "liberated" by Soviet troops. Moscow recognized the new "government," which was, obviously, set up by the Soviet itself. It was headed by the Finnish Communist leader, O. W. Kuusinen. Kuusinen had been a member of the Finnish Red government in 1918, had fled to Russia after the revolt collapsed, and had risen to the high office of Secretary of the Comintern Executive Committee. He now expected to return to his native Finland, after an exile of twenty-one years, to complete the task begun in 1918. His "government" at once proceeded to provide justification for the Soviet invasion by announcing that the Red army had crossed the frontier "at the request" of the Kuusinen government. "It will depart . . . as soon as the People's Government asks it to leave." The Red army had come to aid the Finns. "Only the Soviet Union, which rejects in principle the seizure by force of territory and the enslavement of nations, could agree to use its armed might not for the purpose of attacking Finland or enslaving its people, but for securing its independence." [3]

[3] Statement printed in *Pravda*, December 4, 1939. Quoted in Jakobson, *The Diplomacy of the Winter War*, p. 168.

The Terijoki puppet government concluded a treaty with the USSR on December 2. It set forth still other boldly phrased fictions. As a result of "the heroic struggle of the Finnish people and through the exertions of the Red Army [the] real focus of war infection which the former plutocratic government in Finland had created on the frontiers of the Soviet Union for the benefit of the imperialist powers" would be destroyed. And the Finnish people having "created their own democratic republic, which derives its support entirely from the people, the time has come to establish good relations of friendship" between the two countries, "and with united forces to protect the security and inviolability of our nations," by concluding a "treaty of mutual assistance."

The treaty provided for "certain adjustments" of the frontier on the Karelian Isthmus and for the cession or sale to the USSR of the Hanko Peninsula and islands in the Gulf of Finland. In return, the Soviets agreed that "areas in Soviet Karelia" amounting to "70,000 square kilometers" would be "incorporated into the territory of the Finnish Democratic Republic." The USSR was to pay 120 million Finnish marks for "railway inventory now on the Karelian Isthmus which is to be removed to the Soviet Union." The treaty, concluded for a period of twenty-five years, also included provisions for a mutual assistance arrangement operative in the event that "any European power attacks or threatens to attack the Soviet Union through Finnish territory."

The publication of the treaty made it clear in Finland that the purpose of the war was to destroy the republic and to introduce a Communist regime headed by the veteran revolutionary Kuusinen. The Soviet leaders appear to have expected that the formation of the Terijoki puppet government and the treaty of December 2 would be welcomed by the common folk in Finland and bring them over to the "liberators." The reaction of the workers was quite the contrary. It was clearly shown by the joint statement issued by the Finnish Social Democratic party and the Confederation of Trade Unions, which read in part: "The desire of the Finnish working class for peace is sincere. However, if the invaders do not respect our will to peace, the working class of Finland is left with but one choice, and that is to fight, weapon in hand, against aggression and in defense of democracy, peace, and the right of our country to remain its own master."

The Soviet war aims commitment implicit in the setting up of the Terijoki "government" suggested that a compromise agreement with the USSR was virtually impossible. The Finnish government nevertheless continued the effort to bring the war to an end, preliminary to a resumption of discussions with Moscow. The attempt to enlist the aid of the League of Nations in finding a way out of the dilemma was a conspicuous illustration of the effort.

The Finnish case was submitted to Secretary General Avenol on December 3 in a letter which stated in part that "Finland has never done anything against its powerful neighbor and has neglected no effort in its endeavor to live in peace with its neighbor." This had been to no avail, however. "Making use of fabricated border incidents and alleging that Finland is unwilling to contribute to the security of Leningrad, the USSR has repudiated the nonaggression pact and rejected the proposal of the Finnish Government which provided for mediation by an impartial power." In the light of the situation that had developed because of the Soviets' resort to arms, Finland asked that the Assembly be convoked for the purpose of taking measures necessary to end the attack of the USSR.

The League acted quickly. The Assembly convened on December 9 and the Council on December 11, but to no purpose. The USSR, having been invited to appear, refused to attend. In replying to the League's invitation to send representatives to Geneva, Molotov contended that "the Soviet Union is not at war with Finland, nor does it threaten the people of Finland with war. . . . The Soviet Union maintains peaceful relations with the Finnish Democratic Republic. Its government concluded on December 2 a treaty of friendship and mutual assistance with the Soviet Union. This treaty has settled all the questions" regarding which the USSR had negotiated "unsuccessfully with the former government of Finland now ousted from office." The Soviet reply also stated that the Kuusinen-led government had asked for Soviet military assistance in order to destroy as speedily as possible and in cooperation with Soviet forces the "most dangerous seat of war" allegedly created by "the former rulers of Finland."

The result of League action was most modest and had no effect upon the course of the war. Having looked into the facts, the Assembly "solemnly condemned the action of the Soviet Union against Finland" and appealed to the members of the League to extend to Finland "material and humanitarian" aid, to the extent of their resources, "and to refrain from any action calculated to reduce Finland's ability to resist." On December 14 the Assembly stated that the Soviet Union had placed itself, by its own action, outside the League of Nations—an evasive way of saying that the USSR had ceased to be a member of the League. Seven of the fifteen members of the Council had the courage to vote for the statement; the remainder abstained. Britain, France, and Belgium were the only European states ready to stand up and be counted; Finland's Scandinavian neighbors and the rest of Europe found silent abstention congenial. Only the Union of South Africa, Egypt, Bolivia, and the Dominican Republic stood forth with the British, the French, and the Belgians as the guardians of mankind's conscience.

Finland's astonishing resistance to the Russian invasion aroused the sympathies of the civilized world from the first day of the war. Friendly concern and admiration were in evidence everywhere except in the ranks of the Communists. Winston Churchill's was merely the most eloquent expression of the appreciation of Finland's position in the outside world, when he remarked on January 20, 1940: "Finland alone—in danger of death, superb, sublime Finland—shows what free men can do. The service that Finland has rendered humanity is magnificent," he continued, and added that "if the light of freedom" in the Scandinavian North should finally be extinguished—as it would be if Finland were defeated—"it might well herald a return to the Dark Ages." Numerous as expressions of good will and encouragement were, they did not mean, however, readiness to offer the Finns real aid. The feeble action of the League members at the Assembly and Council meetings in December had indicated the difficulties involved in providing material and military assistance to the victim of aggression.

It was only after certain changes in the Western Allies' plans of action had emerged that Britain and France decided to give Finland direct military support. The war against Hitler had been, in the idiom then frequently used, a "phony war" since the end of September when Poland had been divided by Hitler and Stalin. The situation created by the Soviet attack on Finland appeared to provide an opportunity to strike at Germany, at least indirectly. With this in mind, the Supreme War Council agreed on December 19 upon "the importance of rendering all possible assistance to Finland." It was contemplated that Norway and Sweden would also aid the Finns, the Allies to contribute substantial forces to the enterprise. The basic purpose of the plan, not revealed at the time, was to reduce or end the export of Swedish iron ore from Narvik in north Norway to Germany, thereby extending the Allies' economic blockade of Germany, and in the process to create, if possible, another fighting front against the Nazis.

At the turn of the century, Narvik had been the home of a handful of fishermen. Because of the immense importance of the rich iron ore mined at Kiruna in Swedish Lapland and the fact that the nearest seaports, at the head of the Gulf of Bothnia, were ice-free only during the summer months, a railroad had been constructed by 1902 from the mines to Narvik two hundred miles away. The great natural harbor at Narvik became the main outlet of the ore traffic amounting to some 9,000,000 tons annually. Narvik itself grew into a prosperous city with 12,000 inhabitants.

Winston Churchill had urged drastic action to stop the transportation of ore from Narvik because large quantities of it were carried to Germany by ships using Norwegian territorial waters. On December 22, 1939, the British Cabinet decided upon a strong diplomatic protest to Norway against the misuse of her territorial waters. By December 28, the Swedish government had been persuaded to reduce shipments to Germany by making use of "technical obstruction," in order not to arouse German enmity. Plans were also drawn for the landing of British forces, sent to aid Finland, at Narvik. The problem of the Swedish iron ore and the plan to assist Finland had become two aspects of an effort the basic purpose of which was to serve the Allies' war plans against Germany.

The success of the plan required Norwegian and Swedish cooperation on a scale and in a manner the two countries refused to grant. The Allies' requests that armed units and matériel be given free right of transit to Finland were resolutely rejected. The reason for the refusal was the firm conviction that to accommodate the Allies would expose both countries to German retaliation and result in bringing them into the great war. Undaunted, the Allies persisted. The Supreme War Council approved a joint Anglo-French plan for a Scandinavian expedition on February 5. The expedition was to take over Narvik and establish control over the Swedish iron ore fields, denying their use to the Germans. Some 150,000 men were to be assigned to the enterprise. This was to be no minor diversionary move but a major operation which would have turned all of Scandinavia into a theater of war and in all probability would have led to a full-blown military alliance between Germany and the USSR.

The refusal of Norway and Sweden to allow free passage did not cause the Allies to abandon the plan. They appear to have been convinced that, once the expedition was ready, the two neutrals would yield to suasion and pressure and permit the Allied troops to pass through. Norway was informed by the Allies on March 2 that Britain was "in a position to send force to secure" Trondheim, Bergen, and Stavanger within four days of Norway's grant of passage, and that "the forces for Finland and those destined for the support of Sweden" could arrive in Norway on March 20 if Norway accepted the plan "within the next few days." The Allies also prodded the Finns to present a formal request for British and French aid and to second their effort to gain passage through the reluctant neutrals.

While these plans were being elaborated by the Allies, the Finns had continued their effort to bring the war to an end. Within a few days of the beginning of the war, the Foreign Relations Committee of the Ryti Cabinet concluded that German mediation seemed to offer the best chance of success. Soundings were therefore taken in Germany and through the German minister in Helsinki, Wipert von Blücher. The first informal discussions revealed, in the words of Blücher, that Germany "had no part in the Finnish war" and had no interest in the attempt to persuade the Soviets to resume discussions with Finland. Finnish hopes of German assistance in the attempt to establish liaison with the USSR were dissipated on

January 19 when Blücher informed the Finnish government that
"the German government is of the opinion that for the moment
there are no prospects of settling the conflict." Later discussions
merely confirmed the Finnish impression that Germany was unwilling or unable to open the door to Moscow.

Attempts were also made to reach the Kremlin through Stockholm. Sweden offered mediation, after certain efforts sponsored by
private individuals had seemingly produced no results, on January
25. Thanks to Sweden's good offices, Finland learned that the
Soviets were prepared—despite the earlier ostentatious commitment
to the Kuusinen "government" at Terijoki—to negotiate with the
Ryti Government, whose legal existence it had previously denied.
Four days later Moscow made it known that Finland was expected
to make territorial cessions larger than those discussed in October–
November. In the course of the next six weeks, Finland attempted
to obtain satisfactory assurances regarding (1) the amount and time
of arrival of the armed assistance offered by the Allies; (2) the
attitude of Sweden and Norway regarding the knotty problem of
transit of Allied troops; (3) the possibility of obtaining direct aid
from Sweden in the form of volunteers and military supplies; and
(4) the peace terms insisted upon by the Soviets.

During the long weeks of discussion and weighing of possibilities
it became clear that Allied aid would at best be inadequate and too
late; that Sweden could not be counted on to furnish the military
assistance needed, despite the good will and moral support of the
Swedish people; that, notwithstanding the exceptional success of
the Finnish forces in resisting the Russian invasion, the superiority
of Soviet forces and equipment would ultimately breach the Finnish
lines and expose the country to the dangers of military occupation;
and that Russian terms would therefore have to be accepted while
a chance for negotiation still existed.

Negotiations with Moscow began on March 8. The Soviet demands were received the next day. Their receipt created a particularly difficult dilemma, for Helsinki had received, on March 7, a
communication from Premier Eduard Daladier of France stating
that the Allies had expected for several days a Finnish appeal for
aid, that Russia feared the Finns would request Allied assistance and,

desirous of avoiding "a catastrophe," was ready to negotiate "in order to be able to destroy" Finland later. "I assure you once more, we are ready to give our help at once. The airplanes are ready to take off. The operational force is ready." Requesting a speedy reply, the statement contained a thinly veiled threat: "If Finland does not now make her appeal to the Western Powers, it is obvious that at the end of the war [the Allies] cannot assume the slightest responsibility for the final settlement regarding Finnish territory." Daladier indicated that a reply was expected by March 12 at the latest.

After carefully weighing the alternatives, the government decided that the stiff demands of the USSR had to be accepted. The terms of the Moscow peace treaty were signed on the evening of March 12, 1940, the day fixed by Daladier as the deadline for the reply to his communication.

The Peace of Moscow was a dictated peace involving no give-and-take proposals and counterproposals. It specified the cession not only of the areas demanded in the Karelian Isthmus during the discussion in October–November but of all southeastern Finland along the line drawn in the peace of 1721. In addition, it provided for the surrender of the Salla district along the northeast frontier and the leasing of the Hanko area, for a Soviet naval base, for thirty years. Finland also agreed to construct a railroad—"if possible during 1940"—in the north, connecting the then Finnish railhead at Kemijärvi with the Soviet frontier to the east, thus providing a rail connection between Soviet Kandalaksha and, through north Finland, the Swedish border. The treaty also provided that the two states would undertake no aggression against each other and would abstain from "concluding any alliances or entering any coalitions" directed against the other signatory.

THE SECOND PHASE OF THE WAR, 1941–1944

Disappointing as the harsh terms of the Moscow peace were, they did not have a paralyzing effect on the Finnish people. It was felt that the country had given an exceptional, admirable account of itself in the war. The independence of the nation and the freedom of its citizens had been saved. The cost of having demonstrated before the world that even a small nation can stand erect among the free had been great, to be sure. The number of those killed on the front was 23,150. The number of wounded was 47,550, of whom 9,560 became permanent invalids. Including the civilians killed in bombings of cities and villages, the war had cost Finland 24,900 in dead alone. Over 420,000 people had lost their homes and livelihood by voluntarily choosing to leave the ceded areas and moving to truncated Finland. The problem of the displaced persons seemed insoluble at the time. Yet it was not difficult for the Finns to feel, as they began to enjoy the lengthening sunny days of the early spring in 1940, that the future could not well deny the nation, whatever the course of the Great Power war still in progress would turn out to be, the rewards due a people who had demonstrated its stubborn determination to do or die for freedom.[4]

The fact that the nation's freedom had been saved—miraculously saved, it seemed, in view of the intentions of the Soviets at the beginning of the war—and the realization that attempts to evade the Moscow peace would invite new dangers and, possibly, spell national disaster account for the resolve to accept the verdict of the treaty in full. The determination to do so was demonstrated not only by the evacuation of the ceded areas but also by the ready acceptance of the complications and great costs of providing for the displaced persons. They numbered about 11 percent of the total population of the country. Laws providing for the allocation of land for the displaced farmers and other relief measures were enacted in April–May, 1940. A substantial once-for-all property tax ranging from 2.5 to 20 percent was levied on the whole nation in order to provide necessary funds for reconstruction. A land distribution bill was enacted on June 6, 1940, providing for the establishment of

[4] The question has been frequently raised, why did the USSR decide to end the war before the Finnish lines were broken and the country was open to military occupation? The question is especially interesting in view of the Soviet sponsorship of the Kuusinen puppet government. That "government" was quietly abandoned by the USSR, leaving the impression that it had originally been established merely as a tactic in the effort to bring Finland to surrender. Be that as it may, the reasons for the Soviet failure to press its potential advantage in March, 1940, must remain, in the absence of documented explanations, a matter of conjecture.

38,900 new farm holdings. The acreage involved was taken, in large part, from existing arable or cultivable land in the hands of owners deemed able to contribute part of their holdings. Another law afforded compensation for wartime property losses, ranging from 100 percent in the case of losses up to $6,500 and 10 percent for those of $1,000,000. The number of the evacuated receiving state aid had been reduced, because of the government's speedy action, from 350,000 in May, 1940, to 177,000 in June, 1941. The various measures taken to speed the process of postwar reconstruction were carried through with exceptional dispatch, partly because of the desire to preserve and strengthen one of the most impressive achievements during the dramatic months of the war, namely, the singular spirit of unity and concord that had bound the people together more firmly than any earlier national experience.

The many-sided and exacting effort to repair the ravages of war and to stabilize the nation's economy under the exceptional difficulties which the world war imposed had barely begun when it became clear that Finland's trials were by no means over and that the peace of March, 1940, left much to be desired. Ultimately, the period of peace became only a fifteen-month truce between the Winter War and the second phase of the war that began in June, 1941. Within a few weeks of the signing of the treaty in March, 1940, the Soviet Union began to insist upon additional advantages and concessions. The new exactions were revealed by a lengthening list of demands relating to certain aspects of Finland's foreign policy and internal affairs and new economic and other concessions for the Soviets. They showed that Moscow considered Finnish sovereignty and security as concepts subject to Soviet interpretation and caprice.

The peace treaty imposed no reparations obligation on Finland. The USSR insisted, however, upon compensations equivalent to reparations in all but name. Claiming that Finland had "illegally" removed private and public property from the areas ceded to the Soviets and that compensation must be provided for property destroyed in the areas in question during the war, the USSR demanded restitution in an amount that varied from 95 to 145 million gold rubles. Scores of industrial plants therefore had to be equipped anew and considerable amounts of railroad rolling stock and the like turned over to the Soviets. The Russians also attempted to obtain the valuable Petsamo nickel mine, before the war leased to an English subsidiary of the International Nickel Company of Sudbury, Ontario, but the matter was still pending when war broke out in June, 1941.

The lengthening list of Soviet exactions during Finland's "ordeal by peace" included demands for a variety of other advantages as well. Instances of open interference with some aspects of Finnish foreign policy or internal political and economic matters also occurred. The Soviets insisted on and forced through the demilitarization of the Åland Islands under Russian supervision. They demanded on June 27, 1940, without any treaty or other right, and obtained on September 9, 1940, transit rights on south Finnish railroads from the Soviet border to the Hanko naval base area (possibly, some held at the time, because Sweden had granted in July approximately analogous transit rights on certain Swedish railways to the Germans, although obviously there was no causal connection between the two concessions). Nor was foreign policy immune to interference. Shortly before accepting the peace terms in March, Finland raised the question with Sweden and Norway whether they were inclined to consider a joint agreement for mutual defense. The replies were favorable. Nothing came of the plan, however, because the Soviets insisted on considering it as a design for an aggressive Scandinavian alliance directed against the USSR. By becoming a member of it, the Russians alleged, Finland would violate the peace treaty. Sweden and Norway were bluntly warned by Molotov on March 29 that their participation "in an alliance with Finland would mean that these countries have abandoned their traditional policy of neutrality for a new foreign policy from which it would be impossible for the USSR not to draw the obvious conclusions."

The plan was abandoned. The occupation of Denmark and Norway by Hitler's forces in April removed the scheme from the realm of the possible. The occupation of the two countries placed both Sweden and Finland in an exceptionally isolated position and exposed them to new dangers from the USSR or Germany. Faced by the precarious situation, Finland proposed that a Swedish-Finnish defense treaty be considered. The ensuing discussions indicated that larger areas of common concern than mere defense would have to be recognized; at least partly common foreign and economic policies would likewise be required. These plans also the USSR interpreted as the beginning of a conspiracy designed to violate the March peace treaty. The scheme therefore collapsed in the preliminary discussion phase.

Meanwhile several instances of Soviet interference in Finnish internal affairs were recorded. Certain cabinet members—V. Tanner among them—resigned in August because of continued Soviet attacks insisting that the ministers in question were working against or disturbing "good" Finnish-USSR relations. On the eve of the December, 1940, presidential elections, Moscow made it clear that, if any one of four named men were chosen President, the election would be interpreted by the Kremlin as an indication of Finnish resolve not to observe the March treaty. Numerous evidences of Communist espionage and Soviet military activity in the summer suggested the possibility that the stage was being set for Finland's "voluntary" inclusion in the Soviet Union by the use of techniques—military occupation followed by "elections"—employed in bringing Estonia, Latvia, and Lithuania into the fold in June–July (they were formally brought into the Soviet Union on August 3–6, 1940).

Soviet extortion of special concessions and interference in the nation's internal affairs, and the failure to obtain Swedish support because of Soviet opposition, had left Finland by the autumn of 1940 ominously exposed to further exactions by her eastern neighbor. The only power conceivably able to give aid, Germany, seemed solidly committed to its partnership with the USSR. That partnership had cleared the decks for the invasion of Poland in 1939 and had given the Soviets a free hand in the Baltic countries and in invading Finland. Hitler had remained neutral during the Winter War, but Germany's neutrality had yielded no advantage to Finland, while it enabled the USSR to wage war without interference. Germany as a counterweight to the Soviets thus seemed an unlikely prospect.

The situation changed during the summer of 1940. Cautiously scanning the international horizon for hopeful signs, the Finns were heartened by certain developments in August. One was the release by Germany of considerable Finnish arms cargoes in transit through Norway at the time of the Germans' invasion of Norway and confiscated by them. The arms cargoes were now allowed to proceed to Finland, as were similar cargoes that had been detained in Denmark. Some of the munitions involved were actually German or German war booty, but they were masked, for the sake of secrecy, as Finnish cargoes held by the Germans. A contract for arms purchases in Germany was also signed in August. In connection with this important transaction the Germans raised the question of transit of German troops, through Finland, to and from north Norway, citing the Swedish grant of similar accommodation on July 5 as pertinent precedent.

Two main considerations argued for the German proposal. To have rejected it would have destroyed the chance to obtain much-needed munitions from the only country able to sell munitions in sufficient quantities. Secondly, it was assumed that if the transit right were granted it would necessarily lead to a concrete German interest in the situation in Finland that could be counted upon to act as a potential counterweight to further Soviet pretensions. Nor was the German use of west and north Finnish ports, railroads, and roads seen as a possible occupation threat, as was the case with the Russian demand for transit rights to Hanko, first broached by the Soviets on July 9. After consultations involving President Kallio, Commander-in-Chief Mannerheim, and others, the German proposal was accepted. A preliminary agreement was signed on September 12 and a final agreement ten days later. By the latter date, the transit traffic was already under way. The agrement was expanded later as a result of discussions on November 19–22.

When the members of Parliament were informed of the arrange-ments with Germany, the news was received with relief. Public opinion likewise appears to have approved. Sweden, England, and the USSR were informed of the agreement immediately after it had been concluded. The USSR offered no objections; official quarters in Sweden offered congratulations; and while the British presented a formal protest, private statements made it clear that the reasons for the arrangements were understood in London.

Unknown to Finland and to the world at large, Germany's attitude toward Finland was gradually changing and by the end of November it had come to mean resistance to further Soviet operations in the republic. This was disclosed during the Molotov-Ribbentrop discussions on November 10–12 in which Hitler himself participated. Molotov asserted that the USSR intended to solve the Finnish problem by annexing the country and took for granted that Germany still recognized the Soviets' full liberty of action in Finland and would therefore withdraw the "transit troops" from the country. He was given no satisfaction. Instead, he was told that, while the USSR had "political interests" to care for in Finland, Germany was interested in Finnish nickel and timber products important for the war and did not want the Baltic area to become a theater of war that might result in the British using Finnish air bases against Germany. Germany had no political aims in Finland—an area, Hitler pointed out, which had been identified as a Soviet sphere of influence—but assumed that the USSR would properly recognize Germany's economic needs and interests. Molotov's attempts to obtain Hitler's approval for the reduction of Finland to the status of a satellite or worse had failed. Germany's refusal to accommodate the USSR in this matter appears in retrospect to have been one of the early indications of the Hitlerite plans leading to the attack on the Soviets in June, 1941.[5]

Hitler's refusal to accept Moscow's purposes regarding Finland did not reflect an interest in Finland's safety or welfare as such. Probably early in December he gave orders for the drafting of plans for an invasion of the USSR and undoubtedly was committed, in his own mind, to this enterprise when parrying Molotov's moves in Berlin. The main outline of "Operation Barbarossa" was ready by the end of December. The invasion plan, finally set in motion on June 22, 1941, was top secret and became fully known only after the war ended. As regards Finland, German plans remained unknown but alert observers sensed by March–April that Hitler had changed course. The impression was strengthened by the first

[5] The Berlin discussions are conveniently summarized in Alan Bullock's *Hitler* (2d ed.), pp. 616–21. The evidence clearly shows that nothing short of Soviet occupation of Finland was intended.

cautious German effort in May to arrange military cooperation with Finland.

Upon the invitation of Germany, a Finnish delegation headed by Marshal Mannerheim's chief-of-staff, General E. Heinrichs, visited the German high command at Salzburg on May 25 and Berlin, where the discussions were concluded, on May 26. The Germans reported considerable concentrations of Soviet forces along the western border of the USSR, necessitating German countermoves, but it was pointed out (contrary to facts revealed after the war ended) that Germany had no intention of starting a war. In the event that the Soviets should attack, however, Germany would be forced to undertake operations in the far north involving the sending of a division through Finland to Norway. The Finns having made it clear that they had no authority to discuss, negotiate, or agree to any commitment, and in view of the repeated statements by President Ryti and others that Finland would not under any circumstances launch an unprovoked attack on the USSR, the Salzburg discussions were limited to a weighing of hypothetical alternatives based on the premise of an attack initiated by the USSR. No agreement defining or calling for military cooperation was presented by the Germans or accepted or signed by the Finns. The Germans did not mention Operation Barbarossa. The German interest in Finland, illustrated especially by the invitation to the Salzburg conversations, appeared to justify the surmise that Germany's policy toward the Soviet Union had changed in a manner that meant potential readiness to assist the Finns in facing future Soviet demands. The specific meaning of the change of policy could not be divined because of contradictory rumors and guesses. A measure of the uncertainties of the situation is offered by the instructions President Ryti gave Minister Kivimäki in Berlin on May 30. The envoy was directed to inform Germany that the negotiations with the USSR, carried on by Germany with the Soviets at the time, would result, Helsinki hoped, in guarantees of Finland's independence and, if possible, in a restoration of Finland's boundaries of 1939, modified to leave in the USSR's hands areas considered by the Russians vital to the defense of Leningrad. These and other Finnish suggestions turned out to be useless because at the time the Germans were not, contrary to their statements to the Finns, carrying on any negotiations with the USSR relating to these questions. The fact that the instructions were forwarded three weeks before the German invasion of the Soviets offers a measure of Finland's ignorance of Hitler's real purposes.

The Finns became aware that something was afoot in the second week of June when the number of Germans in north Finland suddenly increased. A division stationed in Norway was moved through Sweden—a special permission for the transfer was obtained from Sweden on June 15—to north Finland, and another, ostensibly moved through Finland to Norway, remained in north Finland. These developments, together with increasing concentrations of Russian and German troops along the new western borders of the USSR, suggested an impending crisis and led the Finns to order partial mobilization on June 10, carried out on an expanded scale on June 18. The deployment of forces along Finland's eastern border was strictly defensive.

When the German armies launched the attack on June 22, the Finns had no obligation or inclination to join the invasion of the USSR. Finland remained neutral. Her neutrality was recognized as a fact by Britain, Sweden, and others, Germany included. By June 25, however, the Soviet air attacks and land operations, begun on the twenty-second, the first day of the war, had assumed dimensions which led the government to announce in Parliament that a state of war had been imposed upon the country by the military aggression of the USSR. The government stated that, the country having been attacked, Finland would defend herself with all available means. The Premier's statement was unanimously endorsed by a vote of confidence, signalizing the unity of the nation when the second phase of the war began.[6]

[6] It has been alleged that Finland had entered into a secret agreement with Germany providing for military cooperation against the USSR, some time before June 22, 1941, and was, for all practical purposes, Hitler's partner in aggression. I have found no evidence to support the contention. Professor Korhonen's objective study, the excellent biography of Mannerheim by General Heinrichs, and other accounts of German-Finnish relations, as well as Finnish military operations well into July, 1941, suffice to deny the allega-

The Finnish government maintained from the first days of the war that the nation had been driven into the war by unprovoked Soviet aggression; that, while Finland was, by force of circumstances not of her own choosing, a cobelligerent of Germany, she was not involved in the Great Power war and was less still a "satellite" of Germany; and that she was fighting only for her own, limited objectives. The Allies refused to accept this contention. The United States also rejected it, even before the "day of infamy" at Pearl Harbor. Washington chose to see Finland as a mere handmaiden of Hitler, serving the aims of the dictator. In November, 1941, Secretary of State Hull raised the question to what extent Finnish military measures included combined operations with the Germans "vitally to injure Great Britain and her associates and to threaten the northern supply lines over which Russia is now receiving supplies and assistance from Great Britain and the United States to aid Russia in resisting the Hitler forces," and to what extent Finland's policy "is a menace to all America's aims for self-defense." After Pearl Harbor, the attitude of the United States stiffened. Intermittent efforts were made to persuade Finland to withdraw from the war. They failed. The reason was that no workable alternative guaranteeing Finnish independence or giving assurances against further Soviet aggression was offered.

The difficulties involved in the effort to take Finland out of the war were illustrated by the reception of the American-British-Soviet declaration in May, 1944. It invited Finland and the "satellites" to withdraw from the war, to cease all cooperation with Germany, and to resist "the forces of Nazism by every possible means." By heeding the advice of the Allies, they would shorten the war, reduce their own sacrifices, and contribute to the victory of the Allies. If they continued to fight, so much the worse for them. The "present

tion. The Germans pressed for an alliance agreement throughout the war. The Finns finally yielded when the Finns' war was about to end, on June 26, 1944. Its terms bound Finland not to make a separate peace with the USSR. Hitler's statement on June 22 that the Germans were fighting "side by side with their Finnish comrades" embarrassed the Finns because it implied the existence of a treaty providing for Finland's participation in the staging of the war against the USSR which Germany alone had begun and for which, therefore, Germany alone was responsible.

politics" of Finland, it was contended, merely contributed to the "strengthening of the German war-machine and did not aid in getting the country out of the war."

Despite the worsening position of Finland as a result of the rising tide of Soviet victories over German forces—on the whole, all had been quiet on the Russo-Finnish front since December, 1941, leaving the Finns in positions they considered advantageous—and the conclusion of the Finnish high command as early as February, 1943, that the Germans had lost the war, the Allied admonition went unheeded. The reason was obvious. Because of the absence of any guarantees of Finnish independence the only alternative to continued fighting that was being offered was the acceptance of Russian conquest, the dreaded prospect of which had led the Finns to take up arms in the first place. The May declaration and similar earlier Allied endeavors appear in retrospect to have been markedly inept and unrealistic because the effort underscored the unimportant and the obvious and therefore had no persuasive or coercive effect, or skirted around the really vital matter, the readiness of the USSR to accept a peace that would safeguard Finland's independence. Without such a guarantee Finland could see no choice but to continue fighting.

However resolutely the Finns attempted to carry on in a manner calculated to convince the outside world that theirs was a separate war, as the Winter War had been, and that Finland was neutral in the Great Power conflict—was, in other words, not serving German purposes—the course of events soon blurred the line the Finns tried to keep sharp and clear between the Finnish-Soviet war and the world war. Nine days after Finland had begun offensive operations against the USSR on July 10, Hitler demanded that Finland break off diplomatic relations with Britain in order to remove the danger that British diplomatic personnel might indulge in espionage for the benefit of the Soviets. The situation was handled with marked ineptness by Foreign Minister R. Witting and resulted in the closing of the consular services of both countries.

Because of German pressure for a binding alliance and Finnish resolve to avoid such an agreement, Finland signed in 1941 another treaty that was considered to have no practical significance and therefore was less objectionable. The treaty was the Anti-Comintern Pact.

The Anti-Comintern Pact had originally been signed by Germany and Japan on November 17, 1936. Italy signed it a year later, on November 6, 1937. Its ideological objective was the defeat of the Communist "world conspiracy." Its main provisions were stated in a secret protocol which bound the signatories to conclude no political treaties with the USSR; in the event of an attack by the Soviets, they agreed "to take no measures" that might aid the Soviets. It was expected that the pact would be accepted by other countries as well. Hitler himself disregarded it in the August 23, 1939, treaty with the USSR. During World War II, Hitler decided that a renewal of the original pact would demonstrate, if properly staged, the "unity" of Europe created under German auspices. The occasion was arranged for November 25, 1941, when nine European nations, Japan, and Manchukuo signed the pact in Berlin. Denmark and Finland were among the signers, neither country having, obviously, a free choice in the matter. Ciano, the Italian Foreign Minister, also a signer, confided to his diary: "The Germans were the masters of the house and they made us all feel it. . . . There is no way out of it. Their European hegemony has now been established. Whether this is good or bad is neither here nor there. . . . Consequently, it is best to sit at the right hand of the master of the house."

Finland had decided to sign (despite the realization that doing so probably would be interpreted abroad as a step toward joining the Axis) in order to avoid raising a troublesome issue with Germany in the midst of the war and probably also because the government felt it essential not to select a seat on the wrong side of "the master of the house." That the possible negative implications of signing the treaty were clearly seen by the Finns was shown by the attempts made to challenge them in advance. The leading Social Democratic daily, the *Suomen Sosialidemokraatti*, commented on the day following the signing of the pact: "The Pact does not . . . limit Finland's freedom of action; it does not change our relations with other countries; it does not tie us to any foreign ideology; it does not impose any political obligations on us. . . . Our war also remains the same as before: our war against Russia is separate from the World War and is waged only for our own freedom and security." A few days later (December 5) the paper called attention to the fact that the pact had not prevented the Ribbentrop-Molotov treaty in August, 1939, or the cooperation of the two dictatorships until the summer of 1941. It was not "considered in any way detrimental to the relations between the two countries, and at times it was half jokingly remarked that the USSR might worm its way into membership in the Pact."

Neither the signing of the Anti-Comintern Pact nor Finland's increasing dependence upon Germany for food and armament changed the Finns' claim that theirs was a separate war.[7] The difficulty of making the claim good and of ending the war on acceptable terms was illustrated early in 1943.

THE END OF THE WAR AND THE PEACE SETTLEMENT

The Finnish government and military leadership concluded in February, 1943, that an attempt should be made, especially in view of the worsening of Germany's position, to get out of the war. Using Sweden as an intermediary, soundings were taken in Moscow but to no avail. The effort was supported by the press and public opinion. The executive committee of the Social Democratic party adopted a resolution on February 15 which underlined a view repeatedly stated during the war:

Finland's present war, a continuation of the Winter War, is a defensive war into which our people were forced against their will. Its purpose is solely to safeguard the freedom and independence of our country. It is, therefore, a separate war; we have no part in the war between the Great Powers. . . . The fact that Finland and Germany are fighting the same enemy, Russia, does not alter this fact. Finland is, therefore, free to decide on withdrawing from the war whenever a favorable moment appears and her freedom and independence are guaranteed.

[7] Finland at war as a cobelligerent of Germany found herself in a situation involving basic, sharply defined contradictions. Germany had deliberately launched an invasion of the Soviet Union intended to carry the Hitlerite dictatorship toward full European hegemony; Finland was defending her territory already once despoiled by the Soviets. Finland's purpose was to remain an independent nation; Hitler's aim was to eliminate the USSR as an obstacle to the triumph of the Nazi order of things.

The problem of getting out of the war was gradually translated from declarations of readiness and intent to a concrete question of ways and means after March 20, 1943, when the government received an American offer of good offices to assist in establishing peace between Finland and the USSR. In considering the offer, the government asked the American chargé d'affaires for information regarding Soviet terms and guarantees to be given to Finland. It was also decided to inform Germany and to explain why the American offer could not be rejected out of hand without exploring its possibilities for peace. Foreign Minister A. Ramsay visited Berlin on March 26 to discuss the matter. Ribbentrop expressed strong disapproval and stated that, if Finland concluded a separate peace, "extreme conclusions" would be drawn by Germany. To avoid further difficulties, Finland was advised to conclude an alliance with Germany providing among other things that neither signatory would make a separate peace. The suggestion was rejected by Finland, as were later proposals urging a pact. It was not until June, 1944, when Finland's position had greatly deteriorated, that a special agreement was accepted.

Meantime no information regarding Soviet terms or possible guarantees was received through American or other channels, and it became clear that the United States stood ready to act merely as an intermediary to get negotiations under way. The Finnish reply to the American offer, therefore, stated that, no indication of the bases of negotiation or of Russian willingness to discuss peace having been received, Finland was unable to take advantage of America's good offices and saw no other possibility but to continue her defensive war. The relations with the United States slowly deteriorated thereafter.

A large-scale Soviet offensive on the Karelian Isthmus began on June 9, 1944. It resulted within two weeks in the loss of the main Finnish line of defense and the threat of further Soviet advance. The important city of Viipuri was lost on June 20; while the Finnish lines were stabilized by the middle of July, all of the western and central areas of the isthmus had fallen into Soviet hands. Meanwhile Finnish units on Soviet soil east of Lake Ladoga were exposed to increasing pressure and were forced to withdraw behind the Finnish border. The exacting withdrawal of the forces was completed with success and enabled the Finns to concentrate large numbers of men on the isthmus, with the result that no Soviet breakthrough occurred. The fact that the Finnish lines held did not, however, obscure the precariousness of the situation, especially in view of the continued German defeats and retreat in the USSR. The government therefore decided once again to attempt to end the war. An emissary was sent to Stockholm on June 22 to inform the Soviets, through a Swedish Foreign Office intermediary, that Finland was ready to discuss peace and sever her relations with Germany and now desired to know the Soviet peace terms.

Finland had received, as early as November, 1943, through Stockholm, intimations of possible Soviet readiness to grant terms and had decided to pursue the leads obtained by suggesting that the boundaries of 1939, adjusted in some respects in favor of the USSR, the removal of Soviet bases from Finnish territory, and assurances of no violation of Finland's sovereignty would serve as a basis for negotiations. The reply to the Finnish soundings was that the boundaries defined in March, 1940, were final and that other matters could be discussed later. Finland's unwillingness to accept the formula suggested temporarily ended the conversations without further clarification of Soviet peace terms. Direct contact with the USSR was established, however, on February 16, 1944, when a Finnish emissary met the Soviet minister to Sweden, Mme Kollontay, in Stockholm. Soviet armistice terms were received in Helsinki on February 19. Some of the terms were to be accepted at once and the rest after discussion.

The terms to be accepted immediately called for a severance of relations with Germany, the ousting or interning of all German forces in Finland (Soviet forces to assist if the task was too difficult for the Finns), and full acceptance of the 1940 treaty. Three main questions were left to later discussion: partial or total Finnish demobilization, reparations, and the Petsamo territory. The terms were reported to Parliament on February 29, with the government recommendation that the efforts to obtain peace be continued despite the ominous conditions put forth by the USSR. Parliament approved the government's stand. The government thereupon replied to the Soviet proposals by urging that Finland be given an opportunity to discuss the terms but received the answer that the terms were "obvious minimum terms" that had to be accepted before discussion to end hostilities could be begun. After considerable hesitation, the USSR was informed that Finland could not "accept in advance the terms in question, which profoundly affect the fate of the nation, without even knowing definitely their content and meaning."

The Finnish reply was followed by a Soviet suggestion that Finland send "one or two delegates" to Moscow for "an explanation of the armistice terms" proposed by the USSR. Two delegates left for Moscow on March 25. The ensuing discussions ended on March 29 when the final armistice terms were handed by Molotov to the Finns. They provided for (1) severance of relations with Germany and the ousting or internment of the Germans in Finland by the end of April at the latest; (2) restoration of the 1940 boundary and withdrawal, during April, of all Finnish forces from Russian soil; (3) immediate return of prisoners of war; (4) reduction of the Finnish army to a peacetime footing during June–July, half of the demobilization to be completed by the end of May; (5) reparations in the amount of $600,000,000 "to be paid in commodities in six years"; (6) cession of Petsamo; (7) return of Hanko to Finland if the preceding six conditions were accepted.

The terms were carefully considered. Parliament gave the government a unanimous vote of confidence and endorsed its decision not to accept because the Soviet terms "would . . . destroy the possibilities for Finland to exist as an independent nation and, experts agree, would place a burden on the Finns which is far beyond their ability to bear." The reparations bill would have meant annihilating economic servitude and the ousting of the Germans within one month an obligation impossible to fulfill, inevitably leading to default and Russian occupation. There was therefore no choice but regretfully to reject the terms, on April 18.

Such was the background of the peace problem which the military situation in the summer of 1944 insistently brought to the fore. The Soviet offensive launched on June 9 was slowed down and halted after ten days of heavy and costly fighting. While the prospects therefore began to look somewhat brighter, further peace efforts were undertaken through Stockholm on June 22. Word was received on the next day that the USSR stood ready to conclude peace but that Finland must first surrender. Before the alternatives imposed by the military situation and the Soviet demand for surrender could be fully considered, an additional complication arose. Germany entered the picture.

German Foreign Minister Ribbentrop arrived in Helsinki on June 23, the day Finland received the Soviet reply. He demanded assurances that Finland remain in the war to the end; if such assurances were not forthcoming, further military aid would be stopped at once. Unless surrender to the Soviets was decided upon, the only choice confronting the government was the acceptance of a political agreement with Germany—frequently demanded by Ribbentrop during the preceding two years—in order thereby to secure continued military and other material assistance. Knowing that Parliament would agree to no political treaty and fearing that a pact concluded in a normal way would have long-range significance that could only be harmful, President Ryti had recourse to another device. He composed a personal letter to Hitler, dated June 26, 1944, carrying no countersignature by any cabinet member, which stated in part:

Referring to conversations which have taken place I want to express my satisfaction that Germany intends to fulfill the wishes of the Finnish Government concerning military assistance . . . by sending German troops and material. . . . In this connection I beg to assure you that Finland has decided to wage war side by side with Germany until the danger that threatens Finland from Russia is removed.

Taking into consideration the aid . . . which Germany is giving to Finland in her present difficult position, I declare that as the President of Finland I shall not make peace with the Soviet Union except in agreement with the German Reich and will not permit the Government of Finland, appointed by me, or any other person, to take steps toward negotiations concerning peace, or any negotiations that might serve that purpose, except in agreement with the German Reich.[8]

[8] This extraordinary document was actually meaningless. The President could not constitutionally give the commitment formulated in the statement and carry it through without inviting a major political upheaval resulting in his being forced to resign. It was meaningless in another sense also. By resigning, Ryti

When the Ryti statement was presented at a cabinet meeting, several members opposed its content and implications. The situation was considered sufficiently precarious, however, to prevent resignations that undoubtedly would have been the result of Ryti's action under anything like normal conditions. The Social Democratic parliamentary group expressed a view generally held when it contended, in a statement issued on July 1, that, while the Socialists took exception to Ryti's letter because it did not reiterate the fact that Finland's war was a separate war and had not been submitted to Parliament, resignation of Socialists from the cabinet could not be considered because "the defense of our country . . . is the most important responsibility at this time and must be supported by all classes."

The German military and other aid which again flowed to Finland after the "Ribbentrop letter" had been delivered was smaller than expected and did not give permanent relief. The news of the Ryti commitment also precipitated diplomatic complications abroad. Washington, for example, chose to see in it formal admission by the Finnish government "that it has now entered a hard and fast military partnership with Nazi Germany" and claimed that "German infiltration into the councils" of the government had reduced Finland to a mere puppet of Germany. The United States therefore ended diplomatic relations with Finland on June 30. Within a few days of the Ryti agreement, it was becoming clear that the letter had to be repudiated and further moves leading to peace made.

The first step in the process was the resignation of President Ryti on August 1 and the cancellation, not long thereafter, of the Ribbentrop agreement. Ryti was succeeded by Marshal C. G. Mannerheim on August 4. These changes in the presidency meant, in accordance with well-established procedure, the resignation of the cabinet and the appointment of a new government. It had been assumed, during the discussions precipitated by the critical situation in June, that a new government, free from whatever objections the Soviets might have against certain Finnish leaders, would gain easier access to and

would leave the road open for whatever choices or decisions his successor and a later government might prefer to make. He did in fact resign on August 1. His successor as President, Marshal Mannerheim, shortly disregarded the Ryti commitment.

possibly obtain better terms from Moscow. A coalition cabinet, headed by Premier A. Hackzell, assumed office on August 8. It was formed, as its predecessor also had been formed, for the specific purpose of getting Finland out of the war. Newly elected President Mannerheim informed Germany on August 17, through Marshal Wilhelm Keitel, that the Ribbentrop agreement was no longer considered binding.

The discussions with Moscow began seriously on August 30 when it was learned that the USSR would receive a Finnish delegation provided, and only if, Finland publicly severed relations with Germany and agreed to demands that Germany withdraw her forces in Finland by September 15 if they had not left by then. Significantly the communication did not insist upon military surrender as a condition for peace discussions. The Soviet Union changed its communication shortly to an ultimatum, insisting that the conditions be accepted by the close of September 2, the alternative being the end of further preliminary discussions and the occupation of Finland. Parliament voted on September 2 to comply, and the government thereupon forwarded a proper communication to Berlin and an affirmative answer to Moscow. A cease-fire was agreed to on September 4 and an armistice and preliminary peace was signed in Moscow on September 19.

The provisions of the preliminary peace operated from the date of signing until the final peace treaty was concluded in Paris, nearly two and a half years later, on February 10, 1947. The preliminary treaty was for all practical purposes the real peace treaty—all of its basic provisions were carried over into the Paris treaty—despite the fact that it was signed only by the USSR, while the Paris treaty was signed by the USSR, Britain, Australia, Canada, Czechoslovakia, India, New Zealand, and the Union of South Africa, all of whom, it was declared, had been "at war with Finland." The Byelorussian Soviet Socialist Republic and the Ukrainian Soviet Socialist Republic also were among the signatories.

The treaty consisted of a preamble, thirty-six articles, and six annexes.[9] The preamble stated that Finland, "having become an ally

[9] The *Treaty of Peace with Finland* (1947), distributed by the U.S. State Department, contains the official text in Russian, English, French, and Finnish;

of Hitlerite Germany" and having fought against the Allied and Associated Powers, had ceased military operations and had withdrawn from the war in September, 1944. Finland had thereupon broken off relations with Hitler's Europe and had signed an armistice. The armistice terms had been loyally carried out by the Finns, it was declared, but no specific mention was made of the fact that Finland had declared war on Germany and, having fought the Germans for over half a year, had become a cobelligerent of the Allies.

The treaty reestablished, with one exception, the frontiers laid down by the peace of March 12, 1940. The exception was the province of Petsamo, which was ceded to the Soviet Union. The areas lost to the USSR approximated 17,760 square miles in all. The Soviet claims to the Hanko enclave included in the March, 1940, treaty were abandoned. The Porkkala area, twelve miles west of Helsinki, was leased to the USSR for fifty years for a naval base. It comprised about 152 square miles. The Soviet Union also obtained the use of Finnish railways, waterways, roads, and air routes for the transportation of personnel and goods to and from the USSR to Porkkala.

The treaty authorized a Finnish army of 34,400 men, roughly the standing army before 1939. The navy was limited to 4,500 men and a tonnage of 10,000 and the air force to 3,000 men and 60 aircraft. The reduction of the services was to be completed within six months from the coming into force of the treaty. Ownership of or experimentation with atomic weapons or any self-propelled or guided missiles was forbidden, as was excess war matériel.

The section dealing with the reparations provisions imposed on Finland by the treaty of 1947 stated in part that, "taking into consideration that Finland has not only withdrawn from the war against the United Nations, but has also declared war on Germany and assisted with her forces in driving German troops out of Finland, the Parties agree that compensation [to the Soviet Union] will be

the map is Russian. Finland had actually been at war only with the USSR, only nominally with the non-Soviet signatories, and not at all with the United States, France, or the other members of the United Nations. James F. Byrnes's *Speaking Frankly* (New York, 1947) should be consulted for background. See Appendix G.

made by Finland not in full, but only in part, namely in the amount of $300,000,000 payable over eight years from September 19, 1944, in commodities." The payments were to be calculated in American dollars.

The treaty imposed two new exactions. All German assets in Finland were transferred to the Soviet Union. No compensation was provided for Finnish assets in Germany or for the destruction wrought by the Germans in Finland during the Finnish-German war. Also, Finland assumed responsibility for the surrender of or compensation for property belonging to nationals of the United Nations. This meant a liability of some $53,000,000. Finland "waives all claims of any description against the Allied and Associated Powers . . . arising directly out of the war or out of actions taken because of the existence of a state of war" since September 1, 1939, "whether or not the Allied and Associated Power was at war with Finland at the time." Pending the conclusion of commercial treaties, the individual United Nations were granted most-favored-nation treatment in dealings between them or their nationals and Finland.

To the onerous territorial clauses were added others "guaranteeing" the enjoyment of basic human rights such as the right of free speech, press, and assembly. The treaty thus ostentatiously "secured" freedoms and rights that had in fact long been fully established in Finland. The real intention of such provisions was to give the Communists a free hand. Full citizenship was restored to Finnish Communists who had fled to Russia during or after the war in 1918. Finland also agreed to the capture and surrender for trial of persons accused of war crimes and of nationals of any Allied or Associated Power charged with "having violated their national law by treason or collaboration with the enemy during the war."

THE COSTS OF THE WAR

When the USSR attacked Finland in November, 1939, it struck at a prosperous nation. Finland's economic advance had been exceptional since 1918. Industrial production had doubled, foreign trade had grown rapidly, and the standard of living had risen appreciably.

The national debt was modest; the foreign debt, rapidly reduced during the 1930s, was only some $12.1 million in 1939. Approximately 5 percent of the annual national income was being allocated to the costs of an ambitious social reform and welfare effort for the benefit of the "forgotten man." The nation's over-all record and prospects discernible before World War II appeared to promise steady economic, social, and political progress unimpeded by the difficulties of foreign relations.

The two-phase war of 1939–44 profoundly changed the situation. Its results imposed exactions upon the people that seemed to mean servitude destructive of the accustomed ways of life before 1939. The economic consequences alone of the "Continuation War" in particular appeared to impose burdens beyond the nation's capacity to bear.

The costs of the 1941–45 war were vastly greater than those of the Winter War. The number killed was 53,740; the number wounded, 59,450. Nearly 2,000 persons lost their lives on the home front as the result of bombings of cities and villages. The total losses of human lives in 1939–45 came to 85,550. Over 90 percent of the soldiers killed were in the 20- to 39-year age category. The war against the Germans in north Finland in September, 1944–April, 1945, was less demanding of human life. It resulted in 774 deaths and 2,900 wounded; later, in 1945–48, when the Finns removed some 64,400 mines used by the Germans during their retreat to Norway in mining roads, buildings, bridges, and the like, 72 persons were killed and 142 wounded. The total loss of life caused by the war exceeded the normal annual population growth for two years.

The war bequeathed another legacy of suffering and want that imposed heavy long-range burdens on the nation. A survey in 1947 disclosed that the war had left 50,000 orphans, most of whom were under five years of age at the time of the father's death. The number of war widows came to 24,000. Approximately 15,000 oldsters, previously dependent upon sons or other relatives who had lost their lives in the war, had been cast adrift and required public care and assistance. Special children's allowances paid to all orphans until the age of seventeen, widows' pensions (in addition to allowances for children), free vocational training financed by public funds, and expanded old age and invalidity pensions were provided by a series of laws enacted in 1941–44 and in 1948. The costs the outlays involved, gradually increasing over the years, came to well over $22,000,000 in 1959 and over $38,000,000 in 1961.

The direct economic losses were staggering. The ceded areas represented about 12 percent of the area of Finland before the war. Approximately 12 percent of the forest resources, 17 percent of railroad trackage, 25 percent of the water-power resources, and 12 percent of the industrial capacity were lost (the equivalent of some 13 percent of the national wealth). The obligation to pay reparations meant additional economic bloodletting the full meaning of which could only be guessed at in 1945; its real magnitude had not been fully measured when the last reparations payments were made in 1952 and probably never will be fully measured. About $30 million were added to the costs as a result of compensation for property allegedly taken from Soviet territory and the loss of various Finnish assets in Germany. By comparison with these huge losses, the devastation of north Finland at the hands of the Germans during the months they were retreating from Finland seems trivial: 16,500 houses destroyed, 230 railroad bridges and 510 ordinary bridges wrecked or blown up, and other extensive property damage caused by systematic and unrelenting application of a scorched-earth policy. The Germans' destruction of property in Lapland was estimated at $120,650,000.

The population of the ceded areas represented still another aspect of the costs of the war. Practically the whole population of the areas left in Soviet hands in 1940—some 425,000 persons—abandoned their homes and most of their property and chose the lot of the displaced rather than accept life under communism. Roughly two thirds of the evacuees had returned by the spring of 1944 to their old homes in the areas that were again turned over to the Russians after the preliminary peace in September, 1944, and thus faced the hard lot of the displaced for the second time. The costs of providing for them after 1945 called for a prodigious effort especially difficult during the years 1945–52 while reparations payments continued.

Reparations payments, various indirect costs included, were estimated, by the time payments were completed in 1952, at somewhat over $1,000 million.

IN RETROSPECT

The decisions that led to Finland's involvement in the war were obviously the Soviet Union's. Finland's refusal to accept the demands of the USSR implied no threat of war or other aggression against the Soviets. The refusal was announced before it became clear that the Russians were determined to use force once suasion had failed to produce the results Moscow desired.

Was the Soviet 1939 war against Finland necessary? Unless we accept the absurd Communist claim that Finland began the war by violating Soviet territory, the answer must be an unqualified no. No evidence has yet been brought forth or is likely to emerge to challenge the conclusion that Finland, left alone, would have remained neutral and, as a neutral nation, no menace to the safety of the USSR. If German-Soviet collusion in August, 1939, had not given the USSR a free hand in Finland and if the country had remained untouched by the blight of Soviet aggression, the republic as a nonwarring neutral would no doubt have represented a greater security factor for the Soviets than a Finland compelled to defend herself because she was invaded. A neutral Finland not violated by the USSR would in all likelihood ultimately have meant, if Germany had attempted to use Finland after June, 1941, against the Soviet Union, a country under German military occupation. The country would have been in a situation analogous to that of Denmark and Norway after they had fallen victim to Hitler's invasion. Finland would in all probability have been an ally against the Germans and not, as Soviet aggression decreed, a nation fighting the USSR.

In attempting to force the Finns to yield during the discussions in October–November, 1939, the Soviet representatives committed several errors. One was in maintaining the notion, apparently accepted without hesitation by the Russians, that the Finns harbored aggressive designs upon the USSR and stood ready, as the hirelings of Western "imperialists," to carry them out at the first opportunity. Another was the failure to evaluate accurately the resolve of the Finns to fight if attacked. The Russians appear to have felt confident that the Soviets' power position was enough to soften the Finns to the point where they would see the "justice" of the Soviet demands. Yet the USSR did not, curiously enough, make use of an ultimatum. An ultimatum would have shown that war was the only alternative to yielding. Instead of thus defining the choices, the USSR had recourse, in launching the invasion on November 30, to a clumsily staged border incident.

The errors committed in dealing with Finland pale into insignificance, needless to say, when compared with the mistakes of the Kremlin's policy toward Hitler's Germany. Stalin's gains in east Poland and the Baltic republics would in all probability have remained merely a brief and unprofitable interlude if the Soviets had been left alone to face the consequences of Hitler's invasion in 1941. And if Allied aid to the Soviets had been limited to the modest assistance extended to the USSR before the massive contribution of the United States balanced the scales and ultimately tipped them in favor of the Allies, the results of the invasion would no doubt have been disastrous, to say the least. The failure correctly to interpret Finland's position and purposes was a humiliating and costly annoyance. The error committed when the Soviets joined hands with Hitler in August, 1939, and thereby accepted partnership in common aggression with Germany, led the USSR to the brink of catastrophe. Without minimizing the staying power and military prowess of the Soviets, we can say that the USSR was saved from disaster by circumstances and developments largely outside Moscow's control. The circumstances that ultimately brought succor offer a revealing measure of the mistakes and shortcomings of Soviet policy.

The early stages of the Russo-Finnish War in 1939–40 showed that the Russians had completely misjudged the Finns' ability to fight. Mass, numbers, and the weight of equipment appear to have meant everything to them; spirit, the immense sustaining power of the sense of being right, of fighting for a just cause morally unassailable because the fight was purely a defensive fight, seems to have been lost on them. This is not to say that the Soviet troops were poor fighters. The record shows quite the contrary. They learned quickly the essentials of fighting under the conditions that prevailed on the Finnish fronts and soon earned the respect, especially when engaged in defensive fighting, of their opponents.

Another error disfigures the Soviet record of the war: the setting up of the Kuusinen "government" and the sophomoric make-believe of the bold-faced claim that the USSR was not at war with Finland because it had concluded a treaty with Kuusinen's regime. Only exceptionally faulty intelligence could have led the Kremlin to conclude that such a "government" would be accepted by the Finns or that it would at least find many supporters among them. Kuusinen, one of the leaders of the Red revolt in 1918, known as a hard-boiled top-rank Soviet Communist since 1918, now the Kremlin's hand-picked stooge chosen to lead the new order of things tailored for Finland by the master craftsmen of the USSR, could not conceivably have succeeded in the role assigned to him, unless and until the Finns had been beaten to their knees. If the intention was, as it clearly appears to have been, to persuade the Finns to overthrow the legal government of the country and rally to the red banner held aloft by Kuusinen, to pull the renegade out of the Soviet bag of tricks more than sufficed to damn the Communist effort at the start.

It is clear that the Finns could have avoided war by meekly accepting the territorial demands of the USSR in 1939 or if they had hoisted the white flag in response to the Soviets' military action in June, 1941. To have complied in 1939 or surrendered in 1941, however, would in all probability have meant loss of independence and absorption in the Soviet Union (witness the fate of Estonia, Latvia, and Lithuania in 1939–40). In putting the matter this way, we are admittedly indulging in a surmise. No fact can be cited, however, that successfully challenges the surmise, while the events in the Baltic republics in 1939–40 and Soviet expansion elsewhere impressively support it.

Given the unprovoked Soviet attack in 1939, the situation created by Soviet policy and procedures in Finland between March,

1940, and June, 1941, and Hitler's attack on the USSR, it is difficult to see how Finland could have avoided becoming involved in the 1941–44 phase of the war. Involvement came not by choice or as the result of a prior conspiracy or alliance with the Germans, committing Finland to wage war. It came as a consequence of circumstances for which, making full allowance for Hitler's machinations and aggression, the USSR must assume the main responsibility.

It bears repeating that the Finns were committed to unqualified neutrality in 1939. Finland was not a whit less firmly determined to remain neutral than her Scandinavian neighbors. It was Soviet aggression that tore Finland from her anchorage in neutrality, just as Germany's invasion of Denmark and Norway cast them adrift on the sea of war and destruction while Sweden alone remained sufficiently favored by circumstances to enable her to stay neutral. The interlude between the end of the Winter War in March, 1940, and Hitler's attack on the USSR in June, 1941, gave Finland no real peace and prevented the country from enjoying the advantages that neutrality presumably again offered after the 1939–40 war had ended. Instead, this period accumulated a lengthening record of further Soviet demands pointing to the purposes Molotov disclosed in Berlin in November, 1940. During his conversations with Hitler, Molotov stated that it was the Soviets' intention to apply "a settlement on the same scale as in Bessarabia" to Finland (Bessarabia had been annexed by the USSR five months earlier, in June, 1940). While the Finns were unaware of this Soviet purpose at the time, they had good reason for fearing the worst. It was during these months of "ordeal by peace" that they witnessed the first signs of German moves—for instance, the German interest in the transit agreement—that were hopefully seen as indications of possible outside counterweights to further Soviet exactions.

Despite great handicaps—the huge disparity in the strength and resources of Finland and the USSR, except in spirit, moral strength, and psychological staying power, in which the Finns were more than a match for the Russians—the Finns fought long enough and well enough to prevent their country from being occupied and to make it possible to ensure peace by treaty instead of having to accept terms as a satellite, under the conqueror's heel. This result

of Finland's fight cannot be explained away by claiming that the
Soviets could have occupied the country had they only been so
minded, and that occupation was avoided not because of the Finns'
performance as fighters but because the USSR had magnanimously
chosen to stay its hand. There is no doubt but that the USSR intended to crush Finland once and for all—Molotov had made that
clear in Berlin—and that annexation would have been carried
through if the Finns had not fought appears certain. That independence was saved by fighting is equally clear. This basic fact is
an indelible part of the record. It will not be eradicated by the
pretentious adroitness of the sophisticates, the distortions of special
pleaders, the bumblings of the ignorant, or the facile improvisa-
tions of the opportunists more delicately attuned to the promise of
profitable tomorrows than to the compelling verities of yesteryear.

XIV

Economic Developments since 1945

THE REPARATIONS PROBLEM

The February 10, 1947, peace treaty, "which, conforming to the principles of justice"—to cite part of the preamble—provided for Finland's reparations obligation, repeated part of the armistice agreement signed by Finland on September 19, 1944. Article 11 of the armistice terms and an annex attached to it specified the payments of reparations in the amount of $300,000,000, in kind. The same article also stated that the details regarding type of deliveries and delivery schedules would be defined in a later special agreement and that the price of the goods and commodities to be delivered would be calculated in terms of American gold dollar prices of 1938.

The special agreement was signed in Helsinki on December 17, 1944. It provided that the war indemnity was to be paid in six years, in six equal amounts of $50,000,000 annually. The payments period was extended to eight years, however, by another agreement signed on December 31, 1945. The new agreement meant that reparations payments, if successfully made by Finland, would end on September 19, 1952, and that the annual payments were reduced, except for the first year, from $50,000,000 to $37,500,000 for the remaining seven years. Ships and metals industry products were to be priced at a level 15 percent higher than that prevailing in 1938, and other reparations goods 10 percent above that level.

These concessions did not appreciably lighten the reparations burden. The rise in prices that set in after 1938 resulted in an increase of about 20 percent in the cost of producing reparations by

1944. The rise continued after 1945. Thus the American wholesale price level, for example, rose by some 33 percent between 1938 and 1944, by 20 percent between 1944 and 1946, and higher still by 1948. Finland was especially hard hit by the general price trend during the first three years after 1944, which, as we can readily see, meant a widening margin between the true postwar dollar and the "indemnity dollar" used to establish the price of the commodities specified by and delivered according to the reparations schedules. The reparations payments during the first indemnity year were about 46 percent more than current market prices in 1944–45 would have called for: Finnish deliveries during the year, calculated in 1938 gold or "indemnity dollars," came to $51,750,000, while the actual value of the deliveries—that is, value according to prices then current—was about $75,500,000.

The widening gap between the nominal reparations amount imposed by the 1944 armistice and the 1947 treaty and the real value of deliveries made was substantially narrowed in 1948. The Soviet Union offered an important reduction in the payments as of July 1, 1948—the offer was widely interpreted at the time as an attempt to influence the 1948 elections—by canceling one half of the payments still due. The cancellation amounted to $73,500,000 or 24.8 percent of the original reparations amount of $300,000,000. The "reparations year" was redefined at the same time, making it begin on July 1 instead of September 19 as originally fixed. The practical effect of the change was to shorten the fourth reparations year and to lengthen the last by about two and a half months. It also reduced the annual payments for the fifth, sixth, and seventh years to $17,500,000 and increased the last or eighth year's sum to $21,000,-000. These figures reflect the fact that Finland had paid, at the end of the fourth reparations year, 67.5 percent of the sum due, leaving only one third of the total for the last four years.

By the end of August, 1952, 99.5 percent of the total indemnity had been paid. The remaining fraction was paid off in time to free the country, as of September 19, from the burden which, at once tremendous and ominous, had weighed down the nation for years and had at times appeared to lead to a servitude from which there might be no return. The magnitude of the accomplishment registered between 1944 and 1952 can be suggested by a closer look at some of the details of the grim ordeal the reparations imposed on the nation.

The reparations provisions were, at first glance, simple. They called for the payment of a specific sum divided into eight equal parts payable annually. Each annual payment in turn was divided into twelve equal monthly payments. To ensure prompt and regular deliveries, a 5 percent monthly fine was specified whenever deliveries fell below the monthly quotas. The fine applied to each category of commodities and not to the total of monthly deliveries. Even a minor failure to deliver brought, as experience was to show, the imposition of the fine. Excess deliveries in one category of goods could not be used to make up for failure to fill the quota in another.

The strict monthly and annual schedules were particularly exacting because of the nature and distribution of the commodities specified. Timber and the products of the woodworking industry together with paper and pulp—the strongest sector of Finland's industry—amounted to only 28 percent of the total reparations deliveries, while machinery, ships, and the products of the cable and wire industries accounted for the rest or 72 percent. The machine and related industries had furnished less than 3 percent of the nation's exports before 1939, while the share of paper, pulp, timber, and wood products in general had varied from 81 to 86 percent annually. Finnish industry that had served only the domestic market or, as was true of shipbuilding, for example, had not been geared to the huge demands required by reparations was now called upon to produce at a tempo and in quantities undreamed of before the war.

What the demands placed upon these relatively minor sectors of Finnish industry meant is suggested by the fact that no less than 164 categories of commodities out of a total of 199 specified by the reparations schedules consisted of goods produced by the machine and metals industry. Finland had to deliver, among other things, complete industrial plants including not only machinery needed for production but all essential auxiliaries such as power plants, storage and handling facilities for raw materials, and the like for three sulphite mills, four paper mills, three mechanical pulp mills, six works for producing plywood, seventeen factories turning out prefabricated houses, and two cardboard factories. The list also included 500 steam locomotives, 200 electric locomotives, and 5,500 railroad cars. The specifications for the steam locomotives alone exceeded forty items; and the spare parts required (they were listed by groups of five locomotives) numbered 50 separate categories, most of which included over 10 and some as many as 20 to 60 different units or series. A relatively minor but telling illustration of how the reparations requirements at times worked out is given by the 90 wooden, 300-ton ocean-going schooners included in the schedules. Their price was fixed at $15,000 each. The cost of producing them, however, came to $180,000 per schooner.

The difficulties involved are further illustrated by the situation at the close of the third or 1947 reparations year. The failure to obtain essential raw materials from the United States and Great Britain because of work stoppages caused by strikes in the coal industry and of the dock workers led to unavoidable delays in deliveries. Default with resulting penalties appeared unavoidable. However, on September 18, the last day of the reparations year, the Finns succeeded in clearing 694 carloads of reparations goods at the Soviet boundary stations. The last of the trains, consisting of 109 freight cars, did not cross the border until 4:15 A.M. on the twentieth. Default was avoided by a Soviet ruling that the 1947 reparations year did not end until 6 A.M. on the twentieth. The deliveries were accepted without the imposition of fines.

Clearly the cost of reparations was very much greater than the sum called for by the armistice agreement and the treaty. To recapitulate part of the record: in the first reparations year deliveries amounted, in terms of current market prices, to $75,500,000, for which sum Finland earned $51,750,000 on the reparations account; in the second year, the corresponding figures were $65,100,000 and $36,800,000; and in the third year, $75,000,000 and $38,800,000. While these figures and those indicating actual costs for the eight reparations years as a whole are only approximations, they are accurate enough to justify the conclusion that the total direct costs of reparations—that is, exports for which no equivalent was received from the USSR—came to about $570,000,000.

A detailed study of the reparations problem points out among other things that if Finland had "purchased the commodities delivered to the Soviet Union in the United States market" the reparations sum of $226,500,000 (after the reduction of the original total amount in 1948) "would have been depleted before the fourth year of reparation deliveries. . . . Finland would have needed . . . about $546,000,000 at the 1952 dollar value to purchase the required commodities." [1] To this sum must be added others. Some of them can literally not be measured—for instance, the actual costs of the huge investments in plant and raw materials that had to be obtained abroad regardless of cost—while others, especially minor ones, are duly recorded. The Soviet Control Commission, for example, added $10,000,000 to the expense of keeping deliveries rolling. The Finnish War Reparations Industries Commission, an organization that ably supervised the production of reparations commodities and that ultimately employed as many as 400 people, required an outlay of $8,000,000. Adding such relatively minor tangibles and other large unmeasured outgo to the estimated costs of reparations, Professor Bruno Suviranta, the leading student of the problem during 1945–52, concluded that the final reparations figure was probably well over $700,000,000.[2] In terms of the total state expenditures, the reparations came to 16.1 percent in 1945 and varied from 14 percent to 10.2 percent in 1947–49. In the last year, the percentage had dropped to 5. The maximum payments, expressed in percentages of the annual gross national product, occurred in 1945 (6.4 percent), 1946 (5.3 percent) and in 1947–48 when the percentage was between 4 and 5. A major economic bloodletting had thus been involved.

THE PROBLEM OF THE EVACUEES

Immense as the reparations costs were, they fell far short of covering all the economic losses sustained by the Finns as a result of

[1] J. Auer, *Suomen Sotakorvaustoimitukset Neuvostoliittolle* (Helsinki, 1956), p. 336. This excellent survey contains a 26-page summary in English.

[2] B. Suviranta has written extensively on the reparations problem. I am indebted especially to his *Suomen Sotakorvaus ja Maksukyky* (Helsinki, 1948) and articles in *Unitas*, 1948, pp. 1–7; 1952, pp. 1–7, *Index* of Svenska Handelsbanken (Supplement, March, 1947), pp. 3–44.

World War II. Conspicuous among the other major items in the long list of economic burdens imposed upon the country by the 1944 armistice and confirmed—purely nominally, to be sure—by the 1947 peace treaty was that relating to the ceded areas and the population of these areas that voluntarily chose to abandon their homes and move within the new borders of Finland.

The property in the ceded territories was estimated, after the war, at $450,000,000 in terms of 1944 prices and considerably higher, because of postwar inflation, by 1952. Directly connected with this cost figure was the value of the property that the USSR arbitrarily considered as "belonging" to the ceded territory and insisted should be "returned." The value of the property in question, ranging from railroad rolling stock and industrial equipment to houses, miscellaneous farm buildings, machinery, and the like, was fixed at $24,-000,000 (according to 1944 prices).

To this figure were added certain others. All Finnish property owned by German persons or corporations in Finland, estimated at $8,000,000, and sums owed by Finland to Germany—as a result of wartime economic aid, munitions deliveries, etc.—fixed at $44,-000,000, were to be turned over to the USSR. No deductions were allowed for Finnish-owned property in Germany, estimated at $5,-000,000, also assigned to the USSR.

Added to the reparations payments, these amounts compounded into a huge total. Their effect upon Finland's post-1945 development, both before the completion of the reparations payments in 1952 and after, was formidable. They were in fact closely connected with still another economic consequence of the 1939–44 war period, that of providing homes, jobs, and compensation for the losses sustained by the 420,000 evacuees from the ceded areas. The social, economic, and legal problems involved in the prodigious undertaking called insistently for a solution at a time when the reparations burden was at its heaviest and the general need for speedy postwar reconstruction allowed little or no delay.

The displaced persons problem was complex. It required immediate measures connected with the moving of hundreds of thousands of individuals, plus the property they succeeded in taking with them, into localities where they could be housed. An elaborate social welfare program had to be devised practically overnight to care for the evacuees while the details of resettlement were worked out. Finally the question of whether and to what extent direct, large-scale economic aid should be given had to be faced. The government and nation unhesitatingly resolved that the evacuees be compensated for the property losses sustained because of their decision not to remain in the areas left under Soviet domination.

The decision to compensate rested on the conviction that considerations of justice and the requirements of a sound social policy demanded compensation. There appeared to be only one way to assist the evacuees to a new start in life, and that was to turn them as quickly as possible into job holders or property owners. It was essential, however, to accomplish this purpose without placing too heavy demands upon the economy of the country, already faced with the immense demands of the reparations payments. Nor could restitution be attempted in such a way as to accelerate unduly the process of inflation lest the dire consequences of a rapidly depreciating currency be added to the other dangers facing the nation.

The laws necessary for the legal framework for the huge project were speedily enacted. The first was passed in June, 1940, and a second in May, 1945. The 1940 and 1945 Compensation Acts defined in detail the evaluation of losses sustained and the amount of compensation to be granted. The former provided for compensation calculated on the basis of the 1939 price level, while the latter accepted—because of a 129 percent price rise due to inflation since 1939—the price level of 1944 as the guide.

The financing of the program was accomplished by means of a special levy on property, state-owned as well as privately owned. Because of the magnitude of the project, ten-year government bonds were also issued as part payment and were thus combined with the expropriation of property to create the resources needed for the compensation program. The 1940 law provided for a capital levy to be carried through in 1941–46, and the 1945 law prescribed a levy for 1946–50. Thus the first part of the second levy came in the same year in which the last portion of the first levy fell due. In principle, all taxpayers liable to the income tax had to surrender part of their property. The levy was progressive. As defined in

1940 it meant 2.5 percent on the lowest category (property of 40,000 marks) and 20 percent on the highest, that is, properties of 41,000,-000 marks or over.[3] The 1945 law revised the rates upward: 2.4 percent on property of 30,000 marks and 21 percent on property worth 10,000,000 marks or more. The taxpayer's property liable to the levy was reassessed annually in order to ensure contributions called for by the law and to prevent the property owner from benefiting by rising prices caused by inflation.

The compensation program required substantial increases in taxes. This is merely one way of saying that it involved a redistribution of wealth: individuals and enterprises that had escaped the property losses sustained by the evacuees were asked to share the losses, each according to his earnings or resources, by contributing to the common fund from which the evacuees were compensated.

It is clear that to ascertain the losses sustained and to determine the levels to which taxes had to be raised in order to achieve the purposes sought involved great difficulties. More often than not, the alleged losses could be fixed only by the claims of the evacuees themselves. The evacuees' estimates probably tended to be overgenerous. The decisions of the Compensation Boards, set up to handle the knotty problem of defining acceptable estimates, appear in general to have resulted in awards that came only to some 40 percent of the evacuees' claims. Farmers fared better on the whole than other groups of claimants. Large property owners and corporations suffered the greatest losses, and owners of forest lands more than owners of arable land. The evacuees themselves ultimately bore not less than one third of the losses, although neither the losses nor the costs of the huge program can be measured accurately enough to permit final calculations.

About 85,000 out of the 420,000 displaced persons were from the urban communities in the ceded areas. Of the 335,000 who comprised the rural folk among the evacuees, some 29,000 had chosen, by 1947, to settle in cities. Over a quarter of the evacuees had thus added, within two years of the end of the war, to the city population of the country, and the drift to the cities continued thereafter.

[3] One dollar was the equivalent of 49.35 marks in December, 1939, 86.30 marks in May, 1945, and 231 marks in 1952.

The ultimate result was that over 10,000 families of the 40,000 families entitled to compensation as farmers—that is, entitled to land allotments and other compensation appropriate or necessary to farming—voluntarily failed to take advantage of the type of compensation which the law prescribed.

The extent to which transfer of land was involved is shown by the following figures. By the time the second phase of the war began in June, 1941, approximately 500,000 acres of land had been allocated to the Karelian evacuees. The recapture shortly thereafter of the areas ceded to the USSR in 1940 led to the abandonment of the land redistribution effort and the return of large numbers of Karelians to their former homes. The policy of redistribution was resumed, however, in 1944, after the war had ended and Finland was forced to surrender not only the areas defined in the March, 1940, treaty but others as well. The second Compensation Act of May, 1945, therefore contained extensive provisions for land transfers for the benefit not only of the evacuees but also of war veterans and certain other groups. The redistribution of land under the law ultimately involved about 5,000,000 acres. About one half of the acreage was taken from the state, or the communes and parishes, 20 percent from corporations, and 30 percent from private owners. In terms of arable land, however, the distribution was different: one quarter was owned by the state or other public bodies, 10 percent by corporations, and about 65 percent by private owners. Approximately one half or 2,500,000 acres of the land involved in the redistribution went to the evacuees, and of this amount one third was arable or suitable for farming.

The combined payments under the 1940 and 1945 Compensation Acts reached, by the end of 1951, approximately 42 billion marks. This indicated, however, only the nominal sum involved. To it must be added the amounts resulting from the fact that the value of the compensation bonds, used as part payment of compensation awards, was tied to the price index. The increase in the price levels had added, by 1952, about 25 percent to the sum mentioned above, bringing the total to well over 50 billion marks. An indication of the burdens the compensation program imposed on the taxpayer is given by the fact that in the first year of the special capital levy,

1941, the yield of the levy amounted to 79 percent more than the income and property taxes collected. The corresponding percentage was 62 in 1942 and 53 in 1946, and varied between 17 and 19 thereafter.

While the majority of the displaced persons appear to have held that the compensation received was unreasonably low, only 12 percent of the awards made resulted in appeals to proper authorities. The program carried through an extensive redistribution of property which contributed substantially to the economic independence of the evacuees. The economic consequences of the ambitious plan, however, turned out to be partly different from those originally envisioned. Extensive as was the transfer of land and other property from the owners to the evacuees, it fell short of providing adequately for them. It therefore became necessary to obtain additional funds. This meant, unavoidably, heavier income and property taxes in the postwar years and, in a real sense, a continuation of the process of redistributing wealth which it had originally been assumed would be accomplished once and for all by the property levies defined by the Compensation Acts of 1940 and 1945. The process therefore became ultimately costlier and more difficult, but it quickened and carried forward a significant, peaceful social and economic transformation which, we like to think, can be successfully accomplished only in a genuine democracy.

THE AGRICULTURAL SCENE

The decline in the relative importance of farming during the interwar years continued after 1945. This was true despite the fact that the acreage under cultivation grew both before the outbreak of the war in 1939 and after the war had ended. Between 1920 and 1939, about 1,500,000 acres of new land were brought under the plow. The farm land lost to the USSR as a result of the 1944 territorial cessions came to half this figure. Additional new land was brought under cultivation after 1944, with the result that arable land in 1959 came to about 6,582,000 acres or slightly more than the figure for 1938. The acreage was very unevenly distributed, as might be expected: 90 percent of it was found in the southern half of the country, the upper or northern half having, primarily because of climate, only one tenth of the total.

Finland remained after World War II what she had been before the war, namely, a nation of small farmers. Only 5 percent of the cultivated acreage belonged in 1950 to farms of 125 acres or more; those of 10 acres or less accounted for 41 percent, while those of 10–25 acres came to 40 percent and those between 25 and 50 acres to 14 percent. The term "large farm" was therefore practically meaningless in Finland after 1945, as it had been, in fact, before 1939. The relatively large land transfers under the 1945 Compensation Act noted above did not change this aspect of the farmer's world any more than they changed the position of farming in the general economic life of the country. In 1959 there were only 237 farms whose arable land was 250 acres or more; their total paid labor force numbered 2,750.

The experiences of World War I in Finland and the rest of the North were such as to make it seem not only desirable but necessary that measures be taken after the war to secure the greatest possible degree of national self-sufficiency in food and other basic essentials. Pre-1914 production of grain, sugar, and other commodities was frequently cited as an illustration of failure to achieve levels of production sufficient to meet the requirements of a decent standard of living. Protective tariffs, export subsidies, and increasing imports of fodder and fertilizers indicated during the two decades before World War II the effort to decrease dependence on the outside world and avoid the consequences of a war and blockade that had brought the nation to the brink of starvation in the closing months of World War I.

The harsh war years 1939–44 amply demonstrated the inadequacies of the pre-1939 measures designed to enable the nation to carry on during years of war. Paradoxically, the war years also demonstrated a larger capacity for self-sufficiency than could have been predicted before the war, but was made possible only by a drastic reduction in consumption and living standards that threatened to become catastrophic by the time Finland got out of the war. It would in fact have come close to being fatal had it not been for the imports of basic food and other essentials from Germany—other foreign sources of supply were closed, for all practical purposes, by the summer of 1944—that saved the country from a disastrous food shortage by the time the armistice with the USSR was concluded in September, 1944.

The years after the war recorded notable agricultural changes and advances. Relatively extensive mechanization, marked reduction in the production of some crops and increase in the cultivation of others, and a substantial growth in the domestic consumption of certain products resulting in the virtual disappearance of some dairy commodities from the list of leading exports of earlier years testified to the emergence after 1945 of a farm economy in many respects different from that before the war.

A significant indicator of the transformation of the old and the emergence of the new was the development between 1950 and 1960. During the decade the part of the population that depended upon agriculture and forestry as the main source of income decreased by 266,000 or about 16 percent. If we take note only of the individuals in agriculture who were active breadwinners or workers—that is, if we exclude dependents not part of the agricultural labor force— the decrease was 21 percent. By the decade of the 1960s agriculture, while still a basic part of the nation's economy, had clearly ceased to be, by a wide margin, the major economic activity of the republic and yielded a livelihood to only about one fourth of the population.

The marked decline in the importance of agriculture had occurred despite substantial mechanization after the mid-forties. The number of horses declined by one third between 1938 and 1961. (Sheep, incidentally, decreased by two thirds, while chickens increased by one third.) Tractors, on the other hand, had become increasingly common. No tractors were listed in the official *Statistical Yearbook* before 1939; in 1959 they numbered 74,600. Threshing machines (141,000 in 1960), mechanical spreaders, combines and milking machines were used by the tens of thousands by the closing fifties. They played a significant part in increasing production and therefore contributed to national self-sufficiency in food. Yet the greater self-sufficiency made possible by them was partly illusory, for while tractors and other mechanical aids to agricultural production were produced at home, gasoline and other necessary liquid fuels and lubricants were not. Dependence on the outside world remained an inescapable fact: greater national self-sufficiency in food meant greater dependence on foreign sources for essentials without which the increased self-sufficiency in food could not have been achieved.

Some of the main aspects of the agricultural sector of the economy are indicated by the production trends during the past quarter-century. While the traditional crops, rye, barley, oats, potatoes, hay, and vegetables, remained the primary staples—except that rye lost a good deal of its earlier importance; its production in the late 1950s was less than one half of that of 1938—some new items appeared in the list and others grew substantially in volume. Sugar beet production was insignificant before World War II. Its production reached 37,100 tons in 1945. It had grown to 358,400 tons in 1954 and 456,100 tons in 1961. Sugar production (excluding confectionery and the like) reached 53,800 tons in 1958 and somewhat less in 1959–60.

Wheat production offered another measure of the changing world of agricultural production. During the last "normal" year before the outbreak of war in 1939, Finland produced about 197,000 tons of spring wheat. The figure dropped to 148,000 in 1945 but rose rapidly thereafter. It had reached 197,500 tons by 1954 and 199,000 tons in 1958. A new high was recorded in 1961 when 410,500 tons of spring wheat were grown (and 50,000 tons of winter wheat). These amounts appear to have met approximately 70–75 percent of the domestic consumption during the late fifties. Butter and cheese production showed the same trend. Dairy-produced butter came to 34,300 tons in 1938, had declined to 15,100 tons in 1945, and climbed to 51,000 tons in 1954. Four years later, the figure stood at 74,500 and reached 92,200 in 1961. During the years in question, butter exports showed a substantial decline, most of the production being used at home—one fact among many indicating an improvement in the standard of living after the war. Annual exports in 1956–61 varied from 25,000 to 17,500 tons. Cheese production in the meantime rose from 11,000 tons in 1938 to 22,800 tons in 1954 and 32,600 tons in 1961, about one half of these amounts going to foreign markets.

Approximately 90 percent of the nation's dairies were cooperatives by the closing 1950s. Their main central organization, the Valio, had been organized in 1905. These cooperatives account for nine tenths of the butter production and three fourths of the cheese production of the country. Other cooperatives handling meat products, eggs, and the like have existed since the first decade of the century. During the past two generations, the farmer's cooperatives have supplied him with a wide variety of services and accommodations. They range all the way from organizations that produce or sell agricultural machinery to mills that grind his flour and experimental agricultural stations that help him chart his future programs of production.

Many of the farmers' cooperatives or other organizations have enjoyed the direct or indirect support of the public treasury since the last war. Some of the support programs go back to the depression years of the early 1930s. Price supports, export subsidies, government purchase and storage of "surplus" production, and other measures designed to help the farmer indicate that basic agricultural problems in Finland and in the Scandinavian North are in some respects similar to those of the United States.

THE GROWTH OF INDUSTRY

Finland faced the postwar years with two seemingly insuperable difficulties. One was the fact that the nation's main industrial resource, the forest lands, had been seriously depleted as a result of loss of territory to the Soviets. The other was the obligation to pay reparations in amounts that seemed paralyzing, to put it mildly. Both of these difficulties, however, turned out to be less serious than was assumed during the bleak half-dozen years after 1945.

The areas ceded to the USSR contained 12–13 percent of the nation's timberland and had provided about 11 percent of the annual forest increment before the war. The productive capacity of the industrial plant had also been substantially decreased because some

10–14 percent of the nation's paper, pulp, plywood, and related factories had been lost. The loss of factories, to be sure, could be made good, in time, by building additional plants. The loss of forest acreage, on the other hand, appeared permanently to fix timber resources at a level substantially below that before the war, thereby imposing a formidable handicap upon the nation's economy.

A closer look at the situation showed that it was better than had been expected. During the war years the annual fellings of timber had been a good deal less than in normal times. Wartime forest fires resulting from "natural" causes, enemy incendiaries, and shelling had destroyed considerable acreage but not enough to mean a permanent loss. Most important, an extensive inventory of forest resources in 1951–53 disclosed the encouraging fact that the standing timber and annual growth increment lost by the cessions of territory had been largely made up by an increase of the resources still available after the war. The annual growth—the determinant of the amounts that could be felled without depleting the "capital" needed to keep the forests going—turned out to be approximately 45,000,-000 cubic meters (1 cubic meter equals 1.308 cubic yards) as against about 46,000,000 cubic meters in the middle 1930s. The paper, plywood, pulp, prefabricated housing, and other industries dependent on wood could therefore draw on substantially greater raw material resources than had been assumed to exist at the end of the war. Their traditional prominence among the nation's industries thus appeared to be secure.

The end result of the reparations payments also turned out to be, once the huge costs involved had been met, a substantial long-range economic advantage. We have seen that approximately four fifths of the reparations goods delivered to the USSR consisted of the products of the shipbuilding and machinery and metals industries. When the reparations deliveries began, these industries were far from ready to produce the amounts and types of commodities required. They therefore had to be expanded, no matter what the cost. By the time the last payments were made in September, 1952, these industries had undergone a transformation that had raised them to a level few could have foreseen in 1939.

The transformation was, broadly speaking, threefold. First, it meant a great increase in the volume and diversity of production. Secondly, the reparations schedules had been such as to impose exacting quality requirements previously largely unknown in these branches of Finnish industry. In order to meet them, up-to-date machinery, tools, and equipment in general had to be provided— again, no matter what the cost—and new methods of production devised. Thirdly, the eight long reparations years yielded an accumulation of new managerial experience and valuable know-how regarding foreign trade and markets that the modest pre-1939 industries in this category had largely lacked.

These and related factors go a long way toward explaining the direction and magnitude of industrial development after 1945 and especially after 1952. The record shows a general industrial expansion unmatched in the earlier history of the country. Some of its main details are indicated by Table 28. In interpreting the figures

TABLE 28

VOLUME OF INDUSTRIAL PRODUCTION, 1938–1962
(1938 = 100)

Main industries

Year	Total industry	Wood	Paper	Metals	Chemicals	Textiles	Food processing	Mining
1938	100	100	100	100	100	100	100	100
1939	91	78	85	96	96	95	86	107
1941	75	53	49	99	104	68	93	121
1944	84	58	52	120	152	71	87	111
1948	133	109	93	200	228	97	124	153
1953	174	115	113	236	383	142	226	194
1959	247	131	203	329	599	180	314	335
1961	310	161	276	430	738	200	368	393
1962	328	150	290	471	796	203	383	415

of the table, we must recall that economic advance during the half-dozen years before 1939 had been very substantial. The base of comparison therefore stands for a high-level economy. We must also note that, except for metals, chemicals, and mining, the low-water mark of production was reached in 1941, the first year of the second phase of the war. It was from the low levels of 1944 that the nation proceeded to forge ahead, burdened by the economic losses inflicted by the territorial cessions and the huge reparations payments defined in the armistice.

General industrial production during the period increased more than threefold and more than fourfold over the wartime low in 1941. The "old" industries, well established long before the Russian attack in 1939—that is, paper, pulp, plywood, and the like—grew relatively less rapidly, or from 50 to nearly 300 percent, although paper production expanded considerably. It decreased to barely one half of the 1938 volume in 1941 and then rose to nearly six times the 1941 figure in 1962. Mining recorded a sixfold growth; food processing multiplied by about four and textiles by about three. Chemicals and metals production multiplied by about seven and four respectively, thus impressively highlighting the trend. That the trend was steadily upward even during the years when the nation was straining its resources in paying the huge reparations bill was no less impressive than the advance after the ransom imposed by the USSR had been fully paid.

The developments noted were also reflected in the growing number of people who depended on industry for a livelihood. They barely topped 220,000 in 1937 and numbered 247,400 when the war ended in 1945. Their ranks grew steadily thereafter. In 1950 industry employed 300,000 people; in 1955 the figure had risen to 364,300; it was 396,000 in 1960 and reached 415,200 in 1961. Meanwhile the annual value of industrial production—leaving the war years aside —had risen at an even faster pace, testifying to increasing mechanization and expanding modernization in general.

Industries not included in Table 28 also registered substantial advance. The annual production of the leather and rubber goods industries was 80 percent higher in 1962 than in 1938. The manufacture of machinery expanded at a greater rate; its volume had nearly doubled by 1948, and the 1962 production volume was well over four times that of the last normal year before the war. Electrical machinery, appliances, and the like belonged in the same category although the rate of expansion was even more marked: the production of 1962 was nearly eight times larger than that of 1938.

The metals industry had provided some 80 percent of the reparations deliveries to the USSR. When the reparations payments were completed in September, 1952, the prospects of the industry seemed anything but bright. Some observers—especially foreign observers —held that the end of reparations deliveries would paralyze or possibly deal a mortal blow to the industry. Not a few analysts went so far as to contend that the metals industry, having expanded because of the requirements of the reparations schedules, had become by 1952 an ominous weakness in the nation's economy which the USSR could and would use at will in the pursuit of its political and economic aims, obviously to the detriment of Finland. Such pessimistic conclusions and alarmist predictions have, however, been proved unwarranted by the record since 1952.

The record shows that, while the metals industry owed its rapid growth after 1945 to the forced draft provided by the requirements of the reparations schedules, the industry was able to stand on its own feet after reparations deliveries ceased. Not only has it held its own since 1952, as Table 28 shows, but its output was doubled, broadly speaking, between 1952 and 1962. The industry flourished because of the fact that the domestic market absorbed ever-greater quantities of its products. It is thus obvious that however significant the Soviet "market" had been before 1952—it was a market that provided Finland with no equivalents for the reparations commodities delivered to it—the metals industry as a whole could exist and develop independent of it.

While the market at home played a decisive part in the growth of the metals industry, foreign markets remained a factor worthy of note. The bloc of eastern states, especially the Soviet Union, accounted for most of the sales abroad. The exports of the industry amounted to approximately 17 percent of its total annual production. Of this amount, the USSR bought about seven tenths (the average percentage for 1954–62 was 70). The other nations of the eastern bloc accounted for 2–5 percent.

Other major aspects of economic growth merely underline the

circumstances illustrated by the various branches of the metals and machinery industries. Table 29 throws light upon developments of importance not only for metals, machinery, and the like but for the economy as a whole.

TABLE 29

IRON AND STEEL PRODUCTION, 1938–1960
(in tons)

Year	Pig iron	Steel	Rolled products
1938	26,000	76,500	97,000
1946	73,300	90,000	73,300
1950	63,400	99,400	77,400
1953	79,800	147,900	119,400
1955	114,800	186,800	177,700
1959	107,600	225,600	159,400
1960	136,600	245,800	195,300

The annual demand for steel in 1959 was about 500,000 tons. Domestic production therefore supplied approximately one half of the amount needed. Pig iron production rested, and continues to rest, mostly on foreign ore. The most important domestic metal product is copper, production of which became significant after 1945. In 1950, production was 13,600 tons. It rose to 21,400 tons in 1954, 32,600 tons in 1959, and dropped to 31,000 tons in 1960. These amounts met most of the domestic demand for copper.

A further indication of the place of the metals industry in the general economy is given by the fact that during 1945–61 its production grew, annually, by 7.1 percent, which was only a fraction less than the figure for industry as a whole. Employment increased by about 2.1 percent per year, which compared favorably with the over-all percentage for industry. The capacity of the industry to grow even after the hothouse conditions provided by reparations deliveries had become a thing of the past is indicated by the fact that it employed 87,500 workers in 1952 and provided employment for 119,000 persons in 1961 (out of a total of about 415,000 for industry as a whole).

Industrial expansion after 1945 resulted in changes in the size and relationship of the various categories of the "economically active" population. The changes recorded in 1950 and in 1960 indicate the trend. During the ten-year period, the number of persons engaged in agriculture decreased, because of the continuing movement out of agriculture to industry or other occupations, by about 24 percent. Meantime the industry category grew by 8.5 percent, construction by 43.5 percent, transport and communications by 20.7 percent, commerce by 47.4 percent, and the service trades by 32.8 percent.[4]

The result was that, out of the total population of 4,446,200 in 1960, the farmer group—including all members of families as well as "economically active" individuals—accounted for 1,118,500. The decade of the sixties thus began with an emphatic accent upon the industrial and other nonagricultural aspects of the economy.

FOREIGN TRADE

We have noted earlier that foreign trade was of utmost importance for the nation during the interwar years. Several circumstances combined to make foreign trade even more essential after 1945. First, the large segment of industry dependent on wood produced paper, pulp, wallboard, plywood, furniture, prefabricated houses, etc., in quantities greatly in excess of the needs of the home market and at prices low enough for successful competition in foreign markets. Secondly, the standard of living had reached levels, long before the 1940s, that led to the consumption of commodities that were produced at home only in insufficient quantities or not at all and therefore had to be imported. Food products, fruits, automobiles, and many other goods belonged in this category. Thirdly, a considerable number of raw materials, feeds, fertilizers, and machinery had been indispensable underpinnings of industry and agriculture alike for decades before 1939. The greater degree of self-sufficiency imposed by the war years had demonstrated with unmistakable finality that a marked reduction or cessation of foreign

[4] The number of "economically inactive independent persons" doubled between 1950 and 1960 and reached 478,000 by the latter date. All nonemployed persons over 65 years of age are included in this category because the national old age pension and supplementary payments available to all over the age of 65 are sufficient for a minimum, independent livelihood.

trade meant a drastic lowering of the general standard of living and a virtual collapse of whole industries (the textile industry, for example). In a word, to sell abroad and to buy abroad, vitally important in normal times, became a matter of economic life or death during the exceptionally trying years after 1945, especially because of the reparations obligation.

A measure of wartime contraction of essential foreign trade and of the distance to be traveled before the country could return to a "normal" economy is suggested by the fact that in 1945 both exports and imports had declined to about 18 percent of the 1935 figures. "Free exports"—that is, exports outside the reparations payments—in 1946 were less than one half of those of the mid-thirties but rose to about 80 percent by 1949. After the completion of the reparations deliveries in 1952, the situation improved rapidly. The trend in the main categories of Finnish exports and imports in 1949–60 is given by Tables 30 and 31.

Professor Erik Dahmén of the Stockholm Graduate School of Business and economic adviser to the well-known Enskilda Bank of Stockholm remarks in a recent study that "Finland's speedy economic development since World War II is impressive when we contemplate the point from which the process began and the difficulties created, among other things, by the cessions of territory and the reparations payments. Finland stands out well indeed in comparison with other nations." Tables 30 and 31 throw a flood of light upon the recovery since the war. They show the extent to which, especially after the mid-fifties, "the rise of the standard of living depended upon the expansion of the country's foreign trade." [5] This is merely one way of saying that Finland succeeded in reentering and in staying in markets that had been of outstanding importance before the war. Marked success had also been recorded in the effort to capture markets—especially in the USSR—that had been nonexistent before 1939.

It will be recalled that the separation from Russia in 1917–18 resulted in a significant change in Finland's foreign trade relations. Before World War I, Russia had accounted for approximately one

[5] The quotations are from Erik Dahmén, *Suomen Taloudellinen Kehitys ja Talouspolitiikka* (Helsinki, 1963), pp. 124–25.

TABLE 30

Exports, 1949–1960

(in millions of marks)

Year	Total	Paper industry	Wood products	Means of transportation	Metals and metal goods	Food products	Machinery and appliances
1949	65,606	26,578	31,047	1,315	978	1,591	568
1951	186,883	98,504	73,232	2,301	2,205	2,034	2,617
1953	131,555	48,541	53,076	11,077	3,109	2,232	6,733
1955	181,259	76,298	69,905	14,589	2,953	2,658	7,194
1957	212,385	98,073	63,928	15,785	3,473	8,803	11,037
1959	267,322	119,052	77,097	19,222	6,816	11,073	18,049
1960	316,474	133,732	84,132				
						53,996	

Source: Tables 30 and 31 are based on Tables 12B, 13A, and 13B on pp. 158–61 of Erik Dahmén, *Suomen Taloudellinen Kehitys ja Talouspolitiikka* (Helsinki, 1963).

TABLE 31

IMPORTS OF SELECTED MAIN COMMODITIES, 1949–1960

(in millions of marks)

Year	Total	Machinery and appliances	Metals and metal products	Means of trans- portation	Oil	Minerals	Grain	Chemicals[a]
1949	66,278	9,045	11,859	2,635	4,644	4,865	3,337	1,900
1951	155,464	15,734	22,646	10,092	11,742	15,719	9,827	5,077
1953	121,860	18,335	13,999	9,335	10,352	10,562	10,283	3,318
1955	176,960	25,810	23,694	13,901	12,251	15,673	9,693	13,275
1957	227,927	33,940	33,613	16,767	24,593	23,878	11,115	16,148
1959	267,300	54,846	37,189	26,199	20,508	16,575	11,430	24,344
1960	340,300		113,291		34,360			30,877

[a] The figures for 1955–60 include the products of "chemical and related industries"; those for 1949–53 are limited to raw materials.

third of the exports and imports of the country; Germany had been more important as a source of Finnish imports, while Britain had been the main buyer of goods sold abroad. By the 1930s, Britain had become Finland's main foreign trade partner, while the USSR remained a negligible quantity both as a buyer and as a seller. During the war years after 1939 Germany captured, for reasons easy to understand, a dominant position in the rapidly and ominously contracting area of foreign trade. By 1943, Germany accounted for well over two thirds of both exports and imports. Sweden and Denmark were the second and third on the list, while trade with the other Western states ceased altogether. The situation changed after the war had ended. Germany disappeared from the picture for several years, Britain quickly resumed most, although not all, of her pre-1939 role, and the Soviet Union emerged as a factor more important than before 1939: Soviet imports of Finnish commodities accounted for 1.3 percent of Finland's exports in 1938, about 15 percent in 1949, 16.8 percent in 1959, and 13.7 percent in 1961.

The geographical distribution of foreign trade in 1949–61, in percentages of exports and imports, is shown by Table 32. We should note that 1953 was the first postwar year when reparations payments statistics no longer distorted the record of Finland's foreign trade position.

Table 32 underscores the fact that Finland's foreign trade is overwhelmingly Western-oriented. In recent years, approximately 75 to 80 percent of the country's exports, for example, have gone to the free West, while the USSR has generally accounted for substantially less than 20 percent. These figures do not tell the whole story, however. Widespread postwar foreign exchange controls, licensing policies, restriction or prohibition of certain imports and exports, subsidies and export premiums, and the like have complicated and limited international commercial exchange in a manner that has given Finland's trade with the Soviet Union a special significance. Forest industry products—accounting, as we have seen, for some 80 percent of Finland's exports—go to Western markets and play only a minor part in the trade with the USSR. The exports to the Soviets consist largely of the products of the metal and shipbuilding industries; imports consist of grain, oil, scrap iron, coal, cotton,

TABLE 32
DISTRIBUTION OF FOREIGN TRADE, 1949–1961
(percentages of the total)

	1949		1953		1956		1959		1961	
	Exports	*Imports*	*Exports*	*Imports*	*Exports*	*Imports*	*Exports*	*Imports*	*Exports*	*Imports*
Pound sterling area	30.5	22.9	24.5	16.3	25.3	21.3	26.7	16.3	24.5	15.7
Other OEEC nations in Europe	34.5	42.8	29.8	36.2	31.4	39.1	36.5	49.4	46.4	55.2
United States and Canada	7.6	7.7	7.3	5.2	6.7	6.7	5.8	5.4	4.5	6.0
Eastern bloc	19.8	19.2	31.3	34.5	27.6	25.0	23.5	24.5	18.1	19.4
USSR's share	15.2	11.3	25.5	21.4	19.2	13.9	16.8	17.8	12.1	13.7
Others	7.6	7.4	7.1	7.8	9.0	7.9	7.5	4.4	6.6	3.7

Source: Tables 11A and 11B, in E. Dahmén, *Suomen Taloudellinen Kehitys ja Talouspolitiikka*, pp. 154–55, and Table 124 in *S.T.V.*, 1962, p. 126.

sugar, automobiles, etc. Speaking in general terms, the export-import relationship between the two countries gives Finland a twofold advantage. First, while the metals and machine industries are by no means exclusively dependent on the exports to the Soviet market, their products can in general be sold there more easily and in larger quantities than in the West. Relatively short transport, especially ease of railroad transportation—both states have the same broad-gauge railroad trackage—accounts for part of the advantage. Secondly, while the commodities imported from the USSR could also normally be readily obtained from the West, their purchase would involve foreign exchange difficulties. The trade with the USSR reduces the dimensions of the foreign exchange problem and therefore eases the nation's foreign trade position.

It has been contended that Finland's dependence on the Soviet market places the country in a dangerous position because Soviet refusal to continue to purchase Finnish commodities would paralyze the nation's economy and thereby undermine its freedom. This claim rests, it would seem, on no solid factual foundation. It also ignores the important fact that Soviet observance of trade agreements with Finland since 1945 has been, possibly because of prestige considerations, meticulously correct. The record of Finnish-Soviet trade relations since 1952, when reparations deliveries ended, appears fully to justify the conclusion that the trade contacts between the two countries rest wholly on considerations of mutual economic advantage.

PRIVATE AND PUBLIC ENTERPRISE

Finland's economy before 1939 was a free enterprise economy, and it has remained such since World War II. Public enterprise, however, is of considerable dimensions if the term is used to cover the whole range of economic activity and services involving national and local governmental authorities.[6]

[6] See R. Talaskivi, in P. Renvall, ed., *Suomalaisen Kansanvallan Kehitys* (Helsinki, 1956), pp. 283–93; J. S. Melin, "Public Enterprise in Finland," in Bank of Finland, *Monthly Bulletin*, March, 1964; and *S.T.V.*, 1962, Tables 111–13.

The reasons for the relatively significant public sector in Finland's economy are simple and obvious. Socialization for the sake of socialization, in response to preconceived conceptions regarding the "harmfulness" of private enterprise on the one hand or the "advantages" of public enterprise on the other, is not the main explanation. The explanation is lack of capital. The lack of private capital for enterprises deemed essential has led to many public undertakings in areas normally left to private enterprise. Where private capital could not provide for large-scale investment needs, the state has stepped in, raised the necessary funds, and of course provided the security foreign capital has required. The construction of railroads from the middle decades of the 1800s to the end of the century and beyond is a good illustration of the essential facts: nearly all of the public debt during this period represented investment in railroads for which private capital was not available.

Mining presents another example, the Outokumpu copper mine being a case in point. The ore deposit, discovered by the Geological Survey of Finland, was at first exploited by a private company. The state purchased the company in the 1920s when the private operators of the mine were unable to obtain the necessary capital for further development. In more recent years, the exploitation of the country's iron ore deposits, on a major scale, has been made possible only by government interest and investment. Certain industrial plants belong in the same category. Outstanding among them is the Enso-Gutzeit Company, originally Norwegian-owned. The majority of the stock in the company—76 percent—was purchased by the state in 1918, and the state has remained the principal owner since that time. Some other companies, deemed to be of special national interest, have also become the beneficiaries of state financial assistance when the lack of necessary capital threatened difficulties. Finally, certain public utilities, such as water, electricity, harbor installations, gasworks, and the like, have long been considered of such a nature and importance as to call for public ownership and management. They are usually managed by the municipality and are, in fact, public utility monopolies run according to approved business practices. The State Alcohol Corporation, which has been, since the repeal of prohibition in 1932, the sole importer, manufacturer, and seller of alcoholic beverages in the country, belongs, for obvious reasons, in a category by itself. The same applies to the State Broadcasting Company.

The share of the public sector in the nation's economy varies. In the broad area of agriculture, it is wholly negligible, or 1.5 percent of the gross domestic product, and in industry 16 percent (figures for 1962). The latter figure reflects the fact that national defense industries were organized as state industries in the thirties. Several of them were later reorganized as the State Metal Industry (Valmet), which employed almost 9,500 persons in 1962. Its production includes a variety of nondefense commodities. The percentage also reflects the fact that pressure of reparations deliveries after 1945 led to state involvement in shipbuilding and some other industries. As we might expect, in view of the fact that the railroads, the postal service, and the telegraph are state-owned, the share of private enterprise in the transport and communication areas is the smallest: 51.3 percent. Construction likewise involves a relatively large public sector, or 25.9 percent. This figure is inflated by the fact that it includes road and waterways construction, normally a government enterprise, and also municipal housing programs. In forestry, private companies account for 83.9 percent. The 16.1 percent public sector reflects, among other things, the relatively large state and municipal ownership of forests, and especially the state ownership of the Enso-Gutzeit Company that operates eleven factories and a power plant and employs some 18,800 persons.

State-owned enterprises or companies which the government partly owns vary a good deal as regards salaries, the status of the employees, the general manner of management, and the importance of the profit motive. The state railways, for example, are operated on the same basic principles as state administration in general. Upkeep, investments, and profits are matters for the government budget; the employees are civil servants; wages, salaries, and terms of employment are those provided by civil service regulations. State-owned corporations, on the other hand, are managed, as a law of 1931 puts it, "according to sound business principles" with the best interests of the state in mind and "with due respect to profitability." The state companies enjoy no special privileges in competition with private enterprises. They are subject to the same tax rates, corporation laws, and normal accountancy rules and requirements as private enterprises. They are run, in other words, as if they were private businesses. Their place in the economy and the problems involved in their control and supervision continue to be subjects of discussion and debate, but it is unlikely that the general pattern of this area of the nation's economy will substantially change in the foreseeable future.

XV

Government and Politics since 1945

THE LAY OF THE LAND

When the Russian government proceeded, two generations ago, to destroy the constitution of autonomous Finland, a large number of the leaders of the Western civilized world rallied to Finland's defense. Over one thousand prominent representatives of the intellectual elite of Britain, France, Italy, Holland, Germany, the Scandinavian countries, and other lands pleaded, through an address forwarded to St. Petersburg, that the sanctity of law not be violated. That the plea was in vain was, in a sense, unimportant. That illustrious men and women had raised their voices in behalf of justice and right was important. It was an impressive illustration of the ethical concerns of an age long since buried in oblivion by a generation seemingly less adequately attuned to the imperatives that led men of sensibility to become petitioners in behalf of moral principle and law. Their readiness to stand up and be counted strengthened the Finns' resolve and capacity to breast the tide of Russification.

Less than two decades later the perils of Russification seemed to have become a part of history and the nation could proceed to the tasks of setting its political house in order as an independent people. That a civil war had been fought before independence had been fully secured was a reminder of an aspect of the process that was, in retrospect, not only tragic but unnecessary. Yet the material and other costs of the war were not great enough to impede or paralyze the upbuilding of the new republic. Less still was the nation required to labor after 1918 under burdens comparable to the servitudes imposed by Soviet exactions in 1944. The years between the wars recorded, as we have seen, exceptional progress along all lines. By the end of the thirties, the events of 1918 had become past history and the nation stood united when the unprovoked Soviet invasion began in November, 1939.

When the war ended in 1944, the Finns faced a future more ominous by far than the future that loomed on the horizon at the turn of the century or in 1918. The armistice in general and the reparations exactions in particular appeared to force the country to the brink of permanent disaster. In contemplating the new perils, the Finns found themselves left alone to face the future. Looking westward beyond the confines of their own land they searched, largely in vain, for friends able to recognize Soviet aggression and its consequences, ready to call aggression and its attendant evils by their right names, and willing to offer at least moral support to the hard-pressed nation. The West did not yet correctly identify the threats embedded in Soviet expansionism and understandably centered its attention on the enormously pressing and complex problems of national and international reconstruction.

Finland thus had to adjust herself, with only nominal outside aid —Sweden's assistance was, in the circumstances, of almost incalculable value—to the exactions defined by the armistice of 1944. The results of the grim effort were reflected in government, the political situation in general, and in the economy that was geared amazingly quickly and efficiently to the needs of the hour.

THE POLITICAL PARTIES

The end of the war and the difficult years that followed left the pre-1939 political party constellation on the whole intact. Two main changes occurred: the Communists reappeared on the scene and the rightist IKL disappeared.

The Communist party of Finland (the SKP), which had been outlawed by Parliament in 1930, was legalized according to one of the provisions of the armistice of September, 1944. The party was formally organized and registered under the Associations Act on October 31, 1944. At the time of the armistice its membership was reported to be approximately 1,200. The party proceeded at once to make political hay while the Soviet sun was shining at its brightest.

One of the early achievements of the Communists was the Finnish People's Democratic Association (the SKDL), organized in November, 1944. Its purpose was to serve as the common, central organ of the Communists, left-wing Socialists who had either quit or had been expelled from the Social Democratic party, and other like-minded elements. In other words, it was not intended to be a regular political party. The original purpose of the SKDL failed, however, and the organization was thereupon turned into a political party pure and simple. It provided a political home, especially during the first few years after 1945, to fellow travelers as yet unwilling or unready to join the SKP. The Communist party as such joined the SKDL, thus bringing into its ranks the program and local and national organization of the party. The leadership of the SKDL therefore fell into the hands of the Communists and became for all practical purposes identical with the Communist party. That it must be identified as a Communist group is shown by the fact that Communists sought electoral victories and other political advantages exclusively under the banner or as the candidates of the SKDL. In other words, the Communists pursued their objectives under the presumably insulated cover of the SKDL.

Another change in the party constellation after 1944 was the disappearance of the IKL (the Patriotic People's Movement). The party had emerged in 1933, it will be recalled, as the result of the anti-Communist movement of the preceding three years. Its membership and especially its leadership included individuals unreservedly committed to fascist ideology. It could therefore be labeled not only rightist but antidemocratic. The party had never become a significant power factor in Finnish politics. In the 1933 election it captured 14 seats out of the 200 seats in Parliament, held its own in the 1936 election, and dropped to 8 seats in 1939. It thus commanded only 4 percent of the votes in the legislature and could not be considered a threat to the democratic institutions of the country. Article 21 of the armistice, however, called for the dissolution of all "fascist" organizations. The IKL was one of the organizations placed in this category—many of them were classified thus quite arbitrarily—and ceased its activities in September, 1944.

The other parties represented the groupings familiar to us from our survey of political developments during the interwar years. On the right we find the conservative National Union party. It may be compared to the Högern in Sweden, the Høyre in Norway, and the Konservative Folkeparti in Denmark. The center continued to be represented by the Agrarian party and the Finnish People's party (since 1951, the successor of the Progressive party). The latter corresponds approximately to the Folkpartiet in Sweden, the Venstre in Norway, and the Radikale Venstre in Denmark. The Agrarian party occupies the same area in the political spectrum as the Centerpartiet (previously Bondeförbundet) in Sweden, the Venstre in Denmark, and the Senterpartiet in Norway. The Swedish People's party remained the party of the heterogeneous Swede-Finn population groups. The Social Democratic party continued to represent politically organized labor on a platform originally accepted in 1903 when the party was founded. Its brand of socialism is that embraced by the parties of the same name in Sweden and Denmark and the Arbeiderpartiet in Norway.[1]

A close look at the parties' programs, membership, success in electoral contests, and the like reveals a number of facts essential to an understanding of the Finnish political scene since the end of the war.

The membership of the parties has not been fully recorded during the past two decades. Available estimates suggest that in the late 1950s the Agrarians had approximately 300,000 members, the Social Democrats slightly over 100,000, the SKDL about 137,000, the Communists, who also appear on the SKDL roster, 48,000, the conservative National Union party nearly 78,000, the Swede-Finn party about 52,000, and the progressive Finnish People's party 18,000. These figures do not reveal, however, the extent to which parties were supported by the voters in national or local elections. An

[1] See Göran von Bonsdorff, "The Party Situation in Finland," in Finnish Political Science Association, ed., *Democracy in Finland* (Helsinki, 1961), pp. 18–19.

estimate of the voting results of the 1958 election indicates that party members accounted for the following percentages of the total number of votes obtained: Agrarians 67 percent, Social Democrats 21 percent, the SKDL 30 percent, the National Union party 26 percent, the Swede-Finns 40 percent, and the Progressives 16 percent. In other words, all the parties obtained a much larger number of votes than membership in the party indicated, the Agrarians being the least successful in recommending programs and candidates to the nonmember voters. The Social Democrats, on the other hand, received nearly four "non-Socialist" votes for every party membership. The small Progressive group did even better.

The conservative National Union party offers a good illustration of the subtleties and complexities of Finnish politics. An investigation of the results of the 1948 election disclosed among other things that the party had been supported by a broad segment of the population; it had obtained 320,400 votes, 17.1 percent of the total, and had captured 33 seats in Parliament. About 27 percent of its supporters were small farmers, 22 percent factory workers, 3 percent other laboring folk, 26 percent "middle class" voters, and some 22 percent belonged in the upper professional categories. About one fourth of the votes the party received thus came from factory hands who by ordinary definition belonged on the left, and one fourth came from small farmers whose affiliation should have been, again by usual definition, Agrarian. The heterogeneity of the support of the party, normally labeled the most conservative and at times branded by its opponents as the reactionary party in the country, underlines the failure of many a voter to choose or reject political alternatives according to criteria—economic advantage and the like —usually accepted as decisive by political historians and commentators.

Similar incongruities—if incongruities they are—characterized the support of other parties as well. The 1948 analysis mentioned above also showed that roughly one quarter of the voters who supported Social Democratic candidates came from nonlabor groups. In the case of the SKDL the nonlabor proportion was about one fifth. While the Agrarians received some 90 percent of their support from the farming segment of the population, the votes came in fact from farmer groups that varied a good deal as regards size of farm, ownership of property in general, or social and educational status, and whose interests and objectives differed quite enough to challenge conventional textbook explanations.

Ever since the parliament reform and the introduction of universal and free suffrage in 1906, the outcome of elections has been determined by the d'Hondt proportional representation device. The result is that the larger parties tend to get greater representation than the votes received justify, while the smaller parties receive fewer seats; the former parties are, in other words, overrepresented and the latter underrepresented. The Agrarians have been, since 1945, the main beneficiaries of the system. In the 1945 election, for example, they received six seats, in the 1948 election seven seats, and in the 1954 election five seats more than the number of votes received would have yielded if they had been distributed on a mathematical basis. The small Finnish People's party, on the other hand, lost from one to three seats in the same elections.[2]

NATIONAL AND LOCAL ELECTIONS

One of the conspicuous features of Finnish politics after World War II was a marked increase in voter participation in national and local elections. During 1919–39, approximately 55–62 percent of the citizens entitled to vote went to the polls in parliamentary elections. In only one election, that of 1919—the first election after the 1918 war—did the figure reach 67. Since the first postwar election in 1945, the percentage has not dropped below 74; in 1954 it reached 79.9. Four years later it stood at 75.0, but in 1962 it rose to an all-time high, 85.1 percent.

The record of municipal elections showed a similar increase in interest in political contests. Local elections before 1939 never enticed more than 48 percent of the voters to the polls; the figure usually varied between 42 and 45. After 1945 the percentage stayed well

---

[2] During the interwar period, the Agrarians were, in general, overrepresented by a five-seat margin, and the Social Democrats also benefited by the system. The appearance of the SKDL in 1944 created a situation that robbed the Socialists of their pre-1939 advantage.

over 50. It was 71.4 in 1953 and rose to 75.5 in 1960. The Electoral Colleges, responsible for the election of the President, registered the same trend. The first Electoral College, that of 1925, was chosen by 39.7 percent of the voters, the second (1931) by 47.3 percent, the third, in 1937, by 57.8 percent. The first postwar election in 1950 recorded 63.8 percent participation. The second, in 1956, raised the percentage to 73.4. That of 1962 was higher still, 78.8.[3]

The greater political activity suggested by the increased participation in elections has raised the question of what it portends in terms of present meanings and long-range implications. The question has not been sufficiently explored to permit definitive conclusions, but it has been ascertained that classes or groups high or relatively high in the economic and social scale vote more readily and more often than others; the lowest strata register the smallest degree of participation. Other factors, however, such as certain political crises and uncertainties of the postwar years, were no doubt also involved. A marked improvement in general standards of living since 1944 does not by itself explain why the number of Finns who went to the polls after 1945 was consistently greater than before the country fell victim to Soviet invasion in 1939.

The results of national elections in 1945–63 are given in Tables 33–35. Table 33 shows the distribution of votes according to parties, Table 34 the relative strength of the parties expressed in percentages of the votes received, and Table 35 the number of seats in Parliament captured by each party. The period witnessed an almost uninterrupted increase in the number of voters: the figure was 1,710,000 in 1945, 2,019,000 in 1954, and 2,310,000 in 1962 (1958 registered a total of some 60,000 less than 1954).

The outcome of the elections shows clearly that the general political constellation remained virtually unchanged after the war.

[3] *S.T.V.*, 1958, Table 351; 1962, Tables 365–72. The total membership of the local councils, urban as well as rural, elected in 1960 for a four-year term, was 12,408. Of this number the SKDL accounted for 2,410 (19.4 percent), the Social Democrats 2,260 (18.2 percent), and the dissidents 263. The non-Socialist groups included 7,442 members or 76.8 percent (74.4 percent in 1957–60). It is therefore clear that in this area no less than on the larger area of national politics and government the Communist and fellow-traveler elements had failed, by a wide margin, to capture the citadels of power. *Ibid.*, 1962, Table 373.

TABLE 33

DISTRIBUTION OF VOTES IN PARLIAMENTARY ELECTIONS, 1945–1962

Year	Social Democrats	Agrarians	SKDL Communists	National Union	Swede-Finns	Progressives	Social Democrat Opposition	Others
1945	425,900	362,700	398,600	255,400	134,100	87,900		33,800
1948	494,700	455,600	375,800	320,400	144,300	73,400		15,700
1951	480,800	421,600	391,400	264,000	137,200	102,900		14,900
1954	527,000	483,900	433,500	257,000	140,130	158,300		8,200
1958	450,200	448,400	450,000	297,100	130,900	114,600	33,900	18,600
1962	448,900	530,600	507,100	346,600	147,700	146,000	100,400	74,600

Source: *S.T.V.*, 1962, Table 366.

TABLE 34

VOTERS' PARTY CHOICES IN NATIONAL ELECTIONS, 1945–1962
(percentages of votes cast)

Year	Social Demo-crats	Agrar-ians	SKDL Commu-nists	National Union	Swede-Finns	Pro-gres-sives	Social Demo-crat Opposi-tion	Others
1945	25.1	21.3	23.5	15.0	7.9	5.1		1.5
1948	26.3	24.2	20.0	17.1	7.7	3.9		0.8
1951	26.5	23.2	21.6	14.6	7.6	5.7		0.8
1954	26.2	24.1	21.6	12.8	7.0	7.9		0.4
1958	23.2	23.1	23.2	15.3	6.7	5.9	1.7	0.9
1962	19.5	23.1	22.0	15.1	6.4	6.3	4.4	3.2

Sources: J. Nousiainen, *Suomen Poliittinen Järjestelmä* (Helsinki, 1961), tables on pp. 13–14; *S.T.V.*, 1962, Table 368. The tables contain a few fractional discrepancies which do not change the over-all conclusions.

TABLE 35

DISTRIBUTION OF SEATS IN PARLIAMENT, 1945–1962

Year	Social Demo-crats	Agrar-ians	SKDL Commu-nists	National Union	Swede-Finns	Pro-gres-sives	Others	Women
1945	50	49	49	28	14	9	1	17
1948	54	56	38	33	14	5		24
1951	53	51	43	28	15	10		29
1954	54	53	43	24	13	13		30
1958	48	48	50	29	14	8	3	28
1962	38	53	47	32	14	13	2	27

Source: *S.T.V.*, 1962, Table 366.

One aspect of it reminds us, quite strikingly, of the dominant feature of the political picture in 1919–39: marked stability and the absence of landslides. The reappearance of the Communists on the political arena caused, to be sure, an important shift in the party balance. The Social Democrats, whose position as the leading party in the legislature had been hardly challenged before World War II—they held 85 out of the 200 seats in 1939—lost their leading position as a result of defections to the SKDL. The party was reduced to the same level as the Agrarians and the SKDL. To make matters worse for the Social Democrats, their ranks were severely depleted in the late 1950s by internal rivalries and dissension. On the eve of the 1962 election, thirteen members of the party's parliamentary group had gone over to the opposition and, while the dissidents succeeded in capturing only two seats in 1962, the party nevertheless suffered a serious defeat. It was reduced to 38 seats, the smallest number in its entire history since 1907.

The cause of progressivism also suffered a decline. The Progressive party had played a decreasing role in Finland no less than in Western democracies in general during the two decades after 1919. Although it had furnished a substantial share of the top leadership in government and politics, as we have seen, the Progressive party did not succeed in resisting the forces that continued to make inroads upon it after the end of World War II. On the contrary, its decline continued—it received only five seats in 1948—and led to the dissolution of the party in 1951. Its successor, the Finnish People's party, fared but little better. It has had to accept, broadly speaking, a minority position similar to that of the Swede-Finn party.

The relative prominence of women representatives in Parliament both before 1918 and during the interwar years continued more or less unchanged in the postwar period. The majority of the women members belonged to the labor and agrarian parties, as has been the case ever since women gained the right to vote and sit in the legislature in 1906. They did not stand out as contenders for causes or policies outside the commitments of the parties to which they belonged; they were, obviously, fully on a par with their male colleagues in serving the purposes and contending for the goals the party had defined as important.

THE PRESIDENTIAL ELECTIONS

During the discussions and debates that preceded the adoption of the republican constitution in 1919, some groups favored direct election of the president, without the intermediary of an electoral college, while others preferred election by Parliament. The Great

Committee of the legislature, however, recommended indirect election—that is, election by a specially chosen Electoral College acting on behalf of the "people of Finland"—and the constitution makers ultimately accepted its recommendation. The assumption was that the procedure would mean a way of selecting the President free from the distractions and limitations of ordinary political contests. The Electoral College of 300, chosen on January 15–16 of the presidential election year, assembles in Helsinki, under the chairmanship of the Prime Minister, on February 15. During the balloting, there is no open or formal discussion of the merits of the presidential nominees—the nominations are made by the political parties in whatever manner they find congenial—and the voting is by secret ballot. A simple majority—151 or more out of 300—suffices to elect. The constitution defined only one qualification for a presidential candidate: he must be a native-born Finnish citizen.

An interesting area of Finnish politics is illumined by a comparison of the success of the various parties in regular parliamentary elections on the one hand and the strength they showed in elections to the Electoral College on the other. Table 36 shows the situation

TABLE 36

ELECTORAL COLLEGE AND GENERAL ELECTIONS, 1948–1962
(party votes, in percent of total)

	1948 General Elections	1950 Electoral Elections	1954 General Elections	1956 Electoral Elections	1962 General Elections	1962 Electoral Elections
Social Democrats	26.3	21.8	26.2	23.3	19.5	13.1
Agrarians (and allied groups in 1962)	24.2	19.6	24.1	26.9	23.1	44.3
SKDL	20.0	21.4	21.6	18.7	22.0	20.5
National Union	17.1	22.9	12.8	18.0	15.1	14.0
Progressives	3.9	5.4	7.9	4.5	6.3	....[a]
Swede-Finns	7.7	8.8	7.0	6.9	6.4	5.1
Others	0.8	0.1	0.4	1.7	7.6	3.0

Sources: *S.T.V.*, 1962, Table 369, and J. Nousiainen, *Suomen Poliittinen Järjestelmä* (Helsinki, 1961), pp. 153–55.

[a] Included in the National Union's 14 percent share of the total.

between 1948, the last general election before the 1950 presidential election, and the parliamentary and presidential elections of 1962. We note that the general election percentages are somewhat higher than the Electoral College percentages.

The important fact noted above in connection with postwar national elections was repeated in elections to the Electoral College. The voters went to the polls to select the Electoral College in substantially larger numbers than before 1939. The last prewar presidential election in 1937 enticed only 57.8 percent of the qualified voters. In 1950 the figure was 63.8 percent. In 1956, when President U. Kekkonen was chosen for his first term, the figure rose to 73.4, and his second-term victory in 1962 was registered in a contest in which nearly four out of every five potential voters (78.8 percent) took the trouble to vote.

In general, presidential elections disclosed interesting deviations from the position of the parties as defined by regular parliamentary elections. The conservative National Union party and the numerically small Progressives have normally scored better in the Electoral College elections than in elections to the legislature. Conversely, the Agrarians have done markedly less well, and the Social Democrats have also lagged behind. The reason appears to be that the conservatives and the liberals have been able to put into the field a number of potential candidates of recognized prominence and ability. The conservative Paasikivi (he had been the leader of the National Union party for a number of years before 1945) after the end of the war or his fellow conservative Svinhufvud or the liberals Ryti or Ståhlberg before the war probably seemed superior, in the eyes of most Finns, to Agrarian hopefuls or potential Social Democratic candidates. U. Kekkonen's victory in 1956 may be said to have registered the first emergence of an Agrarian leader of a stature sufficiently commanding to give him wide support outside of his own party, although special political circumstances, stemming from certain foreign policy considerations, also played a part in determining the outcome of the 1962 contest.

No party represented in the Electoral College was large enough to enjoy a dominating position in the College. It is therefore obvious that, while party preferences did not vanish into thin air when the members of the College assembled to perform their task, they could not proceed to their election merely on the basis of narrow partisan allegiance. Compromise and bargaining unavoidably determined the final choice. The wide margin of discussion and adjustment is suggested by the fact that, as Table 36 shows, only the 1962 coalition of Agrarians, Progressives, and some others obtained somewhat over two fifths of the votes in the Electoral College, and only once was a party successful in getting slightly over one fourth of the votes. It happened in 1956 when the Agrarian candidate, U. Kekkonen, was elected President.

The majorities by which the Presidents were chosen by the Electoral College varied a good deal (Marshal K. G. Mannerheim was designated President by a special law enacted by Parliament on August 4, 1944). J. K. Paasikivi received 159 votes out of 300 in 1946 and 171 when chosen for his second term in 1950. U. Kekkonen had to be satisfied with 151 votes (as against 149 for his rival, the Social Democrat K. A. Fagerholm) in his first election in 1956, but was given a more comfortable winner's margin in his second election in 1962 when he received 199 votes.

GOVERNMENTS SINCE 1945

The number, composition, and political coloration of the cabinets and their leadership in 1945–62 are given by Table 37.

In contemplating the political situation after 1945 we are at once struck by the fact that the preponderant feature of the years before 1939 was carried over into the period after the war: coalition cabinets dominated. Only the first Fagerholm Government (July, 1948–March, 1950) could be called a one-party cabinet, and even it included one minister who served as a nonparty expert. The Sukselainen Cabinet (January, 1959–July, 1961) can be placed in the same category. It included two experts. The Von Fieandt caretaker cabinet (November, 1957–April, 1958) was a pure nonparty group intended to serve as a stopgap and nothing more. All three were minority cabinets able to function at best only so long as the parliamentary majority which they could not automatically control chose

TABLE 37

MEMBERSHIP OF CABINETS, 1945–1962

Prime Minister	Party affiliation	Term of service	National Union	Progressive	Swede-Finn	Agrarian	Socialist	SKDL	Nonparty expert	Total
Paasikivi[a]	Conservative	November 17, 1944– April 17, 1945		1	2	4	4	4	3	18
"	"	April 17, 1945– March 26, 1946		1	1	4	4	5	2	17
Pekkala	SKDL	March 26, 1946– July 29, 1948			1	5	5	6	1	18
Fagerholm	Social Democrat	July 29, 1948– March 17, 1950					15		1	16
Kekkonen	Agrarian	March 17, 1950– January 17, 1951		2	3	10				15
"	"	January 17, 1951– September 20, 1951		1	2	7	7		1	18
"	"	September 20, 1951– July 9, 1953			2	7	7		3	19
"	"	July 9, 1953– November 17, 1953			3	8			6	17

Composition by parties

			4[b]	3[b]	2[b]					
Tuomioja	Progressive	November 17, 1953– May 5, 1954							1	10
Törngren	Swede-Finn	May 5, 1954– October 20, 1954			1	6	6		1	14
Kekkonen	Agrarian	October 20, 1954– March 3, 1956				6	7		1	14
Fagerholm	Social Democrat	March 3, 1956– May 27, 1957		1	1	6	6		1	15
Sukselainen	Agrarian	May 27, 1957– November 29, 1957		3	4	6			1	14
"	"	After July 2, 1957		4			9			13
"	"	After September 9, 1957		2		6		5[c]	2	15
Von Fieandt	Swede-Finn	November 29, 1957– April 26, 1958					13			13
Kuuskoski	Civil Servant	April 26, 1958– August 29, 1958		1[b]			9	4[c]		14
Fagerholm	Social Democrat	August 29, 1958– January 13, 1959	3	1	1		5	5		15
Sukselainen	Agrarian	January 13, 1959– July 14, 1961			1[b]		13		1	15

Source: Condensed from Table 18 in J. Nousiainen, *Soumen Poliittinen Järjestelmä*, p. 188.

[a] While Premier Paasikivi was no longer a member of the conservative National Union party in the 1940s, he may be said to have been close enough to it to warrant the label "Conservative."

[b] Served as expert, not as party's representative.

[c] Members of the Social Democratic Opposition.

to give its support or abstained from delivering a repudiating vote.

During the seventeen years covered by Table 37, seventeen cabinets held office. Three of the seventeen changes were caused by presidential elections—in 1946, 1950, and 1956—and five (if the March, 1945, election is included) by general parliamentary elections. Thus eight out of the seventeen changes in government were caused by the mandate of custom, which has decreed, since the founding of the republic, that presidential and national elections automatically result in the resignation of the cabinet and the appointment of a successor. This rule has been followed even upon the reelection of a President. It is therefore clear that cabinet changes were caused—in fact, frequently caused—not by parliamentary votes of lack of confidence but by other factors. The reasons for resignations can be suggested by noting that in 1918–58, when a total of forty-four cabinet changes occurred, the causes were, in broad terms, as follows:[4]

Changes in the presidency	9
Legislature's decision against cabinet proposals	9
National elections	8
Foreign policy problems or difficulties	5
Specific vote of lack of confidence	4
Dissension within the cabinet	3
Conflicts with the President	2
Other reasons	4
Total	44

Clearly, cabinet instability was not the result of repeated friction or conflicts between the government and Parliament. Nor did differences of opinion between the two always mean that the cabinet, even when it resigned, had suffered defeat at the hands of a parliamentary majority. Some categories of laws require, according to the Finnish constitution, that under certain circumstances a legislative proposal must receive the support of two thirds, or in some cases of five sixths, of the members. If a government proposal in these categories fails to obtain the necessary majority, it has obvi-

[4] J. Nousiainen, *Suomen Poliittinen Järjestelmä* (Helsinki, 1961), pp. 190–96, offers an illuminating discussion of the problem.

ously been defeated, not necessarily by a majority but possibly by a small minority. Yet the cabinet may choose to consider the defeat as reason for resignation.

Problems of foreign policy or foreign relations have on occasion led to partial or complete cabinet changes. A notable instance occurred in 1922 when Foreign Minister Rudolf Holsti resigned after Parliament had repudiated his attempt—the only attempt of its kind after Finland became independent—to bring Finland into a defensive alliance arrangement against the Soviets, a move sponsored by Poland. The U. J. Castrén Government resigned on November 11, 1944, because two of its members held that the cabinet—it was composed of six Social Democrats, four Agrarians, three nonparty experts, and one each from the Conservative, Progressive, and Swede-Finn parties—was not making headway in the effort to establish satisfactory relations with the USSR. The cabinet led by Social Democrat K. A. Fagerholm from August, 1958, to January, 1959— its majority consisted of five Social Democrats and five Agrarians and included three Conservatives—resigned because his government allegedly failed to meet with favor in the eyes of Moscow. The collapse of the Fagerholm Cabinet was precipitated, specifically, by the resignation of the Agrarian members (among them Foreign Minister J. Virolainen). Their withdrawal was explained as unwillingness to serve in a ministry no longer able, in the Agrarian view, properly to safeguard Finland's interests in the area of relations with the USSR.

As might be expected, questions of internal policy have been, directly or indirectly, the most frequent cause for change. Two illustrations will suffice. On April 26, 1958, the Von Fieandt caretaker government was brought down as a result of an adverse vote in Parliament that repudiated certain intended measures for the price supports of agricultural products. A similar situation toppled the A. Karjalainen Cabinet on August 30, 1963. The cabinet had been formed on April 14, 1962, after lengthy discussions and negotiations prolonged by seemingly insuperable difficulties. The difficulties had ultimately been solved by the use of a surprising device: the inclusion of three members who represented not political parties but the Confederation of Finnish Trade Unions (the SAK). The three SAK members ultimately opposed the Agrarian decision to raise certain agricultural prices and were released from their cabinet posts. An internal cabinet controversy thus led to the resignation of the Karjalainen Government—the resignation came, after several changes in the membership of the cabinet, on December 18, 1963—without the problem being submitted to the arbitrament of Parliament.

Another aspect of the political configuration invites comment. The SKDL-Communist group was one of the Big Three that dominated the scene during the years 1945–48. The other two were the Social Democrats and the Agrarians. Among them they were responsible for the first phase of the carrying out of the terms of the 1944 armistice and the 1947 peace treaty. It was during this "period of peril" that the SKDL rode the crest of the wave. The premiership belonged to the party, and the party held six ministerial portfolios, including that of the Interior. It appeared to be headed toward continuing and dominant leadership, but this trend was changed when the ascendancy of the Communists suddenly ended in 1948. The Fagerholm Socialist-dominated cabinet that assumed office after the July, 1948, election marked the end of SKDL-Communist participation in governments. Despite their ability to hold on to 21.5–25 percent of the seats in the national legislature, the two groups have not reached the seats of power since 1948. The indications at the time of writing (January, 1964) are that they have been permanently assigned to the minority position defined by their position in Parliament and underscored by the negative appraisal of their long-range purposes by the non-Communist elements in and outside of the legislature.

The frequent cabinet changes before 1939 and after have been interpreted as a measure of the weakness of government and of the handicaps under which a parliamentary system operates in a multiparty state. That Finland has illustrated some of the difficulties involved is undeniable. This appears to be true especially in connection with matters and projects the nature of which calls for long-range planning and commitment. But however serious the situation might seem in theory, the difficulties appear to be considerably smaller in Finland than alleged.

While cabinet changes have been frequent, real changes of policy have been relatively small and often nonexistent. Just as national elections have witnessed no landslides, so the resignation of one ministry and the appointment of another has normally recorded no sharp change. Marked continuity and not sudden veering to the right or the left—or up or down, for that matter—has been the rule. Several circumstances have combined to produce this result: (1) the relatively long term of office of the President—six years—and the important role he plays in the field of foreign affairs; (2) the fact that the higher civil service, always an important factor in matters of policy as well as administration, is immune to the swings of the political pendulum and therefore constitutes a stabilizing, continuing influence; (3) the extreme right in Parliament having at no time had a decisive say in policy matters in Parliament, and the SKDL-Communists having also been confined to the sidelines since 1948, the center parties and the parties relatively close to them have been in a position to plan and execute on a basis relatively free from paralyzingly divisive imperatives; (4) "ministries change but the ministers remain." A newly appointed government normally includes members of the preceding government, often in key posts. Continuing competence in the handling of cabinet matters is thereby usually ensured. The Liberals, the Social Democrats, the Agrarians, and the Swede-Finns have all been, in varying degree, contributors to a relatively small group of men of "ministerial timber" who serve in successive governments. The same foreign minister served in six cabinets in 1944-50; the Agrarians have usually held the Agriculture portfolio; before he became President in 1946, J. K. Paasikivi had been a member of the Ryti Cabinet in 1939–40 and Prime Minister in 1944–46 (also Prime Minister in 1918); before U. Kekkonen was elected President in 1956, he had served as Minister of Justice in 1936–37, of the Interior in 1937–39, again of Justice in 1944–46, Foreign Minister in 1954, and Prime Minister in 1950–53 and 1954–56. Similar illustrations abound and indicate that continuity of service and policy was a great deal more marked than a hasty consideration of the roster of cabinets or ministers suggests.

Continuity of policy was also ensured, especially in the all-important area of foreign affairs, by the fact that the two incumbents of the office of President since World War II followed the same policy. They were, in fact, co-authors of the essentials of the policy tenaciously and successfully followed by the nation: unbending, strict neutrality in general and unqualified friendship and good-neighbor relations with the Soviet Union. Paasikivi hewed to this line until the end of his second term in 1956, and Kekkonen made it fully his own—he had in fact formulated its essentials while the war was still going on, in 1943—during his presidency after 1956.

The composition and function of cabinets revealed still another feature we must note. While the three leading parties—the Social Democrats, the Agrarians, and the SKDL—joined hands and controlled the governments between 1944 and 1948, the informal coalition that had held them together fell apart in July, 1948, and has not been revived. The elimination of the SKDL from the cabinets since 1948 has already been noted. A definite shift toward the right —to use a term which often fails to describe, except in very broad terms, a specific political program or group—was thus recorded. The trend was thrown into sharper relief by the fact that Social Democrats did not participate in six out of the fifteen cabinets between March, 1950, and January, 1959 (not including the reshuffling of the Kuuskoski Ministry in 1957 or the members of the Social Democratic Opposition). It was further underlined after 1959 when the Agrarian leadership committed itself to a policy of deliberate avoidance of cooperation with the Social Democrats on the alleged grounds that cooperation with them exposed Finland's relations with the USSR to difficulties and, possibly, to serious damage. The result was a mainly centrist coloration of the cabinets, especially after 1957, and even a minor shift to the right of center that would have been unthinkable in the middle and late forties.

TWO DECADES OF PROGRESS

The two decades after 1944 witnessed a number of events of utmost importance to the nation. The paralyzing economic exactions imposed by the reparations schedules ended in 1952. The withdrawal of the Allied (Soviet) Control Commission in September, 1947, after the ratification of the Paris peace treaty, removed an organization that in some ways had functioned as an occupation authority. The recovery of the Porkkala enclave in 1956 erased a galling and dangerous territorial servitude. Membership in the Nordic Council in 1955 and subsequent active participation in expanding Scandinavian cooperation represented enlarged opportunities welcomed by all Finns except the Communists and accented the nation's membership in the brotherhood of the Nordic democracies. Membership in the European Free Trade Association in 1961 signalized an affiliation important not only in an economic sense but because it meant a congenial association with a part of the world of which Finland had been an integral part since time immemorial. Meantime the situation within Finland itself was stabilized in a manner and to a degree that removed the danger of economic stagnation, the likelihood of social upheavals, and the threat of a Communist take-over.

The manner and extent of the political stabilization achieved since the mid-1940s cannot be fully perceived without a detailed record of the eventful years after the 1944 armistice. The essential contours of the developments can be suggested, however, by noting some of the political trends before the end of 1948 and by summarizing the elections of 1948, 1954, 1958, and 1962.

The Communist party and the SKDL had barely appeared in the political arena in the fall of 1944 when they appeared to be forging ahead in a manner that suggested far-reaching changes on the broad front of labor, politics, and government. The attempt to establish Communist control of the Social Democratic party and to create a united front with the party was one illustration of Communist purposes.

The first postwar party congress of the Social Democrats was held on November 25–29, 1944. The delegates were divided as regards the question of the country's policy during the war and what pronouncement regarding it the conference should formulate. The majority of the executive committee of the party was by then composed of members who viewed cooperation with the Communists and a repudiation of those Social Democrats identified with the leadership of the country during the war as minimum essentials for a "sound" policy for the future. Despite the strenuous efforts of the opposition elements to persuade the conference to accept a common-front policy regarding the Communists, it chose an executive committee composed of a majority of old-line Social Democrats who opposed a common front.

The conference also accepted a resolution emphasizing the importance of party unity and repudiating the effort, favored by dissident radicals within the party, to indict Social Democrat leaders for their activities during the war. A number of the opposition group thereupon left the party and found a congenial political home in the SKDL. An attempt by the SKDL to persuade the Social Democrats to accept a common ticket in the March, 1945, elections failed because of Socialist aversion to cooperation with Communists and fellow travelers.

In the March election, as we recall, the Social Democrats suffered substantial losses. They were therefore forced to inventory the political situation anew. The result was the acceptance of an SKDL proposal for cooperation between the three main parties, the SKDL, the Agrarians, and the Socialists. A statement announcing the agreement to cooperate was signed by the Big Three on April 13, 1945. It condemned as harmful the foreign policy of the preceding years and endorsed "a clear and resolute stand against fascism and all forms of reaction." The civil service and especially the army and the police were to be "cleansed" and "democratized," and the socialization of essential sectors of the nation's economy was also urged.

Despite periodic friction and difficulties, the Social Democratic–SKDL common front continued on the whole unchanged until 1947. The local elections in December, 1947, indicated a new trend, however. The uncertainties and fears of the first two years following the end of the war were slowly dissolving by then, and Social Democrats had been returning in increasing numbers to their old views and conceptions that repudiated communism and all its works. That the scales were turning in the Socialists' favor was shown by the distribution of votes in the elections: 24.9 percent for the Social Democrats and 20.4 percent for the SKDL. By the end of 1948 the front had collapsed, not the least because of the defeat suffered by the Communists when the Communist Interior Minister, Y. Leino, was forced to leave his post in May, and the SKDL suffered a serious setback in the parliamentary elections in July.

While the Communists failed to capture the Social Democratic party, the party emerged from the developments of 1944–48 seriously divided. Some of its former leaders and many of its members were lost to the SKDL or the Communists. The party's electoral record after 1948 reflected the extent to which internal dissension weakened it and prevented it from recapturing the leadership of the laboring man it had conspicuously and successfully held before the war. The personal rivalries and other causes for the fragmentation of the Social Democrats became especially marked after 1958; at one time a dissident group was created that held 13 of the seats the Socialists captured in the 1958 election, only to subside to a feeble two-member contingent after the election in 1962.

The Communists also had to accept far less than complete success in their effort to gain control of organized labor. To be sure, they seemed in 1946 to be on the way to capturing the leadership of the SAK (Confederation of Finnish Trade Unions). The SAK had grown rapidly during the preceding two years. The membership in 1944 was 106,000; by the early part of 1946 it had reached 300,-000. Many of the new member unions of the organization had been taken over by the Communists and the expectation appears to have been, by late May, 1946, when the SAK conference was about to meet, that the majority of its members would vote for a Communist-controlled executive committee. The day was saved by the decision of the incumbent executive committee to postpone the conference till 1947. By the time the conference met in May of that year, the attempt to maintain a common Social Democratic–Communist front had seemingly failed and would soon be abandoned. The Social Democrats numbered 170 out of the 300 members of the conference and succeeded in remaining at the helm. The capture of some of the member unions by the Communists far from made up for the failure to obtain control of the executive committee of the SAK and, through it, of the federation itself. The disruption of the SAK and the setting up of a rival, fellow traveler–Communist-controlled organization fell far short of the goal the Communists had originally set for themselves.

Symptomatic of the situation during the years of Communist ascendancy was the manner in which the signing of the 1947 peace treaty was observed. On February 10, the day of the signing of the treaty, flags were flown throughout the country at the order of public authorities. Mass meetings were held, special radio programs were put on the air, and in Helsinki the government was host at a gala gathering attended by Finnish, Russian, and other dignitaries. The keynote was celebration and rejoicing over the long-delayed formal ending of the war. No critical comment on the treaty or any part of it was made in public. No direct reference to Russian aggression as the cause of the war, and therefore the cause of the suffering and losses it had imposed on the nation, was hazarded. The staging, the script, and the day's performance conformed to the demands of the hour, which prohibited, as everyone with a modicum of common sense could readily understand, realistic discussions of the whys and wherefores of the war and/or of the immediate and long-range consequences of the peace.

A telling illustration of the spirit of the day and especially of the obsequiousness of some elements even outside the hard-shell Communists was the address delivered on the evening of February 10 by Premier M. Pekkala. Most of the speech was devoted to abusing the Finns and their leaders since 1918. The Premier contended among other things that the signing of the peace treaty did not mean a defeat. "Our day of defeat," asserted Pekkala, "came about thirty years ago when we struck out on the path of foreign policy that led us astray. And defeat was ours," he continued, "on the day when we lost the peace, that is to say, when we no longer reposed our confidence in the possibilities . . . of negotiation but put our trust in the treacherous might of arms and went to war."

The Communists did not miss the chance to be heard. They gave clear indication of resolve to make full use of the newly won opportunities to serve the cause. The Communist Minister of the Interior, Y. Leino, held that the war between Finland and the USSR had been caused by the Finns' desire to gain territory at the expense of the Soviets. In his view, the military defeat suffered by Finland was not a defeat suffered by the Finnish people. They had, in fact, won a victory. Defeat had been suffered only by "the wrong orientation in Finland, the wrong prophets of the nation, and the wrong social system that had prevailed in the country." These errors and shortcomings had been the real enemies of the people. They had now been eliminated, and the nation could proceed to build a new, "more democratic and more progressive society" on the ruins of the old. The reparations obligations were a mere minor detail by comparison with the destruction and impoverishment the nation had imposed upon itself as a result of its past errors. A Communist newspaper proclaimed that "all talk about a crushing peace means nothing less than a distortion of the magnificent picture of the future filled with beautiful promise for the years to come." [5]

Barely a year after the Paris peace treaty had been signed, the Communists suffered a serious setback when they were forced to surrender the all-important Ministry of the Interior, headed by Y. Leino since 1945.

Y. Leino was one of the leading members of the Communist party. To the public at large he was, however, an unknown name at the time of his appointment as Vice-Minister for Social Affairs in the first Paasikivi Cabinet in November, 1944. Long involved in the illegal operations of the SKP before the war, he had served time for his activities. He had quickly become one of the Communist luminaries after the war, during which he had been an underground operator. His prominence was considerably enhanced by the fact that he was married to Hertta Kuusinen, the daughter of O. W. Kuusinen, one of the leaders of the 1918 revolt and a top-ranking Communist in the USSR ever since his escape to Russia in 1918. Leino reached the real seat of power when he became Minister of the Interior in April, 1945. His wife had meantime become, after the preceding March national election, the leader of the Communist group in Parliament.

During the following two years, Communist influence and control was extended to the political police and gradually to the regular police force as well. Leino's own activities included the surrender

[5] Quoted in *Helsingin Sanomat*, February 11, 1947.

(in 1945), on the order of the Soviet Control Commission, of twenty émigré Russians to the USSR. Ten of the émigrés were Finnish citizens. Leino had acted on his own, without discussion or decision by the cabinet as a whole. Later the matter came to the attention of President Paasikivi, who concluded, after discussions with the foreign minister, that Leino had had, in view of the Control Commission's order, no choice in his action.

There the matter rested till March, 1947, when the facts in the case came to the attention of Parliament. The parliamentary Committee on the Constitution investigated the problem, heard Leino's side of the story, and tentatively concluded that the officials involved in the surrender of the émigrés had been in error. The Pekkala Government considered the question on June 4, 1947, and unanimously found for Leino.

Leino and the Communists in general thus seemed to face no serious obstacles as they proceeded along the path which, they hoped, would lead to a victory for their cause. The fate of Czechoslovakia and the Mutual Assistance and Friendship pact signed on April 6 appeared to augur well for the cause. Rumors of a Communist coup were rife. Preparations were undertaken by the authorities to forestall any attempt to destroy the legal order in Helsinki, where, presumably, the coup would begin.

This was the state of affairs when the Leino case of 1945 once again took the center of the stage. Parliament's Committee on the Constitution had thoroughly surveyed the question submitted to it. Its report held that Leino had committed an illegal act, although, considering all the facts in the case, Parliament was not obligated, in the committee's view, to bring charges against Leino in the State Court. The report was taken up for discussion in Parliament on April 19, less than two weeks after the signing of the pact with the USSR, in the midst of the uncertainties and surmises of the moment. After lengthy debate the matter was dropped. It was immediately revived, however, in connection with a consideration of the cabinet's account of its stewardship during the year 1945. The discussion led once again to a reconsideration of Leino's policies and undertakings. It culminated in a vote of lack of confidence. Leino was relieved of his cabinet post on April 22, 1948, in a letter by President Paasikivi which specifically stated that Leino was being dismissed because he no longer enjoyed the confidence of Parliament. Noisy and threatening protests from the SKDL were of no avail. Leino's dismissal marked the end of Communist membership in government. The "wave of the future" of 1944–48 thus turned out to be a temporary upsurge destined to subside because of the failure of a leader of the new dispensation.

The defeat of the Communists in the Leino case was merely preliminary to another defeat in July. The July, 1948, election resulted in substantial Communist losses; the SKDL group in Parliament was reduced from 49 to 38 seats, while the Social Democrats captured 54 seats and the Agrarians 56.

Not the least significant result of the election was the government that took office after the new Parliament convened on July 22. The government appointed on July 27 was headed by the Social Democrat K. A. Fagerholm; its whole membership came from the Social Democratic ranks. The fact that the cabinet was a minority government existing on the sufferance of elements in the legislature that it could not directly control was in itself an interesting illustration of prevailing political conditions. More important, however, was the fact that the Communists were ousted from the seats of power, despite dire predictions in some quarters of the dangerous consequences of such "bold" action.

The decision in July, 1948, not to admit Communists within the gates of government has been maintained since. At the present time (Spring, 1965) the Communists are still knocking at the door through which they freely walked during the "years of danger" but which has remained closed for over a decade and a half despite continuing efforts to open or to unhinge it.

The fall of Leino and the subsequent loss of ground by the Communists in the July election reduced but by no means eliminated the dangers that had been perceived by many Finns during the preceding four years. The lengthening distance separating Finland in the fifties and the sixties from the uncertainties of the mid-forties was shown, clearly enough, by the elections in 1954, 1958, and 1962.

The March, 1954, election followed a split between the two largest parties, the Social Democrats and the Agrarians, who had formed a coalition government in January, 1951. By the summer of 1953 they were hopelessly divided by pressing economic difficulties caused by a decline in the price abroad of certain vital Finnish export commodities. The Socialists withdrew from the government, whereupon the Premier, U. Kekkonen (Agrarian), attempted to carry on without a parliamentary majority. He introduced a budget in September designed to reduce government expenditure, and offered tax relief to interests hardest hit by the drop in export prices. By the beginning of November his cabinet was in difficulties that ultimately led to defeat and resignation.

The attempt to form another coalition government failed, and an interim caretaker cabinet of experts was accepted by all concerned. It took office on November 17, 1953, headed by Mr. S. Tuomioja, governor of the Bank of Finland. The new government was composed mostly of members of the liberal Finnish People's party and of the Conservatives. It marked the first return to cabinet posts of the Conservatives since the war. Contrary to some predictions, their comeback did not disturb Finland's relations with the USSR. The Tuomioja Government concluded a new trade agreement with the Soviets within two weeks of taking office, and in February negotiated another pact which improved Finland's trade situation with the USSR by providing for the payment in gold or in Western currencies for exports to the Soviet Union.

On the recommendation of the new government, the date of elections for a new Parliament, normally held in July, was advanced to March 6–7. The election campaign was in full swing for three months. Internal issues held the center of the stage. Only the Communists attempted to emphasize foreign policy; they contended that Finland's main problem was a choice between "friendship" with the USSR or membership in the line-up of Western "imperialists." The other parties took the stand generally accepted for years: Finland must remain outside all Big Power conflicts, avoid measures and policies that might seem inimical to the USSR, and maintain normal, friendly relations with all countries. The Communists labored hard to recapture the ground they had lost between 1945 and 1951 and hoped to gain sufficient following to entitle them to ministerial portfolios. The non-Communist parties did not hesitate to label the

Communists as tools of a conspiracy designed to destroy democracy and to rivet a dictatorship on the nation. The non-Communist press had been consistently and effectively critical of communism since the late forties and in the weeks before the elections attacked the Communist party program and candidates in strong terms. The Conservative party, for example, inserted a large advertisement in the leading Finnish liberal daily enumerating and condemning a long list of Communist undertakings, especially those of the years 1945–48 when the "People's Democrats" held important cabinet posts and controlled a substantial part of organized labor. The attack on the Communists by the Social Democrats was especially skillful, persistent, and undisguised.

When the ballots were counted, it was shown that some 2,020,000 voters, or 80 percent of those registered, had gone to the polls. New and young voters appeared to have turned out in larger numbers than usual. The new Parliament differed but slightly from its predecessor. Broadly speaking, there was a shift toward the left, illustrated by the loss of four seats by the Conservatives (from 28 to 24), the gain of one seat by the Social Democrats (from 53 to 54), and the relatively substantial increase in the strength of the liberal Finnish People's party (from 10 to 13 seats). The Communists succeeded in holding their 43 seats. The trend was also underscored by the increase in the strength of the Agrarians by two seats.

There was a good deal of post-election comment to the effect that the non-Socialist parties had scored well enough to prevent a "leftist majority" in that the Social Democrats and the Communists together held 97 seats or four short of an absolute majority. Such interpretations are largely meaningless because of the incompatibility of the Social Democrats and the Communists. The Socialists had borne the main brunt of the anti-Communist campaign for the preceding half-dozen years, and deep-seated animosities divided the two representatives of the "left" in Finland as elsewhere. They give every promise of retaining irreconcilable antipathies. To measure the results of the 1954 election in terms of a "balance" between "right" and "left" is a sterile exercise.

The July, 1958, elections resulted, as we have seen, in a coalition cabinet headed by the veteran Social Democrat leader, K. A. Fagerholm. The Fagerholm Ministry included no Communists; all other parties were represented in it. The foreign minister was J. Virolainen, an Agrarian. President U. Kekkonen was a former leader of the same party. Thus two of the main architects of foreign policy had the same party background.

Shortly after Fagerholm became Premier, his government ran into difficulties. He was frequently attacked by the Communists. They charged over and over again that the "rightist" cabinet of Fagerholm could not possibly succeed in convincing the USSR that Finland's policy of friendship toward her eastern neighbor would be continued unchanged. When the Soviet ambassador left Helsinki and did not return to his post, Communist critics interpreted the situation as an indication of Soviet displeasure over the political situation in Finland. Trade negotiations carried on at the time with the USSR were not speedily concluded; according to noisy Communist claims, the reason was Soviet rejection of the "reactionary" and "dangerous" policies of the Fagerholm Ministry, whose foreign policy was labeled irresponsible and destructive of good relations with the USSR.

These claims and interpretations were soon echoed by the Soviet press and radio. Fagerholm and other Finnish leaders made repeated and emphatic statements to the effect that the government and the parties represented in it would under no circumstances deviate from a genuine good-neighbor policy, all to no avail. President Kekkonen stated in a radio address that Finnish-Soviet relations "dominate everything else in the field of our foreign affairs. This question is our only real foreign relations problem and upon it depends the future of our people." Nothing must be done that could in any way be considered to imply purposes or action "directed against the USSR, and we must convince our eastern neighbor that this is our firm resolve." The press of the country spoke with one voice in support of these views, as it had for years before 1958. Spokesmen of every party subscribed to them but appeared to make no impression in Moscow.

The result was the collapse of the Fagerholm Government. Apparently seriously disturbed by continuing Communist attacks and allegations, the foreign minister and his Agrarian colleagues resigned on November 27, 1958. Premier Fagerholm thereupon offered his resignation. He was succeeded on January 13, 1959, by V. J. Sukselainen, who headed a purely Agrarian minority cabinet that commanded only 48 out of 200 seats in Parliament.

The Soviet purposes in the situation were suggested less than two weeks later by Premier Nikita S. Khrushchev. Speaking in Leningrad during an "unofficial" visit by President Kekkonen, he reviewed recent Finnish-Russian relations. Professing not to desire any interference in the internal affairs of Finland, he claimed that a "freeze" had set in with the coming of the Fagerholm Cabinet, led and backed as it was by Social Democrats "who are known for their hatred of the Soviet Union." The statement seemed to make it clear that it was the composition of the Fagerholm Government and not its policies that was the reason why the USSR "could not expect anything good" for Finnish–Soviet relations to come from the Fagerholm Ministry. "Certain Finnish newspapermen and publications" were also tarred with the brush of disapproval because they were "possibly" in the pay of "outside powers interested in worsening" the relations between the two countries. If these "negative influences" were to continue to operate in Finland, "a great deal of damage" to Finnish–Russian relations would result. If contemporary accounts can be taken literally, President Kekkonen appears not to have challenged or repudiated Khrushchev's charges. Khrushchev's speech precipitated uneasy comment in all segments of Finland's press except that of the Communists.

It is clear that neither the 1954 nor the 1958 election meant a defeat of the Communists in the sense of freeing the country from further exposure to their attempts to persuade, subvert, and coerce. The same holds true of the election of 1962. All three contests showed, however, that the choice of the voters in these free elections was spelled out in terms that relegated the SKDL and its supporters to a continuing and seemingly permanent minority position.

The 1962 election was scheduled for July. It was held on February 4–5, however, because of the Soviet note in the preceding October (see pp. 454–57). It appeared obvious that, if Moscow had had complete confidence in Finland's continuing resolve to observe fully the terms of the 1948 pact, the Kremlin would not have been concerned to the extent of suggesting the need of consultations. It therefore seemed necessary to offer, as quickly and convincingly as possible, full support of President Kekkonen and the government then in office and to reaffirm once again the nation's unqualified commitment to neutrality. The February election involved in the first instance a verdict in the foreign policy area and illustrated the fact that, as had been repeatedly contended by Paasikivi and his successor since 1945, "foreign policy questions take precedence over domestic policies."

The result was, as we have seen, exceptionally active voting; 84.5 percent of the qualified voters went to the polls. The Communists lost 3 seats and got 47, the Agrarians won 53, a gain of 5, the Social Democrats 38 (the dissident Socialists lost 12 and had to be satisfied with 2), the Conservatives 32, the Swede–Finns 14, and the Progressives—the Finnish People's party—13. The new cabinet, headed by Dr. A. Karjalainen, included representatives of all parties except the Social Democrats and the Communists. Agrarians held five seats, the Conservatives three, the Swede-Finns two, the Finnish People's party two, and three nonparty members represented the trade unions (an innovation in Finnish politics). Once again the SKDL was excluded from cabinet membership and the influence ministerial posts imply. On the whole the general political configuration of the country remained unchanged. The repudiation of the dissident Socialists by the voters, coupled with the failure of the Communists to gain additional strength, appeared to hold out a promise that the Social Democrats might return to something like "normal" strength in the not too distant future. Continuing political stability and not approaching political disturbances was the verdict in 1962, as it had been of every election since 1948.

XVI

Foreign Relations since 1945

FINLAND AND THE USSR

The territorial expansion of the Soviet Union in Europe since World War II and the extension of Soviet influence through the satellite nations represent the most impressive advance yet made by the Communist cause in the West. The USSR stands, for all practical purposes, in the very heart of the European continent. The posture it has assumed there indicates that it will not be readily dislodged or pushed back to Russia's western borders before 1939.

It has been fashionable in some quarters to see in this westward expansion merely a post-1939 illustration of an inevitable "historical process" that has worked its way through Russian history, especially during the past two centuries. This view was accepted by many immediately after the close of the last war, when belief in the possibility of "friendly coexistence" had not yet been challenged by the harsh realities of the cold war period.

The fact is, however, that a fundamental difference exists between the pre-1914 territorial conquests in the Baltic area, for example, and those engineered since 1939 by the Soviet rulers. Westward advance in the days of Peter the Great and later under his imperial successors proceeded without any long-range plan or scheme, and without the benefit, it might be added, of a mysterious historical "law" or "process." This has been pointed out with enviable clarity by Professor Michael T. Florinsky in his *Russia: A History and an Interpretation*. The undertakings that brought backward Muscovy in the 1700s to the shores of the Baltic and transformed Russia into a great power by 1914 issued from no specific program of conquest tenaciously followed from century to century but from differing circumstances, opportunities, and choices made by succeeding generations of Russia's policy makers.

The objectives pursued by the Soviet policy makers are a different matter. Since 1919 their basic aim has been, as far as we can tell, to overthrow the "international bourgeoisie" and to create a Sovietized world order by whatever means necessary, "including the use of force" (in the words of the charter, never revised, of the Communist International, accepted in 1919). This objective has been as openly defined as Hitler's expansionist plans were before he became chancellor in 1933. It has remained a basic purpose and has dictated the varying procedures used, in differing circumstances, to persuade, subvert, and coerce. Both the purposes and the procedures are illumined by Finland's relations with the USSR since 1944.

One of the consequences of World War II was the apprehension and trial of a large number of persons classified as war criminals or charged with having collaborated with the enemy. In the countries occupied by German forces—the Netherlands, Belgium, France, Denmark, and Norway in particular—liberation meant the capture of quislings large and small and the meting out of punishment to collaborators ranging from jail terms to execution. Even individuals in high places who could be charged with having disregarded the needs of national defense before the war, and others allegedly guilty of having failed to resist the Germans after invasion, were held up to public censure and wrathful condemnation.

In Finland, the problem turned out to be quite different. There the effort to identify and punish individuals allegedly responsible for the nation's suffering and losses in 1941–44—the effort was sparked by the Allied (Soviet) Control Commission—led to grotesque results: not traitors and collaborators with the enemy but outstanding patriots and statesmen were placed in the dock and ultimately found guilty of crimes none had committed or could have committed.

Article XIII of the September 19, 1944, armistice agreement stated that "Finland undertakes to collaborate with the Allied Powers in the apprehension of persons accused of war crimes and in their trial." At the time, the Allies had not yet defined "war crimes" or identified in other ways the individuals or groups to which Article XIII applied. The matter was clarified by the "Agreement Concerning the Prosecution and Punishment of the Major War Criminals of the European Axis" accepted by the Allies in London on August 8, 1945. It defined war crimes as "violations of the laws or customs of war." It also identified, in broad terms, "crimes against peace": planning of aggressive war, preparation or starting of such, or wars in violation of international agreements or participation in a common plan or conspiracy regarding such a war.

The apprehension and trial of a number of Finns under Article XIII produced results unique in the postwar effort of the victorious Allies to punish individuals guilty according to the definitions of the London agreement. The machinery of retribution was set in motion before the London agreement and independent of the limits which the agreement placed, by implication, upon arbitrary detention and punishment contrary to sound principles of law and justice.

The Allied Control Commission in Helsinki—the Commission was, for all practical purposes, a Soviet organ, despite its name— demanded on October 19, 1944, that the Finnish government apprehend sixty-one military personnel, allegedly guilty of war crimes. Twoscore of them were put behind bars and other arrests followed. These developments were ominous indications of Soviet purposes, but they paled into insignificance beside the "war responsibles" problem that emerged early in 1945 and developed into the most sensational case in the legal history of the country.

The case of the "war responsibles" concerned an effort to label several of the leading personages of the war years as war criminals and policy makers responsible for Finland's involvement in the war. The effort was supported by Finnish Communists and by an assortment of individuals in stations high and low who felt, for a variety of reasons, that Finland had no choice but to act on Moscow's suggestions and demands that the "war responsibles" be identified, apprehended, tried, and punished. The Paasikivi Government, then in office—it included three Communists—yielded to the pressure. It introduced a bill in Parliament on August 23, 1945, providing that persons "who had decisively influenced, in the Government, Finland's involvement in the war in 1941 . . . or had acted during the war to prevent the reestablishment of peace shall be sentenced to a jail term of not more than eight years or, if the circumstances are especially aggravating, to hard labor for a specified term of years or for life."

The law was accepted, by a vote of 129 to 12, on September 11 and promulgated the next day. The Allied Control Commission had issued a public statement on the eleventh, before the vote was taken, contending that the category of "war criminals" mentioned in the armistice and preliminary peace of September, 1944, included persons who belonged in the group suggested by the words cited.

Soviet coercion had thus resulted in a law that was clearly unconstitutional. It was unconstitutional because it was retroactive; it classified as punishable acts not punishable by any law at the time when violations of the law had allegedly occurred. That the Communists, ready to do the bidding of the Kremlin, had played a conspicuous and noisy part in setting the stage for a decision that all but Communists considered a travesty of justice merely accentuated the exceptional conditions that prevailed in Finland at the time. The law lacked all moral sanction, except among the faithful followers of the gospel of St. Marx, Soviet version.

The list of "war responsibles" was made public on November 6. It included eight names. Among the accused was former President Risto Ryti. Two former Premiers, four former cabinet ministers, and the wartime Finnish envoy in Berlin accounted for the rest.

The defendants were tried by a court that was also clearly unconstitutional. It was composed of fifteen members. Three were specifically designated by the law of September 12: the Chief Justice of the Supreme Court, the President of the Supreme Administrative Court, and a member chosen by the Faculty of Law of the University of Helsinki. The remaining twelve members were chosen according to the party situation in Parliament: three Communists, three Agrarians, and three Social Democrats, and one Conservative, one Progressive, and one Swede-Finn, chosen by Parliament.

The trial began on November 15, 1945, and the verdict was delivered on February 21, 1946. Former President Ryti was given ten years; the other sentences ranged from two to eight years. In each case the court divided eight to seven. The accused served approximately half of their respective sentences. The verdict of guilty and the sentences imposed did not brand the defendants but rather increased their prestige and enhanced the esteem in which they were held. V. Tanner, for instance, reentered politics in 1951 and was elected to Parliament, where he had sat since 1907. He was chairman of the Social Democratic party until 1963, long attacked by Communists at home and abroad. E. Linkomies, a distinguished scholar who had been Premier in 1945, returned to his duties at the University of Helsinki and served as Rector Magnificus of that institution after 1956. These leaders and the other defendants found guilty in the trial earned distinction and not moral or legal opprobrium by becoming the victims of the greatest miscarriage of justice in modern Scandinavian history.

Finland's international position reflected in various ways the consequences of the cold war after 1945. The question of participation in the Marshall Plan in the summer of 1947 illustrated the difficulties at the time. Twenty-one nations, Finland included, were invited to Paris to discuss questions involved in joining the plan. The parliamentary Foreign Relations Committee considered the invitation on July 10. The majority of its members were in favor of sending a representative to Paris but the final decision was nevertheless in the negative. The official statement held in part that "the Marshall Plan having become the source of serious differences of opinion among the Big Powers, Finland, desiring to remain outside the areas of conflict in Big Power politics, regrets that it does not find it possible to participate in the said conference."

The reasons for the decision are not difficult to find. The USSR and the Communists elsewhere in Europe opposed the plan. The Finnish Communists, faithfully echoing the pronouncements of Moscow, contended that participation would move Finland over "into a camp politically inimical to the Soviet Union. . . . The retention of a Soviet confidence, of our own right to decide for ourselves, and the retention of our independence, are much more important than a few crumbs off Truman's and Marshall's table."

Finland's firm determination to avoid, in her foreign policy, every-thing that might offend the USSR was illustrated in other ways. In 1947–48, when the Scandinavian democracies were discussing the question of forming a neutral bloc free from all Big Power affilia-tions, the Soviets chose to see in the plan a military coalition serving Western "imperialist" purposes. Finland's participation was espe-cially objectionable to Moscow. The result of the Soviet attitude was the conspicuous absence of Helsinki from the negotiations. Finland's unambiguous Scandinavian orientation before the war had thus been diluted. Under anything like the conditions before 1939 Finland would undoubtedly have been in the forefront of efforts to work out security arrangements for the Scandinavian North.

A new element was added to Finnish-Soviet relations in 1948 when President J. K. Paasikivi received a communication from Stalin on February 23. It referred to pacts signed by Moscow earlier in the month with Rumania and Hungary and stated that Finland presumably was interested, as the two countries allegedly had been, in concluding "a mutual assistance pact with the USSR against possible German attack." Stalin suggested that "in the event Finland has no objection" the proposal be discussed by appropriate repre-sentatives of the two countries.

The proposal caused extensive discussion in Finland after it had been made public on February 28. The discussions proceeded against the somber background of the events in Czechoslovakia, where an internal political crisis a week earlier had set the stage for a Com-munist coup. Public opinion of all shades—the Communists excepted —was apprehensive and opposed to a pact. Consultation with the cabinet and parliamentary leaders led President Paasikivi to accept Stalin's suggestion, there obviously being no other alternative with-out the risk of arousing Soviet suspicions and enmity. Negotiations culminated on April 6 in the signing of a ten-year "Agreement of Friendship, Cooperation, and Mutual Assistance." [1]

The treaty provided that, if Finland "or the Soviet Union through Finnish territory" was attacked by Germany or any state allied with Germany, "Finland will . . . fight to repel the attack . . . within

[1] See Appendix H.

the frontiers of Finland . . . and, if necessary, with the assistance of . . . the Soviet Union." The treaty also stated that the question of when Soviet aid might be necessary or might be given was to be decided by "mutual agreement." In the event that a threat of military attack emerged, the two signatories were to "confer with each other." The two countries agreed "loyally to participate" in all measures for keeping the peace in accordance "with the aims and principles" of the United Nations. Alliances or coalitions directed against the other party were forbidden. Both governments pledged themselves "to observe the principles of the mutual respect of sovereignty and integrity and that of non-interference in the internal affairs" of the other signatory.

The 1948 mutual assistance pact has frequently been mentioned as the cornerstone of Finland's foreign policy. Its meaning and implications have been scrutinized often and with care. Especially during the years immediately after 1948, some observers concluded that the treaty made Finland a member of the Soviet-dominated East European bloc; that the USSR's and not Finland's interpretation of "attack," "assistance," "through Finnish territory," and other elastic phrases would prevail to the detriment of Finland; and that Soviet pledges of noninterference in Finland's internal affairs are worthless guarantees upon which no reliance can be placed.

The events since 1948 have clarified the matter in many important respects. It has become clear that the earlier pessimistic analysis and surmise were wide of the mark. The treaty appears to have changed no significant aspect of Finland's position in the postwar period. That Finland would fight against Germany or any other power in the event of an armed attack is clear, treaty or no treaty. There is nothing in Finland's record to date that challenges this conclusion. The provision in the treaty that "Finland will fight" therefore spells out no commitment at variance with what would happen anyway if an invasion were attempted. As regards possible Soviet assistance after "mutual agreement," it is probably safe to say that this provision added nothing of substance to the situation that has existed since 1944. Either "mutual agreement" will furnish the basis for cooperation in repelling an invader, or Finland will have been reduced, by developments antecedent to the moment of invasion, to a position that leaves the decision altogether in Soviet hands.

The pact forestalls Finnish military commitments to the West, but it does not limit other relations with Western nations. Finland's neutrality remains intact and her control of the army and general foreign policy unimpaired. The treaty emphasized a fact which Finnish leaders have regarded as a basic reality since World War II: the Soviet Union's interest in Finland is dictated, fundamentally, by defense considerations. It is therefore vitally important to convince the USSR that Finland's territory will not be used by any Power, directly or indirectly, as a base for an attack upon the Soviets. If an attempt were made to launch an attack on the USSR through Finland, Finland would fight the aggressor. Fighting to defend her own territory would obviously mean fighting in defense of the USSR as well, quite apart from treaty commitments and the like.

The 1948 treaty—it was extended for twenty years in 1955—differs in an important respect from other similar treaties concluded by the Soviet Union. It called for no discussions or consultations regarding political or international questions in general (the obligation to engage in such discussions and consultations would in all probability result in serious limitations upon freedom of action in foreign affairs) and it left Finland free to pursue a strict neutrality policy in all actual or potential instances of USSR military conflicts that do not involve the territory of Finland.

For thirteen years the treaty added no new problems or complications to Finnish-Soviet relations. Finland's sovereignty remained as inviolate as it had been before the spring of 1948. A Moscow note of October 30, 1961, however, appeared to introduce a new aspect in the relations of the two states.

The important, decisive antecedents of the note lay outside of Finland, in the larger area of the cold war that has involved, for years, East Germany, Berlin, and the North Atlantic Treaty Organization. Well over nine tenths of the note consisted of a lengthy indictment of the Western "warmongers and imperialists" and included critical references to NATO members Denmark and Norway and to neutral Sweden. Moscow claimed that West German militarists were guilty of creating and expanding the military potential of the Federal Republic, that Norway and Denmark were assisting in the revival of a militarized Germany threatening the peace of Europe, and that certain Swedish munitions manufacturers and other "interests" were also involved. As a result, Moscow contended, a situation was emerging that threatened the security of Finland and the USSR. In view of the threat, the Soviets proposed consultation on the basis of the 1948 treaty.

The note precipitated extensive discussion and comment in Finland and abroad. It led to a proposal by President U. Kekkonen that the questions raised by it be discussed by Premier Khrushchev and himself. The suggestion was accepted. The results of the two statesmen's exchange of views were stated in a Finnish-Soviet communiqué dated November 25, 1961. According to the communiqué, Khrushchev "had a high regard for the political experience of the Finnish President and in his good will and ability to maintain and strengthen" Finland's strict neutrality policy, which "had the support" of the Soviet Union. The USSR could therefore "put off the military conversations it had proposed." The Soviet government also expressed the wish that the Finnish government "would closely follow the development of the situation in Northern Europe and in the Baltic area and, if necessary, would transmit" to the USSR "its views on any measures that might be called for" by future events.

The long-range implications and meanings of the note and of the agreement of November 25 will in all probability depend upon the course and intensity of the cold war. In Finland, the October note ultimately led to the dissolution of Parliament in December and new elections in February, 1962. As regards its actual consequences for Finland's foreign relations position, it did not change the nation's commitment to unbending neutrality any more than the April, 1948, treaty. One thing is abundantly clear. Neither the treaty nor the note prevented an uninterrupted strengthening of the nation's democratic institutions and elements or the stability of her general international position. It is altogether unlikely that they will in any way modify the conviction of the nation that friendly relations with the Soviet Union are the alpha and the omega of Finland's foreign policy.

RELATIONS WITH THE NORTHERN DEMOCRACIES

Denmark, Finland, Norway, and Sweden represent a unique area in north Europe. Taken together, they illustrate a degree of homogeneity that stands out in sharp contrast to factors and circumstances that divide the other Western peoples. Their economic development has followed much the same general pattern. Political institutions have long functioned in a way that shows these nations to be tested and tried democracies. The history of law and the administration of justice reveal the same fact. Educational developments, especially during the past century, and the position and functions of the national churches likewise disclose large areas of basic similarities and conformities in handling the problems of man and his society.

The implication of these all-important similarities is not, needless to say, that past historical development or the requirements of the passing hour have erased the lines that divide Scandinavia into four states.[2] Quite the contrary is true. Especially since the first half of the last century, some of the differences have become more rather than less deeply etched: each has its own distinct political structure; linguistic differentiation is in some ways growing rather than decreasing; and each of the four peoples considers itself the possessor of a separate culture and "national character." This basic fact has not been blurred by the important and growing area of intra-Scandinavian cooperation, itself a most fascinating development that spans the decades since World War I, that has expanded since the end of World War II in a manner that is gradually creating what might well be called the first beginnings of common citizenship for the nationals of the four countries. The expanding area of collaboration—much of it unofficial but no less important than that sponsored by the governments and other public authorities—has been particularly significant for Finland since 1945. Extensive and complex in

[2] While the verdict of geography separates Iceland from the other four Nordic lands and the small size of her population (about 180,000 in 1961) also places her in a separate category, Iceland obviously belongs in the family of these democracies.

the variety of its forms but simple and obvious in its basic purposes, it has given sharp relief to a unique foreign policy relationship that Finland shares with her sister democracies of the North.

Scandinavian cooperation emerged as a significant trend about a century ago. It began to assume real importance, however, only after World War I. The reasons were many. Outstanding among them was the emergence of Norway as a fully sovereign state in 1905 and of Finland as an independent republic in 1917–18. By the closing 1930s, continuing cooperation within a large field of common interest and concern had become an arresting fact. It covered cultural matters, significant aspects of social policy, health services, communications, regulation of travel, and the like. Collaboration in foreign affairs was limited to the pursuit of policies designed to maintain peace and friendly relations with all nations. No defense alignment or alliance had been formed by the time World War II began.

The war years 1939–45 exposed the four nations to different experiences: Finland threatened with extinction as a result of Soviet aggression, yet emerging from the war with independence intact; Denmark and Norway exposed to brutal Nazi occupation for five long years; and only Sweden, sufficiently favored by good fortune, able to enjoy the blessings of a neutrality policy that all of the four democracies had equally proclaimed and were equally resolved to observe in 1939. However, the different experiences did not prevent the emergence of a strong feeling of solidarity once peace had been established. The decade after 1945 witnessed a broadening field of intra-Scandinavian cooperation. It led to a careful consideration of two basic problems in particular that had been left almost wholly untouched before the war, namely, common defense and common economic policies.

The problem of common defense turned out to be especially difficult for reasons that lay largely outside the choice or control of the four democracies. In the spring of 1940, Finland, Sweden, and Norway contemplated a mutual defense arrangement. The idea was abandoned because Moscow chose to see in the plan a potential anti-Soviet alliance. In the autumn of the year, after Denmark and Norway had fallen victim to Nazi invasion, Sweden and Finland discussed a mutual defense arrangement. In the course of the preliminary discussions it became clear that not only a military pact but some form of political affiliation or union would have to be contemplated in order to achieve the defense purposes considered essential. The USSR interpreted the intended plans as a potential conspiracy directed against the Soviets and insisted that Finland's participation in them meant a clear violation of the March 12, 1940, treaty that ended the Winter War. The project was therefore abandoned.

In 1947–48, Denmark, Norway, and Sweden gave thought to the establishment of a neutrality bloc that would place Scandinavia clearly outside all Big Power conflicts and combinations. Finland, obviously most actively interested in increasing the security and neutrality of the Scandinavian area, did not participate in the discussions because once again the Soviets chose to see in the contemplated plan an anti-Soviet military scheme. Norway and Denmark ultimately joined NATO, while Sweden and Finland remained neutral, Finland's neutrality being defined, as we have seen, with especial emphasis in the April, 1948, treaty with the USSR. The search for a common defense formula thus led to a result that divided rather than united the four nations.

The attempt to map out a common economic policy and orientation turned out to be more successful. The idea of economic cooperation within the Scandinavian group of nations emerged and was discussed well over a century ago, and some advance in this area had been recorded by 1900. World War I, and such earlier developments as the dissolution of the Norwegian-Swedish union in 1905, offered a serious setback to the hopes of further progress. Wartime experiences, however, demonstrated the usefulness of and the need for cooperation. This was shown in 1919 when the governments of Denmark, Norway, and Sweden initiated a joint investigation of ways and means for promoting economic cooperation. While the work of the committees then set up yielded no concrete results at the time, the climate favoring cooperation improved during the 1930s, especially after 1932. By that time the difficulties caused by the depression had been fully recorded in many sectors of Scandinavia's national economies.

World War II again interrupted developments that might have led to systematic and expanding programs of cooperation. But the war years also accented the need of measures leading to a common market and common trade policies. In the spring of 1948, a Joint Scandinavian Committee for Economic Cooperation was set up by Denmark, Norway, Iceland, and Sweden (Finland was as yet unable to participate). Its main task was to examine the possibilities for a common tariff as a basis for a Scandinavian customs union. It held that the elimination of intra-Scandinavian tariff walls and the introduction of uniform customs duties on imports from non-Scandinavian countries would benefit the North's national economies, and that the establishment of a Scandinavian customs union would be wholly compatible with the plans, then being discussed, for the economic reconstruction of Europe. Its formal report, however, concluded that "for the present" a full customs union comprising the peoples of the North could not be launched.

But like Banquo's ghost, the idea would not down. After the Nordic Council began to function in 1953, the question was tackled anew. The result was that plans for a common Nordic market comprising Denmark, Finland, Norway, and Sweden were extensively discussed and were considered in detail at the session of the Council in Helsinki in February, 1957.

Before the Scandinavian program had reached the stage of final political decision making by the national governments, the Scandinavian common market project was overtaken by the plan to set up more extensive common market areas in west and central Europe. The Rome treaty establishing the continental common market of the Six was signed on March 25, 1957, and the European Economic Community became a fact on January 1, 1958. Meanwhile the efforts to create a free-trade area had also continued. They made little progress, however, whereupon the idea of establishing a European Free Trade Association (EFTA or the Outer Seven) emerged. It took shape early in 1959, and by the summer of the same year Britain, Denmark, Norway, Sweden, Switzerland, Portugal, and Austria had agreed to form such an association. An agreement was signed on January 4, 1960, and went into effect four months later.

The abandonment of the original plan for a Scandinavian common market and the subsequent establishment of EFTA posed special problems for Finland. They derived partly from the desire of the Finns to see to it that their trade with the east European bloc would not be adversely affected, and that nothing was undertaken that might be interpreted by Moscow as a deviation from a policy of strict neutrality in all matters. On the other hand, a large part of Finnish foreign trade—approximately one third—consisted of trade with the seven EFTA nations. It was therefore natural that Finland would carefully explore the possibilities of devising, in cooperation with the EFTA members, ways and means whereby the republic's vital economic interests in this area could be safeguarded. The result was a special convention with EFTA, signed on March 27, 1961. It provided for affiliation with EFTA as of July 1, 1961. The convention created a new free-trade area within which Finland enjoys the same rights and assumes the same obligations (with some exceptions) as the other nations have assumed with respect to each other. The agreement went into effect on the date specified.

The emergence in 1962 of the possibility that Britain and Denmark, and possibly other EFTA nations as well, would become affiliated with the Common Market added new complications. They involved economic interests of considerable magnitude, as the following figures clearly show. During the first half of 1961 (before Finland's affiliation with EFTA had gone into effect, and therefore before the advantages of affiliation had been recorded in growing exports) the Common Market and EFTA nations combined absorbed 65 percent of Finnish exports. The Common Market alone accounted for 30 percent of the total exports. Britain was once again Finland's best customer and accounted for 67 percent of the EFTA total. Incidentally, the eastern bloc markets—including the USSR—accounted for 17 percent of the exports, as against 19 percent in 1960. These figures indicate the extent to which Finland's trade continued to be overwhelmingly Western-oriented after 1945.

Meantime the Finland-EFTA group moved toward the abolition of all tariff dues in trade between the members. The Finnish tariff reductions brought the basic duties, on May 1, 1964, to 40 percent of the original. The remaining levies will be abolished, according to the tariff timetable accepted by the members, by the close of 1969.

The most striking and important post-1945 achievement in the field of Scandinavian collaboration was the establishment of the Nordic Council in 1952. The idea of a Scandinavian council had been put forth by Foreign Minister P. Munch of Denmark in October, 1938, but did not lead to concrete results before World War II began less than a year later. The proposal was revived during the defense league discussions in 1949. The meeting of the Scandinavian Inter-Parliamentary Union—the Union dated from 1907—in Stockholm in August, 1951, however, responded favorably to the Danish effort by appointing a committee to draft a statute for a council. The draft statute brought forth was endorsed by the representatives of Denmark, Iceland, Norway, and Sweden. The Finnish representatives abstained because of foreign policy considerations that seemed compelling at the time. The foreign ministers of Denmark, Iceland, Norway, and Sweden, meeting in Copenhagen in March, 1952, agreed to submit to their respective Parliaments the proposal of the Scandinavian Inter-Parliamentary Union. The legislatures of the four countries approved the draft statute in May–June, 1952, with substantial majorities. The Nordic Council began to function in 1953.

Finland took no official part in the first three sessions of the Council in 1953–55 and followed developments by means of an informal observer. In October, 1955, the government proposed and the Parliament approved full and official membership in the Council. Finland's representatives attended the fourth session of the Council in Copenhagen in January, 1956, and Finland was host to the Council for the first time in 1957.

The statutes of the Nordic Council define it as an organization "formed for the purpose of consultation" among the Parliaments of Denmark, Finland, Iceland, Norway, and Sweden, "as well as the Governments of these countries, in matters involving joint action by any or all of these countries." [3] The Council concerns itself, in principle, "only with current problems, that is, with problems con-

[3] The second quotation is from F. Wendt, *The Nordic Council and Cooperation in Scandinavia* (Copenhagen, 1959), p. 107.

sidered suitable for immediate and specific action." The Council should, in pursuing its objective, "abstain from making declarations regarding future goals" for which "no immediate measures can be proposed." The Council is purely consultative, but it may propose and often has proposed measures for adoption by the individual legislatures and governments.

The membership is composed of representatives elected by the Parliaments and of cabinet ministers appointed by the governments. Each national Parliament elects sixteen members, and that of Iceland five. Each parliamentary delegation is composed of representatives of the legislature chosen on the basis of party representation in the national legislature. To this total of sixty-nine are added the cabinet ministers, who have no vote. The 1953 session was attended by fifteen ministers; since the 1953 session, the number has been in the neighborhood of thirty. The prime ministers and the foreign ministers are normally among the cabinet members present.

Since its founding in 1952, the Nordic Council has initiated or has participated in the growth of a many-sided body of intra-Scandinavian legislative and other measures that have notably expanded the area of collaboration among the four nations and Iceland. The results have been such as to enable a Dane, Finn, Norwegian, and Swede to enjoy, while living in a Scandinavian country other than his own, many of the benefits and advantages originally provided by his country for its own nationals. The abolition of passports (in 1952) and a free labor market (after 1954) meant, as regards travel and employment, the elimination of the boundaries that divide the four nations into separate sovereignties. A convention accepted in 1956 provided that social security benefits enjoyed by the citizens of one country must "in principle be extended to citizens of the other Nordic country living in that country"; the costs of such mutuality of sickness, accident, maternity, old age, and other similar benefits are borne by the country of residence and not by the beneficiary's native country. By the end of 1961 the Council had accepted and forwarded to the national governments a total of 186 recommendations dealing with matters that ranged from education to legal questions, from taxation to research in various fields of science, from radio and television to the employment of nurses and midwives, from the regulation of road and railroad traffic to problems of foreign exchange, from questions involving the Lapps to atomic energy and inter-Scandinavian water-power problems, and many others. The number of specific subjects covered was 241. Of these, 59 had been fully and 49 partly carried through, while the purpose of 17 others had been reached without government action. Approximately one third of the recommendations dealing with economic and social policy questions, and well over one half of those dealing with legal or traffic matters, have been favorably acted upon.

The resolve to work together for common purposes was impressively shown in 1962. At the annual session of the Nordic Council in Helsinki (March 17–23)—the session marked the tenth anniversary of the Council—Denmark, Finland, Iceland, Norway, and Sweden signed an agreement (the Helsinki Convention). The agreement, later ratified by the Parliaments of the five nations, defined and described broad areas of existing cooperation and laid down guidelines for future cooperation. The forty articles of the convention dealt with law and the rights of the citizen; cooperation in the field of cultural and educational matters, ranging from more effectively coordinated programs in school and university to the utilization of the opportunities offered by radio and television; social legislation extending from regulation of the common labor market to matters of health and sanitation; economic cooperation involving continuing discussions and consultation for the purpose of encouraging increased intra-Scandinavian production and investment and rational regional division of both; and further planning and effort to stimulate and expand intra-Scandinavian traffic, communications, and travel. The agreement also provided that a citizen of one Nordic country could, in certain circumstances, make use while abroad of the foreign service facilities of a northern country other than his own.[4]

The fact that Norway and Denmark (and Iceland) are members of NATO while Sweden and Finland pursue a strict neutrality policy within differing frameworks fashioned for them by developments since 1945 indicates the extent to which the Nordic nations

[4] See Appendix I.

take different views of the changing international situation and its requirements. These differences do not, however, prevent them from cooperating in the area of foreign policy. Marked unanimity of view and purpose in fact prevails. The essence of the matter has been stated by a Danish observer in a manner that underscores the factors which are especially significant for Finland, whose membership in the Nordic Council signalizes nothing more than a resumption of the foreign policy orientation toward the other Scandinavian nations interrupted by World War II:

The explanation must be sought largely in the cooperation that unites the Nordic peoples in so many other fields. But another factor of no less importance is that it is only in approach and not in objectives that the Nordic countries hold different views in foreign policy. Their fundamental attitude . . . is identical. They have one overriding interest and one goal: to preserve peace. This is a traditional policy for the Nordic countries, but their experience since 1939 has made it a matter of life and death for them. . . . They must therefore contribute as much as they can to the security of the world. . . . In the present constellation of powers each [Nordic country has] taken the position it finds best for its own safety, for the cause of peace and for the interests of the other Nordic peoples. And the resolve to work for peace and democratic ideals is identical in all five states.[5]

RELATIONS WITH THE UNITED STATES

Finland's relations after 1945 with the Western democracies outside of Scandinavia were reestablished without friction or difficulty. The speed and ease with which normal relations were established were strikingly illustrated by the manner in which the United States and Finland resumed diplomatic and other contacts.

The first definite steps leading to the resumption of normal relations were announced in January, 1945, four months after Finland had signed the armistice ending the second phase of the Russo-Finnish War and some four months before the end of the war in Europe. On January 12, President Roosevelt assigned Mr. Maxwell

[5] Wendt, *The Nordic Council,* p. 235.

M. Hamilton as United States representative in Finland, with the personal rank of minister. Pending Mr. Hamilton's arrival in Helsinki, Mr. L. Randolph Higgs, who had served in Helsinki before 1940 and had handled Finnish affairs in the State Department during the war, was placed in charge of the United States mission in Finland. The mission—it did not as yet constitute a resumption of "formal diplomatic relations"—was established in Helsinki a few days later. The USSR and Great Britain were "fully informed" regarding the assignment of Mr. Hamilton to his new post and the designation of Mr. Higgs.

The next step came in August of the same year. At the Berlin Conference, the three powers had agreed that they would in due time examine, separately, the question of establishing normal diplomatic relations with Finland. The Secretary of State announced, on August 21, that the United States had acted upon this agreement, and that, the Finnish government formed after the March elections having been found to be "broadly representative of all democratic elements in Finnish political life," the United States government had instructed its representative in Helsinki to propose the establishment of diplomatic relations between the two republics. This was done, and the first Finnish postwar minister to Washington, K. T. Jutila, presented his credentials on November 21, 1945.[6] The two ministries were raised to embassy rank in the fall of 1954, and Ambassador Jack K. McFall assumed his ambassadorial duties in Helsinki in January, 1955.

During the years since 1945, American policy toward Finland has been a part of the evolving policy increasingly defined by the rising menace of Soviet-led world communism. It has been a part of the policy of containment elaborated since 1947 and continued through the cold war. Its main element has been the determination to limit Soviet expansionism in Europe by means of an

[6] The political "means test" that Finland had to meet before relations with the United States could be normalized is an interesting illustration of wartime views in Washington. Actually all Finnish elections since the founding of the republic had resulted in governments "broadly representative" of the democratic elements in the nation. The March, 1945, elections did add a new element to Finnish political life, however. They enabled the Communists to reassert themselves, before being excluded from cabinet posts in 1948.

armed Western alliance and other corollary undertakings, without a commitment to offensive moves designed to force the USSR to recede beyond the boundaries of 1947 or 1939. Economic aid, in order to speed recovery and create conditions that would increase resistance to Communist infiltration and Soviet advance, has been a part of the policy of containment since it was first formulated by Secretary of State Marshall in June, 1947.

Specifically, American policy has recognized the realities of Finland's position since 1944 for what they are. Finland's cautious and restrained Western foreign policy commitments and attitudes have been accepted without reading into them either indifference to American purposes or subtly disguised resolve to oppose them. This circumstance has been understood in Washington, where it has been seen that the outcome of the last war and the conflict between the Western democratic world and Soviet imperialism have placed Finland in a precarious position, and that it is in America's interest to assist Finland in maintaining her republican institutions and democratic way of life. It is significant that, during the early and specially difficult years of the reparations payments when Finland was subjected to various political and economic pressures, American aid was given to Finland on several occasions. During the crucial period 1946–48, sorely needed credits were extended, through the Export-Import Bank, in the amount of more than $80,000,000. The figure ultimately came to approximately $120,-000,000. Some $38,000,000 was granted in 1949–52 through the International Bank for Reconstruction and Development, an agency of the United Nations. About $23,000,000 was allocated later to Finland for the purchase of war surplus materials, in addition to smaller sums for special purposes.

Other measures were also taken to help the Finnish people "to maintain their free institutions and their national integrity" (to use a phrase from the Truman doctrine) during these years. Thus the State Department announced in December, 1947, that the United States would not invoke, as it might well have done, the status of a "third-party beneficiary" under Article 29 of the Finnish peace treaty, which would have enabled the United States to avoid paying compensation for Finnish ships seized during the war. This decision permitted Finnish shipowners ultimately to collect about $4,475,000 for tonnage that had been requisitioned by the United States in 1941–42. A commercial air service between the United States and Finland was authorized in April, 1947, and a formal air transport agreement was signed in March, 1949. The trade agreement signed in Helsinki on May 7, 1955, was another example of American readiness to assist in keeping Finland's economy sound. It provided for the purchase by Finland of $5,250,000 worth of American cotton and tobacco, much of which was paid for by Finnish-made prefabricated houses. The arrangement was intended to provide a safeguard against the consequences of possible heavy decreases in Soviet purchases of Finnish industrial goods.

Not the least significant illustration of this policy came in January, 1949, when the United States Advisory Commission on Educational Exchange recommended that future Finnish payments on the World War I debt be used to pay for the education of Finnish citizens in the United States and for American educational materials for use in Finland. Acting upon this recommendation, Congress provided, in a Joint Senate-House Resolution of August 24 of the same year, that future payments on Finland's debt be used for a reciprocal educational exchange program between the two republics. The first funds became available when Finland paid its December, 1949, installment ($264,585). The program will continue till 1984.[7] On July 2, 1952, the United States and Finland signed another agreement which extended the Fulbright educational exchange program to Finland. It provided annual expenditures for five years of not over $250,000 (that is, the equivalent of this sum in Finnish currency) for study, research, and teaching purposes. The program was financed by means of certain funds made avail-

[7] The schedule of payments, accepted in 1923 when the Finnish debt funding agreement was made, calls for gradually decreasing annual payments by Finland. The sum available to the educational exchange program therefore becomes smaller, year by year. It was $210,910 in 1959, will be $151,060 in 1969, only $66,605 in 1979, and $12,075 in the last year, 1984. The 1923 funding arrangements, schedules, etc., are conveniently found in the 1922–26 *Combined Annual Reports of the World War Foreign Debt Commission* (Washington, 1927), pp. 118–29.

able to the United States by the sale of surplus American property in Finland. By 1955, over 300 Finns had come to the United States to pursue studies financed by the funds provided by this agreement.

The spirit reflected in the policy of economic and other aid was also shown in additional ways. Finland has served for several years as an illustration—Sweden also belongs in the same category—of what may be called nonalignment or neutralism. Faced with the threat inherent in the Soviet policy of subversion and penetration, Finland has followed a policy of staying clear of Big Power groupings and has in general displayed deliberate caution in all commitments in order not to assume a posture or become involved in action that could be construed as something other than neutrality. To hold internal communism in check and to remain in all respects fully outside the Iron Curtain have meanwhile been a prime concern. The success of this policy is demonstrated by the fact that the country has remained free and democratic. Appropriate to Finland's needs, this policy accounts in no small measure for the significant circumstance that, while the USSR has been able since 1939 to push hundreds of miles westward in central and southeastern Europe, the only dent in the North made by the Soviets is that represented by the southeastern and northern Finnish areas ceded in 1940 and 1944. The rest of the border line of 1939 still holds fast and now represents a northern dike against communism that will not be breasted except by the use of overwhelming force. The Finnish policy of neutrality has thus played a part in denying to the Soviet Union a key area which seemed, at the end of the war, to be exceptionally exposed to Communist advance. It has served the same ends as the American policy of containment.

President Truman, in urging the Congress in 1947 to provide funds to be used for economic and military aid for Greece and Turkey, stated in part that one of the primary purposes of United States foreign policy

is the creation of conditions in which we and other nations will be able to work out a way of life free from coercion. . . . We shall not realize our objectives, however, unless we are willing to help free peoples to maintain their free institutions and their national integrity against aggressive movements that seek to impose upon them totalitarian regimes. This is no more than a frank recognition that totalitarian regimes, imposed on free peoples, by direct or indirect aggression, undermine the foundations of international peace and hence the security of the United States. . . . It must be the policy of the United States to support free peoples who are resisting attempted subjugation by armed minorities or by outside pressures.[8]

Since 1947 the Marshall Plan, NATO, and other developments have exemplified, in varying degree, the expansion in Europe of American commitments. Nowhere, however, have the commitments been such as to translate fully into action the extravagant idiom which Truman used in his statement to Congress. American policy toward Finland, for example, has not shown readiness to consider the precarious aspects of Finland's position—clearly the consequence of Soviet aggression and designs—a circumstance that undermines the security of the United States and should therefore be frankly recognized as a vital concern of the United States. There has been, obviously and understandably, no commitment to help the Finns "maintain their free institutions and their national integrity" against possible Soviet aggression. Specific American commitment has, clearly, been limited to the Western military alliance and related undertakings. In the Scandinavian North, Denmark and Norway are within the area which, presumably, the Soviet Union can penetrate only at the risk of inviting military action by NATO, while Sweden and Finland are—again presumably —outside of it.[9]

[8] *Congressional Record,* 80 Cong., 1 sess. (March 12, 1951), p. 1981.
[9] While the Truman doctrine was uncritically generous in suggesting ample limits for American interest and assistance, the post-1949 expansion of United States commitments has not resulted in a clear-cut identification of those areas in Europe (outside NATO) which, in the event of war, will be defended or those which will be abandoned. Finland and Sweden will be involved in the choice, if and when it comes. The choice presents a serious dilemma. It would seem that if readiness to meet aggression is the best way to prevent aggression—a concept which lies at the basis of the vast American defense program of the past years—it will serve no useful purpose to abandon in advance the defense potential of the eastern Scandinavian area.

THE POLICY OF NEUTRALITY

Finland's pre-1939 foreign policy of "friendship toward all and entangling alliances with none" had not prevented the country from falling victim to Soviet aggression. After 1945 it was more than obvious that, even if Finland had had an inclination to seek anchorage in a different policy, neutrality and friendly relations with the USSR were an overriding must. All the considerations that supported neutrality before 1939 made it clear that any other policy except strictest neutrality would not only be risky but in all probability would threaten the independence of the republic. This policy and reasons for it were repeatedly put forth by presidential statements, the spokesmen of all the political parties, discussions in Parliament, and countless editorial and other newspaper comment. The only pressing foreign policy problem of these years has been to convince the Soviet Union of the Finns' firm resolve to maintain cordial and friendly relations with it.

Occasionally the readiness to emphasize the unquestioned acceptance of this policy and no other has led to the claim or implication that Finland had followed an aggressive anti-Soviet policy before 1939, that the tragic war years were a direct result of this policy, and that since 1945 Finland, defeated by the Soviet Union, has merely been atoning for her past errors and sins. The post-1945 so-called Paasikivi-Kekkonen neutrality line, which allegedly is the only real guarantee of the nation's freedom and sovereignty, has frequently been presented as a new departure different from the policy pursued before 1939. Actually it is new only in that its spokesmen have propounded neutrality and friendship toward the USSR more frequently and more loudly than formerly—and often more anxiously—in the hope that Finland's good faith and pacific intentions be fully accepted by Moscow.

The nature and purpose of neutrality before 1939 was summarized by Urho Kekkonen—later Prime Minister and elected President in 1956—in a speech in Stockholm in 1943. Commenting on the fact that the USSR's demands and invasion in 1939 had "wantonly violated Finland's rights," Kekkonen raised the question "whether, merely in terms of her own interest, Russia's attack was necessary." The answer was in the negative. He asserted that "Finland's policy of neutrality in the 1930s was, as far as it related to the USSR, a serious commitment, and Finland would have continued to adhere to it no matter what turn the world war might have taken. Finland would have stood ready to defend by arms any attack, no matter who the aggressor, upon her neutrality and sovereignty. We held then, and still hold, that Finland's geographical position and well-equipped army would have given us a chance to remain neutral and to ward off attacks upon it." Referring to the claim, occasionally put forth by foreign commentators, that "some elements among our citizens had found National Socialism congenial," Kekkonen stated that "the overwhelming majority of the Finnish people" unqualifiedly embraced democratic principles and practices and that no responsible groups in Finland had considered it even remotely possible that "Finland could have become, as a result of some 'fifth column,' a staging or support area for Germany's attack. Such notions held abroad can rest only upon a complete unfamiliarity with the situation in our country." [10]

Kekkonen's speech was delivered on July 12, 1943, when the end of the war was not yet in sight. He nevertheless undertook to reflect upon the probable situation at the end of the war and the demands it would in all likelihood impose. He saw neutrality as the only defensible and useful policy: "I believe that the goal of our national policy, after peace has been established and even while we get ready for peace, should be to return to the policy of neutrality from which the unfortunate course of events forced us to deviate in 1939." [11] Membership in any alliance or power combination could only mean placing the country's vital interests in jeopardy, for Finland, a small country, could not possibly expect to have a decisive voice in questions dealt with according to Big

[10] K. Vilkuna, ed., *Maan Puolesta* (Helsinki, 1955), pp. 205–6.
[11] "Unfortunate course of events" ("händelsernas olyckliga utveckling") was a strange way of referring to the Soviet invasion. It foreshadowed some of the post-1945 idiom Finnish speakers and writers have found congenial in their attempts to avoid giving offense by calling things and events by their right names.

Power considerations. In the event of war, the destruction of the nation would be certain. And in no event would it be safe to rely upon the quarrels and conflicting purposes of the Big Powers to be resolved in such a way as to safeguard the interests of Finland. Neutrality, in a word, was not a matter of tactical choice or adjustment to changing circumstances but indispensable for national survival.[12]

After the signing of the armistice in September, 1944, the purposes and preferences delineated by Kekkonen were translated into a program and performance dictated by the consequences of a lost war. Among them were two of overriding importance.

The first was spelled out by the requirements of the armistice itself, including partial demobilization, the ousting of the Germans, evacuation of the ceded areas, the trial of the "war responsibles," the payment of reparations, etc. The second was of a subtler kind. It may be suggested by saying that, as Kekkonen remarked in a radio address a week after the armistice, "The main problem created by Finland's new situation will be to eliminate the suspicions and distrust that have prevailed in the relations between Finland and the USSR." National interests required that good relations between the two neighbors be established. Especially while the terms of the armistice were being carried out—and while failure or default might well have been assumed to result in added burdens, including occupation—it was of utmost importance to convince the Russians of the resolve to meet, in full, the requirements of the treaty. The armistice was, after it had been ratified, the law of the land. Because of its importance, it took precedence over other laws.

It is thus clear that post-1945 policy involved, in part, a sustained effort to convince the USSR of Finland's resolve to hew undeviatingly to a line of complete neutrality. After the terms of the armistice and the 1947 peace treaty had been fully met by 1952, the same neutrality policy continued as the dominant feature of the foreign policy of the republic. The "Paasikivi-Kekkonen line" was accepted by all parties and groups. It was interpreted, especially after 1946, as requiring more than official pronouncements,

[12] See also E. S. Repo, ed., *Urho Kekkonen* (Helsinki, 1960), pp. 142–43.

mere observance of treaties, however meticulous, or occasional demonstrations of good intentions. President Paasikivi, before he left his high office in 1956, and President Kekkonen, after he became chief executive in that year, repeatedly insisted, in discussing foreign policy, that the purposes and undertakings of all officials should "be clearly reflected in everything that is done." Even the ordinary citizen was invited and enjoined to serve the cause of neutrality by abstaining from words or deeds that might create suspicion and distrust in Moscow.

The effort to persuade and convince the USSR induced, shortly after the war ended, an arresting interpretation of Soviet purposes regarding Finland. It was presented by the then Prime Minister, Paasikivi, in a lengthy newspaper interview in December, 1945, and has been repeated and elaborated on many occasions since. In substance, he stated that the Soviets have only a military or strategic interest in Finland. Considerations of defense pure and simple account for the views held and the purposes sought by Moscow. It therefore follows that Finland can contribute to Soviet security by impressing on the USSR the firm determination of the country never to assume, directly or indirectly, a policy or posture inimical or dangerous to the Soviets. By making this contribution to Soviet security, Finland will directly add to her own safety and security.

Helpful as this interpretation is in the effort to clarify the problem that the "Paasikivi-Kekkonen line" is intended to solve, it ignores ominous realities sharply etched in the record since 1917 and especially since 1939. Specifically, it loses sight of the wide range of Soviet purposes which were summarized some years ago, by a Columbia-Harvard Research Group, as follows: The USSR "is committed to work by all possible means toward the conversion of non-Communist states, toward their inclusion in the 'Socialist camp' and toward their ultimate transformation along the lines of the Soviet model. This must be taken as fundamental, as constant for the immediate foreseeable future, and as a basic factor in any aspect of the international situation." [13] The fate of Estonia, Latvia, and Lithuania as well as other parts of east and central Europe il-

[13] *A Study Prepared at the Request of the Committee on Foreign Relations, United States Senate. . . .* Under the Administration of Columbia University, February 14, 1960, Henry L. Roberts, Director, p. 53.

lustrates the correctness of the conclusion offered by the Research Group and challenges the adequacy of the Paasikivi view of Soviet goals.

However overly optimistic the Paasikivi interpretation is, there is no doubt but that the "Paasikivi-Kekkonen line" has been strikingly successful. During the exceptionally difficult years 1944–48, the Finns managed to create a political atmosphere and to establish a record of accomplishment that reassured the leaders in the Kremlin. The temporary limitations on the sovereignty of the country were removed surprisingly quickly. The Porkkala enclave, leased to the USSR for fifty years, was returned to Finland in 1955–56. A galling and dangerous territorial and economic servitude was thus ended. Finland's membership in the Nordic Council in 1955 and in the Outer Seven (EFTA) free-trade organization in 1961 recorded other important gains in the recapture of full freedom of action that could hardly have been predicted or been taken for granted a decade earlier.

Against these and other successes in the most difficult and trying area of Finland's foreign policy, some observers of the passing scene have placed the pact of 1948 or the Khrushchev note of October, 1961. The contention or the implication has been that the pact and the note demonstrate Soviet readiness to bring Finland to heel whenever the purposes of the USSR require it and that both illustrate dangerous meddling in the affairs of a friendly neighbor. In order to place these events in their proper relationship to the neutrality policy of the forties and the fifties, note must be taken of still another aspect of the "Paasikivi-Kekkonen line."

Not the least significant feature of this neutrality policy is the fact that its basic purpose is hidden under the extensive comment and interpretation the "line" has caused since the end of the war. The basic purpose is simple: to prevent Soviet aggression or invasion. The Finnish effort—and a genuine effort it is—to create and maintain friendly, good-neighbor relations with the USSR is merely a means, however important and worth while by itself, to an end.[14]

[14] In the large amount of literature on the subject that has come to my notice, no mention is made of this fact. Yet it seems quite obvious that to avoid war is the real objective, that is, to avoid anything and everything that might invite Soviet aggression.

Not to provoke, not uncritically to challenge, not to act contrary to the provisions of treaties or the mandates of common sense, in order to avoid situations endangering neutrality, has been an expression of the tenacious effort to do everything possible to avoid falling victim once again to Soviet aggression.

President Paasikivi repeatedly urged his countrymen to recognize the realities of the world after 1945, and exhorted them to understand and accept the dictates of the situation into which Finland had been placed by the war. Well over a year before the pact of 1948, he had occasion to contemplate the possibility that Finland might be invaded by an enemy of the Soviet Union. He concluded that "if some Power would try in the future to attack the USSR through Finland, we would have to fight, together with the Soviets, as hard and long as possible." This was merely one way of saying that Finland would fight, in such a situation, to protect her own sovereignty and territory. The pact of April, 1948, added nothing of substance, as far as Finland was concerned, to the realities involved, for it appears safe to say that, pact or no pact, the Finns would fight any invader attempting to violate their territory. President Kekkonen stated in January, 1952 (he was Prime Minister at the time) that "Finland's position in the present international situation is completely clear. We have voluntarily concluded, in order to protect our own peace and the policy of peace in the North, a treaty of friendship and mutual assistance with the Soviet Union." Kekkonen also pointed out that the pact was strictly limited in the application of its military clauses: military cooperation with the USSR would be involved only if Finland were attacked or if the Soviet Union were attacked (by Germany or by a power allied with Germany) through Finland.

It is clear that, if an international crisis appeared leading the USSR to proceed to military action in Finland in violation of the 1948 treaty, the situation would undoubtedly be such as to mean Soviet invasion in any case, treaty or no treaty. The treaty does not by itself expose Finland to new dangers. It has become part of the area of cooperation within which the "Paasikivi-Kekkonen neutrality policy line" has successfully operated, and it appears to have played a significant part in convincing the USSR that the Finns' "friendship and good-neighbor policy" can be depended on. In view of the strange and distorted conceptions the Soviets have held, on occasion, regarding Finland's relations with the USSR and the outside world in general, the task has at times been far from easy. It promises to be a central concern of the Finns well into the future. The continued effort will be easier because of the success in creating the right kind of image in Moscow. It will also be aided by the attitude of the press. Since the war, the non-Communist press in Finland has displayed conspicuous restraint in commenting on the USSR, its government, politics, economic development, and the like. The resulting sobriety of approach and idiom reflects a high degree of self-imposed discipline which makes for a greater objectivity and is in itself an illustration of and a contribution to "friendly" relations. Domestic communism and its leaders, on the other hand, enjoy no immunity. Their purposes and undertakings are exposed to continuing observation and appraisal quite sufficient properly to identify them as the purveyors of an alien ideology.

FINLAND AND THE UNITED NATIONS

Finland did not qualify for membership in the United Nations until the Paris peace treaty had been signed in 1947. The Parliament accepted in July, 1947, by a unanimous vote, the government's proposal for membership. The application for membership was stymied for eight years by Great Power conflicts of interests and purposes; the Soviet Union repeatedly vetoed Finland's membership because several Communist states—Albania, Bulgaria, Hungary, and others—had been refused admission by the Western states. It was not until December 14, 1955, that Finland was admitted, together with fifteen other nations. The Great Power tug-of-war, the setting in of the cold war, the war in Korea, and other developments had demonstrated, by 1955, that the United Nations would not be the forum where, after due and seemly debate and argument, friendly suasion would author solutions for international problems or, specifically, make war unnecessary or impossible.

To say that the successful functioning of the United Nations depends in the last analysis on the recognition, by the members, of common interest is to state the obvious. During the decade that followed the signing of the Charter in 1945 and the years that have lapsed since Finland became a member in 1955, it has become abundantly clear that the national interests of the members and not "common interests," however loosely defined, have furnished the real motive force activating the members. Merely to mention NATO, the Warsaw Powers, Cuba, and the cold war in general, to say nothing of the impressive number of newly independent African and Asian nations now on the roster of the United Nations, is to suggest the immense complexities and potential dangers inherent in the pursuit of "national interests" by well over fivescore nations that have accepted, upon becoming members of the organization, certain obligations dictated by the "common interests" of all.

Finland's policy in the United Nations is merely an aspect of the country's general foreign policy. Its solid bases are the peace treaty of 1947 and the April, 1948, treaty with the Soviet Union. Both have been discussed above. Another important area of foreign policy concern and commitment is defined by the membership in the Nordic Council and EFTA. Writ large over these arrangements is the resolve, as we have seen, to observe at all times the requirements of strict neutrality, and an equally unambiguous determination to maintain friendly relations with all nations. Membership in the United Nations has not altered the firm policy of remaining outside the conflicts and controversies of the Great Powers. Speaking in general terms, Finland has displayed conspicuous caution in regard to certain questions and problems on the United Nations agenda. Matters involving military policy or commitments have been avoided; regarding them, and also regarding questions relating to conflicting Great Power interests or purposes, the rule has been "hands off." The same applies to some other problems. In general, the record shows that Finland has preferred to support realistic plans for peace, disarmament, and other progressive endeavors while shying away from high-flown proclamations or purposes that offer no possibility of concrete achievement. In the words of the able Finnish ambassador to the United Nations, Ralph Enckell, spoken on November 3, 1960, Finland's "well-known policy of refraining from conflicts of interest between the Great Powers" has been dictated "by the conviction that we . . . should do nothing . . . that might make it more difficult than it apparently already is for the Powers principally concerned to find a basis for continued negotiations."

Finland has likewise abstained from supporting propositions or resolutions that contain mere "moral indictments" or involve votes against governments or condemnation of the internal policies of member states. Votes supporting such proposals have been considered more likely to aggravate situations and increase international discord than to provide remedies desired. This was the Finnish view regarding the Union of South Africa, for example, during the General Assembly session in November, 1959. In this instance, and in some others, Finland held that the United Nations has no authority "to intervene in matters which are essentially within the domestic jurisdiction of any state or shall require the members to submit such matters to settlement under the present Charter" (Paragraph 7 of Article 2 of the Charter). Finland has strictly adhered to this article, unwilling to subscribe to the view that, as has been implied by the preferences of many members, it can be invoked or ignored at will.

It is thus the strict neutralist policy followed in the United Nations as well as outside that accounts for Finland's votes for or against (and also the abstentions from) the proposals and resolutions on the agenda since the republic became a member of the organization. It also explains the readiness for close cooperation within the United Nations between Finland and her sister democracies of the North. This cooperation covers a wide variety of United Nations business and concerns. It involves regular and at times daily consultation between the representatives of the five nations (Iceland is naturally included). Among the evidences of their cooperation are the frequent meetings of the foreign ministers at which decisions are formulated and common positions agreed upon regarding United Nations matters. The use of a single Scandinavian delegate, also frequent, to present proposals or offer statements on behalf and in the name of all the four nations—or five as the case may be—testifies to their sense of unity and the similarity of their purposes. In all but certain political questions their voting pattern, while by no means fixed, is practically uniform and underlines the fact that Finland is a charter member of the Scandinavian democracies.

APPENDIX A

Alexander I's Act of Assurance,

Porvoo Diet, March, 1809

We, Alexander I, by the Grace of God Emperor and Autocrat of all the Russias, etc., etc., etc., Grand Duke of Finland, etc., etc., etc., do make it known: That Providence having placed Us in possession of the Grand Duchy of Finland, We have desired, by the present Act, to confirm and ratify the religion and fundamental laws of the Land, as well as the privileges and rights which each Estate in the said Grand Duchy in particular, and all the inhabitants in general, be their position high or low, have hitherto enjoyed according to the Constitution. We promise to maintain all these benefits and laws firm, unchanged, and in full force. In confirmation whereof We have signed this Act of Assurance with Our own hand.

Given . . . March 15, 1809.   Alexander

Decree of April 4, 1809

We, Alexander I . . . do make it known: That when We convoked Finland's Estates to a General Diet, and received their oath of allegiance, We desired, on that occasion, by means of a solemn Act . . . proclaimed in the sanctuary of the Supreme Being, to confirm and secure to them the maintenance of their religion and fundamental laws, together with the liberties and rights that each Estate in particular, and all of Finland's inhabitants in general, have hitherto enjoyed.

In hereby promulgating the Act mentioned above to Our faithful Finnish subjects, We also desire to inform them that We having agreed to conform to and to maintain the traditional customs of this land, We consider the oath of allegiance, of the Estates in general, and of the Deputies of the Estates of the Peasants in particular, taken in the name of their fellows as well, to be good and binding on all the inhabitants of Finland, without exception.

Fully convinced that this good and loyal people will ever cherish toward Us and Our successors the same fidelity and firm affection which has ever distinguished it, We shall for Our part not fail to give this nation, with God's aid, continuing proof of Our constant fatherly solicitude for its happiness and prosperity.

Treaty of Peace Between the Republic of Finland and the Socialist Federal Republic of Russia, October 14, 1920

The Government of the Republic of Finland and the Government of the Socialist Federal Republic of Russia, in view of the fact that Finland declared itself an independent Republic in 1917 and that Russia has recognized the independence and sovereignty of Finland, within the borders of the Grand Duchy of Finland, and desiring to end the war that later broke out between the two states, and to establish permanent peaceful relations between themselves, and definitely to clarify the relationships that derive from the earlier political union between Finland and Russia, have decided to conclude a treaty for these purposes . . . and have agreed as follows:

Article 1

From the date when this treaty goes into effect, the state of war between the two signatories ends, and the two Powers agree henceforth to maintain mutual peace and good-neighbor relations.

Article 2

[Defines the boundaries between Russia and Finland.]

Article 3

[Defines the territorial waters of the signatories in the Gulf of Finland areas.]

Articles 4 and 5

[Defines the boundaries of the Petsamo area in the north, and provides for the withdrawal of all Russian forces from Petsamo within forty-five days of the coming into force of the treaty; and for a boundary commission that will fix the details of the boundary within nine months.]

Article 6

Finland agrees not to maintain any men of war or other armed vessels in [her territorial Petsamo waters, except ships up to 400 tons], or submarines or armed aircraft [and likewise agrees not to maintain other military or naval establishments for ships larger than those mentioned above].

Article 7

[Defines the fishing rights of the nationals of the signatories in the waters of Petsamo and adjacent areas.]

Article 8

1. The Russian state and Russian citizens shall enjoy the right of free transit, through the Petsamo territory, to and from Norway.

2. [Goods transported from and to Norway or Russia, through Petsamo, pay no duties or tolls.]

3. Russian citizens who travel through Petsamo to and from Norway are entitled to free passage with passports issued by proper Russian authorities.

4. [Unarmed Russian planes have the right to maintain air traffic between Russia and Norway.]

5. [Agreements regarding the use of roads in Petsamo and the establishment of consular services there will be concluded after the peace treaty goes into effect.]

Article 9

Russian citizens residing in the Petsamo area automatically become Finnish citizens; those over eighteen years of age may opt for Russian citizenship within one year of the coming into force of the peace treaty. . . . Individuals who opt for Russia may freely leave the area and take all their movable property with them without any charges or levies. They retain full rights to real estate property they leave in Petsamo.

Article 10

Finland will withdraw, within forty-five days of the coming into force of the peace treaty, her military forces from the Repola and Porajärvi parishes, which will be reunited with the Russian state and will form, in union with the Karelian population of Archangel and Aunus, the autonomous East Karelian area that enjoys rights of national self-determination.

Article 11

As regards the more specific conditions under which Repola and Porajärvi, the communes mentioned in the preceding article, will be united with the autonomous East Karelian area, it has been agreed, for the benefit of the local population, that:

1. The inhabitants of the communes will be granted a complete amnesty in accordance with the provisions of Article 35 of the peace treaty.

2. The maintenance of peace and order within the area of the communes will be, for two years after the peace treaty has gone into effect, in the hands of a militia organized by the local population.

3. The inhabitants of the communes are guaranteed the rights of their movable property within the communes, as well as the free right to dispose of or use the cultivated land owned by them, as well as real estate, within the limits of the laws in force in the autonomous East Karelian area.

4. All inhabitants who desire to do so have the right, within a year after the peace treaty has gone into effect, freely to move to Russia. Their property rights remain as defined above, in part 3.

5. Finnish citizens and companies who have timber-felling contracts entered into before June 1, 1920, will continue to enjoy the right, for one year after the peace treaty has gone into effect, to cut and transport the timber.

Article 12

The two signatory powers accept in principle the neutralization of the Gulf of Finland and of the whole Baltic Sea, and bind themselves to work in behalf of this purpose.

Article 13

Finland will militarily neutralize her islands in the Gulf of Finland . . . by not constructing or maintaining on them fortifications, batteries, observation posts [except, as regards such posts, Someri and Narvi islands], military harbors or stores, or military personnel except such forces as are essential to maintain order.

Article 14

Immediately after the peace treaty has gone into effect, Finland will take steps militarily to neutralize the Suursaari [Hogland] island, under international guarantees. [Neutralization means: no military installations, stores, or forces on the island.] Russia agrees to support the efforts to obtain the international guarantees mentioned.

Article 15

Finland agrees to remove, within three months of the coming into force of the peace treaty [the firing, sighting, etc., mechanisms of the cannon at Ino and Puumala and to raze these fortifications within a year after the treaty goes into effect], and also agrees not to construct at Seivasto and Inonniemi, within twenty kilometers of the coast, any [batteries, etc., capable of firing beyond the limits of Finland's territorial waters].

Article 16

[The signatories agree not to maintain, either on Lake Ladoga or on its rivers or the Neva, offensive military installations; ships of less than one hundred tons armed with cannon or no more than forty-seven millimeters are permitted.] In the event that the neutralization of the Baltic Sea is carried through, Lake Ladoga will also be neutralized.

Article 17

Russia agrees to grant Finnish ships a free right of navigation on the Neva between Lake Ladoga and the Gulf of Finland, on the same conditions as Russian ships. Finnish ships are, however, forbidden to carry military material or property. [Both signatories agree, if requested, to undertake discussions within a year regarding a convention embodying the details involved in applying this article.]

Article 18

The level of the water in Lake Ladoga shall not be changed without previous agreement between Finland and Russia.

Article 19

Questions regarding customs inspection, fishing, navigation installations, the maintenance of order outside the territorial waters in the Gulf of Finland, the removal of mines in said waters, the establishment of uniform pilotage rules, and such matters will be submitted to Finnish-Russian mixed commissions.

Articles 20 and 21

[Immediately after the coming into force of the peace treaty, passport, customs, and border traffic matters will be arranged by special agreements, and the signatories will also proceed to provide for traffic on rivers that run through or into the territories of both.]

Article 22

Russian state-owned property in Finland is turned over to the Finnish state, without compensation. The same principle applies to Finnish state-owned property in Russia. Both reserve to themselves, for diplomatic and consular purposes, three city properties, with lot and buildings.

Article 23

The government of Finland agrees to deliver to Russia, immediately after the peace treaty has gone into effect, Russian ships left in Finland in 1918. . . . Russia agrees to return to Finnish citizens or corporations ships requisitioned without compensation by the Russian government during the World War. . . .

Article 24

Neither signatory will claim from the other compensation for its war costs. Finland assumes no part of the costs caused by the World War, 1914–1918, to Russia.

Article 25

Neither signatory is responsible for the public debt or other commitments of the other signatory.

Article 26

[Russia's debts and other obligations to Finland, and Finland's debts and other obligations to Russia, are mutually canceled. . . .]

Article 27

[Russia admits that Finland is not obligated to compensate the citizens of third states for losses] suffered by them in Finland as the result of the action of Russian authorities during the World War, before Finland became independent. Claims regarding such losses shall be addressed to the government of Russia.

Article 28

[Finnish citizens and corporations having property in Russia or claims against the Russian state have, regarding such property and claims, the same rights as those granted by Russia to the most favored nations.]

Article 29

[Provides for the mutual exchange of the archives and documents of public institutions and offices relating wholly or mainly to the other signatory or its history.]

Article 30

[Finland agrees to reserve, for ten years, half of the beds in Halila hospital for the inhabitants of greater Petrograd, on the same terms as apply to the Finns.]

Article 31

After the peace treaty has gone into effect, economic relations between the two states will be resumed. . . .

Article 32

Until a commercial treaty has been concluded, temporary arrangements will be employed which either party can end on six months' notice. [The temporary arrangements included provisions regarding uniform, nondiscriminatory freights and charges, the use of shipping, railroads, coastal navigation, etc., and provided that] Finnish agricultural, handicraft, and industrial products can be exported to Russia without any customs or other charges.

Article 33

Immediately after the peace treaty has gone into effect, the signatories will proceed to take measures essential for the organization of railroad traffic between Finland and Russia in such a way that direct traffic, without reloading or change of trains by passengers, becomes possible. . . .

Article 34

The postal and telegraphic connections between Finland and Russia will be established and a special agreement entered into regarding the matter, after the peace treaty has gone into effect. [Finland agreed, until the end of 1946, to the use, by Russia, of three cables that connect Petrograd, through Finland, with Stockholm, Newcastle, and Fredericia.]

Article 35

Russian citizens in Finland and Finnish citizens in Russia are allowed to return to their own country after the peace treaty has gone into effect, unless they have been arrested for serious crimes. Prisoners of war and other detained persons shall be freed and returned to their own country as soon as possible. Citizens detained for reasons involving attempts to restore national self-rule, or charged with such activity, will be released at once.

Article 36

The signatories will establish diplomatic and consular relations immediately after the peace treaty has gone into effect. . . .

Article 37

[A mixed Finnish-Russian commission will be set up to arrange for and to take care of questions that may arise in connection with the carrying out of the peace treaty.]

Article 38

The present treaty has been drafted in Finnish, Swedish, and Russian; each text is equally authentic. In connection with the exchange of ratifications, the signatories will sign a French text of the treaty which will likewise be authentic.

Article 39

This treaty shall be ratified. Ratifications will be exchanged in Moscow. The treaty will go into effect immediately upon the exchange of ratifications.

In witness hereof the Plenipotentiaries have signed the present treaty and affixed their seals.

The original done in Dorpat on the fourteenth day of October, 1920, in the languages mentioned above. . . .

[The treaty contained two annexes, listing the ships and other vessels to which reference is made in Article 23.]

[Before signing, the leader of the Russian delegation offered three declarations. One of them related to the autonomy of East Karelia and is given on pp. 307–8.]

Treaty of Nonaggression and

Pacific Settlement of Disputes

Between Finland and the USSR,

January 21, 1932

The President of the Republic of Finland, of the one part, and

The Central Executive Committee of the Union of Soviet Socialist Republics, of the other part,

Actuated by the desire to contribute to the maintenance of general peace;

Being convinced that the conclusion of the undertakings mentioned below and the pacific settlement of any dispute whatsoever between the Republic of Finland and the Union of Soviet Socialist Republics is in the interests of both High Contracting Parties and will contribute towards the development of friendly and neighborly relations between the two countries;

Declaring that none of the international obligations which they have hitherto assumed debars the pacific development of their mutual relations or is incompatible with the present treaty;

Being desirous of confirming and completing the General Pact of August 27, 1928, for the Renunciation of War;

Have resolved to conclude the present treaty and . . . have agreed upon the following provisions:

Article 1

1. The High Contracting Parties mutually guarantee the inviolability of the existing frontiers between the Republic of Finland and the Union

of Soviet Socialist Republics, as fixed by the Treaty of Peace concluded at Tartu [Dorpat] on October 14, 1920, which shall remain the firm foundation of their relations, and reciprocally undertake to refrain from any act of aggression directed against each other.

2. Any act of violence attacking the integrity and inviolability of the territory or the political independence of the other High Contracting Party shall be regarded as an act of aggression, even if it is committed without declaration of war and avoids warlike manifestations.

PROTOCOL TO ARTICLE 1

In conformity with the provisions of Article 4 of the present treaty, the Agreement of June 1, 1922, regarding measures ensuring the inviolability of the frontiers shall not be affected by the provisions of the present treaty and shall continue to remain fully in force.

Article 2

1. Should either High Contracting Party be the object of aggression on the part of one or more third Powers, the other High Contracting Party undertakes to maintain neutrality throughout the duration of the conflict.

2. Should either High Contracting Party resort to aggression against a third Power, the other High Contracting Party may denounce the present treaty without notice.

Article 3

Each of the High Contracting Parties undertakes not to become a party to any treaty, agreement, or convention which is openly hostile to the other Party or contrary, whether formally or in substance, to the present treaty.

Article 4

The obligations mentioned in the preceding articles of the present treaty may in no case affect or modify the international rights or obligations of the High Contracting Parties under agreements concluded or undertakings assumed before the coming into force of the present treaty, in so far as such agreements contain no elements of aggression within the meaning of the present treaty.

Article 5

The High Contracting Parties declare that they will always endeavor to settle in a spirit of justice any disputes of whatever nature or origin which may arise between them, and will resort exclusively to pacific means of settling such disputes. For this purpose, the High Contracting

Parties undertake to submit any disputes which may arise between them after the signature of the present treaty, and which it may not have been possible to settle through diplomatic proceedings within a reasonable time, to a procedure of conciliation before a joint conciliation commission whose powers, composition, and working shall be fixed by a special supplementary Convention, which shall form an integral part of the present treaty and which the High Contracting Parties undertake to conclude as soon as possible and in any event before the present treaty is ratified. Conciliation procedure shall also be applied in the event of any dispute as to the application or interpretation of a Convention concluded between the High Contracting Parties, and particularly the question whether the mutual undertaking as to nonaggression has or has not been violated.

Article 6

The present treaty shall be ratified and the instruments of ratification shall be exchanged at Moscow.

Article 7

The present treaty shall come into force on the exchange of the instruments of ratification [ratified on August 9, 1932].

Article 8

The present treaty is concluded for three years. If it is not denounced by either of the High Contracting Parties after previous notice of not less than six months before the expiry of that period, it shall be deemed to be automatically renewed for a further period of two years.

Article 9

The present treaty is drawn up in duplicate in French, in the town of Helsinki, the 21st day of January, 1932.

In faith whereof the Plenipotentiaries have signed the present treaty and have thereto affixed their seals.

[The treaty was renewed, until December 31, 1945, on April 7, 1934.]

Convention of Conciliation Between
Finland and the USSR, April 25, 1932

In accordance with the provisions of Article 5 of the Treaty of Non-aggression and Pacific Settlement of Disputes concluded on January 21, 1932, between Finland and the Union of Soviet Socialist Republics . . . Finland and . . . the Union of Soviet Socialist Republics have decided to conclude a Conciliation Convention and have . . . agreed upon the following provisions:

Article 1

The High Contracting Parties mutually undertake to submit to a Conciliation Commission for amicable settlement, in accordance with the provisions of the present Convention, all disputes of whatsoever nature which may arise between them on account of circumstances occurring after the signature of the Treaty of Nonaggression and Pacific Settlement of Disputes between Finland and the Union of Soviet Socialist Republics and which cannot be settled within a reasonable time through the diplomatic channel. This undertaking also refers in particular to any possible differences regarding the interpretation and enforcement of conventions which have been or may hereafter be concluded between the High Contracting Parties.

Article 2

The Conciliation Commission provided for in Article 1 shall consist of four members, of whom each of the High Contracting Parties shall appoint two from among its nationals for each session of the Commission.

Either High Contracting Party shall be entitled to have recourse to experts appointed by itself, who may sit on the Commission in an advisory capacity. Either High Contracting Party may also, if both Parties on the Commission agree, arrange for persons, whose evidence it may consider useful, to be heard.

Each session shall be presided over by one of the members of the Commission who is a national of the country in whose territory the Commission is sitting.

Article 3

It shall be the duty of the Conciliation Commission to clear up the questions at issue which have been submitted to it, to collect all necessary information for that purpose, and to make such proposals for the settlement of disputes as it may consider equitable, and it shall recommend the High Contracting Parties to accept such proposals through the diplomatic channel.

Should the Conciliation Commission, during a session, fail to agree on a joint proposal concerning a question submitted to it, and should the High Contracting Parties subsequently fail to reach an agreement for the settlement of the dispute within a reasonable time, it is understood that the dispute may, on the request of either High Contracting Party, be again submitted to a procedure of conciliation.

Article 4

The Conciliation Commission shall meet at the request of either High Contracting Party communicated to the other through the diplomatic channel, on a date to be fixed by mutual agreement between the High Contracting Parties.

The Commission shall meet not later than one month after the receipt of the said application.

As a general rule, the Commission shall not meet oftener than once a year, except in urgent cases. In such event, the government which had proposed the holding of one urgent session shall inform the other government of the circumstances giving rise to such application.

The session shall not normally last longer than fifteen days, unless the High Contracting Parties jointly decide otherwise.

The Commission shall sit alternately at Moscow and Helsinki. The first meeting shall be held at Moscow.

Article 5

Not less than fifteen days before the meeting of the Conciliation Commission, each High Contracting Party shall communicate to the other, through the diplomatic channel, a list of the questions which it desires to have examined by the Commission at that session.

Article 6

Unless the High Contracting Parties jointly decide otherwise, the Conciliation Commission shall itself determine its procedure.

Article 7

The Commission of Conciliation shall be deemed to form a quorum only if all the members duly convened are present.

Should any member be unable to attend the proceedings of the Commission, the High Contracting Party concerned shall appoint a substitute for him within not more than thirty days after his inability to attend has been ascertained.

The decisions of the Commission shall be taken by the unanimous agreement of its members.

Article 8

The High Contracting Parties undertake to assist the Conciliation Commission in carrying out its tasks, and more particularly to supply it, as far as is possible, with all necessary information and documents.

Article 9

The Conciliation Commission shall draw up a report on the disputes which have been submitted to it. This report shall be supplied before the end of the session during which the questions at issue have been examined, unless the High Contracting Parties decide by mutual agreement to extend that time-limit.

The report shall contain proposals for the settlement of every question at issue submitted to the Commission, if such proposals have been accepted by all the members of the Commission.

Should the Commission fail to agree on joint proposals, the report shall contain the proposals of both parties on the Commission.

Article 10

The Conciliation Commission's report shall be signed by all its members. It shall be communicated at once to each High Contracting Party.

Article 11

Each High Contracting Party undertakes to inform the other, within a reasonable time-limit, which shall in no case exceed three months, whether it accepts the Commission's joint proposals contained in its report.

Article 12

The Conciliation Commission's report may not be published, either in full or in part, without the consent of both High Contracting Parties.

Article 13

The emoluments of members of the Conciliation Commission and of the experts or other persons employed by each High Contracting Party shall be paid by the Party concerned.

All other expenses arising out of the working of the Commission shall be paid in equal shares by each Party.

Article 14

While the conciliation procedure is in progress, the High Contracting Parties undertake to refrain from any steps in their power which might have a prejudicial effect on the Conciliation Commission's proposals regarding the questions submitted to it.

Article 15

The present Convention shall constitute an integral part of the Treaty of Nonaggression and Pacific Settlement of Disputes concluded on January 21, 1932, between Finland and the Union of Soviet Socialist Republics and shall be regarded as ratified by the actual fact of the ratification of the aforesaid treaty.

It shall come into force simultaneously with the said Treaty of Non-aggression and shall remain in force for the same period as that Treaty.

Article 16

The present Convention is drawn up in French, in duplicate, at Helsinki, the 22nd day of April, 1932.

In faith whereof the Plenipotentiaries have signed this Convention and have thereto affixed their seals.

APPENDIX E

Resolution of the Assembly of the
League of Nations, December 14, 1939

THE ASSEMBLY:

I

Whereas, by the aggression which it has committed against Finland, the Union of Soviet Socialist Republics has failed to observe not only its special agreements with Finland but also Article 12 of the Covenant of the League of Nations and the Pact of Paris;

And whereas, immediately before committing that aggression, it denounced, without legal justification, the Treaty of Nonaggression which it had concluded with Finland in 1932, and which was to remain in force until the end of 1945:

Solemnly condemns the action taken by the Union of Soviet Socialist Republics against the State of Finland;

Urgently appeals to every Member of the League to provide Finland with such material and humanitarian assistance as may be in its power and to refrain from any action which might weaken Finland's power of resistance;

Authorizes the Secretary-General to lend the aid of his technical services in the organization of the aforesaid assistance to Finland;

And likewise authorizes the Secretary-General, in virtue of the Assembly resolution of October 4, 1937, to consult non-member States with a view to possible cooperation.

II

Whereas, notwithstanding an invitation extended to it on two occasions, the Union of Soviet Socialist Republics has refused to be present at the examination of its dispute with Finland before the Council and the Assembly;

And whereas, by thus refusing to recognize the duty of the Council and the Assembly as regards the execution of Article 15 of the Covenant, it has failed to observe one of the League's most essential covenants for the safeguarding of peace and the security of nations;

And whereas it has vainly attempted to justify its refusal on the ground of the relations which it has established with an alleged government which is neither *de jure* nor *de facto* the government recognized by the people of Finland in accordance with the free working of their institutions;

And whereas the Union of Soviet Socialist Republics has not merely violated a covenant of the League, but has by its own action placed itself outside the Covenant;

And whereas the Council is competent under Article 16 of the Covenant to consider what consequences should follow from this situation:

Recommends the Council to pronounce upon the question.

Resolution of the Council of the League of Nations, December 14, 1939

THE COUNCIL,

Having taken cognizance of the resolution adopted by the Assembly on December 14, 1939, regarding the appeal of the Finnish Government,

1. Associates itself with the condemnation by the Assembly of the action of the Union of Soviet Socialist Republics against the Finnish State, and

2. For the reasons set forth in the resolution of the Assembly,

In virtue of Article 16, paragraph 4, of the Covenant,

Finds, that, by its act, the Union of Soviet Socialist Republics has placed itself outside the League of Nations. It follows that the Union of Soviet Socialist Republics is no longer a Member of the League.

APPENDIX F

Treaty ot Peace Between the Republic of Finland and the Union of Soviet Socialist Republics, March 12, 1940

The government of the Republic of Finland on the one hand and

The Presidium of the Supreme Soviet of the Union of Soviet Socialist Republics on the other hand,

Desiring to put an end to the hostilities which have arisen between the two countries and to create lasting peaceful relations between them,

And being convinced that the creation of precise conditions for reciprocal security, including the security of the cities of Leningrad and Murmansk and of the Murmansk Railway, corresponds to the interest of both contracting parties,

Have to this end found it necessary to conclude a peace treaty and have . . . agreed upon the following:

Article 1

Hostilities between Finland and the USSR shall cease immediately in accordance with procedure laid down in the protocol appended to this treaty.

Article 2

The national frontier between the Republic of Finland and the USSR shall run along a new line in such fashion that there shall be included in the territory of the USSR the entire Karelian Isthmus with the city of

Viipuri and Viipuri Bay with its islands, the western and northern shores of Lake Ladoga with the cities of Kexholm and Sortavala and the town of Suojärvi, a number of islands in the Gulf of Finland, the area east of Märkäjärvi with the town of Kuolajärvi, and part of the Rybachi and Sredni peninsulas, all in accordance with the map appended to this treaty.

A more detailed determination and establishment of the frontier line shall be carried out by a mixed commission made up of representatives of the contracting powers, which commission shall be named within ten days from the date of the signing of this treaty.

Article 3

Both contracting parties undertake to refrain from any attack upon the other and to make no alliance and to participate in no coalition directed against either of the contracting parties.

Article 4

The Republic of Finland agrees to lease to the Soviet Union for thirty years, against an annual rental of eight million Finnish marks to be paid by the Soviet Union, Hanko Cape and the waters surrounding it in a radius of five miles to the south and east and three miles to the north and west, and also the several islands falling within that area, in accordance with the map appended to this treaty, for the establishment of a naval base capable of defending the mouth of the Gulf of Finland against attack; in addition to which, for the purpose of protecting the naval base, the Soviet Union is granted the right of maintaining there at its own expense the necessary number of armed land and air forces.

Within ten days from the date this treaty enters into effect, the government of Finland shall withdraw all its military forces from Hanko Cape, which together with its adjoining islands shall be transferred to the jurisdiction of the USSR in accordance with this article of the treaty.

Article 5

The USSR undertakes to withdraw its troops from the Petsamo area which the Soviet state voluntarily ceded to Finland under the peace treaty of 1920.

Finland undertakes, as provided in the peace treaty of 1920, to refrain from maintaining in the waters running along its coast of the Arctic Ocean warships and other armed ships, excluding armed ships of less than one hundred tons displacement, which Finland shall be entitled to maintain without restriction, and also at most fifteen warships or other armed ships, the displacement of none of which shall exceed four hundred tons.

Finland undertakes, as was provided in the same treaty, not to maintain in the said waters any submarines or armed aircraft.

Finland similarly undertakes, as was provided in the same treaty, not to establish on that coast military ports, naval bases, or naval repair shops of greater capacity than is necessary for the above-mentioned ships and their armament.

Article 6

As provided in the treaty of 1920, the Soviet Union and its citizens are granted the right of free transit across the Petsamo area to Norway and back, in addition to which the Soviet Union is granted the right to establish a consulate in the Petsamo area.

Merchandise shipped through the Petsamo area from the Soviet Union to Norway, and likewise merchandise shipped through the same area from Norway to the Soviet Union, is exempted from inspection and control, with the exception of such control as is necessary for the regulation of transit traffic; neither customs duties nor transit or other charges shall be assessed.

The above-mentioned control of transit merchandise shall be permitted only in the form usual in such cases in accordance with established practice in international communications.

Citizens of the Soviet Union who travel through the Petsamo area to Norway and from Norway back to the Soviet Union shall be entitled to free transit passage on the basis of passports issued by the appropriate officials of the Soviet Union.

Observing general directives in effect, unarmed Soviet aircraft shall be entitled to maintain air service between the Soviet Union and Norway via the Petsamo area.

Article 7

The government of Finland grants to the Soviet Union the right of transit for goods between the Soviet Union and Sweden, and, with a view to developing this traffic along the shortest railway route, the Soviet Union and Finland consider it necessary to build, each upon its own territory and in so far as possible in the year 1940, a railway which shall connect Kantalahti (Kandalaksha) with Kemijärvi.

Article 8

Upon the coming into force of this treaty economic relations between the contracting parties shall be restored, and with this end in view the contracting parties shall enter into negotiations for the conclusion of a trade agreement.

Article 9

This treaty of peace shall enter into effect immediately upon being signed, and shall be subject to subsequent ratification.

The exchange of instruments of ratification shall take place within ten days in the city of Moscow.

This treaty has been prepared in two original instruments, in the Finnish and Swedish languages and in Russian, at Moscow this twelfth day of March, 1940.

[A separate protocol, appended to the peace treaty, provided for the cessation of hostilities and the details regarding the withdrawal of troops from the various sectors of the front and the turning over of the ceded areas to the USSR.]

APPENDIX G

Treaty of Peace Between the Allies and Finland, February 10, 1947

The Union of Soviet Socialist Republics, the United Kingdom of Great Britain and Northern Ireland, Australia, the Byelorussian Soviet Socialist Republic, Canada, Czechoslovakia, India, New Zealand, the Ukrainian Soviet Socialist Republic, and the Union of South Africa, as the states which are at war with Finland and actively waged war against the European enemy states with substantial military forces, hereinafter referred to as "the Allied and Associated Powers," of the one part, and Finland, of the other part;

Whereas Finland, having become an ally of Hitlerite Germany and having participated on her side in the war against the Union of Soviet Socialist Republics, the United Kingdom, and other United Nations, bears her share of responsibility for this war;

Whereas, however, Finland on September 4, 1944, entirely ceased military operations against the Union of Soviet Socialist Republics, withdrew from the war against the United Nations, broke off relations with Germany and her satellites, and, having concluded on September 19, 1944, an armistice with the governments of the Union of Soviet Socialist Republics and the United Kingdom, acting on behalf of the United Nations at war with Finland, loyally carried out the armistice terms; and

Whereas the Allied and Associated Powers and Finland are desirous of concluding a treaty of peace which, conforming to the principles of justice, will settle questions still outstanding as a result of the events hereinbefore recited and will form the basis of friendly relations between them, thereby enabling the Allied and Associated Powers to support Finland's application to become a member of the United Nations and also to adhere to any convention concluded under the auspices of the United Nations;

Have therefore agreed to declare the cessation of the state of war and for this purpose to conclude the present Treaty of Peace, and have accordingly appointed the undersigned Plenipotentiaries who . . . have agreed on the following provisions:

PART I. *TERRITORIAL CLAUSES*

Article 1

The frontiers of Finland . . . shall be those which existed on January 1, 1941, except as provided in the following article.

Article 2

In accordance with the Armistice Agreement of September 19, 1944, Finland confirms the return to the Soviet Union of the province of Petsamo (Pechenga) voluntarily ceded to Finland by the Soviet state under the peace treaties of October 14, 1920, and March 12, 1940. . . .

PART II. *POLITICAL CLAUSES*

Section I

Article 3

In accordance with the Armistice Agreement, the effect of the peace treaty between the Soviet Union and Finland concluded in Moscow on March 12, 1940, is restored, subject to the replacement of Articles 4, 5, and 6 of that treaty by Articles 2 and 4 of the present treaty.

Article 4

1. In accordance with the Armistice Agreement, the Soviet Union confirms the renunciation of its right to the lease of the Peninsula of Hanko, accorded to it by the Soviet-Finnish Peace Treaty of March 12, 1940, and Finland for her part confirms having granted to the Soviet Union on the basis of a fifty years lease at an annual rent payable by the Soviet Union of five million Finnish marks the use and administration of territory and waters for the establishment of a Soviet naval base in the area of Porkkala-Udd as shown on the map annexed to the present treaty. . . .

2. Finland confirms having secured to the Soviet Union, in accordance with the Armistice Agreement, the use of the railways, waterways, roads, and air routes necessary for the transport of personnel and freight dispatched from the Soviet Union to the naval base at Porkkala-Udd, and

also confirms having granted to the Soviet Union the right of unimpeded use of all forms of communication between the Soviet Union and the territory leased in the area of Porkkala-Udd.

Article 5

The Åland Islands shall remain demilitarized in accordance with the situation as at present existing.

Section II

Article 6

Finland shall take all measures necessary to secure to all persons under Finnish jurisdiction, without distinction as to race, sex, language, or religion, the enjoyment of human rights and of the fundamental freedoms, including freedom of expression, of press and publication, of religious worship, of political opinion, and of public meeting.

Article 7

Finland, which in accordance with the Armistice Agreement has taken measures to set free, irrespective of citizenship and nationality, all persons held in confinement on account of their activities in favor of, or because of their sympathies with, the United Nations or because of their racial origin, and to repeal discriminatory legislation and restrictions imposed thereunder, shall complete these measures and shall in future not take any measures or enact any laws which would be incompatible with the purposes set forth in this article.

Article 8

Finland, which in accordance with the Armistice Agreement has taken measures for dissolving all organizations of a Fascist type on Finnish territory, whether political, military, or paramilitary, as well as other organizations conducting propaganda hostile to the Soviet Union or to any of the other United Nations, shall not permit in future the existence and activities of organizations of that nature which have as their aim denial to the people of their democratic rights.

Article 9

1. Finland shall take all necessary steps to ensure the apprehension and surrender for trial of:

(a) Persons accused of having committed, ordered, or abetted war crimes and crimes against peace or humanity;

(b) Nationals of any Allied or Associated Power accused of having violated their national law by treason or collaboration with the enemy during the war.

2. At the request of the United Nations government concerned, Finland shall likewise make available as witnesses persons within its jurisdiction, whose evidence is required for the trial of the persons referred to in paragraph 1 of this article.

3. Any disagreement concerning the application of the provisions of paragraphs 1 and 2 of this article shall be referred by any of the governments concerned to the heads of the diplomatic missions in Helsinki of the Soviet Union and the United Kingdom, who will reach agreement with regard to the difficulty.

SECTION III

Article 10

Finland undertakes to recognize the full force of the Treaties of Peace with Italy, Rumania, Bulgaria, and Hungary and other agreements or arrangements which have been or will be reached by the Allied and Associated Powers in respect of Austria, Germany, and Japan for the restoration of peace.

Article 11

Finland undertakes to accept any arrangements which have been or may be agreed for the liquidation of the League of Nations and the Permanent Court of International Justice.

Article 12

1. Each Allied or Associated Power will notify Finland, within a period of six months from the coming into force of the present treaty, which of its prewar bilateral treaties with Finland it desires to keep in force or revive. Any provisions not in conformity with the present treaty shall, however, be deleted from the above-mentioned treaties.

2. All such treaties so notified shall be registered with the Secretariat of the United Nations in accordance with Article 102 of the Charter of the United Nations.

3. All such treaties not so notified shall be regarded as abrogated.

PART III. *MILITARY, NAVAL, AND AIR CLAUSES*

Article 13

The maintenance of land, sea, and air armaments and fortifications shall be closely restricted to meeting tasks of an internal character and local defense of frontiers. In accordance with the foregoing, Finland is authorized to have armed forces consisting of not more than:

(a) A land army, including frontier troops and antiaircraft artillery, with a total strength of 34,400 personnel;

(b) A navy with a personnel strength of 4,500 and a total tonnage of 10,000 tons;

(c) An air force, including any naval air arm, of 60 aircraft, including reserves, with a total personnel strength of 3,000. Finland shall not possess or acquire any aircraft designed primarily as bombers with internal bomb-carrying facilities.

These strengths shall in each case include combat, service, and overhead personnel.

Article 14

The personnel of the Finnish Army, Navy, and Air Force in excess of the respective strengths permitted under Article 13 shall be disbanded within six months from the coming into force of the present Treaty.

Article 15

Personnel not included in the Finnish Army, Navy, or Air Force shall not receive any form of military training, naval training, or military air training as defined in Annex II.

Article 16

1. As from the coming into force of the present Treaty, Finland will be invited to join the Barents, Baltic, and Black Sea Zone Board of the International Organization for Mine Clearance of European Waters and shall maintain at the disposal of the Central Mine Clearance Board all Finnish minesweeping forces until the end of the postwar mine clearance period, as determined by the Central Board.

2. During this postwar mine clearance period, Finland may retain additional naval units employed only for the specific purpose of minesweeping, over and above the tonnage permitted in Article 13.

Within two months of the end of the said period, such of these vessels as are on loan to the Finnish Navy from other Powers shall be returned to those Powers, and all other additional units shall be disarmed and converted to civilian use.

3. Finland is also authorized to employ 1,500 additional officers and men for minesweeping over and above the numbers permitted in Article 13. Two months after the completion of minesweeping by the Finnish Navy, the excess personnel shall be disbanded or absorbed within the numbers permitted in the said Article.

Article 17

Finland shall not possess, construct, or experiment with any atomic weapon, any self-propelled or guided missiles or apparatus connected with their discharge (other than torpedoes and torpedo launching gear comprising the normal armament of naval vessels permitted by the present treaty), sea mines or torpedoes of noncontact types actuated by influence mechanisms, torpedoes capable of being manned, submarines or other submersible craft, motor torpedo boats, or specialized types of assault craft.

Article 18

Finland shall not retain, produce, or otherwise acquire, or maintain facilities for the manufacture of, war material in excess of that required for the maintenance of the armed forces permitted under Article 13 of the present treaty.

Article 19

1. Excess war material of Allied origin shall be placed at the disposal of the Allied Power concerned according to the instructions given by that Power. Excess Finnish war material shall be placed at the disposal of the governments of the Soviet Union and the United Kingdom. Finland shall renounce all rights to this material.

2. War material of German origin or design in excess of that required for the armed forces permitted under the present treaty shall be placed at the disposal of the two governments. Finland shall not acquire or manufacture any war material of German origin or design, or employ or train any technicians, including military and civil aviation personnel, who are or have been nationals of Germany.

3. Excess war material mentioned in paragraphs 1 and 2 of this article shall be handed over or destroyed within one year from the coming into force of the present treaty.

4. A definition and list of war material for the purposes of the present treaty are contained in Annex III.

Article 20

Finland shall cooperate fully with the Allied and Associated Powers with a view to ensuring that Germany may not be able to take steps outside German territory towards rearmament.

Article 21

Finland shall not acquire or manufacture civil aircraft which are of German or Japanese design or which embody major assemblies of German or Japanese manufacture or design.

Article 22

Each of the military, naval, and air clauses of the present treaty shall remain in force until modified in whole or in part by agreement between the Allied and Associated Powers and Finland or, after Finland becomes a member of the United Nations, by agreement between the Security Council and Finland.

PART IV. *REPARATION AND RESTITUTION*

Article 23

1. Losses caused to the Soviet Union by military operations and by the occupation by Finland of Soviet territory shall be made good by Finland to the Soviet Union, but, taking into consideration that Finland has not only withdrawn from the war against the United Nations, but has also declared war on Germany and assisted with her forces in driving German troops out of Finland, the Parties agree that compensation for the above losses will be made by Finland not in full, but only in part, namely in the amount of $300,000,000 payable over eight years from September 19, 1944, in commodities (timber products, paper, cellulose, seagoing and river craft, sundry machinery, and other commodities).

2. The basis of calculation for the settlement provided in this article shall be the United States dollar at its gold parity on the day of the signing of the Armistice Agreement, i.e., $35 for one ounce of gold.

Article 24

Finland, in so far as she has not yet done so, undertakes within the time-limits indicated by the government of the Soviet Union to return to the Soviet Union in complete good order all valuables and materials removed from its territory during the war, and belonging to state, public or cooperative organizations, enterprises, or institutions or to individual citizens, such as: factory and works equipment, locomotives, rolling stock, tractors, motor vehicles, historic monuments, museum valuables, and any other property.

PART V. *ECONOMIC CLAUSES*

Article 25

1. In so far as Finland has not already done so, Finland shall restore all legal rights and interests in Finland of the United Nations and their nationals as they existed on June 22, 1941, and shall return all property in Finland of the United Nations and their nationals as it now exists.

2. The Finnish government undertakes that all property, rights, and interests passing under this article shall be restored free of all encumbrances and charges of any kind to which they may have become subject as a result of the war and without the imposition of any charges by the Finnish government in connection with their return. The Finnish government shall nullify all measures, including seizures, sequestration, or

control, taken by it against United Nations property between June 22, 1941, and the coming into force of the present treaty. In cases where the property has not been returned within six months from the coming into force of the present treaty, application shall be made to the Finnish authorities not later than twelve months from the coming into force of the treaty, except in cases in which the claimant is able to show that he could not file his application within this period.

3. The Finnish government shall invalidate transfers involving property, rights, and interests of any description belonging to United Nations nationals, where such transfers resulted from force or duress exerted by Axis governments or their agencies during the war.

4. (a) The Finnish government shall be responsible for the restoration to complete good order of the property returned to United Nations nationals under paragraph 1 of this article. In cases where property cannot be returned or where, as a result of the war, a United Nations national has suffered a loss by reason of injury or damage to property in Finland, he shall receive from the Finnish government compensation in Finnish marks to the extent of two thirds of the sum necessary, at the date of payment, to purchase similar property or to make good the loss suffered. In no event shall United Nations nationals receive less favorable treatment with respect to compensation than that accorded to Finnish nationals.

(b) United Nations nationals who hold, directly or indirectly, ownership interests in corporations or associations which are not United Nations nationals within the meaning of paragraph 8 (a) of this Article, but which have suffered a loss by reason of injury or damage to property in Finland, shall receive compensation in accordance with subparagraph (a) above. This compensation shall be calculated on the basis of the total loss or damage suffered by the corporation or association and shall bear the same proportion to such loss or damage as the beneficial interests of such nationals in the corporation or association bear to the total capital thereof.

(c) Compensation shall be paid free of any levies, taxes, or other charges. It shall be freely usable in Finland but shall be subject to the foreign exchange control regulations which may be in force in Finland from time to time.

(d) The Finnish government shall accord to United Nations nationals the same treatment in the allocation of materials for the repair or rehabilitation of their property in Finland and in the allocation of foreign exchange for the importation of such materials as applies to Finnish nationals.

(e) The Finnish government shall grant United Nations nationals an indemnity in Finnish marks at the same rate as provided in subparagraph (a) above to compensate them for the loss or damage due to special measures applied to their property during the war, and which were not applicable to Finnish property. This subparagraph does not apply to a loss of profit.

5. All reasonable expenses incurred in Finland in establishing claims, including the assessment of loss or damage, shall be borne by the Finnish government.

6. United Nations nationals and their property shall be exempted from any exceptional taxes, levies, or imposts imposed on their capital assets in Finland by the Finnish government or any Finnish authority between the date of the armistice and the coming into force of the present treaty for the specific purpose of meeting charges arising out of the war or of meeting the costs of reparation payable to any of the United Nations. Any sums which have been so paid shall be refunded.

7. The owner of the property concerned and the Finnish government may agree upon arrangements in lieu of the provisions of this article.

8. As used in this article:

(a) "United Nations nationals" means individuals who are nationals of any of the United Nations, or corporations or associations organized under the laws of any of the United Nations, at the coming into force of the present treaty, provided that the said individuals, corporations, or associations also had this status at the date of the armistice with Finland.

The term "United Nations nationals" also includes all individuals, corporations, or associations which, under the laws in force in Finland during the war, have been treated as enemy;

(b) "Owner" means the United Nations national, as defined in subparagraph (a) above, who is entitled to the property in question, and includes a successor of the owner, provided that the successor is also a United Nations national as defined in subparagraph (a). If the successor has purchased the property in its damaged state, the transferor shall retain his rights to compensation under this article, without prejudice to obligations between the transferor and the purchaser under domestic law;

(c) "Property" means all movable or immovable property, whether tangible or intangible, including industrial, literary, and artistic property, as well as all rights or interests of any kind in property.

Article 26

Finland recognises that the Soviet Union is entitled to all German assets in Finland transferred to the Soviet Union by the Control Council for Germany and undertakes to take all necessary measures to facilitate such transfers.

Article 27

In so far as any such rights were restricted on account of Finland's participation in the war on Germany's side, the rights of the Finnish government and of any Finnish nationals, including juridical persons, relating to Finnish property or other Finnish assets of the territories of the Allied and Associated Powers shall be restored after the coming into force of the present treaty.

Article 28

1. From the coming into force of the present treaty, property in Germany of Finland and of Finnish nationals shall no longer be treated as enemy property and all restrictions based on such treatment shall be removed.

2. Identifiable property of Finland and of Finnish nationals removed by force or duress from Finnish territory to Germany by German forces or authorities after September 19, 1944, shall be eligible for restitution.

3. The restoration and restitution of Finnish property in Germany shall be effected in accordance with measures which will be determined by the Powers in occupation of Germany.

Article 29

1. Finland waives all claims of any description against the Allied and Associated Powers on behalf of the Finnish government or Finnish nationals arising directly out of the war or out of actions taken because of the existence of a state of war in Europe after September 1, 1939, whether or not the Allied or Associated Power was at war with Finland at the time, including the following:

(a) Claims for losses or damages sustained as a consequence of acts of forces or authorities of Allied or Associated Powers;

(b) Claims arising from the presence, operations, or actions of forces or authorities of Allied or Associated Powers in Finnish territory;

(c) Claims with respect to the decrees or orders of Prize Courts of Allied or Associated Powers, Finland agreeing to accept as valid and binding all decrees and orders of such Prize Courts on or after September 1, 1939, concerning Finnish ships or Finnish goods or the payment of costs;

(d) Claims arising out of the exercise or purported exercise of belligerent rights.

2. The provisions of this article shall bar, completely and finally, all claims of the nature referred to herein, which will be henceforward extinguished, whoever may be the parties in interest.

3. Finland likewise waives all claims of the nature covered by para-

graph 1 of this article on behalf of the Finnish government or Finnish nationals against any of the United Nations whose diplomatic relations with Finland were broken off during the war and which took action in cooperation with the Allied and Associated Powers.

4. The waiver of claims by Finland under paragraph 1 of this article includes any claims arising out of actions taken by any of the Allied and Associated Powers with respect to Finnish ships between September 1, 1939, and the coming into force of the present treaty, as well as any claims and debts arising out of the convention on prisoners of war now in force.

Article 30

1. Pending the conclusion of commercial treaties or agreements between individual United Nations and Finland, the Finnish government shall, during a period of eighteen months from the coming into force of the present treaty, grant the following treatment to each of the United Nations which, in fact, reciprocally grants similar treatment in like matters to Finland:

(a) In all that concerns duties and charges on importation or exportation, the internal taxation of imported goods and all regulations pertaining thereto, the United Nations shall be granted unconditional most-favored-nation treatment;

(b) In all other respects, Finland shall make no arbitrary discrimination against goods originating in or destined for any territory of any of the United Nations as compared with like goods originating in or destined for territory of any other of the United Nations or of any other foreign country;

(c) United Nations nationals, including juridical persons, shall be granted national and most-favored-nation treatment in all matters pertaining to commerce, industry, shipping, and other forms of business activity within Finland. These provisions shall not apply to commercial aviation;

(d) Finland shall grant no exclusive or discriminatory right to any country with regard to the operation of commercial aircraft in international traffic, shall afford all the United Nations equality of opportunity in obtaining international commercial aviation rights in Finnish territory, including the right to land for refueling and repair, and, with regard to the operation of commercial aircraft in international traffic, shall grant on a reciprocal and nondiscriminatory basis to all United Nations the right to fly over Finnish territory without landing. These provisions shall not affect the interests of the national defense of Finland.

2. The foregoing undertakings by Finland shall be understood to be subject to the exceptions customarily included in commercial treaties

concluded by Finland before the war; and the provisions with respect to reciprocity granted by each of the United Nations shall be understood to be subject to the exceptions customarily included in the commercial treaties concluded by that state.

Article 31

1. Any disputes which may arise in connection with Articles 24 and 25 and Annexes IV, V, and VI, part B, of the present treaty shall be referred to a Conciliation Commission composed of an equal number of representatives of the United Nations government concerned and of the Finnish government. If agreement has not been reached within three months of the dispute having been referred to the Conciliation Commission, either government may require the addition of a third member to the Commission, and, failing agreement between the two governments on the selection of this member, the Secretary-General of the United Nations may be requested by either party to make the appointment.

2. The decision of the majority of the members of the Commission shall be the decision of the Commission and shall be accepted by the parties as definitive and binding.

Article 32

Articles 24, 25, 30, and Annex VI of the present treaty shall apply to the Allied and Associated Powers and France and to those of the United Nations whose diplomatic relations with Finland have been broken off during the war.

Article 33

The provisions of Annexes IV, V, and VI shall, as in the case of the other annexes, have force and effect as integral parts of the present treaty.

PART VI. *FINAL CLAUSES*

Article 34

1. For a period not to exceed eighteen months from the coming into force of the present treaty, the heads of the diplomatic missions in Helsinki of the Soviet Union and the United Kingdom, acting in concert, will represent the Allied and Associated Powers in dealing with the Finnish government in all matters concerning the execution and interpretation of the present treaty.

2. The two heads of mission will give the Finnish government such

guidance, technical advice, and clarification as may be necessary to ensure the rapid and efficient execution of the present treaty both in letter and in spirit.

3. The Finnish government shall afford the said two heads of mission all necessary information and any assistance which they may require for the fulfilment of the tasks devolving on them under the present treaty.

Article 35

1. Except where another procedure is specifically provided under any article of the present treaty, any dispute concerning the interpretation or execution of the treaty, which is not settled by direct diplomatic negotiations, shall be referred to the two heads of mission acting under Article 34, except that in this case the heads of mission will not be restricted by the time limit provided in that article. Any such dispute not resolved by them within a period of two months shall, unless the parties to the dispute mutually agree upon another means of settlement, be referred at the request of either party to the dispute to a Commission composed of one representative of each party and a third member selected by mutual agreement of the two parties from nationals of a third country. Should the two parties fail to agree within a period of one month upon the appointment of the third member, the Secretary-General of the United Nations may be requested by either party to make the appointment.

2. The decision of the majority of the members of the Commission shall be the decision of the Commission, and shall be accepted by the parties as definitive and binding.

Article 36

The present treaty, of which the Russian and English texts are authentic, shall be ratified by the Allied and Associated Powers. It shall also be ratified by Finland. It shall come into force immediately upon the deposit of ratifications by the Union of Soviet Socialist Republics and the United Kingdom of Great Britain and Northern Ireland. The instruments of ratification shall, in the shortest time possible, be deposited with the government of the Union of Soviet Socialist Republics.

With respect to each Allied or Associated Power whose instrument of ratification is thereafter deposited, the treaty shall come into force upon the date of deposit. The present treaty shall be deposited in the archives of the government of the Union of Soviet Socialist Republics, which shall furnish certified copies to each of the signatory states.

[The List of Annexes contains six items: (1) a map of Finland's new frontiers and of the areas mentioned in Articles 2 and 4; (2) definitions of military, etc., training; (3) definition and lists of war materials; (4) special provisions relating to certain kinds of property; (5) contracts, etc.; and (6) prize courts and judgments.]

In faith whereof the undersigned Plenipotentiaries have signed the present treaty and have affixed thereto their seals.

Done in the city of Paris in the Russian, English, French, and Finnish languages this tenth day of February, one thousand nine hundred forty-seven.

[Signed by the USSR, Britain, Australia, Canada, India, the Union of South Africa, New Zealand, the Byelorussian SSR, Czechoslovakia, the Ukrainian SSR, and Finland.]

Agreement of Friendship, Cooperation, and Mutual Assistance Between the Republic of Finland and the Union of Soviet Socialist Republics, April 6, 1948

The President of the Republic of Finland and the Presidium of the Supreme Soviet of the USSR;

Desiring further to develop friendly relations between the Republic of Finland and the USSR;

Being convinced that the strengthening of good neighborhood relations and cooperation between the Republic of Finland and the USSR lies in the interest of both countries:

Considering Finland's desire to remain outside the conflicting interests of the Great Powers; and

Expressing their firm endeavor to collaborate towards the maintenance of international peace and security in accordance with the aims and principles of the United Nations Organization:

Have for this purpose agreed to conclude the present agreement and have . . . agreed to the following provisions:

Article 1

In the eventuality of Finland, or the Soviet Union through Finnish territory, becoming the object of an armed attack by Germany or any state allied with the latter, Finland will, true to its obligations as an independent state, fight to repel the attack. Finland will in such cases use all its available forces for defending its territorial integrity by land, sea, and air, and will do so within the frontiers of Finland in accordance with obligations defined in the present agreement and, if necessary, with the assistance of, or jointly with, the Soviet Union.

In the cases aforementioned the Soviet Union will give Finland the help required, the giving of which will be subject to mutual agreement between the Contracting Parties.

Article 2

The High Contracting Parties shall confer with each other if it is established that the threat of an armed attack as described in Article 1 is present.

Article 3

The High Contracting Parties give assurance of their intention loyally to participate in all measures towards the maintenance of international peace and security in conformity with the aims and principles of the United Nations Organization.

Article 4

The High Contracting Parties confirm their pledge, given under Article 3 of the Peace Treaty signed in Paris on February 10, 1947, not to conclude any alliance or join any coalition directed against the other High Contracting Party.

Article 5

The High Contracting Parties give assurance of their decision to act in a spirit of cooperation and friendship towards the further development and consolidation of economic and cultural relations between Finland and the Soviet Union.

Article 6

The High Contracting Parties pledge themselves to observe the principle of the mutual respect of sovereignty and integrity and that of non-interference in the internal affairs of the other state.

Article 7

The execution of the present agreement shall take place in accordance with the principles of the United Nations Organization.

Article 8

The present agreement shall be ratified and remains in force ten years after the date of its coming into force. The agreement shall come into force upon the exchange of the instruments of ratification, the exchange taking place in the shortest time possible in Helsinki.

Provided neither of the High Contracting Parties has denounced it one year before the expiration of the said ten-year period, the agreement shall remain in force for subsequent five-year periods until either High Contracting Party one year before the expiration of such five-year periods in writing notifies its intention of terminating the validity of the agreement.

In witness hereof the Plenipotentiaries have signed the present agreement and affixed their seals.

Done in the city of Moscow on the sixth day of April, 1948, in two copies, in the Finnish and the Russian languages, both texts being authentic.

APPENDIX I

Agreement for Cooperation Between Denmark, Finland, Iceland, Norway, and Sweden, March 23, 1962

The governments of Denmark, Finland, Iceland, Norway, and Sweden, desirous of developing further the close unity that exists among the Nordic nations in matters cultural, conceptions of law and society, and wanting to carry forward cooperation among the people of the North;

striving for uniform rules and regulations among the four nations over the widest possible areas;

desiring to achieve, in all fields where opportunities therefor exist, expedient and practical division of labor among the five countries;

and desiring to continue the cooperation important to all our nations, within the Nordic Council and other organs of cooperation,

have agreed to the following.

INTRODUCTORY PROVISION

Article 1

The signatories shall attempt to preserve and develop further cooperation between themselves in the field of legal matters, in cultural, social, and economic areas, as well as in matters relating to traffic.

COOPERATION IN LEGAL MATTERS

Article 2

The contracting parties shall continue to work for the establishment of the greatest possible legal equality between the citizens of a Nordic country who reside in another Nordic country, and the citizens of the country where they reside.

Article 3

The contracting parties shall attempt to make it easier for citizens of one Nordic country to acquire citizenship in another.

Article 4

The contracting parties shall continue their cooperation in matters pertaining to law in order to achieve the greatest possible uniformity in the field of civil law.

Article 5

The contracting parties should strive for uniform provisions regarding crimes and punishments therefor. It should be possible, over a wide range of cases, to investigate and prosecute crimes committed in one Nordic country even in another Nordic country.

Article 6

The contracting parties should attempt, even in areas other than the ones mentioned, to achieve coordination in legislation whenever coordination seems to serve a useful purpose.

Article 7

Each contracting party should endeavor to bring about regulations which permit the carrying out of one Nordic nation's court verdicts, or decisions by some other authority, within the jurisdiction of the other signatories.

CULTURAL COOPERATION

Article 8

In each of the Nordic countries, the teaching and instruction given in schools should include, in appropriate degree, instruction in the languages of the other Nordic nations, as well as instruction concerning their culture and general social conditions.

Article 9

Each signatory should maintain and expand, in its educational institutions, opportunities for study, and for taking examinations, for students from the other Nordic countries. Preliminary examinations passed in one country should be accepted, to the greatest possible extent, toward meeting final examination requirements in another.

Fellowship and scholarship aid should be granted without reference to the country where studies are pursued.

Article 10

The contracting parties should introduce such uniformity in their public instruction as is intended to afford competence in a given trade. Such instruction should be recognized as giving, as far as possible, the same competence in all of the Nordic countries. If special national considerations require it, additional training might, however, be required.

Article 11

In areas where cooperation will serve useful purposes, the development of educational establishments should be coordinated by means of continuing cooperation in planning and execution.

Article 12

In the field of research, cooperation should be directed in a manner that will coordinate and ensure the most effective use of available funds and other resources, *inter alia*, by establishing common institutions.

Article 13

In order to support and strengthen cultural development, the signatories shall support the free education of the people, as well as to foster exchanges within the areas of literature, art, music, the theater, the moving pictures, and other fields of cultural endeavor. The possibilities offered by radio and television should therewith be utilized.

Article 14

The signatories should preserve and expand further the common Nordic labor market, along the lines drawn by earlier agreements. Labor exchanges and vocational guidance should be coordinated; the exchange of trainees should be free. Attempts should be made to render uniform the national rules and provisions regarding the protection of workers and such matters.

Article 15

The signatories should labor to the end that the citizen of a Nordic country, while residing in another, will enjoy to the fullest possible extent the social benefits available to the natives.

Article 16

The signatories shall develop further their cooperation in the fields of health, the care of the sick, children and youth, as well as efforts on behalf of temperance.

Article 17

Each signatory should strive for a medical, technical, and suchlike system of inspection and control in a manner that certification in one country can be accepted in the other Nordic countries.

ECONOMIC COOPERATION

Article 18

The contracting parties shall, in order to promote economic cooperation in various fields, discuss questions dealing with economic policy. Attention should be given therewith to the possibility of coordinating measures intended to stabilize business conditions.

Article 19

It is the intention of the signatories to promote as extensively as possible cooperation between their countries in the areas of production and investment, and in this connection to create favorable circumstances for direct cooperation between enterprises active in two or more of the Nordic countries. In their effort to develop further their cooperation, as part of large international cooperation, they should strive for a practical division of labor, among themselves, in matters of production and investment.

Article 20

The signatories shall labor for the greatest possible freedom for the movement of capital between the Nordic countries. Attempts will be made to find common solutions for other payments and foreign exchange problems that interest them all.

Article 21

The signatories will endeavor to strengthen existing cooperation designed to remove obstacles to trade between the Nordic countries, and agree to develop and strengthen this cooperation as far as possible.

Article 22

The signatories shall attempt to promote, each for himself and also together, Nordic interests when international commercial questions are involved.

Article 23

The contracting parties shall endeavor to coordinate the technical and administrative customs regulations and to bring about such simplification of customs arrangements as will contribute to easier traffic between them.

Article 24

Regulation of trade in the areas adjacent to the boundaries shall be such as to cause the least possible trouble to the inhabitants.

Article 25

Whenever necessary and when the essential prerequisites for the economic development of the areas close to the border belonging to two or more signatories exist, they will attempt to cooperate in promoting such development.

COOPERATION IN THE AREA OF TRAFFIC AND COMMUNICATION

Article 26

The contracting parties shall attempt to expand the cooperation that already exists between them in the field of traffic and communication and will attempt to develop it in order to improve connections and the exchange of goods between them, and in order to solve the problems that still may exist in this area.

Article 27

The development of traffic connections involving the territory of two or more of the contracting parties shall be undertaken on the basis of consultation between the parties concerned.

Article 28

The signatories shall attempt to retain and develop further the cooperation which has turned their territories into a single passport control area. The control of travelers who cross the borders of the Nordic countries shall be further simplified and rendered uniform.

Article 29

The signatories will coordinate the efforts to increase the safety of traffic.

OTHER FORMS OF COOPERATION

Article 30

Whenever possible and practical, the contracting parties shall consult with each other regarding questions of common interest that are considered in international organizations and at international conferences.

Article 31

A signatory's foreign service officer who is serving abroad, outside the Nordic countries, shall assist, in so far as it is in keeping with his responsibilities in discharging his duties, citizens of another Nordic country if it lacks representation in the area in question.

Article 32

The contracting parties shall coordinate, whenever it is possible and practical, their efforts to aid and to work with underdeveloped countries.

Article 33

Measures intended to publicize and to increase knowledge of the Nordic countries and Nordic cooperation should be undertaken in close cooperation between the contracting parties and their informational organization abroad. Whenever convenient, the five countries should act and appear together.

Article 34

The contracting parties shall endeavor to render uniform the various branches of their official statistical services.

THE FORMS OF NORDIC COOPERATION

Article 35

In order to achieve the purposes mentioned in this agreement the contracting parties shall continue to consult one another and when necessary undertake action in common.

This cooperation shall take place, as has been the case hitherto, at meetings of Cabinet members, within the framework of the Nordic Council and its organs, according to the directives of the Statute of the Council, and in various other organizations for cooperation, or between appropriate officials.

Article 36

The Nordic Council shall be given an opportunity to express itself regarding the principles of Nordic cooperation except when, because of the time element, this is not possible.

Article 37

Accords that have been entered into as the result of the cooperation of two or more of the contracting parties cannot be changed by one party, except upon notice to the others. Notice is not required, however, in matters that demand quick action, or are of no particular importance.

Article 38

The authorities and officials of the Nordic countries may correspond with each other in regard to matters other than those which, because of their nature or other reasons, must be handled by and through the Ministry for Foreign Affairs.

Article 39

This agreement will be ratified and the instruments of ratification shall be deposited, as soon as possible, with the Ministry for Foreign Affairs of Finland.

The agreement becomes effective on the first day of the month following the deposit of ratifications by all of the contracting parties.

Article 40

[The agreement can be canceled upon written notice, given to the government of Finland, and becomes effective six months after notice.]

In witness whereof [we have] signed this agreement,

Signed in Helsinki, in one copy done in Danish, Finnish, Icelandic, Norwegian, and Swedish, each of which text is equally authentic, the twenty-third of March, nineteen hundred and sixty-two.

Select Bibliography

Ahava, I., *et al.*, eds. *Kaksikymmentä Vuotta Suomen Itsenäisyyttä*. Helsinki, 1927.

Ailio, L., *et al.*, eds. *Politiikkaa ja Merkkimiehiä*. Helsinki, 1935.

Auer, J. *Suomen Sotakorvaustoimitukset Neuvostoliitolle*. Helsinki, 1956.

Aurola, E. *Suomen Tehtaankoulut*. Helsinki, 1961. Historiallisia Tutkimuksia, Vol. LXI.

Bank of Finland. *Monthly Bulletin*. Helsinki, 1929—

Bergh, E. *Finlands Statsrättsliga Utveckling efter 1808*. Helsinki, 1889.

Bonsdorff, Carl von. *Gustav Mauritz Armfelt*. Vols. I–III. Helsinki, 1930–32.

—— *Opinioner och Stämningar i Finland, 1808–1814*. Helsinki, 1918.

Bonsdorff, Göran von. *Suomen Poliittiset Puolueet*. Helsinki, 1957.

Bonsdorff, L. G. von. *Den Ryska Pacificeringen i Finland, 1808–1809*. Helsinki, 1929.

Borgman, F. W. *Der Überfall der Sovietunion auf Finland, 1939–1940*. Berlin, 1943.

Brotherus, K. R. *Katsaus Suomen Valtiollisen järjestysmuodon Historialliseen Kehitykseen*. Porvoo, 1948.

Castrén, Liisa. *Adolf Ivar Arwidsson Isänmaallisena Herättäjänä*. Helsinki, 1961.

Coon, Carlton S. *The Races of Europe*. New York, 1939.

Dahmén, Erik. *Suomen Taloudellinen Kehitys ja Talouspolitiikka*. Helsinki, 1963.

Danielson, J. R. *Finlands Inre Självständighet*. Helsinki, 1892.

—— *Finland's Union with the Russian Empire*. Porvoo, 1891.

Danielson-Kalmari, J. R. *Ahvenanmaan Asia Vuosina 1914–1920*. Helsinki, 1920.

—— *Tien Varrelta Kansalliseen ja Valtiolliseen Itsenäisyyteen*. I–III. Porvoo, 1928–30.

Deutsch, Babette. *Heroes of the Kalevala*. New York, 1940.

530   Select Bibliography

Donner, K., *et al.*, eds. *Suomen Vapaussota*. Vols. I–VIII. Jyväskylä, 1921–28.
Enckell, Carl. *Poliittiset Muistelmani*. Vols. I–II. Helsinki, 1959–60.
Erfurth, W. *Der Finnische Krieg, 1941–1944*. Wiesbaden, 1950.
Estlander, E. *Friherre Viktor Magnus von Born*. Helsinki, 1931.
Finnish Political Science Association, ed. *Democracy in Finland*. Helsinki, 1961.
—— *Finnish Foreign Policy*. Helsinki, 1963.
Frietsch, C. O. *Suomen Kohtalonvuodet*. Helsinki, 1945.
Furuhjelm, E. *Ur Finlands Kulturhistoria under 1840–1870 talen*. Vol. I. Helsinki, 1902.
Gadolin, C. A. J. *Finland av i går och i dag*. Stockholm, 1938.
Generalguvernör Bobrikoffs Berättelse öfver Finlands Förvaltning från Sept. 1898 till Sept. 1902. Helsinki, 1905.
Gripenberg, G. A. *En Beskicknings-Chefs Minnen*. Vol. I. Helsinki, 1959.
—— *London-Vatikanen-Stockholm*. Helsinki, 1961.
Gummerus, Herman. *Jääkärit ja Aktivistit*. Translated by E. Voionmaa. Porvoo, 1928.
—— *Sverige och Finland 1917–1918*. Helsinki, 1936.
Hallendorff, Carl, and Adolf Schück. *History of Sweden*. Stockholm, 1929.
Halsti, Wolf H. *Suomen Puolustuskysymys*. Kuopio, 1954.
—— *Suomen Sota, 1939–1944*. Vols. I–III. Helsinki, 1957.
Haltsonen, S., *et al.*, eds. *Juhlakirja Rafael Koskimiehen Täyttäessä 60 Vuotta 9. 2. 1958*. Helsinki, 1958.
Hankins, Frank H. *The Racial Basis of Civilization*. New York, 1926.
Hannula, J. O. *Suomen Vapaussodan Historia*. 5th ed. by A. Korhonen. Porvoo, 1956.
Hansen, R. *Finlands Medeltidsurkunder*. Vol. I. Helsinki, 1910.
Harmaja, L. *Effects of the War on Economic and Social Life in Finland*. New Haven, 1933.
Havu, T. *Lauantaiseura ja sen Miehet*. Helsinki, 1945.
Heinrichs, Erik. *Mannerheim Suomen Kohtaloissa*. Vols. I–II. Helsinki, 1957, 1959.
Hellner, H. *Memorandum Rörande Sveriges Politik: Förhållande till Finland under tiden från Finlands självständighetsförklaring till det finska inbördeskrigets slut*. Stockholm, 1936.
Heporauta, F. A., and M. Haavio, eds. *Kalevala, Kansallinen Aarre*. Helsinki, 1949.
Herlin, P., *et al.*, eds. *Metalliteollisuus Suomen Kansantaloudessa*. Helsinki, 1963.
Hermanson, R. *Suomen Valtiosääntö Pääpiirteittäin*. Translated by K. Kaila. Porvoo, 1928.

Hertzberg, R. *Helsingfors.* Helsinki, 1888.
Hirvikallio, Paavo. *Tasavallan Presidentin Vaalit Suomessa, 1919–1950.* Helsinki, 1958.
Hornborg, Eirik. *Finlands Historia.* Helsinki, 1963.
Hultin, T. *Taistelun Mies.* Helsinki, 1927.
Huuhka, K. *Talonpoikaisnuorison Koulutie . . . 1910–1950.* Helsinki, 1955. Historiallisia Tutkimuksia, Vol. XLIII.
Hyvämäki, L. *Vaaran Vuodet.* Helsinki, 1954.
Idman, K. G. *Diplomatminnen.* Helsinki, 1954.
—— *Maamme Itsenäistymisen Vuosilta.* Helsinki, 1953.
Ignatius, H., K. Grotenfelt, *et al.*, eds. *Suomen Vapaussota Vuonna 1918.* Helsinki, 1922.
Jaakkola, J. *Suomen Myöhäiskeskiaika.* Vols. I–II. Porvoo, 1950.
—— *Suomen Sydänkeskiaika.* Porvoo, 1944.
—— *Suomen Varhaishistoria.* Porvoo, 1935.
—— *Suomen Varhaiskeskiaika.* Porvoo, 1938.
Jaakkola, J., and John H. Roos, eds. *Vuoden 1616 Valitusluettelot.* Helsinki, 1936.
Jackson, J. Hampden. *Finland.* New York, 1940.
Jakobson, Max. *The Diplomacy of the Winter War.* Cambridge, Mass., 1961.
Järvinen, Y. A. *Suomalainen ja Venäläinen Taktiikka Talvisodassa.* Porvoo, 1948.
Joustela, K. E. *Suomen Venäjän-kauppa . . . vv 1809–1865.* Helsinki, 1963.
Jutikkala, Eino. *A History of Finland.* New York, 1962.
—— *Suomen Talonpojan Historia.* Helsinki, 1958.
Kalevala, The. Compiled by Elias Lönnrot. Prose translation by Francis Peabody Magoun, Jr. Cambridge, Mass., 1963.
Kallinen, Y. *Hälinää ja Hiljaisuutta.* Helsinki, 1958.
Kannisto, A., *et al.*, eds. *Suomen Suku.* Vols. I–II. Helsinki, 1926–28.
Kansallinen Kokoomus. *Suomalainen Konservatismi.* Tampere, 1958.
Kare, K., *et al.*, eds. *J. K. Paasikivi.* Hämeenlinna, 1960.
Kerkkonen, M. *Peter Kalm's North American Journey.* Helsinki, 1959. Studia Historica, Vol. I.
Ketonen, O., and U. Toivola, eds. *Introduction to Finland 1960.* Porvoo, 1960.
Killinen, K. *Demokratia ja Totaalinen Sota.* Porvoo, 1956.
Kilpi, Sylvi-Kyllikki. *Lenin ja Suomalaiset.* Helsinki, 1957.
Knoellinger, C. E. *Fackföreningar och Arbetsmarknad i Finland.* Helsinki, 1959.
—— *Labor in Finland.* Cambridge, Mass., 1960.
Kohtamäki, J. *Ankara Puutarhuri.* Helsinki, 1956.

Korhonen, Arvi. *Barbarossa Suunnitelma ja Suomi*. Porvoo, 1961.
Korhonen, Arvi, ed. *Suomen Historian Käsikirja*. Vols. I–II. Helsinki, 1949.
Korhonen, K. *Suomen Asiain Komitea*. Helsinki, 1963.
Koskinen, Y. *Suomen Kansan Historia*. 3d ed. Helsinki, 1933.
Krohn, E., *et al.*, eds. *Juhlakirja Lauri Viljasen Täyttäessä 60 Vuotta*. Porvoo, 1960.
Krohn, K. *Kalevalan Runojen Historia*. Helsinki, 1903.
Kurjensaari, M. *Suuntana Suomalainen*. Helsinki, 1955.
Kuussaari, E. *Suomen Sota, 1941–1945: Karjalan Kannaksen Valtaus Kesällä 1941*. Helsinki, 1951.
Laati, J. *Sosialinen Lainsäädäntö ja Toiminta Suomessa*. Helsinki, 1939.
Laine, Y. K. *Suomen Poliittisen Työväenliikkeen Historia*. Vols. I–III. Helsinki, 1946–51.
Lehmusto, H. *J. V. Snellman ja Suomalaisuus*. Jyväskylä, 1935.
Lehtinen, E. *Hallituksen Yhtenäistämispolitiikka 1600-luvulla*. Helsinki, 1961.
Lindman, Sven. *Parlamentarismens Genomförande i Finlands Statsförfattning*. Uppsala, 1935.
—— *Studier Över Parlamentarismens tillämpning i Finland, 1919–1926*. Turku, 1937.
Lizelius, A. *Suomenkieliset Tieto-Sanomat 1775–1776*. Turku, 1959.
Lundborg, H. *Svenska Folktyper*. Stockholm, 1919.
Lundin, C. Leonard. *Finland and the Second World War*. Bloomington, Ind., 1957.
Mannerheim, C. G. E. *Memoirs*. Translated by Eric Lewenhaupt. London, 1953.
—— *Minnen, 1882–1946*. Vols. I–II. Helsinki, 1951–52.
Manninen, I. *Suomensukuiset Kansat*. Porvoo, 1929.
Mead, W. R. *An Economic Geography of Scandinavia and Finland*. London, 1958.
—— *Farming in Finland*. London, 1953.
Mörne, A. *Axel Olof Freudenthal*. Helsinki, 1927.
Nervander, E. *Blad ur Finlands Kulturhistoria*. Helsinki, 1900.
Niemi, A. R. *Kalevalan Kokoonpano*. Helsinki, 1898.
Niukkanen, J. *Talvisodan Puolustusministeri Kertoo*. Porvoo, 1951.
Nivanka, E., ed. *Pysy Suomessa Pyhänä*. Helsinki, 1961.
Nordenstreng, S. *Borgarståndets Historia*. Vols. I–V. Helsinki, 1920.
Nousiainen, J. *Suomen Poliittinen Järjestelmä*. Helsinki, 1961.
Nurmio, Y. *Suomen Itsenäistyminen ja Saksa*. Porvoo, 1957.
Nyström, A. *Karl XII*. Stockholm, 1928.
Odhe, T. *Finland: A Nation of Co-operators*. Translated by John Downie. London, 1931.

Öhquist, H. *Talvisota.* Porvoo, 1950.

Oittinen, R. H. *Työväenkysymys ja Työväenliike Suomessa.* Helsinki, 1948.

Paasikiven Linja. Vols. I–II. Porvoo, 1956.

Paasikiven Muistelmia Sortovuosilta. Vols. I–II. Porvoo, 1957.

Paasikivi, J. K. *Toimintani Moskovassa ja Suomessa 1939–1941.* Vols. I–II. Porvoo, 1953.

Paasivirta, J. *Plans for Commercial Agents and Consuls of Autonomous Finland.* Turku, 1963.

—— *Suomen Itsenäisyyskysymys V. 1917.* Vols. I–II. Helsinki, 1948–49.

—— *Suomi Vuonna 1918.* Porvoo, 1957.

Paavolainen, O. *Synkkä Yksinpuhelu.* Vols. I–II. Porvoo, 1946.

Palmén, E. G. *Suomen Valtiopäiväin Historia.* Porvoo, 1910.

Paloposki, T. J. *Suomen Talonpoikaissäädyn Valtiopäiväedustus Vapaudenajalla.* Helsinki, 1961.

Peitsara, T. *Suomen ja Venäjän Talvisota 1939–40.* Helsinki, 1941.

Pietilä, A. J. *Daniel Juslenius.* Porvoo, 1907.

Pipping, H. *Finlands Näringsliv Efter Andra Världskriget.* Helsinki, 1954.

Platt, Raye E., ed. *Finland and Its Geography.* London, 1957.

Pohjanpoika, P. *Punainen Valhe.* Helsinki, 1962.

Pohjolan-Pirhonen, H. *Suomen Historia, 1523–1617.* Helsinki, 1960.

Procopé, H. J. *Fällande Dom som Friar.* Stockholm, 1945.

Puntila, L. A. J. K. *Paasikiven Linja.* Lahti, 1957.

—— *Ruotsalaisuus Suomessa.* Helsinki, 1944.

—— *Suomen Poliittinen Historia 1809–1955.* 2d ed. Helsinki, 1963.

Rantanen, S. H. *Kuljin S K P:n Tietä.* Helsinki, 1958.

Rasila, V. *Suomen Torpparikysymys Vuoteen 1909.* Helsinki, 1961.

Reade, A. *Finland and the Finns.* London, 1916.

Renvall, P. *Kuninkaanmiehiä ja Kapinoitsijoita Vaasa-kauden Suomessa.* Turku, 1949.

Renvall, P., ed. *Suomalaisen Kansanvallan Kehitys.* Helsinki, 1956.

Repo, E. S., ed. *Urho Kekkonen.* Helsinki, 1960.

Reuter, J. N. *"Kagalen."* Vols. I–II. Helsinki, 1929–30.

Rintala, Marvin. *Three Generations: The Extreme Right Wing in Finnish Politics.* Bloomington, Ind., 1962.

Ruuth, Y. O. *Självständighets Politiken och Jägarrörelsens Uppkomst.* Translated by R. Numelin. Helsinki, 1919.

Schauman, A. *Från Sex Årtionden i Finland.* Vols. I–II. Helsinki, 1892–93.

Schybergson, M. G. *Henrik Gabriel Porthan.* Vols. I–II. Helsinki, 1910, 1911.

Seitkari, O. *Vuoden 1878 Asevelvollisuuslain Syntyvaiheet.* Helsinki, 1951.

Siilasvuo, H. *Suomussalmen Taistelut.* Helsinki, 1940.

534 Select Bibliography

Smith, C. Jay, Jr. *Finland and the Russian Revolution, 1917–1922.* Atlanta, 1958.

Söderhjelm, H. *The Red Insurrection in Finland in 1918.* London, n.d.

Söderhjelm, W. *Johan Ludvig Runeberg.* Vols. I–II. Stockholm, 1929.

Soini, Y. *Kuin Pietari Hiilivalkealla.* Helsinki, 1956.

—— *Kuulovartiossa.* Helsinki, 1960.

Sosiaalipoliittinen Yhdistys. *Heikki Waris ja 15 Tohtoria.* Porvoo, 1961.

Ståhlberg, K. J. *Grunddragen av Finlands Förvaltningsrätt.* Translated by H. Koroleff. Helsinki, 1947.

—— *Puheita, 1919–1925.* Helsinki, 1925.

Suolahti, Gunnar, et al., eds. *Suomen Kulttuurihistoria.* Vols. I–IV. Jyväskylä, 1933–36.

Suomen Historiallinen Seura. *Historiallinen Arkisto.* Vols. LVII–LVIII. Helsinki, 1961–62.

—— *Juhlajulkaisu Carl von Bonsdorffin Kunniaksi . . . 1947.* Helsinki, 1947.

—— *Juhlajulkaisu, 1875–1925.* Vol. I. Helsinki, 1925.

—— *Juhlajulkaisu Einar W. Juvan Kunniaksi.* Turku, 1962.

—— *Juhlajulkaisu H. G. Porthanin Kunniaksi . . . 1939.* Helsinki, 1939.

—— *Juhlajulkaisu K. R. Melanderin Kunniaksi . . . 1938.* Helsinki, 1938.

Suomen Tilastollinen Vuosikirja—The Statistical Yearbook of Finland. Helsinki, 1920–62.

Suvanto, S. *Suomen Poliillinen Asema . . . 1483–1497.* Helsinki, 1952.

Suviranta, Bruno. *Finland and the World Depression.* Helsinki, 1931.

—— *Suomen Sotakorvaus ja Maksukyky.* Helsinki, 1948.

Svetshnikov, M. S. *Vallankumous ja Kansalaissota Suomessa 1917–1918.* Translated by O. Kostiainen. Helsinki, 1925.

Swento, R. *Työmies ja Talonpoika.* Helsinki, 1937.

Talas, O. *Ei Se Niin Tapahtunut.* Hämeenlinna, 1949.

Tanner, Väinö. *Itsenäisen Suomen Arkea.* Helsinki, 1956.

—— *Kuinka Se Oikein Tapahtui.* Helsinki, 1948.

—— *Olin Ulkoministerinä Talvisodan Aikana.* Helsinki, 1950.

—— *Suomen Tie Rauhaan.* Helsinki, 1952.

—— *Tarton Rauha.* Helsinki, 1949.

—— *The Winter War.* Stanford, 1957.

Tarkiainen, V. *Mikael Agricola.* Forssa, 1958.

Teljo, J. *Suomen Valtioelämän Murros, 1905–1908.* Porvoo, 1949.

Toivola, U., ed. *Introduction to Finland 1963.* Helsinki, 1963.

Tokoi, O. *Maanpakolaisen Muistelmia.* Helsinki, 1947.

—— *Sisu, "Even Through a Stone Wall": Autobiography.* New York, 1957.

Tommila, P., ed. *Itsenäisen Suomen Ulkopolitiikan Alkutaival.* Porvoo, 1962.

Tuominen, A. *Sirpin ja Vasaran Tie.* 7th ed. Helsinki, 1957.

Van Cleef, E. *Finland—the Republic Farthest North.* Columbus, Ohio, 1929.

Vilkuna, K., ed. *Maan Puolesta.* Helsinki, 1955.

Vuorela, T. *Suomensukuiset Kansat.* Helsinki, 1960.

Waris, Heikki. *Siirtoväen Sopeutuminen.* Helsinki, 1952.

—— *Suomalaisen Yhteiskunnan Rakenne.* Helsinki, 1948.

—— *Suomalaisen Yhteiskunnan Sosialipolitiikka.* Helsinki, 1961.

Wendt, F. *The Nordic Council and Co-operation in Scandinavia.* Copenhagen, 1959.

Westermarck, E. *Memories of My Life.* Translated by Anna Barwell. New York, 1929.

Wuorinen, John H. *The Finns on the Delaware.* New York, 1938.

—— *Nationalism in Modern Finland.* New York, 1931.

—— *The Prohibition Experiment in Finland.* New York, 1931.

Wuorinen, John H., ed. and trans. *Finland and World War II, 1939–1944.* New York, 1948.

Files of the daily press, especially of *Helsingin Sanomat, Hufvudstadsbladet, Suomen Sosialidemokraatti, Uusi Suomi, Maakansa, Kansan Uutiset, Päivän Sanomat.*

Index

Committee on Publications
The American-Scandinavian Foundation